The Human Odyssey
Volume 2
Our Modern World, 1400 to 1914

Contributing Writers

Tamim Ansary

Robin Currie

Susan Hitchcock

Rebecca Jones

Mara Rockliff

Michael Stanford

Academic Reviewers

Richard B. Barnett *University of Virginia*

Douglas Cope *Brown University*

Helen Delpar *University of Alabama*

Benjamin A. Elman *Princeton University*

Gregory L. Freeze *Brandeis University*

J. Matthew Gallman *University of Florida*

Robert Geraci *University of Virginia*

Raymond Grew *University of Michigan*

Ronald Herzman *State University of
New York at Geneseo*

Morton Keller *Brandeis University*

Patrick Manning *Northeastern University*

Byron McCane *Wofford College*

Theodore K. Rabb *Princeton University*

Robert Rotberg *Harvard University*

Michael Stanford *Arizona State University*

Sheldon M. Stern *Former Historian,
John F. Kennedy Presidential Library*

Isser Woloch *Columbia University*

Staff for This Volume

John Agnone *Project Manager*

Jeff Burridge *Text Editor*

Laura Seuschek *Art Director*

Steve Godwin *Art Director*

Jayoung Cho *Senior Designer*

Chris Raymond *Designer*

Bill Gordon *Designer*

Charlotte Fullerton *Illustrations Editor*

Connie Gelb *Illustrations Researcher*

Jane A. Martin *Illustrations Researcher*

Betsy Woodman *Research Editor*

Martin Walz *Map Editor*

Mark Wentling *Indexer*

Patricia Pearson *Teaching Specialist*

Bud Knecht *Clean Reader*

Lisa Dimaio Iekel *Production Manager*

Volume 2

The Human Odyssey

Our Modern World, 1400 to 1914

Edited by Mary Beth Klee, John Cribb, and John Holdren

K12

Cover Images

Front cover and title page:

Top: *The Journey of the Magi to Bethlehem* by Benozzo Gozzoli, c. 1459

Bottom: The St. Louis World's Fair of 1904

These two images contrast important aspects of the human odyssey between 1400 and 1914. The painting at top shows Lorenzo the Magnificent (in gold on horseback) and other members of Florence's powerful Medici family mounted on horses and reenacting the biblical journey of the three kings. With the great fortune they made in banking, the Medici supported the arts and at times acted like kings during the Renaissance. At bottom, a photograph from the early twentieth century depicts a new and different part of the journey—a growing middle class traveling by car. Once luxury items, automobiles were becoming affordable in the early 1900s. More and more people used them to travel to new forms of mass entertainment, such as the World's Fair depicted here.

Back cover top: Sixteenth-century ivory pendant from the African kingdom of Benin. Masters of sculpture in brass and ivory, artisans from Benin carved this image depicting the mother of one of their rulers.

Back cover bottom: *The Great City of Tenochtitlán* by Diego Rivera, 1945. In this painting, a great modern Mexican artist imagined what the capital of the Aztec Empire may have looked like before its fall to Spanish conquerors in the sixteenth century.

Library of Congress Cataloging-in-Publication Data

The human odyssey / edited by Mary Beth Klee, John Cribb, and John Holdren.
    p. cm.
  Includes index.
  ISBN 978-1-931728-56-0
 1. World history--Juvenile literature. I. Klee, Mary Beth, 1953- II. Cribb, John. III. Holdren, John, 1954-
  D20.H88 2004
  909--dc22

2004007909

Printed by Quad Graphics, Versailles, KY, USA, May 2019, Lot 042013

Contents

Prologue: The Human Odyssey: Our Modern World 8

Part 1

Introduction: The World in 1400: A Backward Glance 14

Chapter 1: Europe Reborn: Rediscovering Greece and Rome 24
    A Page from the Past: Dear Cicero 34

Chapter 2: Cities Spur Change 36
    Historical Close-up: Gutenberg and the Printing Press 45

Chapter 3: The Flowering of Genius in Florence 50
    Historical Close-up: Leonardo da Vinci's Early Years 61

Chapter 4: Rome Revived 66
    A Page from the Past: Michelangelo and Julius: A Stormy Relationship 75

Chapter 5: Of Courtiers and Princes: Politics of the Renaissance 80
    Historical Close-up: Leonardo, the Ultimate Renaissance Man 90

Chapter 6: The Renaissance Beyond Italy 94
    A Page from the Past: Thomas More's Utopia 104

Chapter 7: The Reformation Splits Christendom 106
    A Page from the Past: Luther's Ninety-five Theses 112

Chapter 8: The Counter-Reformation and the New Face of Europe 120
    Historical Close-up: Teresa of Avila 131

Chapter 9: Three Islamic Empires 136
    A Page from the Past: Finding the "Path of Truth" in History 148

Chapter 10: Ming China and Feudal Japan 150
    A Page from the Past: The Closing of Japan 163

Chapter 11: Russia Rising 164

Conclusion: Looking Back on the Early Modern World 176

Part 2

Introduction: A New Spirit of Exploration and Inquiry 192

Chapter 1: Portugal, Spain, and the Age of Exploration 196
    A Page from the Past: From the Log of Christopher Columbus 208

Chapter 2: Still Seeking the Indies and Filling In the Map 210
    A Page from the Past: The Discovery of a Westward Passage 220

Chapter 3: Old Civilizations in a New World 222
    Historical Close-up: Better Than Gold: Hiram Bingham
    and the Lost City of the Inca 235

Chapter 4: Clash of Civilizations: Conquistadors in the New World....... 238
    A Page from the Past: The Death of Montezuma....................... 246

Chapter 5: The Spanish and Portuguese Build Empires................. 250
    A Page from the Past: "Nothing more detestable or more cruel" 257

Chapter 6: Songhai, Benin, and the New Slave Trade 262

Chapter 7: Elizabethan England and North American Initiatives 272
    Historical Close-up: At the Globe with Shakespeare 285

Chapter 8: England: Civil War and Empire 290

Chapter 9: The Scientific Revolution 308
    A Page from the Past: Galileo's Celestial Observations.................. 314

Chapter 10: The Enlightenment: An Age of Reason 322
    A Page from the Past: From John Locke's Two Treatises of Government... 327
    Historical Close-up: Benjamin Franklin and the Spark of Reason.......... 334

Conclusion: Expanding the Known World........................... 338

Part 3

Introduction: An Age of Democratic and Industrial Revolution.......... 348

Chapter 1: The World Turned Upside Down: The American Revolution ... 352
    A Page from the Past: Paine Offers Common Sense 360

Chapter 2: Liberty, Equality, Fraternity: The French Revolution.......... 368
    *A Page from the Past: The Declaration of the Rights of Man
    and of the Citizen* 375

Chapter 3: Napoleon: Revolution and Empire....................... 384
    A Page from the Past: Napoleon Rallies His Troops 386

Chapter 4: Latin American Independence Movements 400
    Historical Close-up: Father Hidalgo's Cry for Freedom.................. 412

Chapter 5: The Russia of the Romanovs............................ 416
    A Page from the Past: Catherine Proposes a New Code of Laws........... 425

Chapter 6: Romantic Art in an Age of Revolution..................... 430

Chapter 7: Britain Begins the Industrial Revolution.................... 444
    A Page from the Past: From Adam Smith's The Wealth of Nations 450

Chapter 8: A Revolution in Transportation and Communication......... 458
    Historical Close-up: Samuel Morse Invents the Telegraph 469

Chapter 9: Strife and Struggle: Hard Times and New Ideas During
the Industrial Revolution... 474
    A Page from the Past: Hard Times in Industrial England................. 479

Chapter 10: Slavery in a Changing World 490
    A Page from the Past: Aboard a Slave Ship 496

Conclusion: Revolutions Change the World. 508

Part 4

Introduction: An Age of Outreach and Overreach 518

Chapter 1: Italy and Germany: Nationalism and the New Map of Europe . 522
    A Page from the Past: The Oath of Young Italy. 526

Chapter 2: Civil War in the United States: A House Divided and Reunited 538
    A Page from the Past: The Gettysburg Address. 548
    Historical Close-up: A Big Day at Promontory Point 553

Chapter 3: An Age of Innovation 558
    Historical Close-up: Guglielmo Marconi: Father of Radio. 568

Chapter 4: The New Imperialism. 572

Chapter 5: Organizing for Change: Cities, Workers, and Women 592
    Historical Close-up: Louis Pasteur: Fighting Disease 600

Chapter 6: Reaching Millions 610
    Historical Close-up: Henry Ford: Motor Cars for the Multitudes. 621

Chapter 7: Culture Shocks: Questioning Reason and Reality 626
    A Page from the Past: Émile Zola Depicts Life in the Slums 631

Chapter 8: Rising Expectations in Waning Empires 640
    A Page from the Past: Gandhi's Nonviolent Resistance 649

Chapter 9: Linking the Seas and Reaching for the Skies 654

Conclusion: Big Ambitions in a Shrinking World 668

Epilogue: Looking Back, Looking Forward 678

Appendix: Geographic Terms and Concepts 682

Atlas 690

Pronunciation Guide 712

Glossary 713

Text Credits and Permissions 720

Illustrations Credits 721

Index 726

Odysseus returns home, as imagined by an artist of the early 1500s.

The Human Odyssey:
Our Modern World

*L*ong ago, when the valiant Greek warrior Odysseus finished fighting on distant shores, he sheathed his sword and sailed for home. The battle-weary soldier longed to see his wife and son again. But, as the old myth tells us, Odysseus struggled for ten years to make his way home. Angry gods stirred the seas against him. A one-eyed giant tried to eat him. Sea monsters lay in wait for him on the shoals of narrow passages. Through wit and bravery, Odysseus finally found his way home. The story of his ten-year trek became known as the *Odyssey*. Today we use the word *odyssey* to refer to any great journey.

History, the human journey through time, is a kind of odyssey. The human odyssey is much longer and grander than Odysseus's decade-long voyage. Some scientists think

Above: This African prehistoric rock art dates from about 4500 to 2500 B.C. It depicts a herd of domesticated cattle and the herdsmen who tended them.

Below: The Parthenon, a huge temple, stands atop the Acropolis in Athens, Greece. It remains a powerful symbol of the classical civilization of ancient Greece.

the human story goes back as far as two million years or more. The written record of human adventures begins some six thousand years ago. We human beings have been journeying for a very long time.

Where have we come from? Where are we headed?

A Backward Glance

In the first volume of *The Human Odyssey*, we charted the human adventure beginning with prehistory, the time before written records. We saw how human beings began as hunters and gatherers, nomads who followed their prey.

Later they became farmers and city-builders. In the river valleys of

Mesopotamia, Egypt, India, and China, we watched people develop the first civilizations. They invented the first systems of writing, codes of laws, and forms of government. They built great and lasting monuments—ziggurats in Mesopotamia, pyramids in Egypt, and the Great Wall in China.

From these ancient civilizations we moved on to examine the classical world, the civilizations of ancient Greece and Rome. Homer's *Odyssey*, the epic poem about the homeward voyage of Odysseus, is one of the great literary works from the classical world. We witnessed the development of democracy in Greece and republican government in Rome.

We learned about the birth of philosophy. We saw how, from early times, human beings sought meaning for their lives. We witnessed the emergence of major world religions still with us today—Hinduism, Buddhism, Judaism, Christianity, and Islam.

Finally, we toured the Middle Ages, the thousand-year period after the fall of Rome. We explored trading kingdoms in Africa, a great Mongol empire in China, and new centers of scholarship in Arabia. We studied the feudal system in Europe, with

lords in castles, knights on horse-back, and serfs in the fields. Also in Europe, we watched the Christian Church grow in power and influence, and we saw learning begin to revive in thriving new universities.

What Does "Modern" Mean?

In this second volume of *The Human Odyssey*, our story continues as we journey into modern times. This book takes you on a voyage from the fourteenth century to the early twentieth century. This part of the human journey may be the most exciting to you. Recent centuries help explain many things about the world we now inhabit. In fact, the word *modern* comes from the Latin root *modo*, meaning "recently" or "just now."

If "modern" means "just now," but this book begins in the 1300s, then why do we say this book is about "our modern world"? What's so modern about the fourteenth century? That was more than six hundred years ago! Was the world really "modern" way back then?

Historians say, "Yes, indeed." True, six hundred years ago, people didn't have what we take for granted in the twenty-first century—cars and computers, e-mail and antibiotics, jet planes and cell phones. But these technologies are just part of our modern story. The events and ideas that made them possible started back in fourteenth-century Europe and rippled through history to the present.

The modern world began more than six hundred years ago when people in Europe questioned some of their main assumptions about the

During the modern era, people began to investigate the natural world in new ways. Here, sixteenth-century astronomers study the sky.

world. They gained new confidence in human abilities and a new curiosity about the natural world. Their confidence and hope made them feel as if the world were being reborn. That time of "rebirth" or revival in Europe is known as the Renaissance (REH-nuh-sahns), and it set much of humanity on a new path. The Renaissance marked the beginning of our modern world.

What's New?

In this volume, we'll begin our journey in the Renaissance. Here's a preview of some big ideas we'll explore along the way.

- People began to focus on human potential. They began to see that

Help with Pronunciation

In this book you will encounter words that may be new to you. To help you pronounce those words, we have respelled them to show how you say them. For example, the word *Renaissance* is respelled as (REH-nuh-sahns). The capital letters indicate which syllable to accent. For a closer look at how to pronounce the respelled words, see the Pronunciation Guide on page 712.

Right: Civilizations meet as the ruler of Calicut, on India's southwest coast, receives a newcomer, the Portuguese explorer Vasco da Gama, who had sailed all the way to India. Here da Gama presents a letter from the king of Portugal to the Indian ruler.

Below: Eighteenth-century English scientists demonstrate a device that showed the motion of the planets in the solar system. The light shining on the onlookers' faces comes from a lamp that represents the sun.

human beings can achieve marvelous things. As the Renaissance progressed, people created great art and great literature. They also began to question many long-held beliefs about their religions and religious leaders.

- Europeans embarked on bold voyages of exploration. By the end of the sixteenth century, human beings had charted the globe. More and more, they moved from one continent to another. Civilizations long kept apart met head-on—sometimes with disastrous consequences.

- People began to focus on the here and now. They gained confidence in the power of human reason to understand and improve the world. Curious people probed and explored the natural world, and developed science as we know it.

- The city-states, kingdoms, and empires of old times gradually became modern-day nations. The small manors and fiefdoms that dotted Europe in the Middle Ages disappeared. Old empires fell apart. Powerful nation-states with their own governments, industries, and laws emerged. The most powerful nations colonized peoples in distant lands. Colonized peoples longed for independence, and often fought for it.

- Back in the Middle Ages, lords, princes, kings, and emperors had been in charge. But if ordinary people had the potential to think well and choose wisely, why should they bow to those rulers? More and more people began to

insist that they had rights, that governments should protect those rights, and that government should represent the people. Some nations began to follow democratic principles and experiment with republican government—that is, government by leaders chosen by the people.

- As nations followed democratic principles and embraced new ideas about human dignity, people began to speak about—and sometimes fight for—liberty and human rights.

- New ideas about freedom led to new ideas about business, trade, and profit. More people asked, "Why should kings, queens, and powerful governments set all the economic rules and enjoy most of the rewards?" In some lands, businesses took the lead in changing lives and reshaping the world.

- Science and industry made huge and rapid strides. New machines harnessed powers that helped people accomplish more than ever. New technologies sped up transportation and communication, so that what happened in one part of the world rapidly affected another. These technologies also changed the way many people lived and worked, bringing both progress and problems for millions.

In this book, we'll make our way to 1914, a very important year. It's the year in which, in a sense, the world grew smaller. In 1914,

the Panama Canal opened, offering a speedy shortcut between the Atlantic and Pacific Oceans. From one hemisphere to the next, people, goods, and ideas moved faster than ever before. The year 1914 also marked the beginning of the First World War, an international catastrophe of huge proportions. Nations collided and the terrible results changed almost everyone's life.

In this book, we'll walk right up to the edge of that catastrophe. The story to that point is often one of optimism, progress, and confidence, as well as some *hubris*, or overconfidence. Pride, as they say, goeth before a fall.

The big ideas that help explain our modern world emerge into sharp focus between the fourteenth and the twentieth centuries. This six-hundred year period in our human odyssey introduces us not just to life as it was, but to life as it is.

Suffragists march through the streets of London in 1908 to demand the right to vote. The women's suffrage movement was one of many modern movements to extend basic political rights to all citizens.

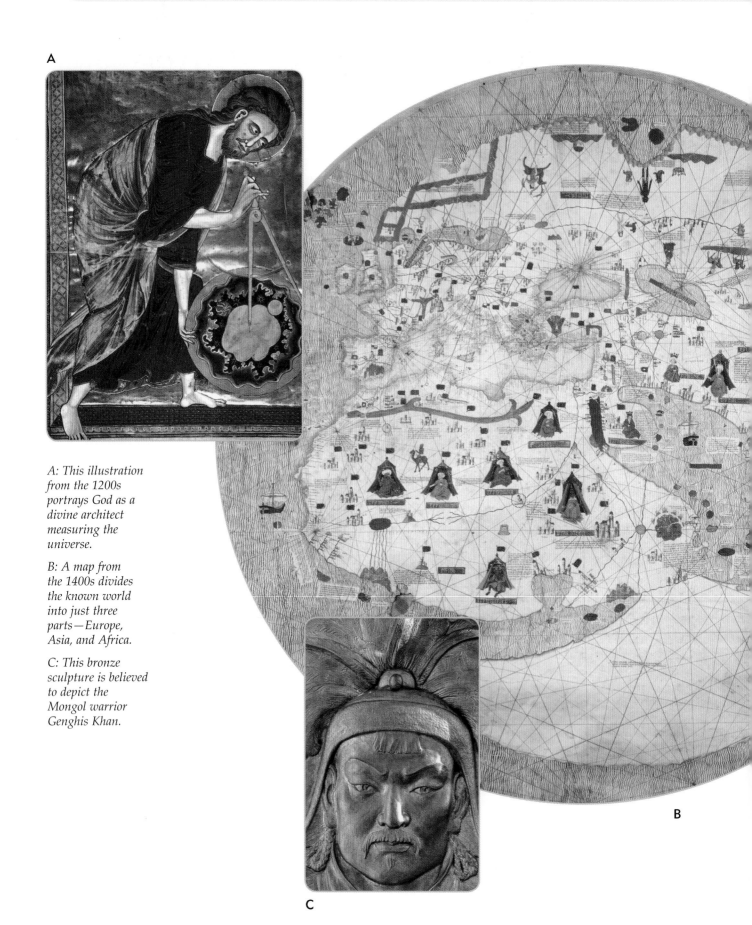

A: This illustration from the 1200s portrays God as a divine architect measuring the universe.

B: A map from the 1400s divides the known world into just three parts—Europe, Asia, and Africa.

C: This bronze sculpture is believed to depict the Mongol warrior Genghis Khan.

The World in 1400: A Backward Glance

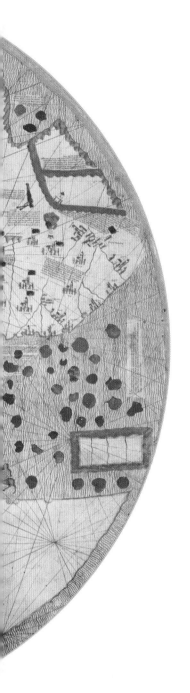

A wise novelist once wrote, "The past is a foreign country: they do things differently there." He was right. Imagine you had a time capsule that could carry you to any place on the globe in 1400. You'd find a world that looks, in some ways, much like ours today—the same seas, continents, mountains, and rivers. But if you zoomed back six hundred years to the exact place you are living now, you'd find different language, different dress, different buildings, different borders, different customs, different laws, different problems, and different hopes.

What was this past world like? In the last volume of *The Human Odyssey*, we learned that the medieval period was an "age of faith." In large parts of the world, religion was the bond that united people. To understand many of the important borders, buildings, customs, and hopes in 1400, you need to know how the course of events was shaped by two major religions—Christianity and Islam.

The Christian faith united most people in Europe. Islam united much of Arabia, as well as parts of Asia and Africa. Let's tour the domains joined by those faiths, and then look at a great empire beyond their borders.

The Realm of "Christendom"

In the late Middle Ages, western Europe was divided like a jigsaw puzzle, with some big pieces, and many small. There were a few large kingdoms and empires. There were many small territories ruled by princes and dukes. And there were a handful of independent city-states and republics.

Rival kings sat on the thrones of France, England, and Spain.

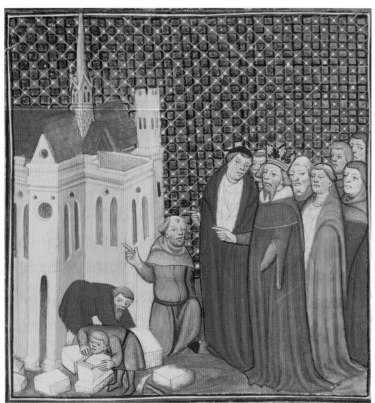

A blue-robed king and a group of Church officials supervise construction of a monastery north of Paris. During the late Middle Ages, the Church oversaw construction of many monasteries and cathedrals in Europe.

A Holy Roman Emperor ruled German and Austrian lands. Merchant families headed city-states in Germany and Italy.

But an invisible thread bound these realms to each other, and back to ancient Rome. That thread was the Christian faith.

Christianity, the religion based on the life and teachings of Jesus Christ, had become the official religion of the Roman Empire by the end of the fourth century. When Rome fell, Christianity's influence grew. Amid the chaos of war waged by Germanic tribes, Christian missionaries spread the gospel or "good news" of their religion.

Fanning out through Europe, monks started monasteries and schools. They protected ancient manuscripts from nomadic tribes roaming the land and fighting for territory. Bishops oversaw the building of cathedrals. Priests worked among common folk on manors and in cities. For leadership, bishops and priests looked to the city of Rome. There, the pope headed the growing Christian Church.

As time went on, the importance of the Christian Church grew, though not all Europeans in 1400 were Christian. Jewish communities thrived in some places. And parts of southern Spain lay under Muslim rule. But most Europeans at this time were Christians. In fact, most people did not speak of living in "Europe." Instead, they referred to this vast region as "Christendom" (KRIH-suhn-duhm).

In 1400, Christendom stretched from Portugal and Spain in the west

The Realm of Christendom, c. 1400

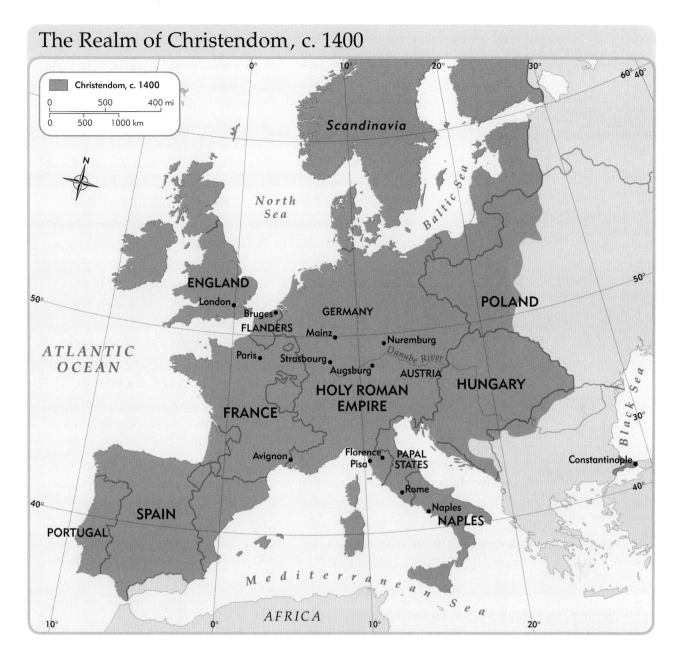

Christendom, c. 1400

to Poland and Hungary in the east. It reached from Scandinavia in the north to Naples at the heel of the Italian peninsula in the south.

The leader of the Christian Church, the pope, grew very powerful. Kings, princes, and dukes listened to what the pope had to say. The pope had his own court and secretaries. He even ruled a large territory on the Italian peninsula known as the Papal States.

By 1309, the papacy—that is, the office of the pope—had grown too powerful to suit some of Europe's royalty. The French king wanted more influence in Church affairs, so he managed to move the papacy from Rome to the city of Avignon (ah-vee-NYAHN), at the edge of France. For more than 75 years, popes resided at Avignon under the watchful eyes of the French court. It was the first time in more than a thousand years that western Europe's Christian Church was not centered in Rome.

When a pope finally managed to move back to Rome, the French

Sometimes, as in the title of the map above, you will see the abbreviation *c.* before dates. It stands for the Latin word *circa*, meaning "about" or "around," and indicates that a date is approximate.

king decided to create a *second* pope. For four decades, two popes—one in Avignon and one in Rome—argued about who was the real leader of the Christian Church in Europe. A Church council tried to settle the dispute and ended up creating a third challenger. This split, called the Great Schism (SKIH-zuhm), lasted until 1417 and weakened the Church.

• On the map on page 17, note the extent of Christendom. Locate Rome and Avignon.

At the end of the Middle Ages, Christendom was a troubled realm. The Christian Church, supposedly the heart of unity, squabbled over its leaders—one pope in Avignon, another in Rome, a third in the Italian city of Pisa (PEE-zuh).

To make matters worse, famine stalked the continent; many people died of starvation. And Europe was just recovering from a deadly plague that had wiped out a third of the continent's population. Cities had been hardest hit by this "Black Death." In many towns, more than half the people had died because of this terrible epidemic.

War raged too, as England and France fought their Hundred Years' War. These two kingdoms had learned about gunpowder, which had been invented by the Chinese. The English and French soon introduced cannons into their battles. Once invincible castles now crumbled into rubble.

All of these events—famine, plague, warfare, and religious infighting—shook the medieval world to its core. Some people believed that these catastrophes showed God's displeasure with man. They worried about the state of Christendom.

But western Europe was not the only Christian domain.

The Flickering Light of Byzantium

To the east of Europe lay another center of Christian life and culture—the Byzantine (BIH-zn-teen) Empire, also known as Byzantium. Byzantium rose to power during the early Middle Ages, when the vast Roman Empire split into two parts—east and west. The eastern part became the Byzantine Empire.

The Byzantine Empire straddled Europe and Asia. Ambitious emperors, such as Constantine and Justinian, expanded the empire. At one time Byzantium included Asia Minor, Greece, the eastern Mediterranean, and parts of southern Italy. Greek was the dominant language in this part of the world.

Anguished survivors mourn relatives killed by the plague in this detail from a stained glass window at Canterbury Cathedral in England.

The Byzantine Empire, c. 1025–1400

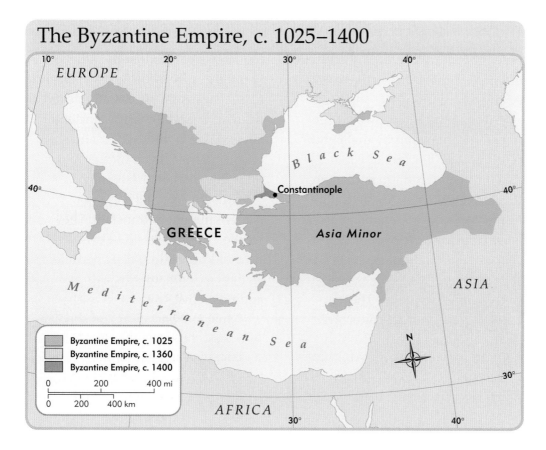

The Byzantine Empire became a center of trade. The markets and bazaars of the capital city, Constantinople, boasted silk, spices, and gems from far parts of the world.

Scholarship thrived in Byzantium. When nomadic tribes threatened western Europe in the early Middle Ages, many learned men moved east to Byzantium. Later, when Muslim armies pressed from the south and east, more scholars fled to Byzantium. Between the ninth and eleventh centuries, Byzantium stood as a great protective barrier, shielding western Europe from Muslim armies.

Byzantium's founding emperor, Constantine, had been the first Roman emperor to convert to Christianity. The Christian faith spread in the region. But in time, the bishop of Constantinople, called the patriarch, insisted that he—not the pope in Rome—was the leader of the eastern Church.

In 1054, the eastern and western branches of the Christian Church split. The eastern branch became known as the Eastern Orthodox Church, headed by the patriarch in Constantinople. The western branch became known as the Roman Catholic Church, headed by the pope in Rome.

The map above shows the Byzantine Empire. By 1400, the empire was very much reduced in size. Constantinople and a small area to its west were all that remained of Byzantium. Much of the once mighty empire had been taken over by warriors inspired by another faith—Islam.

The Muslim World

The religion of Islam was born in the early Middle Ages. This religion, based on the life and teachings of the

Catholic means "universal." The title was more a hope than reality. People often called the Christian Church in Europe "the Roman Church" or "the Latin Church" to distinguish it from the Eastern Church.

seventh-century leader Muhammad, united several warring tribes of the Arabian Peninsula.

At first, the Islamic world centered on Arabia. But by the eighth century, the followers of Islam, called Muslims, dominated an area that stretched from Arabia to Palestine, Syria, Mesopotamia, Persia, North Africa, and Spain.

Religious and political rulers called caliphs (KAY-luhfs) headed the dynamic new faith. They encouraged art and architecture. Under the Abbasid (uh-BA-sid) dynasty, Muslims moved their capital to the city of Baghdad on the Tigris River.

Islam was a religion that prized learning. By the ninth century, Baghdad rivaled Constantinople for its scholarship and wealth. In the House of Wisdom, Baghdad's famous library, Muslim, Jewish, and Christian scholars translated texts from all over the world—ancient Greek texts in philosophy and science, Indian texts on mathematics, Persian works on astronomy.

Muslim scholars were not content merely to translate. They worked hard to advance every field of knowledge. They became leaders in mathematics, astronomy, and medicine.

Muslim translation and scholarship was not limited to Baghdad. Among the many Muslim cities with large research libraries were Damascus in Syria, Timbuktu in Mali, and Cordoba in Spain. The Muslim world helped keep learning alive at a time when much of Europe endured chaos and warfare.

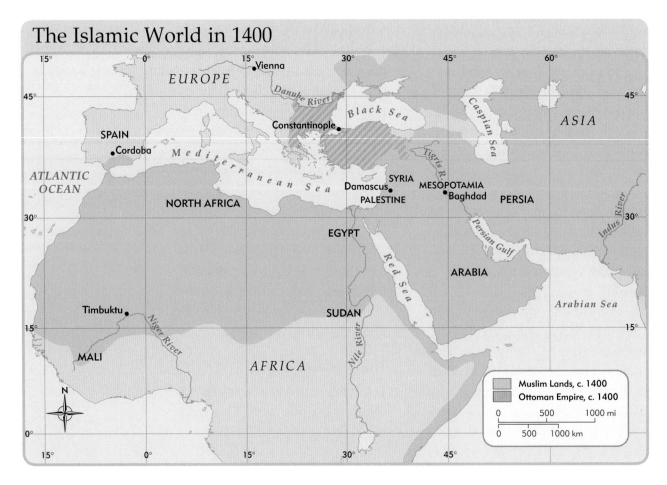

The Islamic World in 1400

EUROPE
Vienna
Danube River
Black Sea
Caspian Sea
ASIA
Constantinople
SPAIN
Cordoba
Mediterranean Sea
ATLANTIC OCEAN
SYRIA
Damascus
MESOPOTAMIA
Baghdad
PERSIA
Tigris R.
Indus River
NORTH AFRICA
PALESTINE
EGYPT
Persian Gulf
Red Sea
ARABIA
Arabian Sea
Timbuktu
Niger River
SUDAN
Nile River
MALI
AFRICA

N

Muslim Lands, c. 1400
Ottoman Empire, c. 1400

0   500   1000 mi
0   500 1000 km

The vast Islamic Empire included a large swath of northern Africa. Farther south, the great warrior federation of Mali embraced Islam as well. In 1400, Timbuktu, a great Muslim city on the Niger River, boasted a research library and a fine mosque. On the east African coast, Egypt and the Sudan traded with the Muslim world and counted many followers of Islam.

- On the map on page 20, locate the following cities in the Islamic world: Baghdad, Damascus, Timbuktu, and Cordoba.

Crusades and Conflicts

The spread of Islam sparked resistance from the Christian world. In 1095, the pope called for Christians to join in a holy war against the Muslims. Thus began a series of wars called the Crusades. For two hundred years, Christians and Muslims engaged in a terrible and bloody tug-of-war, with no real winner.

In 1400, the borders of the Islamic world were changing. In the west, the Spanish and Portuguese were struggling to expel the Muslim conquerors they called "Moors." But in other parts of the Mediterranean and in the east, Muslim power was growing. Turkish Muslim tribes competed for power, and a new tribe called the Ottoman Turks was building a strong empire. You'll learn more about the Ottoman Empire later in this book.

By 1400, the Ottoman Turks were eating away at what remained of the Byzantine Empire. They made

Europeans nervous by threatening the great cities of Constantinople and Vienna. And they were making another group nervous—the Mongols.

The Mighty Mongols

In the early thirteenth century, fierce horsemen came thundering out of the grassy plains of Mongolia behind their leader, Genghis Khan (JEHNG-gihs KAHN). Soon they were conquering an empire.

The Mongols pounded into northern China, breaching the Great Wall. They became the first foreigners to conquer the Chinese. Under Kublai Khan (KOO-bluh KAHN), one of Genghis Khan's grandsons, the Yuan (you-EN) dynasty ruled a huge east Asian empire. It included China and Korea. Kublai Khan's armies also invaded Burma and Vietnam.

While an adult visitor looks on, a cane-wielding teacher instructs students in a mosque, or Muslim house of worship. Islam places a high value on education.

The Mongol Empire, c. 1400

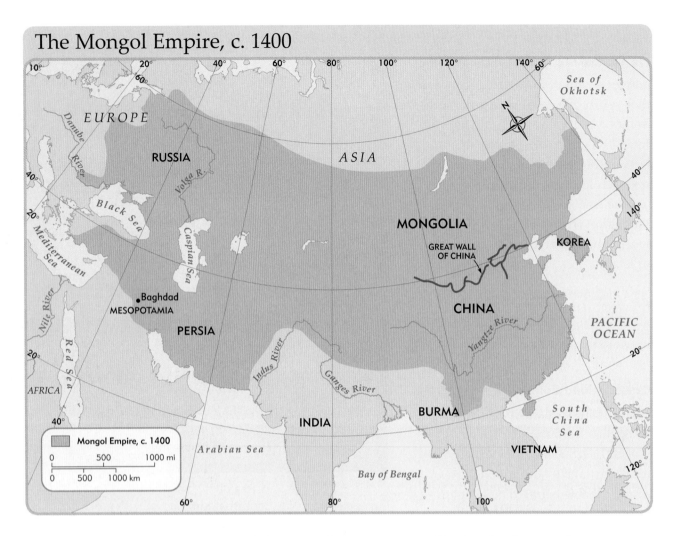

The Mongols began pushing west. They charged into Russia, destroying whole towns in their path. The Russians called these invaders "Tatars" (TAH-tuhrz).

The unstoppable Mongols also swept into Muslim lands to the west. They overwhelmed Persia and Mesopotamia. In 1258, they captured Baghdad, slaying the caliph and hundreds of thousands of his followers. By 1350, the mounted warriors ruled the largest land empire in all of history—before or since.

The Mongols' empire did not last long. They had a hard time ruling their vast domain. Unlike the Romans centuries before, they weren't skilled at running the machinery of government.

During the fourteenth century, the Mongols faced challenges in all parts of their empire. The Chinese expelled the Mongol Yuan dynasty. The Russians plotted to overthrow their Tatar masters. Ottoman Turks in Asia Minor grew restless under Mongol rule.

Meanwhile the Europeans, who were recovering from a terrible century of war and plague, prayed that Mongol horsemen would not get past the Danube River. They got their wish. By the beginning of the fifteenth century, the huge Mongol Empire had fallen apart.

- On the map above, note the extent of the Mongol Empire by about 1400. Locate Mongolia.

On the Eve of Change

Our quick glance back at the Middle Ages reveals a time of both disasters and triumphs.

Christians clashed with Muslims in long and bloody wars. Mongol warriors spread destruction wherever their horses carried them. In Europe, England and France clashed in the Hundred Years' War. Indeed, war was a constant fact of life in the Middle Ages. Besides the constant fighting, both famine and plague spread death across Europe in the fourteenth century.

At the same time, great cathedrals and new universities rose in Europe. Despite the plague's devastation, cities were showing new signs of life in Italy, Germany, and other regions. They were turning into bustling centers of business, trade, and learning. Merchants moved between Europe, North Africa, the Middle East, and Asia, carrying both goods and new knowledge wherever they traveled.

Great tragedies and triumphs almost always change civilizations in profound ways. That's what happened in Europe during the fourteenth century. That era's upheavals and achievements set the stage for changes that would profoundly affect world history.

Let's turn now to meet two people who lived and worked at the end of the Middle Ages. Their work tells us much about what mattered to people of the times, and in what way Europe was about to be reborn. The continent was moving from the Middle Ages to the age we call the Renaissance.

The spires and stone saints of Italy's Milan Cathedral soar into the night sky. By the end of the Middle Ages, cathedrals had become a symbol of the Christian faith throughout Europe.

Italian artist Sandro Botticelli celebrated the theme of new life or rebirth in Primavera (Spring). *The Renaissance painting was inspired by a myth from classical Greece and Rome.*

Europe Reborn: Rediscovering Greece and Rome

Renaissance—say it aloud. It's a melodic word. It seems full of newness, promise, and hope. We use the term *Renaissance* to identify an important period in the history of Europe, from the late 1300s to the early 1600s, a time of extraordinary artistic and literary creativity.

Renaissance is the French word for "rebirth." What was reborn in Europe during the Renaissance? For one thing, a keen interest in something very old—the classical civilizations of Greece and Rome.

That reborn interest in ancient civilizations led people to learn and create in new ways. Eager scholars hunted for lost Greek and Latin works. Poets wrote elegant verse inspired by ancient Greek and Latin models. Architects, painters, and sculptors created a new world by studying an old one that had been long forgotten. From something old, something new was born.

In history, however, "newness" rarely happens overnight. New directions and big changes build slowly. And in this case, the newness of the Renaissance had been building through the 1300s.

The fourteenth century was in many ways a calamitous time, with its wars and plagues. But it was also a century of creativity and change.

In this chapter, we'll look at two brilliant individuals who stood between the medieval and modern worlds—Dante Alighieri (DAHN-tay ah-luh-GYEH-ree) and Francesco Petrarca, known to history as Petrarch (PEH-trahrk). Their work pointed back

This chapter focuses on Europe at the outset of the Renaissance.

Dante Alighieri stands at the threshold of a new era. The book he holds may well be his literary masterpiece, The Divine Comedy.

to what was old and forward to something new. They ushered in the Renaissance and showed the ways in which the world was changing.

Dante: Banished and Searching

"In the middle of my life, I came to a dark wood." Those words begin one of the greatest books of all time, *The Divine Comedy*, by the Italian poet Dante Alighieri.

The Divine Comedy tells the story of a spiritual journey, an imagined voyage from hell to heaven. Why a "comedy"? Because back then a comedy was any work with a happy ending, and Dante's poem had a joyful conclusion indeed.

The Divine Comedy is much more than one poet's ideas about the afterlife. It reveals a great deal about the times in which Dante lived. They were in many ways "a dark wood."

Dante Alighieri grew up in the Italian city-state of Florence, a town the poet's Roman ancestors had helped to found. Dante loved Florence and its civic life. Like many educated men of his time, he wanted to serve his city. In 1300, he held a high government office.

But politics got him into trouble. When Florentines suspected the ambitious pope of trying to extend his reign over Florence, they sent

Dante to Rome as an ambassador. Pope Boniface (BAHN-uh-fuhs) VIII did have designs on Florence. He held Dante in Rome against his will, while the pope's friends gained control of Florence.

Dante's rivals banished him from Florence and condemned him to death should he return. Deeply saddened, Dante spent the rest of his life in painful exile from the city-state he loved.

At 37, Dante had lost his home and his career. An outlaw, he had to travel from town to town. The bleak mountain roads were dangerous, overgrown with thickets, briars, and trees that hid thieves. Many times Dante did not even understand the people around him, for no common language united the people of Italy, who spoke more than 36 different dialects.

Still, Dante's exile was not without its blessings. For years he had been writing beautiful verse. Now poetry became his passion. He turned his exile into a life of writing poetry.

As he wandered lonely paths, Dante wondered if he was like the ancient Roman hero Aeneas (ih-NEE-us). Aeneas was the hero of the *Aeneid* (uh-NEE-id), an epic by the greatest poet of ancient Rome, Virgil (70–19 B.C.). Educated men of Dante's time were well acquainted with the *Aeneid*. They knew the story of how Aeneas fled the burning city of Troy after the Trojan War, how he set forth on uncharted waters, how he endured many trials and eventually did something great—he founded the city that would become Rome.

Dante did not know if greatness was in store for him, but he wanted

Dante's Comedy: Why "Divine"?

When Dante wrote his great poem, he gave it the title *La Commedia*, which means "The Comedy" in Italian. People loved the work so much that they began calling it "The Divine Comedy," a name that has stuck throughout history.

to find meaning in his exile and in his life. He found that meaning through poetry.

Writing *The Divine Comedy*

Dante was no stranger to verse. He came from a noble family and enjoyed a good education. He grew up studying Christian thinkers as well as Roman writers such as Livy, Cicero, and the great Virgil. Dante knew Latin well and spent hours absorbing its rhythm and form.

The young man had also experienced something very important for writing poetry—he had fallen in love! Long before his exile, he wrote love poetry about a beautiful young woman from Florence named Beatrice, whom he had met when they were both children.

Dante saw Beatrice only twice in his life. She died before Dante was exiled, and the poet idealized her for the rest of his life. He called her "a creature come from heaven to earth." His thoughts turned to Beatrice in dozens of verses, including his masterpiece, *The Divine Comedy*.

Around 1308, Dante began writing that great work. Like most Europeans, Dante was a Christian who placed his hope in eternal life. But in times so evil, who would gain eternal life? Greedy officials of the Church? Scheming politicians and self-seeking bankers? For a dozen years or more, Dante wrestled with those questions in *The Divine Comedy*.

The "comedy" certainly does not begin happily. Its first part is called *Inferno*. Dante finds himself lost in a dark wood, frightened by savage beasts. Mysteriously, the ancient Roman poet Virgil appears and offers to be his guide. In Dante's poem, Virgil embodies the power of reason. Together the two poets descend into the Inferno, or Hell.

There Dante and Virgil meet souls eternally condemned for the sins they had committed during their earthly lives. They meet traitors,

The Divine Comedy *tells the story of Dante's imagined journey from hell to heaven. In this illustration from* Inferno, *the first part of the book, the poet encounters some wild beasts. Behind him stands his guide, the Roman poet Virgil.*

murderers, robbers, liars, heretics, and more. Some are tossed about in the dark air, some imprisoned in fiery tombs, some stranded in hot, dry deserts. Others suffer a constant storm of snow and hail, or roll huge rocks this way and that.

Many of the sinners are figures from history, such as Brutus and Cassius, two of the ancient Romans who killed Julius Caesar. Dante also put many people from his own day into his poem's Hell, including corrupt popes, politicians, and merchants.

The second part of *The Divine Comedy* is called *Purgatorio* (puhr-guh-TOHR-ee-oh), or Purgatory, which comes from a Latin word meaning "to purify." In Dante's time, all Christians believed that Purgatory was a place between Heaven and Hell for souls that were not yet ready to go to Heaven. In Purgatory, Dante and Virgil climb a mountain and meet souls being purified of their sins so that they might enter Heaven.

On the mountain's summit, Dante bids farewell to Virgil, who has brought him as far as reason can go. Now, in the third part of Dante's poem, *Paradiso* (pah-rah-DEE-zoh), or Paradise, Dante's childhood love, Beatrice, becomes his guide. Beatrice leads Dante up through the stars to a world of light where saints and angels dwell. Then even she must bid Dante farewell, as a great medieval saint named Bernard leads Dante to God.

Dante's radiant Heaven is a place of perfect happiness and peace where souls behold God. It is the complete satisfaction of all desires. Dante, who knew so little of the perfect happiness he imagined, died within weeks of writing the final verses of his great poem.

Dante's Legacy

When *The Divine Comedy* first appeared in 1321, scholars immediately recognized its brilliance. They said Dante was *il poeta divino,* the poet from heaven.

The Divine Comedy dealt with matters that were important to thoughtful people of the late Middle Ages. It showed a deep Christian faith in a life after death. Virgil's Aeneas left his beloved Troy to found a new earthly city, Rome. Dante, banished from Florence, looked for his reward in a *heavenly* city. Like most medieval Christians, Dante saw life as a trial to be endured, and heaven as the goal of earthly strivings.

But in writing his great poem, Dante was not just looking to heaven. He was also taking some bold new steps in this earthly world. To begin with, Dante wrote in Italian. He was from the Italian city-state of Florence, so why is it surprising that he wrote in Italian? Because during the Middle Ages, all philosophical writing was in Latin. Dante, however, had walked his native land and heard its many dialects. He believed that Italian was a beautiful tongue, worthy of great poets.

Dante and the Italian Language

In Dante's time, the people of Italy spoke many different dialects, or versions, of the Italian language. *The Divine Comedy* helped change that. People all over Italy read and loved the poem, which was written in a Florentine dialect. Its popularity helped make the Florentine dialect into what we now know as the Italian language.

What else was new about *The Divine Comedy*? In most early medieval poems, the characters were abstract figures that represented virtues or vices. For example, there might be characters named Beauty and Knowledge, or Gluttony and Envy. But Dante's characters are individuals, real people with their own pasts. Dante paints each character in colorful detail. He shines a light on recognizable people and problems of his age. We meet scheming politicians, and popes who sought to win land rather than souls.

Dante may have looked on earthly life as a trial and a prelude to eternal life, but he also took the things of this life very seriously. His use of Italian, his rich portrayal of recognizable individuals, and his denunciation of the evils he saw

around him were all part of a new attitude in the late Middle Ages—a heightened concern for this world, for the here and now.

Giotto: An Artist Between Two Worlds

Like Dante, the artist Giotto di Bondone (JAWT-toh dee bohn-DOH-nay) stood between two eras. A fellow Florentine, he painted during the same period in which his friend Dante penned *The Divine Comedy*. And like Dante, he came to be known by just his first name—Giotto.

Giotto's paintings show an artist breaking away from old styles. Like all the great medieval artists, he chose religious subject matter. He painted scenes from the Bible and from the lives of the saints. His figures wore glowing halos and radiated a quiet calm.

Much medieval art depicted flat figures. The faces in these paintings showed little expression or individual personality. But Giotto took a different approach. He painted rounded, lifelike figures. His subjects were individuals. He placed them in natural-looking settings and showed realistic details, such as the folds of clothing.

Just as Dante's characters were real, fleshed-out individuals, Giotto's subjects revealed recognizable human emotions in their stance and in their faces. Whether weeping, questioning, or seeking counsel, they breathed life from the canvas.

In his art Giotto celebrated nature and the human form. He is often hailed as the pathbreaker for Renaissance painting.

The Lamentation of Christ, *painted about 1305, shows Giotto's realistic style.*

Petrarch Seeks Classical Wisdom

One name more than any other stands for the time of change in Europe from the Middle Ages to the Renaissance—Francesco Petrarca, or Petrarch, as the name has been translated. Petrarch was nearly 40 years younger than Dante. Like Dante, his family had been exiled from Florence during one of the city-state's many vicious feuds.

Petrarch was born in 1304 in a small town in Italy. A few years later he moved with his family to the pope's court, which was then in Avignon. Petrarch's father, a lawyer, was determined to see his son take up his profession. At age 12, Petrarch found himself studying law. But the young scholar loved nature and the great outdoors, and he soon fell under the spell of classical poetry and literature.

Petrarch lived in an exciting time. Scholars were discovering translations of classical works that had been lost for centuries. Petrarch was drawn to the great Roman poets. He spent all his money on books of Latin poetry and any works he could find by the Roman statesman Cicero. The young man was enchanted by classical writers' use of language. Latin was still the language used in many documents, but medieval Latin seemed clumsy and stiff next to classical works. Petrarch loved the precision and power of classical Latin.

Petrarch's father did not share this passion for the classics. When he discovered his son's treasures, he threw the books into a fire. Petrarch's sobs moved his father to rescue two volumes from the flames, one by the poet Virgil and the other by Cicero. "Here," said the father to his son, "keep this one for the sake of a little recreation now and then, and this other one to help you study the law."

When Petrarch's father died, the young man quickly abandoned his legal studies. A year after his father's death, when Petrarch was 23 years old, he caught sight of a beautiful young lady in church. At once he fell in love with her. But it seems that the woman, named Laura, was already married. So, just as Dante had written about his unattainable Beatrice, Petrarch had to content himself with writing poems about his distant idol, Laura.

Eventually, Petrarch decided to become a priest. Being a clergyman gave him the opportunity to travel, study classical literature, and write for the rest of his life. Over the years, even after he became a priest, he wrote hundreds of love poems, some in Latin but most, like Dante's

Petrarch sits with a crown of laurel leaves on his head and one of his beloved books on his lap in this fifteenth-century portrait. Following a custom from classical times, the Roman Senate awarded Petrarch the crown in honor of his poetry.

Where Were the Classical Texts Coming From?

In the late 1200s and 1300s, more and more ancient Greek and Latin texts were becoming available in Europe. As Spanish and Portuguese armies drove the Moors off the Iberian peninsula, Christian scholars inherited Muslim libraries full of classical manuscripts. As the Ottoman Turks pressed on Byzantium, Greek scholars fled west, especially to Italy, carrying classical texts with them. And many classical works had been in European monasteries all along. Scholars now read them with a new, appreciative eye.

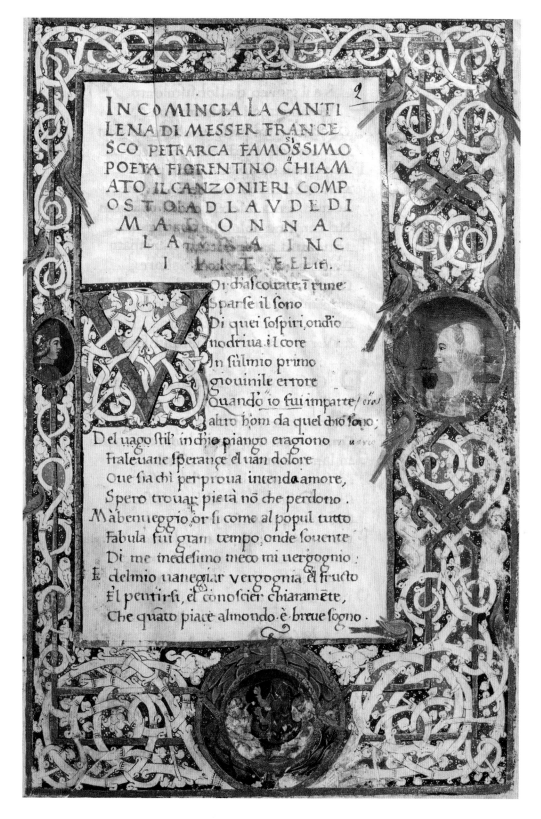

IN COMINCIA LA CANTI
LENA DI MESSER FRANCE
SCO PETRARCA FAMOSSIMO
POETA FIORENTINO CHIAM
ATO IL CANZONIERI COMP
OSTO AD LAVDE DI
MADONNA
LAVRA INC

An elaborately illustrated page from a book of Petrarch's poems depicts a beautiful young woman named Laura. Petrarch first saw her in church and immediately fell in love with her. He penned hundreds of love poems, most of them in Italian.

verses, in Italian. He wanted to make contemporary Italian as eloquent as ancient Latin.

Petrarch wrote poems praising Laura's beauty and grace. He wrote poems about the beauty of nature. Inspired by the classical past, he wrote biographies about the heroes of ancient Rome. The more he wrote, the more his reputation spread.

In 1341, Petrarch traveled to Rome to be honored by its citizens. The Roman Senate awarded him a prize for his poetry, a crown of laurel leaves. Crowning heroes with wreaths of leaves was a custom from classical times. Petrarch gave a speech calling for a rebirth of classical wisdom and poetry. He then carried his wreath through the city and laid it on the tomb of Saint Peter—a gesture that showed his debt as a scholar to both Christian and classical heritages.

On the Move

Petrarch was a man who made friends easily, and that made him an excellent diplomat. He traveled from city to city—Milan (muh-LAHN), Naples, Venice, Florence, Verona—on errands for bishops and princes. "I am always on the alert," he wrote, "for new and uncalled-for undertakings, so distasteful to me is sleep and dreary repose."

Petrarch worked for the pope and was deeply discouraged with what he saw. "You can see with your own eyes what this new Babylon really is," he wrote of the papal court at Avignon. It was "seething, obscene, terrible. Whatever perfidy and fraud, whatever cruelty and arrogance, whatever shamelessness and unbridled lust you have heard of … you may see heaped up there."

Although he hated the corruption of the papal court, Petrarch still undertook difficult missions for the pope. In 1348, one of the years the Black Death devastated Italy, Petrarch traveled the Italian peninsula on a papal mission.

He saw many around him die and learned that the plague had killed his beloved Laura.

Petrarch's experiences saddened him. Increasingly, he found comfort by turning to his favorite classical writers. He wrote letters to the ghosts of Cicero, Virgil, Homer, and other ancient figures he loved. To the historian Livy, he wrote, "I would wish that I had been born in your age."

Surely, he did his best to recover that glorious classical age. Traveling gave Petrarch the chance to search for ancient manuscripts with the zeal of a treasure-hunter. He concentrated on finding missing Latin texts. Petrarch loved visiting monastery libraries and scouring the musty shelves. He found and copied long-lost works of Cicero and Livy. More and more, he became convinced that the ancient thinkers of Greece and Rome could help restore wisdom and virtue to his troubled world.

The Father of Humanism

Petrarch proposed a new educational program that emphasized the classics and became known as "humanism." Humanism emphasized the value of the classics—for example, the epics of Homer and philosophic writings of Plato. Petrarch believed that in the search for virtue and truth, all knowledge was useful, including the wisdom of the classical writers. No one, said Petrarch, had ever surpassed the ancient writers' mastery of grammar, rhetoric, poetry, history, and philosophy.

Petrarch, a devout Christian, believed that even though the

Babylon was the capital of the kingdom of Babylonia and one of the great cities of the ancient world. Over time, the term *Babylon* also came to mean a city where people care mainly about riches and pleasure.

classical writers lived before the time of Christ, their works could help educate good Christians. In fact, he believed that the ancients—with their respect for human abilities and potential—often taught the path to virtue better than Church leaders.

Petrarch saw no conflict between two views. He held the Christian view that this world is a place in which to prepare for the life to come. At the same time, he held the classical view that humans are noble creatures. Petrarch believed that God had endowed human beings with the ability and freedom to accomplish great things.

In Petrarch's humanistic view, God had created the world and set humans at the very center to do great things until they passed on to the next life. In these verses, Petrarch describes what he believed God had given to human beings:

> Thou hast given him a visage commanding and serene, and a spirit that may know thee and contemplate that which is celestial.
>
> Thou hast added innumerable arts whereby life may be adorned;
>
> Thou hast given also the hope of eternal life.

Petrarch went on traveling, studying, and working until he was an old man. In 1374, he passed away in his study, his head resting on a manuscript by the Roman poet Virgil.

Petrarch's reputation continued to grow after his death. His fascination with the wisdom of classical

The Greek philosopher Plato is depicted in this fourth-century B.C. marble bust. Plato and other classical thinkers inspired Renaissance humanism.

civilizations spread through Italy. Others on the Italian peninsula began to take up his call to use the light of the past as a guide to a new future.

The Meaning of Humanism

Humanism represented a new concern with human nature and potential. It looked to the classical past for insights about human abilities. It stressed the dignity of man and placed confidence in human potential.

Dear Cicero

Petrarch admired the classical age so much that he often wrote letters to Homer, Virgil, Livy, and other Greek and Roman writers of antiquity. During one of his travels, Petrarch unearthed a lost volume of letters by the Roman statesman Marcus Tullius Cicero. He was delighted. Here are excerpts from letters that Petrarch wrote in 1345 to Cicero. Though Cicero had died some 1400 years before Petrarch's time, the Roman statesman was, in Petrarch's mind, a living presence.

A Page from the Past

Your letters I sought for long and diligently; and finally, where I least expected it, I found them. At once I read them, over and over, with the utmost eagerness. And as I read I seemed to hear your bodily voice, O Marcus Tullius, saying many things, uttering many lamentations, ranging through many phases of thought and feeling. I long had known how excellent a guide you have proved for others; at last I was to learn what sort of guidance you gave yourself. O great father of Roman eloquence! Not I alone but all who deck themselves with the flowers of Latin speech render thanks unto you. It is from your wellsprings that we draw the streams that water our meads. You, we freely acknowledge, are the leader who marshals us; yours are the words of encouragement that sustain us; yours is the light that illumines the path before

Meads are meadows.

Petrarch often wrote letters to Cicero and other figures from classical times.

us. In a word, it is under your auspices that we have attained to such little skill in this art of writing as we may possess....

You have heard what I think of your life and your genius. Are you hoping to hear of your books also; what fate has befallen them, how they are esteemed by the masses and among scholars? They still are in existence, glorious volumes, but we of today are too feeble a folk to read them, or even to be acquainted with their mere titles. Your fame extends far and wide; your name is mighty, and fills the ears of men; and yet those who really know you are very few, be it because the times are unfavorable, or because men's minds are slow and dull, or, as I am the more inclined to believe, because the love of money forces our thoughts in other directions.

Consequently right in our own day, unless I am much mistaken, some of your books have disappeared, I fear beyond recovery. It is a great grief to me, a great disgrace to this generation, a great wrong done to posterity. The shame of failing to cultivate our own talents, thereby depriving the future of the fruits that they might have yielded, is not enough for us; we must waste and spoil, through our cruel and insufferable neglect, the fruits of your labors too, and of those of your fellows as well, for the fate that I lament in the case of your own books has befallen the works of many another illustrious man.

*Renaissance city-states were lively places.
Venice, a port city on the Adriatic Sea, drew
merchants, scholars, bankers, and eager
businessmen. The grand palace of the doge,
the city's ruler, stands in the background.*

Cities Spur Change

Dante, Giotto, Petrarch—these three giants who pointed the way to the Renaissance had something important in common. They were all city-folk.

Dante grew up in Florence. During his exile he traveled from city to city, venturing as far as Paris. Giotto painted not just in Florence, but also in Rome, Assisi (uh-SEE-see), Padua (PAH-dyou-wuh), and Naples. Petrarch visited many great European cities—Avignon, Rome, Florence, Venice, and Paris.

If the medieval world had been shaped by the manor, the Renaissance world was forged by cities. Most of these cities lay in northern Italy, surrounded by ruins of the ancient Roman Empire. Renaissance Italy was a patchwork quilt of city-states. Many were centers of trade and commerce, linked to distant lands by that all-important waterway, the Mediterranean Sea.

Farther north, cities also prospered, including Paris in France and Bruges in Flanders. German city-states like Augsburg, Nuremberg, and Mainz (miynts) grew at the junctions of rivers. They were connected to each other and to the Italian peninsula by well-traveled roads.

At the end of the Middle Ages, cities had grown rapidly. Some sprouted outside castle walls. Most began as trading posts established by merchants along rivers or seas. The merchants bought charters for the towns from local landholders. These charters guaranteed the towns the right to form their own governments.

By the fourteenth century, ambitious traders, craftsmen, and businessmen were running the towns, independent of local lords. The towns became booming

> The region once called Flanders includes parts of modern-day Belgium, France, and the Netherlands. The adjective *Flemish* means of or having to do with Flanders.

Italian City-States, c. 1450

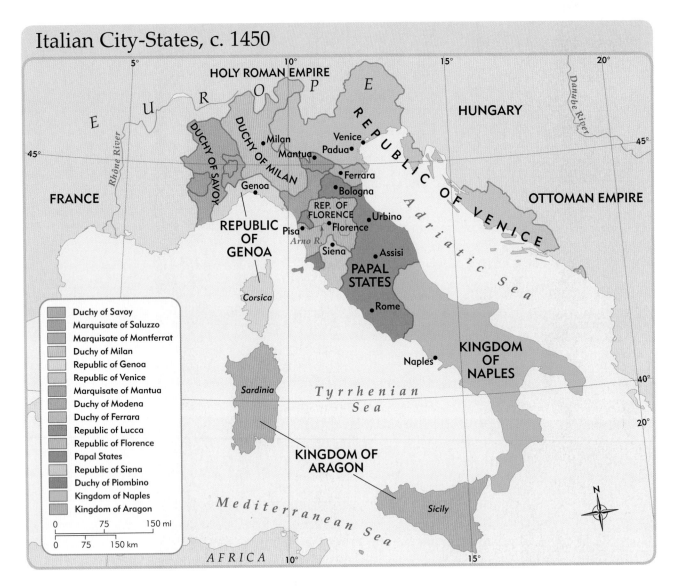

centers of commerce and craftsmanship. They created the conditions for major change.

Europe's Revived Cities

Europeans had long traded with Byzantium and Asia for silk, paper, perfume, gems, and spices. But by the late Middle Ages, European craftsmen were making many things they had once imported.

In Florence, workmen made fine woolens and exquisite silk. In Venice, artisans crafted glass goblets, gleaming mirrors, and eyeglasses. Europe's first paper mills sprang up. Foundries in German cities forged cannons and iron guns. European merchants exported these products to other European cities and to the East.

As trade grew, more people flocked to the cities. Laborers came to build city walls. Cask makers, cart builders, blacksmiths, and

What's a City-State?

A city-state consisted of a principal city where most people resided and the land around it that they claimed. Some city-states were ruled by kings, as in ancient Sumer. Others, such as Athens in ancient Greece, were democracies. Italian city-states in the Renaissance were often republics led by powerful merchant families.

Typical craftsmen and artists of an Italian city are depicted in this mid-fifteenth-century painting. At left (top to bottom) a scribe, two clock-makers, and armorers apply their trades. In the middle, beneath a banquet scene, two cooks prepare food at an oven. At right, a painter, a sculptor, and an organ-maker go about their tasks.

shipwrights plied their trades. Farmers and herders came to cultivate the land and tend their flocks outside the town walls.

At the center of each city, the market square hummed with activity. The shops of tailors, furriers, and barbers lined the square. Bakers, brewers, and butchers sold their treats and meats. In the shadow of the church, troops marched in formation, while nearby, passersby jeered at prisoners in the stocks.

Above all, Renaissance cities were places of business. Money changed hands rapidly and constantly. Craftsmen and merchants wanted to make even more money, so they tried to improve their products or sell something no one else had. Florentine weavers, for example, invented new techniques for dying and weaving wool. Italian and German merchant families came up with new systems of banking. Ambitious merchants and shop-owners competed with each other and with other city-states.

The owners of these businesses and trading ventures grew rich. In many city-states, wealthy families began to build elegant homes. Some patronized artists—that is, they supported the artists by buying their works or paying them to create new works. They were proud of their towns and eager to display their own wealth and importance. So they started to fund town projects, such as a new statue, town hall, or fresco for a chapel. Wealthy merchant families often took a special interest in making their city's church the finest around.

But the great families were never completely sure of their future. Early Renaissance cities were dangerous places. They were crowded, dirty, and unsanitary—conditions just right for the plague. Thieves lurked in wait. And at any given moment, people who were *not* in power were hatching deadly schemes to get rid of people who were in power.

A man carefully measures out gold on a scale while his wife, distracted from her prayer book, looks on in The Banker and His Wife, *painted in 1514 by a northern European artist. Moneylenders helped finance new business ventures and encouraged trade in Europe's thriving cities.*

Guilds and Power Plays

As you've seen with Dante's Florence, self-government was not a peaceful affair. The early charters granted merchants the right to govern as they wished. Some city-states remained republics, electing their leaders. As each city grew, the wealthy competed for power and the chance to run the city-state.

Since medieval times, merchants and tradesmen had organized themselves into associations called "guilds" that set standards for their work and protected their interests. In Florence, wool merchants had one guild, silk weavers another, while druggists, furriers, and bankers each had their own guild. Often important families controlled a single guild. Guild representatives maneuvered for power in city government.

Why did guilds want to influence the city governments? Because those governments decided what improvements to make in churches, markets, town squares, and guild halls. They decided which walls to build, what size militia to raise, which moats and canals to extend, and which roads to pave. All of these decisions would direct wealth to some and away from others. Important families and guilds were willing to fight each other for control over such decisions.

These city-dwellers didn't just fight among themselves. They fought most fiercely against other city-states. Nothing could stop the bickering among Florentines faster than a threatening move by neighboring Siena (see-EH-nah) or Milan. Venetians, who specialized in sinister plots against each other, would

Left: A winged lion—symbol of St. Mark, patron saint of Venice—adorns the city's fifteenth-century clock tower. The Venetians loved lions. Some citizens even kept real ones in their gardens until laws forbade such pets.

Below: The Venetians developed a high-quality, clear glass similar to crystal. This ornate goblet is an example of the fine Venetian glassware that was eagerly sought by wealthy Europeans.

rapidly band together against arch-rival Genoa (JEH-noh-uh).

Let's take a closer look at some of the major city-states in Europe in the 1400s. Most were on the Italian peninsula, but we'll also look at an important city in southern Germany. They were all places of competition, innovation, and dynamic change.

Venice: Lion of a City

Lions were everywhere in Venice—that is, lions carved in stone or covered with gold. That's because the lion was the symbol of the city's patron saint, Saint Mark, the writer of one of the four Christian gospels. Sculptures of lions with pen in paw reminded Venetians of both the might of their empire and the importance of the written word.

Venice was a floating city, a collection of about 120 islands in a sheltered lagoon. Crisscrossing canals served as streets and avenues, all of them pouring into the sea. From its perch on the Adriatic Sea, Venetians could easily

sail to Byzantium and farther east. Venetian ships had once carried supplies to Crusaders and returned home with silk, spices, and gems.

- On the map on page 38, locate Venice.

At the end of the fourteenth century, the Lion City had defeated its rival city-state of Genoa in a series of wars. In the next half-century, wars with Bologna (boh-LOH-nyah) and Milan further expanded Venice's territory. The Venetian empire included trading posts all along the shores of the Adriatic and Mediterranean. Like stepping stones, they reached all the way to the Black Sea. Venice had a monopoly on trade with Byzantium and the Muslim world.

Venetians did not merely import goods. Their workshops turned out beautiful glass for export. To guard the secrets of fine glassmaking, the city moved its entire glass industry to the island of Murano

The Venetian court receives ambassadors from abroad. Venetian prosperity depended on trade, so the city's rulers tried to maintain good relations with other city-states and kingdoms.

(myoo-RAH-noh), where talented artisans turned out richly colored pieces, including glass lanterns gilded with phrases from the Qur'an, for use in mosques in Muslim lands.

The ruler of Venice, called the doge (dohj), negotiated trading agreements with Byzantine and Muslim representatives. The term *doge* comes from the Latin word *dux*, meaning "leader." Since Venice was a republic, its citizens elected the doge, usually from one of the wealthy merchant families. There were about 150 great Venetian families, and the competition among them was fierce, because the stakes were so high. The doge commanded a trading empire. He sent Venetian ambassadors far and wide.

From the east, Venetian ships brought not just luxuries but also scholars. When the Ottoman Turks conquered Constantinople in 1453, many Greek scholars fled west to the welcoming city of Venice. They carried precious ancient manuscripts. In Venice, they found speakers of every language imaginable. Venice was a center of learning, translation, and printing. From all over Europe, eager students of the classics, such as Petrarch, came to see what literary treasures they could find in Venice.

Marco Polo, Son of Venice

The most famous son of Venice was the medieval traveler Marco Polo. He spent more than two decades in the East, but when he returned to Venice in 1295, a life of ease did not await him. The Venetian navy recruited him to fight against Genoa. The Genoese captured him and made him a prisoner.

While in jail, Marco Polo told his cellmate marvelous tales of his journeys to China, India, and beyond. The cellmate persuaded him to put his stories into writing. The result was Marco Polo's famous book, *Description of the World.*

Florence: City on the Arno

A little Roman settlement along the Arno River grew to become the great city-state of Florence. Florence ignited the flame of Renaissance renewal. Like Venice, it was home to nearly a hundred thousand people.

In the 1300s, the city endured fire, flood, and repeated bouts of plague to become the wealthy center of Europe's wool and silk industry.

- On the map on page 38, locate Florence.

As water flows from a fountain, creative genius poured from Florence. Dante was a son of Florence. So was the young painter Giotto, whose lifelike figures opened new possibilities for artists. Petrarch's family, too, had come from Florence.

The Florentine republic was poised for greatness largely because of the efforts of one family—the Medici (MED-uh-chee). The talented and ambitious Medici made their first fortune in cloth manufacture. They imported wool from England and turned it into fine fabric. Their shops wove smooth finished pieces and dyed the rich fabric in vivid shades of scarlet, blue, and crimson.

The Medici turned their profits to good use in another business—banking. By 1422, the Medici operated the largest bank in Europe, with branches in Venice, Rome, Avignon, Bruges, and London.

Throughout the Renaissance, Florence remained a republic, but a republic ripe with plots and infighting. The Medici family competed with rival families. Sometimes members of these rival families tried to assassinate each other.

Each wealthy Florentine family wanted to set itself above the others. They all competed to display their wealth and magnificence. In some ways, this competition was good for Florence, because it spurred the wealthy families to patronize the arts, learning, and many building projects in their beloved city-state.

In the fifteenth century, visitors to Florence remarked on things that Florentines took for granted—the city's high and secure walls, its fine streets paved with stone. At night, the streets glowed with a new form of lighting—wall-mounted torches. Visitors noticed the new library and elegant palaces, or *palazzi* (pah-LAHT-zee). They saw hospitals and almshouses, buildings the city fathers had constructed to care for the sick and the poor. The citizens of Florence, visitors observed, adorned themselves with the finest linens, silks, and brocaded velvets.

You'll read more about Florence in the next chapter.

Rome and the Papal States

In central Italy lay a region called the Papal States. The leader of the Christian Church, the pope, ruled this area. At the heart of the Papal States

Classical arches and columns flank a courtyard in Florence's Palazzo Vecchio, or "Old Palace." Construction of the palace, which became the seat of government for the Florentine republic, began about 1300.

stood the city of Rome, capital of the old Roman Empire and historic center of Christendom.

- On the map on page 38, locate Rome and the Papal States.

In 1400, Rome was in shambles. Large parts of the city had decayed while the popes lived in exile in Avignon. Weeds grew in the Roman Forum. Goats grazed on Capitoline hill. Sewage flowed in the Tiber River. Mighty aqueducts that had once carried water to public baths lay in ruins. After Petrarch unearthed Cicero's letters, more architects, artists, and scholars came to Rome, but the old city remained a mere shadow of its former greatness.

In 1417, when the pope officially returned to Rome, a dramatic turn-around took place. One pope after another set about rebuilding the fallen capital and restoring it to its former glory. These popes wanted to rival doges, kings, and merchant tycoons in splendor. The remains of the Colosseum, the Pantheon, and the aqueducts served as inspiration to both Church leaders and artists. (In a later chapter, you'll read more about the revival of Roman glory.)

Officially, the pope in Rome ruled such nearby cities as Ferrara (fehr-RAH-rah), Bologna, and Urbino (uhr-BEE-noh). But sometimes these cities shrugged off papal rule. Their leading families set up their own courts and considered themselves fairly independent. The popes did not hesitate to remind these cities that they were *Papal* States. Occasionally a pope would even send troops to reclaim these cities.

Two Renaissance popes chose names especially appropriate for their role as conquerors. When Rodrigo Borgia (roh-DREE-goh BOR-juh) became pope in 1492, he took the name Alexander VI, in honor of the conquering warrior of classical times, Alexander the Great. Pope Julius II chose his name because of his admiration for Julius Caesar. Julius (whom you'll read more about later) even led his own troops and became known as "the warrior pope."

North of Italy

North of the Italian peninsula, other important cities grew and prospered during the Renaissance. Paris and London were national capitals under strong French and English kings. In German lands near rivers, towns prospered as trade revived after the plague. City-states such as Augsburg, Nuremberg, and Mainz thrived. These self-governing city-states had their wealthy merchant families, their rival guilds, and their industries. German foundries cranked out cannons and

The city of Nuremberg in southern Germany is depicted in this 1552 engraving. At the time, Nuremberg was a major center of commerce and culture, thanks to its position astride four important trade routes.

guns. Nuremberg was famous for its metal-working and toys.

- On the map on page 17, locate Paris and London. Locate Augsburg, Nuremberg, and Mainz.

The city of Augsburg was important throughout the Renaissance. By 1400, there was a brisk textile trade. The wealthiest families in the region also turned to banking, mining, and the jewelry business. All this fortune became Augsburg's good fortune as the wealthy families patronized the arts and built numerous monuments and buildings.

Gutenberg and the Printing Press

Just as in Italy, wealthy men in German lands were always looking for good ways to invest their money. In the mid-fifteenth century, word spread among German merchants that in the city-state of Mainz a fellow named Johannes Gutenberg (yoh-HAHN-uhs GOOT-uhn-burg) had invented an amazing machine. Let's read about Gutenberg's machine and see what German investors did with it.

Historians don't know much about the details of Johannes Gutenberg's life. But by using available records, they have been able to piece together the story of how he invented his printing press.

Historical Close-up

Books are so common today that we rarely think of them as *special*. But 600 years ago a book was a *very* special thing, a treasured possession that most people could not afford. In the early 1400s, few individuals treasured books more than Johannes Gutenberg.

Born about 1395 in the town of Mainz, Gutenberg had always loved to read. His father was wealthy enough to buy a small collection of books, and we can picture young Johannes curled up by a window of the family home, enjoying tales about heroes from times past. But he must have quickly run out of books. For Johannes's father, as wealthy as he was, could not possibly have owned enough volumes to satisfy the boy.

In Gutenberg's day, books were called *manuscripts*, a term that comes from Latin words meaning "written by hand." Scribes copied every volume, word by word, with goose-feather quill pens. Copying by hand took a long time— many months for a single book. The slow process made books very expensive. In fact, a good collection of books could cost as much as a medium-sized farm. Little wonder that Johannes could never get his hands on enough to read. The local monastery had some books, but many were so precious that they were chained to reading tables.

If only more books were available! There had to be a faster, cheaper way to make them, Johannes told himself.

When Johannes finished school, he began to work with his father at the town mint, the place where coins were made. The building that housed the mint stood on the market square just two minutes' walk from the Gutenberg home. Johannes was a good metal worker. He was keen to learn all he could about engraving from the older employees. But busy as he was, he never forgot about books.

Then one day a thought occurred to him. The process of minting used a machine to stamp images onto coins. Maybe he could make a machine to stamp words onto paper—over and over again—to make books, copy after copy.

Johannes Gutenberg was not the first person to try printing words on paper. Perhaps as early as the sixth century, Chinese craftsmen had carved characters onto blocks of hard wood, scraping away excess material so that only the characters stood out. They then applied ink to the raised characters and pressed them against paper to make prints.

Gutenberg also tried to work with wood. He found the results unsatisfactory. The wood was soft and the edges did not stay sharp. From his experience in the mint, he knew that metal was a more durable material. He began to cast separate metal letters, known as movable type. He arranged these letters in different combinations to form words. Then he spread ink evenly over the letters and placed paper on them. He pressed firmly so the letters transferred onto the parchment.

Seated at their slanted desks, medieval monks copy manuscripts by hand in the monastery's scriptorium, *a writing room set aside for the use of scribes.*

The young man was disappointed with the results. No matter how meticulous he was, the letters came out crooked on the printed page. And if one of his metal letters was just a little bit shorter than the others, it did not get enough ink to print well. He *had to* find a better way to print words.

One day when Gutenberg was in his early twenties, he visited a paper-making shop that had just opened in Mainz. Fascinated, he watched as the paper makers made paper from cloth rags and water, beat to a pulp in a huge vat. He saw how they scooped out the paper pulp by dipping screen-covered molds into the vat. Then they placed each wet pulp sheet on a piece of felt. Next came the part that really interested Gutenberg. The paper makers used a mechanical wooden press to squeeze water from the pulp sheet.

A press! Maybe that was the answer. Instead of using a press to force water *out*, maybe he could use one to force print *in*—by pushing a single piece of paper hard against ink-covered metal type.

Gutenberg thought about it more and more—but not in Mainz. His family got caught up in a political squabble with a rival guild. The rivals won, so Gutenberg fled to Strasbourg and continued his experiments there. He hired a carpenter to build a press. It had a large wooden screw that, when cranked with a handle, pushed the paper onto inked type held in a boxlike frame. Gutenberg was convinced that such a machine could make perfect impressions over and over again.

By 1442, his machine and metal letters could make a hundred, or even a thousand, identical copies of the same page. He hoped to print more books in a few days than the scribes at the local monastery could make during the rest of their lives. But much work remained. The penniless Gutenberg dreamed of the day when his press would make him wealthy.

Working on his invention cost Gutenberg everything he owned. He had to hire assistants, pay the carpenter, and purchase materials. Ink and metal cost him a small fortune. The ink had to be wet enough to coat the type, yet thick enough to stick without running. He finally found the right ink in a mixture of linseed oil and fine soot. As for the metal used to make the type, he had first tried lead. But this soft metal wore out quickly. He tried mixing other metals with lead and finally came up with the right combination.

All this experimenting took time—and money. Gutenberg had to take out loans and find partners. In 1450, after he had moved back to Mainz, he met a backer with plenty of money, Johann Fust (foost), a wealthy lawyer. With his support, Gutenberg ordered several more presses and lots of materials. After working on his experiments for nearly 30 years, he was ready to print his first book. Gutenberg, now in his fifties, had no doubt what it would be—the Bible, the most widely read book in Europe.

In 1454, Gutenberg printed about 180 copies of the Bible, each with 1,282 pages. If a single letter was blurred, Gutenberg threw away the whole page and set about making a new piece of type. Each page had to be sharp and clear, or it did not go into his Bible.

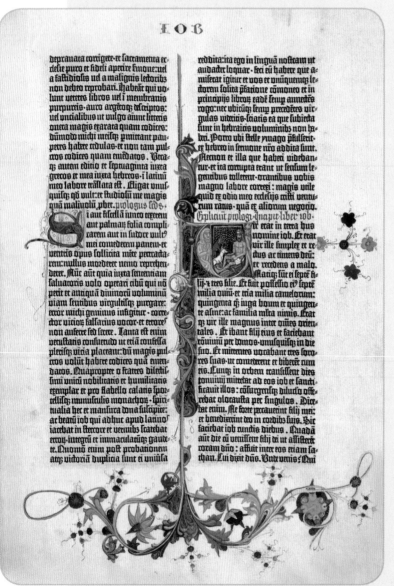

The Gutenberg Bible featured text printed with movable type and hand-painted illustrations. This page from the Book of Job depicts Job in the rounded capital V.

Gutenberg's partner showed less patience. During this time, Fust took the inventor to court. He sued Gutenberg, claiming the printer had not repaid his loan on time. The judge ruled in Fust's favor. Gutenberg had to surrender his press shop, his tools, and his nearly completed Bibles to Fust!

News of Gutenberg's remarkable invention spread. People traveled to Mainz to see the machine and learn how it worked. Some of them made their own printing presses. German printers traveled to other lands—Italy, France, Spain, and beyond—where they set up presses. German bankers funded them. By the end of the fifteenth century, hundreds of busy printers were churning out books across Europe.

Many printers and presses went to Venice, a city where scholarship flourished, money abounded, and people treasured the written word. Only a year before Gutenberg printed his Bible, Venice had been flooded with Greek scholars fleeing the Ottoman Turks in Constantinople. The scholars brought ancient texts with them. German bankers were happy to fund Venetian printers. The printers in Venice and other cities produced texts in Latin and Greek. They published works of Cicero and Plato. They printed books about medicine, philosophy, art, and much more.

Books, now less expensive, traveled from one end of Europe to another. More people learned how to read. Never before had so many ideas traveled so quickly.

And what of Johannes Gutenberg? The unfortunate printer made little money from his invention. In fact, at first many people gave Johann Fust credit for producing the first printed Bible. But today Gutenberg is rightly honored as the father of modern printing. The Gutenberg Bible is considered the first printed book in the Western world. Forty-seven of those Gutenberg Bibles exist today, cherished treasures from a man who, since his boyhood days, thought of books as the most valuable of possessions. 🌿

Johannes Gutenberg proudly displays a sample of his work. The inventor had high standards. The letters on every page had to be perfect to be included in his Bible—the first printed book in the Western world.

What Do We Mean by "Western"?

When we say that the Gutenberg Bible is considered the first printed book in the Western world, what do we mean by *Western*? Geographically, west is a direction: the sun sets in the west. To a historian, "the West" is more than a direction. It is also a collection of ideas. Today, when historians refer to "Western civilization," they are thinking of a body of ideas generally shared in Europe and the Americas. These ideas have their roots in the ancient Hebrews and Greeks. Among these root ideas are the importance of law and the worth of human beings as individuals. Western civilization is sometimes contrasted with Eastern civilization, made up of the shared ideas of India, China, Japan, and other countries. But this is a general contrast, because there are many ideas common to both East and West.

*Filippo Brunelleschi's glorious cathedral dome
has become a symbol of Renaissance Florence.*

The Flowering of Genius in Florence

Florence, the Italian city-state on the Arno River,

had suffered many trials in the fourteenth century

but rose above them all. On the city's bell tower, a new relief

sculpture told the tale. The winged figure of Daedalus

pushed off from his earthly perch and took to the skies. Daedalus, a hero from Greek mythology, was both a craftsman and inventor. While a prisoner, he made wax-and-feather wings for himself, and then flew to freedom. Florence, the sculpture seemed to say, would soar as well, past war, past famine, past plague.

When Julius Caesar founded the city on the river's edge in 59 B.C., he named it *Florentia*. The word meant "blossoming." It was a fitting name. Fifteenth-century Florence became the first flower of the Renaissance. Wealth and ingenuity came together, sparking a rebirth of learning and art that rekindled all Europe. Florentines gloried in the classical past and heartily savored the humanism of

the present. They put scholarship, art, and architecture on a new course.

Why Florence?

Florence was not the biggest city-state in Italy. It had no great seaport. Its army was not large or powerful. Yet its people were resourceful and ambitious. They had good heads for business and could drive a hard bargain. By 1400, even after the ravages of the plague, the little city-state was prosperous and its people confident. Why? Florentine merchants and craftsmen had learned that making luxury goods could make them rich.

At a time when most Europeans wore wool, Florence clothed much

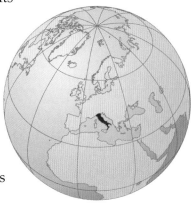

The next three chapters focus on Italy, birthplace of the Renaissance.

of the continent. By the late Middle Ages, fleece from as far away as England and Spain arrived daily at riverside docks on the Arno. Florentines spun, dyed, and wove the fleece, turning it into smooth woolen cloth that they shipped to buyers in Rome, Naples, Constantinople, and London. The city began to specialize in other luxury goods as well—creamy silks, gold jewelry, and tooled leather.

Florentine merchants grew wealthy, but one family prospered above all others—the Medici. Giovanni de' Medici (joh-VAHN-nee d'MED-uh-chee) made his first fortune in textiles. He then turned to banking, and the family fortune multiplied. Giovanni's son, Cosimo (KAW-zee-moh), was a banking genius. Cosimo managed the pope's finances and received many favors in return. Before long Medici banks were the most powerful in Europe.

The Medici financed trading expeditions, made loans to popes, and even loaned money to dukes and princes to pay for their wars. The Medici made Florence a hub of Mediterranean commerce.

Gold *florins*—coins minted in Florence—were good anywhere merchants traveled. Florentines liked to tell a story about the duke of Milan showing off his treasure to an ambassador from Florence. The ambassador scooped up a handful of the duke's florins. "Every one of them stamped with a lily, the emblem of Florence," he remarked. "Just think how many *we* have, since we are the ones who make them."

Wealth was not the city's only reason to be proud. In the early part of the fifteenth century, Florence conquered the neighboring state of Pisa, and so got access to the coast. It won a military victory against mighty Milan to the north and later absorbed strategic Siena, which controlled the road to Rome.

Florentines could also boast that their city-state was a republic, like ancient Rome. While princes and kings

Straddling the Arno River where Julius Caesar founded the city, Florence was the first flower of the Italian Renaissance. This late fifteenth-century painting shows a prosperous city that had grown rich from its trade in wool, silks, jewelry, and other luxury goods.

FIORENZA

ruled other regions, Florentines believed they were heirs to one of the greatest treasures of classical times— government by the people. True, sometimes Florence didn't seem like a republic. The wealthiest families, such as the Medici, directed much of the city's affairs. Guilds scrapped for power. And Florentines had been known to murder for control of the government. Still, the people of Florence were proud of their city-state.

The wealthiest citizens of Florence prized the finest workmanship. They wanted the best for themselves and their city-state. So the city council hired architects to build magnificent offices and churches. They paid sculptors to fill the city's public squares and guild halls with statues. They commissioned artists to create stunning paintings and frescoes.

Cosimo and Lorenzo

As the threat of plague and famine receded, a new generation of Florentines began to celebrate the here and now. The wealthy Medici became enthusiastic humanists and patrons of art and learning. Cosimo de' Medici spent fortunes on paintings and sculpture to adorn Florentine monasteries, convents, and chapels. He sponsored expeditions to collect classical manuscripts, statues, and coins. He employed dozens of scribes to copy Latin and Greek texts for the family library. He also established the first public library in Italy, filled with thousands of ancient manuscripts, and open free of charge to scholars and students.

Cosimo attracted numerous classical scholars to Florence and established an academy for the study of classical texts, especially the writings of the ancient Greeks. He even persuaded the University of Florence to offer the study of Greek for the first time in seven centuries.

Cosimo's grandson, Lorenzo, became the most famous Medici of all. "Lorenzo the Magnificent," as he became known, surrounded himself with art and learning. He was a poet himself, and he brought the most brilliant painters, sculptors, and scholars to Florence. As one admirer noted, Lorenzo "loved exceedingly all who excelled in the arts, and he showered favors on the learned."

Lorenzo followed the example of Cosimo. He surrounded himself with humanists to discuss classical ideas and debate philosophical issues. He named his group the Platonic Academy, after the famous school in Athens run by the Greek philosopher Plato. Lorenzo once remarked that he wished he could spend his entire fortune on books.

With such energy, wealth, and devotion to the arts, little wonder that Florentines looked at their city and saw the grandeur of Athens and Rome reborn.

Sculptors Inspired by the Past

In fifteenth-century Florence, the art of sculpture was revived by keen interest in classical civilizations. Centuries earlier, Greeks and Romans had sculpted in marble and bronze to express their admiration for the human form. Could such efforts be matched by Florentine artists?

They would try. In 1401, the wool merchants of Florence decided to adorn a church known as the Baptistery with

Lorenzo de' Medici, known as "the Magnificent," was a great patron of the arts and learning in Renaissance Florence.

a set of gilded bronze doors. They sponsored a contest for the commission and seven sculptors competed. According to one biographer, two men won—Lorenzo Ghiberti (luh-REN-zoh gee-BEHR-tee) and Filippo Brunelleschi (fee-LEEP-poh broo-nehl-ES-kee). Brunelleschi refused to share the honor with anyone, and he turned down the prize. Ghiberti was unperturbed. "I had surpassed everyone," he gloated.

Ghiberti spent the next 21 years filling the Baptistery doors with scenes from the Bible, retelling in bronze Old Testament stories as well as scenes from the life of Christ. Just as Giotto had transformed painting, now Ghiberti's work seemed to breathe life into sculpture. His rounded and natural-looking figures sang the beauty of the human form. They captured movement and individual expression as never before. Ghiberti made each scene leap forth: Abraham raises a knife to his son, while Isaac cowers in fear; a startled Mary receives an urgent message from an angel.

The proud artist made sure to include a portrait of himself on the Baptistery doors. This was something new. Artists were beginning to think of themselves not as anonymous workmen, but as individual creators, worthy of recognition. The cloth merchants were so pleased that they ordered a second set of doors, which took Ghiberti another 27 years to finish.

Another great Florentine sculptor, Donatello (dahn-uh-TEL-oh), worked as Ghiberti's assistant before striking out on his own. The kindhearted artist was said to have kept his earnings in a basket hanging from his ceiling so that his friends could take money whenever they needed it.

Donatello was proud of Florence, but he knew that the ancient masters of his craft had worked in Rome. So he headed south to study the remains of sculpture there.

His hard work paid off. Cosimo de' Medici hired Donatello to create a bronze statue for his courtyard. Cosimo chose a subject from the Bible—David, slayer of the giant Goliath. Why David? Because the proud Florentines saw themselves as standing firm in their wars against neighboring city-states, especially their large neighbor, Milan. They saw their little city as a kind of David, a slayer of giants.

Donatello's heroic David was the first free-standing nude statue in western Europe since classical times. It was a symbol of Florentine courage against tyrants. The statue was also a celebration of man. It showed the grace of the human form and breathed confidence in human abilities. That confidence was reflected in other arts as well.

To the Florentines, Donatello's bronze statue of the Biblical hero David represented their own brave little republic. Like David challenging Goliath, Florence stood up to powerful neighboring city-states.

Building for the Ages

The wealthy merchants of Florence were determined to build offices, churches, and public squares that reflected their pride, hope, and confidence. They kept hundreds of artists and craftsmen busy turning the city on the Arno into a showcase.

One of the greatest of these architects was Filippo Brunelleschi, a native of Florence who started his career by training as a goldsmith and sculptor. In 1401, he entered the contest to see who would make the bronze doors for the city's Baptistery. He was certain he had come up with the best design, but when the judges

The Revival of the Nude

In ancient Greece and Rome, sculptors often depicted the unclothed human body. In art, a depiction of a human figure without any clothes is called a *nude*. In the Middle Ages, artists generally did not depict nude figures because the Church considered such art to be shameful. But Renaissance artists revived the nude as a proper subject for art. Like the artists of classical times, Renaissance artists saw beauty, grace, and strength in the healthy human form.

declared two winners—Brunelleschi and his rival Ghiberti—Brunelleschi walked away. If he could not have the project all to himself, he wanted nothing to do with it. He decided to turn his talents to architecture, and with his close friend Donatello, he headed for Rome.

The grandeur of the ruins of ancient Rome fired Brunelleschi's imagination. The sixteenth-century historian Giorgio Vasari (JOR-joh vah-ZAH-ree) reported that the young architect stood before the dome of the Pantheon "so engrossed in thought that he seemed to be beside himself with amazement." He measured the crumbling walls

Brunelleschi's innovative design for the dome of Florence's cathedral took 16 years to complete. In the drawing below, scaffolding surrounds the "lantern," a structure that lets light into the top of the dome.

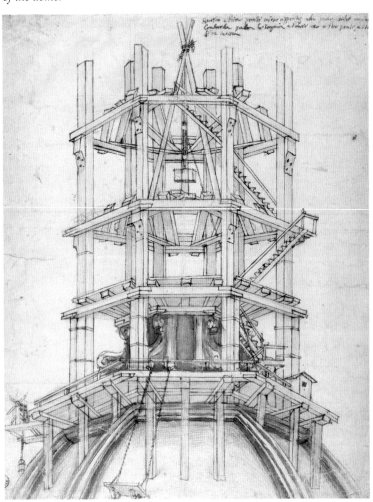

of temples and palaces. He filled his notebook with sketches of old Roman columns and arches. He studied classical writings on architecture.

In 1418, officials in Florence announced a contest to see who could come up with a way to construct a dome for the city's cathedral. For more than a century Florentines had toiled on their cathedral. They wanted to make it bigger and better than neighboring Siena's. But no one had been able to figure out how to build the massive dome they needed to finish the structure. Some said it could not be done. Not since the sixth century, when the Emperor Justinian built Hagia Sophia in Constantinople, had such a huge dome been attempted. Cathedral officials knew what they wanted their dome to look like. But they didn't know how to build it.

Brunelleschi leaped at the opportunity. He had new ideas from his studies in Rome. He built a model of brick and submitted it. Skeptics laughed and called him a madman. These bricks, they said, would rain down on the heads of people below! But the judges, who included Cosimo de' Medici, were intrigued. Brunelleschi won the commission, and the architect forged ahead. During the next 16 years, he built the dome of all domes. (See page 50.)

Brunelleschi used an ancient Roman technique to build two interior shells of brick in a herringbone pattern. He used a system of rib supports to lessen the weight of the heavy dome on the building's foundation. The busy architect invented hoists to raise materials into the sky.

Florence's skyline is a medieval and Renaissance creation. Construction of its cathedral began in 1296. The tall bell tower or campanile *(at left in the picture) was built in the fourteenth century. The cathedral's huge dome dates to the fifteenth century.*

He even equipped scaffolds with kitchens so builders could work and eat hundreds of feet in the air.

By 1436, Brunelleschi's dome was complete. It dominated the city. Florentines declared that the world had never seen such a glorious structure. Not even Rome's Pantheon could compare.

All over Florence, architects attempted to build in the style of the classical past. Like the temples of ancient Greece and Rome, new buildings boasted arches, columns, pilasters (rectangular columns set into the wall), and friezes (ornamented bands running above the columns). Their walls reflected the classical love of proportion and balance. Upon seeing the churches, palaces, and public buildings in Florence, one architect wrote, "I seem to see again the noble buildings that were once in Rome. It seems to me that on seeing those noble buildings I have been reborn."

Painters Pay Tribute to Old and New

During the Renaissance, the inspiration of the classical past spread beyond Florentine sculptors and architects. Painters, too, were drawn to works from ancient Greece and Rome. They admired the realism of the ancient works. They marveled at the balance, proportion, and graceful lines of classical sculptures and buildings. Renaissance painters tried to incorporate these elements and make their paintings lifelike and almost sculptural.

Their efforts marked a break with medieval tradition. The subject matter for painters was still mainly religious—scenes from the Bible or from the lives of the saints. But Renaissance painters treated religious topics in new ways. They wanted to direct attention not so much to the hope of salvation in the next life, but to the beauty of creation in the here and now. They looked carefully at nature—sunlight on buildings, trees in the countryside, horses galloping in a field, the human body at rest or in motion—so they could recreate that beauty on their canvases.

Above all, Renaissance artists tried to depict human beings as living individuals. They filled their notebooks with drawings of the human figure. They followed the advice of a Florentine scholar who wrote in a book on painting, "Begin with the bones, then add muscles, and then cover the body with flesh in such a way as to leave the position of the muscles visible." Painters strived to give each figure its own unique identity. Florentine patrons liked seeing themselves in important works, so artists often painted leading figures of the day into ageless scenes.

The trailblazer for the new methods of painting was Masaccio (mah-ZAHT-choh). He earned the nickname "Simple Tom" because of his absentmindedness and untidy appearance. But there was nothing scattered or untidy about his painting. Masaccio was an admirer of the classics, and along with his contemporary Florentines Donatello and Brunelleschi, he made the trek to Rome. There he studied ancient works and tried to put principles of proportion, balance, and above all, human dignity into his painting.

Masaccio's *The Tribute Money* was the first great example of the new humanism in painting. He painted the work for a chapel in Florence in 1427. The painting depicts an

Masaccio's The Tribute Money *tells a story. In the center, Jesus directs Peter to pay the toll collector with a coin from the mouth of a fish. At left, Peter finds the coin, and to the right, he pays the gatekeeper. Masaccio's use of realism, perspective, and light earned him the title "Father of Renaissance Painting."*

episode from the Bible. When Jesus and his followers arrived at the city of Capernaum, the gatekeeper demanded that they pay a toll. Jesus told his disciple Peter to catch a fish and that he would find in its mouth a coin to pay the tribute.

Masaccio painted this scene with extraordinary detail and realism. The citizens of Florence were startled at the way he used light and shadow to make his dramatic figures look dignified and solid. They marveled at how he carefully arranged his images to make some appear closer to the viewer, and some farther away. (Artists call this giving a painting *perspective*.) Masaccio gave each disciple his own unique face and character—Peter wary, Jesus authoritative, Judas impatient. And the artist set the scene on the familiar streets of fifteenth-century Florence! Florentines felt almost as if they were witnessing the scene. Masaccio's work changed painting forever.

Masaccio's life was tragically short. He died just short of age 27

while on a return visit to Rome. But he became known as the "Father of Renaissance Painting," and other artists followed in his daring footsteps.

One of those followers was a Florentine named Sandro Botticelli (SAHN-droh boht-ih-CHELL-ee). Botticelli often turned to classical mythology for inspiration. His *The Birth of Venus*, painted around 1485, is one of the most famous paintings of the Renaissance. It portrays an ancient legend about the birth of the Roman goddess of love. Venus rises out of the sea on a shell as two wind gods blow her to shore and a nymph waits to give her a cloak.

In another important work, Botticelli captures the new spirit of the age. His *Primavera*, or *Springtime*, shows a female goddess of spring or rebirth, flanked by the Roman gods Cupid, Mercury, and Zephyr. Botticelli filled his painting with

graceful lines and carefully balanced shapes that recall the harmony and beauty of classical art. (See page 24.)

Ghiberti, Donatello, Brunelleschi, Masaccio, Botticelli—these Florentine artists, inspired by the classical past, turned their city into the first shining jewel of the Renaissance. While Botticelli was putting the final touches on *Primavera* around 1478, an eager 25-year-old named Leonardo da Vinci (lay-uh-NAHR-doh duh VIN-chee) was opening his own studio in Florence. You'll read about him at the end of this chapter.

Bonfire of the Vanities

As Florence displayed its glorious art and architecture, most people marveled, but some were less pleased. One man was outraged—an eloquent and quick-witted friar named Girolamo Savonarola (jee-ROH-lah-moh SAH-voh-nah-ROH-lah). The priest

In Sandro Botticelli's The Birth of Venus, *the goddess of love rises from the sea on a huge shell. Zephyrus and Aura—the spring wind and the goddess of breezes— blow her ashore, where a waiting nymph prepares to wrap Venus in a flowered cloak.*

A *friar* (from the Latin *frater*, meaning "brother") is a member of a religious order dedicated to teaching and serving the poor.

worried that the people of Florence were distracted from God by their wealth and many possessions. Savonarola could be charming and humorous, but he was also a fiery and single-minded preacher. He saw himself as a prophet.

In his sermons, Savonarola attacked the new emphasis on worldly goods and the glorification of human abilities. Florentines, he warned, should focus on God and their souls. Savonarola took aim at the humanists' fondness for classical writers. He rejected Petrarch's simultaneous embrace of classical wisdom and Christian faith. The ancients, fumed Savonarola, had known nothing of Christ. "Plato, Aristotle, and the other philosophers are fast in hell!" he roared. "Any old woman knows more about faith than Plato."

Savonarola hurled accusations left and right. The Medici, he said, were corrupt rulers, the bankers were stealing from the people, and the priests were more concerned with power and wealth than saving souls. When Lorenzo the Magnificent died, Savonarola hailed it as a sign from God. "Behold the sword of the Lord," he shouted, "swift and sure over the peoples of the earth!"

As Savonarola's influence grew, unrest spread. In 1494, the French invaded Italy, and Florence fell into chaos. Florentines drove the Medici from the city. A mob ransacked the Medici palace, stealing and destroying all the priceless art they could find. Now Savonarola held the upper hand in Florence. The city was pulled between the new spirit of humanism and medieval Christian ideals.

"Vanity of vanities," says the preacher in the book of Ecclesiastes in the Bible, "all is vanity"—meaning that all earthly effort is useless and empty. Savonarola urged Florentines to collect their "vanities"—cosmetics, playing cards, dice, carnival masks, paintings of women, books of poetry, musical instruments—and throw them onto a huge bonfire while church bells rang. The raging flames of this "bonfire of the vanities" moved many people and frightened others. Botticelli even stopped painting Venuses for a while.

Powerful merchants and political leaders were not the only ones who felt Savonarola's sting. The priest even lashed out at the pope. He denounced Pope Alexander VI as immoral and corrupt. He warned that God would visit judgment on Italy for sinfulness.

Alexander finally had enough of Savonarola. He ordered Florentine leaders to silence the popular preacher. They arrested Savonarola. A crowd gathered in the main public square to watch as the monk and two followers were hung and their bodies burned.

The Medici returned to Florence and resumed their role as leaders of the city-state. Some of them guided Florence wisely, some foolishly. Florence never regained its position as Italy's cultural leader. Still, the spirit of the Renaissance, which had flowered along the banks of the Arno during the fifteenth century, was by no means dead. On the contrary, it was alive and well, and, as we'll soon see, spreading throughout Italy and beyond.

Leonardo da Vinci's Early Years

Painter, sculptor, architect, engineer, scientist, philosopher, visionary—the Florentine genius Leonardo da Vinci is perhaps the most fascinating figure of the Renaissance. In many ways, his life and his work sum up that era of creativity and achievement. Let's learn about the first part of his life in Florence. (You'll read more about Leonardo in a later chapter.)

Historical Close-up

Vinci. That is the name of the tiny hillside village near Florence where Leonardo was born in 1452. Leonardo's family took its name from the place. *Leonardo da Vinci* means "Leonardo of Vinci" in Italian.

It must have been a wonderful place to be a boy. Fields, forests, olive groves, and vineyards lay around the village, all waiting to be explored. Leonardo spent his earliest years wandering the rocky mountain slopes, gazing down at the distant Arno River and coming to know the rocks, trees, and flowers.

But Leonardo wasn't destined to spend his life in a remote village. His father was a well-to-do businessman, and eventually the Vinci family moved to Florence. There young Leonardo studied reading, writing, music, and geometry, but more than anything else he loved to draw. When he was about 15, his father apprenticed him to Andrea del Verrocchio (anh-DREH-ah del vahr-ROHK-kyoh), a renowned sculptor, goldsmith, painter, and engineer.

Verrocchio's busy workshop seemed like paradise to Leonardo. Verrocchio and his assistants turned out all kinds of wonders—paintings for churches, tapestries for palaces, banners for festivals, costumes for grand parties, plates and bowls for wealthy merchants' tables. Leonardo learned to grind colors, make brushes, draw, paint, and create sculptures in clay, bronze, and marble. He soon proved to be the workshop's most gifted apprentice, and Verrocchio—whose name meant "true eye"—did not fail to see his talent.

Around the year 1472, Verrocchio allowed Leonardo to help finish a painting of Saint John baptizing Jesus. Verrocchio had nearly completed the work and asked his young apprentice to paint one of the angels. Legend says that when Verrocchio saw Leonardo's angel, he was so stunned by its beauty that he broke his own paintbrush and declared that he would never paint again.

In his spare time, Leonardo roamed the streets of Florence, the bustling hub of the Renaissance. He looked up at Brunelleschi's dome, a symbol of the city's confidence and pride. He saw elegant new *palazzi*—palace-like homes. He visited churches filled with paintings. He knew the works of sculptors who were studying long-lost Roman statues, and of scholars who had unlocked the secrets of dusty, ancient manuscripts.

In Florence, Lorenzo the Magnificent often invited humanists and artists to visit the Medici palace. Leonardo, now in his twenties, found himself among that lucky group. He soaked up knowledge from the philosophers he met, though his mind sometimes wandered during their long discussions about the nature of the soul. Leonardo possessed a practical mind. He wanted to know about the nature of the world he could see with his own eyes.

Meanwhile, Leonardo continued to paint. After several years of learning from Verrocchio, he set up his own studio. His career got off to a slow start. Although rich merchants were eager to hire him, he had trouble finishing paintings. He enjoyed sketching and planning pictures, but he seemed to become bored or distracted when it came to the long process of applying the paint.

In 1481, some monks in Florence hired Leonardo to paint a picture to hang above an altar in their monastery. He chose to depict a scene described in the Bible—the wise men who traveled from afar to see the infant Jesus. As Leonardo covered sheet after sheet of paper with sketches, a work of genius began to emerge. After months of sketching and painting, however, he simply stopped. Even in its unfinished state, the *Adoration of the Magi* is one of the great works of the Renaissance.

Leonardo decided to leave Florence for the city-state of Milan to the north. Milan was ruled by Ludovico Sforza (loo-doh-VEE-koh SFORT-sah), an arrogant, ambitious duke always scheming to increase his power and prestige. He lived in an immense fortress where, like other Renaissance nobles, he gathered artists and scholars about him.

Ludovico constantly made war with other Italian city-states. Leonardo, ever practical, wrote the duke a letter in which he offered to design fighting machines. Leonardo wrote that he could build "very strong but light bridges, extremely easy to carry," and that he could "dry up the water of moats" during sieges. He claimed that he knew "methods of destroying any citadel or fortress, even if it is built on rock." He could dig tunnels under enemy lines, as well as make bombs, covered assault wagons, and catapults. And in his spare time, Leonardo added, he could sculpt, paint, and design buildings for Milan.

We don't know what Ludovico thought of this letter, but Leonardo soon had a contract to paint a picture of Mary and Jesus for a church in Milan. The monks of the church told Leonardo exactly what they wanted the painting to show. Leonardo ignored them and painted the image that *he* had in mind. *The Virgin of the Rocks*, as the painting is known, became of the talk of Milan.

Leonardo's talents caught Ludovico's eye, and the duke of Milan soon put him to work. Busy years followed. Leonardo—said to have a wonderful voice—sang and played music at court. He painted portraits. He decorated

In Leonardo da Vinci's unfinished Adoration of the Magi, *the wise men gather around the Virgin Mary to worship the infant Jesus.*

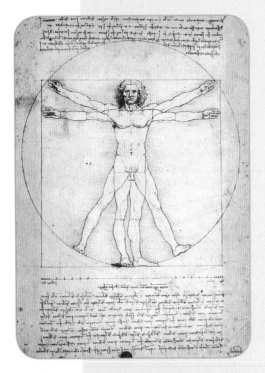

Ludovico's castle, made cannons, built canals, and planned pageants for court celebrations.

The court of Milan saw Leonardo as a charming and witty man, always able to supply a riddle or an amusing story for the duke's pleasure. In truth, Leonardo preferred to be alone. He spent his solitary hours thinking about the world around him. All subjects fascinated Leonardo. He saw fossils of shells and fish on mountaintops and concluded that those rocks once lay beneath the sea. He threw a pebble into the water and, watching the ripples, wondered if light and sound also traveled in waves. He spent long nights cutting into corpses in hospital morgues—in part to learn how the body works, and in part so he could paint the human figure more accurately.

When alone, Leonardo often wrote in his note-books. He filled thousands of pages with his ideas and observations—sketches of plants and animals, plans for inventions, studies of the human body, mathematical problems, notes on painting and architecture. Leonardo was left-handed and found it easier to write backward, from right to left. To read his famous notebooks, you must hold the pages up to a mirror.

At last Ludovico gave Leonardo a job the artist had long wanted—to create a huge bronze statue of Ludovico's father on a horse. Leonardo worked on the project, on and off, for some 12 years. He filled his notebooks with sketches of horses and planned the largest bronze sculpture the world had ever seen. He even invented a new method for casting such a huge statue. After 10 years of work, he built a full-size clay model of the horse. All of Milan gaped in wonder. Leonardo gathered 70 tons of bronze and prepared to cast the statue. But the duke went to war again and decided to use the bronze to make cannons instead. The great horse was never cast.

Top: Leonardo's inventive mind came up with this design for a flying machine.

Above: This ink sketch shows Leonardo's understanding of the proportions of the human body. "Man," he declared in his notes, "is the model of the world."

During Leonardo's stay in Milan, Ludovico gave him another commission—to paint a wall in the monks' dining hall in one of Milan's churches. Leonardo's painting, called *The Last Supper*, depicts the last meal that Jesus shared with his disciples. Leonardo showed the moment when Jesus announced that one of his followers would betray him. He painted the disciples reacting with shock and despair. No artist had ever achieved such drama in a mural. People began to speak of Leonardo as one of the greatest artists of his age.

Yet even in this triumph, Leonardo tasted failure. To create *The Last Supper*, he had developed a new method of applying paint on the wall. The procedure proved flawed. Soon after he finished it, Leonardo's masterpiece began to show tiny cracks. Eventually it started to flake off the wall.

Leonardo did not have long to lament his painting's fate. In 1499, King Louis XII of France invaded Milan and forced Ludovico to flee. "The duke lost his states, his personal fortune, and his freedom, and none of his projects came to fruition," Leonardo wrote. French soldiers used the model of the great clay horse for target practice and reduced it to rubble. After 17 years in Milan, Leonardo packed his belongings and left the city, his mind fixed on the future.

Among the most famous paintings in the world, Leonardo's The Last Supper *has undergone many restorations.*

St. Peter's Basilica in Rome was rebuilt during the 1500s on the site of an older church. Much of Rome saw a glorious revival during the Renaissance.

Rome Revived

*I*n the early 1400s, Florentine artists such as Donatello, Brunelleschi, and Masaccio hunted for classical treasures in the ruins of Rome. They filled their notebooks with sketches of broken columns, collapsed arches, and fractured statues.

Then they returned home to Florence to recreate the glory of the ancient capital.

If Florence was the polished jewel of the early Renaissance, Rome was its diamond in the rough. The walls of the Colosseum were crumbling. The once-magnificent stadium housed scores of filthy taverns. Thieves lurked in the ancient baths. On Capitoline Hill, the old center of Roman government, vines grew over the benches of senators. One humanist lamented that the Roman Forum, once the heart of an empire, had turned into "a neglected desert, here the home of pigs and wild deer, and there a vegetable garden."

By the mid-fifteenth century, however, the city by the Tiber River was springing to new life. Sculptors, painters, architects, thinkers, and writers poured into the city. They were answering the call of a new and tireless patron, the pope. With the pope back in his historic home, the ancient capital revived. The center of Renaissance activity now shifted from Florence to Rome.

The Popes Restore Rome

Rome was the historic center of the Christian Church. Here, according to Christian tradition, the apostle Peter was buried. Peter's successors, the bishops of Rome, had directed the Church's affairs in western Europe for most of the Middle Ages. During the fourteenth century, French kings had forced popes to live in the town of Avignon. But by the early fifteenth century, Rome once again became the official home of the pope, who faced the enormous task of restoring the fallen city.

Each pope knew the glory of Florence to the north—the palace-like homes, the new sculpture and painting, the courts full of poets and philosophers. No pope wanted to be left behind. Each determined to bring equal glory—no, more glory—to Rome.

The leader of the Christian Church had the money to do it— more money than even the Medici family in Florence. All over Europe, kings, princes, the Holy Roman Emperor, and ordinary folk gave money to the Church as a sign of their faith. Much of that money flowed to the pope in Rome.

For the next two hundred years, one pope after another worked at reviving the ancient city. Like the wealthy merchants of Florence, Renaissance popes lived as princes and became patrons of the arts. They ordered workers to clear the rubble from Capitoline Hill and clean up sewage in the Tiber River. They replaced crumbling columns and arches with magnificent new churches and palaces. They turned broken streets into wide avenues and barren ruins into magnificent gardens.

Many Renaissance popes were keenly interested in the revival of classical learning. They took advantage of the city's location in the heart of the old Roman Empire. They organized teams to find ancient statues rumored to be buried in the vicinity. They collected coins, books, and other relics of the ancient past. They transformed the Vatican— the headquarters of the Church in Rome—into a vast palace complex to display some of Europe's finest treasures. Poets, philosophers, and scholars were welcomed by the Vatican. And a new papal library housed a growing collection of Latin and Greek texts.

Renaissance popes were often more concerned with politics, power, and luxury than spiritual leadership. For example, Pope Sixtus IV show-ered the Church's gold on his rela-tives and gave five of his nephews powerful positions in the Church. He fought a war against Florence and plotted against Lorenzo de' Medici. Sixtus often presided over rich banquets where guests dined on roasted boar and plundered small castles made of sweets.

Despite these excesses, Sixtus IV also worked hard to revive Rome's splendor. He built new roads, repaired aqueducts, and restored the city's walls. He sought out ancient Greek, Latin, and Hebrew writings, and added more than a thousand volumes to the Vatican

Why Is It Called the "Vatican"?

Vaticanus was the Latin name for one of the hills in Rome. There the Christian Church located its main church building. The church and about 100 acres of land around it are now known as Vatican City, or "the Vatican." Nowadays the Vatican is both the headquarters of the Roman Catholic Church and the smallest independent country in the world. It is ruled by the pope and located entirely in the city of Rome, Italy.

library. His crowning achievement was to build a new chapel in the Vatican called the Sistine Chapel, named after Sixtus himself. He hired the best artists in Italy, including Botticelli, to paint scenes from the lives of Moses and Christ on its walls. To pay for these projects, Sixtus did what Dante had condemned in *The Divine Comedy*—he sold Church offices and privileges.

Julius II: An Army unto Himself

During the Renaissance, each new pope tried to outdo the pope before him. Each pope tried harder to restore power to the papacy and bring glory to Rome. None tried harder than Giuliano della Rovere (jool-YAH-noh del-lah roh-VEH-reh). This nephew of Sixtus IV became pope in 1503 after bribing Church officials to elect him to the office. He chose the name Julius, after the great Roman general, Julius Caesar.

Julius was 60 years old when elected pope but he had the energy of a man half his age. He was impulsive and strong-willed, with strong opinions matched by a strong temper. He sometimes flew into rages, thrashing anyone within reach. No wonder he was known as *il papa terribile*, the "terrifying pope." "It is virtually impossible to describe how strong and violent and difficult to manage he is," wrote an awestruck ambassador from Venice. "In body and soul he has the nature of a giant."

Julius was a man of large appetites—physical and political. He gorged on eels and caviar, washed down with Greek wine. He declared

An enthroned Sixtus IV appoints a new head of the Vatican Library, who kneels before him and points to an inscription praising the pope's enterprises in Rome. Around Sixtus stand his nephews, including the future Pope Julius II in the red robe at center.

the papal apartments unworthy and built himself three palaces.

Like his namesake Julius Caesar, Julius II wanted firm control of his domain. He was determined to put down anyone who challenged his rule of the Papal States. Julius wasn't content to let others fight his battles. In 1506, he astonished Rome by announcing that he would lead an army against the rebel cities of Perugia and Bologna.

The "Warrior Pope," as he came to be known, departed Rome with a force that included five-hundred mounted knights, several thousand foot soldiers, twenty-six cardinals (high officials in the Church), and the choir from the Sistine Chapel. His enemies fled, and the people of Perugia and Bologna threw open their city gates. As bells tolled,

In this ancient statue based on a Greek myth, sea serpents attack the priest Laocoön and his twin sons. Laocoön had warned the city of Troy not to accept the wooden horse left by the Greeks. Gods favoring the Greeks sent the serpents to punish Laocoön.

bonfires blazed, and crowds cheered, Julius was carried through the streets in his papal chair.

When he was not at war, Julius focused on rebuilding Rome. He ordered workers to pave streets, replace ancient sewers, and dredge the Tiber River so ships could come and go more easily. He attracted scholars to the city. He collected books and purchased classical art. When some men working in a vineyard unearthed the *Laocoön* (lay-AH-kuh-wahn)—a famous Greek statue that had been transported to Rome in ancient times and then lost for centuries beneath the city's rubble—Julius paid a fortune for the sculpture.

To help beautify Rome, the pope hired the best painters, sculptors, and architects in Italy.

He was determined to turn the Vatican into a showplace with new courtyards, fountains, a theater, sculpture garden, and even an arena for bullfights.

Within the Vatican lay what Christians considered the holiest church in Europe—St. Peter's Basilica. (A basilica is a church of historical significance that plays an important part in the religious life of a particular region.) Twelve centuries earlier, Christians had brought the bones of Peter to the spot beside the Tiber River where he was believed to have been crucified. There they had built the basilica over a tomb. By the time of the Renaissance, the church's walls were leaning and threatening to collapse. In 1505, Julius stunned many

The Swiss Guard

During the Renaissance, Swiss soldiers were renowned for their military skill. In 1510, Julius II requested an elite guard of 250 Swiss soldiers to protect him. The Swiss Guard have been bodyguards to the pope ever since. Their uniform is said to have been designed by Michelangelo.

when he decided to demolish the ancient basilica and erect a huge new St. Peter's, one to rival any church in Christendom.

Julius planned to place his own magnificent marble tomb inside this grand church, close to the bones of St. Peter himself. To carve his tomb, Julius turned to a brilliant young sculptor from Florence, Michelangelo Buonarroti (miy-kuh-LAN-jeh-loh bwaw-nahr-RAW-tee).

Michelangelo Makes His Mark

Michelangelo and Julius II were both temperamental, arrogant, and demanding. They often infuriated each other. But the stormy relationship between this artist and his patron led to some of the finest art the world has known.

Michelangelo was born in a mountain village east of Florence. The nurse who cared for him was the wife of a stonecutter, so he grew up hearing the ring of hammer and chisel on stone. Around age 10 Michelangelo entered school in Florence, but he loved drawing more than studying. When he announced to his family that he wanted to be an artist, like Masaccio or Donatello, his angry father answered that painters and sculptors were no better than common laborers. But Michelangelo convinced his father to let him become an apprentice in an artist's studio. There he learned how to paint in fresco, that is, on wet plaster.

Soon Lorenzo de' Medici learned of the boy's talent, and invited him to study sculpture at his palace. Young Michelangelo lived at the Medici palace, often eating alongside the poets, philosophers, and artists whom Lorenzo the Magnificent invited to his table. From these humanists Michelangelo learned to admire human abilities and the classical past. He learned to write poetry. He loved Petrarch's sonnets.

Most of all, he loved sculpting in marble, as the ancient Greeks and Romans had done. He burned to depict the human form in stone.

To sculpt the human body, Michelangelo needed to understand it. He began making secret visits to a nearby hospital where he cut open dead bodies to study the positions of muscles and veins. He spent hour after hour learning to chisel arms, legs, and heads out of stone. When sculpting, Michelangelo thought of little else—he could work for weeks without bothering to change clothes. He was never happier than when covered in fine white marble dust.

For all his talent as an artist, Michelangelo possessed little skill for making friends. He was moody, sharp-tongued, and often short-tempered. He once quarreled with a fellow student who, in a fit of envy, struck him on the nose. The blow left Michelangelo with a crumpled nose for the rest of his life.

In 1496, Michelangelo, at age 21, traveled to Rome for the first time. The young genius stood breathless in the presence of so many ancient statues and monuments. Soon he would equal if not surpass the ancient masters.

In Rome, an elderly French cardinal commissioned Michelangelo to carve a marble statue of the Virgin

In Michelangelo's Pietà, *sculpted around 1499, the Virgin Mary cradles the body of her crucified son. The sculpture's exquisite details convey both agony and solemn resignation.*

Mary holding the dead Christ in her arms. Such a scene was called a pietà (pee-ay-TAH), which means "pity" in Italian. Michelangelo worked feverishly for more than a year, hardly sleeping at all, gnawing only pieces of bread when his stomach demanded.

Michelangelo's finished *Pietà* awed all who saw it. The young man from Florence had managed to capture every fold in Mary's robe, every vein and muscle in Christ's arms, as well as the immeasurable sorrow

in Mary's face. No one, not even the ancient Greeks, had sculpted with such skill.

Michelangelo returned to Florence to take up a new challenge. The young artist had his eye on a huge block of marble that had been sitting near the city's cathedral for more than 30 years. The giant stone was said to be flawed and unusable for making a statue. Michelangelo convinced the city's leaders to give him a chance to turn it into a symbol of Florentine greatness.

The council agreed. Michelangelo erected a shed around the great block so he could work in privacy. For two years, Florentines heard the sculptor chiseling away. Finally he revealed his finished work—a 14-foot-tall statue of the biblical David about to do battle with Goliath.

Seventy years earlier, Michelangelo's predecessor, Donatello, had sculpted a graceful and slender David as a symbol of Florence. (See page 55.) Now, in 1504, Michelangelo gave the city his boldly different version. Michelangelo's David had the heroic strength and vital intensity of an ancient Greek sculpture. Florentines admired it and put it in a public square. Church bells rang and crowds paraded through the streets as the statue was set on its pedestal for all to see.

Michelangelo and the Sistine Ceiling

By 1505, Michelangelo was the most famous sculptor in Italy. So when Pope Julius wanted a sculptor to carve a grand tomb in which the Warrior Pope would eventually be buried, he summoned Michelangelo to Rome. Michelangelo sketched a design for a colossal monument that would include 40 life-size statues. Julius was delighted, and Michelangelo rushed to a mountain quarry to choose the finest blocks of marble.

But even before the marble arrived in Rome, Julius started thinking about other projects. One day he led Michelangelo into the Sistine Chapel and pointed up at the blue vaulted ceiling. He announced that he wanted the young sculptor to cover the ceiling with frescos. "But painting is not my trade!" Michelangelo protested. Julius paid no attention. It was not wise to disobey a pope, so Michelangelo agreed to paint the chapel's ceiling.

The work took four agonizing years. Michelangelo himself designed a scaffold that allowed him to paint some 60 feet above the floor. He began the work with assistants. But he soon grew dissatisfied with their work and sent most of them away.

Day after day he stood with head and shoulders pulled sharply back,

Michelangelo sculpted his magnificent 14-foot-tall statue of David from a single block of marble. The sculpture seemed to sum up Florence itself—noble, daring, and full of confidence.

In the middle of the great fresco Michelangelo painted on the Sistine Chapel ceiling, God reaches out and imparts life to Adam. Biblical characters and scenes cover the other sections of the ceiling.

his beard, as he said, pointed toward heaven. Paint dripped from his brush into his eyes. He hauled a mattress onto the high platform and often slept there. "I live here in great toil and great weariness of body, and have no friend of any kind and do not want any, and haven't the time to eat what I need," he wrote to his brother.

Michelangelo had to paint the curved ceiling with enormous figures so they would be visible from far below. Occasionally Julius stole into the chapel and rapped on the floor with his cane. "When will you finish?" the impatient pope would call up to Michelangelo. "When I am able!" the stubborn artist would shout back. Julius threatened to have the artist thrown from the scaffolding if he did not finish his work. Finally,

in 1512, Michelangelo declared the work complete.

Excited crowds gathered to see what the artist had done. Michelangelo had painted nearly 350 magnificent human figures teeming with such life and energy that they looked as though they had been sculpted into the ceiling. Biblical scenes from the creation of the universe to the flood of Noah covered the massive space. Near the center loomed an image of God giving the divine spark of life to a near-perfect Adam. Even Julius gazed up in awe. Surely, people whispered, the great sculptor Michelangelo had proven that he was also the finest painter alive.

A few months later, Julius died. Michelangelo set his heart on finishing the pope's grand tomb. But in the years that followed, other popes and merchant princes demanded the artist's services. To Michelangelo's bitter disappointment, of the forty statues he had envisioned for Julius's tomb, he managed to carve only three.

Meanwhile, another of Julius's ambitious projects lay unfinished— the building of a new St. Peter's Basilica. For 40 years, an army of builders and engineers had labored on the giant church. When Michelangelo was 71 years old, a pope named Paul III appointed him to be architect of St. Peter's. (See page 66.)

The sculptor devoted the last 17 years of his life to the building. He designed a lofty dome to crown the church—a dome to rival any from ancient times. Every day, through blistering heat or freezing rain, the aging artist made his way to St. Peter's to oversee the work. He refused to accept any pay. He said that he did it for the good of his soul.

Michelangelo lived to see the framework of his dome rising against the sky. One February afternoon in 1564, he started to go to St. Peter's but found his legs too weak to mount his horse. Five days later, a few close friends stood around his bed as he spoke of "dying just as I am beginning to learn the alphabet of my profession." His friends carried his body back to Florence, where adoring citizens lined the streets to bid Michelangelo farewell.

Michelangelo and Julius: A Stormy Relationship

Julius hired Michelangelo to sculpt his tomb, but the pope was an infuriating patron. Michelangelo complained that the pope was often slow in paying for the project. In 1506, when Julius appeared to lose interest in the tomb and payments lagged, the sculptor left Rome in disgust and returned to his home of Florence. Julius sent an ambassador to bring him back. Here is Michelangelo's reply, addressed to an architect employed by the pope. The letter gives a glimpse of the relationship between the stubborn artist and his equally headstrong patron.

A Page from the Past

Florence, May 2, 1506

    MAESTRO GIULIANO, Architect to the Pope

Giuliano, I learn from a letter sent by you that the Pope was angry at my departure, that he is willing to place the money at my disposal and to carry out what was agreed upon between us; that I am to come back and fear nothing.

As far as my departure is concerned, the truth is that on Holy Saturday I heard the Pope, speaking at table with a jeweler and the Master of Ceremonies, say that he did not want to spend another bajocco [a small coin] on stones, whether small or large, which surprised me very much. However, before I set out I asked him for some of the money required for the continu-

Michelangelo and Julius II admired each other, but they often argued. The pope commissioned Michelangelo to sculpt his tomb. When the artist had trouble getting paid, he quit the project and returned to Florence — until the pope called him back to Rome.

ance of my work. His Holiness replied that I was to come back again on Monday: and I went on Monday, and on Tuesday, and on Wednesday, and on Thursday — as his Holiness saw. At last, on the Friday morning, I was turned out, that is to say, I was driven away: and the person who turned me away said he knew who I was, but that such were his orders. Thereupon, having heard those words on the Saturday and seeing them afterwards put into execution, I lost all hope. But this alone was not the whole reason of my departure. There was also another cause, but I do not wish to write about it; enough that it made me think that, if I were to remain in Rome, my own tomb would be prepared before that of the Pope. This is the reason for my sudden departure.

Now you write to me on behalf of the Pope, and in similar manner you will read this letter to the Pope. Give His Holiness to understand . . . that if he really wishes to have this tomb erected it would be well for him not to vex me as to where the work is to be done, provided that within the agreed period of five years it be erected in St. Peter's, on the site he shall choose, and that it be a beautiful work, as I have promised: for I am persuaded that it will be a work without equal in all the world if it be carried out.

If His Holiness wishes to proceed, let him deposit the said money here in Florence with a person whose name I will communicate to you. . . . I beg of you to let me have an answer, and quickly. I have nothing further to add.

Your Michelangelo,

Sculptor, in Florence

Raphael: The Prince of Painters

While Michelangelo was the stubborn, moody loner, another great Renaissance painter, Raphael Sanzio (RAHF-ee-uhl SAHNT-syoh), was known throughout Italy as a gentle, courteous man who could get along with just about everyone. It was said that Raphael was "so full of nobility and kindness that even the animals loved him."

Just as Raphael's character differed from Michelangelo's, so did his style of painting. While Michelangelo created figures that brought to mind strength, struggle, and determination, Raphael painted in a soothing, elegant style. Raphael and his paintings were so popular that he was called "the prince of painters."

The son of an artist, Raphael was born in the city-state of Urbino and grew up learning to draw and paint. When he was about 20 years old, he moved to Florence to study the works of Masaccio and Leonardo da Vinci. Raphael soon made a reputation for himself by painting lifelike portraits of wealthy Florentine merchants.

Raphael's most popular works were his paintings of Mary and the infant Jesus, known as Madonnas. Raphael's Madonnas feature gentle faces, soft lines, and delicate colors. The careful balance in the paintings show the artist's love of the classical ideal of order.

While Michelangelo was painting the ceiling of the Sistine Chapel, Julius II heard of Raphael's genius and summoned the young painter to Rome. His first commission from the pope was to decorate the walls

of the pope's private rooms in the Vatican. Raphael had never tackled such a huge project, but he went straight to work designing frescos.

Julius loved the classics, so in the pope's library Raphael painted a fresco called *The School of Athens*. For this grand painting, Raphael imagined all the great philosophers of ancient Greece gathered in one spot. Plato and Aristotle stand at the very center. Plato (the bearded figure with his right hand pointing up)

Raphael painted this Madonna *around 1505.* Madonna, *a word often used to refer to Jesus' mother, Mary, comes from the Italian words* ma donna, *meaning "my lady."* Madonna *eventually became a term for any statue or painting showing Mary with the child Jesus.*

On a First Name Basis

Two artists of the Renaissance, Michelangelo Buonarroti and Raphael Sanzio, made such unique contributions that no one could mistake them for anyone else. The two have historically been referred to only by their first names—Michelangelo and Raphael.

Above: Raphael looks straight out at us in this detail from his painting called The School of Athens. *It's as if he is asking, "How do you like my painting?"*

Right: In The School of Athens, *Raphael depicts the great philosophers of ancient Greece gathered together in the unfinished basilica of St. Peter's. At the center stands a red-robed Plato, whom Raphael painted with the features of Leonardo da Vinci.*

looks very much like Leonardo da Vinci. Raphael may have painted the resemblance as a tribute to the great Renaissance artist. Raphael also painted himself into the scene. Look for him in the lower group of figures on the far right—the youth looking pensively at us, second from the right.

Raphael charmed just about everyone he met, except Michelangelo, who trusted almost no one. Michelangelo thought that Raphael was too quick to copy others' techniques. He grew jealous of the young painter's ability to make friends. The two often traded barbs with each other.

Yet Raphael recognized Michelangelo as a genius. When he saw the Sistine Chapel ceiling, he was overcome with awe. He soon added another figure to *The School of Athens*, the thinker seated in the foreground, looking alone and lost in thought as he writes. Raphael said it was a reclusive Greek philosopher named Heraclitus. But this figure, unlike others in the painting, wears leather boots and a more modern coat. His nose is broad and flattened. It appears to be Raphael's tribute to his rival, the great Michelangelo.

Raphael spent the last 12 years of his life in Rome. He lived only until age 37, but still he left behind scores of portraits, Madonnas, and frescos.

By the time Raphael died in 1520, Rome was indeed a city revived. Raphael and Michelangelo had been part of a gigantic outburst of creativity that restored the city to its historic splendor. Meanwhile, as we'll see in the next chapter, Renaissance ideas in art, architecture, and learning were spreading far beyond Rome and Italy.

Ludovico Gonzaga, ruler of the city-state of Mantua, sits surrounded by his family and courtiers. Renaissance princes filled their courts with artists, scholars, and advisors.

Of Courtiers and Princes: Politics of the Renaissance

Florence, Rome, Venice, Milan, Urbino, Mantua, Naples—sixteenth-century Italy had many centers of power. In each you could find ambitious rulers, such as the Medici in Florence, the pope in Rome, or the doge in Venice.

Each of these rulers wanted his city-state to outshine the others. Each tried to fill his palaces with marble statues, his libraries with ancient manuscripts, his churches with giant frescoes. And each ruler knew that his success greatly depended on the people who advised him. So rulers surrounded themselves with brilliant courtiers, well-educated people who served a ruler at court.

Some courtiers were scholars, some were artists, and many were nobles. What did a courtier do? A prince might ask a courtier to give advice on how to build a new palace, repair a cathedral, fix a canal, or construct defensive walls. He might order the courtier to take a message to a rival court, negotiate a treaty with a neighboring city-state, or lead troops into war. The prince might need a courtier to translate an ancient Greek manuscript, or to discuss philosophy, astronomy, or mathematics. Often the prince simply wanted someone to tell an amusing story or sing a ballad.

The best courtiers needed a wide range of knowledge, talents, and skills. In the sixteenth century, people who wanted to be effective courtiers turned for advice to one man above all others—Baldassare Castiglione (bahl-dahs-SAHR-ay kahs-tee-LYOH-nay).

Castiglione: *The Book of the Courtier*

In 1478, when the Renaissance was well underway, Baldassare Castiglione was born to a poor but

Castiglione helped shape the tastes and culture of the Renaissance in The Book of the Courtier. *Raphael painted this portrait of his friend Castiglione in the early 1500s.*

noble family in the city-state of Mantua. As a boy he studied Greek, Latin, and the classics. He had a knack for just about everything—music, art, literature, athletics—and possessed a gift for getting along with people. "A young man well-favored in person," the bishop of Mantua wrote his father, "learned, elegant, discreet, of the utmost integrity, and so gifted by nature and fortune that if he continues as he has begun he will have no equal."

Little Mantua sat between the powerful city-states of Venice and Milan, so the ruling family of Mantua, the Gonzagas (gohn-DZAH-gahz), was always on the lookout for talented advisors. The young Castiglione became a courtier to Francesco Gonzaga, the prince of Mantua. Castiglione followed Gonzaga to war against Naples. Later he served the duke of the small city of Urbino, which lies in the mountains of central Italy.

- On the map on page 38, locate Mantua, Venice, Milan, and Urbino.

The Code of Chivalry

In the Middle Ages, the code of chivalry spelled out rules of honorable conduct for knights to follow. A good knight, said the code, was loyal to the Christian Church and to the lord he served. He fought bravely and was expected to protect the poor and the helpless, and all women and children. The code of chivalry called upon the knight to be fair, just, truthful, generous to all, and merciful to his enemies. The code described an ideal knight. It set high standards that few knights actually met.

Urbino may have been remote, but the duke's court was a lively place. Scholars, soldiers, counts, and cardinals came and went. The duke invited poets, painters, sculptors, and musicians to his court, and Castiglione met them all. The young courtier often traveled on behalf of the duke of Urbino. His duties as a diplomat gave him the chance to meet such figures as the king of England and Pope Julius II. During his stay in Rome, he worked with the artist Raphael on a report about how to preserve the city's ancient buildings and monuments.

In every court he visited, Castiglione observed how various courtiers served their princes, and he listened in on their conversations. Soon he began to write down his reflections on what he saw and heard. Eventually he put his observations into a book called *The Book of the Courtier*.

Published in 1528, *The Book of the Courtier* was a how-to guide for graceful behavior. It described how a courtier should act while serving at court, and how he could best serve his prince. Castiglione based *The Book of the Courtier* partly on the writings of the ancient Roman statesman Cicero. The medieval code of chivalry also helped form the book's ideals of gentlemanly behavior.

But Castiglione wrote for a new age. No longer were battles mainly fought by knights wielding axes and javelins. The Renaissance was a time when new weapons were appearing on battlefields, such as bronze cannons that fired iron shot hundreds of feet into enemy lines. Military victory now required more than brute strength. It also needed the intellectual strength of men who knew how to build weapons, design fortifications, plan battles, and lead troops. Renaissance princes wanted good strategists, engineers, and advisors. Education and intelligence mattered.

Castiglione recognized these changes. He believed that a good Renaissance courtier still needed some qualities of the chivalrous knight, such as courage, horsemanship, and good swordsmanship for battle at close range. He thought that courtiers should also know how to wrestle, swim, jump, and run, since such skills often helped a man win a good name.

But Castiglione believed that a good Renaissance courtier needed to be more than a warrior or athlete. The courtier, said Castiglione, needed a much broader education than the medieval knight ever did. A courtier should know "not only Latin, but Greek as well," he wrote. "Let him be versed in the poets,

as well as in the orators and historians, and let him be practiced also in writing verse and prose." He should be able to discuss art and philosophy with his prince, as well as draw, paint, dance, and play some musical instruments.

Renaissance courtiers were supposed to possess, among other traits, the qualities of a knight—bravery, honor, and skill in battle.

Humanism and the Humanities

Many Renaissance courtiers were humanists. As you've learned, humanism was an educational program that emphasized the classics. It included the study of writing, persuasive speaking, poetry, history, and philosophy. Scholars still call such branches of learning the *humanities*.

The ideal courtier should also be a man of good character. "You ought to obey your lord in all things profitable and honorable to him, not in those that will bring him harm and shame," Castiglione advised. The courtier should have many talents and skills but be modest about them. He should be witty in conversation, but never crude or impolite. Under all circumstances, he should be calm.

Furthermore, said Castiglione, the courtier should have the quality of *sprezzatura* (spreht-zah-TOOR-uh)—that is, he should be able to display his skills with ease. "Whatever is done or said," Castiglione declared, should "appear to be without effort."

Few people, if any, could actually acquire all the knowledge and traits that *The Book of the Courtier* described. But Castiglione wanted his book to paint an image of the perfect courtier, the ideal man of Renaissance times. In this era of excitement about human potential and new knowledge, the most admired men possessed education and abilities in many different areas. To this day, to be a "Renaissance man" means to be a person of wide and varied knowledge and skills.

Castiglione's book became a favorite of rulers and courtiers throughout Europe. The Holy Roman Emperor Charles V kept it by his bedside. Generations of noblemen consulted *The Book of the Courtier* to find out how to excel at court. Wealthy merchants studied it to brush up on their manners and know how to act when rubbing elbows with princes and dukes. In England, it helped define the idea of a gentleman. *The Book of the Courtier* still gives us the most complete description of the ideal Renaissance courtier.

Isabella d'Este: A Court of Her Own

North of Urbino, where Castiglione spent so many fruitful years, lay Castiglione's birthplace, Mantua. The Gonzaga family had ruled Mantua for four centuries and developed a court that became a place of great learning. In the early 1500s, the most remarkable Gonzaga of them all was a woman who married into the family. She became one of the outstanding figures of the Renaissance. Her name was Isabella d'Este (DES-tay).

Isabella grew up in the city of Ferrara. Thanks to her father, who believed in the equality of boys and girls, she received an excellent education. Isabella's intelligence and abilities continually amazed her teachers. By her mid-teens, she could read Greek and Latin. She could play the lute, sing, dance, and discuss politics. Blond-haired, dark-eyed, and

Castiglione's Advice to Ladies at Court

Castiglione wrote that women at court should possess many of the same virtues he recommended for men. They should be magnanimous, prudent, and self-restrained. "Everything men can understand, women can too," he wrote in *The Book of the Courtier*. Castiglione also advised women at court to "know how to entertain graciously every kind of man with charming and honest conversation, suited to the time and the place and the rank of the person with whom she is talking."

Isabella d'Este helped
turn Mantua into
a leading center of
culture. Her learning,
diplomacy, and leader-
ship skills made her
a true "Renaissance
woman."

always elegantly dressed, Isabella d'Este became a charming, shrewd, and very determined young woman.

At about the age of 16, Isabella's parents arranged a marriage for their brilliant daughter. They decided that she would marry Castiglione's former prince and the ruler of Mantua, Francesco Gonzaga. Francesco was by no means a handsome man, and Isabella's sister was appalled at the engagement.

But the marriage proved successful for Isabella. Francesco shared Isabella's passion for the arts. Francesco was more soldier than politician, so in situations that called for skillful diplomacy, he often sought his wife's advice. When problems arose, Francesco often had a two-word solution: "Ask Madame."

Isabella knew how to navigate the whirl of plots, schemes, and intrigue in Mantua's court. In 1509, a war with Venice tested her abilities. The Venetians took Francesco prisoner, and little Mantua faced terrible danger. Isabella rallied her people, rooted enemies out of her court, and took command of the army.

Isabella paid careful attention to every detail at court. "Not a leaf stirs without her consent," observed one of her officials. She knew how to stand firm in troubled times. At one point the Venetians sent word that they would release Francesco only if Isabella sent them her son Federico. Francesco agreed to risk his son becoming a hostage, but Isabella refused. Instead, she worked hard to gain support from powerful leaders, including Pope Julius II, the king of France, and, as she put it, "all the other reigning heads and potentates of Christendom."

Isabella Stands Firm

In response to the Venetian demand that she send her son as a hostage, Isabella wrote to her imprisoned husband, "I would rather lose our State, than deprive us of our children." She advised Francesco, "Have patience! You can be sure that I think continuously of your liberation and when the time comes I will not fail you, as I have not relaxed my efforts.... If it were *really* the only means of setting you free, I would not only send Federico but all the other children as well. I will do everything imaginable."

Isabella eventually managed to secure her husband's release, but soon afterwards he fell ill and retired to a country villa. Isabella governed Mantua on behalf of Francesco until his death in 1519. After that, she governed on behalf of her son, Federico.

Isabella had read Castiglione's *The Book of the Courtier* and possessed many of the talents he outlined. She became a dedicated patron of the arts and kept her own personal museum in a suite of 16 rooms she called her "paradiso." There she amassed the treasures of her court—paintings, statues, and rare books. Even her dishes were works of art, each adorned with a different scene from classical mythology or the Bible.

Although her city-state was less powerful than Florence or Rome, Isabella made Mantua a center of learning and art. Her wit, charm, and commanding presence drew acclaimed writers and artists to her court. Even the great Leonardo da Vinci visited Mantua and made a sketch of Isabella.

The Florentine writer Niccolò Machiavelli lived in a time of invasions and wars in Italy. He came to believe that Italy needed princes who could maintain strong, secure city-states.

Isabella was not content to collect the works of others. She made her own drawings and wrote her own poems. She also penned hundreds of letters to friends, family, princes, and artists all over Europe. Many contained her thoughts on politics and war.

In a time when men held most of the power and privilege, Isabella d'Este was a striking exception. She was a doer and a thinker, a true "Renaissance woman."

Machiavelli Studies Princes

Two issues were always on the minds of princes in Renaissance Italy—politics and war. In the early sixteenth century, one writer began to address these important issues in a new way. His writings transformed the world of politics. His name was Niccolò Machiavelli (neek-koh-LOH mah-kyah-VEL-lee).

Machiavelli was a native of Florence, a place he loved until his dying day. His family did not have much money, but they did have the treasure Gutenberg had made possible—books. We can imagine young Machiavelli bent over his books in his house near the city, studying Latin, reading about Caesar's campaigns, and learning what he could about Greek philosophy.

In Machiavelli's time, Italy was a war-torn peninsula. In 1494, when Machiavelli was 25 years old, the

French army invaded Italy. The people of Florence used the occasion to drive out the Medici. Meanwhile, Spanish soldiers marched into Italy. Troops from Germany and Switzerland appeared as well, not as invaders but as mercenaries—that is, they fought for whichever city-state paid them the most money. In central and northern Italy, popes battled to bring various parts of the Papal States under their rule.

In this time of strife and struggle, Machiavelli went to work for the government of Florence. He often traveled to other city-states or nations. He saw that strong nations like France and Spain considered the Italian city-states weak. They invaded at will. Machiavelli started to think that Italy needed princes who could make their city-states respected and secure.

In 1502, Florence sent Machiavelli on a mission to Rome. There he met Cesare Borgia (CHAY-zahr-ay BOR-juh), the illegitimate son of Pope Alexander VI and a leader of the armies of the Church. Cesare was strong, arrogant, and ruthless.

In the three months he spent with Cesare, Machiavelli carefully observed how the cunning prince wielded power. Pope Alexander VI had given Cesare the task of crushing towns and cities that had rebelled against papal rule. Machiavelli watched the young tyrant march his army through the Papal States, seizing one mutinous town after another. He defeated his enemies not so much by military might, but through trickery and sheer terror.

Machiavelli studied Cesare Borgia to learn how princes use power. The ruthless Borgia led papal armies against the enemies of Rome.

Machiavelli observed how Cesare Borgia dealt with disloyalty. Once Cesare hired local lords and their armies to fight for him. When they plotted against Cesare, the prince acted decisively. He invited the plotters to a banquet, promising to extend his forgiveness and renew their friendship. The rebels arrived unarmed and without guards. Cesare quickly seized and executed them.

Machiavelli left Cesare Borgia wondering if such a leader—a man who would stop at nothing to achieve his ends—could bring order to war-torn Italy. But Pope

Machiavelli and the Classics

Writing, Machiavelli said, made him feel as though he could "enter the courts of the ancients and [be] welcomed by them ... and there I make bold to speak to them and ask the motives of their actions, and they, in their humanity, reply to me. And for the space of ... hours I forget the world ... I pass indeed into their world."

Alexander soon died, and Cesare ended up in prison. And in 1512, Machiavelli's career in politics came to an abrupt end when the Medici returned to power in Florence. Machiavelli lost his position and was forced into exile in the countryside.

Despite all his efforts, Machiavelli had not become an important figure in his beloved native city. Few ordinary Florentines even knew his name. Exiled to the old family estate, where he could see the dome of Florence's cathedral just 10 miles away, he turned from the practice of politics to writing a how-to book for princes. In the process he made himself the father of modern political science—the study of politics and government.

The Prince

Machiavelli titled his book *The Prince*. In it, he laid out bold new guidelines for creating and maintaining a secure state. He drew on lessons learned in his study of classical history. He also drew on the lessons he learned by studying the triumphs and defeats of Cesare Borgia and others.

Machiavelli knew that Cesare was a wicked man. But he believed that the time in which he lived—a time when Italy's city-states suffered invasions and war—required a certain kind of leader. The time called for a cunning prince willing to do whatever it took to protect his state and make it an orderly place. In Machiavelli's view, anyone who wanted to know

Machiavelli's ideal prince had to be a powerful figure, ready to use the sword—a man who inspired not just admiration, but fear.

how "to destroy one's enemies, to secure some allies, to win wars, whether by force or by fraud, to make oneself both loved and feared by one's subjects … cannot hope to find, in the recent past, a better model to imitate than Cesare Borgia."

Machiavelli startled his readers by rejecting certain ideals of the Middle Ages. Medieval philosophers had written that a ruler should exercise power virtuously for the common good of his people, and that he should base his actions on Christian principles. But Machiavelli argued that a good ruler should do whatever it took to secure and unite his state. In Machiavelli's eyes, those who expected rulers to act honestly and virtuously in every instance were living in "an imaginary world." It was better, he said, for a prince to use harsh measures when needed to maintain his kingdom and secure his state.

To hold on to power, Machiavelli declared, a prince must act as circumstances required. If this meant breaking his promises, so be it. If it meant committing cruel acts, then that was the price to pay for a well-ordered and secure state. In short, the ends justified the means.

According to Machiavelli, the world of politics was a jungle. Only a savage beast—part lion, part fox—could survive as the king of that jungle.

For such rulers there could only be one answer to the question, "Is it better to be loved or to be feared?" In Machiavelli's words, "The reply is that one ought to be both … but as it is difficult for the two to go together, it is much safer to be feared than to be loved." Machiavelli wrote: "When a ruler is at the head of his army and has a vast number of soldiers under his command, then it is absolutely essential to be prepared to be thought cruel; for it is impossible to keep an army united and ready for action without acquiring a reputation for cruelty."

Despite his hopes, Machiavelli never returned to political office. He hoped that the Medici would call upon him, but that call never came. Instead, his matter-of-fact presentation of how a prince should govern a state shocked many readers.

Machiavelli's ideas spread well beyond Florence and Italy. Soon after his death, *The Prince* was translated into several foreign languages. Princes and courtiers all over Europe read it. The book gave Europe's rulers new ideas—some good, some bad—about how to govern. Not everybody agreed that human beings were basically wicked and self-centered. But the book made rulers and their counselors think less about abstract ideals and more about actual human conduct and likely results. That is why many people consider Niccolò Machiavelli to be the founder of modern political science.

Was Machiavelli Machiavellian?

Machiavelli was by all accounts an upright citizen and good man. But his advice to rulers, often summed up as "the ends justify the means," has given us the English word *Machiavellian*. Though it probably would have surprised Machiavelli himself, his name has come to stand for secrecy, treachery, and intrigue.

Leonardo, the Ultimate Renaissance Man

Like Machiavelli and Castiglione, Leonardo da Vinci was a courtier. Earlier you read how he learned to draw, paint, and cast bronze in Florence, and then joined the court of Ludovico Sforza, the duke of Milan. When a French army invaded Milan in 1499, Leonardo fled his home of 17 years. Let's rejoin this "Renaissance man" now.

Leonardo bid goodbye to Milan, the city where he had spent so many years. He traveled to the little city-state of Mantua, where he visited the court of Isabella d'Este and made a charcoal drawing of the strong-willed duchess. Then he moved on to Venice. The Venetians were alarmed by an approaching Turkish army. Leonardo advised them to flood a nearby river valley to prevent their enemies from reaching the city. Venice's leaders doubted that such an unusual defense could work. A few weeks later, Leonardo was on his way home to Florence. Luckily for Venice, the Turkish army did not attack the city.

Leonardo lived in a time when the rulers of Italy constantly fought each other. Every year, it seemed, one city-state or another raised an army to march against its neighbors. Leonardo soon found himself caught up in the fighting. In 1502, he entered the service of Cesare Borgia, the ruthless son of Pope Alexander VI.

Leonardo da Vinci sketched this tank, or armored car, in his notebook.

Borgia was determined to conquer central Italy, and for a year Leonardo traveled with his army to strengthen fortresses and make maps. Leonardo described war as "bestial madness," but he filled his notebooks with ideas for new military machines—a tank, an exploding bomb, even a kind of machine gun.

During his military travels, Leonardo became friends with Niccolò Machiavelli, who was studying Borgia's treacherous tactics. After two years, Leonardo left Borgia's military campaigns and returned to Florence.

The Florentines welcomed Leonardo as an honored native son. But it was a different city than he had known as a boy. Lorenzo the Magnificent was dead. While

Leonardo was in Milan, Savonarola had convinced the Florentines to burn their books and paintings on a bonfire of the vanities. The angry preacher was now dead, while the Renaissance lived on in Florence. But now a new generation of artists was making its mark.

Among them was Michelangelo. Leonardo and Michelangelo did not like each other. Leonardo had once called sculpting a dirty, sweaty "mechanical exercise." Michelangelo had insulted Leonardo on the streets of Florence. "You made a model of a horse you could never cast in bronze and which you gave up, to your shame," he taunted the older artist.

The Florentines loved a good rivalry, and they made sure they got one. They invited each artist to paint a wall in the city's council chamber. Leonardo set to work painting the battle of Anghiari (ahng-GYAH-ree), in which Florence had defeated Milan 60 years before. Michelangelo was to paint the battle of Cascina (kah-SHEE-nah), fought between Florence and the city-state of Pisa in 1368. All of Florence looked forward to the contest between these two great artists.

Leonardo decided to try an ancient Roman technique of painting with oils. He covered his wall with soldiers and horses clashing in the storm of battle. He then proceeded to dry the paint with coal fires. But the process did not work. The colors ran down the wall, ruining the painting. Leonardo did not have the heart to start over. He abandoned the project. Michelangelo never finished his painting either. He soon left for Rome, where he ended up painting the ceiling of the Sistine Chapel for Pope Julius II.

About the time Leonardo painted the battle of Anghiari, he also threw himself into the dream of building a flying machine. He filled his notebooks with studies of birds' wings and flight patterns.

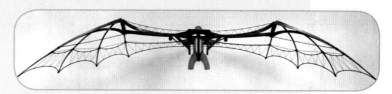

A model of a flying machine follows Leonardo's original design.

"The bird is an instrument functioning according to mathematical laws, and man has the power to reproduce an instrument like this with all its movements," he wrote.

The Mona Lisa *has become Leonardo's most famous painting. Viewers have long been intrigued by the dark-eyed gaze and half-smile of the face in this extraordinary portrait.*

Over the years he sketched designs for several machines, including one similar to a modern hang glider, and another like a helicopter. Legend says that an assistant strapped himself into one of the flying machines without Leonardo's knowledge, jumped off a cliff—and tumbled to the ground.

While in Florence, Leonardo began work on a painting that has become one of the best known paintings in the world—the *Mona Lisa*. Historians were long unsure of the identity of the lady in this famous picture, but many now believe she was the wife of a merchant living in Florence. Her mysterious smile and the misty landscape behind her have intrigued onlookers for centuries.

In 1506, Leonardo received an invitation to return to Milan, which the French now ruled. He journeyed north, looking forward to seeing again the city where he had lived for nearly two decades.

Leonardo's second stay in Milan was one of the happiest times of his life. The French rulers welcomed him as a prince. They admired him for always seeking new knowledge and creating things of beauty. Leonardo spent time making geological studies, tackling mathematical problems, studying the human body, and improving the city-state's canals. But a few years later, yet another war broke out. A Swiss army forced the French to abandon Milan. In 1513, 61-year-old Leonardo packed his bags yet again and moved to Rome.

Leonardo spent only about three years in Rome. He threw himself into studies of mathematics, motion, plants, and the body. Pope Leo X gave him the task of draining the swampy countryside around Rome. Leonardo also began to build an enormous curved mirror, perhaps to use as part of a huge telescope.

Leonardo created this self-portrait in red chalk around 1512, seven years before his death.

He never completed the mirror. He did not feel at home in Rome, and his stay there turned bitter. Younger artists were winning praise for their work. Leonardo, on the other hand, seemed to be falling out of fashion. He was an old man with a long white beard. His health was beginning to fail. He spent much time alone, pursuing his studies and strolling Rome's streets to look at ancient monuments.

At this sad time of his life, Leonardo received one last summons. King Francis I invited him to come live in France. Leonardo packed his notebooks, gathered three paintings—including the *Mona Lisa*—and in 1516 left Italy for France.

Francis considered Leonardo to be the most learned man alive. The king gave him a handsome house and income, and installed him in his court as "first painter, architect, and mechanic of the king." Francis delighted in Leonardo's conversation and in his architectural skills. In no time he had Leonardo designing his palaces, or *chateaux* (sha-TOH). French chateaux began to look more and more like Italian *palazzi*. Ill health kept the aging Leonardo from painting anymore, but he spent his last years pursuing his studies, drafting architectural plans, and arranging his notebooks.

Leonardo died at age 67 in 1519. The biographer Giorgio Vasari, writing a few decades later, reported that Da Vinci died with the king of France at his side. Leonardo, he said, was patiently observing and describing the nature of his own illness to the very end. That report may or may not be true, but it is not hard to imagine that up to the moment of death, Leonardo continued his lifelong passion for learning.

After Leonardo died, his precious notes were scattered throughout Europe. Much of his artwork disappeared. Many of the projects he had started were never finished, so they faded from people's memories. Monks even cut a door into the wall on which Leonardo had painted *The Last Supper*.

For centuries people remembered Leonardo da Vinci as a fine Renaissance artist. Only when modern-day scholars began to collect and examine his notebooks did the public appreciate his genius. No one else had ever attempted to do so much in so many areas, or shown such an unlimited desire for knowledge. Leonardo da Vinci was indeed the ultimate Renaissance man.

Hans Holbein the Younger's painting of two French ambassadors to the English court illustrates how the Renaissance love of learning spread beyond Italy. The men are posed with symbols of their interests, including globes, books, and musical instruments.

The Renaissance Beyond Italy

When Leonardo da Vinci moved to the court of the French king, he helped export the Renaissance beyond Italy. Italians were good at exporting both products and ideas to other places. They exported fine luxury goods from Florence, Venice, and Rome. They exported classical Greek and Latin texts printed in Venice. They also exported modern works, such as Machiavelli's *The Prince* and Castiglione's *The Book of the Courtier.*

Italian ideas spread in other ways. Sometimes armies invaded Italy and hauled Italian artwork home. Merchants who journeyed throughout Europe spread the word about Italian accomplishments. Scholars traveled from monastery to monastery carrying Italian ideas with them.

As word of Italy's achievements reached the cities of northern Europe, people began to wonder: "What is going on down south?

Do these Italians know something we need to know?"

Renaissance ideas were on the move. It was not long before thinkers and rulers in distant lands found themselves inspired by the ideas that had sparked a rebirth in Italy—the new admiration for classics, the new curiosity about human abilities, the new love of lifelike painting and sculpture, and the new principles of architecture. These ideas spread beyond Italy and began to influence northern European art, religion, and thought.

This chapter focuses on the spread of Renaissance ideas beyond Italy.

Europe's Strong Monarchs

By 1500, England, France, and Spain had come under the rule of

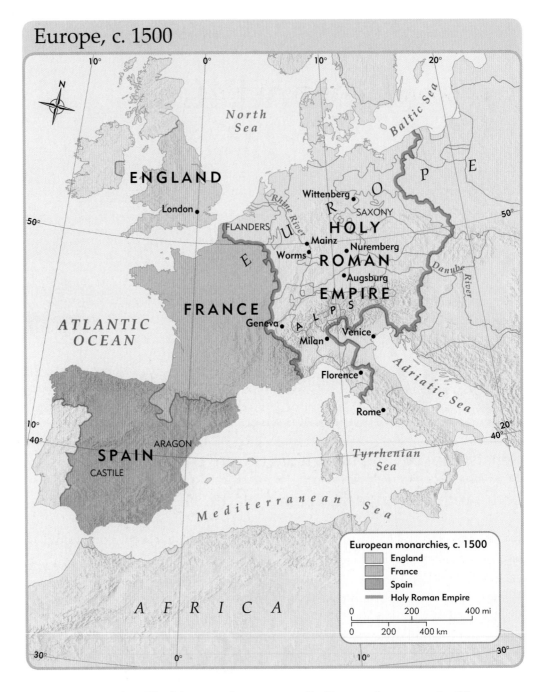

Europe, c. 1500

European monarchies, c. 1500
- England
- France
- Spain
- Holy Roman Empire

0   200   400 mi

0   200   400 km

strong monarchs. The kings and queens of these lands were bent on expanding their power. Even before Machiavelli wrote *The Prince*, these monarchs acted according to the principle that "the ends justify the means." What means did they use to gain power? For starters, they bribed their rivals with land, threatened them with war, threw them into prison, or simply cut off their heads.

In France, for example, King Louis XI came to be known as the Spider King because he was constantly spinning a web of schemes. Louis and later French kings changed France from a territory of warring states into a strong monarchy.

In Spain, King Ferdinand of Aragon and Queen Isabella of Castile joined their kingdoms by marrying each other in 1469. Spain soon had the strongest royal government in

Europe, as well as the best army. Across the English Channel, strong kings were taking charge. Beginning with King Henry VII, a royal family called the Tudors brought the English nobility under control.

- On the map on page 96, locate the monarchies of England, France, and Spain (Aragon and Castile).

While strong monarchs ruled England, France, and Spain, other parts of Europe remained fragmented. For example, east of France lay the vast Holy Roman Empire, covering the lands known today as Germany and Austria. There a family called the Habsburgs built a powerful dynasty by marrying into other wealthy landowning families. The Habsburg ruler called himself an emperor, but his Holy Roman Empire was really a hodgepodge of duchies and city-states filled with stubborn dukes and rich merchants who ran affairs as they saw fit. (A duchy [DUH-chee] is a small territory ruled by a duke.)

- On the map on page 96, locate the Holy Roman Empire and the city-states of Mainz, Nuremberg, and Augsburg.

Kings, queens, and the Holy Roman Emperor amassed large armies, and they were not afraid to use them. Armies from France, Germany, and Spain often invaded Italy. The invading kings and their courtiers found themselves enchanted by the artwork of Milan, the gardens of Florence, and the palaces of Venice. They hauled wagonload after wagonload of glittering treasures back home—Italian paintings, Italian books, Italian ideas and attitudes.

Northern European monarchs became patrons of Renaissance art. We've seen that in France, King Francis I fell in love with all things Italian. Francis, who ruled from 1515 to 1547, lured Leonardo da Vinci from Italy and sought his advice on architecture. The king and his nobles built splendid castles patterned on Italian designs. They collected Italian

King Ferdinand of Aragon and Queen Isabella of Castile greet Christopher Columbus, whose voyages they sponsored. The king and queen united their kingdoms to make Spain the most powerful monarchy in Europe.

artwork and sent agents to Italy to buy ancient manuscripts. Francis started a university for the study of humanist ideas. He invited artists and scholars to live at his court. He even married his son into the Medici family.

Such patrons—whether kings, dukes, or wealthy merchants—supported artists throughout northern Europe.

The Renaissance in Northern Europe

While Masaccio, Leonardo, and Michelangelo were painting and sculpting in Italy, artists in northern Europe were creating masterpieces

Jan van Eyck painted his Giovanni Arnolfini and his Bride *on a wood panel using slow-drying oil paints, which allowed him to add much wonderful detail to the painting.*

of their own. With a little practice you can spot differences between Renaissance art from Italy and art from northern Europe, especially in paintings.

Italian painters emphasized the beauty of the human body. They wanted to show the ideal human form and face. Leonardo and Raphael created beautiful Madonnas, while Michelangelo painted bold, athletic figures that seem to spring to life.

Artists in northern Europe, on the other hand, painted with great attention to detail, even if the detail was not flattering. If a merchant had a wart on his face, a northern European artist was likely to include that wart. For the northern European painter, capturing the ideal was less important than rendering the real in great detail.

Jan van Eyck: An Eye for Detail

One of the most influential northern European artists was Jan van Eyck (yahn van IYK), who painted in the early fifteenth century. He worked in Flanders. Van Eyck was one of the first artists to paint on wood panels with colors mixed in oil. Italian artists often painted in fresco—that is, onto freshly spread plaster. Fresco painters had to work quickly to finish before the plaster dried. But oil paint dries slowly. That gave Van Eyck time to add more detail to his pictures. He could paint layer upon layer of detail.

One of Van Eyck's most famous paintings is called *Giovanni Arnolfini and His Bride.* He painted this portrait of an Italian merchant and his wife in 1434. Van Eyck was probably a witness to the marriage, and he has tried to show us everything as it appeared to his eye. The picture is filled with details—the glittering chandelier, the fruit sitting on the window sill, the shoes on the floor. It is almost as if Van Eyck is holding a mirror to the scene. In fact, if you look very carefully in the round mirror on the wall, you can see Van Eyck himself standing in the room.

The picture also contains realistic details that Renaissance viewers would have understood as symbols. For example, the dog represents the married couple's faithfulness to each other. The single lit candle on the chandelier stands for their Christian faith.

Dürer: The "Leonardo of the North"

The busy German town of Nuremberg produced one of the great geniuses of the Renaissance—Albrecht Dürer (AHL-brekt DYOUR-ur). Dürer's father, a goldsmith, taught his son how to carve delicate designs onto hard pieces of metal. The boy showed an astonishing gift for drawing.

As a young man, Dürer traveled to Flanders to see the paintings of Van Eyck. Then he went to Germany and Switzerland. Everywhere he went, he heard about the new Italian artists who, inspired by the classics, were beautifully portraying the human form.

In 1494, Dürer made his first trip across the Alps to Venice. He loved what he saw. For a few months, and then again on a return trip 10 years later, he soaked up all he saw

In his self-portrait of 1500, Albrecht Dürer appears as a Christ-like figure. German-born Dürer became one of the Renaissance's most brilliant artists— the "Leonardo of the North."

in Italy—idealized figures, accurate perspective, bold color.

In Italy Dürer read Latin poetry and studied geometry. A Venetian painter taught him how to draw a perfectly proportioned human body. Italian painters, meanwhile, marveled at Dürer's ability to paint minute details realistically. Shortly before returning to Nuremberg, Dürer wrote, "Oh, how I shall long for the sun!" He could not take the Italian sun with him, but he did take home his knowledge of Italian art.

The young artist applied his new learning to a subject near at hand—himself. With painstaking detail, he painted remarkable self-portraits. His self-portrait of 1500 shows an idealized, Christ-like figure.

Dürer's most important works were not paintings but engravings. To produce an engraving, the artist cut an image into a copper plate, rubbed the plate with ink, and then pressed the plate against paper.

a pond at sunset, a wildflower growing beside the road, ladies on the streets of Venice.

By the time he died in 1528, Dürer had produced almost 200 paintings, over a thousand drawings, and hundreds of woodcuts and engravings. "Would to God it were possible for me to see the work of the mighty masters to come!" he wrote with Renaissance optimism for the future.

Hans Holbein: Portrait Master

Another great northern European artist, Hans Holbein (hahns HOHL-biyn) the Younger, was born in Augsburg in southern Germany. Holbein is known as "the Younger" because his father, who was also a painter, had the same name.

Like Dürer, young Holbein spent time in Italy studying the works of master artists. Later he lived in Switzerland, where he painted portraits of wealthy merchants and other important people.

This was an age before cameras, so kings, popes, and rich merchants eagerly sought artists who could create lasting records of what they looked like. When King Henry VIII of England heard of Holbein's talent, he called the painter to London to create portraits of the royal household.

Holbein's portraits made him famous throughout Europe. His faithful brush captured accurate likenesses. But his portraits also seemed to reveal each subject's personality. (See page 94.)

When Italian artists saw paintings by Van Eyck, Dürer, Holbein, and other northern masters, they

Dürer, who was not only a painter but also an engraver, set his Nativity *in his own time. Mary kneels before the infant Jesus while Joseph fetches water. But the eye is first drawn to the fine details of the rundown buildings.*

Printers could make many copies of a single engraving and even put them in books. Before long, Dürer's beautiful engravings were known across Europe.

Dürer's boundless curiosity and energy made him a true Renaissance man—the "Leonardo of the North," as he is sometimes called. He invited humanists and scholars into his home. He wrote about theories of proportions, model cities, and ideal beauty. Wherever he went, he made sketches of everything he saw—

Germany's Hans Holbein the Younger won fame as a gifted portrait painter. Henry VIII commissioned him to paint this portrait of the king's only son, Edward VI.

were amazed at the lifelike details and vivid colors. Knowledge of northern techniques traveled to Italy, where artists began to experiment with oil paints and incorporate more detail. German and Flemish influences spread south, just as Italian influence spread north.

Christian Humanism

Like the humanists of Italy, the humanists of northern Europe were inspired by the wisdom of ancient Greek and Roman writings. The northern humanists also shared the Renaissance faith in the ability of human beings to reason and improve themselves. But the northern humanists differed from their southern counterparts in one important way. They were more interested in using ancient texts to further their understanding of Christianity's teachings.

The scholars of northern Europe are often known as Christian humanists. They read Plato and Aristotle, but they studied early Christian writings with even greater zeal. They mastered ancient Greek and Hebrew so they could read the Bible as well as the letters of Paul and other Church fathers.

The Christian humanists were worried about the Church. They were alarmed by the poor training of many priests—some couldn't even read. They disapproved of high-ranking Church officials who were more concerned with money, power, and land than people's souls. They criticized the bishops and the pope in Rome for spending fortunes to collect art while neglecting to spread Christ's message. The Christian Church, they said, needed to put its house in order.

Erasmus Sees Folly

One learned Dutch monk looked around and shook his head at the folly of his fellow men, especially his fellow churchmen. His name was Desiderius Erasmus (DEH-sih-DEER-ee-us ih-RAZ-mus). Erasmus decided to leave the monastic life behind to travel, study, teach, and write. He lived all over Europe—in France, England, Germany, Switzerland, and Italy. He especially loved Rome. "There," he wrote, "one enjoys sweet liberty, rich libraries, the charming friendship of writers and scholars, and the sight of antique monuments."

But in Rome Erasmus also saw much to trouble him—worldly cardinals, power-hungry priests, Church officials building themselves grand palaces, even a pope, Julius II, who strapped on armor to gain control of nearby city-states.

Erasmus left Rome for England. There he wrote a book to protest

Holbein's painting of Erasmus shows the great scholar working on his new edition of the New Testament. In another book, The Praise of Folly, Erasmus criticized the foolish behavior of Church officials.

the wrongs he had seen in Rome, and to offer sharp observations on various failings of human conduct. The book, published in 1509, is called *The Praise of Folly*.

In his book, Erasmus speaks through the voice of a character named Folly, or foolishness. Folly tells how she runs the world. "If you please," says Folly, "let us look a little into the lives of men, and it will easily appear not only how much they owe to me, but how much they esteem me even from the highest to the lowest." Scholars, princes, courtiers, merchants, hunters—few escape the sharp barbs hurled by Folly.

But Erasmus saved his sharpest criticism for monks, priests, cardinals,

and other officials of the Church. As for "those that commonly call themselves the religious and monks," says Folly, they are "most false in both titles, when ... a great part of them are farthest from religion."

The printing press made *The Praise of Folly* widely available. It soon became one of Europe's best-selling books.

Erasmus was deeply versed in classical learning. He studied ancient Greek texts of the Bible to prepare a new edition of the New Testament in Latin. He went back to the ancient texts because he wanted to get a better understanding of the teachings of Jesus.

In 1523, Erasmus's friend Hans Holbein painted a portrait of him writing at his desk. The portrait shows us what a thoughtful, scholarly man he was. He believed in the power of human beings to improve their lives through faith, reason, and education.

More Seeks Utopia

Erasmus wrote *The Praise of Folly* at the London home of his good friend Thomas More. More was England's greatest Christian humanist. Erasmus even dedicated his book to More.

In about 1527, Hans Holbein the Younger painted a portrait of More. Holbein's picture shows us a dignified man who seems to have much on his mind. He clutches a book in his hands and looks as though he's eager to jump up and put the words of the book into action.

Thomas More was a man of learning and a man of faith. He

Books Spread Ideas

The printing press played an important role in spreading Renaissance ideas. By 1500, there were more than a thousand printing presses in Europe. As Europeans produced more and more books, ideas traveled faster than ever before.

loved to read classical literature and the Bible. He made translations of Greek authors and wrote poems in Latin. King Henry VIII of England loved to invite him to the royal dining table to talk about astronomy, geometry, and the classics.

Like his friend Erasmus and other Christian humanists, Thomas More believed that the Church leaders and royalty of his day were often greedy and power-hungry. In 1516, More wrote a book to highlight the problems of Europe. The title of the book is *Utopia* (yoo-TOH-pee-uh). More made up the word from the Greek terms *ou-topos*, meaning "no place."

More's Utopia is an imaginary island governed entirely by reason. In this perfect world, there are no rich or poor, powerful or weak. The citizens of Utopia run their city-state not by competing for power, riches, and fame, but by cooperating, sharing, and dealing fairly with one another. Everyone has what they need. Everyone works nine hours a day, no matter what their job. For the rest of the day, they are "free to do what they like—not to waste their time in idleness or self-indulgence, but to make good use of it in some congenial activity."

Utopia was soon translated into most European languages. Everyone knew that such a perfect world would never exist. Still, *Utopia* made people think about how *imperfect* their world was—especially the Christian Church. After all, Christ had told people to love and help their neighbors. In an age when popes and bishops lived like kings and fought each

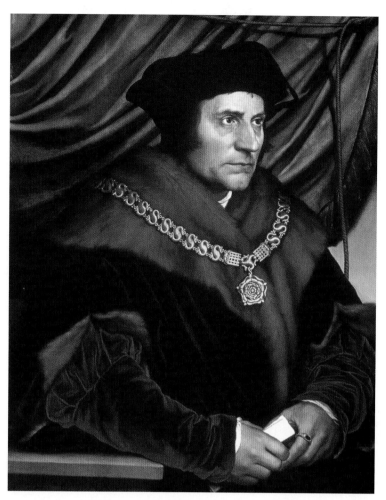

other for power, something seemed very wrong.

Soon after *Utopia* was published, Thomas More entered the service of King Henry VIII of England. As we'll see in the next chapter, the ideas of More, King Henry, and the pope in Rome were on a collision course.

Erasmus's friend, Thomas More, was another leading humanist thinker. Holbein's portrait of More shows an intense man who dreamed of an ideal world—a utopia—in which there was justice for all.

The Meaning of "Utopia"

The title of More's book, *Utopia*, has become a word in the English language. People now use the word utopia to refer to any vision of an ideal society. Sometimes people use the adjective *utopian* to refer to ideas that seem impractical and out of reach.

Thomas More's Utopia

In Utopia, Thomas More described an imaginary island where no one is poor, justice reigns, and land-hungry kings have no place—a far cry from the reality of sixteenth-century Europe. Here is a brief selection from More's book.

A Page from the Past

The island contains fifty-four city-states, all spacious and magnificent, identical in language, traditions, customs, and laws. They are similar also in layout and everywhere, as far as the nature of the ground permits, similar even in appearance…. The lands are so well assigned to the cities that each has at least twelve miles of country on every side, and on some sides even much more…. No city has any desire to extend its territory, for they consider themselves the tenants rather than the masters of what they hold….

Though [each city-state's farmers] are more than sure how much food the city with its adjacent territory consumes, they produce far more grain and cattle than they require for their own use. They distribute the surplus among their neighbors….

The streets are well laid out both for traffic and for protection against the winds…. On the rear of the houses, through the whole length of the block, lies a broad garden enclosed on all sides by the backs of the blocks. Every home has not only a door into the street but a back door into the garden. What is more, folding doors, easily opened by hand and then closing of themselves,

More's imaginary island of Utopia was home to well-ordered and contented city-states.

give admission to anyone. As a result, nothing is private property anywhere. Every ten years, they actually exchange their homes by lot....

Every thirty families choose annually an official whom in their ancient
language they call a syphogrant.... The whole body of syphogrants ... having
sworn to choose the man whom they judge most useful, by secret balloting
appoint a governor.... Whatever is considered important is laid before the
assembly of the syphogrants who, after informing their groups of families,
take counsel together and report their decision to the senate....

As for clothes, these are of one and the same pattern throughout
the island and down the centuries, though there is a distinction
between the sexes and between the single and married. The garments
are comely to the eye, convenient for bodily movement, and fit for wear
in heat and cold....

Gold and silver, of which money is made, are so treated by them
that no one values them more highly than their true nature deserves.
Who does not see that they are far inferior to iron in usefulness
since without iron mortals cannot live any more than without fire
and water? ... While [the Utopians] eat and drink from earthenware
and glassware of fine workmanship but of little value, from gold
and silver they make chamber pots and all the humblest vessels for
use everywhere....

War, as an activity fit only for beasts and yet practiced by no kind of beast
so constantly as by man, they regard with utter loathing.... They know that
the common folk do not go to war of their own accord but are driven to it by
the madness of kings....

They have no more than thirteen [priests] in each city.... The reason for
having few and exceptional priests is to prevent the dignity of the order, which
they now reverence very highly, from being cheapened by communicating the
honor to many....

In Utopia, where everything belongs to everybody, no one doubts ...
that the individual will lack nothing for his private use.... In Utopia
there is no poor man and no beggar. Though no man has anything,
yet all are rich.

German monk Martin Luther burns a papal bull, or decree, on a bonfire outside the town of Wittenberg to show his followers that he rejects the authority of the pope in Rome.

The Reformation Splits Christendom

*I*n the early 1500s, the Christian humanists Desiderius Erasmus and Thomas More called for the Church to put its house in order. But even as far back as the 1300s, the scholar Petrarch had criticized the practices of the Christian Church. He described the papal court in Avignon as a "new Babylon." He meant that Church leaders cared more about luxury, wealth, and pleasure than the spiritual life of the people.

These early critics wanted to clean up the corruption in the Church. In the sixteenth century, this desire to clean up the Church took on a new intensity. Critics within the Church launched a movement known as the Reformation. *Reformation* comes from the word *reform*, which means "to improve, to make better." The Reformation began as an attempt to make changes that would lead to a better Christian Church. But before it was over, the Reformation expanded into a vast movement that split Christianity, divided a continent, triggered bloody wars of religion, and changed the world forever.

The Worldly Church Challenged

In the Renaissance, some high officials of the Church were more concerned with worldly power and luxury than spiritual matters. Many bishops and cardinals wanted to live like princes, so they built their own *palazzi*, or palaces. Pope Sixtus IV and Pope Julius II reasoned that if wealthy merchants lived in splendor, then why should the head of the Church settle for anything less?

Some Christians began to question such reasoning. "Has the Church always been this way?" they asked. To find answers, scholars turned to the Bible and the writings of early Church leaders. These texts were written mostly in Greek. Since the Renaissance had popularized the study of classical Greek, many Biblical scholars were prepared to plunge into the early Greek texts of the New Testament.

In these texts they rediscovered a Christianity unconcerned with worldly power and material goods. In the gospel of Matthew, they read Christ's caution: "No one can serve two masters…. You cannot serve God and mammon"—that is, you cannot be devoted to both God and money. The Renaissance scholars also read about how early Church leaders made personal sacrifices and cared for the sick and the needy.

The humility and charity described in ancient texts seemed worlds away from the Renaissance clergy's grasping for wealth and power. More and more people began to talk about the need for churchmen to change their ways. Their voices grew louder in 1513 when Julius II died and a new pope, Leo X, took office.

Leo X: The "Indulgent" Pope

Pope Leo X was the son of Lorenzo de' Medici. Like his father and great-grandfather Cosimo, Leo adored the arts. He often seemed more interested in the paintings of Raphael than the teachings of the Gospel. It is said that he once remarked, "Let us enjoy the papacy since God has given it to us."

Leo set his heart on finishing the rebuilding of St. Peter's Basilica. Construction on the grand church was proving to be very expensive, and Leo needed more funds. He had an idea. Why not raise money through a special "indulgence"?

What was an indulgence? To answer that, we have to look at some specific beliefs of Christians during the Renaissance. At that time, most Christians believed that if a person confessed his sins to a priest before he died and was truly sorry, he received forgiveness for those sins. After he died his soul would go to heaven, but only after spending time in a place called purgatory. (You may

Renaissance popes such as Leo X often seemed more interested in power and splendor than in spiritual matters. Raphael painted this portrait of Leo X, who used a special indulgence to raise money to rebuild St. Peter's Basilica.

remember that the Italian poet Dante set one of the three books of *The Divine Comedy* in purgatory.)

The term *purgatory* comes from a Latin word meaning "purge" or "burn out impurity." Purgatory, Christians believed, was a place where sinners were punished for their sins. Even if a sinner had been forgiven, he still had to endure punishment for sins in order to be purified for heaven. Medieval and Renaissance engravings show souls in purgatory burning for their sins. The Church taught that after a painful time in purgatory, a purified soul would be ready to go to heaven.

The idea of spending a painful period in purgatory frightened many people. Because they feared the pain of purification, people welcomed the idea that they could do something to shorten their stay in purgatory. They listened eagerly when priests told them that they could shorten the time of their punishment by performing acts of prayer or charity *before* they died.

In return for a good act, the Church could grant an indulgence. An indulgence was a kind of privilege—specifically, the privilege of shortened time in purgatory. These indulgences were written on official pieces of paper, stamped with a red cross, and emblazoned with the papal coat of arms.

One deed that merited an indulgence was giving money to the Church. Such giving was considered an act of charity. Rich and poor alike saved to donate money to the Church. They hoped the indulgences gained through these donations would help them pass quickly through purgatory and go to heaven.

How many indulgences were enough to free a soul from punishment in purgatory? That depended on how bad your sins were. It was said that one German prince acquired enough indulgences to eliminate 1,443 years in purgatory! Some of the more costly indulgences not only promised to shorten the time of punishment for past sins but also to eliminate future punishment for sins not yet committed. People could even donate money and get indulgences for dead loved ones suffering in purgatory.

In 1517, Pope Leo, who needed a great deal of money to finish St. Peter's, encouraged Church officials to make more indulgences available for money than ever before. Church officials asked a friar named Johann Tetzel (yoh-HAHN TET-suhl) to preach about indulgences in the German states. Tetzel was a great showman and a persuasive preacher. He rode around the countryside selling indulgences in a kind of traveling sideshow, complete with price lists for different sins. Buy an indulgence or two, he urged, so that "when you

Jan Hus Condemns Indulgences

In the early 1400s, a priest named Jan Hus (yahn hoos) criticized the sale of indulgences as a corrupt money-making scheme. He argued that Christians could not substitute the payment of money for repentance. In 1415, the Church tried Hus as a heretic. He was condemned and burned at the stake. The memory of Jan Hus's fate was never far from the minds of the critics of the Church.

die the gates of punishment shall be shut, and the gates of the paradise of delight shall be opened."

To some people, Tetzel's preaching sounded like cheap salesmanship. Angry critics scoffed: "As soon as the coin in the coffer rings, the soul from purgatory springs." And, as critics pointed out, poor peasants had little if anything to spare for indulgences.

No one was more repulsed by the sale of indulgences than a young German monk who taught university classes in the small town of Wittenberg. His name was Martin Luther.

- On the map on page 96, locate Wittenberg.

Luther Looks for Answers

Martin Luther's father, a prosperous copper miner, hoped his son would become a lawyer. Martin had the temperament for it—he was tough-minded and argumentative. So in 1501, the young man enrolled in a German university. But he found little satisfaction in legal matters. What really interested him was theology, the study of God.

At 18, Martin Luther was a tormented young man. The Church constantly reminded Christians that they were sinners. Weekly sermons urged the faithful to reflect on their many failings. Luther became overwhelmed by a sense of his own sinfulness and feared he would never be saved.

Luther decided to set aside his legal studies and instead become a monk. Later in his life, he described the dramatic events that led to his decision. In 1505, as Luther recalled,

he was traveling back to the university after a visit home. Suddenly a sharp thunderclap rang out and lightning struck beside him, hurling him to the ground. He wrote, "I was walled around with the terror and agony of sudden death." In desperation, he made a promise that if he survived, he would become a monk.

Some have questioned whether Luther was in fact struck by lightning. In any case, he *did* decide not to become a lawyer. Although his father was furious, the young man entered a monastery and plunged deep into theological studies. Still he felt haunted by a sense of his own sinfulness.

In 1510, Luther traveled to Rome on Church business. He was eager to see the holy city. He said that he rushed around like a "frantic saint" visiting all the holy places. But what he saw troubled him.

Luther saw the construction underway on St. Peter's Basilica, and he knew that so magnificent a building must cost a fortune. He saw corrupt cardinals living in luxury. He saw a pope who spent Church funds on paintings, statues, and feasts. Luther returned home discouraged. "Everything is permitted in Rome except to be an honest man," he observed.

Luther became a professor of biblical studies at the University of Wittenberg in the German province of Saxony. He continued to wrestle with his own conscience. He made long lists of his sins and worried he had forgotten some. He did penance, fasted, gave alms, and kept hoping to find peace.

Martin Luther gave up his legal studies to become a monk and, later, a university professor. He began to question some Church activities and the behavior of some Church leaders.

A small crowd watches as the monk Luther nails his Ninety-five Theses to the church door in Wittenberg. His theses, or arguments, criticized the Church's sale of indulgences.

Then one day he was struck by six words in a letter of St. Paul: "The righteous shall live by faith." Luther said those words acted as "flashes of lightning, frightening me each time I heard them."

He meditated on the words and came to a bold conclusion. Luther concluded human beings were so sinful that they could never earn forgiveness by their own actions. Instead, to be saved, he thought, Christians had to live by faith alone and depend on the mercy of God. Salvation, he insisted, came only through God's mercy, and could not be gained through any penance or fast or indulgence.

That conclusion brought Martin Luther new peace. The 32-year-old monk continued to teach, but with renewed spirit.

Luther's Ninety-five Theses

One day some citizens of Wittenberg came to Luther with indulgences sold by Johann Tetzel. They asked Luther if the promises of shortened time in purgatory were true. Luther was furious. He knew how poor many German peasants were. He was convinced that the sale of indulgences was just a vile money-making scheme.

He took up his pen and wrote out 95 theses, or arguments, explaining why indulgences were wrong. He wrote in thesis number 37, "Any true Christian, whether living or dead, participates in all the blessing of Christ and the Church; and this is granted him by God, even without indulgence letters."

According to tradition, Luther nailed his Ninety-five Theses to the church door in Wittenberg on October 31, 1517. In those days placing such a letter on the church door was like pinning a notice on a public bulletin board. The Ninety-five Theses were soon translated from Latin into German. Thanks to Gutenberg's printing press, Luther's writings began to spread throughout Germany. The fervent German monk was openly challenging the Church to reform itself. The Reformation—the great upheaval that changed Christendom forever—had begun.

Luther's Ninety-five Theses

Martin Luther once said, "I am hot-blooded by temperament and my pen gets irritated easily." You can see some of his passion in the following selections from his Ninety-five Theses concerning the sale of indulgences.

A Page from the Past

They preach only human doctrines who say that as soon as the money clinks into the money chest, the soul flies out of purgatory. (Thesis 27)

Those who believe that they can be certain of their salvation because they have indulgence letters will be eternally damned, together with their teachers. (Thesis 32)

Any true Christian, whether living or dead, participates in all the blessings of Christ and the church; and this is granted him by God, even without indulgence letters. (Thesis 37)

Christians are to be taught that he who gives to the poor or lends to the needy does a better deed than he who buys indulgences. (Thesis 43)

Christians are to be taught that he who sees a needy man and passes him by, yet gives his money for indulgences, does not buy papal indulgences but God's wrath. (Thesis 45)

A Split Becomes a Fissure

Johann Tetzel greeted the Ninety-five Theses with glee. "Within three weeks I shall have the heretic thrown into the fire," he promised, referring to the fate that sometimes awaited those who clung to beliefs that went against Church teachings. Tetzel probably thought this troublesome monk would back down when he heard the threat. But Tetzel did not know Martin Luther.

Although Luther was troubled by many Church practices, he did not intend to break away from the Church. For the moment, all he cared about was ending the sale of indulgences. He wanted to make the Church a better, more spiritual institution.

But Church leaders warned Luther to cease his criticism. In 1518, the monks relieved Luther of some of his duties. Luther was pleased. Now he had more time to think and teach.

He kept teaching in Wittenberg. Students flocked to his lectures,

Christians are to be taught that, unless they have more than they need, they must reserve enough for their family needs and by no means squander it on indulgences. (Thesis 46)

Christians are to be taught that if the pope knew the exactions of the indulgence preachers, he would rather that the basilica of St. Peter were burned to ashes than built up with the skin, flesh, and bones of his sheep. (Thesis 50)

Injury is done to the Word of God when, in the same sermon, an equal or larger amount of time is devoted to indulgences than to the Word. (Thesis 54)

Let him who speaks against the truth concerning papal indulgences be ... accursed. (Thesis 71)

But let him who guards against the lust and license of the indulgence preachers be blessed. (Thesis 72)

[Indulgences cause people to ask questions such as:] "Why does not the pope, whose wealth is today greater than the wealth of the richest ... build this one basilica of St. Peter with his own money rather than with the money of poor believers?" (Thesis 86)

and he delivered sermons to local monks. Within a year, Martin Luther took a big step. He questioned whether the Christian Church even needed a pope! This was too much for Pope Leo. Heresy proceedings began in Rome.

Local printers could not get their hands on Luther's writings quickly enough. A printer's apprentice often sprinted through the streets of Wittenberg, carrying Martin Luther's latest writings under his arm. Presses

Luther, shown here preaching, wanted to reform the Roman Church, but his criticisms led to a split within the Church.

churned out copies of Luther's words, mostly in pamphlets six to eight pages long.

These pamphlets traveled to towns across Europe, even to Rome itself. Luther criticized the Church for hiding the true meaning of the gospel from ordinary people. He called on the German princes to establish a reformed German church with no pope at its head.

Standing Firm at the Diet of Worms

Leo X could not ignore such statements. In 1520, he issued a papal bull, or decree, saying that if Luther did not recant, his writings would be burned. Luther and his students responded by throwing the papal bull and books of Church law onto a bonfire outside the walls of Wittenberg. Leo, in turn, excommunicated Martin Luther and ordered his publications burned.

Meanwhile, the Holy Roman Emperor, an ally of the pope, watched the uproar Luther was causing. He summoned the combative monk to a meeting called the Diet of Worms.

A *Diet of Worms*? It wasn't what you might think. A diet is a special meeting, and Worms is a city in Germany. The Diet of Worms was a general assembly of the princes of Germany. The Holy Roman Emperor himself attended. So did representatives of the pope. It was a last chance for the monk from Wittenberg to say that he was wrong and take back the heresies that he had been spreading.

- On the map on page 96, locate Worms.

At the meeting in April 1521, Luther refused to recant. He said all of his beliefs were inspired by sacred scripture and by reason. The Bible, he emphasized, was the heart and soul of Christianity. All beliefs and actions, he said, needed to be measured against the gospel.

To *recant* is to take back or reject something one has said earlier.

At the Diet of Worms, Luther defends himself before the Holy Roman Emperor and officials representing the pope. When ordered to recant his criticisms, Luther declared, "I cannot and I will not recant anything."

Luther argued that the practices of the Church and actions of the pope had "condemned the gospel." He claimed that his own teachings were all inspired by a clear understanding of the Bible. "Unless I am convicted by Scripture and plain reason," he said to those gathered at Worms, "my conscience is captive to the Word of God. I cannot and I will not recant anything, for to go against conscience is neither safe nor right. God help me. Amen."

An Outlaw Translates the Bible

Luther's words rang out like a declaration of war against the Church. The Holy Roman Emperor understood as clearly as anyone. He fumed, "A single friar who goes counter to all Christianity for a thousand years must be wrong."

Luther made enemies of the pope and the emperor. But many German princes, nobles, and knights sided with him. Ordinary folk rallied behind him, too. "Nine tenths of the people are shouting 'Luther!'" one of the pope's representatives wrote from Worms. "And the other tenth shouts 'Down with Rome!'"

In Rome, Luther was condemned as a heretic and an outlaw. He quickly set off for Wittenberg, but he never made it. Outside Worms, armed horsemen seized him and spirited him away. No one knew what had happened to the outspoken monk. Had the emperor's soldiers arrested him? Had he been killed? The great German artist Albrecht Dürer wept when he heard the news. "O God," he despaired, "if Luther is dead, who now will teach us the holy Gospel?"

Armed horsemen seize Luther on his return from Worms and carry him off to the safety of Wartburg castle. The horsemen were sent by Prince Frederick of Saxony, who chose to protect the monk from the Holy Roman Emperor.

But Luther was very much alive. The armed horsemen did not belong to the emperor. They were the soldiers of Prince Frederick, who ruled Saxony, the province in which Luther taught. Frederick resented the emperor threatening one of his subjects. He ordered his men to carry Luther to the safety of a nearby castle. There Luther lived in hiding for almost a year, disguising himself as a country gentleman.

During this time Martin Luther began his life's greatest work. He translated the Scriptures from their original Hebrew and Greek into German, the everyday language of his countrymen. Before Luther's time, most Bibles were printed in Latin, which only very educated people could read. Now anyone who read German could read the Bible. The combination of the printing press and translation into German made the Bible available to thousands of people.

Luther wanted ordinary people to be able to read the Bible, and not have to rely on the Church to interpret it for them. He denied the importance of priests in interpreting the Bible. He claimed there was a more important priesthood—"the priesthood of all believers." Believers had only to read the Scriptures, Luther said, and they would understand the truth.

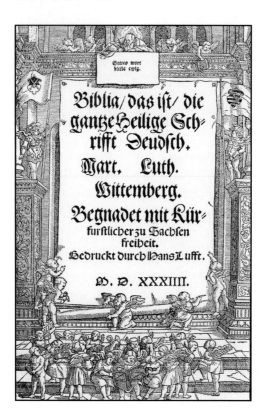

During the year or so he spent in hiding at Wartburg castle, Luther began to translate the Bible into German. He believed that German-speaking people should be able to read the Scriptures in their own language.

The Bible in the Vernacular

Vernacular means the native language of a place. Well into the Renaissance, legal documents and formal works were written in Latin, which only highly educated people could read. Dante broke with this tradition by writing *The Divine Comedy* in Italian, the vernacular of Italy. Likewise, Martin Luther translated the Bible from Latin into the vernacular of Germany. By creating a German Bible, he gave many people a chance to read scripture for the first time.

After nearly a year, Luther decided to risk returning to Wittenberg. In the emperor's eyes, he was still an outlaw. All subjects of the empire were forbidden to deal with him. Indeed, anyone who saw Luther was supposed to seize him and turn him in to the authorities or, if that proved too difficult, kill him on sight.

But Luther refused to hide or be silent. He continued to preach and write. He insisted on the need to return to the original teachings of the Bible. Prince Frederick continued to offer his protection.

As more and more people responded to Luther's message, a new branch of Christianity emerged, one that did not recognize the leadership of the pope. It came to be called Lutheranism. German kingdoms began to split. On one side were those who supported the pope. On the other side were those who backed Luther. All across Europe, people began to take sides.

Catholic and Protestant

Luther's ideas spread quickly. As far north as Scandinavia, the kings of Denmark and Norway made Lutheranism the official religion of their realms.

Reformed churches, following the teachings of Martin Luther, began to spring up across Europe. They were known as Protestant churches because their members *protested* the practices of the Church based in Rome.

The Roman Church, headed by the pope, began to call itself the Roman *Catholic* Church. The Church

Left: Protestant ideas soon spread to other countries in Europe. These French Huguenots followed the teachings of another leader of the Reformation, John Calvin.

Below: Calvin was a gifted scholar who turned Geneva into a kind of "Protestant Rome." His ideas, called Calvinism, took root in the Netherlands, Scotland, and central Europe, as well as in Switzerland and France.

had always considered itself "catholic," a word that means "universal," because the Church taught a message it said was for everyone. Early Church documents speak of "the catholic faith we teach." Officials in Rome began to refer to the "Roman Catholic Church" because the Church was headquartered in Rome, and because they wanted to emphasize its universal authority.

In time, Christians simplified the label and began to refer to the Roman Catholic Church as simply the Catholic Church.

Protestantism Spreads: Calvin Speaks Up

In France, where Luther's ideas attracted many followers, a young scholar named John Calvin took up the cause of the Reformation. Calvin had studied Greek and Latin at the University of Paris. But the French king was a devout Catholic and persecuted Protestants in his country. So Calvin moved to Switzerland.

Under Calvin's guidance, the city of Geneva became a dynamic center of the Protestant faith—"the most perfect school of Christ on earth," one of his followers said. Others were not impressed. In Geneva, Calvin banished some who disagreed with him and supervised the execution of others.

Calvin's teachings spread to the Netherlands, Scotland, and central Europe. Calvin, like Luther, stressed the "priesthood of all believers." Calvin wanted to organize churches differently. He said churches should not be run by priests but instead by a board of "elders" chosen from the congregation.

In Scotland, Calvin's followers became known as Presbyterians, a term that comes from *presbyteros*, the

ancient Greek word for "elder." In his homeland of France, Calvin's followers were called Huguenots (HYOO-guh-nahts). In England—and later in the American colonies—Calvin's followers became known as Puritans.

England Champions Protestantism

In England, King Henry VIII heard reports of Martin Luther's protests. In 1521, after Luther had posted his Ninety-five Theses, Henry wrote a pamphlet denouncing the German monk. The pope, in turn, honored Henry with the title "Defender of the Faith." So for a while, it seemed as though the king of England and the pope of the Roman Catholic Church were on the same side. But history was about to take a strange twist.

As a young man, Henry had married Catherine of Aragon, a Spanish princess. Within a year the royal couple had a baby boy, and all of England rejoiced. But the infant died at three months. Catherine bore five girls, four of whom died. Henry was distraught that he had no male heir. He wanted a son to carry on the family name and dynasty. So he made up his mind to take a new wife.

In the sixteenth century, it was not easy to end a marriage. Christians had to get permission from the Church. So Henry pressed the pope to set aside his marriage to Catherine. The pope refused to grant Henry's request. Henry's advisors suggested that England should break from the Roman Catholic Church and establish its own official church. That way, the new Church of England could authorize an end to Henry's marriage. The king agreed.

So it was that in 1534 England became a Protestant nation. England's Parliament declared the king "the only supreme head on earth of the Church of England." The pope no longer led the English church. Now Henry could give himself permission to take a new wife. Anyone who disagreed with his decision to break from the pope and the Roman Catholic Church risked punishment by death.

One man you've met, Thomas More, England's greatest Christian humanist, firmly disagreed with the break from the Catholic Church. More at this time was England's Lord

King Henry VIII of England disagreed with the teachings of Martin Luther. But after the pope refused to give him permission to divorce, Henry formed his own Protestant Church of England, declaring himself its head.

Chancellor, one of the king's top offi-cials. While More agreed that Catho-lic Church leaders were often greedy and power-hungry, he believed that the Catholic Church represented the only true Christian faith. Thus More did not agree that Henry had the authority to end his marriage.

King Henry and Thomas More each tried to get the other to see things his way. Neither would change his mind. Henry demanded that More sign an oath recognizing the king as the head of the Church of England. More refused. In his heart, he believed that only the pope could lead the Church. More knew what the consequence would be. In 1535, he was beheaded.

Luther's Legacy

Martin Luther, the man who started the Reformation, continued to teach theology at Wittenberg, but he left the priesthood. He married and had six children—three sons and three daughters. He also wrote music, including the famous hymn "A Mighty Fortress Is Our God."

In 1546, Martin Luther died knowing that he had triggered a great split in the Christian Church, but feeling at peace with the God that he had tried to serve.

While Luther died at peace, he left behind a troubled continent. As Protestantism continued to spread, some European rulers made Protes-tant churches the official churches of their realms. In other lands, rul-ers stayed with the Roman Catholic Church. Soon the continent was divided between Protestant and Catholic states. Western Europe was no longer united by a single faith. "Christendom" was no more.

Thomas More's daughter visits her imprisoned father in the Tower of London. When More refused to support Henry's break with Rome, the king threw him in prison, and later had him beheaded.

*Bishops and other Catholic Church leaders
meet at the Council of Trent. Their efforts to
strengthen the Church were part of a movement
called the Counter-Reformation.*

The Counter-Reformation and the New Face of Europe

T he kings and nobles of Europe often fought for land and power, but for nearly a thousand years they had one thing in common—their religion. Despite all their differences, the people of Europe thought of themselves as

part of "Christendom," bound by their shared religion. But in the 1500s, religious quarrels split Europe apart.

Christianity divided into Catholics and Protestants. The new teachings of Martin Luther, John Calvin, and other Protestant leaders attracted many Christians. In northern Europe, many rulers made the new Protestant faiths their official religions. In England, King Henry VIII divorced his Spanish wife, Catherine of Aragon, and broke with the pope in Rome. Henry's England later supported the Protestant cause, while Spain, under the zealous leadership of King Philip II, defended the Roman Catholic Church.

The Reformation, the movement launched by Martin Luther, marked a crisis for the Roman Catholic Church. As many Christians turned to embrace new Protestant beliefs, the Catholic Church responded by launching its own *Counter*-Reformation, or, as it is sometimes called, the Catholic Reformation. Catholic leaders set out to correct bad practices and clarify the teachings of the Catholic Church. They also tried to reverse the spread of Protestantism in Europe.

Let's look at how the Counter-Reformation came about.

Looking Inward and Taking Stock

Martin Luther, John Calvin, and other Protestant reformers criticized the Roman Catholic Church. They went on to establish their own churches. Other reformers, such as the Christian humanists Erasmus and Thomas More, also criticized some practices of the Catholic Church. But they decided to stay with the Church and try to improve it from within.

For a time their efforts seemed useless. In 1534, however, a new pope was elected in Rome. This pope, who became known as Paul III, saw the need for change. His time as pope marked a turning point for the Catholic Church.

In some ways Paul III was like other Renaissance popes. He came from a wealthy and powerful Italian merchant family, and he made sure his relatives got important positions within the Church. He was a man of culture and an admirer of the classics. He had studied under humanist

Pope Paul III recognized that the Catholic Church needed reform. He convened the Council of Trent to help address problems facing the Church.

scholars in the palace of Lorenzo de' Medici in Florence.

But this pope also realized that too many clergymen hungered for money, power, and other worldly things. He understood that if the Catholic Church did not reform itself, people would continue to leave it for the new Protestant faiths.

Pope Paul III made a number of improvements. He tried to find good, honest men to act as bishops of the Catholic Church. He encouraged the faithful to become monks and nuns and devote their lives to caring for the sick, helping the poor, and preaching Jesus' message of love for one's neighbor.

But Paul III knew that the Catholic Church needed to do much more. It needed to take a hard look at its beliefs, its practices, and its plans for the future. He decided to bring together a special gathering of bishops, called a council. This gathering took place in the small Italian city of Trent, so it is known as the Council of Trent.

• On the map on page 123, locate the city of Trent.

The Council of Trent

The Council of Trent was not a single meeting but rather a series of meetings—25 in all—held between the years 1545 and 1563. At Trent, the pope and other leaders set out to answer a number of questions about the beliefs of the Roman Catholic Church. What are the teachings of the Catholic Church? What beliefs must all Catholics share? What beliefs are heretical—that is, what

Europe, c. 1600

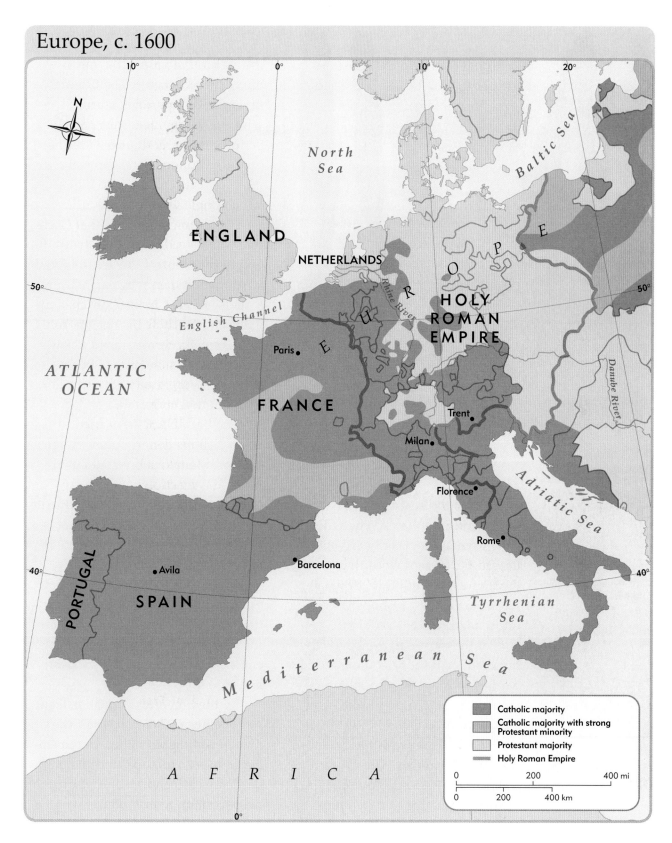

beliefs violate basic Catholic teachings? Paul III believed that it was important for the Council of Trent to answer such questions so that people would know exactly what it meant to be a Roman Catholic.

Sometimes the debate between the bishops grew heated. One

The Council of Trent opens at the cathedral of Trent in northern Italy on December 13, 1545. The Council agreed on a new statement of beliefs for the Catholic Church.

account says that a bishop grabbed another by the beard and pulled out a handful of hairs! When the Holy Roman Emperor heard about the scuffle, he sent word that if the Council did not calm down, he would have a few bishops thrown into a nearby river to cool off.

For the most part, however, the hundreds of bishops at the Council worked hard to solve problems facing the Church. For example, while the Council defended indulgences, it denounced the way they had been used to raise money. The Council challenged bishops to correct this practice. The pope said no more indulgences would be granted for money.

The Council of Trent affirmed the long-standing belief that the pope should lead the Church. It also affirmed that only the Church had

the authority to judge the meaning of the Scriptures. The Council denounced "unbridled spirits" who engage in "distorting the Holy Scriptures in accordance with [their] own conceptions, [and] presume to interpret them contrary to that sense which [the] Church … holds."

The Council also said that God's will was revealed through the tradition of the Church, the accumulated wisdom of writings by early Church leaders, decrees of the Church, and gatherings such as the one at Trent. The Council commissioned a new catechism, or statement of beliefs, to summarize the teachings and rules of the Catholic Church.

The Council of Trent tried to bring bishops closer to their congregations. Many bishops had fallen into the habit of living far away from the people they were supposed to be serving. The Council told these bishops to stick close to their cathedrals and preach every Sunday.

Church critics complained that many priests knew little about Christianity, so the Council set guidelines for schools to educate priests. It encouraged priests to live modestly and care for the poor.

By the time the Council of Trent wrapped up its work in 1563, the message of the Catholic Church was clear. Priests, bishops, and the pope needed to focus on people's spiritual needs, not on money and power.

A New Piety

In response to the Council of Trent, some priests and bishops tried to lead more devout lives. The archbishop of Milan, for example, gave all his money to the poor. When a plague struck Milan in 1576, he refused to flee the city. Instead he remained behind to tend the sick and the dying. The archbishop died of the plague eight years later. He was only 46 years old.

In many Catholic countries more men and women became monks or nuns so they could devote their lives to the care of the sick, the hungry, and the old. Spain's King Philip II encouraged the practice and did all he could to support them.

A nun named Teresa of Avila (AH-vih-luh) inspired many Spaniards. In the mid-sixteenth century, Teresa founded many new convents. At a time when many Church leaders lived in comfortable, even luxurious, surroundings, Teresa encouraged the nuns in her convents to lead lives of self-denial and service to others. (See page 131.)

Ignatius of Loyola and the Jesuits

Spain produced another Catholic reformer, Ignatius of Loyola (ig-NAY-shus of loy-OH-luh). Ignatius had been a wild youth, his head full of tales of medieval knights and courtly romance. He dreamed of glory on the field of battle, and he decided to become a soldier. But his dreams vanished during a battle against the French when a cannon blast shattered one of his legs.

It took a long time for Ignatius to recover from his wounds. It was a difficult period for this man of action. To help pass the time more quickly, he read. In the castle where he was staying, he could find only two books—one about the life of Jesus, and the other about Christian saints.

As Ignatius read, new thoughts occurred to him. He knew that his injuries had ended his military career. But, he thought, perhaps that was for the best. All his life he had thought only of gaining glory for himself. Now he wondered if he should seek another kind of glory.

When he could walk again, Ignatius set off for a monastery near the city of Barcelona, Spain. After much prayer in a church there, he hung his sword next to the altar. From now on, he told himself, he would serve God and the Church.

Ignatius knew he needed more education before he could begin his service. He needed to learn languages, history, and the theology of the Church. So he began to study at the University of Paris.

At the university, a small group of followers gathered around Ignatius. He and some of his university friends vowed to pursue lives of poverty and chastity. After they

Ignatius of Loyola (often called simply Ignatius Loyola) founded a new order of priests called the Society of Jesus, better known as the Jesuits. The Jesuits worked hard to reclaim parts of Germany and eastern Europe for Catholicism.

became priests, they traveled to Rome to tell Pope Paul III that they wished to help convert Muslims to Christianity.

The pope, however, was not thinking about Muslims. Instead, he wanted to enlist Ignatius and his followers in the effort of the Counter-Reformation. So in 1540, a new order of priests was born. Its name was the Society of Jesus, and its members became known as "Jesuits."

The Jesuits organized themselves like an army. At first the former soldier Ignatius used military terms, calling himself "the general" and his men "the Company of Jesus." The general did not hesitate to say that

The Jesuits were great educators. Jesuit colleges such as this one in Munich trained priests and scholars.

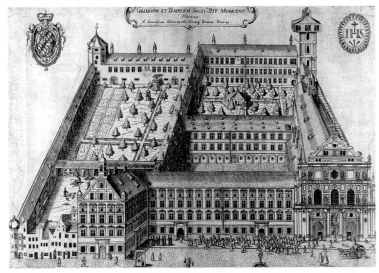

his followers needed to engage in "conflict for God." He did not mean military battle. He meant winning the conflict of beliefs between Catholics and Protestants.

The Jesuits were highly disciplined and completely obedient to the pope. Ignatius told his followers, "We must praise all the commandments of the Church, and be on the alert to find reasons to defend them, and by no means in order to criticize them." To emphasize his point, he added: "What seems to me white, I will believe black if the … Church so defines."

To oppose the advance of Protestantism, the Jesuits established schools to educate the young. The scholarly Jesuits also began teaching in Catholic universities. They preached to the public and performed works of charity for the poor. Their efforts helped restore Catholicism to parts of Germany and Eastern Europe.

The Jesuits also took the Christian message far beyond Europe. Hundreds of Jesuit missionaries traveled to Africa, China, Japan, India, and the newly discovered Americas.

One of the most energetic missionaries was a Jesuit from Spain named Francis Xavier (ZAYV-yur). For more than a decade he carried the gospel to India and the Far East. Everywhere he visited, he preached simple sermons in the local languages. He baptized thousands of Christian converts. In 1552, Xavier died of fever while trying to enter China. By then the Jesuits were at work in distant parts of the globe, from Ethiopia to Brazil.

To Be Called a "Jesuit"

Ignatius Loyola never called his followers "Jesuits." Before the 1500s, the term was an insult. It referred to people who used the name of Jesus too frequently and tried to call attention to their holiness. Critics used it to mock the most zealous members of Ignatius Loyola's band. But eventually, members of the Society of Jesus adopted the name and gladly called themselves Jesuits.

The efforts of reformers like Teresa of Avila, Ignatius Loyola, and Francis Xavier were paying off. Not only was the Catholic Church recovering from a long decline, it was also expanding its reach.

The Index of Forbidden Books and the Inquisition

To hold back the rising tide of Protestantism, the Catholic Church tried to reform itself and to expand its reach. Some Catholics thought the Church should take more extreme steps to stamp out new Protestant ideas. They pointed to the thousands of books and pamphlets that were spreading Protestant ideas across Europe. Many Catholic leaders said these new ideas were dangerous and

wrong, so they banned the books that contained them.

Church leaders drew up an Index of Forbidden Books, a list of publications that loyal Catholics should not read. It included the works of Martin Luther and other Protestant reformers, as well as writings by "dangerous" Catholic philosophers and theologians, such as Erasmus. Machiavelli's *The Prince* was on the Index of Forbidden Books. Even Teresa of Avila, who sometimes clashed with Catholic Church officials as she pushed for reforms, worried that her writings would end up on the list.

To stop the spread of ideas considered heretical, the Catholic Church also arrested people and brought them before the Inquisition.

As depicted in a Japanese paper screen, Francis Xavier arrives in Japan in 1549. The Jesuit missionary carried the Christian message to Asia for more than 10 years.

The word *inquisition* means "examination" or "investigation." The Inquisition was the name of the Church court that examined people and punished those whose beliefs went against Church teachings.

The courts of the Inquisition had been around since the Middle Ages. Back in 1431, a court of Inquisition had condemned Joan of Arc, the maiden who claimed to hear voices from heaven and led French troops in the Hundred Years' War. But after the Reformation, the activities of the Inquisition grew. In France, Germany, Italy, and Spain, Catholic officials called more and more people to explain their beliefs to the Church judges, called inquisitors. The Inquisition was most ruthless and active in Spain, where King Philip II vigorously championed the Catholic Church.

Inquisitors used methods that seem barbaric to us today. The inquisitors did give those accused of heresy a chance to explain their beliefs. But if the judges decided those beliefs violated Church doctrines, then they required the accused to confess their heresies. If they confessed and informed on other heretics, they might face only imprisonment. If they refused to confess, the inquisitors showed them instruments of torture that included red-hot irons and the rack, which stretched a victim's limbs.

Faced with agonizing pain, many of the accused agreed to say whatever their inquisitors wanted to hear. Those who refused to confess suffered the most terrible forms of torture. Inquisitors said that unless a heretic recanted, his soul could not be saved. They claimed they were torturing the heretic in order to save him. Many people who refused to renounce their beliefs were burned at the stake.

While the Inquisition resorted to some horrible practices, these practices were not unique to the Roman Catholic Church. Many cruel punishments, including branding and burning at the stake, were common to all European judicial systems at the time.

Religion Splits the Continent

Since the Reformation, the Catholic Church had taken a series of decisive steps. At the Council of Trent, it defined what it meant to be Catholic. It eliminated the outright sale of indulgences. It drew up the Index of Forbidden Books. It encouraged the work of the Jesuits and other reformers, such as Teresa of Avila, who spread the Catholic faith. And it granted perhaps too much power to its sometimes ruthless Inquisition.

While all these efforts provided new direction for the Catholic Church, they did not stop the growth of Protestantism. The war of ideas between the Catholic Church and Protestant reformers led to a split in Europe. The rulers of various nations chose sides, some Protestant, some Catholic.

These rulers were not concerned about religious beliefs alone. In every European kingdom, the Catholic Church owned property—a *lot* of property. If a ruler decided to break away from the Catholic Church, then he could seize all Church properties in his country.

So a great deal of land and money was at stake in this religious quarrel.

The split was especially severe in the German lands of the Holy Roman Empire, where many peasants and princes favored the teachings of Protestantism. The war of ideas eventually erupted into real and bloody wars. These wars changed the map of Europe in the sixteenth century.

In Germany, the Holy Roman Emperor led Catholic forces against a league of Protestant states. At first he was victorious on the battlefield. But Protestant states quickly recovered and fought back. In 1555, the battle-weary emperor agreed that each German prince could choose his state's official religion, Protestant or Catholic.

In France, a civil war pitted Catholics against the Protestant minority known as the Huguenots. Between 1562 and 1598, fighting broke out across the country nine times. The conflict peaked with the massacre of more than 10,000 Huguenots in 1572. Many Huguenots left France to practice their religion in neighboring Protestant countries.

Those accused of heresy went before a special Church court called the Inquisition. The accused wore pointed caps approximately three feet high. These corozas were the origin of what we now call dunce caps.

War and Disease

The wars of religion during the sixteenth century were long and brutal. People on both sides became convinced that heretics polluted the earth. They often tossed the bodies of those executed for heresy—both Protestant and Catholic—into rivers. They thought this would "cleanse" their villages, but in fact the practice increased the possibility of disease.

One of those countries was the Netherlands. This region had long been ruled by Catholic Spain. But Protestants in the north waged a long and bloody revolt. They wanted both political independence and religious freedom. Eventually they set up an independent Protestant Dutch state.

Meanwhile, the English nation was beginning to flex its muscles. As you learned, King Henry VIII had divorced Catherine of Aragon and set up a new Anglican Church with himself at the head. After Henry, England swung back and forth between Protestantism and Catholicism, depending on the king or queen in power. England's Queen Mary wed Philip II of Spain and tried to turn England back to Catholicism. Because she ordered the execution of so many Protestants, she became known as "Bloody Mary." But after Mary, Henry's

The *Anglican Church* is another name for the Church of England.

daughter, Elizabeth, became queen, and under her rule England became a solidly Protestant nation.

Protestant England fought a series of wars with Catholic Spain. The two nations became bitter enemies. Their hostility seemed to represent the religious division that now fractured the continent.

- On the map on page 123, note Catholic and Protestant regions. Locate England, France, Spain, the Holy Roman Empire, and the Netherlands.

By 1600, the Christian faith that was once a common bond in Europe had become a source of rivalry and division. As we'll see in coming chapters, the rivalry spread beyond the continent as English, Dutch, Spanish, and Portuguese explorers ventured across the seas in service of God and country.

French Catholics slaughtered their Protestant countrymen in the St. Bartholomew's Day Massacre in Paris on August 24, 1572. Wars of religion raged throughout Europe in the decades after the Reformation.

Teresa of Avila

At a time when many clergy and nuns enjoyed wealth, ease, and power, Teresa of Avila encouraged a simple, disciplined religious life and service to others. Here is her story.

Growing up in the Spanish city of Avila, little Teresa had only to look around to see its medieval past. Thick stone walls, 40 feet tall, encircled the city. Soldiers in even taller watchtowers scanned the mountainous horizon for enemy invaders. A proud cathedral stood within the city walls, for Avila, in the center of Spain, was very much a Roman Catholic city. It was called the "City of Knights" because during the Crusades many Christians set out from its gates to fight Muslim foes in what they considered to be holy wars.

In 1522, seven-year-old Teresa trudged up a hillside above Avila, ready to lay down her life. She was accompanied by Rodrigo, her favorite of nine brothers. Battles between Christians and the Muslim conquerors of Spain, called Moors, had raged for years. If the Moors captured her, Teresa thought, she would become a martyr, someone who died for her faith, and surely go to heaven.

Teresa and Rodrigo did not get very far. Their uncle found them marching bravely along the road and took them home. From that day on, Teresa kept seeking the path that might take her to heaven.

Teresa's mother died when she was about 14, so there was no one to give her womanly advice about romance and courtship. She was very pretty, and her father worried that she was getting too wild, so he sent Teresa to school in a convent. Nuns in convents, like monks in monasteries, prayed often, attended many church services, and tried to focus their thoughts on God. After Teresa finished her education, she became a nun at the convent.

The convent was not a grim place. Many of the sisters from noble

Teresa was born in Avila in 1515. The city's turreted walls date to the eleventh century.

families had lovely apartments. Teresa was of noble birth, so her apartment had two floors and its own kitchen. There she could entertain family and friends. She also went home frequently. Teresa was a lively woman, and she gathered a devoted group of friends around her.

But inner conflicts tormented her. She wondered whether she lived a life of too much worldly ease. She fell ill and got so sick that she lapsed into a coma. Her family believed she was dead. The nuns dug her grave outside the convent chapel. Luckily, Teresa awoke before they tried to bury her. But she remained paralyzed for three years. She prayed for hours at a time. When she finally was able to crawl, she praised God.

About this time Sister Teresa began hearing voices and having visions. She said that as she sang a hymn one day, she heard these words: "I will have thee converse now, not with men, but with angels." Another day, she believed that she saw Jesus clearly in front of her. She told the nuns and the chapel priest about her experiences. They told her not to believe what she saw. They said she must not act like Protestants who claimed to have direct contact with God through their reading of the Bible.

Later, during prayer one day, Teresa said she had a vision of an angel. "He was not tall, but short, and very beautiful," she wrote years later. She said the angel carried "a long golden spear" with "a point of fire." With this spear, she wrote, he seemed to "pierce my heart several times" and "left me completely afire with a great love for God."

Not long after, Teresa met a priest who was part of a group called the Discalced (dihs-KALST) Franciscans. They followed the example of St. Francis of Assisi (uh-SEE-see), who wanted his followers to travel around teaching and living simple lives. They also went barefoot. (*Discalced* comes from a Latin term that means "without shoes" or "barefoot.") They rejected all worldly comforts and embraced poverty, hunger, and physical hardships.

Teresa, who was now in her 40s, decided to begin a new group of nuns, the Discalced Carmelites. She planned for her nuns to live austere lives of prayer. Teresa spent years seeking help to start her new convent at Avila. Her brother-in-law helped buy a building where the nuns could live and pray. In 1562, her Convent of St. Joseph, home of the Discalced Carmelites, opened with just four nuns in residence.

Austere means severely simple, without any comforts.

Around 1650, the great Italian sculptor Gian Lorenzo Bernini created this dramatic depiction of Teresa of Avila and her vision of an angel.

Teresa and the other nuns wore plain robes of rough brown cloth and slept on beds of straw. They gave up all worldly possessions. There were no class distinctions among them. All lived in great simplicity. They spent hours alone in prayer and silent meditation, and had almost no contact with the world beyond their convent walls. What little money they needed came through donations from city residents.

Life in St. Joseph's was stricter and less comfortable than in many other convents and monasteries—and that is how Teresa wanted it. She believed that worldly things distracted from prayer. Through prayer and suffering, she said, her sisters could come closer to understanding why Jesus Christ endured tortures on the cross.

Once St. Joseph's was established, Teresa felt driven to establish more convents and monasteries throughout Spain. She moved from town to town, finding old buildings, befriending nuns and priests who shared her principles, and convincing wealthy citizens to fund her projects.

Between 1567 and her death in 1582, Teresa traveled all over Spain. She founded more than a dozen new convents and monasteries. She wrote extensively about her life and beliefs.

There is a famous story about Teresa toward the end of her life. She was 66 years old when she set out through wintry weather to start a new convent in Burgos in northern Spain. She traveled in a mule-drawn cart and felt every bump in the road. Cold rain turned to sleet, and Teresa fell off the cart and into a ditch.

Teresa formed a new order of Carmelite nuns who lived simply and prayed tirelessly.

"Why, God?" she asked. "Do you do this to torment me?" She told others that a familiar voice responded, "This is how I treat my friends." Teresa responded, "If this is how you treat your friends, no wonder you have so few of them!"

Teresa had always suffered from a bad back, stomach ailments, and sore throats, and these conditions grew worse as she aged. She was 67 years old when she set out in the fall of 1582 to bless the newborn daughter of a generous duchess. By the time she reached the duchess's town, she was near death. She blessed the baby and passed away in the arms of one of her dearest fellow nuns.

Even those who doubted her visions recognized what Teresa left behind—an inspiring example of service and self-denial, a new religious order, and fresh inspiration for the Catholic Church.

In 1622, Teresa was declared a saint and was later given the title "Doctor of the Roman Catholic Church" for her religious writings. She is one of only 33 people to hold that honor.

Süleyman the Magnificent, a gifted lawgiver and military leader, ruled the Ottoman Empire from 1520 to 1566. Europeans called him "the Magnificent" because of his taste for beauty and the splendor of his court.

Three Islamic Empires

When little Teresa of Avila marched up a hillside near her home with her brother, she imagined herself going to convert the Muslims, known as Moors, who had conquered parts of Spain. Teresa lived at a time when Muslim empires stretched along the southern and eastern borders of Europe.

In Teresa's time—the 1500s—Muslim empires were on the rise, springing back from centuries of hardship. Like Europe during the Middle Ages, the Islamic world had suffered years of trouble and turmoil.

You learned that during the thirteenth century, Mongol armies from Central Asia swept into the Muslim heartlands of Persia and Mesopotamia. The Mongols were not Muslim. Everywhere they rode, Mongol horsemen looted, pillaged, and killed. They burned priceless books and works of art. They demolished mosques, the Muslim places of worship. In 1258, Mongols took Baghdad itself, nearly destroying the city.

The Mongol invasions marked a dark period in Islamic history. But at about the same time Europe experienced its Renaissance, the Islamic world recovered, too. Between the fourteenth and seventeenth centuries, three new Muslim empires appeared—the Ottoman (AH-tuh-muhn) Empire, centered in Asia Minor; the Safavid (sa-FAH-vuhd) Empire of Persia; and the Mughal (MOO-guhl) Empire of India.

Together these three empires brought Islam to a new height of power and influence. Let's back up to the late Middle Ages and see how this happened.

This chapter focuses on the Ottoman, Safavid, and Mughal Empires.

Islamic Empires

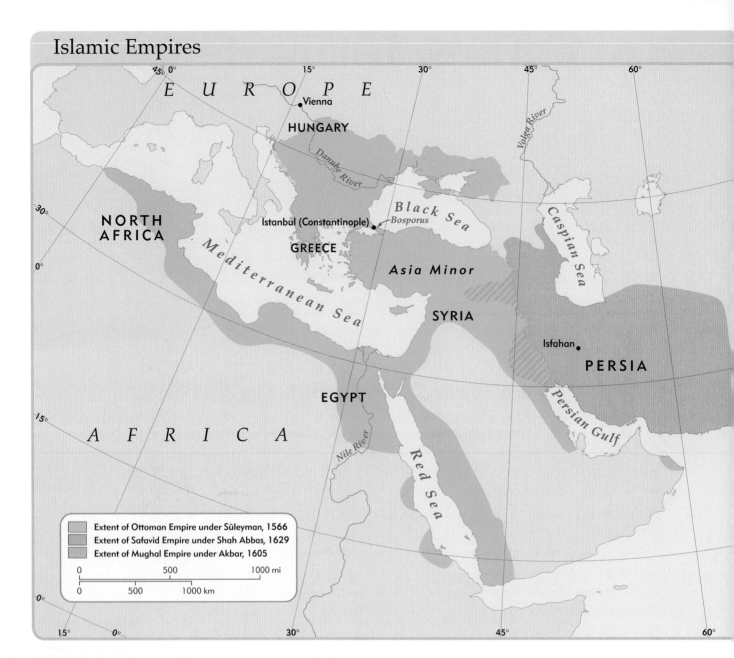

Map legend:
- Extent of Ottoman Empire under Süleyman, 1566
- Extent of Safavid Empire under Shah Abbas, 1629
- Extent of Mughal Empire under Akbar, 1605

Scale: 0 — 500 — 1000 mi / 0 — 500 — 1000 km

Map labels: EUROPE, Vienna, HUNGARY, Danube River, Volga River, NORTH AFRICA, Istanbul (Constantinople), Bosporus, Black Sea, Caspian Sea, GREECE, Mediterranean Sea, Asia Minor, SYRIA, Isfahan, PERSIA, EGYPT, AFRICA, Nile River, Red Sea, Persian Gulf

Osman I dreamed of empire. "Ottoman" comes from Osman.

Osman's Dream of Conquest

In about 1260, a boy named Osman (os-MAHN) was born into a tribe of Muslim nomads living in present-day Turkey. When he grew up, Osman had a strange dream. He dreamed that a great tree grew out of his body. The tree kept growing till its branches spread for thousands of miles, shading the continents of Europe, Asia, and Africa. Osman decided the dream prophesied that he would lead his people to conquer lands on all three continents.

Inspired by this vision, Osman and his followers set out to defeat their neighbors. Osman's men were fierce warriors. Like the Mongols, they were skilled at firing arrows from horseback. Before long, they had taken over most of Asia Minor.

After Osman died, his son and grandson continued his conquests. Their people became known as Ottomans, or "people of Osman." The ruler of the Ottomans was called the sultan. Whenever a new sultan came to the throne,

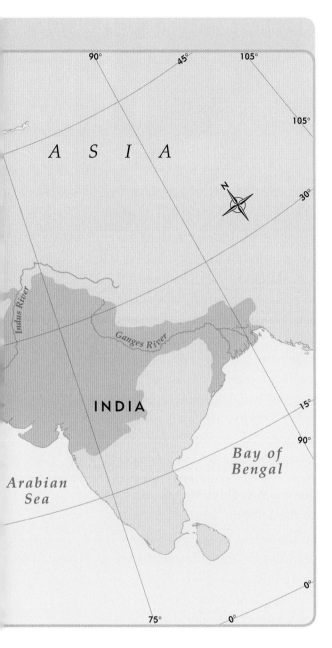

the people cried, "May he be as good as Osman!"

After the Ottomans had conquered all of Asia Minor, they turned west to invade Europe. Portions of eastern Europe had been part of the once-powerful Byzantine Empire. Now that empire was weak and crumbling, and the Ottomans took advantage of its weakness. By the middle of the fifteenth century, they had conquered much of eastern Europe, including present-day Macedonia, Bulgaria, and Serbia.

One great prize remained to be captured—Constantinople, the capital of the Byzantine Empire. The beautiful old city overlooked the Bosporus, the narrow body of water separating Asia and Europe.

- On the map above, locate Constantinople. Locate the Bosporus.

In 1453, the Ottomans laid siege to Constantinople. The people of Constantinople peered down from the city's walls and saw 300,000 of the sultan's soldiers surrounding them. Even more frightening were the Ottomans' gigantic cannons.

Ottoman troops lay siege to the walled city of Constantinople. When the Ottoman sultan captured the Byzantine capital, he declared it a Muslim city and renamed it Istanbul.

The Ottomans turned Byzantium's largest Christian church, Hagia Sophia, into a mosque. At each corner they added minarets, towers used to call Muslims to prayer.

The largest was 28 feet long, and so heavy it had to be pulled by 30 oxen.

For two months, Ottoman cannons rained destruction on the city. Its inhabitants rallied around their leader, the Byzantine Emperor Constantine XI, who battled from the city walls and refused to surrender.

The sultan ordered a great assault on Constantinople. Wave after wave of soldiers attacked the walls, but the defenders beat them back. Finally the sultan ordered his finest troops—the janissaries (JA-nuh-sehr-eez)—to attack. They rushed forward, blowing trumpets and banging on cymbals to create a terrifying noise.

> The name *janissaries* comes from Turkish terms meaning "new army."

The janissaries fought their way through one of the city gates. The rest of the Ottoman army poured in behind them. Seeing them come, the Byzantine emperor drew his sword and led his soldiers in a hopeless charge. The Ottoman soldiers cut him down. Soon after their emperor's death, the exhausted people of Constantinople surrendered.

The victorious sultan rode to Hagia Sophia, the city's largest Christian church. There he offered thanks to Allah and gave orders that the church be transformed into a mosque. He decreed that Constantinople was now a Muslim city, the capital of a Muslim empire, and renamed it Istanbul. The Byzantine Empire was no more.

Janissaries: Slave Warriors of the Sultan

In the century after the fall of Constantinople, the Ottomans went on to win even more victories in Europe. They conquered the lands now known as Greece and Hungary. At the same time they pushed south, conquering Syria, Egypt, and the coastline of North Africa. By the middle of the sixteenth century, Osman's dream had come true. His descendants ruled a vast empire that stretched across the three continents of Europe, Asia, and Africa.

- On the map on pages 138–39, locate the Ottoman Empire.

What made the Ottoman army almost invincible? In the days of Osman, the sheer fierceness of his nomadic warriors proved to be a

From "Constantinople" to "Istanbul"

The Ottoman Turks shortened the name Constantinople to something they could easily pronounce. They changed Constantinopolis (the city's Greek name) to *Istanbul.*

powerful advantage. As the Ottoman Empire grew bigger and richer, its army became better equipped and organized. The wealthy Ottoman sultans could afford the most up-to-date weapons, like the giant cannons at the siege of Constantinople.

But the Ottomans' most important advantage may have been the discipline of their army. One Italian writer pointed out that European soldiers often acted in wild and uncontrolled ways. By contrast, he said, the Ottoman troops "obey their commanders promptly; they never show the least concern for their lives in battle; [and] they can live a long time without bread and wine, content with barley and water."

The janissaries—the Ottoman troops who led the final charge at Constantinople—stood out as the most disciplined of all. They were the best trained and most respected of all the sultan's soldiers. In their fine uniforms and tall white hats, the janissaries swaggered proudly through the streets of Ottoman cities.

Yet, strangely, every one of these proud soldiers was a slave. Just as strangely, every one had been raised as a Christian. Each year the sultan sent his officers to Christian villages in eastern Europe. The Ottoman soldiers selected the strongest boys in each village and took them away as slaves. They forced the young boys to convert to Islam and trained them to become janissaries.

By taking the boys away from their homes and families, the sultan created a group of soldiers loyal to

him alone. He even forbade the janissaries to marry or have children. The life of a janissary was hard and dangerous, but the soldiers were richly rewarded and honored. Some Christian families even volunteered their sons, since becoming a janissary was a route to riches, power, and status in the Islamic empire.

Süleyman the Magnificent

In the middle of the sixteenth century, the Ottoman Empire stood at the height of its power and

This elaborately attired soldier is a janissary. The janissaries, the fiercest troops in the Ottoman army, led the final assault on Constantinople.

prosperity. The empire's millions of subjects paid taxes that flowed to Istanbul to enrich the sultan's government. At the same time, people from all over the empire—Greeks, Jews, Arabs, Africans—flocked to the capital city to seek their fortune. For the most part, these groups got along well.

From 1520 to 1566, the empire enjoyed the rule of the greatest of all the sultans, Süleyman (SOO-lay-mahn) I. A brilliant military leader, Süleyman led his troops against Europeans to the west and Persians to the east. Visitors were awed by the wealth and splendor of Süleyman's court. One European ambassador described "the immense crowd of turbaned heads, wrapped in countless folds of the whitest silk … and everywhere the brilliance of gold, silver, purple, silk and satin." He added, "A more beautiful spectacle never was presented to my gaze." Because of the sultan's taste for luxury and beauty, Europeans called him "Süleyman the Magnificent." (See page 136.)

Süleyman set out to make Istanbul the most beautiful city in

the world. He hired a brilliant architect named Mimar Sinan (see-NAHN) and asked him to design new buildings for the city. Perhaps Sinan's greatest building was the mosque named after the sultan—the Süleymaniye (soo-lay-MAHN-ee-yeh). This magnificent building looks like a mountain made of domes of different shapes and sizes. Nearby stand four graceful minarets, towers used to call Muslims to prayer.

Over the door of the Süleymaniye mosque were carved the words "Maker of the Imperial Laws." The phrase is a good reminder of how Süleyman's subjects saw him. Only foreigners called the sultan "Süleyman the Magnificent." The Ottomans themselves called him "Süleyman the Lawgiver."

To maintain order, the sultan decreed a vast new set of laws for his empire. These laws—hundreds of them—governed life in Süleyman's Ottoman Empire. There was even a law about how to fold a turban. The new legal code was good for most of

Süleyman's architect, Mimar Sinan, designed the Süleymaniye mosque using the old plans for the Hagia Sophia.

the sultan's subjects. It meant that everyone had to follow the same set of rules. If someone thought he had been treated unjustly, he could appeal to the sultan himself. Travelers from abroad praised the fairness of the empire's laws and the honesty of its judges.

Persia's Safavid Empire

To the east of the Ottoman Empire lay its rival, Persia. In the early sixteenth century, a group of Muslim nomads from the north, called the Safavids, conquered Persia. Their leader, Ismail (iss-mah-EEL), declared himself shah, or emperor, of Persia and began to conquer even more lands.

The shah made the mistake of invading Asia Minor, the heartland of the Ottoman Empire. Süleyman sent out a great army to meet the invaders. The Safavid warriors fought bravely. But like the defenders of Constantinople, they could not withstand the discipline of the sultan's janissaries, or the firepower of his cannons. The Safavids suffered heavy losses. After Ismail himself was wounded, he ordered his army to retreat.

The Ottomans and the Safavids became bitter enemies, partly because each empire wanted to expand into the other's territory. But there was also a religious reason for the conflict.

Both the Ottomans and the Safavids were Muslims. But the Ottomans belonged to the Sunni (SOO-nee) branch of Islam, and the Safavids belonged to the Shi'ite (SHEE-iyt) branch. Shah Ismail declared Shi'ism to be the state religion of his empire, and he

Shah Ismail, seated at left, was the emperor of the Safavid people of Persia. The Safavids were Shi'ite Muslims, while the Ottomans were Sunni Muslims. Shah Ismail launched an unsuccessful invasion of the Ottoman Empire in the early 1500s.

Sunnis and Shi'ites

Not long after the prophet Muhammad's death in A.D. 632, Muslims disagreed about how to choose his successor. One group believed that the leader should always be someone from Muhammad's family. Muhammad left no son, so this group rallied around his son-in-law, Ali, and Ali's descendants. Ali's supporters were called the Shia Ali ("the party of Ali"), or Shi'ahs (SHEE-ahs) for short. They are often referred to as Shi'ites.

Other Muslims said it was wrong for the leadership of Islam to stay in Muhammad's family. They said the most capable Muslim should lead, and that he should rule following the Qur'an and the example of Muhammad. In Arabic, "example" is *sunna*, so these Muslims are called Sunnis. Over the centuries, there has been much conflict between the Sunni and Shi'ite Muslims.

The Safavid Empire reached its peak during the reign of Shah Abbas I. Above, the shah extends a cup of welcome to a visiting ruler, while dancers and musicians entertain their foreign guest.

persecuted Sunni Muslims who refused to change their faith. The Ottomans resented the shah's cruel treatment of their fellow Sunnis.

Shah Abbas, Warrior and Builder

For the next century, the Ottomans and Safavids fought an on-again, off-again war. Under Süleyman the Magnificent, the Ottomans seized large territories from the Safavids. But in 1587, a new leader came to power in Persia, Shah Abbas I.

Abbas decided that the only way to beat his enemies was to learn from them. So he copied the Ottoman way of making war. He captured slaves for his army and trained them to be loyal to him alone, as the janissaries were loyal to the sultan. He equipped his troops with the latest weapons—muskets and cannons. With his powerful new army, he won back most of the lands his people had lost to the Ottomans.

- On the map on pages 138–39, locate the Safavid Empire.

Shah Abbas ruled his empire as brilliantly as he led his armies. Under him, the Safavid Empire reached its highest peak of power and influence. Persian merchants and craftsmen prospered, and trade connected the empire to the rest of the world. Wealthy people in Europe eagerly purchased costly Persian carpets with their intricate designs. Other Persian craftsmen produced beautiful pieces of pottery. The shah himself loved the arts, and he supported poets and painters.

Persian artists of this time were bold and original. In the early days of Islam, religious teachers laid down the rule that no living creatures, humans or animals, could be shown in art. Only Allah, they said, could make a living thing. So if an artist depicted something living, he was showing excessive pride by trying to be like Allah.

Although they were Muslims, Persian painters did not accept this idea. They made pictures full of images of living things. In their paintings, horses pranced, lions roared, and legendary heroes battled their enemies.

During the time of Shah Abbas, merchants brought copies of European paintings into Persia. The Renaissance was underway in Europe, where artists had discovered new techniques such as perspective. By studying these techniques, Persian painters made their pictures more lifelike.

To celebrate the glory of his empire, Abbas built a new capital city, Isfahan (is-fah-HAHN). Right in the center of the city, his architects laid out a huge rectangular park. Here people could come to celebrate festivals or watch polo matches.

On two sides of the park in Isfahan stood bazaars—big buildings full of bustling stores. A magnificent mosque rose over one end of the park. The mosque's gracefully swelling dome glittered with blue tiles—a favorite Persian decoration. Beyond the park and the mosque, the city sprawled. Trees shaded its wide streets. Fountains played in its gardens. Travelers from all over the world came to admire the shah's beautiful, well-planned city. In Isfahan, all the wealth of Safavid culture was on display.

India's Mughals

In the 1520s, while Süleyman ruled in Istanbul and the Reformation fractured Christendom, a Muslim chieftain from Central Asia invaded northern India. His name was Babur (BAH-bur), and he founded a dynasty of rulers known as the

Left: Though Muslim, Persian artists did not hesitate to paint living things. Here noblemen play polo, a game invented in Persia and now played all over the world.

Below: A stunning blue-tiled dome tops a mosque in Isfahan, capital of the Safavid rulers.

Mughals. Babur's grandson Akbar (AK-bur) went on to conquer most of northern and central India. Under Akbar in the second half of the sixteenth century, the Mughals built a large and powerful empire.

- On the map on pages 138–39, locate the Mughal Empire.

This third Muslim empire was very different from the Ottoman and Safavid Empires. In the homelands of those two empires—Asia Minor and Persia—the great majority of people were Muslims. But the Mughals conquered India, a land where people practiced the religions of Hinduism and Buddhism. Most Indians were Hindu. So Akbar faced a difficult problem. How could he get the Hindu majority to accept rule by Muslims?

Akbar solved this problem by treating the Hindus well. He appointed Hindus to high office. He took Hindu women as wives (Muslims could marry more than one woman), allowing them to practice their religion in his palace. He did away with the tax that non-Muslims had to pay in Muslim countries. He even banned the killing of cows, an animal sacred to Hindus.

Akbar thought that every religion had something good to teach. He brought Muslim, Hindu, Jewish, and Christian scholars together in his palace. He spent hours asking them about their religious ideas and trying to learn from them.

Later, Akbar's son boasted of his father's acceptance of other faiths: "He associated with the good of every race and creed and persuasion…. This was different from the practices in other realms, for in Persia there is room for Shi'ahs only, and in Turkey … there is room for Sunnis only."

Sometimes Akbar's actions shocked his Muslim subjects. The emperor, who loved the arts, employed more than a hundred painters to make pictures for him. Among their paintings were portraits of the emperor and his nobles. Some people complained about the portraits. Making pictures of the

The Mughal emperor Akbar hunts tigers from the back of his horse. The emperor built a mighty Islamic empire in northern and central India. He too believed that artists should be able to paint the human figure.

Akbar Meets the Jesuits

The energetic Jesuit missionary Francis Xavier traveled to India in the 1540s. He started schools and converted more than 10,000 people to Christianity, leaving an active mission there. The Mughal leader Akbar invited Jesuits to his court so he could learn about their religion. The Jesuits wrote glowing reports about Akbar's tolerance and curiosity.

Akbar's grandson, Shah Jahan, built one of the most famous examples of Muslim architecture in the world. The Taj Mahal, constructed in the 1630s as a tomb for Shah Jahan's wife, is a triumph of Mughal culture.

human body, they said, violated the teachings of Islam. This could not be true, responded the emperor. Allah made the human body, so surely Allah would be pleased to see its beauty reflected in art.

Akbar's painters learned their realistic way of painting from the artists of Safavid Persia. The Mughals respected the brilliant culture of the Safavids and learned from it in many ways. For example, Mughal architects built mosques with swelling domes and decorated them with colored tile, so that they resembled the mosques in Isfahan.

From 1300 to 1600, while the Renaissance energized European nations, the Islamic empires on Europe's borders stood as rival centers of power and culture. The Ottoman, Safavid, and Mughal Empires stretched from the Mediterranean Sea to the Bay of Bengal. Their achievements and cultures had a lasting effect on that part of the world.

Meanwhile, farther to the east, other civilizations flourished. In our next stop on the human odyssey, we'll look at two Asian lands—China and Japan.

Finding the "Path of Truth" in History

A Page from the Past

Ibn Khaldun (IH-buhn kahl-DOON) was a Muslim scholar from North Africa who lived in the fourteenth century. He wrote a seven-volume study of world civilization that is considered one of the greatest works of that age. Ibn Khaldun was a pioneer in thinking about how historians should approach the past. He stressed that they should base accounts of the past not on legends, hearsay, or religious beliefs, but on accurate and reliable information. In the introduction to his world history, Ibn Khaldun said that students of history must try to distinguish fact from fiction.

Students often happen to accept and transmit absurd information.... Al-Masudi, for instance, reports such a story about Alexander. Sea monsters prevented Alexander from building Alexandria. He took a wooden container in which a glass box was inserted, and dived in it to the bottom of the sea. There he drew pictures of the devilish monsters he saw. He then had metal effigies of those animals made and set them up opposite the place where the building was going on. When the monsters came out and saw the effigies, they fled. Alexander was thus able to complete the building of Alexandria.

It is a long story, made up of nonsensical elements which are absurd for various reasons. Thus [Alexander is said] to have taken a glass box and braved the sea and its waves in person. Now, rulers would not take such a risk. Any ruler who would attempt such a thing would work his own undoing and provoke the outbreak of revolt against himself, and be replaced by the people with someone else. That would be his end. People would not wait one moment for his return from the risk he is taking....

Were one to go down deep into the water, even in a box, one would

Ibn Khaldun on the Rise and Fall of Empires

Ibn Khaldun pondered the question: Why do empires rise and fall? According to Ibn Khaldun, most empires are founded by warlike tribes that follow inspiring leaders. After a tribe sets up an empire, it settles down to a life of peaceful ruling. Over a few generations, the tribe loses its fighting spirit and its loyalty to its leaders. Finally it falls to an invading warlike tribe. And so the cycle continues.

Ibn Khaldun's idea seems to fit the Ottoman, Safavid, and Mughal Empires. All three were founded by nomadic warriors. All three declined after two or three hundred years, overtaken by more warlike enemies.

have too little air for natural breathing…. Such a man … would perish on the spot.

Al-Masudi reports another absurd story, that of the statue of the starlings in Rome. On a fixed day of the year, starlings gather at that statue bringing olives from which the inhabitants of Rome get their oil. How little this has to do with the natural procedure of getting oil!

Another absurd story is reported by al-Bakri. It concerns the way the so-called "Gate City" was built. The city had a circumference of more than a thirty days' journey and had ten thousand gates. Now, cities are used for security and protection. Such a city, however, could not be controlled and would offer no security or protection.

Then there is also al-Masudi's story of the "Copper City." This is said to be a city built wholly of copper in the desert of Sijilmasah…. The gates of this city are said to be closed. When the person who climbs its walls, in order to enter it, reaches the top, he claps his hands and throws himself down and never returns. All this is an absurd story. It belongs to the idle talk of storytellers. The desert of Sijilmasah has been crossed by travelers and guides. They have not come across any information about such a city. All the details mentioned about it are absurd. They contradict the natural facts that apply to the building and planning of cities. Metal exists at best in quantities sufficient for utensils and furnishings. It is clearly absurd and unlikely that there would be enough to cover a city with it….

To establish the truth and soundness of information about factual happenings … it is necessary to investigate whether it is possible that the [reported facts] could have happened…. If we do that, we shall have a … method for distinguishing right from wrong and truth from falsehood in historical information…. We shall have a sound yardstick with the help of which historians may find the path of truth and correctness where their reports are concerned.

A fifteenth-century stone warrior stands guard at the tombs of the Ming emperors. China flourished under the Ming, the country's "brilliant" dynasty.

Ming China and Feudal Japan

*I*n the early thirteenth century, the Mongol leader Genghis Khan conquered much of China. His grandson Kublai Khan finished the job in 1279 and established the Yuan dynasty to rule China. For decades the Chinese suffered under Mongol rule. They paid high taxes, had little say in their government, and endured terrible famines.

By the middle of the fourteenth century, the Chinese people had had enough of foreign rule. They struggled to overthrow the Yuan. No one played a greater role in that struggle than a poor peasant from southern China named Zhu Yuanzhang (joo you-en-jahng).

The Peasant Turned Emperor

From an early age, Zhu knew first-hand the sufferings of his people. His parents and three older brothers had starved to death when, after a drought, a swarm of locusts devoured the few crops remaining in the family's fields. Zhu managed to survive by joining a Buddhist monastery. But the Mongols burned the monastery to the ground. Soon Zhu joined a band of rebels battling to drive the hated Mongols out of his land.

Zhu proved himself a natural leader. He quickly began to recruit followers. Again and again he led his men to victory against the Mongols. In 1355, he assembled an army and conquered the southern Mongol city of Nanjing (nahn-jing), which eventually became the capital.

Zhu's army was just one of several competing rebel armies in China. Over the next decade, he fought more battles against Chinese rivals than against the Yuan rulers.

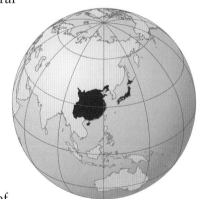

This chapter focuses on Ming China and feudal Japan.

China and Japan

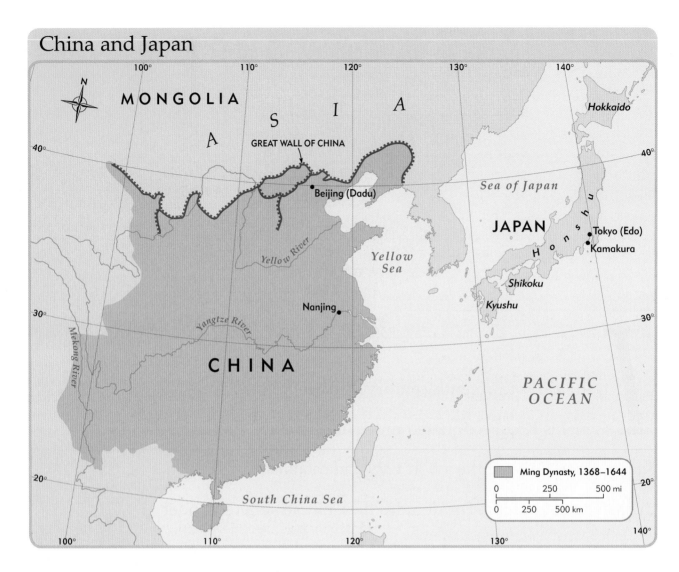

MONGOLIA

ASIA

GREAT WALL OF CHINA

Beijing (Dadu)

Yellow River

Yellow Sea

Sea of Japan

JAPAN

Hokkaido

Honshu

Tokyo (Edo)
Kamakura

Shikoku

Kyushu

Nanjing

Yangtze River

Mekong River

CHINA

PACIFIC OCEAN

South China Sea

Ming Dynasty, 1368–1644

0   250   500 mi
0   250   500 km

Zhu Yuanzhang founded the Ming dynasty and became its first emperor.

By 1368, Zhu had defeated both the Mongols and his Chinese rivals in the south. He established himself as ruler over most of southern China and proclaimed a new imperial dynasty.

For the first time in China's long history, a man born a peasant sat on the imperial throne. Zhu gave his dynasty an impressive name. He called it the *Ming*, which means "brilliant." The brilliant new emperor then set out to capture the northern part of China.

Never before had northern China been ruled by an emperor from the south. But the Ming emperor knew he could count on the support of people all over China who hated living under Mongol rule. Soon after setting up his new dynasty, Zhu gathered an army and marched on the city of Dadu (dah-doo), the Mongol capital.

The Yuan emperor who ruled in Dadu was a far cry from the great Mongol conquerors Genghis Khan and Kublai Khan. He spent most of his days in the imperial palace making clocks. As Zhu's army approached, the clock-making emperor decided to flee rather than fight. He abandoned Dadu and escaped across the frontier to the safety of Mongolia.

The Ming, China's "Brilliant" Dynasty

Zhu had conquered an empire. Now it was time to rule it.

For centuries Chinese emperors had employed thousands of smart, talented men to help run their empire. These men made up the civil service, and they helped run the government. Mongol emperors had ended the Chinese civil service and instead hired Mongols and other foreigners to help them rule. Zhu decided to restore China's civil service. He began to recruit capable men. He found candidates in schools that taught the wisdom of the ancient philosopher Confucius. These candidates took rigorous exams that included tests in Confucian classics. Candidates who passed the exams could enter government service.

Under the Ming—the "brilliant" dynasty—Chinese arts and crafts flourished. Craftsmen wove beautiful rugs and carpets. Architects designed graceful bridges, temples, and tombs. Imperial artisans became famous for their fine designs carved on lacquered trays, bowls, and boxes—leaping deer, roaring dragons, peaceful mountain scenes.

Perhaps the most brilliant of Ming era artworks was the superb porcelain, a form of ceramics that had been perfected by the Chinese in earlier centuries. Traditionally, porcelain was white and translucent. Under the Ming, imperial workshops began to use other pigments as well, especially blue. Artisans painted delicate designs on the ceramic. Flowers, birds, phoenixes, and dragons adorned plates and vases.

In the early 1400s, one of Zhu's successors decided to move the capital from Nanjing in the south to the old Yuan city of Dadu. This new northern capital became known as Beijing (bay-zhing). It remains the capital of China to this day.

Ming artisans created this fine porcelain bowl, decorated with a dragon, and this lacquered tray. Lacquer is a liquid resin that comes from the lacquer tree. Artists painted layer after layer of lacquer until they created a smooth hard surface that was deep enough to be carved.

- On the map on page 152, locate China under the Ming dynasty. Locate the city of Beijing.

At the emperor's command, the Chinese rebuilt much of Beijing. The emperor was determined to make it more magnificent than it had ever been. He ordered hundreds of thousands of workers to labor on the project for a period of 14 years. Engineers laid out the splendid new capital in a huge grid of streets. At its heart lay an area few Chinese and almost no foreigners were permitted to see—the Forbidden City.

The *civil service* is the body of government officials appointed to help run a government. A country's civil service does not include its elected officials or its judges.

The Ming palace complex in Beijing was known as the Forbidden City, a place where few Chinese and no foreigners were allowed to visit. Over the centuries, the Forbidden City was home to 24 different emperors.

The Forbidden City

Surrounded by walls and a moat, the Forbidden City was a private world, set apart for the imperial court. Across its 178 acres spread temples, palaces, gardens, courtyards, carved stone bridges, and elaborate ceremonial halls.

The main entrance was the imposing Meridian Gate. Standing nearly 125 feet high, it became a symbol of imperial power. Visitors and subjects were supposed to feel puny as they stood before it.

Beyond the gate lay a large courtyard, through which the Golden River ran in a majestic arc. Five white marble bridges spanned the river, leading toward the 75 buildings that made up the Forbidden City. Each of the buildings faced south, the direction from which benevolent spirits were believed to come.

But should evil forces also make their way to the Forbidden City, the emperor and his court had taken many precautions. On the ground, fearsome lions of gilded bronze stood guard. Carved dragons entwined themselves around tall columns. And on the rooftops sat fanciful earthenware creatures, said to protect the city. In the Forbidden City, the most important buildings had the greatest number of animal figurines perched on their roof ridges.

No building was more important than the Hall of Supreme Harmony. Measuring 210 feet by 122 feet, the hall was the heart of the royal court. There the emperor sat on his dragon throne for the most important state occasions, such as the celebration of the New Year or his birthday.

Farther north lay the imperial living quarters. Beyond the living quarters sprawled colorful gardens and winding paths. In the center of the gardens rose a temple called the Hall of Imperial Peace, a secluded retreat where the emperor could withdraw for quiet contemplation.

The Forbidden City was the emperor's home, office, and retreat. Everything about it was designed to show the might of the emperor, the importance of the Ming dynasty, and the insignificance of just about everything else!

Zheng He Sets Sail

In the early fifteenth century, the Ming emperors who ruled China from the Forbidden City dispatched great fleets of sailing ships to explore distant lands. The most renowned of their sailors was an admiral named Zheng He (choung huh).

Zheng He, who came from a Muslim family, had been taken captive by Chinese forces when he was just 10. The Chinese put the boy into their army, where he worked hard and rapidly rose through the ranks. Eventually his abilities caught the attention of the imperial court.

Zheng had been in the military for about 20 years when the emperor selected him to lead a voyage of exploration. He spent the next 28 years sailing the seas in the emperor's service, partly in pursuit of trade and partly in search of knowledge.

In all, Zheng embarked on seven separate expeditions. Some of the ships he sailed were more than 400 feet long with four decks and

Zheng He explored the "western oceans" in the service of the Ming emperor.

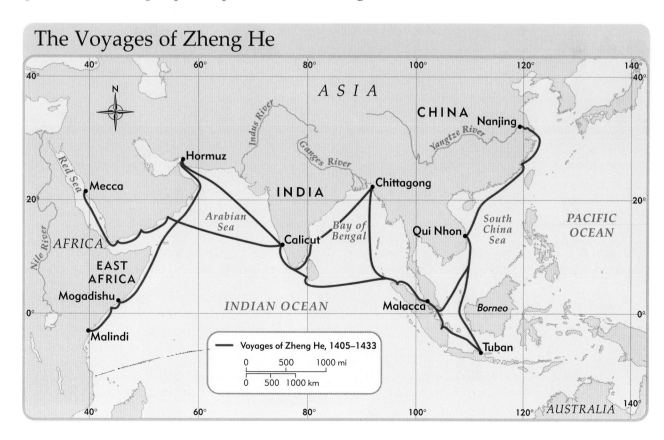

The Voyages of Zheng He

Voyages of Zheng He, 1405–1433

0   500   1000 mi

0   500   1000 km

watertight compartments. Almost 90 years before Columbus began his famous voyage to the Americas with three tiny vessels, Zheng explored the oceans with a fleet of no fewer than 62 large ships, 225 small ones, and about 27,000 men.

Zheng's journeys took him into distant, uncharted waters. Navigating by compass, he explored the coasts of Southeast Asia and India. He ventured across the Arabian Sea to East Africa, and up the Red Sea. He pushed south to Borneo, and perhaps close to Australia. It is even possible that about 70 years before European sailors managed it, some Chinese ships achieved the remarkable feat of sailing around the southern coast of Africa.

- On the map on page 155, locate the voyages of Zheng He.

From his seven voyages, Zheng brought back visitors or captives from 36 different countries. These foreigners presented the emperor with exotic gifts such as ostriches, zebras, and giraffes. A whole world seemed to lie within China's reach.

But after 1433, the expeditions ceased. Zheng died in 1435, and the Ming emperors turned increasingly inward. They decided that they did not need to explore faraway parts of the world. They came to distrust foreigners. They feared that outsiders, especially Christian missionaries, wanted to change traditional Chinese practices and beliefs. Eventually, the emperors even banned the construction of oceangoing ships and forbade their merchants from leaving Chinese waters.

Why? Around the time of Zheng's death, Ming emperors had a reason to turn their attention away from the sea and focus it elsewhere. They faced a new threat from the north. The Ming's old enemies, the Mongols, were on the move again.

Building Walls

In the mid-fifteenth century, new Mongol raids began in the north of China. So the Ming undertook an old project with new vigor. They began to rebuild the Great Wall.

- On the map on page 152, locate the Great Wall of China.

Back in the third century B.C., the Chinese had begun building the Great Wall to keep out invaders from the north. But the wall had fallen into disrepair, and it had not stopped the Mongols in the thirteenth century. By the 1400s, much of the Wall was in bad shape. When their northern neighbors again threatened China's frontiers, the Ming decided to fortify the barrier.

The Ming rebuilt the Great Wall of China and its watchtowers to keep out Mongol invaders from the north. Most of the wall that we see today dates from the time of the Ming.

The Great Wall they inherited was built of beaten earth. To strengthen it, Chinese workers added stone slabs and bricks. In some places they made the wall wide enough for five horsemen to pass abreast. On top they erected watchtowers, generally 200 yards apart. From these towers, defenders could unleash arrows and spears on attackers. The watchtowers also served as signal stations to help warn of invasions. The army divided the long wall into nine zones, each placed under the control of a different commander.

Ming rulers used countless thousands of laborers to strengthen and extend the Great Wall during their reign. Eventually the wall snaked thousands of miles inland from the Yellow Sea along China's vulnerable frontier. It was one of the greatest engineering feats ever undertaken.

The Chinese also built walls around their cities. All this wall-building worked. The Ming dynasty repelled invaders and ruled China for nearly 300 years, from 1368 to 1644.

China's Influence on Japan

In various ways, Japan felt the influence of its much bigger neighbor to the west, China. In the second millennium B.C., the Chinese had developed a system of writing, which the Japanese adapted for their own purposes. As early as the fourth century, Japan's scholars read the great Chinese philosopher, Confucius. His moral teachings about justice, diligence, and respect appealed to the Japanese and had a lasting impact on their values. From the Chinese the Japanese also learned the art of calligraphy, beautiful writing as an art form.

Across the Sea of Japan

About 500 miles off the east coast of China lies another land that the Mongols tried to conquer—Japan.

Japan is made of four large islands and thousands of smaller ones. Honshu (HAWN-shoo), the main island, is home to most Japanese and the major cities. To the south lie the islands of Shikoku (shee-KOH-koo) and Kyushu (KYOO-shoo). And to the north lies Hokkaido (hoh-KIY-doh), which was not claimed by the Japanese until the nineteenth century.

- On the map on page 152, locate Japan. Locate the four main islands—Honshu, Shikoku, Kyushu, and Hokkaido.

For most of its early history, Japan's isolated location protected it from invaders. The mountainous islands offered only a limited amount of good farming land, which the people mostly used to grow rice. But Japan's 17,000 miles of coastline provided abundant seafood.

The native religion of Japan was Shintoism (SHIN-toh-ih-zuhm). Shinto followers believe that all things in nature have spirits, called *kami* (kah-mee). To Shintoists, kami are everywhere in nature—in the sun, the sea, mountains, animals, trees, rocks, and wind. Shintoists offer prayers and devotion to their kami, and they honor them by building shrines, or holy places. Large shrines have a sacred entrance gate called a *torii* (tor-EE-EE). These beautiful wooden gates have become a symbol of the Shinto religion.

In the sixth century, missionaries from mainland Asia brought another religion that the Japanese also made their own—Buddhism (BOO-dih-zuhm). Buddhism (as you might recall if you read Volume 1 of *The Human Odyssey*) is a major world religion begun in the sixth century B.C. by the Indian prince Siddhartha Gautama (sid-DAHR-tuh GOW-tuh-muh). During the Middle Ages, Buddhism spread from India east to China. From China the faith spread to other parts of Asia, including Japan.

Buddhism emphasized detachment from worldly goods and rising above temptations. Many Japanese were drawn to the wise teachings of the Buddha. In time, Buddhist shrines were rising alongside Shinto gates.

Japan's best-known symbol of Buddhism is the Great Buddha of Kamakura (kah-mah-KOOR-ah) in the country's ancient capital. This bronze statue, which was cast in 1252, weighs more than 120 tons and towers 44 feet high. It shows the Buddha in a seated position. The faithful believe that the Buddha was sitting this way under a tree in his native India when he gained enlightenment.

The face of the Buddha of Kamakura, itself more than eight feet long, is a picture of serenity. Upon its head lie 656 curls. And in the forehead, above the half-closed eyes, sits a third eye of silver. That eye symbolizes the light of Buddhist teaching, which is said to illuminate the universe.

The Great Buddha of Kamakura is the best-known symbol of Buddhism in Japan. The statue's hands form a triangle in the lap, symbolizing meditation.

The Age of the Samurai

By A.D. 1000, Japan, like much of Europe, was a land divided among many different rulers. The society was organized on the principles of feudalism—the system in which rulers grant land to those who pledge their loyalty and military service in return. At the top of the feudal

Shintoists built sacred gates like this one to welcome the spirits, or kami.

structure stood the shogun (SHOH-guhn), the military dictator of Japan. The shogun granted fiefs (parcels of land) to local lords who were known as daimyo (DIY-mee-oh). The daimyo built castles on their land and, in return for the fiefs, pledged their political and military support of the shogun.

The daimyo held the real power in feudal Japan. Like the lords of European manors, they exercised almost total control over their own territories. They commanded their own private armies and often waged war with one another. To protect and control their territories, they called upon the services of skilled samurai (SA-muh-riy).

The word samurai means "one who serves." The samurai were originally personal attendants. Over time, the term came to apply to professional warriors employed by a lord. The samurai's first loyalties were to his daimyo. Indeed, it was the duty of the samurai to die for his lord if necessary. In exchange for such dedicated service, the samurai received their own grants of land. Over the course of four centuries, these warriors fought battles on behalf of various lords seeking to dominate Japan.

Apprenticed at an early age, samurai served with masters who taught archery and swordsmanship. As part of their apprenticeship, they endured hardships such as barefoot marches through the snow and prolonged fasts. The samurai of Japan lived according to a strict code of behavior, much like the knights of medieval Europe. This code was called bushido (BOU-shee-doh), which means "the way of the warrior." The code required devotion to duty and absolute bravery and loyalty.

The samurai were an impressive and intimidating sight. Before battle, some blackened their teeth and put

This suit of armor was worn by a samurai, one of Japan's professional warriors. It weighs about 25 pounds and could be folded for easy travel. The helmet has a mask with a boar's hair mustache designed to scare enemy warriors.

powder on their faces. After tucking their hair into a topknot, they strapped on their armor, picked up their weapons—a bow, a short sword, and a long sword—and headed into the fight.

Unlike the heavy metal armor worn by European knights, the samurai's armor was composed of many small, thin scales made of iron or leather, all coated in a thick lacquer. These scales were laced together with leather thongs. Such armor combined strength with flexibility, essential for warriors who fought on foot as well as horseback.

On his head the samurai wore a helmet of iron, often with an elaborate crest in the shape of horns, an eagle, or a dragon. Many helmets also had a mask to cover the face and flaps to protect the ears and neck. Some masks even sported a large moustache made of boar's hair, which was meant to frighten the enemy. Large rectangular shoulder guards acted as shields against arrow attacks, and shin guards protected the lower legs. Around the neck, a throat guard protected against a favored samurai attack—decapitation with the long sword.

Many samurai practiced Zen, a form of Buddhism imported from China. Zen Buddhism grew popular during the thirteenth and fourteenth centuries. The religion appealed to warriors because it stressed discipline, self-control, and self-reliance. Such qualities were all-important to the samurai, who fought not only for the spoils of battle but also for honor and glory.

The Tokugawa Shogunate

For many years, powerful warlords struggled for rule of Japan. Some managed to control particular areas, but none was ever able to dominate

The Divine Wind

In 1274, many samurai fought to protect their country against a Mongol invasion. With 900 ships, 25,000 soldiers, and several thousand sailors, the mighty Mongol leader Kublai Khan invaded Japan. When the khan's troops landed, they were met by only a few thousand Japanese soldiers. By sunset, the Mongol warriors had killed most of the Japanese.

But then help came to the Japanese in the form of a mighty weapon that even Kublai Khan could not defeat—the weather. As night fell, the island on which the khan's troops had landed was struck by the lashing winds and driving rain of a typhoon (a hurricane). The storm churned the sea and smashed ships to pieces. By the next morning, the fury of the typhoon had driven the Mongols out of Japan.

The shogun ordered new defenses in case of another Mongol attack. Workers built many small fast ships, as well as a long stone wall to protect the coastline of the island of Kyushu.

Sure enough, in 1281 Kublai Khan launched his second attack on Japan. This time he had organized 140,000 soldiers and about 4,400 wooden ships. On land and on sea, the Japanese fought the Mongols for almost two months. Then one August night, the clouds darkened and the winds began to howl. Once again, a typhoon came to the aid of the Japanese. The storm sank perhaps as many as 4,000 of the Mongol ships, and the rest sailed back to China in defeat.

The Japanese people came to call typhoons the "kamikaze" (kah-mih-KAH-zee), which means "divine wind." (*Kami*, you recall, are the spirits of the Shinto religion.) Thanks to the kamikaze, the Mongols gave up trying to conquer Japan.

Right: Japanese warlords, or daimyos, built towering castles and fought each other for control of Japan.

Below: Ieyasu eventually managed to unite Japan under his rule. He established a capital at Edo (modern-day Tokyo) and founded the Tokugawa shogunate, which ruled Japan from 1603 to 1867.

the whole land. In the early 1600s, however, one man vanquished all the other warlords. He came from the Tokugawa (toh-kou-GAH-wuh) family, and his name was Ieyasu (ee-yeh-yah-soo).

Ieyasu was powerfully built and renowned for his thunderous battle cry. By 1603, he succeeded in uniting the country under his rule. He had himself appointed shogun and moved his headquarters to the castle town of Edo (AY-doh). In the years that followed, power passed to Ieyasu's descendants, thus forming a dynasty known as the Tokugawa shogunate. The city of Edo became known as Tokyo, Japan's center of power.

Japan prospered under the Tokugawa shogunate. The country enjoyed a 250-year period of peace. The shogun at last controlled the quarrelsome daimyo. The once powerful warlords now found themselves subject to the laws of the shogun.

The Tokugawa also imposed their will on the Western traders and Jesuit missionaries who were beginning to visit Japan. In 1600, a Dutch ship sailed into Japanese waters, and soon more and more Europeans began to arrive. The Tokugawa grew alarmed at the number of Japanese people converting to Christianity. They also feared that European nations might someday threaten their rule. They expelled many Christian missionaries and began to persecute Japanese Christians.

By the 1630s, the Tokugawa had closed Japan's borders to all but a handful of foreign traders. Like its great neighbor China on the Asian mainland, the island nation of Japan turned its back on much of the outside world.

The Closing of Japan

Early in the seventeenth century, the Tokugawa shogunate began to suspect that European powers might eventually try to control Japan. So Japan's rulers took steps to end all missionary efforts and restrict the movement of foreigners visting Japan.

The following excerpts are from a Japanese law known as the Act of Seclusion of 1636.

*A Page
from the Past*

- Japanese ships shall by no means be sent abroad.

- No Japanese shall be sent abroad. Anyone violating this prohibition shall suffer the penalty of death, and the ship owner and crew shall be held up together with the ship.

- All Japanese residing abroad shall be put to death when they return home.

- All Christians shall be examined by official examiners.

- Informers against Christians shall be rewarded.

- The arrival of foreign ships must be reported … and watch kept over them.

- The Namban people [Spaniards or Portuguese] and any other people … propagating Christianity shall be incarcerated in the Omura prison as before.

- Everything shall be done in order to see that no Christian is survived by descendants, and anyone disregarding this injunction shall be put to death, while proper punishment shall be meted out to the other members of his family according to their deeds.

- Children born of the Namban people [Spaniards or Portuguese] in Nagasaki and people adopting these Namban children into their family shall be put to death; capital punishment shall also be meted out to those Namban descendants if they return to Japan, and their relatives in Japan, who may communicate with them, shall receive suitable punishment.

- The samurai shall not purchase goods on board foreign ships directly from foreigners.

To *incarcerate* is to put into prison.

An *injunction* is an order.

Nagasaki is a major port city on the island of Kyushu.

The domes of St. Basil's Cathedral glow against Moscow's night sky.

Russia Rising

Wedst of China and Japan lay another civilization that turned inward—the giant land of Russia. Russia is the largest country in the world. Like a great bear, it sprawls across two continents, Europe and Asia.

The Baltic Sea washes Russia's northwestern tip. The Black Sea and Caspian Sea lie to the southwest. The Pacific Ocean marks the country's eastern edge. The icy Arctic Ocean stretches across Russia in the north.

- On a globe or world map, locate the modern-day country of Russia. Locate the Baltic Sea, Black Sea, Caspian Sea, Pacific Ocean, and Arctic Ocean.

Russia has not always been as gigantic as it is today. It began as a much smaller region of city-states that were often at odds with each other. By the end of the sixteenth century, it had become a powerful empire. Let's see how that empire got its start.

From Vikings to Vladimir

Russia is a land of flat, wide-open spaces. Vast, treeless plains make up much of the country. The open spaces allowed peoples from eastern Europe called Slavs (slahvz) to settle along the network of great rivers crossing the land. But if it was easy for the Slavic tribes to move in, it was also easy for others to follow.

The Vikings, warlike mariners from Scandinavia, plundered much of Europe during the Middle Ages. They sailed out of the frigid north to raid the Christian empire of Byzantium and steal its glittering treasures. One group of Vikings known as the

This chapter focuses on the rise of Russia, from the Middle Ages to the sixteenth century.

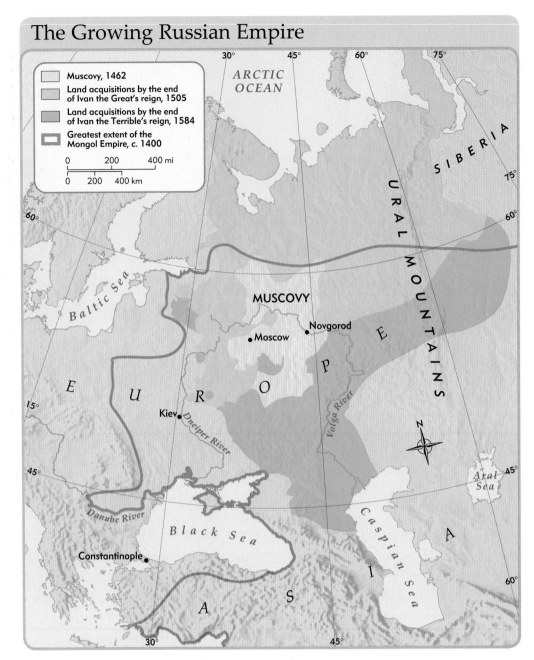

The Growing Russian Empire

Muscovy, 1462

Land acquisitions by the end
of Ivan the Great's reign, 1505

Land acquisitions by the end
of Ivan the Terrible's reign, 1584

Greatest extent of the
Mongol Empire, c. 1400

0   200   400 mi
0   200   400 km

ARCTIC
OCEAN

SIBERIA

URAL MOUNTAINS

Baltic Sea

MUSCOVY

• Moscow   • Novgorod

E   U   R   O   P   E

Kiev • Dnieper River

Volga River

Aral Sea

Danube River

Black Sea

Caspian Sea

Constantinople •

A   S   I   A

Viking longships nose their way along a river through "the land of the Rus." Eventually, the Vikings established permanent settlements next to these river routes and lived alongside the area's earlier inhabitants, the Slavs.

Varangians or Rus (roos) reached Byzantium by traveling along a series of rivers that ran through a flat landscape. The area later came to be called "the land of the Rus," and eventually, Russia.

The Vikings settled down beside the Slavs in cities all along the river routes. Kiev (KEE-ehf), an important city to the south, became the region's capital. In the north, the city of Novgorod (NAWV-guh-rahd) attracted merchants eager to buy

and sell goods such as honey, wax, and furs.

• On the map above, locate Kiev and Novgorod.

Each city had its own prince as well as landowning nobles called boyars (BOH-yahrz). The prince of Kiev was less a monarch than a leader of a loose alliance of squabbling city-states.

In 980, a young man named Vladimir (VLAD-uh-mihr) became

the grand prince of Kiev. At that time, Russia was a land of many religions. Vladimir realized that his realm would be more unified if his people shared a single faith. He decided to choose an official state religion.

Vladimir sent agents to neighboring lands to investigate the religions of Judaism, Islam, and Christianity. His agents were dazzled when they visited Constantinople, the home of the Eastern Orthodox Church. "We knew not whether we were in heaven or on earth," they reported after seeing the Cathedral of Hagia Sophia. "For on earth there is no such splendor or such beauty, and we are at a loss to describe it." Around the year 988, Vladimir converted to Orthodox Christianity and ordered his subjects to do the same.

Soon the Eastern Orthodox Church flourished in Russia. By the twelfth century, Kiev had four hundred churches in the Byzantine design, decorated with frescoes, mosaics, and painted icons.

Russia was still a land divided among many local rulers. These

The eleventh-century Cathedral of St. Sophia is said to be the oldest church in Russia. It is located in the city of Novgorod, an important trading center in early Russia.

rulers split their land among their sons, breaking the country into smaller bits with each generation. Brothers and cousins often quarreled over what they inherited. Princes treated each other as rivals. Even when fierce Mongol horsemen began to appear on Russia's frontiers, the Russian princes failed to join forces against them.

The Mongols Invade Russia

In the early thirteenth century, huge armies of Mongols charged across Russia. These warriors, who came to be called Tatars, destroyed one town after another. One Russian account stated, "The churches of God they devastated, and in the holy altars they shed much blood. And no one in town remained alive: all died equally and drank the single cup of death."

In 1240, a grandson of the famous warrior Genghis Khan led a Tatar army against Kiev, leveling the city, looting its treasure, and massacring its people. Many other towns shared Kiev's fate. In one city, when the people took shelter in a church, the Tatars set the building on fire. Everyone inside perished.

This policy of terror had exactly the effect the Tatars wanted. Russians who survived the attacks saw

Paying Tribute

Throughout history some conquerors have been content to let the people they defeat manage their own affairs as long as they pay the conquerors a certain amount of money every year or so. Giving such money to conquerors is called "paying tribute."

their conquerors as invincible. The Tatar army was free to move on, leaving only thirty thousand soldiers in Russia. In time, the Mongol Tatars slightly loosened their grip on Russia. As long as a Russian prince paid tribute to his Tatar rulers and drafted soldiers for their armies, they left him alone.

The Tatars Meet Ivan the Great

Most Russian princes paid the tribute and tried not to anger their Tatar rulers. But in 1462, a prince named Ivan III came to the throne of a powerful city-state called

Ivan the Great

Muscovy (MUHS-kuh-vee). Ivan had no intention of remaining under Mongol rule. His achievements made him a Russian hero known as Ivan the Great.

Muscovy lay far to the north and east of Kiev. Its capital, Moscow, was a thriving center of trade. But Ivan wanted more than Muscovy. He wanted to rule all of Russia.

• On the map on page 166, locate Muscovy and Moscow.

Two obstacles stood in Ivan's way. First, there were the rival Russian princes. Second, there were the Tatar overlords.

Ivan turned first to his rivals. A clever and ruthless politician, he used any means he could to bring their territories under his control. Sometimes he bought their land.

Sometimes he persuaded or forced dying princes to leave their territories to him instead of to the rightful heirs. Most often, he won territory by waging war.

Through war, Ivan won the important city of Novgorod. His actions after conquering Novgorod reveal the scope of his ambitions. Unlike the Tatars, he was not content to let local rulers keep their power as long as they paid him tribute. When a boyar opposed him, Ivan deported the troublemaker—that is, he sent the boyar to a far end of the realm.

Ivan killed Novgorod's mayor and abolished the town assembly. He wanted to make sure the city's people could not easily organize against him. So he tore down the bell that called the citizens of Novgorod together and carted it off to Moscow. Ivan took millions of acres from the boyars and gave the land to men who served in his army and government. These new nobles kept their land only as long as they pleased Ivan.

With land and nobles under his control, Ivan turned his thoughts to freeing Russia from the Tatar khans. He stopped sending tribute to the Tatar court. In 1480, he announced that he would no longer give his allegiance to the Tatar empire. The Tatar khan sent an army to crush the troublemaker. Ivan the Great met it with his own army.

Ivan the Great tears a letter from the Tatar khan demanding tribute payments from Muscovy. By this act, Ivan declared that Muscovy would no longer remain under Tatar, or Mongol, rule.

The two armies sat for weeks on opposite sides of a broad river, neither daring to attack. Finally, the river froze. Expecting the enemy to charge, the Russian forces retreated and waited. To their surprise, the Tatars turned and rode away. Russia was free of its foreign masters.

Ivan the Great's Great Ambition

Now Ivan took steps to unify his realm. He used the pride that Russians took in their religion as a way to make them feel like one people. Two and a half centuries of Tatar rule had limited communication with Eastern Orthodox Christians in other regions. So the Russians had gradually developed their own version of Christianity. They conducted church services and read scripture in Russian, rather than in the Greek used in the Eastern Orthodox Church. They came to see their church, which they called Russian Orthodox,

Russian artists painted icons such as this depiction of the Virgin Mary and the infant Jesus. Ivan the Great encouraged Russians to view the Russian Orthodox Church as Christianity's one true church.

as the one true church, especially after the Byzantine Empire fell to the Turks in 1453.

Ivan the Great encouraged his people to believe that Moscow had replaced Rome and Constantinople as the new center of Christianity. He married a Byzantine princess, the niece of the last Byzantine emperor. Ivan believed that this marriage made him the heir to the fallen Byzantine Empire. He thought that Moscow now surpassed Constantinople in power and influence. In Ivan's view, Moscow was the "Third Rome."

Ivan took a title that recalled the might of ancient Rome. He called himself the tsar (also spelled *czar*) of all Russia. The word comes from the Latin word *Caesar*. By calling himself tsar, Ivan proclaimed that he was as powerful and important as Julius Caesar, the great Roman conqueror and ruler. Later Russian rulers also called themselves tsars.

While Ivan the Great was gaining power in Russia, the Renaissance was changing Europe. Literature, learning, and the arts flourished in Italy, France, Germany, Britain, and beyond. By 1462, when Ivan took the throne, a 10-year-old Italian village boy named Leonardo da Vinci was learning how to paint and sculpt. Michelangelo was born while Ivan was busy conquering Novgorod.

Tatar rule had left Russia largely cut off from the new ideas and changes sweeping Europe. But Ivan heard of the rebirth underway in the West. His wife Sophia helped Ivan attract scholars, painters, and architects to Moscow. Ivan's court soon played host to many masters of the Italian Renaissance. Ivan himself was not a lover of the arts and sciences, but he was interested in power and glory. He wanted a splendid court to show the world Russia's glory—and his own.

Ivan Rebuilds the Kremlin

Moscow was no longer just a bit of territory in a Mongol empire. It was the capital of the independent kingdom of Muscovy and the center of Russian Orthodox Christianity. Ivan the Great wanted to stage royal ceremonies and spectacular religious festivals in Moscow. So the city needed a splendid new seat of government to demonstrate its importance.

Ivan turned his attention to Moscow's old and crumbling kremlin. In Russian, the word *kremlin* means "fortress." In medieval times, walled fortresses, or kremlins, often protected Russian cities. Kremlins were usually located near a river, and their ramparts, moats, and towers provided a place of refuge. Sometimes they enclosed cathedrals or palaces.

By the fifteenth century, Moscow's kremlin was a sorry sight. The triangular enclosure's brick walls were cracking, and the moats no longer ran with water.

To help reconstruct Moscow's kremlin, Ivan summoned the most talented builders in Russia. He knew that Italy was home to Europe's best architects and engineers, so he hired Italian builders as well. New walls rose. Towers sprang up. A broad moat joined the waters of two rivers.

The Italian architects designed a magnificent group of buildings,

Ivan the Great strengthened Moscow's kremlin by building new walls, towers, and a moat. The fortress became a symbol of Russia's growing power.

Кремль при Іоаннѣ III—мъ

known as *the* Kremlin. Three great stone cathedrals rose inside the Kremlin's walls. It was all that Ivan could have hoped—a mighty fortress, a symbol of Russia's power, and a bustling court full of artists and scholars from all over Europe.

Ivan the Great accomplished much of what he wanted in his life. He shook off Tatar domination. He made Moscow the center of both the Russian church and state. He won many military triumphs and extended his rule far beyond the bounds of Muscovy. But he did not wield absolute power over Russia. He passed that ambition

A Truly Towering Tower

The Ivan the Great Bell Tower is the tallest structure in the Kremlin in Moscow. In 1505, Ivan hired an Italian architect to help him build this famous onion-domed tower. The bell tower not only sounded the hours, it also served as a watchtower. If you climb the bell tower on a clear day, you can see for miles in any direction.

on to his grandson, Ivan IV, better known as Ivan the Terrible.

Ivan the Terrible

Ivan IV was only three years old when his father died in 1533, so his mother ruled Russia in his name. This haughty woman ran the country as she wished, ignoring the opinions of the boyars. Five years into her reign, she suddenly died—poisoned, or so her son believed.

Publicly, the boyars bowed before young Prince Ivan. Privately, they bullied and neglected him while they schemed against each other to control the throne. Greed and suspicion ruled. The powerful boyars used their influence to funnel wealth to family and friends. They imprisoned, exiled, or murdered rivals who got in their way.

Surrounded by cruelty, Ivan learned to be cruel. He liked to ride horseback through the streets of Moscow, slashing with his whip at anyone he passed. It was said that if he happened to see a man whose face he didn't care for, he commanded his servants to lop the man's head off on the spot.

At the age of 13, Ivan had a powerful leader of the boyars seized and killed. Four years later, in 1547, the head of the Russian Orthodox Church crowned young Ivan tsar of all Russia. Ivan himself planned every detail of the coronation and made sure the ceremony was full of pomp and pageantry.

Ivan's reign got off to a rocky start. The teenage tsar did not

from God for his cruelty and violence. He had a moment of remorse. The tsar walked 38 miles in bare feet, threw himself to his knees in the center of Moscow, and promised to rule in the interests of his people.

But Ivan had no intention of looking after the interests of the boyars. Like his grandfather, he resented the nobles and their influence. He flew into a fury when they interfered with his plans. He never forgot that when he was a young prince, the boyars had treated him with contempt. And he was sure they had poisoned his mother.

Many Russians suffered during the reign of Ivan IV, or as he is better known, Ivan the Terrible. He humiliated the boyars, the country's once-powerful nobles. And he forced Russian peasants to stay on the land where they were born, reducing many to the status of serfs.

Ivan and the Peasants

Ivan also made little effort to look after the interests of Russia's peasant farmers. Russian peasants were poor, but at least they had a little freedom. If they could pay off their debts to their landlord, they could move and work on someone else's land.

This freedom to move presented a problem for the landowners who served in Ivan's army or government posts. It was hard for them to be away from their estates when the peasants who worked their land could pick up and leave.

Ivan responded by taking steps to force peasants to stay on the land where they were born. Eventually Russian peasants were no longer free workers but serfs, legally bound to remain on the land of their lord.

tolerate any challenge or criticism. When a group came to complain about the governor he had appointed for their city, Ivan reportedly poured boiling wine on them and burned their beards off with a candle.

Not long afterwards, a dreadful fire broke out in Moscow and burned down much of the city. Thousands burned to death. Mobs rioted. Ivan believed the fire was a punishment

Peasant Life in Russia

Most Russians were poor peasants. Their lives were hard and short. They scratched out a living on estates controlled by boyars. A peasant family

Peasants, like those shown in this fifteenth-century manuscript, made up most of the Russian population. By law, they were free workers. But Russian peasants were so tied to the estates of the great landowners that they became little more than property of the rich.

might own a few rough pieces of furniture, some chickens, a cow, and perhaps a little house, but few had more than that. One bad harvest could lead to starvation. In years of crop failures, thousands of peasants survived by eating grass, straw, tree bark, or whatever else they could find.

Russian peasants were overwhelmed by taxes and heavy rents they had to pay the landowners. On certain days they had to work in the landowner's fields. They owed him not only their labor but also payments in cash, grain, honey, beeswax, or other produce. They often fell into debt to boyars and spent the rest of their lives struggling to pay what they owed.

In theory, Russian peasants were free workers. In reality, their crushing debts made it difficult for them to leave the estate where they worked. Often the peasants were treated as if they were the property of the landowner. If the owner sold the estate, the peasants went to the new owner, just as the land did.

In desperation, many peasants— sometimes whole villages—fled to the forests or the remote region known as Siberia. The boyars were determined to keep the workers who remained behind, and they passed harsher laws restricting peasant movements.

By the time of Ivan the Terrible, many of Russia's peasants had become serfs. They were practically slaves. They led miserable lives from which they could rarely escape except by death.

In much of western Europe during the sixteenth century, the old feudal system of serfdom was disappearing. But in Russia the number of serfs increased. Under Ivan's rule, more and more peasants became tied to the land. As time went on, serfdom spread and the serfs' conditions only grew worse.

Ivan the Terrible Grows an Empire

Meanwhile, Ivan was busy expanding Russia's borders. He launched raids on the Tatars and added their territories to his growing empire. Then he pushed east into Siberia.

- On the map on page 166, note the extent of the Russian empire by the end of the reign of Ivan the Terrible.

It was at this time that Ivan earned the nickname "the Terrible"—not because of his cruelty or the way he treated his own people, but because he struck fear into the hearts of Russia's enemies.

To celebrate his victory over a region known as Kazan, Ivan ordered the construction of a new cathedral in Moscow. His grandfather, Ivan the Great, had hired foreigners to design his cathedrals, but Ivan the Terrible insisted on a Russian architect. He instructed the architect to build something so new, so radiant, so majestic that it would astonish everyone who saw it.

The architect designed a cathedral made of a main central church, boasting a high tower and eight smaller chapels, each with its own unique dome. Each chapel commemorated a battle that Ivan had fought. Together the chapels formed a giant cross.

Ivan called this glorious building the Cathedral of the Intercession of the Virgin, to remind everyone that he had invaded Kazan on a holiday honoring the Virgin Mary. But people soon began calling the cathedral St. Basil's, after a holy man who lived in Moscow (and who some said had spoken out against the tsar).

With its brilliant colors and its many onion-shaped domes, St. Basil's indeed astonished everyone who saw it. This cathedral is no Renaissance work reflecting the orderliness of classical architecture.

It is, rather, a fanciful feast of swirling shapes and color. (See page 164.)

Ivan Grows More Terrible

As time passed, Ivan's behavior became more and more bizarre. He saw traitors everywhere, especially among the boyars. Anyone who managed to displease him felt the full force of his wrath. Once he invited several of his advisors on a winter trip to the country. Halfway there, he stripped them of their royal robes and forced them to return to Moscow naked, on foot, in the snow.

Ivan's brutal rule became a reign of fear. The tsar's black-hooded secret police roamed Russia on black horses. They terrorized the country, torturing and killing Ivan's subjects by the hundreds. Meanwhile Ivan poured his energy into inventing horrible new tortures.

No one knew who might next fall victim to the tsar's wrath. In a rage, Ivan even struck and killed his oldest son.

By the end of Ivan's reign, a huge portion of the boyar class lay dead. The survivors lived in fear. Russia's serfs spent their lives tied to the land. No one dared question any decision of the tsar. His grip on Russia was cruel, tight, and all-powerful.

When Ivan the Terrible died in 1584, he left behind a vast empire, greatly expanded by his military victories. But his reign of terror left Russia smaller in spirit and largely isolated from the growth of thought and culture in the West.

One of the onion-shaped domes of St. Basil's Cathedral

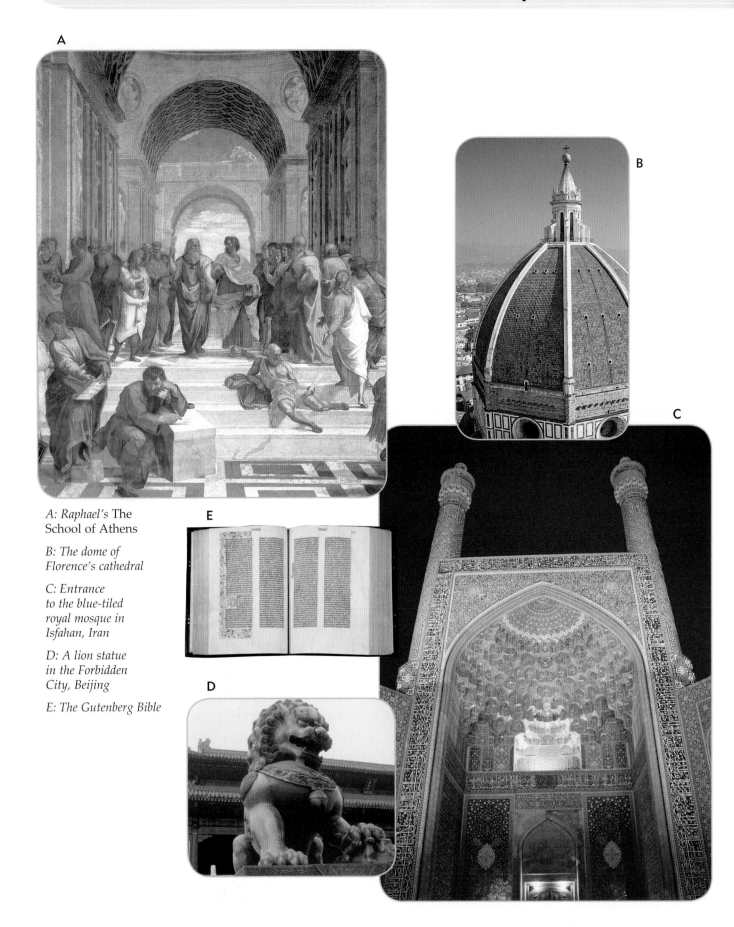

A: Raphael's The School of Athens

B: The dome of Florence's cathedral

C: Entrance to the blue-tiled royal mosque in Isfahan, Iran

D: A lion statue in the Forbidden City, Beijing

E: The Gutenberg Bible

Looking Back on the Early Modern World

*L*et's pause to reflect on some of the major themes and events in our account of the human odyssey so far. We've journeyed to the Ottoman Empire, Ming China, Tokugawa Japan, and Russia. We began, however, by focusing on the great changes that took place in Europe during the Renaissance.

While Europe's Renaissance did not instantly reshape life around the globe, the modern world as we know it had its birth in Renaissance Europe. New ideas, attitudes, and inventions transformed that continent, and eventually transformed the world. What were those developments and how did they shape the course of world history?

A New Appreciation for the Classics

Throughout the Middle Ages, scholars in Europe devoted their attention to theology, the study of God. They also studied the classics, the works of ancient Greek and Roman writers. But many major Greek and Roman works had been lost during the Middle Ages. When long-lost works of classical writers once again became available in Europe in the late Middle Ages, scholars like Petrarch helped turn a new page in history.

In the classics, Petrarch and other scholars found powerful and inspiring ideas. As the fourteenth century drew to a close, Europeans were reeling from a series of calamities—wars, famine, plague. In these troubled times, the classics offered new encouragement and wisdom. The ancient Greeks and Romans had recognized that human beings are, in many ways, like Homer's hero, Odysseus. Though buffeted by

A portrait of Petrarch adorns a book of the great Italian scholar's sonnets. Petrarch's writings helped usher in the Renaissance.

Dante wrote his *Divine Comedy* not in Latin but Italian. Giotto drank in the beauty of the Tuscan hills and painted landscapes that breathed life. The poet and diplomat Petrarch climbed mountains, wrote sonnets, and celebrated the beauty of his homeland.

For Giotto and Petrarch, the earthly life no longer seemed a trial to be endured. The beauty of creation inspired them. The natural world seemed a delight to be celebrated.

Towns and Patrons on the Rise

Invigorated by the classics and the world around them, scholars and artists increasingly captured their new delight in verse, stone, bronze, fresco, and canvas. What made that possible?

Part of the answer was a rising merchant class and increasingly prosperous cities. During the Middle Ages, towns had stood apart from the sheltered world of the feudal manor. Many towns were dangerous places. But by the late 1300s, as trade revived and commerce grew, so did cities. Merchants, bankers, and owners of businesses became leaders of the growing city-states. Wealthy families took a leading role.

In Italy, one important family, the Medici of Florence, led the way in business, then in banking, and then in culture. They used their wealth to support architecture, scholarship, and the arts. Their example inspired other wealthy families in towns across Europe to become patrons of the arts and learning.

Florentines and leaders of other city-states wanted to revive ancient Greek respect for the polis and Roman admiration of civic virtue. They

storms of chance and ill fortune, he survived and even thrived because of his intelligence, creativity, and determination.

The rebirth of interest in the classics gradually changed the way that people thought about their world. The ancient Greeks and Romans had been very curious about the world around them. They focused their attention on this world rather than the next. They saw an ordered beauty in nature. Above all, classical thinkers respected what they regarded as the greatest work in nature—humankind.

As the early champions of the Renaissance turned with renewed interest to Greek and Roman works, they began to celebrate the natural world and human potential. Dante, Giotto, and Petrarch did not turn their backs on the study of God, nor did they lose faith in the Christian promise of the next life. But, inspired by the classics, they trained appreciative eyes on the world around them.

Attuned to the harmony and elegance of his native language,

wanted to make their towns safer places. They wanted to show that cities could be centers of culture.

Ideas on the Move

During the Renaissance, ideas were on the move as never before. Since the fourteenth century, Venetians had been the champions of learning in Europe. When Constantinople fell to the Ottoman Turks in 1453, many Byzantine scholars fled to Venice. A year later, Johannes Gutenberg produced his famous Bible on his newly invented printing press. Businessmen quickly funded presses in Venice, making it the capital of the printed word.

In Florence, the Medici encouraged the spread of ideas. Even before the printing press, Cosimo de' Medici hired scholars to copy hundreds of texts for his library. His grandson, Lorenzo the Magnificent, eagerly reaped the fruits of the printing press. His Platonic Academy gathered scholars to study the works of classical antiquity.

Other city-states joined in the new quest for learning. In Rome, Pope Sixtus IV added more than 1,000 books to the papal library. He and his successors surrounded themselves with some of the finest

Renaissance artists often depicted their patrons in their works. The Journey of the Magi to Bethlehem, *by Benozzo Gozzoli, depicts Lorenzo de' Medici (on the white horse gazing out at us) as one of the three magi. Grandfather Cosimo rides on the brown mule behind him.*

Wealthy families who led Renaissance city-states did not necessarily have noble roots. The Medici began as healers or physicians. Their family crest shows six balls, which many scholars believe are pills, or medicine, to remind family members of their roots.

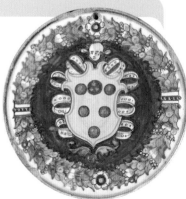

Medici family crest

scholars of the day. In Urbino, Mantua, Milan, Ferrara, and Bologna, ambitious families built not only elegant *palazzi* but also magnificent libraries.

Their shelves held the seeds of a new educational program that became known as humanism. Humanists emphasized the wisdom of the classical past. They celebrated human dignity and human potential. They rejected the idea that earthly life was mostly a trial to prepare for the next life. They saw earthly life less as a struggle to endure than an effort to *create*.

Artists with New Goals

Many artists and architects of the Renaissance were swept up in the tide of new humanist ideas. The renewal of the arts began in

Florence. The city was home to such innovative painters as Giotto, Massaccio, and Botticelli. Their tender, natural, and lifelike portrayals of the human form set art on a new path.

Many of their works treated traditional religious themes, such as biblical stories or the lives of the saints. But they told these stories with a new emphasis on individual emotion and solid human form.

Botticelli and other painters also turned to classical myths for inspiration. Botticelli's *Birth of Venus* and *Primavera* are among the masterpieces of the Italian Renaissance.

Sculptors also showed devotion to classical ideals and humanist thought. In the 1400s, sculptors revived the ancient classical ideal of shaping marble or bronze into lifelike portrayals of the human form. Donatello emerged as master of the craft. He awed Florentines with his elegant *David*, the first male nude sculpture since the fall of Rome.

In fifteenth-century Florence, Ghiberti worked in bronze and gold to create the doors for the city's Baptistery. Most panels showed biblical scenes, but on one panel Ghiberti sculpted his own face. This artist no longer saw himself as an anonymous laborer or an artisan. He was stepping forth as an individual.

While architects of the Italian Renaissance were devoted to classical ideals, they also wanted to surpass their predecessors. When Filippo Brunelleschi went to Rome to study the Pantheon, he came back inspired to do better. For Florence's cathedral he designed and built a double-shelled dome that surpassed any classical model. Also, like the ancient Greeks and Romans, Brunelleschi developed mathematical formulas for showing perspective in drawing and painting. Renaissance artists grew more and more skilled at using perspective to portray space and depth on a flat surface.

One painter who demonstrated complete mastery of perspective—and a great deal more—was Leonardo da Vinci. Leonardo could capture the rough surface of a rock, the icy peaks of distant mountains, a woman's mysterious smile, a mother's graceful hands. He took an interest in everything from art and architecture to weapons, canals, and flying machines. A versatile

Left: Donatello's bronze sculpture David *amazed Florentines with its lifelike depiction of the biblical hero.*

Below: Leonardo da Vinci's Madonna of the Rocks *demonstrates the painter's mastery of perspective.*

Above: A watercolor by Albrecht Dürer captures the detail that was so important to painters of northern Europe. Dürer, Jan van Eyck, and Hans Holbein were leaders of the northern European Renaissance.

Below: Michelangelo covered the ceiling of the Sistine Chapel with frescoes depicting scenes from the Bible.

genius, Leonardo was the exemplary Renaissance man.

Leonardo was one bright star in a dazzling constellation of genius during the Renaissance. In works such as the *Pietà* and *David*, the sculptor Michelangelo depicted the human form and human emotion with breathtaking power and tenderness. The power of his sculpture comes through in his painting as well, especially in the glorious ceiling of the Sistine Chapel.

Michelangelo was not fond of his fellow artist, Raphael, but it was no matter—to the rest of Florence, Raphael was "the prince of painters." He drew his subjects from both the classical world and Christian scriptures. His most

popular works were his Madonnas—warm, delicate, and intensely human paintings of Mary and the infant Jesus.

In northern Europe, the spirit of the Renaissance flowered in the works of artists like Jan van Eyck, Albrecht Dürer, and Hans Holbein. For these northern European painters, capturing the ideal was less important than rendering precise individual expression and startling detail.

Advice for Princes and Courtiers

The Renaissance was a tumultuous time in the life of European city-states and nations. War loomed as a constant threat. Gunpowder, introduced by the Chinese at the beginning of the period, had revolutionized

strangers to warfare, provided inspiration for political writers in the Renaissance. Machiavelli pored over the Roman historian Livy. Machiavelli did not concern himself with writing about an ideal world in which virtuous rulers attempt to govern according to conscience. Instead, in *The Prince*, Machiavelli provided a kind of how-to manual for rulers governing in an imperfect world, a world in which unscrupulous leaders often sought power or wealth at any cost.

How should a prince govern in dangerous and insecure times? Machiavelli's answer shocked many. He said, in effect, that the ends justify the means. To achieve good ends—such as order, stability, or justice—a prince must be prepared to act ruthlessly. Was it better, Machiavelli asked, for a prince to be loved or feared? It was, he replied, best to be both, but if a ruler could only choose one, it was better to be feared.

Italian city-states were governed by powerful rulers like the duke of Mantua, seen here sharing a confidence with a courtier. The duke was a learned leader, a patron of the arts, and a celebrated soldier.

fighting. Ambitious rulers amassed large and powerful armies.

City-states frequently waged war on each other, kidnapping and slaying rival rulers. France routinely invaded Italy. Popes periodically crushed rebellions in towns they controlled. If the Renaissance was an age of creativity and confidence in human prospects, it was also an age of conflict and destruction.

Writings by the ancient Greeks and Romans, who had been no

During the Renaissance, rival city-states often fought against each other. At left, the artist Paolo Uccello depicts a battle between Florence and neighboring Siena.

Martin Luther spoke out boldly against corrupt practices in the Church. Luther at first did not want to break away from the Church. But the Reformation eventually split it into Catholic and Protestant camps.

Baldassare Castiglione wrote a different kind of how-to book. He aimed his advice at the new courtiers who surrounded Renaissance rulers. The ideal courtier, he said, must do many things well—know the classics, read Greek and Latin, offer counsel humbly and discreetly, and make it all look effortless.

The Split in Christendom

For Europeans in the late fifteenth and early sixteenth centuries, the greatest conflict was not military but religious. For nearly a thousand years, most Europeans, who were Christians, thought of themselves as part of "Christendom." They were united by the Church of Rome, led by the pope.

Over time, however, many Church leaders came to devote more attention to political power and worldly wealth than to spiritual pursuits. Many people grew disgusted at the corruption of the Church leaders. The Christian humanists Erasmus and Thomas More criticized the worldly practices of the Church. But Martin Luther, a monk, teacher, and biblical scholar, shook the Church to its very foundations.

In 1517, when Luther posted his Ninety-five Theses criticizing the sale of indulgences, he was trying to reform the Christian Church in Europe. But this Reformation led to a rupture within Christianity. By the 1540s, Christianity stood divided into two camps—the Roman Catholic Church and the Protestant churches. The Protestants

challenged the authority of the pope and broke ranks with Catholicism on many questions of belief.

The religious split quickly became political as well. Spain and France championed Catholicism. England and Scandinavia became Protestant.

The Roman Catholic Church responded to the Reformation with its own Counter-Reformation, also called the Catholic Reformation. The Inquisition and Index of Forbidden Books were part of the effort to put down what the Church regarded as heresy. More positive and constructive efforts came from individuals like Ignatius Loyola, Francis Xavier, and Teresa of Avila, who worked to revitalize the spiritual mission of the Church.

In 1600, Christianity still played an important part in the lives of most Europeans, but it no longer united them. Over time people stopped using the term "Christendom" to describe their realm. Instead, they began using a name the ancient Greeks had given their continent—"Europa," or Europe.

Rivalry and Splendor in the Muslim World

Throughout the Middle Ages, just as Christianity had united most Europeans, Islam united the Arab world. Muslim rulers competed with Christian kings for power and territory in Europe. But during the Renaissance, new rivalries created lasting splits in the Muslim world. During this time, the Ottoman, Safavid, and Mughal dynasties often fought each other.

The Ottoman Turks began as a warrior power. Their disciplined warriors, the janissaries, drove the Mongols from Asia Minor. In 1453, the Ottoman Turks conquered Constantinople. They renamed the city Istanbul, and launched a great empire.

The Ottoman ruler Süleyman I was not only a mighty warrior but also a lawgiver and builder. He

Left: The Spanish nun Teresa of Avila helped rebuild the spiritual life of Catholicism. Many Catholic leaders tried to strengthen the Church and turn back Protestantism—a movement known as the Counter-Reformation.

Below: A European prince pays homage to Süleyman I, ruler of the Ottoman Empire. The Ottoman realm stretched from North Africa across the Middle East to eastern Mesopotamia.

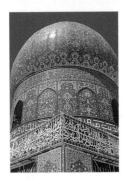

Above: During the Renaissance, European and Muslim architects were both inspired by classical domes. At the Süleymaniye mosque, built by Süleyman in Istanbul, Muslims worshipped beneath a massive dome.

Right: A stunning dome tops this mosque built by the Safavids in the city of Isfahan in Persia, now Iran.

revised the empire's legal code, making it fairer and more efficient. He beautified Istanbul with new fountains, gardens, bridges, and buildings, especially the Süleymaniye mosque.

By the 1600s, the Ottoman Turks dominated the Middle East and the southern Mediterranean. Their empire stretched from Algiers in North Africa to the eastern edge of Mesopotamia. The Ottoman Turks had won much of this expanse from another Muslim power— the Safavids in Persia. These two Muslim dynasties were bitter enemies, divided by religion. The Ottomans were Sunnis, while Persia's Safavids were Shi'ites.

By the seventeenth century, the Safavids, under Shah Abbas, were powerful enough to regain many of their lost lands from the Ottomans. Shah Abbas and other Persian sultans actively supported

the arts. Persian artists were influenced by European Renaissance artists and strove to create lifelike miniatures. Like other Muslim civilizations, the Safavids gloried in architecture. Their accomplishments are still visible at Isfahan, where a blue-tiled dome rises gracefully from a mosque, and where fountains, gardens, and parks grace the expansive boulevards.

South and east of the Safavids lay the Mughal empire of India. This Muslim dynasty from central Asia had conquered India, a mostly Hindu land. Early on, the Mughal ruler Akbar the Great faced the problem of getting a Hindu majority to accept rule by Muslims. His solution was new and striking—religious toleration. He appointed Hindu counselors to high office. He limited the killing of cows, which were sacred to Hindus. He was also eager to meet with Jesuit missionaries, who had landed in India at this time. He believed that every religion had something important to teach.

The Mughals also encouraged the arts and architecture. The Mughal empire's most lasting architectural triumph is the Taj Mahal, built by Akbar's grandson, Shah Jahan, as a mausoleum to honor his wife.

Ming China and Tokugawa Japan

In fourteenth-century China, a peasant revolutionary led a revolt that chased out the Mongols who had long ruled the land. For his dynasty he chose the name Ming, which means "brilliant"—and brilliant it was. The Ming are still remembered for their fine porcelain, their intricately carved lacquer work, and their bronze and stone sculptures. Ming rulers

restored China's Great Wall in an attempt to keep out Mongol invaders from the north. They also restored the civil service system, with rigorous examinations for those who wished to serve in government.

The Ming moved the nation's capital to a northern city, Beijing. There they built the Forbidden City. The imperial palace and grounds—with its temples, carved stone bridges, gardens, and ceremonial halls—covered nearly 180 acres.

One fifteenth-century Ming emperor sent Zheng He to explore the world beyond the Middle Kingdom. But as time went on, the Ming launched no more voyages of

Above: The Taj Mahal is the most lasting architectural triumph of the Mughal empire of India. A Mughal emperor named Shah Jahan built the Taj Mahal in memory of his wife.

Left: A stone sculpture depicts two Chinese officials, one military and one civil, from the time of the Ming dynasty. The Ming also made fine porcelain, lacquer work, and bronze sculptures. Their grandest achievement was rebuilding the Great Wall of China.

Above: Japanese warriors were known as samurai. Like other members of society in feudal Japan, they lived according to a strict code of behavior.

Opposite: European astronomers gather in a town square to observe an eclipse of the sun in 1571. As you'll read in coming chapters, curiosity about the natural world ushered in an age of exploration and scientific achievement.

The Ivans in Russia

The vast land of Russia gradually turned inward as well. In the late fifteenth century, Ivan III—the prince of Moscow who became known as Ivan the Great—drove the Mongol Tatars from Russia. He fortified Moscow's Kremlin. He set Russians on the road to developing their own Russian Orthodox Church.

Ivan the Great's heir, Ivan IV, was known as Ivan the Terrible. This ruthless tsar led a reign of terror. He wanted the boyars, the landowning nobles, to be totally under his control. Ivan the Terrible fought prolonged wars to expand the Russian empire. Under his rule, Russia became fortress-like and turned its back on Renaissance developments in western Europe.

During the reign of Ivan the Terrible, life grew worse for Russia's peasants. Many became serfs, tied to the land. While serfdom disappeared in most of Europe, it persisted in Russia.

The European Moment

At the end of the Middle Ages, western Europe, scarred by battle and weakened by plague, looked like the region least likely to bring about worldwide change. But by the late fifteenth century, western European city-states prospered, and Renaissance thinkers pursued new intellectual and philosophical goals.

They emphasized creative responses to the here and now, stressing human reason, dignity, and ability. Their renewed confidence and their growing curiosity about the natural world launched an era of extraordinary creativity and widespread change.

exploration. They grew suspicious of foreigners and outsiders. The Forbidden City walled the imperial family off from the rest of the world, and even from fellow Chinese.

The Chinese were not the only ones to turn inward. For years the Japanese had fended off attacks from the Mongols and then the Chinese. Japanese feudal society—organized around the daimyo, samurai, peasantry, and a code of bushido—persisted hundreds of years after feudalism had declined in Europe. In the sixteenth century, when Jesuit missionaries sought entry to Japan, they were welcomed at first, but then the Tokugawa dynasty grew suspicious. The Tokugawa sharply limited the entry of foreigners. Jesuits and Christians were expelled from Japan. Emperor Ieyasu wanted Japan only for the Japanese.

But Europeans did not set these changes in motion solely through their art, architecture, or writing. They did it mainly through their explorers, ships, colonies, and science. You'll learn more about these big changes as we proceed in our account of the human odyssey.

Time Line (1300–1600)

1300 // 1400

1321
Dante Alighieri finishes writing *The Divine Comedy*.

c. 1472
Ivan the Great begins rebuilding the Kremlin in Moscow.

1454
The Gutenberg Bible, the first printed book in the Western world, is published.

1436
Filippo Brunelleschi finishes building his dome for Florence's cathedral.

c. 1406
Ming rulers begin to build the Forbidden City.

1453
The Ottoman Turks conquer Constantinople, capital of the Byzantine Empire.

1498
Leonardo da Vinci finishes *The Last Supper*.

1500 ｜

1600 ｜

1512
Michelangelo
completes
his painting
of the Sistine
Chapel ceiling.

1513
Niccolò
Machiavelli
writes
The Prince.

1534
Henry VIII
of England
breaks with the
Catholic Church
and establishes
the Church
of England.

1517
Luther nails his
Ninety-five Theses
to the church door
in Wittenberg.

1545
The Council of Trent
begins its sessions to
clarify the beliefs of the
Catholic Church.

1556
Akbar begins his
reign of the Mughal
Empire in India.

1603
Ieyasu unites
Japan under his
rule as shogun.

1547
Ivan the Terrible is
crowned tsar of all Russia.

1550
Süleyman the
Magnificent
begins building
the Süleymaniye
Mosque in Istanbul.

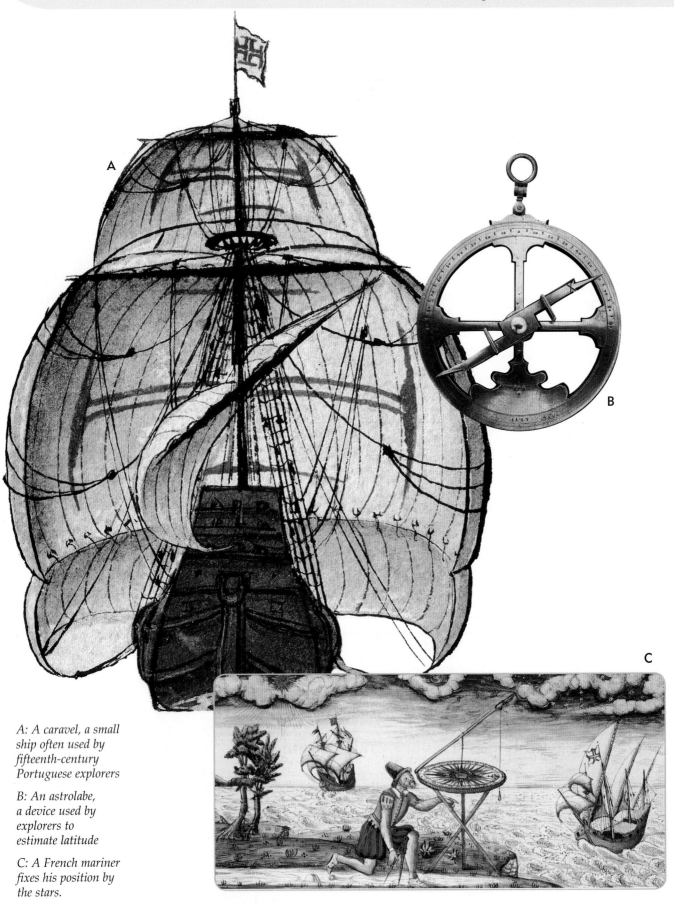

A: A caravel, a small ship often used by fifteenth-century Portuguese explorers

B: An astrolabe, a device used by explorers to estimate latitude

C: A French mariner fixes his position by the stars.

A New Spirit of Exploration and Inquiry

When you think of "the Earth" or "the world," you see a mental picture of a big sphere with blue oceans and seven continents. But if you had lived around the year 1400, you would see a very different mental picture. In those days no one knew what "the world" looked like.

Maps made 600 years ago reveal that for most people, the world was limited to nearby areas. For mapmakers, the world was mainly the region they knew. And because human beings like to be in the center of things, mapmakers put their own regions at the center of their maps.

The Chinese called their land the "Middle Kingdom" and placed it in the middle of their maps. They encircled their kingdom with a vast sea and sprinkled other lands around its edges.

In the Muslim world, maps centered on the Arabian Peninsula. These maps showed Arabia and Europe fairly accurately, but stretched Africa's coast far to the east, beyond India toward China.

In Europe, the most famous medieval map showed the three known continents of Europe, Africa, and Asia as a single landmass, with the holy city of Jerusalem at the center.

In 1400, when people were drawing such maps, important events were taking place all over the globe. But most civilizations had little knowledge of distant peoples. In fact, civilizations in different parts of the world often were unaware of each other. They simply didn't know that other parts of the world existed.

Europeans, Asians, and Africans knew nothing of the Americas. Inhabitants of the Americas did not know that whole kingdoms and continents lay beyond the oceans. All this, however, was about to change.

The monks who created this thirteenth-century English map depicted a bewildering and complex world, with Jerusalem in the center, marked by a cross inside a circle, and above the circle, the figure of Jesus (now barely visible) presiding over all. The map is filled with mythological creatures, imagined peoples, and rumored marvels of the world.

An Age of Exploration

As you've learned, the Renaissance in Europe was a time of intellectual and artistic inquiry. Many people pursued new paths of knowledge. They took a new interest in the world around them.

That same spirit of inquiry made them curious about the larger world, about faraway lands beyond the seas. Europeans began a large-scale effort to explore these distant lands. For the first time in history, humans traveled all the way around the Earth. For the first time, mapmakers began to draw a fairly accurate picture of the whole world. Historians call this period the Age of Exploration.

It wasn't intellectual curiosity alone that motivated Europeans to explore the world. It was also a desire for economic gain. Europeans wanted to trade with the East. On their long journeys by sea, they found continents previously unknown to them. They claimed those lands for their own and settled many colonies. Eager for riches and power, they built empires on a scale the world had never before seen.

Most of the lands that Europeans "discovered" were already inhabited by other peoples. Civilizations that had been unaware of each other's existence suddenly came into contact. Unfortunately, these contacts often turned into conflicts. As you'll learn, the Age of Exploration was a time of great progress—people, ideas, and products moved around the globe as never before—but also a time of terrible destruction.

An Age of Science and Reason

The spirit of curiosity that sparked the Age of Exploration led in the late 1500s to the Scientific Revolution, a time when scholars made many new discoveries about the natural world. Through careful observation, experimentation, and mathematics, scholars began to realize that the universe follows certain laws, and that people can understand those laws. Science, the organized study of how nature works, was born.

Meanwhile, other thinkers began to wonder: If natural laws govern the physical world, are there natural laws that apply to the world of human activity? Can people discover those laws and use them to live together peacefully and happily? As we'll see, the eighteenth century came to be known as the Age of Reason because thinkers were sure that they could use the power of reason to improve people's lives.

Filling in the map of the world. Circling the globe. Using science to understand nature and even control it. Using reason to understand principles of good government. These events and ideas, presented in the following chapters, have had a powerful influence in shaping what we know as our modern world.

By the time this globe was made in Germany in the late fifteenth century, Europeans had begun mapping much of the Earth's surface. Scholars also began to ask questions about the Earth's position relative to the sun and the planets. Such questions helped launch the Scientific Revolution.

In the fifteenth century, Portuguese and Spanish mariners explored a world that was still largely unknown to Europeans. Many people believed that sea monsters awaited ships that sailed too far from shore.

Portugal, Spain, and the Age of Exploration

*I*t was (and still is) one of the smallest countries in the world—slightly smaller than the state of Indiana. In the fifteenth century, it was a poor country of fishermen. Who would have thought that little Portugal would become a world leader?

Portugal sits on the western edge of Europe. It is not quite one-fifth the size of Spain, its neighbor on the Iberian (iy-BIHR-ee-uhn) Peninsula. Portugal is separated from Spain by broken mountains and a barren plateau. Its western edge has the profile of a craggy face, staring out at the vast Atlantic Ocean.

- On a globe or world map, locate the countries of Portugal and Spain.

In the Middle Ages, no one in Portugal or any other part of Europe knew what lay on the other side of the Atlantic. They didn't know that two large continents separated the Atlantic and Pacific Oceans. They knew very little about Africa to the south. When fishermen and sailors took to the sea, they tried to stay within sight of familiar land, and they did not willingly venture into unknown waters.

But all this changed during the Renaissance. In the fifteenth century, Europeans began setting sail across uncharted seas as they sought new ways to reach distant Asian lands to the east.

Why go east? From the time of the Roman Empire, European merchants had imported silk from China. By the Middle Ages, when the explorer Marco Polo made his famous trek, Europeans wanted pearls and gems from India. But the most important item on the shopping list of eastward-bound Europeans was spices.

This chapter focuses on explorations that set out from Portugal and Spain in the 1400s.

The Age of Exploration

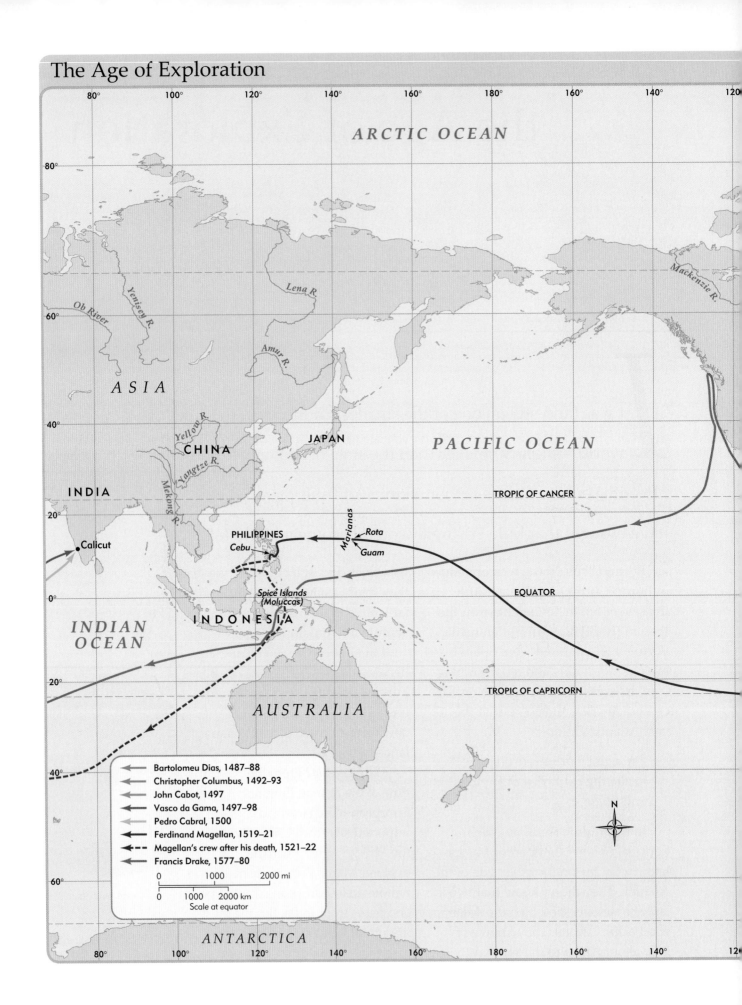

Bartolomeu Dias, 1487–88
Christopher Columbus, 1492–93
John Cabot, 1497
Vasco da Gama, 1497–98
Pedro Cabral, 1500
Ferdinand Magellan, 1519–21
Magellan's crew after his death, 1521–22
Francis Drake, 1577–80

0   1000   2000 mi
0   1000   2000 km
Scale at equator

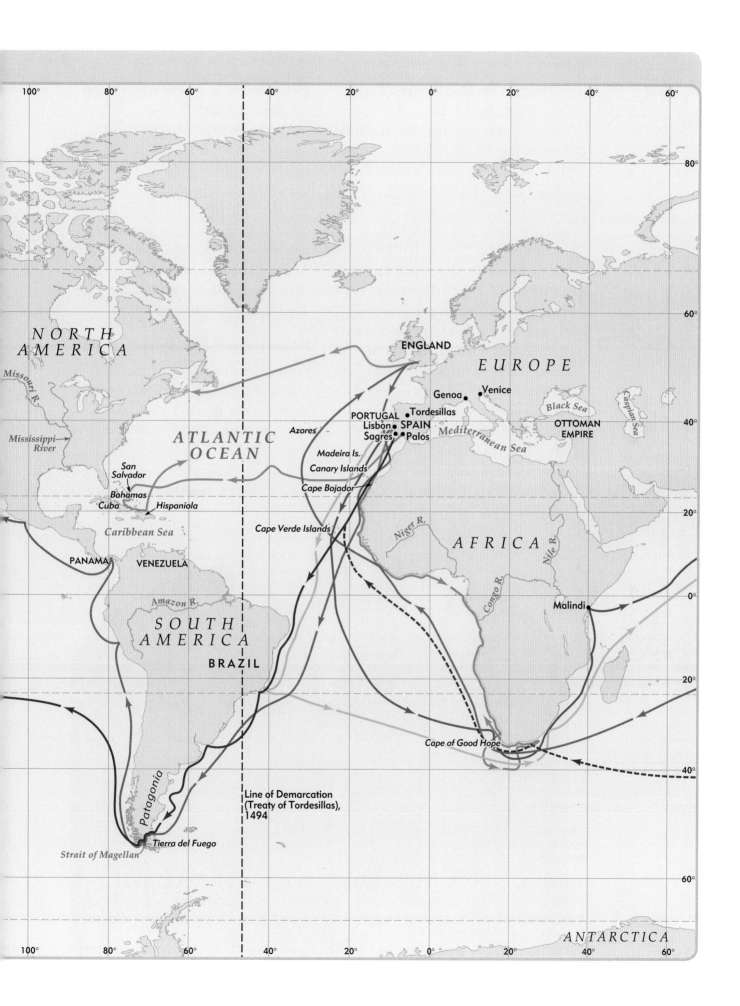

100° 80° 60° 40° 20° 0° 20° 40° 60°

80°

NORTH
AMERICA

Missouri R.

*Mississippi
River*

ATLANTIC
OCEAN

*San
Salvador*

Bahamas
Cuba → *Hispaniola*

Caribbean Sea

PANAMA

VENEZUELA

Amazon R.

SOUTH
AMERICA

BRAZIL

Patagonia

Tierra del Fuego

Strait of Magellan

ENGLAND

EUROPE

Genoa •Venice

PORTUGAL •Tordesillas
Lisbon• SPAIN
Sagres• •Palos

Azores

Madeira Is.
Canary Islands
Cape Bojador

Cape Verde Islands

Mediterranean Sea

Black Sea

OTTOMAN
EMPIRE

Caspian Sea

AFRICA

Niger R.

Congo R.

Nile R.

Malindi•

Cape of Good Hope

Line of Demarcation
(Treaty of Tordesillas),
1494

ANTARCTICA

100° 80° 60° 40° 20° 0° 20° 40° 60°

80°

60°

40°

20°

0°

20°

40°

60°

During the Middle Ages, Crusaders brought back pepper, cloves, cinnamon, nutmeg, and ginger from the East. In the days before refrigeration, those seasonings both flavored and preserved food. They were also used in medicine. For many reasons, then, spices were in great demand in Europe.

By the 1400s, it was getting harder and harder to meet that demand. The Ottoman Turks controlled the Silk Road, the land route from Europe through the Middle East to Asia. In the best of times the overland route had been long and hazardous. Travelers braved mountain passes, desert storms, and bandits. Now the Ottoman Turks were determined to keep the road for their own use. Travel over land became too dangerous for Europeans. So

they asked themselves: Why not set out upon the sea?

In the 1400s, Portugal's lonely seaside perch turned into an advantage. It was the perfect spot for launching what historians often call the Age of Exploration. This tiny country emerged as the center of one of the largest empires in history. And it all began with a curious Portuguese prince who wondered what lay beyond the sea.

Prince Henry the Navigator

Prince Henry was *the* man for his time and place. He made only a few short sea voyages in his life, and he himself never sailed in unknown waters. But he did so much to encourage exploration that, centuries after his death, he became known as Prince Henry the Navigator, the

Prince Henry the Navigator studies a map, planning another voyage for Portugal's sailors. The Portuguese led the way during the early years of the Age of Exploration.

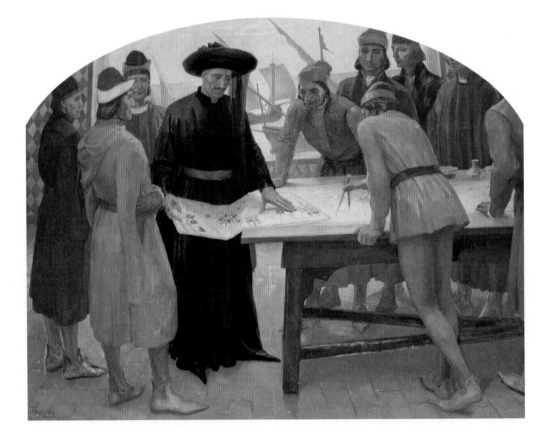

person most responsible for ushering in the Age of Exploration.

In the early 1400s, when Prince Henry was a young man, Portugal was ruled by his family, the House of Aviz (uh-VEEZH). The young prince was full of curiosity and he loved adventure. In 1415, he took part in a campaign that captured a Muslim stronghold in northwest Africa. He fought bravely and was knighted by his father. He took as his motto *talant de bien fere*—"a hunger to perform worthy deeds." He saw nothing worthier than the spread of Christianity.

As the third son of the king, Prince Henry was unlikely to become king, so he turned to his passion— the sea. The sea seemed to call to the prince. He founded a small court in Sagres (SAH-greesh), a village at the southern tip of Portugal. From there, he looked out over the Atlantic Ocean and wondered where it led.

- On the map on pages 198–99, locate Sagres.

Ptolemy's ancient maps could tell Portuguese sailors little about Africa beyond its northern coast. The explorers sent out by Prince Henry added 2,000 miles to maps of the continent.

The World They Knew

Back in the second century, the mathematician and astronomer Ptolemy wrote much about geography. In the early 1400s, his work was rediscovered and translated from Greek into Latin. The new printing press helped spread his map of the world across Europe. It showed only a vague notion of the shape and extent of Africa, and did not include the continents of North and South America. Many people accepted Ptolemy's map (see above) as a true picture of the world.

Henry knew that Africa lay to the south of Portugal. But for Europeans in the fifteenth century, Africa remained a mystery. European ships had sailed along the northern coastline, but no one knew the size or shape of the rest of Africa. Even mapmakers didn't know where the continent ended.

Prince Henry tried to learn as much as he could about Africa and its resources, especially gold. He was fascinated by stories he heard about a legendary African leader named Prester John. No one had ever met Prester John, but it was said he was a Christian who led mighty armies against Muslim troops in northeastern Africa. It was also said that he had more gold, silver, and precious stones than any man in the world.

Did Prester John exist? Or were he, his armies, and his riches just legends? Prince Henry

wanted to find out. And it's likely that he also wanted to learn about a possible sea route to the east. So he started sending Portuguese explorers on sea voyages to Africa.

Prince Henry sent out more than 50 expeditions. None of them ever found Prester John. But the Portuguese did learn a lot about Africa and sailing on the open sea. They also explored and colonized the islands known as the Madeiras (mah-DIR-uhs) and the Azores (AY-zohrz).

• On the map on pages 198–99, locate the Madeira Islands and the Azores.

Swift-Sailing Caravels

As Prince Henry kept track of Portuguese expeditions, he constantly looked for ways to improve their ships and equipment. Most ships in those days were large vessels, built to carry heavy loads. But explorers needed lighter ships that they could maneuver both on the open sea and in shallow waters.

The prince worked with shipbuilders to adapt small sailing ships called *caravels* that rode high

Portuguese mariners sailed light, maneuverable caravels to explore the coasts of Africa. Lateen-rigged caravels like this one had triangular sails that could catch the slightest wind.

on the water. With their small hulls and light weight, caravels could approach unfamiliar coasts without scraping against rocks on the bottom.

While caravels moved easily through the water when the wind and currents were just right, their square sails made them difficult to control in rougher waters. So Portuguese shipbuilders adapted a triangular-shaped sail used by Arab sailors. This sail could catch the slightest wind. One navigator called these ships, known as lateen-rigged caravels, "the best ships that sailed the seas."

The first expeditions that Prince Henry sent out didn't make much progress. Sailors were still cautious because they had heard terrible stories about what they would find farther down the coast—boiling water, sea monsters, and a sun so hot that it charred men's skin. When a ship was blown off course or the sailors became frightened for some other reason, they often turned around and headed back to the safety of Sagres.

The Portuguese in Africa

In 1434, one group of Portuguese sailors achieved a breakthrough by sailing past Cape Bojador (BAH-juh-dohr), the farthest point on the west African coast previously reached by Europeans. As later voyages revealed more of the coast, the Portuguese began to trade with the local people. They bartered horses, wheat, and other products for gold dust and slaves.

Sometimes the Portuguese took captured Africans back to Europe as slaves. Like most people of his time, Henry did not understand or think much about the tragedy of slavery.

Fifteenth-century sailors used navigational instruments like the astrolabe (upper left corner), sextant (below the astrolabe), and compass (bottom right).

Finding Their Way at Sea

Since they had no good means to find their way on the open seas, most sailors feared leaving sight of a shoreline. So even in their swift-sailing ships, Portuguese seamen could not venture far on the ocean. To make longer trips possible, the Portuguese improved navigational equipment so sailors could figure their location at sea.

The Portuguese fine-tuned the astrolabe, a small round instrument that sailors held up to the sky to help them estimate their latitude—their north-south position. For even more accuracy, they used the quadrant, a small quarter-circle fitted with a plumb line and marked with degrees. It took two sailors to use a quadrant—one to line up the quadrant with a star and the other to record the angle of the plumb line. If both sailors did their jobs correctly, and if the ship was not rocking too much, a quadrant would indicate the ship's latitude with some accuracy.

Astrolabes, quadrants, and other navigational equipment kept ships from being lost at sea. They also allowed explorers to keep more accurate records.

He believed that the Africans the Portuguese bought as slaves would be better off than before since they would be baptized as Christians. (A later chapter will examine the difficult issues of slavery in more detail.)

By the time Prince Henry died in 1460, his explorers had added 2,000 miles to maps of Africa. Europeans still didn't know where the continent ended. Portuguese kings continued to send out expeditions that allowed mapmakers to add thousands of miles to maps of the African coast. But there was still no sign of the southern tip of Africa.

Dias Rounds the Cape

In 1487, King John II of Portugal sent an explorer named Bartolomeu Dias (bahr-tou-lou-MAY-ou DEE-ahsh) to find the southern tip of Africa. Dias set sail with two caravels and a supply ship. His ships sailed south for four months until they had gone farther than any ships had gone before. Then they met a terrible storm. The winds blew so fiercely that the caravels had trouble staying afloat.

At first Dias wanted to wait out the storm, but when it didn't let up, he decided to head out to open sea, away from Africa. He left the supply ship behind, and the two caravels sailed for 13 days in the storm.

Finally, the sea calmed, and Dias turned his ships east, back toward Africa. After watching for several days and still not seeing land, Dias tried sailing north. When he spotted land, the coast was running in a new direction. He realized his ships had accomplished the amazing feat of rounding the southern coast of Africa.

Dias wanted to sail on toward Asia, but his crew did not. They were exhausted from the storms, and they worried about going on without their supply ship. Dias and his officers went ashore to discuss the men's complaints. The officers said they agreed with the crew and urged Dias to turn around. He asked them all to sign a statement swearing that Dias wanted to continue but they did not. Every man signed it.

Then Dias told the officers that the ships would continue sailing up the eastern coast of Africa for a few more days but would turn back if they found nothing interesting. The ships sailed on until the crew began to complain again. Finally, with great disappointment, Dias turned back.

King John, however, was not disappointed. It is said that Dias named Africa's southern tip the Cape of Storms. After Dias and his men returned to Portugal, King John renamed the Cape of Storms the Cape of Good Hope, because he finally had hope that Portuguese ships would find their way to Asia.

- On the map on pages 198–99, locate Bartolomeu Dias's route. Locate the Cape of Good Hope.

Christopher Columbus Looks West

Meanwhile an eager Italian navigator named Christopher Columbus was urging Portugal's King John to try a new direction.

Columbus had grown up in the Italian port city of Genoa. He was the son of a wool-weaver and began work as his father's assistant. But the boy was soon drawn to the sea. As a young man, he got a job as a seaman with a convoy of merchant ships. When the convoy rounded the southern coast of Portugal, a French force attacked it. Columbus's ship sank, and he clung to a wooden oar that carried him to shore.

Columbus decided to stay in Portugal, where his brother, a mapmaker, was living. He learned Portuguese and began studying what the Portuguese knew about navigation and open-sea sailing. He studied geography and learned the chartmaker's trade of making maps for sea voyages. In the early 1480s, he sailed on Portuguese ships along the coast of Africa.

Columbus was in Lisbon, the Portuguese capital, when Dias returned. He wasn't surprised when he heard Dias had rounded the tip of Africa. But he was convinced there was a shorter route to Asia. Educated people at that time knew the world was round—which meant that if ships could sail far enough west, they would eventually reach the East, in particular, the lands to the east that Europeans called the Indies.

Columbus's calculations showed that sailing west was the *shortest* route to the East. Why did Columbus think his route to the Indies was the shortest? Because he based his calculations on his favorite readings, including Marco Polo's *Description of the World*. He also read *Image of the World*, a book by a French cardinal and geographer named Pierre d'Ailly. From these works, Columbus calculated both the circumference of the Earth and the size of Europe and Asia. It turns out that he underestimated the

Christopher Columbus was convinced that the quickest way to the Indies and the East was by voyaging west. When Portugal's King John declined to fund an expedition, Columbus took his plan to King Ferdinand and Queen Isabella of Spain.

Earth's circumference and overestimated the size of Europe and Asia.

With his calculations in hand, Columbus went to Portugal's King John and asked for ships to make the westward journey. The king seriously considered Columbus's request. In the end, however, he decided that Portugal should stick to the route around Africa.

Disappointed, Columbus took his plan to the rival Spanish court. King Ferdinand and Queen Isabella of Spain were intrigued. They were growing jealous of Portugal's expanding empire. They imagined the treasures that Portuguese ships would bring from the Indies—spices, gems, silks. Most of their advisors

What Were the Indies?

When fifteenth-century Europeans spoke of "the Indies," they were referring to a large and varied group of lands, including India, China, Japan, Southeast Asia, and the islands of Indonesia.

were against financing Columbus's trip. But one advisor later told the queen she would be missing a grand opportunity. So Queen Isabella offered to sell her jewels to pay for Columbus's voyage.

It turned out that Isabella did not have to sell her jewels; the Spanish government paid for the trip. On August 3, 1492, Columbus and his crew of 90 men left Palos, Spain, in three ships, the *Niña*, the *Pinta*, and the *Santa María*. They sailed to the Canary Islands, where they loaded provisions. When they set sail again, they headed due west, out to the open sea.

Landfall at Last—But Where?

The ships had smooth sailing most of the way. Columbus had good compasses and a crude quadrant to measure latitude. He figured his longitude by dead reckoning, that is, combining compass readings with estimates of the speed and distance his ships had traveled. He knew enough astronomy to keep the ships on course by measuring their relationship to the North Star.

The ships sailed for five weeks. Columbus's men had never sailed so long without seeing land, and they grew nervous. He tried to cheer them on, crying, "Sail on! Sail on!" On October 10, the *Santa María*'s crew threatened mutiny. Columbus promised he would turn back if they didn't see land within the next three days.

Around ten o'clock the next night, Columbus spotted a small light bobbing in the distance. Perhaps it was a torch or a beach fire because a few hours later, around two o'clock in the morning of October 12, 1492, a sailor on the *Pinta* spotted land. It was an island that Columbus later named San Salvador, in the Bahamas.

Columbus soon stood on the beach and claimed the land for Spain. He did not think that the island might belong to those who lived there. He assumed that it was Spain's to claim, since Spain was European, Christian, and thus, in the view of Columbus and his fellow Europeans, superior.

- On the map on pages 198–99, locate Christopher Columbus's route.

Columbus believed he had reached the Indies, and he called the people he saw "Indians." They were not the elaborately dressed people that Marco Polo's journal had led him to expect. He wrote that they were a handsome people, and that he thought they could easily be converted to Christianity.

Columbus and his men sailed from island to island, planting a Spanish flag wherever they went. They hunted for gold and spices, but not successfully. Columbus chanced upon some twigs from Caribbean trees that he considered cinnamon, and took these back to Spain. When he reached the large island now known as Cuba, he was sure it was part of China, so he sent men to present a letter from King Ferdinand and Queen Isabella to the emperor of China. The men never found the emperor, but they did see some people smoking cigars. This was the first time any Europeans had ever seen tobacco.

Columbus and his men had many problems. On Christmas Day

Columbus meets "Indians" on the island of San Salvador in the Bahamas. Columbus traveled from island to island throughout the Caribbean in search of gold and spices.

the *Santa María* was wrecked on a reef on the northwest coast of the island now called Hispaniola (his-puh-NYOH-luh). Columbus decided to found a colony nearby and called it La Navidad (Christmas). In January 1493, he set sail for Spain with the *Niña* and the *Pinta*. He left 40 men behind to hunt for gold.

The return trip was very rough, and the two ships became separated in a storm. At one point the *Niña* came so close to sinking that Columbus packed a written account of his discoveries into a sealed cask and threw it overboard. The *Niña* stayed afloat but was damaged in another storm, just off the coast of Portugal. The ship had to dock in Lisbon for repairs, so Columbus had the satisfaction of telling the jealous King John about his successful voyage.

The *Niña* and the *Pinta* both returned to Palos on the same day, March 15, 1493. King Ferdinand and Queen Isabella gave Columbus a grand reception. He hadn't brought back the spices and gold they had expected, but he had found a route to Asia—or so the royal couple thought.

Two Cultures Meet

The first native people Columbus met were the Taino (TIY-noh). He was curious about their ways, but like many Europeans of the time, he did not consider them his equals. Their lack of clothing made them seem primitive. And their lack of Christianity made them seem, in Columbus's eyes, uncivilized. Columbus's men captured some of the Taino and took them back to Spain to show Ferdinand and Isabella. You'll learn more about such attitudes and actions in the next chapters.

Europeans called the continent between the Atlantic and Pacific Oceans America *in honor of Amerigo Vespucci. The Italian-born explorer is depicted on this detail from a 1507 map.*

Naming America

Columbus never knew he had begun something even more important—he had helped fill in the map of the world. He happened upon a huge landmass separating the Atlantic and Pacific Oceans. Within ten years, Europeans realized the significance of his discovery, but these lands were not named after Columbus. That honor went to Amerigo Vespucci (uh-MEHR-ih-goh veh-SPOO-chee).

Columbus made three more trips across the ocean. On his third trip, in 1498, he landed on the coast of what is now Venezuela in South America. "I believe that this is a very great continent which until today has been unknown," he wrote in his journal. But he still believed that this new continent was in the East and that he had found a route to Asia.

Like Columbus, Amerigo Vespucci was an Italian-born navigator who served both Spain and Portugal and voyaged across the Atlantic Ocean. Around 1502, he wrote a widely circulated letter in which he referred to the recent discoveries as a "New World." Eventually mapmakers put his name on those new lands—America.

From the Log of Christopher Columbus

Columbus kept a daily record of his voyage of 1492. This excerpt from October 11 and 12 recounts a dramatic moment in history.

A Page from the Past

I sailed to the WSW [west-southwest], and we took more water aboard than at any other time on the voyage. I saw several things that were indications of land. At one time a large flock of sea birds flew overhead, and a green reed was found floating near the ship. The crew of the *Pinta* spotted some of the same reeds and some other plants; they also saw what looked like a small board or plank. A stick was recovered that looks manmade, perhaps carved with an iron tool....

After sunset I ordered the pilot to return to my original westerly course, and I urged the crew to be ever-vigilant. I took the added precaution of doubling the number of lookouts, and I reminded the men that the first to sight land would be given a silk doublet as a personal token from me. Further, he would be given an annuity of 10,000 maravedíes [Spanish coins].

About 10 o'clock at night, while standing on the sterncastle, I thought I saw a light to the west. It looked like a little wax candle bobbing up and down. It had the same appearance as a light or torch belonging to fishermen or travelers who alternately raised and lowered it, or perhaps were going from house to house. I am the first to admit that I was so eager to find land that I did not trust my own senses, so I called for Pedro Gutiérrez, the representative of the King's household, and asked him to watch for the light. After a few moments, he too saw it. I then summoned Rodrigo Sánchez of Segovia … and asked him to watch for the light. He saw nothing, nor did any other member of the crew. It was such an uncertain thing that I did not feel it was adequate proof of land.

The moon, in its third quarter, rose in the east shortly before midnight…. Then, at two hours after midnight, the *Pinta* fired a cannon, my prearranged signal for the sighting of land.

I now believe that the light I saw earlier was a sign from God and that it was truly the first positive indication of land. When we caught up with the *Pinta*, which was always running ahead because she was a swift sailer, I learned that the first man to sight land was Rodrigo de Triana, a seaman from Lepe….

At dawn we saw naked people, and I went ashore in the ship's boat, armed, followed by Martin Alonso Pinzón, captain of the *Pinta*, and his brother, Vincente Yanez Pinzón, captain of the *Niña*. I unfurled the royal banner and the captains brought the flags which displayed a large green cross…. After a prayer of thanksgiving I ordered the captains of

Columbus sailed for five weeks across the Atlantic before he saw land.

the *Pinta* and *Niña* … to bear faith and witness that I was taking possession of this island for the King and Queen…. To this island I gave the name San Salvador, in honor of our Blessed Lord.

San Salvador is Spanish for Holy Savior.

Ferdinand Magellan was the first explorer to reach the Indies by sailing west. His expedition was also the first to circumnavigate the globe.

Still Seeking the Indies and Filling In the Map

Christopher Columbus believed that he had found a westward route to the Indies. The news pleased King Ferdinand and Queen Isabella of Spain, who had sponsored his expedition. King John II of Portugal, on the other hand, wondered if he now had a problem on his hands.

Portugal and Spain were rivals in the exploration of the seas. Both nations hoped to establish sea routes to the Indies, so their ships could bring spices, gems, and other goods back to Europe. Both nations wanted to claim distant lands for themselves. Did Columbus's expeditions for Spain mean that Portugal was about to be left behind?

King John II was suspicious of the claim that Columbus had reached Asia. Columbus had brought some native people back to Europe with him, and the king did not think that they looked as if they came from the Indies. He wasn't sure what to make of Columbus's voyage, but he knew one thing—he wasn't going to stand by idly while the Spaniards planted their flags on distant shores. Soon after Columbus's first trip, King John decided to send ships west to claim land for Portugal.

Spain and Portugal Divide the World

When King Ferdinand and Queen Isabella heard about Portugal's plans, they immediately sent a message to King John. They asked him to postpone doing anything "until it was decided by law to whom the said seas and conquests belonged."

Both Spain and Portugal were Catholic nations, so the rulers agreed to let Pope Alexander VI settle the matter. In 1493, the pope drew a line on a map of the Atlantic Ocean.

Pope Alexander VI divided the New World between Portugal and Spain.

Since Bartholomeu Dias had sailed east around the Cape of Good Hope, Portugal could claim lands east of the line. And since Columbus had reached islands by sailing west, Spain could claim everything west of the line.

This line, known as the Line of Demarcation, ran from north to south, 100 leagues (about 320 miles) west of the Cape Verde Islands in the Atlantic Ocean. When King John objected, representatives of Spain and Portugal met in the Spanish town of Tordesillas (tor-day-SEE-yahs) in 1494 and signed a treaty establishing a new line. This new line ran 370 leagues (nearly 1,200 miles) west of the Cape Verde Islands.

Two Nations Divide the World

When the pope drew the Line of Demarcation in the late fifteenth century, European rulers thought of lands on either side of the line as theirs for the taking. It did not occur to them to ask for a vote from those who inhabited the distant shores. To our modern way of thinking, it seems arrogant for two countries to divide the world between them. By what right did Spain or Portugal claim all these lands?

None, really—but that's because the idea of "rights," as we think of them today, developed *later* in history. When Portugal and Spain divided the world between them, it was long before Europeans or anyone else had ideas about the equal rights of all individuals or the rights of nations to rule themselves. (For example, almost 300 years would pass before Thomas Jefferson argued for the rights of "life, liberty, and the pursuit of happiness.")

This doesn't make what Spain and Portugal did right. It just reminds us they saw the world differently. Our modern standards for how nations should behave did not exist at that time.

• On the map on pages 198–99, find the Line of Demarcation. Locate Tordesillas in Spain.

The Treaty of Tordesillas gave Portugal clear rights to its eastward sea route to Asia. After King John II died in 1495, his 26-year-old cousin Manuel became king. King Manuel asked his advisors whether Portugal should go forward with more expeditions to Asia. Many said no. They pointed to the huge expense of new explorations, as well as the risk of conflict with Spain.

King Manuel listened but came to his own conclusion. "I have inherited from my predecessors a sacred mission," he said. "Their labors must not be brought to naught." Dias had sailed past the southern tip of Africa. Now King Manuel wanted Portuguese ships to push farther east—all the way to the Indies.

Vasco da Gama: On to Asia

Almost everyone in Portugal expected Bartolomeu Dias, now 47 years old, to head the next expedition. But King Manuel appointed a young nobleman named Vasco da Gama (VAHS-koh dah GAH-muh).

Da Gama set to work right away. He prepared three caravels for the trip and stocked a fourth ship with supplies. He hired three translators— two spoke Arabic and a third spoke many African dialects. Like earlier Portuguese explorers, he hoisted numerous heavy stone pillars aboard, hoping to place them on various sites he would claim for Portugal.

The ships left Portugal in the summer of 1497. Da Gama wanted to

avoid the coastal storms that had plagued Dias. So he made a great loop south and west, out into the open sea. From there, he took advantage of trade winds that carried him back to the Cape of Good Hope.

The Portuguese ships rounded the Cape and headed north. Along the way they stopped to explore Africa's eastern coast. In some places, they found very friendly people, eager to trade. Vasco da Gama liked one place so much that he named it *Terra de Boa Gente*—Land of Good People. Da Gama and his men placed their stone pillars along Africa's east coast in the lands that most impressed them.

As da Gama's ships sailed up the east African coast, some of the people they met were hostile, but at Malindi (mah-LIHN-dee), in present-day Kenya, the ruler gave the Portuguese a friendly reception. He also provided them with a Muslim pilot who guided them across the Indian Ocean in only 23 days.

In May 1498, more than 10 months after leaving Portugal, da Gama's ships reached the port city of Calicut, India. Up went a stone pillar. The Portuguese were in Asia, ready to trade.

- On the map on pages 198–99, locate da Gama's route to India. Locate Calicut.

Da Gama sent cloth, hats, corals, sugar, and other gifts to the ruler of Calicut. The ruler was insulted and demanded better gifts. But da Gama

Vasco da Gama placed this cross-topped stone pillar at Malindi on the east coast of Africa, in what is now Kenya. The Portuguese later established a trading post at Malindi.

Vasco da Gama sailed from Portugal to India in about 10 months. For this achievement, he was named Admiral of the Indian Sea.

didn't have anything better. He had hoped to sell similar items to Indian merchants and use the money from those sales to buy spices and other treasures that he could take back to Portugal. Now the Indian merchants refused to buy anything from da Gama.

Da Gama sent his crew members to the market to buy what they could. One seaman reported that the Indian merchants "spat on the ground" at them. The Portuguese managed to buy only a few things—just a sampling of what was available.

Still, da Gama was pleased. He had found the route to India, and he was taking useful information about trading back to Portugal. He also took home some valuable spices.

On the trip home, almost 60 sailors died of scurvy, a disease caused by lack of vitamin C. It soon became clear that da Gama did not have enough seamen to crew the three caravels. He burned one of the ships and divided its crew between the remaining two caravels.

Of da Gama's original crew, only about one-third made it back to Portugal alive. Those who did were called *heróis do mar*—heroes of the sea—and Vasco da Gama was named Admiral of the Indian Sea.

Pedro Cabral Stumbles Onto Brazil

Now the Portuguese knew the route to India, as well as the kind of goods Indian merchants wanted. So King Manuel decided to follow quickly with another trip. He chose a nobleman named Pedro Cabral (kuh-BRAHL) to head a fleet of 13 ships.

In the spring of 1500, Cabral was following the route down the coast of Africa. He swung out into the Atlantic Ocean to pick up those helpful trade winds that Vasco da Gama had found. But Cabral sailed farther west than he had intended. Suddenly, his lookouts spotted a mountain rising out of the ocean. Cabral was puzzled. What was a mountain doing in the middle of the ocean? Was it an island?

As the ships drew closer, Cabral saw that the mountain was on land that stretched farther than an island. He realized that it must be part of a continent. In fact, it was the eastern

Scurvy and Vitamin C

When people get the disease called scurvy, their wounds don't heal easily, their joints become weak, and they can die. In the sixteenth century, scurvy plagued sailors because no one knew that the disease was caused by a severe lack of vitamin C. Sailors lived for months on diets of salt beef and biscuit. Without vitamin C from fresh fruits and vegetables—such as oranges, lemons, grapefruit, tomatoes, or broccoli—many sailors got scurvy and died at sea.

coast of South America. He went ashore and told his crew to build a giant wooden cross to stake Portugal's claim on the land now known as Brazil. It was the only part of the Americas that lay east of the Line of Demarcation, so according to the Treaty of Tordesillas, Portugal could claim it.

- On the map on pages 198–99, locate the lands in South America claimed by Portugal. Locate Cabral's route.

Cabral then turned around and sailed to India, following the route that Vasco da Gama had established. At last the Portuguese had a sea route to the East—a route their ships could use to trade for spices, gems, and other treasures from the Indies. King Manuel became known as "Manuel the Fortunate." And Europe was beginning to answer the question that Prince Henry had asked: What lay beyond the ocean?

Ferdinand Magellan: In Columbus's Wake and Beyond

While the Portuguese concentrated on sailing east, Spanish explorers looked west. Christopher Columbus, who had sailed for Spain, went to his grave believing that he had discovered a westward route to the Indies. Europeans soon realized his mistake, but they weren't dismayed. They knew that a giant stretch of land—the continents now called North America and South America—lay on the other side of the Atlantic.

The Spaniards asked themselves two questions: How could they make good use of the new lands they had claimed? And could they find a sea passage through this new land so that Spanish ships could sail west to the Indies, as Columbus had dreamed?

In the next chapters you'll read about how the Spanish conquered and settled the lands Columbus had claimed for them, and about the fate of the native peoples in these lands. But for now, let's continue the story

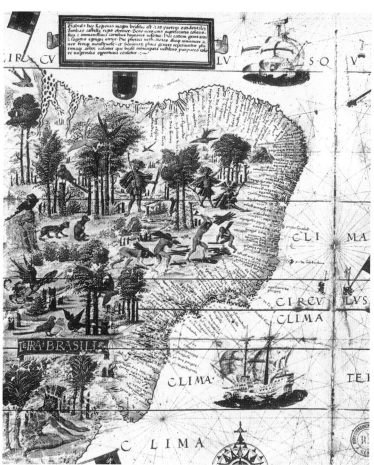

A Portuguese map depicts the coast of Brazil, which Pedro Cabral encountered while sailing farther west of Africa than he intended. Because this part of South America lay east of the Line of Demarcation, Portugal claimed it.

South America: Not Just Spanish Spoken Here

Today the language spoken in most of South America is Spanish, because Spain colonized most of the continent during the Age of Exploration. But the modern nation of Brazil has a different heritage. It was colonized by Portugal. Portuguese is the official language of Brazil.

Ferdinand Magellan set out on his westward journey around the world aboard the Victoria.

of exploration. Could mariners find a sea route through the Americas to the Indies?

To answer that question, Spain turned to an experienced seaman named Ferdinand Magellan (FUR-dn-and muh-JEHL-uhn). Magellan was Portuguese, but he did not get along with Portugal's King Manuel, so he offered his services to the Spanish crown. He was sure that he could find a strait through South America. Once he located it, he planned to keep sailing west to the Indies and the lands known as the Spice Islands.

Ferdinand Magellan was a small, quiet man who often wore a grim expression and limped from an old war wound. Those who saw him for the first time thought that he didn't

look much like a leader. But men who had sailed with him knew better. He was full of grit and resolve. (See the portrait on page 210.)

Magellan was nearly 40 years old when his expedition set sail in September 1519 with some 270 men aboard five ships—the *Trinidad, San Antonio, Concepción, Victoria,* and *Santiago.* The little fleet headed into the Atlantic. They ran into trouble as they sailed along the west African coast. A series of storms lashed the ships, and for weeks the small craft rolled on hostile seas.

When the storms died down, the winds disappeared. The ships drifted for three more weeks while the sun blazed, food rotted, and crewmen fainted in the heat. Sharks circled the fleet. "They have terrible teeth and eat men when they find them alive or dead in the sea," reported Antonio Pigafetta (pee-gah-FAYT-ah), an Italian who sailed with Magellan.

At last the ships made landfall on the east coast of South America. In what is now Brazil, they stopped long enough to taste pineapples, enjoy sunny weather, and trade with the native people for food. Then the explorers headed south. Whenever they spotted a bay or large river, Magellan sent a ship to see if it might be the passage he sought. Each probe met with disappointment.

The coast grew bleak and the weather turned cold as the explorers sailed farther south. They anchored at two islands where they saw what they thought were huge numbers of strange black geese (penguins) and fierce swimming wolves (sea lions).

The Spice Islands

The Spice Islands—that was what Europeans called a tiny group of islands lying near the equator in present-day Indonesia. These islands are now known as the Moluccas (moh-LUH-kuhz). During the sixteenth century, Europeans were willing to pay very high prices for cloves and nutmeg from the Spice Islands.

When Magellan's crew first saw penguins in the South Atlantic, they thought the birds were a type of black geese. The penguins, at left, are known as Magellanic penguins after the explorer.

Magellan announced that the fleet would spend the winter in a gloomy-looking bay and then resume its voyage in a few months. According to Magellan's companion, Pigafetta, the native people they met were gigantic in size. Magellan called them *Patagoni*, or "big feet," and the region is still called Patagonia.

Perhaps because they resented Magellan's Portuguese nationality, a group of Spanish officers mutinied and seized three ships. Magellan managed to regain control of the fleet and punish the rebels. He beheaded one and left two other ringleaders stranded on a cold, desolate shore.

That winter the fleet lost one of its ships when a storm tore the *Santiago* to pieces. Spring arrived, and the four remaining vessels put to sea again. Magellan headed south.

Through a Strait and Across an Endless Sea

The battered fleet edged down the continent seeking the strait that would lead west. Finally the ships came upon a large bay surrounded by cliffs and mountains. Magellan sent the *Concepción* and *San Antonio* to explore it. As soon as the ships entered the bay, a gale rose and swept them out of sight. Two days later, they had not reappeared. Giving them up for lost, Magellan prepared to sail away. Just then, Pigafetta wrote, "We saw the two ships approaching under full sail and flying their banners."

The *Concepción* and *San Antonio* reported that they had been blown into a narrow channel hidden behind a cliff. The channel opened into a second wide bay. Beyond that, another channel led to a third wide stretch of water. Magellan's hopes soared. Surely this was the long-sought passage.

The fleet sailed into the winding strait. The ships passed looming cliffs, snow-covered peaks, thick forests, and giant glaciers. "I think there is in the world no more beautiful strait than that," Pigafetta wrote. Some of the seaman disagreed.

The Concepción, Trinidad, *and* Victoria *sail through the channel at the tip of South America that would later be named the Strait of Magellan.*

The *San Antonio*, the ship carrying the largest store of food, sneaked away and headed back to Spain.

A month after entering the Strait of Magellan, as the passage is known

The Strait of Magellan

The Strait of Magellan, which links the Atlantic and Pacific Oceans, lies between the mainland tip of South America and the group of islands known as Tierra del Fuego, which means "Land of Fire." Magellan's men gave the islands that name because they spotted many fires burning on a large island at night as they sailed past. The fires belonged to the native people who were warming themselves during the frigid nights.

The Strait of Magellan is about 350 miles long and varies from 2 to 20 miles wide. It is still infamous for its stormy weather. During 10 months of the year, from March to December, few people want to sail through the strait.

today, the three remaining ships sailed into open sea. At the sight of ocean waves, the iron-willed Magellan cried for joy. He named this ocean the *Mar Pacifico*, which means "peaceful sea," because it seemed so calm compared to the stormy waves of the Atlantic. We know it as the Pacific Ocean.

- On the map on pages 198–99, locate Magellan's route through the Strait of Magellan to the Pacific Ocean.

Magellan's ships encountered no storms while crossing the Pacific. But it turned out to be much wider than Magellan had ever imagined. For more than three months the ships sailed west-northwest. The food in their holds began to rot. Bread crumbled into dust. The hungry men searched in corners for rats to eat, and then gnawed on leather and swallowed sawdust. Scurvy claimed many of the sailors, and much of the crew grew too weak to work. One by one, they began to die.

The explorers finally encountered two islands, Guam and Rota in the Marianas, where they found fresh food and water. They kept sailing west, and soon many green islands dotted the sea. After crossing 13,000 miles of the Pacific, Magellan had reached the islands now known as the Philippines. He promptly claimed them for Spain.

As the men sailed from island to island in the Philippines, they exchanged gifts and traded with the friendly people. At Cebu (say-BOO), the expedition's chaplain baptized the king and queen and hundreds of others. But one island chief refused to welcome the newcomers and become a Christian. Magellan decided to teach him a lesson by storming his island. It was a disastrous decision.

Magellan sailed to the chief's island with a small group of soldiers. But as soon as they landed, the islanders attacked. The outnumbered Spaniards scrambled onto boats. Magellan and a few of his men tried to make a last stand on the beach, but the angry islanders overwhelmed them. Magellan, the tireless captain, met his doom on April 27, 1521.

They Circled the Globe

The weary sailors continued west without their commander. They did not have enough hands to man all three ships, so they burned the *Concepción*. They sailed among the islands of southeast Asia, always seeking the Spice Islands, which they finally reached in November 1521.

Magellan's men loaded a valuable cargo of cloves, but they were still half a world away from Spain. After trying to reach Mexico, the *Trinidad* returned to the Spice Islands and was captured by the Portuguese. Meanwhile the *Victoria* sailed for home by a western route. The crew battled rotting supplies, a lack of water, and contrary winds as they crossed the Indian Ocean, rounded the Cape of Good Hope, and plodded up the west coast of Africa.

Three years after embarking on its voyage, the *Victoria* returned to Spain with only 18 crew members aboard. They were the first people in history to circle the globe. "I believe that nevermore will any man undertake to make such a voyage," wrote Pigafetta, who was among the survivors.

Although Magellan did not live to see the end of the epic journey, his name is forever linked with that first circumnavigation of the Earth. Not quite 30 years after Columbus's voyage, Magellan's ships had reached the Indies by sailing west.

The Strait of Magellan did not suddenly become a busy seaway for trade. The voyage from Europe—across the Atlantic, through the difficult strait, and then across the Pacific—was simply too long and dangerous for most merchant ships during the sixteenth century.

But Magellan's feat inspired other adventurers. Europeans

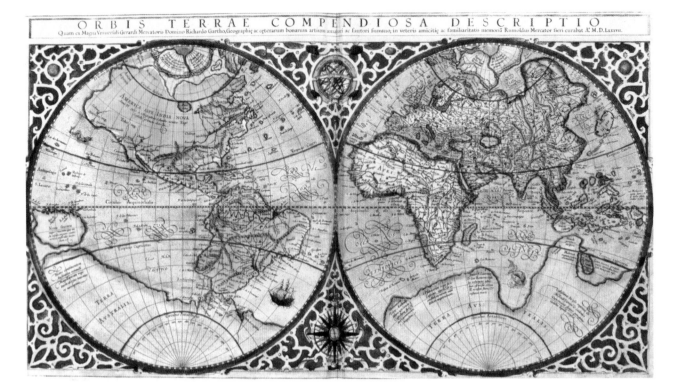

ORBIS TERRAE COMPENDIOSA DESCRIPTIO

A map published 64 years after Magellan's round-the-globe expedition demonstrates how much Europeans knew about the world by the late sixteenth century.

were quickly filling in the map of the world, coming to know the contours of major land masses and important islands. Yes, there were still unknown lands. But da Gama, Magellan, and others showed that the globe would offer up its secrets to those with courage enough to explore. Europeans set their sights on distant lands and dreamed of empires, riches, and glory.

The Discovery of a Westward Passage

A Page from the Past

The young Italian nobleman Antonio Pigafetta wrote a detailed account of Magellan's famous voyage. Here he describes how the explorers came upon what would turn out to be the long-sought passage to the Pacific Ocean—the passage known today as the Strait of Magellan.

Setting course to the fifty-second degree toward the said Antarctic Pole ... we found by miracle a strait which ... is surrounded by very great and high mountains covered with snow. In this place it was not possible to anchor, because no bottom was found.... To most of those in the ships it seemed that there was no way out from it to enter the said Pacific Sea. But the captain-general [Magellan] said that there was another strait which led out, saying that he knew it well and had seen it in a marine chart of the King of Portugal, which a great pilot and sailor named Martin of Bohemia had made.

The said captain sent forward two of his ships, one named *San Antonio* and the other *Concepción*, to seek and discover the outlet of the said strait, which was called the Cape de la Baya. And we with the other two ships (namely the … *Trinidad* and the other, *Victoria*) remained awaiting them in the Baya. And in the night we had a great storm, which lasted until noon of the next day. Wherefore we were compelled to raise the anchors, and to let the ships ply hither and thither in the Baya.

The other two ships had such a passage that they could not round a cape forming the Baya, and trying to return to us they were hard put not to run aground. But approaching the end of the Baya (thinking themselves lost) they saw a small opening, which did not seem an opening but a creek. And like desperate men they threw themselves into it, so that perforce they discovered the strait.

Then seeing that it was not a creek but a strait with land, they went on, and found a bay. Then going further they found another strait, and another bay larger than the first two. Very joyful at this, they at once turned back to inform the captain-general.

We thought indeed that they had perished, first because of the great storm, and then we had not seen them for two days. And while in suspense we saw the two ships approaching under full sail and flying their banners, coming toward us. When near us, they suddenly discharged their ordnance, at which we very joyously greeted them in the same way. And then we all together, thanking God and the Virgin Mary, went forward.

To *discharge their ordnance* means to fire their cannons.

The ruins of Machu Picchu sit high amid the Andes mountains of Peru. The city is the most famous reminder of the achievements of the Inca civilization.

Old Civilizations in a New World

*E*uropeans saw the American continents as a "New World." As the sixteenth century began, the Spanish and Portuguese sent explorers and settlers to this unknown land. But they did not arrive in an uninhabited wilderness.

Cities rose in what seemed to be jungle, and villages dotted the banks of rivers. Millions of native people inhabited North and South America. To them, the "New World" wasn't so new at all.

In this chapter we'll look back at civilizations in the Americas before the Europeans arrived.

A Very Long Time Ago: The Olmec

How long have humans been in the Americas? Archaeologists have long thought that during the most recent Ice Age, about eleven thousand years ago, hunters from Asia arrived in North America. Scholars think these hunters were on the trail of herds of wild horses, caribou, and mammoths, and that they crossed a land bridge hundreds of miles wide, which once linked Siberia to Alaska. According to this theory, these people moved southward from Alaska. Recent archaeological findings suggest that these people may have sailed rather than walked. And there is even evidence that other people may have arrived in the Americas as long as fifty to sixty thousand years ago. Some scholars speculate that these early people may have migrated across the Pacific, or even across the Atlantic.

Archaeologists do generally agree that by 1200 B.C., about the time the Egyptians were building glorious temples and the Greeks

This chapter focuses on the Olmec, Maya, Aztec, and Inca civilizations.

Three Civilizations: Olmec, Maya, and Aztec

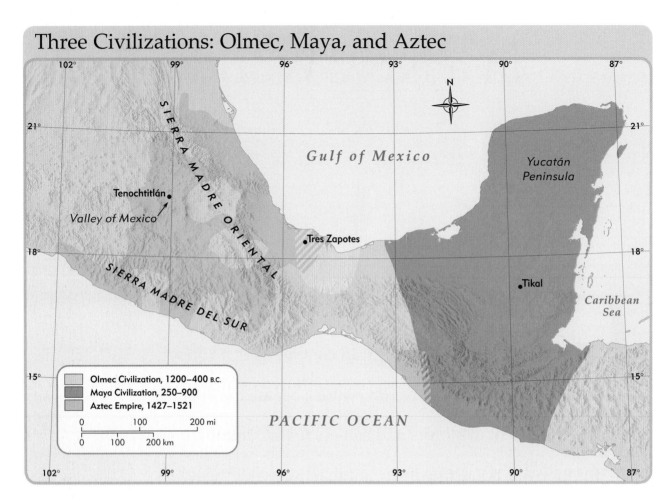

Gulf of Mexico

SIERRA MADRE ORIENTAL

SIERRA MADRE DEL SUR

Tenochtitlán

Valley of Mexico

Tres Zapotes

Yucatán Peninsula

Tikal

Caribbean Sea

PACIFIC OCEAN

Olmec Civilization, 1200–400 B.C.
Maya Civilization, 250–900
Aztec Empire, 1427–1521

0   100   200 mi
0   100   200 km

Archaeologists discovered this nine-foot-tall stone head in Mexico. The Olmec civilization left behind many such heads, which may represent Olmec gods.

were fighting their Trojan Wars, civilization had begun in the Americas. Do you recall the meaning of "civilization"? The English word *civilization* is related to the Latin *civitas*, which means "city." People in a civilization are city-builders. They have learned how to farm and grow a surplus of food. They've learned to divide labor. And they've begun to build cities.

If you've read Volume 1 of *The Human Odyssey*, you know that the world's first civilizations developed near flooding rivers. In ancient Mesopotamia, Egypt, India, and China, annual floods left rich deposits of silt and minerals along the riverbanks, producing fertile land for farming. As you might expect, in

the Americas civilization also began along flooding rivers.

A people called the Olmec (OHL-mehk) established what may have been the earliest civilization in the Americas. Olmec civilization thrived between 1200 and 400 B.C. in the area that is now Mexico's Gulf Coast. The Olmec fished in the rivers and took advantage of the fertile soil left behind by floods. They began to farm, produce a surplus, and build cities.

- On the map above, locate the Olmec civilization.

Archaeologists digging into huge earthen mounds have uncovered ruins that appear to be Olmec religious sites. Archaeologists have also found colossal heads carved out of stone, the largest weighing up to 80,000 pounds. These giant heads probably had a religious significance. Perhaps they represented gods.

The Olmec used a calendar and invented an early form of writing. They worshipped nature spirits and carved jade sculptures of jaguars and serpents. Their artistic influence spread as far south as what is now El Salvador.

Mayan Marvels

The hot, swampy lowlands of modern-day Guatemala might not seem a likely setting for achievement in the arts and sciences. But the area was home to one of history's great civilizations, the Maya (MIY-uh). From about A.D. 250 to 900, Mayan culture spread across a region that today includes southern Mexico, Belize, the Yucatán Peninsula, much of Guatemala, and parts of El Salvador and Honduras.

- On the map on page 224, locate the Yucatán Peninsula and the area inhabited by the Maya.

Many Mayan cities boasted populations in the tens of thousands. One of the biggest and most important cities was Tikal (tee-KAHL) in what is now Guatemala.

Like other Mayan cities, Tikal rose amid the rain forests. The jungle was not far off. The air was hot and sticky. In the distance, city dwellers could hear the cries of howler monkeys, and sometimes even glimpse a jaguar.

On the outskirts of the city, peasants worked the land to grow beans, squash, and corn. Corn was the main food. The Maya ground corn into flour for tortillas, and also used it to make a sweet and spicy drink.

The peasants grew many of their crops on steep, terraced hillsides. Sometimes they drained swamps and turned the land into farmland. Why plant crops in such difficult areas? Wasn't it hard work to drain swamps and shape the hillsides into terraces? Yes, but not as hard as trying to beat back the jungle.

The peasants needed to grow food for themselves as well as for thousands of nobles, priests, and other city dwellers living in Tikal. The city itself was home to more than 60,000 people. On the days of special religious festivals, another 20,000 peasants from the surrounding area made their way to Tikal.

The Maya worshiped many gods and goddesses, each thought to have important powers. The priests performed various rituals to keep the gods happy. It would be disastrous, the Maya thought, if the sun-god or the rain-god refused to bless the fields.

In the great central plaza of Tikal stood a tall and narrow stone pyramid. At the top, a giant stone statue of the Mayan king looked out over the city. Below the sculpture a door led into the temple. A priest would climb the long flight of steps up the side of the pyramid and disappear into the temple to perform the secret rituals.

The city of Tikal had five enormous pyramids,

A Mayan potter fashioned this elegant incense burner in the form of a seated figure. Burning incense may have been one way in which the Maya tried to keep their gods happy.

and they were more than just temples. Like the pyramids of the ancient Egyptians, they also served as tombs where rulers were buried along with their favorite belongings—and their servants—to take with them into the next world.

The Maya call to mind the Egyptians in other ways. The Maya developed a system of writing, one of the important requirements of civilization. The Maya wrote in hieroglyphs, pictures that stood for words or sounds that made up words.

Without a single metal tool, royal sculptors carved towering stone monuments called stelae (STEE-lee). The sculptors covered the stelae with hieroglyphs describing the deeds of leaders and heroes. Modern-day scholars have been able to translate some Mayan hieroglyphs, but much of the complex writing system remains a mystery. When scholars finally crack the code, we will learn much more about this accomplished people.

For their time, the Maya possessed advanced knowledge of astronomy and mathematics. Their priest-astronomers learned to predict eclipses and developed a 365-day calendar more accurate than any known in Europe at the time. In mathematics, the Maya understood the idea of zero as a number. They also understood the idea of positional notation or what you might know as "place value." For example, in the number 373, the value represented by each 3 depends on its position (the first represents 300, and the

A stone pyramid looms over the central plaza of Tikal, one of the most important cities of the Maya. In the foreground stands an ancient stele covered with hieroglyphs, picture words whose meaning, for the most part, still remains a mystery.

Mayan astronomers recorded their calculations on manuscripts like this one, which contains predictions of eclipses and the movements of the planet Venus.

second, just 3). While the use of zero and place value might seem basic today, these were sophisticated ideas in the time of the Maya. They allowed the Maya to make calculations with very large numbers.

By the start of the tenth century, the civilization of the Maya passed its peak. No one is certain why, but people abandoned the great cities in the jungle and moved south to the Guatemalan highlands and north to the Yucatán. Within a few hundred years, the days of Mayan splendor were a distant memory. But in the region that is now central Mexico, a new civilization emerged, one of both dazzling sophistication and startling brutality.

The Aztecs Seek a Home

The people called the Aztecs settled in what is now the Valley of Mexico around the year 1250. Legend says the first Aztecs were nomads who came from somewhere to the north of central Mexico. Their war god Huitzilopochtli (weets-eel-oh-POHCH-tlee) was said to have sent the Aztecs south. There, so the war god said, they would find their new home in a place where an eagle spread its wings as it tore apart a serpent.

As they traveled south, the Aztecs did not meet a warm welcome. City after city chased out the warlike nomads. At last, the legend says, one local lord agreed to let the Aztecs stay, thinking they would intimidate his enemies. He even gave them a piece of land—rocky, barren land that no one in the city used, as it was infested with poisonous snakes. When the Aztecs saw the lethal snakes slithering over their campground, they shrieked with joy. Soon the warriors were dining happily on roasted snake.

Impressed and a little frightened, the lord treated the Aztecs with more respect. Legend has it that he even agreed to let his daughter marry their god Huitzilopochtli in a holy ceremony. But when the lord arrived with fragrant offerings of flowers and incense, he discovered that the Aztecs had prepared the girl for her new status as a goddess by killing her. The enraged father ordered his soldiers to drive the Aztecs into the desert.

Shunned by all, the wanderers at last took refuge on a remote island in the middle of a lake. Little more than prickly pears grew on the deserted island. To keep from starving, the Aztecs ate flies' eggs, worms, and grubs.

One day, says the legend, they saw an eagle land atop a cactus. In its beak, it held its next meal—a wriggling snake. As the eagle spread its wings and devoured its prey, the Aztecs told themselves that the

promise of Huitzilopochtli was fulfilled. In this harsh environment, the Aztecs made their home.

Building the Aztec Empire

Within a few centuries, the Aztecs transformed the deserted island on which they had settled into a glittering metropolis known as Tenochtitlán (tay-nawch-teet-LAHN). And they built a mighty empire stretching across central and southern Mexico. Tenochtitlán, the capital, was the hub of this empire.

- On the map on page 224, locate the Aztec Empire and Tenochtitlán.

The island city of Tenochtitlán was linked to the mainland by wide, straight causeways—roads built above the lake's surface. A second island held a giant market where thousands of people came to buy and sell each day. A bridge connected the two islands. Busy streets and canals crisscrossed the capital. The Aztecs used the canals to carry goods in their canoes to the city's markets. Many smaller towns surrounded Tenochtitlán, some of them built on man-made islands.

In 1500, Tenochtitlán had a population of perhaps 150,000. At the time, only a half dozen cities in Europe had more than 100,000 inhabitants.

Tenochtitlán was not only big but also beautiful. The city was laid out in four neat sections, meeting at a central plaza. Stone monuments and temples filled the plaza. Towering over all was the Great Temple, an enormous pyramid 150 feet high, topped by two temples standing side by side.

The best of everything came to Tenochtitlán. Gold, silver, and

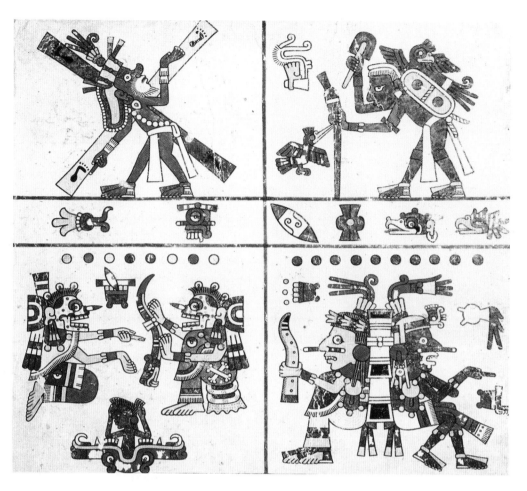

An Aztec manuscript depicts the activities of merchants who traveled far and wide. At top right, a porter carries a cargo of quetzal birds. At top left is the patron god of merchants and travelers.

copper arrived from mines to the north. Skilled metalworkers in the great city fashioned the precious metals into fine jewelry. Craftsmen transformed the brilliant feathers of the quetzal bird, as well as gemstones such as turquoise, into dazzling headdresses, cloaks, and ornaments.

In Tenochtitlán, learning thrived as well. Trained scribes—more like artists than secretaries—painted brilliantly colored books depicting Aztec gods and history. The scribes also kept records of taxes and the territories conquered by the Aztecs.

In Tenochtitlán, the Aztec emperor lived in his royal palace with landscaped gardens and a private zoo filled with exotic animals and birds. The palace itself was ornamented with precious works

Why "Aztec"? Why "Mexico"?

Today the term *Aztec* is generally used to refer to the large empire that developed in the fourteenth and fifteenth centuries in what is now central and southern Mexico. But many different native peoples made up the Aztec Empire. These various peoples spoke the same language, Nahuatl (nah-WAW-tl). The people living in the capital city of Tenochtitlán were the conquerors and ruling class. They referred to themselves as the *Mexica* (may-SHEE-kah).

Legend has it that the Mexica came from a desert region to the north known as Aztlán, which means "White Land." Later, when the Spaniards arrived, they referred to all the different Nahuatl-speaking peoples conquered by the Mexica as Aztec, from the word *Aztlán.* The Spaniards called their new colony and capital city Mexico after its native inhabitants, the Mexica people. (You'll read more about the Spaniards and the Aztecs in the next chapter.)

The Aztecs carved this calendar stone in 1479. The basalt stone measures nearly 12 feet in diameter. It depicts Aztec gods, including the sun-god at center. The calendar also shows the Aztec notion of earlier ages—they believed that the world had been created and destroyed four times before the present era.

of art and the finest gold and silver pieces crafted by Aztec artisans.

The Aztecs had come a long way since their early days. Once homeless wanderers, they went on to build one of the most advanced civilizations in the world. They had done it largely by conquest. The warlike Aztecs subjected neighboring city-states to their will, one by one, making each a part of their vast empire.

Sacrificing to the Gods

At the core of Aztec culture was a frightful practice—human sacrifice on a massive scale. Prisoners captured during frequent wars were sacrificed to the gods.

The Aztecs believed that every night their god Huitzilopochtli battled against darkness and then rose in the morning as the sun. To renew his strength, he had to consume human hearts and blood each day. Otherwise, he would grow weak, the sun would fail to rise, and the earth's people would perish.

To feed their god, the Aztecs practiced human sacrifice. They dragged their living sacrifices to the top of the Great Temple. There, black-robed priests wielding stone knives tore out the victims' beating hearts. Across the plaza stood a grisly altar—a great rack holding thousands of human skulls. For an Aztec warrior, the greatest prize of war was not wealth, land, or slaves, but instead an enemy soldier captured alive to offer in sacrifice to Huitzilopochtli and his fellow gods.

As neighboring peoples saw their treasures looted, their children enslaved, and their bravest warriors butchered to feed an alien god, they came to despise and fear the Aztecs. At the height of their power, the Aztecs saw little reason to worry about the resentment of conquered peoples. But as we'll see in the next chapter, this resentment played a part in the Aztecs' fall.

The Inca

Far to the south, along the spine of the Andes mountains, rose another great civilization that was also rich in silver, gems, and gold. A people called the Inca came to power around 1200. At its height around 1500, the Inca Empire reached nearly the entire length of South America, from the present-day nation of Ecuador to central Chile. It included parts of Peru, Bolivia, and Argentina. More than ten million people lived under Inca rule.

- On the map on page 232, locate the Inca Empire.

The Inca built their capital city of Cuzco (KOOS-koh) in a fertile valley.

From there the Inca emperor ruled his vast realm. Some scholars believe that Cuzco was the Inca word for "navel," a fitting description for a capital that lay near the center of a 2,500 mile long empire.

The Inca were impressive builders and stone masons. A gigantic fortress called Sacsahuamán (sahks-ah-wah-MAHN) dominated a hill overlooking the city of Cuzco. Some of the stones in this fortress weigh 200 tons or more. Thousands of men used ropes and rollers to haul the stones many miles to the construction site. Stone masons chiseled the enormous irregular blocks into shape and polished them against each other with wet sand until they fit together so precisely that the thinnest knife blade could not slip between them. Historians and archaeologists still do not know exactly how Inca stonemasons accomplished their task with such precision.

The Inca devised a remarkable system of roads to link Cuzco with faraway towns in the Andes. Two great roads ran the empire's entire distance—the Coastal Road and the Royal Road. A network of smaller roads also reached much of the Inca's realm. Along the major roads, the Inca set up storage houses full of grain. This grain fed the empire's armies and supplied local communities during years of poor harvests.

The Inca used runners and a relay system to speed news and information over their roads. These messengers did not have to run very far. But they did have to be alert and fast. A runner often spent an entire day waiting in the doorway of his hut. When he spotted another runner coming toward him, he started running, too. The two raced alongside each other while the arriving runner repeated a message. Then the tired runner stopped to

The fortress of Sacsahuamán protected Cuzco, the Inca capital. Below, Sacsahuamán's huge stones dwarf three Peruvian herders and their llamas.

Inca Empire

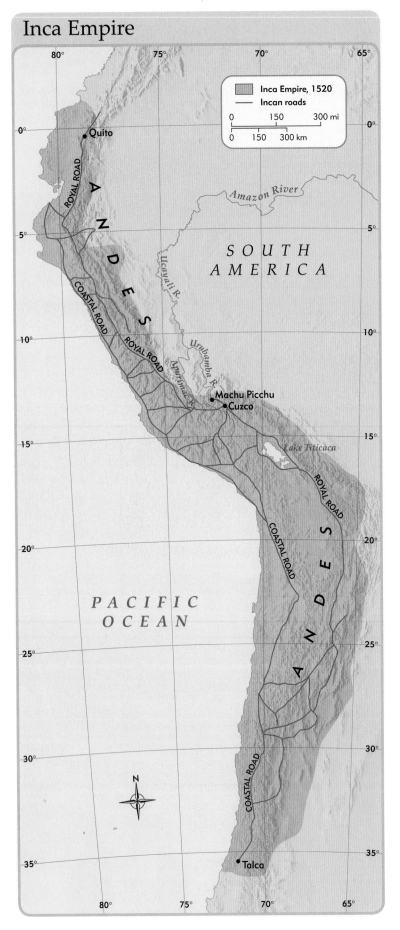

Map legend:
Inca Empire, 1520
Incan roads

0   150   300 mi
0   150   300 km

Quito

ROYAL ROAD

A N D E S

COASTAL ROAD

ROYAL ROAD

Amazon River

Ucayali R.

Urubamba R.

Apurímac R.

S O U T H
A M E R I C A

Machu Picchu
Cuzco

Lake Titicaca

ROYAL ROAD

COASTAL ROAD

A N D E S

P A C I F I C
O C E A N

COASTAL ROAD

N

Talca

rest while the new runner sprinted on to the next station, where he passed along the message. Thanks to this relay system, important news from all over the empire could reach Cuzco in just days.

In the highlands of the Andes, runners had to be agile enough to cross the many bridges spanning rushing rivers and deep canyons. Some bridges were nothing but a rope tied to a tree or rock on either side. At other bridges, a runner crouched in a basket and pulled himself along a rope.

Carrying Khipu for the Emperor

Sometimes runners carried fresh seafood up the steep slopes of the Andes to the table of the emperor in Cuzco. Often runners carried cargo even more important—*khipu* (KEE-poo). Khipu were the records of the Inca Empire. The Inca used them to record numbers—numbers telling everything from how much fine woven cloth was in the royal store-houses to how many Inca soldiers had died in a battle.

A khipu was made of a cord with knotted strings attached. The strings' colors conveyed important information. Red might stand for soldiers, for example, or yellow for gold retrieved from river beds. Everything about the knots—their size, their number, how far apart they were—had meaning. Only those highly skilled in reading khipu could understand the compli-cated system. The knowledge was passed down from father to son. With this system of roads, runners, and khipu, the emperor kept

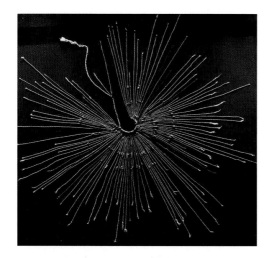

up with what was happening in his realm.

Like most emperors, the Inca ruler reserved the best for himself. All of the realm's gold and silver belonged to him. Inca gold—or "sweat from the sun," as they called it—came not from land mines but from rivers in the north. Finely wrought gold adorned the emperor's stone palace. Skilled artisans crafted fine jewelry for the emperor and his family. If he was in a generous mood, the emperor might give gold nose rings or other jewelry to favored subjects.

The Inca revered their rulers even after death. Like the ancient Egyptians, the Inca mummified their dead. They treated the mummies of deceased emperors as if they were still alive. They brought the mummies to public ceremonies, and a dead ruler's palaces, servants, and riches were still considered his property. A newly crowned emperor had to gain his own sources of wealth by conquering more territories.

Machu Picchu

The most famous reminder of Inca royalty and achievement is probably the mountain city of Machu Picchu

(mah-choo PEE-choo). The name *Machu Picchu* means "old peak." The city perches among the clouds atop a high ridge in the Andes. Towering peaks and plummeting valleys surround the city, hiding it from the outside world. (See page 222.)

At Machu Picchu, the Inca built a fortified military tower and a number of temples and altars. They constructed palaces, plazas, terraces, and more than a hundred flights of steep stone steps, all superb feats of stonemasonry.

Most archaeologists believe that the Inca built Machu Picchu as a summer vacation spot for their

Left: Runners relayed messages throughout the Inca Empire. Sometimes they carried a khipu, a cord with knotted strings attached that recorded amounts of such things as cloth, soldiers, and gold.

Above: One of the most famous bridges in the Inca Empire crosses the Apurímac (ah-poo-REE-mahk) River. Rebuilt yearly, it is made of woven vines and branches. Twisted ropes hold the swaying bridge high above the river.

A flight of stone steps leads to one of the ruined temples of Machu Picchu, the mountain city of the Inca. Before it was abandoned, Machu Picchu may have served as a vacation spot for the nobility as well as a religious center.

nobility and as a religious center. The city lay about fifty miles from Cuzco. When Cuzco suffered from humidity and heat, Machu Picchu offered cool mountain air.

The views in all directions from Machu Picchu were spectacular. Terraced hillsides allowed for cultivation of crops while the royal family was in residence. Sure-legged llamas brought provisions from the valley below. Altars and temples dotted the hillsides.

The Inca eventually abandoned Machu Picchu. Scholars are not sure why. Forgotten by all but the local people, the city remained unknown to the outside world until a traveler from the United States named Hiram Bingham happened on it while exploring 8,000 feet above sea level in the Andes mountains.

Better Than Gold: Hiram Bingham and the Lost City of the Inca

Hiram Bingham III was born to adventure. His grandfather had been a Christian missionary to the island of Hawaii. His American father and mother traveled as missionaries to the Gilbert Islands, more than two thousand miles southwest of Hawaii in the South Pacific. From his father, Hiram learned an exciting skill—mountaineering. Hiram's father was an avid mountain climber. On lush, tropical islands in the Pacific, young Hiram learned to bushwhack his way up mountain slopes, wield a knife against treacherous vines, throw a rope, and scale a sheer cliff.

Historical Close-up

When he was a young man, Hiram left the palm-covered islands of the Pacific to study at Yale University. After graduating, he traveled to Hawaii and worked for a while as a chemist. But the curious young man wanted to know more about history, and about distant cultures and peoples. So he went to Harvard University and became an archaeologist.

Bingham grew fascinated by South America and he led two expeditions there. He and his team followed old trade routes through the Andes mountains, traveling from Argentina to Peru. He published his findings in a book. Before long, Yale hired him to teach history and undertake more expeditions.

Bingham spent each year planning his next expedition to learn more about the vanished civilizations of South America. During his travels on that continent, he kept hearing about Inca gold hidden high in the Andes mountains. Bingham knew that Inca rulers had been rich in jewels, silver, and gold. So he was excited to hear rumors that the rulers had built a mountaintop city so secret and remote that few of their subjects had even known it existed. Were the rumors true? If so, could the city's ruins be found?

Bingham thought so. In July 1911—winter in the Southern Hemisphere—36-year-old Hiram Bingham returned to the mountainous jungles of southeastern Peru. He had climbed these heights many times before, but he had not found what he was looking for. This time, he was determined to discover "the lost city of the Incas," as he called it.

Bingham and a group of hardy scientists picked their way through the dense tropical jungle. Peruvian guides led the way up sheer rock slopes.

*The explorer
Hiram Bingham*

When they finally reached a ridge and could look around, they saw row upon row of spectacular mountain peaks, 20,000 feet tall or more. "I know of no place in the world which can compare with it," Bingham wrote later. He marveled at the "great snow peaks looming above the clouds more than two miles overhead" and the "gigantic precipices of many-colored granite rising sheer for thousands of feet above the foaming, glistening, roaring rapids."

Bingham and his team led their mules and llamas along narrow, rocky paths, keeping watch for poisonous vipers. They crossed bridges made from logs lashed together with jungle vines. A hundred feet below, mountain rivers bounded over massive boulders. Occasionally they met native people living in this awe-inspiring landscape. One said that he knew of Inca ruins nearby. When Bingham asked which way, the man pointed straight up.

Bingham's team hacked through jungle vines and inched across a slippery log bridge. They crawled up a slope so steep and rocky that, as Bingham later recalled, they had to hold on by their fingernails. Soon they met two Peruvians who farmed this remote mountainside high above the clouds. After a meal of roasted sweet potatoes, the farmers showed them how they planted vegetables in broad terraces of soil, held up by rock walls built long ago by human hands.

Bingham followed one terrace along the curve of the mountain. As he later wrote in his book, *Lost City of the Incas*, "Suddenly I found myself confronted with the walls of ruined houses built of the finest quality of Inca stone work. It was hard to see them, for they were partly covered with trees and moss, the growth of centuries, but in the dense shadow, hiding in bamboo thickets and tangled vines, appeared here and there walls of white granite ashlars [squared stones] carefully cut and exquisitely fitted together."

Bingham spied "a cave beautifully lined with the finest cut stone," and then "a semi-circular building [that] followed the natural curvature of the rock." It was, in Bingham's opinion, "the work of a master artist." Soon he and his companions realized that they had come upon an entire city of magnificent buildings. They named the site Machu Picchu, after the ridge on which it was built.

In Machu Picchu, Inca laborers had carved or built some 350 buildings out of granite, including houses, storage buildings, and temples. Stripping away vines and vegetation, archaeologists found more than 100 stairways connecting parts of the city, including a 150-step sidewalk through the city center. Stone-lined ditches carried water to fountains, basins, and gardens.

In the houses, Bingham and his fellow explorers found pieces of bowls, pots, spoons, and jugs, sometimes decorated with geometric designs. They found bronze knives, mirrors, and pins used to fasten shawls.

As they began scouting down the mountain, they discovered dozens of burial caves. In these caves they found skeletons curled knees to nose. Often bits of cloth, bowls, jugs, and pins lay nearby. Some graves also contained the bones of llamas, which the Incas kept as pack animals and used as a source of meat and milk. Bingham even found the skeleton of a little dog buried next to one woman.

In all his searches, Bingham found no gold. But that did not disappoint him, because he considered the "lost city" a discovery even more precious, a treasure of human history. 🌿

Bingham found this bronze knife pendant at Machu Picchu.

In the early sixteenth century, Spanish soldiers known as conquistadors set out to conquer much of the Americas. This statue depicts Francisco Pizarro, who conquered the Inca Empire.

Clash of Civilizations: Conquistadors in the New World

T he year was 1519. It was the eighteenth year of the reign of the Aztec emperor Montezuma II (mahnt-uh-ZOO-muh; also spelled Moctezuma). In the island city of Tenochtitlán, with its massive monuments and towering

temples, a messenger arrived, bearing disturbing news. He reported that a lookout on the coast had spotted "towers or small mountains floating on the waves of the sea."

Those floating mountains were ships. Soldiers packed the decks. They stood gazing at the shore and dreaming of conquest in this New World.

Who were these men and why had they come?

They were Spaniards, and they came to win glory for themselves and new lands for the Spanish crown. They came as crusaders, eager to make converts to Christianity. They came hoping to find valuable spices. But most of all, they came in search of gold.

The Spaniards had a name for a soldier who marched for glory, God, and gold. They called him a conquistador (kahn-KEES-tuh-dor)— a conqueror.

Cortés Seeks Gold and Glory

The motto of the conquistador was *Ir a valer mas*, which means "Go forth to be worth more!" One conquistador named Hernán Cortés (kor-TEZ) took those words to heart—repeatedly.

Cortés was born in Spain to a family that was noble but not wealthy. His parents wanted him to study the law. Instead, he dropped out of school and spent his time loitering in port cities. A close acquaintance wrote that "he was a source of

Routes of Cortés and Pizarro

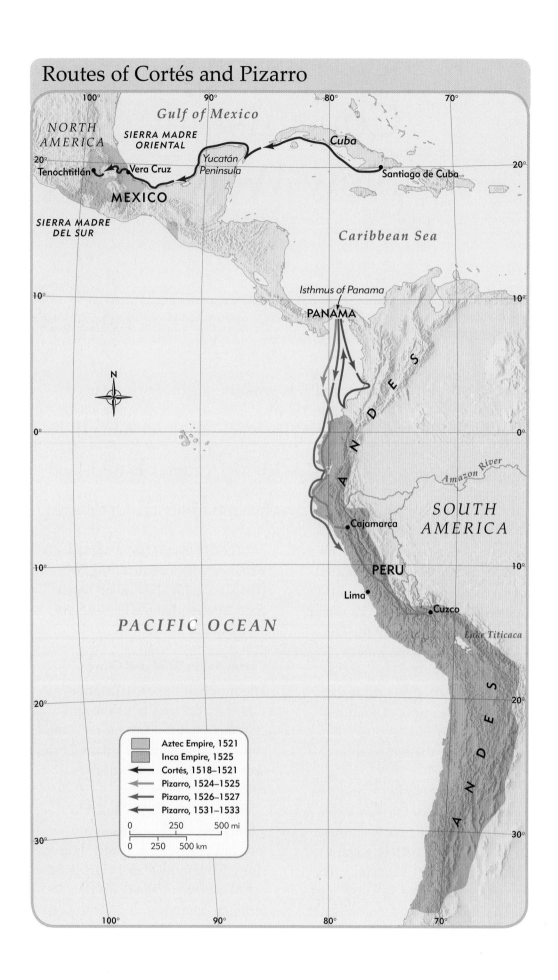

NORTH AMERICA

Gulf of Mexico

SIERRA MADRE ORIENTAL

Cuba

Yucatán Peninsula

Tenochtitlán • Vera Cruz

MEXICO

Santiago de Cuba

SIERRA MADRE DEL SUR

Caribbean Sea

Isthmus of Panama

PANAMA

A N D E S

Amazon River

SOUTH AMERICA

• Cajamarca

PERU

Lima •

• Cuzco

Lake Titicaca

PACIFIC OCEAN

A
N
D
E
S

	Aztec Empire, 1521
	Inca Empire, 1525
←	Cortés, 1518–1521
←	Pizarro, 1524–1525
←	Pizarro, 1526–1527
←	Pizarro, 1531–1533

0   250   500 mi

0   250   500 km

trouble to his parents as well as to himself, for he was restless, haughty, mischievous, and given to quarreling, for which reason he decided to seek his fortune."

In 1504, 19-year-old Cortés took passage on a ship bound for the Spanish island colonies in the West Indies. There he took part in the conquest of Cuba. The Spanish government gave him land and slaves in return for his service.

Eventually, Cortés settled down on a plantation. But he was restless, and still far from wealthy. In fact, he was in debt. What money he had, he squandered on gambling, expensive clothes, and nights out on the town.

Then his luck turned. Spanish sailors landed on the Yucatán peninsula of Mexico and sent back word of an extraordinary find — not tribal villages, but great stone cities, larger even than Seville in Spain. Rumors began to spread among the Spaniards—rumors of a land filled with gold.

The governor of Cuba, a military leader named Diego Velázquez (DYAY-goh vuh-LAHS-kuhs), wrote to Spain asking permission to colonize this new land. Meanwhile, he decided to send out a fleet to explore. Velázquez chose Hernán Cortés to lead the expedition.

Cortés leaped at the chance for gold and glory. He borrowed money to outfit some ships. Eager to look the part of the dashing and gallant captain, he donned a gold-trimmed velvet cloak and feathered plume. News of the expedition spread, and hundreds of adventurers rushed to join.

Some people frowned at Cortés and his take-charge manner. Rivals whispered that his first loyalty wasn't to Cuba's governor or to Spain, but to himself. Velázquez grew troubled and sent orders forbidding the fleet to sail. But Cortés was not about to lose this opportunity. Under cover of darkness, he raised anchor and slipped from port.

Cortés's fleet consisted of eleven ships carrying more than five hundred soldiers, sixteen war horses, attack dogs, and cannons. Also on board were two Spanish monks, whose mission was to convert the native people of the land to Catholicism.

But Cortés was focused on conquest and his own glory. When his fleet reached the coast of Mexico, he made it clear that he was not interested in following orders from Governor Velázquez. He declared that he answered only to the king of Spain, who was an entire ocean away. His men officially named him "Captain General" and agreed to give him one-fifth of the gold they acquired.

Cortés planted the Spanish flag and built a settlement. He gave it a name that summed up his ambitions—Villa Rica de la Vera Cruz, or "Wealthy Town of the True Cross."

Greed for Gold

News of the Spanish arrival soon reached the Aztec capital of Tenochtitlán. Aztec ambassadors arrived in Vera Cruz bringing gifts and greetings from the emperor Montezuma. Cortés said that he would like to meet this emperor and asked if the

Dreams of conquest, gold, and glory drove Hernán Cortés. He found all three in the lands of the Aztecs, and the Aztecs paid a heavy price.

emperor had any gold. Yes, the Aztecs told him. The emperor's palaces were filled with gold.

"Send me some of it," Cortés replied, "because my companions and I suffer from a disease of the heart which can be cured only with gold."

The ambassadors returned to Montezuma with this message, along with alarming stories of the strangers who had landed on their shores. The Aztecs had never seen a horse before. Spanish soldiers on horseback looked to them like monstrous two-headed, six-legged creatures. The Spaniards' sharp steel weapons looked menacing when they glittered in the sun. And when Cortés fired a cannon, the noise and stench of burning gunpowder left the Aztecs weak and dizzy.

Montezuma was no coward. Over the years he had faced many scheming rivals and put down many rebellions. But this news filled him with fear and dread. Who were these beings who commanded wild animals and covered their bodies in a shiny metal that made arrows bounce away? Were these white-skinned newcomers gods? Were they wicked sorcerers?

Whether gods or men, the strangers had made clear what they were after—gold. Montezuma decided to give them what they desired. Perhaps then they would be satisfied and go away.

Montezuma's ambassadors returned to Vera Cruz bearing gifts of precious metals in every form. Two great wheels, seven feet across, one silver like the moon, one golden like the sun. A stunning gold necklace embellished with 183 emeralds. A golden mirror decorated with pearls. Golden shields covered with feathers. A helmet filled with pure gold dust. And there was more, much more.

Montezuma's generosity did not leave Cortés satisfied. Instead, it sparked his greed. When Cortés saw the treasure, he resolved to follow these riches to their source. He must have it all!

Some of Cortés's men balked at the prospect of marching two hundred miles into unknown territory. They remained loyal to Governor Velázquez and wanted to return to Cuba. Cortés responded to this challenge in his usual decisive way. He sank his ships. He spared one ship and explained that it was for those who wanted to go back. After waiting to see which soldiers would choose to get on board, he sank that one, too.

The Path to Conquest

Cortés soon discovered that the mighty Aztec Empire was more fragile than it first seemed. Some sixteen to eighteen million people lived under Montezuma's rule, but many bitterly resented the tribute they were forced to pay. The Aztec emperor's men took not just corn and silver, but sons and daughters to be kept as slaves or sacrificed to the gods.

The people conquered by the Aztecs lived in fear for their lives. Cortés felt certain that they were ripe for revolt. He had found a way to communicate with them, through a woman named Malintzin (mah-LINT-suhn). She had been given to the Spaniards as a slave, but she soon became an invaluable translator and advisor.

The Spaniards began their long trek toward Tenochtitlán. As Cortés marched along, he invited the native peoples he met to join his army. Some readily joined forces with the conquistador. Others resisted. They rained down darts and stones and surrendered only after weeks of bloody battle with the heavily armed foreigners. By the time Cortés and his allies reached Tenochtitlán, their numbers had grown to six thousand.

When they came upon the capital city, an astonishing sight greeted the invaders. A soldier named Bernal Díaz del Castillo (ber-NAHL DEE-ahs del kahs-TEE-yoh) described his first glimpse of Tenochtitlán. "These great towns and temple pyramids and buildings rising from the water, all made of stone, seemed like an enchanted vision," he wrote. "Indeed, some of our soldiers asked whether it was not all a dream."

Everything about Tenochtitlán astounded them—its impressive roads and bridges, wide enough for ten horses to walk abreast; its monumental palaces and temples; and its people—tens of thousands of them, thronging the plazas, crowding on the lake in their canoes, every gaze locked on the army entering their city.

Montezuma himself came out to meet Cortés. He arrived in dazzling finery, shaded by a canopy made of green feathers embroidered in gold and silver and adorned with pearls. Aztec nobles walked ahead, sweeping the path and laying down mats so that the emperor's jewel-encrusted golden sandals never touched the ground.

Montezuma welcomed Cortés and his men with great ceremony. He lodged them in a palace and sent

A model of Tenochtitlán captures the grandeur of the Aztec capital, which was one of the largest cities in the world at the beginning of the sixteenth century. On entering Tenochtitlán, one Spaniard described it as "an enchanted vision."

Two civilizations meet as a conquistador encounters an emperor. Cortés, on the left, wears a heavy suit of armor, while Montezuma is attired in the finery of an Aztec ruler.

servants with Aztec delicacies, such as chocolate. The emperor invited the strangers to explore the city and enjoy his royal zoos and gardens. But Cortés grew more and more uneasy. They were on an island city, vastly outnumbered by the native population. Had he walked into a trap?

Montezuma Captured

Cortés decided that it was time to turn the tables on this mighty leader. He decided to guarantee Spanish safety by taking Montezuma as a hostage.

Perhaps it was the Spaniards' weapons that frightened Montezuma. Perhaps it was their allies, thousands strong, who surrounded the city. Or perhaps the emperor truly believed it was his destiny to yield to this white-faced, black-bearded conquistador.

For whatever reason, when Cortés arrived to take him prisoner, Montezuma did not resist. As the soldiers paraded the Aztec ruler through the streets, he announced to his stunned subjects that he went willingly.

With Montezuma as their hostage, the Spaniards now ruled Tenochtitlán. First they ransacked the royal treasury, melting down priceless works of art for the gold. The conquistadors demanded tribute, and cities across the empire sent gold, silver, and other riches.

Next the Spaniards turned to the Great Temple, "whose great size and magnificence," Cortés said, "no human tongue could describe." The temple's blood-soaked steps and rack of grinning skulls appalled even the ruthless captain and his battle-hardened soldiers. Ever since they came ashore, they had been shocked by the Aztec's sacrifice of human victims. Now the Spaniards removed the images of Huitzilopochtli and other Aztec gods from the temple, and raised a new one—the Virgin Mary. The Aztec priests, horrified at this act, moved the image of

Huitzilopochtli to another shrine, where they worshipped it in secret.

The Aztecs grew increasingly resentful of the invaders. Still they obeyed their imprisoned emperor and did not rise up against the Spaniards. Meanwhile, Cortés had another problem. He received word that 15 more ships had appeared off the coast. He realized that Governor Velázquez had sent troops to bring him back to Cuba.

Cortés left a lieutenant in charge of Tenochtitlán and marched back to Vera Cruz with half his men. They launched a surprise attack against their fellow Spaniards on a rainy night and defeated them. Cortés persuaded most of the governor's soldiers to join his side by promising them a share in the spoils. Trumphantly, he led them back to the capital city.

But in his absence, things had not gone well at Tenochtitlán. Cortés returned to find his men under siege and the palace surrounded by Aztec warriors. The conquistador insisted that Montezuma go up to the roof to plead for peace. The Aztecs answered with a shower of stones.

Did a stone hit the emperor on the head and kill him, as the Spaniards claimed? Or did the Spaniards murder Montezuma, as the Aztecs said, because they had no further use for him? In any case, the once mighty Aztec emperor perished.

Cortés saw he had no choice but to flee. The Spaniards gathered all the treasure they could carry. At midnight, they slipped from the palace.

They didn't make it far before someone sounded the alarm. Spears flew as the conquistadors ran for a bridge to the mainland. But the Aztecs had destroyed the bridges. The desperate men dove into the water. Those who had been greediest in stuffing their clothes with gold and jewels were the first to drown. Half of the Spanish soldiers died that night, along with thousands of their allies. Legend says that after making his escape, Cortés sat under a tree and wept.

The Fall of Tenochtitlán

Ten months later, Cortés and his men, including a large force of native allies, returned and laid siege to Tenochtitlán. They cut off the city's supply of food and fresh water. Like their ancestors, the Aztecs were forced to survive on lizards, worms, and twigs. Still, they fought ferociously and held out for nearly four months.

The Spaniards had an unexpected ally in their fight—disease. During the previous spring, one of the Spanish soldiers had come down with smallpox. The Aztecs had no resistance to this European plague. Thousands of people sickened and died. In the end, disease, starvation, and the steel swords of the Spaniards overwhelmed the Aztecs.

On the ashes of Tenochtitlán, the victorious invaders built Mexico City, the capital of New Spain. Hernán Cortés realized his dream. He became a rich man. The Spaniards realized their dream as well. They gained a huge empire. But the once mighty Aztec civilization was no more.

The Death of Montezuma

*A Page
from the Past*

Bernal Díaz del Castillo was a conquistador who accompanied Cortés in Mexico. Fifty years later he wrote his recollections in a book entitled The True History of the Conquest of Mexico. *Here Díaz gives his account of the death of the Aztec emperor Montezuma.*

Cortés, perceiving how desperate our situation was, determined that Montezuma should address his subjects from a terrace, and desire them to desist from their attacks, with an offer from us to evacuate Mexico…. When this was made known to Montezuma, he burst out into violent expressions of grief saying, "What does he want of me now? I neither desire to hear him, nor to live any longer, since my unhappy fate has reduced me to this situation on his account." He therefore dismissed those sent to him with a refusal, adding … that he wished not to be troubled any more with the false words and promises of Cortés….

Montezuma addresses the Aztec people from the roof of his royal palace.

The enemy continued their attacks, and Montezuma was at length persuaded. He accordingly came, and stood at the railing of a terraced roof, attended by many of our soldiers, and addressed the people below him, requesting, in very affectionate language, a cessation of hostilities, in order that we might quit the city. The chiefs and nobility, as soon as they perceived him coming forward, called to their troops to desist and be silent, and four of them approached, so as to be heard and spoken to by Montezuma. They then addressed him, lamenting the misfortunes of him, his children, and family….

As they concluded their address, a shower of arrows and stones fell about the spot where Montezuma stood, from which the Spaniards … protected the king; but expecting that while speaking to his people they would not make another attack, they left him unguarded for an instant, and just then three stones and an arrow struck him in the head, arm, and leg. The king when thus wounded refused all assistance, and we were unexpectedly informed of his death…. It was said that he had reigned seventeen years, and that he was the best king Mexico had ever been governed by….

After the death of Montezuma, Cortés sent two prisoners, a nobleman and a priest, to inform the new sovereign, Cuitláhuac (kweet-LAH-wahk), and his chiefs, of the event, and how it had happened….

Cortés then caused the body of the king to be borne out by six noblemen, attended by most of the priests, whom we had taken prisoners, and exposed it to public view…. These noblemen accordingly related the circumstances of the king's death to Cuitláhuac, and we could hear the exclamations of sorrow which the people expressed at the sight of his body. They now attacked us in our quarters with the greatest violence, and threatened us that within the space of two days we should pay with our lives the death of their king, and the dishonor of their gods, saying that they had chosen a sovereign whom we could not deceive, as we had done the good Montezuma.

Pizarro Ventures South

Tales of Aztec gold kindled dreams of wealth and glory in many a would-be conquistador, including Francisco Pizarro (puh-ZAHR-oh). Like Cortés, Pizarro took part in Spanish military campaigns at an early age and journeyed to the New World to seek his fortune. In 1513, as part of an expedition led by Vasco Núñez de Balboa (VAHS-koh NOON-yays day bal-BOH-uh) across the Isthmus of Panama, Pizarro became one of the first Europeans to see what would later be called the Pacific Ocean.

In Panama, Pizarro heard rumors of an empire to the south, a land of gold perhaps richer than any other in the New World. He swore to find and conquer this legendary land of gold.

Pizarro joined forces with a fellow soldier and a priest. Together they raised money, recruited volunteers, and made plans for a voyage of exploration down the coast of South America. It was a daring plan—so daring that the people of Panama called Pizarro and his companions "the company of lunatics."

Their first expedition, launched in 1524, proved a costly failure. But Pizarro had no thought of giving up. In 1526, the trio tried again. After a long, storm-tossed journey, they reached the northern edge of the Inca Empire, where the modern-day nation of Ecuador now lies. There they were greeted by a sight to warm their gold-loving hearts—a prosperous stone city filled with men and women wearing stunning ornaments of emeralds and gold.

The people of the city did not share the Spaniards' delight at the

Francisco Pizarro looked on the Americas as a place where he could become fabulously wealthy. He lusted after Inca gold.

The captured Inca emperor Atahualpa negotiates the price of his freedom with Pizarro. They agreed on enough gold to fill the room where Atahualpa was being held, here fancifully depicted in European style.

to the south." Then he stepped across the line.

Thirteen men chose to stay with Pizarro. Together they sailed south and reached Peru. Pizarro encountered a small group of Inca, but the conquistador did not try to conquer them. Instead, he and his men returned to Panama several months later with a few captives, some llamas, clothing, pottery, and gold. But their appetite had been whetted and continued to grow. Pizarro traveled to Spain and received royal approval to conquer the region.

A Treacherous Plan

In 1531, Pizarro set out once more for the Inca Empire. He was in his fifties now, tough, scarred, and single-minded in his desire for power, fame, and fortune.

When the conquistador landed on the coast, he did not find the prosperous towns he expected, but a scene of devastation. In the years since his last voyage, disease and civil war had ravaged the Inca Empire.

The disease was smallpox. It spread with astonishing speed, traveling south ahead of the Spaniards who had brought the lethal virus to the Americas. The Inca emperor himself may well have been one of the epidemic's millions of victims. He left behind two sons—Huascar (WAHS-kahr), a name that meant "Gentle Hummingbird," and Atahualpa (ah-tah-WAHL-pah), or "Wild Turkey." Each son believed he should be the next ruler.

The sons battled each other. Years of bloody conflict ended at last with

encounter. According to the frightened Spaniards, ten thousand warriors assembled along the shore to repel the invaders.

With most of his crew, Pizarro retreated to a nearby island. He dispatched some men to Panama to get reinforcements. But the governor of Panama grew worried that the expedition was on the verge of turning into a disaster. He sent two ships to bring Pizarro and his men back to Panama.

Cold, wet, and starving, Pizarro refused to return. With his sword, he drew a line in the sand. "Friends and comrades!" he said. "On that side are toil, hardship, hunger, the drenching storm, and death. On this side are ease and comfort. There lies Peru with its riches; here, Panama and poverty. Choose as brave Spaniards. I go

Atahualpa on the throne and Huascar in prison. When the Spaniards arrived, Atahualpa's control over his battered empire was still shaky.

Pizarro saw his opportunity. He plunged into the mountains in search of Atahualpa. The conquistadors dragged their cannons and supplies up steep paths and across rope bridges that swayed over yawning chasms. They baked in their steel armor and gasped in the thin air as they marched.

Atahualpa and eighty thousand warriors waited in a valley. The tired little band of fewer than two hundred Spanish soldiers could not have appeared very threatening. But the Inca did not realize how treacherous Pizarro could be.

Pizarro sent messages of peace and friendship to Atahualpa. At sunset, the Inca emperor ventured forth to meet the conquistador in a nearby town. Atahualpa wore an emerald collar and a golden robe. He held a shield of gold with the image of the sun-god. Eighty servants carried him on a litter covered with gold, silver, precious stones, and brightly colored parrot feathers. Dancers and musicians marched ahead of him, singing a song of praise: "O great and very powerful lord, son of the Sun, only ruler, may all the earth obey you."

Most of the Spaniards had hidden themselves in buildings around the town's central square. Suddenly cannons boomed. Soldiers on horseback charged into the crowd, swords flashing. By nightfall, thousands of Inca lay dead, and their ruler had become a hostage.

Atahualpa quickly saw that, beyond anything, the bearded strangers loved gold. He made them an offer. In exchange for his release, he would give them enough gold to fill the room where he was being held, and enough silver to fill two rooms.

The Spaniards agreed. Load by load, the ransom began to arrive from the Inca capital, Cuzco. The desperate Inca sent treasures stripped from temples and the royal palace. Pizarro and his men melted the jewelry and masks, more than 30,000 pounds of gold and silver. But, like Montezuma before him, the Inca emperor misjudged his Spanish captors. The Spaniards broke their promise to release Atahualpa. Instead, they executed him. When news of Atahualpa's death reached the Inca warriors, they scattered.

By 1537, the Inca Empire was in Spanish hands. Cuzco had fallen to Pizarro. The conquistador founded a new capital city named Lima (LEE-muh) on the coast, and there he built his own palace.

To the north, in Mexico, Spaniards controlled the land that had once belonged to the mighty Aztecs. The stage was set for Spain to rule much of the New World.

To ransom their captured leader, the Inca gave the Spanish many tons of gold, including pieces like this golden figure.

A twentieth-century mural by Diego Rivera depicts Spanish colonial masters and Indian laborers in the New World.

The Spanish and Portuguese Build Empires

T he riches of the New World exceeded even the conquistadors' dreams. As the Spanish invaders— and soon after them, the Portuguese—pushed inland, they discovered hidden gold and silver mines. They forced the Indians to dig up the precious metals, which they melted down and shaped into bars. Soon fleets of royal ships were crossing the Atlantic, their cargo holds loaded with fortunes in silver and gold.

This glittering treasure enriched the Spanish and Portuguese rulers, and made others jealous. But the mines provided only a fraction of the riches exported to Europe. The true wealth of the New World lay not under the earth, but on it.

Back in Europe, textile manufacturers wanted the indigo and cochineal that conquistadors found to dye their fine cloth blue and red. Merchants valued animal hides. And hungry Europeans literally gobbled up the bounty of the Americas— cacao beans (used to make chocolate), corn, tomatoes, and potatoes.

Europeans especially clamored for the sweet white crystals made from the juice of sugarcane. Sugarcane is a tall grass that grows best in hot, tropical regions. Parts of the Americas offered the perfect climate and vast stretches of fertile land on which to grow this profitable crop.

Spain and Portugal saw the Americas as an endless stream of gold, silver, sugar, and other goods, constantly flowing to fill royal purses. But the New World lay thousands of miles across the Atlantic from Europe. Spanish and Portuguese kings wanted to make sure they controlled America's riches. So they ruled their new overseas territories with a tight grip.

Indigo is a blue dye obtained from a plant also known as indigo. *Cochineal* (KAH-chuh-neel) is a red dye obtained from the dried bodies of cochineal insects.

The Power of the Spanish Crown

Ferdinand and Isabella's grandson, King Charles I of Spain, took steps to strengthen royal control over his New World possessions. His first action was to replace the troublesome Hernán Cortés. Cortés had become governor of the lands he had conquered. Ruthless ambition made him an effective conquistador, but the king worried that such a headstrong governor would be hard to control. So in 1535, he sent a trusted nobleman, Antonio de Mendoza, to be his viceroy in the New World.

Viceroy means "in place of the king," and that was how Charles expected Mendoza to rule. The viceroy was to watch over the lands and subjects claimed by the king. The viceroy was supposed to increase the king's wealth and carry out his will.

King Charles I of Spain sent explorers to colonize a region in what today is Argentina. In 1536, they founded the walled city of Buenos Aires.

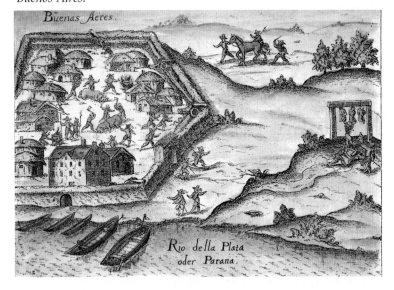

The king eventually divided his New World holdings into two huge sections called viceroyalties. He sent a viceroy to rule each of these territories, which were called New Spain and Peru.

- On the map on page 254, locate the Spanish viceroyalties of New Spain and Peru.
- Locate Brazil, which was a Portuguese colony.

Each viceroy lived like a king. Just as European princes built their splendid palazzi in the Old World, so the Spanish and Portuguese governors in the New World assumed they should do the same.

The viceroys could make a few decisions on their own, but in general they followed orders from Spain. More than 6,000 royal decrees from Spain reached the colonists. These decrees touched every detail of their lives. They told them where and how to build a school. They specified which fruits they might plant—lemons and oranges, yes, but grapes and olives, no (because the king wanted the colonists to keep buying high-priced wine and oil imported from Spain).

Sometimes Spanish colonists in the New World found ways to avoid decrees that didn't suit them. Peru, for instance, produced its own wines and olives. But for the most part, the colonists followed the king's wishes. Even if they disliked a particular decree, they did not question the king's right to rule.

The colonists also obeyed the king because he kept such tight control over American ports. The king and his advisors kept careful records about all the goods going into and out of the viceroyalties. Every load that left the colonies—cacao beans, indigo, or gold—had to be approved by Spain and transported on Spanish ships.

The royal court in Spain also carefully controlled who came to the colonies. Every missionary or government official who sailed for the Americas had to be a trusted subject of the crown. But the king did not rely on trust alone. In fact, he encouraged his officials to spy on each other and send secret reports back to Spain.

A Rigid Class System

The system of government in Spain's Americas colonies had one main purpose—to maintain the king's power over the colonies. The king also maintained control through another means—a rigid class structure.

In the highest class were the men sent to the Americas to represent the king and enforce his will. These men were native Spaniards, born on the Iberian Peninsula, and so they were called peninsulares (pehn-een-suh-LAHR-ehs). The peninsulares held all important government positions in the colonies. The king sent these peninsulares to the colonies for limited terms and then called them home, to make sure their first loyalty remained to Spain.

Ranking beneath the peninsulares were the Creoles (KREE-ohls), members of Spanish families who were born and raised in America. Even though they were of Spanish descent, Creoles seldom held official government positions, except at the lowest levels.

Spaniards and other Europeans at this time placed a high importance on

Merchant ships in Lisbon harbor prepare to depart Portugal for the New World. Such ships brought the wealth of the Americas back to Europe—cargoes of sugar, indigo, silver, gold, and more.

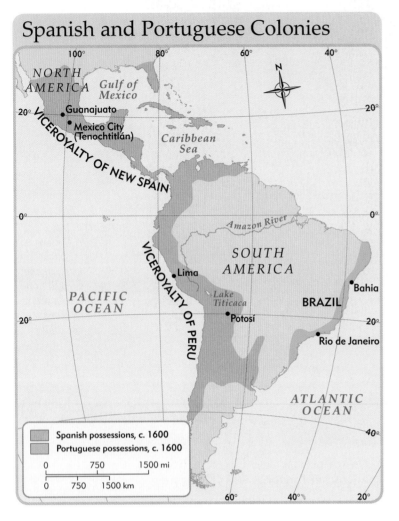

Spanish and Portuguese Colonies

NORTH AMERICA

Gulf of Mexico

Guanajuato

Mexico City (Tenochtitlán)

VICEROYALTY OF NEW SPAIN

Caribbean Sea

Amazon River

SOUTH AMERICA

Lima

VICEROYALTY OF PERU

PACIFIC OCEAN

Lake Titicaca

Potosí

BRAZIL

Bahia

Rio de Janeiro

ATLANTIC OCEAN

Spanish possessions, c. 1600
Portuguese possessions, c. 1600

0   750   1500 mi
0   750   1500 km

mixed race, descended from both Spaniards and native people. As time passed, more and more mestizos populated the colonies. They were generally poor, but they were free to move about and take whatever work they could find. They often learned a trade or craft, such as blacksmithing or carpentry. Many worked for the Creoles, while other mestizos joined the army.

At the bottom of the class structure came the Aztec, Inca, and other native peoples who had survived the Spanish conquest. Under Spanish rule, the Indians were very poor. In the eyes of most peninsulares, Creoles, and mestizos, the Indians existed for one reason—work.

The Encomienda

At first, the Spaniards obtained most of their laborers through the *encomienda* (en-koh-mee-EHN-duh). The term comes from a Spanish word meaning "entrust." The encomienda was a system under which the crown officially "entrusted" a colonist with all the Indians who lived in a particular village or region. The colonist—known as an *encomendero* (en-koh-mehn-DEHR-oh)—forced the Indians to farm the land or work in mines. He was allowed to collect tribute from the Indians, such as a share of the crops. The encomendero was expected to protect the Indians and teach them Christianity and European customs.

Legally, Indians held in encomienda were not slaves but "free" subjects of the crown. In reality, the encomenderos often forced the Indians to work from dawn

a person's place of birth. Creoles might have "pure" Spanish blood, but Spaniards persisted in their prejudice that the Creoles were inferior because they had been born in the "savage" New World. The peninsulares saw the Creoles as lazy, untrustworthy, and even immoral.

Many of the Creoles were grandchildren or great-grandchildren of the conquistadors. They resented the higher social status of the peninsulares. Still, the Creoles did rank near the top of the social pyramid, and they could live quite well in the New World.

Beneath the Creoles were the mestizos (meh-STEE-zohs), people of

Not all Europeans traveled to the New World in search of riches. Catholic missionaries came to spread their religion. Here, a friar baptizes an Aztec leader into the Christian faith.

till dusk so that the colonists could live like Spanish gentlemen of leisure.

Hernán Cortés, who entrusted himself with at least 100,000 Indians, declared, "I did not come to till the land like a peasant." A Brazilian colonist commented, "It is not the style for the white people of these parts, or of any other of our colonies, to do more than command their slaves to work and tell them what to do."

Abuse of the Indians was common. The colonists sometimes beat, tortured, and even murdered the native peoples. If an Indian fled, the colonists tracked him with bloodhounds.

The Indians could not turn to the king's men for help. Royal officials were often just as harsh and cruel as the encomenderos. One early Spanish judge was said to have hanged six Indians for the crime of failing to sweep his path.

The Friars and the Indians

In a Spanish play written in 1600 called *El Nuevo Mundo* (*The New World*), one of the characters says of the conquistadors, "It is not Christianity that leads them on, but gold and greed." While the conquistadors plundered Aztec and Inca treasure, some Spaniards did in fact go to the New World to spread Christianity. They were Catholic friars, members of religious orders who had taken vows of poverty. To the Indians, these early missionaries seemed a different sort of Spaniard. Many deeply cared about the welfare of the Indians.

The first friars arrived barefoot, wearing simple robes. They accepted whatever food they were offered and settled down to live among the Indians.

The friars had no more desire to preserve Indian culture than the colonists did. Their goal was to convert the native people of the Americas to the Catholic faith. That meant

What's a Friar?

The word *friar* comes from the Latin *frater*, meaning "brother." In the late Middle Ages, some men chose to join religious orders that moved about and were devoted to teaching and serving the poor. In 1216, a Spanish priest named Dominic formed such an order. His new friars traveled about preaching, helping the needy, and earning their bread by begging. Many Dominican friars and many Jesuits journeyed to South America.

teaching them a whole new way of life, including faith in a new God and loyalty to Spain's Catholic king.

To communicate with the Indians, the friars learned the local languages and compiled dictionaries and grammars. They studied traditional Indian beliefs, looked for similarities with the Christian faith, and then used those similarities to help explain Christian ideas. Thanks to the friars' efforts, much knowledge of these Indian civilizations was not completely lost.

Bartolomé de Las Casas

The Catholic missionaries did not come to defend the Indians from the encomenderos. Their main concern was not social justice but saving souls. They soon found, however, that widespread mistreatment of the native people made it harder to win converts.

The Indians had seen how many Christians behaved, and it was not with love and kindness. According to a friar named Bartolomé de Las Casas (bahr-toh-loh-MAY day lahs KAHS-ahs), many natives refused to be baptized out of terror of spending eternity with the violent encomenderos.

Las Casas himself had once been an encomendero on the island of Hispaniola. In *A Brief Account of the Destruction of the Indies*, he wrote about the way the Indians of Hispaniola were treated:

> When they have been brought to the very edge of collapse by the labors to which they are put and begin to drop from toil and hunger as they stumble through

the mountains with enormous loads on their backs, the Spanish kick them and beat them with sticks to make them get up and resume their wearisome trudge…. Oh, would that I could describe even one hundredth part of the afflictions and calamities wrought among these innocent people by the benighted Spanish!

Shocked by such brutality, Las Casas gave up his encomienda and became a Dominican friar.

Many missionaries shared his feelings. In a famous sermon, one friar demanded, "Tell me, by what right do you keep these Indians in cruel servitude?… Are these not men? Have they not rational souls?" Las Casas begged the Spanish monarchy to end the encomienda, a system he called "more unjust and cruel than Pharaoh's oppression of the Jews."

"Nothing more detestable or more cruel"

Bartolomé de Las Casas wrote A Brief Account of the Destruction of the Indies *to publicize Spanish mistreatment of the Indians. Most scholars believe that Las Casas may have exaggerated some of his claims in order to prompt reforms. But his accounts of harsh conditions are no doubt generally accurate. In this excerpt, he describes the way Spanish colonists forced natives to dive for pearls.*

A Page from the Past

There is nothing more detestable or more cruel, than the tyranny which the Spaniards use toward the Indians for the getting of pearl. Surely the infernal torments cannot much exceed the anguish that they endure, by reason of that way of cruelty; for they put them under water some four or five ells [15 to 18 feet] deep, where they are forced without any liberty of respiration, to gather up the shells wherein the pearls are; sometimes they come up again with nets full of shells to take breath, but if they stay any while to rest themselves, immediately comes a hangman rowed in a little boat, who as soon as he has well beaten them, drags them again to their labor.

Their food is nothing but filth, and the very same that contains the pearl, with a small portion of that bread which that country affords; in the first whereof there is little nourishment; and as for the latter, it is made with great difficulty, besides that they have not enough of that neither for sustenance; they lie upon the ground in fetters, lest they should run away; and many times they are drowned in this labor, and are never seen again till they swim upon the top of the waves: oftentimes they also are devoured by certain sea monsters, that are frequent in those seas.

Consider whether this hard usage of the poor creatures be consistent with the precepts which God commands concerning charity to our neighbor, by those that cast them so undeservedly into the dangers of a cruel death, causing them to perish without any remorse or pity, or allowing them the benefit of the sacraments, or the knowledge of religion….

Spanish soldiers forced Inca men, women, and children into a life of hard labor. Many Indians literally worked themselves to death on colonial plantations or in gold and silver mines. But more perished as a result of diseases the Europeans brought to the New World, such as smallpox, measles, typhus, chicken pox, and mumps.

Back in Spain, other members of the clergy joined the protest against those who said discovery and conquest gave Europeans the right to do anything they wanted in America. One Jesuit scholar asked: What if the Indians had invaded and defeated Spain? How would the Spanish enjoy losing their land, their freedom, and their way of life?

Indeed, King Charles was eager to get rid of the encomienda, but compassion was not his motivation. The king wanted the riches of the New World to flow directly to him, not to those who controlled the encomienda. And he wanted to prevent the colonists from gaining enough wealth and power to challenge his rule.

In 1542, the king issued a set of "New Laws" that called for reform and set tight limits on the encomienda. Angry protests poured in from the colonies. Faced with the threat of uprisings in the viceroyalties of New Spain and Peru, the king backed down.

Toil and Disease Take Their Toll

Even if the king had not issued his "New Laws," the encomienda was on its way out. There were simply too many Spaniards competing for too few natives. And the natives were dying.

The royal government wanted Indian laborers for sugarcane and rice plantations, and for gold and silver mines. These enterprises enriched the Spanish crown. The Catholic Church—which eventually became the largest single landowner in the New World—wanted Indian laborers to help build monasteries and cathedrals.

Each year more colonists arrived in the Americas. As the Spanish population increased, the native population decreased. In 1519, the year Cortés arrived in Mexico, some sixteen to eighteen million people may have lived under Aztec rule. Fifty years later, barely half that many Indians remained in central Mexico. By 1605, just over one million survived.

What happened to the Indians? Las Casas blamed the harshness and brutality of the encomienda. Savage beatings, never-ending labor, and sheer exhaustion took their toll on the native population.

But an even more destructive force was at work—disease. Colonists brought smallpox, measles, typhus, chicken pox, mumps, and other illnesses from Europe to the Americas. The Indians had no resistance to these diseases. Epidemics swept the land. In one native town of sixteen thousand, a single smallpox outbreak left only four hundred alive.

Often without meaning to, colonists made the situation worse. For example, the government forced Indians living in scattered villages to move into towns. Diseases spread even more quickly since people in the towns lived close to each other.

With fewer strong and healthy people left to work the land, hunger followed. Again, the colonists made a bad situation even worse. They chopped down entire forests for firewood and lumber, leaving hillsides bare. When the rains came, fertile topsoil washed away. The colonists' cows, turned loose to graze, wandered into the Indians' fields, trampling their corn and squash.

Once the Indians had tilled their land to feed themselves and their communities. Now they toiled for strangers who took almost all they grew and left the Indians to starve. With each passing year, fewer and fewer Indians were left to work the land.

Taking Their Land

Under the old encomienda system, colonists controlled the Indian laborers. Officially, the land itself did not belong to the encomendero. It belonged to the Indians, and ultimately to the Spanish crown.

As the colonists came to think of the New World as their permanent home, they wanted to own land. Land was wealth. Land was prestige. Land was something the Creoles could hand down to their children, to keep in the family for generations.

From Tenochtitlán to Mexico City

Before the arrival of the Spanish, Aztec glory and power centered in the dazzling capital city of Tenochtitlán. The Spaniards destroyed Tenochtitlán and on its ruins built Mexico City as the capital of New Spain. By around 1600, Mexico City had a population of 100,000. It was a splendid city in the European style, filled with parks and plazas, universities and churches. An admiring visitor from Spain called it "the Athens of America."

The streets of Mexico City were lined with great stone mansions, houses built to last—and to intimidate. A royal order made this purpose plain. The Spaniards' mansions, said the order, should fill the native people "with admiration ... [so they] will realize that the Spaniards are settling there permanently and not temporarily. They will consequently fear the Spaniards so much that they will not dare to offend them...."

Mexico City became the capital of New Spain.

Indian laborers and Spanish guards lead a caravan of llamas carrying silver from the Potosí mine in Upper Peru. The journey to the coast took three weeks. From there, the silver traveled by ship to the western shore of Panama, then by land across the Isthmus of Panama to the Atlantic. Treasure ships carried the silver over the ocean to ports in Spain.

With the native population waning, the colonists saw their opportunity. They used various tricks to push the surviving natives into smaller and smaller areas and claim their lands. For example, the colonists required Indians to show legal title to the land—something the Indians had no way to do, since before the Spaniards arrived, they had never thought of producing documents to prove their ownership of the land.

The colonists' appetite for land was insatiable. Sometimes a colonist combined multiple plots into a huge estate known as a *hacienda* (hah-see-EHN-duh). A single family might own a million acres. One northern hacienda spread across more than eleven million acres. In Brazil, one huge estate covered more ground than some European states.

Unlike the encomienda, this new system of owning land did not give colonists a legal right to Indian labor. But hacienda owners needed somebody to work their land. And the Indians, who earned little money from farming, had to pay taxes and church fees. Some of them moved onto haciendas. There they worked like serfs in return for meager wages and rations, as well as protection from the demands of government officials. But life in a hacienda could easily turn into a trap. Workers became dependent on their landlords. Sometimes they acquired debts that forced them, and even their children, to remain on the estate permanently.

Mining Gold and Silver

Work on the haciendas was grueling but still preferable to the dangers of working in gold and silver mines. Indian workers toiled for 12 hours a day in dangerous mine shafts. One mine called "the mouth of hell" in Guanajuato (gwah-nah-HWAH-toh) was said to be the deepest in the world at the time. Workers carried 200, even 300 pounds of ore out of the earth on their backs.

By 1600, Spain's colonies had produced at least three times as much gold and silver as the total supply in Europe in 1500. The silver mine of Potosí (poh-toh-SEE), in the mountains of Upper Peru (today, Bolivia), remains one of the richest mines ever found. Brazil produced most of the world's newly mined gold supply during the first half of the eighteenth century.

The Spanish crown claimed one-fifth of all the gold and silver taken out of the earth in its New World colonies, a share known as the *quinto* or the "royal fifth." For such riches, the new king of Spain, Philip II, was more than willing to overlook mistreatment of Indian mine workers. He even allowed the owners of the mines to draft Indians for labor. In

Potosí, each adult male Indian was supposed to serve every seven years for a period of four months. Many died at the task.

Not even the power of the Spanish crown could slow the disappearance of the native labor force. The Indians were dying. Who would harvest sugarcane and tend the cattle on the haciendas? Who would haul the treasure from the mines?

To the Spaniards and the Portuguese, who had once sailed around the Cape of Good Hope, an answer became clear—African slaves.

During the 1500s, more than a third of the world's supply of gold came from South America. Both Inca and Spanish craftsmen made beautiful objects of gold. The mask below depicts one of the Inca gods. Beside it is an ornate Spanish plate made of New World gold.

A brass plaque depicts three chiefs from the kingdom of Benin, one of the great civilizations of West Africa during the fifteenth and sixteenth centuries.

Songhai, Benin, and the New Slave Trade

The Age of Exploration was in many ways a great leap forward in the human odyssey. Adventurers figured out how to travel farther than ever before. They made bold voyages and sailed around the world for the first time in history. Goods and ideas began to move from continent to continent much faster than in the past.

But sometimes great changes also bring tragedy. The coming of the Spaniards and Portuguese to the New World resulted in much misery and death. The conquistadors crushed whole civilizations, and in the decades that followed, millions of native people died.

Across the Atlantic Ocean, a different kind of tragedy unfolded in the sixteenth century—a terrible slave trade that cost millions of people their freedom and often their lives.

Slavery was not new in the sixteenth century. It had existed all over the world in various forms for thousands of years. It had existed in Africa throughout recorded history. But around the year 1520, a new slave trade began to develop in which millions of Africans were taken against their will across the Atlantic Ocean to the Americas.

To understand how this happened, we need to back up in time and see how various factors came together. We will look first at the rise of some great trading kingdoms in Africa. We will then see how the Portuguese encounter with Africa combined with the demand for labor in the Americas to produce one of the most lamentable chapters in human history.

This chapter focuses on West African kingdoms and the beginnings of the transatlantic slave trade.

Sunni Ali of Songhai

Through western Africa, there runs a great river called the Niger (NIY-jur). Stretching about 2,600 miles, the Niger has a shape like a horseshoe.

During the Middle Ages, a people called the Songhai (sahng-GIY) lived along the banks of the Niger. They built their capital city of Gao near the bend in the horseshoe. By the 900s, Gao was growing prosperous by trading with the Islamic lands to the north of the Sahara. The Songhai merchants traded gold and copper. They also traded African slaves, who were in demand throughout the Islamic world. Most of these unfortunate people had been captured in war. African slaves were marched from Ghana (farther west) to Gao, and then across the Sahara to Egypt.

- On the map below, locate the Niger River, Gao, and the Sahara.

Around the year 1000, the king of the Songhai converted to Islam. For the next several hundred years, the Songhai rulers were Muslim. So were many Songhai merchants, as well as people who lived in cities like Gao. But the majority of the Songhai—

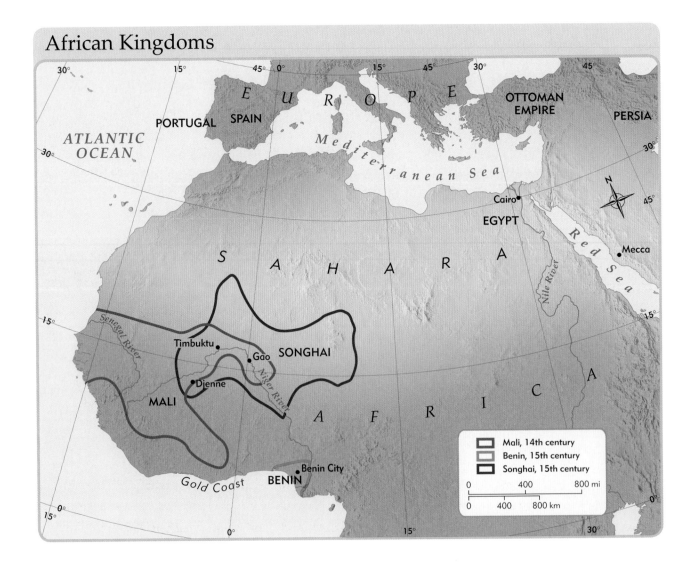

African Kingdoms

Mali, 14th century
Benin, 15th century
Songhai, 15th century

such as the farmers and fishermen who lived in the countryside—never converted to Islam. They went on worshipping the old gods of their people.

To the west of Songhai sprawled the vast Muslim empire of Mali (MAH-lee). Mali had grown rich by controlling the gold trade. In the early 1300s, armies from Mali conquered large stretches of Songhai territory, including the capital city of Gao. For the next few decades, Mali ruled the lands of the Songhai. But eventually Mali's empire began to fall apart. The Songhai regained their independence, and in the 1400s they began to build their own empire.

In 1464, a bold and brilliant warrior named Sunni Ali (sou-NEE ah-LEE) became king of Songhai. He set out to conquer the lands of the crumbling empire of Mali. His skilled cavalry, armed with spears, charged into battle riding horses and camels. His bowmen, dressed in padded armor, fired volleys of poison-tipped arrows. He launched a great fleet of canoes down the river to attack his enemies.

Sunni Ali seemed so invincible in battle that strange rumors about him began to spread. It was said that he was a sorcerer who turned himself into a vulture before battle, and that he gave his men pieces of jewelry that made them invisible to the enemy.

In 1468, Sunni Ali conquered the famed Muslim city of Timbuktu (tim-buhk-TOO). The king was angry with Timbuktu's leaders for allying themselves with enemy tribes. So he allowed his soldiers to burn and loot the city. Some Muslim scholars and holy men were killed; others fled the city.

Later Sunni Ali's forces besieged another important trading city of the old Mali Empire, Djenné (je-NAY). The siege lasted for seven long years. When Djenné finally fell, Sunni Ali proved himself more merciful than he had been at Timbuktu.

The armies of Mali made it a powerful Islamic empire in the early 1300s. Around that time, an artist from Mali fashioned this terra-cotta mounted warrior.

Mali's Mansa Musa

If you read the first volume of *The Human Odyssey*, you met Mali's most renowned leader, Mansa Musa (MAHN-sah moo-SAH), who came to the throne around 1312 and ruled for the next quarter century. He expanded the Mali empire and founded several mosques, libraries, and schools, especially in the city of Timbuktu. Mansa Musa was a Muslim, and in 1324 he made a famous pilgrimage to Mecca, on the Arabian Peninsula. Accompanying him on his pilgrimage were troops, slaves, family members, friends, teachers, and doctors—according to some reports as many as 60,000 people in all. His caravan also included 80 to 100 camel-loads of gold dust, each load weighing about 300 pounds.

He spared the city out of respect for its people's courage. Then, to strengthen the bonds between Djenné and Songhai, he married the mother of Djenné's young king.

Although Sunni Ali was a powerful conqueror, not everyone thought he was a good king. His treatment of the religious scholars of Timbuktu angered many of his Muslim subjects. Writing many years after Sunni Ali's death, Muslim historians condemned him as a cruel and unreasonable ruler. They said that he was always flying into a rage at someone and ordering him to be executed, even if the person had done nothing wrong. It is possible that Muslim historians exaggerated his faults. Whatever the truth, shortly after Sunni Ali's death, another emperor became famous for his devotion to Islam.

Traders and their camel caravans have crisscrossed the Sahara for centuries. Songhai grew rich on trade with the lands north of the desert. Its merchants bought textiles, horses, salt, and cowrie shells. In return, they sold gold, kola nuts, and slaves.

Askia Muhammad: The Devout Emperor

When Sunni Ali died in 1492, his son took charge. Only a year later, a rebellious general overthrew Ali's son. This general, Askia Muhammad (as-KEE-uh moh-HAM-uhd), went on to become the greatest of Songhai's kings.

Under Askia Muhammad, the Songhai empire reached its greatest size, stretching westward all the way to the Atlantic Ocean. Askia seized former territories of Mali and turned towns of the Sahara into colonies of Songhai. Like the old empire of Mali, the empire of Songhai grew rich on trade with the lands to the north of the Sahara. Songhai's merchants imported textiles, horses, salt, cowrie shells, and other goods. They exported gold and kola nuts. And the captives they took in war, they sold as slaves.

Unlike Sunni Ali, Askia Muhammad was known as a devout Muslim. Like Mansa Musa, he went on a famous pilgrimage to Mecca. On the way to the holy city, he stopped at Cairo to visit the caliph of Egypt. (A caliph is a Muslim ruler.) The caliph placed a black turban on Askia Muhammad's head to signify that Askia Muhammad was the rightful Muslim ruler of Songhai. When he arrived in Mecca, Askia Muhammad visited many scholars in an effort to acquire more knowledge about his religion.

Askia Muhammad was away on his pilgrimage for two years. When he came home, he changed the government of Songhai to bring it closer to Islamic law. He made laws based on Islamic teaching and appointed

Muslim judges to the courts. He rebuilt Timbuktu, the city that Sunni Ali had pillaged, into a center of Muslim learning.

Askia Muhammad ran a well-organized and efficient government divided into different departments. Each department had a high official in charge. One official was in charge of fishing, one in charge of farming, one in charge of the army, and so on. The officials reported to the emperor and helped make his reign a time of prosperity for the people of Songhai.

Benin: Kingdom of the Rain Forest

Under Askia Muhammad, the Songhai Empire spread across the vast area south of the Sahara known as the savanna. The savanna is a plain covered with tall grasses, but with very few trees. If a resident of Songhai had traveled hundreds of miles to the south, he would have left the savanna and entered the very different world of the rain forest.

In the African rain forest, gigantic trees soar into the sky and block out much of the light. Unlike the savanna, the rain forest teems with animal life—chattering monkeys, bright-feathered parrots, and frightening snakes such as the python.

In the 1400s and 1500s, as the Songhai Empire rose in the north, another great kingdom called Benin (buh-NEEN) dominated the rain forest and the coastal regions of what today is the country of Nigeria. Benin was inhabited by a people known as the Edo. Like the Songhai, the Edo were fierce warriors and clever traders. But while Islam was a powerful force in the culture of

Askia Muhammad reigned as the greatest of Songhai's kings. He was buried in this pyramid-shaped tomb in Gao, his capital city.

Songhai, it had no influence in Benin, where the people worshipped traditional African gods.

The king of Benin was known as the oba (OH-buh). He lived in a vast palace and stayed largely secluded from his people. The people of Benin, like the ancient Egyptians, worshipped their king as a god. To keep up his godlike image, the oba made sure that his subjects never

Timbuktu Under Askia Muhammad

During the reign of Askia Muhammad, a North African traveler known as Leo Africanus visited Timbuktu. "In Timbuktu," he reported, "there are numerous judges, scholars, and priests, all well paid by the king." Books were so valued that booksellers made more money than any other merchants.

Leo was impressed by the wealth of the city. He reported that instead of coined money the inhabitants used pieces of pure gold, although if they were buying something cheap they paid in seashells.

saw him doing anything merely human, such as eating food. When he left the palace, he rode in the midst of a great procession, surrounded by warriors and musicians. Tame leopards stalked beside him, their leashes held by servants—a symbol of the king's godlike power to control the fierceness of nature.

Brassmakers were highly honored in Benin. One skilled craftsman created this masterpiece depicting the mother of the oba, or king, in the early 1500s.

Under the strong rule of the obas, Benin became a great trading kingdom and a military power that dominated its neighbors. Benin City, the capital, was a large, bustling, well-organized town, surrounded by a high earthen wall seven miles around. In the big central marketplace, people could buy everything from parrots out of the rain forest to cloth from far-off Europe. Broad, straight streets divided the city into different neighborhoods. Everyone who lived in a neighborhood shared the same job or craft. There was a neighborhood of woodcarvers, a neighborhood of weavers, a neighborhood of carpenters, and so on.

• On the map on page 264, locate Benin and Benin City.

The most respected craftsmen in Benin City were the brassmakers. They worked exclusively for the oba himself, casting wonderful images in brass. The walls of the king's palace were adorned with brass plaques depicting scenes of life in Benin—hunters aiming their bows, acrobats twirling on ropes, musicians playing fifes and drums. The brassmakers also created remarkable free-standing statues. Some of the statues depicted animals. These animals usually stood for religious ideas. For example, birds were thought to take messages from the mortal world to the spirit world.

Often an animal sculpture symbolized the oba's power. One Edo artist crafted a pair of regal leopards for the oba. Another fashioned a giant brass python, which the oba placed on the roof of the palace to remind everyone of his power to crush his enemies. (The python squeezes its prey to death.) Still other statues depicted the oba himself or his ancestors. Brass images often showed people wearing a coral headdress with multiple coral necklaces covering their necks and chins (see page 262). The Edo believed that coral had magical power to protect a person from harm.

Today we recognize these richly detailed sculptures as masterpieces of art. The great period of Benin sculpture began around 1500—at the very time when Michelangelo and other artists of the Italian Renaissance were producing some of the greatest works of European sculpture.

The Portuguese Come to Benin

In the 1480s, Portuguese merchants exploring the west coast of Africa started to trade with Benin. The Portuguese traded copper, cloth, wine, and other European goods for ivory and some gold. Soon, however, they became more interested in something else—slaves.

At first the Portuguese weren't interested in shipping slaves to the Americas. Rather, they wanted to trade slaves for gold. The Portuguese wanted to acquire gold from a region in Africa known as the Gold Coast, now the country of Ghana. They didn't always have goods that were acceptable to African traders. But they discovered that if they brought slaves from Benin to the Gold Coast, they could trade the slaves for gold.

Arab and African merchants wanted slaves to work as porters when they crossed the Sahara to the Muslim world. So the Portuguese asked Benin's oba to sell them some slaves, and he agreed. The Portuguese transported these slaves to the Gold Coast and exchanged them for gold.

As Benin sold more and more slaves to the Portuguese, the kingdom became ever wealthier. Benin became one of Portugal's most valued trading partners. Once, the oba sent an ambassador to Lisbon, the capital of Portugal. A Portuguese writer recalled, "This ambassador was a man of good speech and natural wisdom. Great feasts were held in his honor … and he returned to his land in a ship of the king's."

Soon other peoples along the west coast of Africa began selling their captives to the Portuguese. And so, little by little, a new slave trade grew.

Today people sometimes ask how Africans could have sold other Africans into slavery. The answer is that the slaveholders did not think of themselves or their slaves as "Africans." Instead they thought of themselves as Edo, or Songhai, or members of another group. They thought of their slaves as foreigners and inferiors. In the same way, the Spanish,

Left: A brass leopard from Benin symbolizes the power of the oba.

Below: Plaque depicting an oba, or ruler, of Benin

In the 1520s, European ships began to transport African slaves across the ocean to Spanish colonies in the New World. The transatlantic slave trade endured for the next three centuries.

the French, and the English could massacre each other in bloody wars because they thought of themselves as Spanish, French, or English rather than "Europeans."

The Transatlantic Slave Trade Begins

Slavery existed in Africa long before the Portuguese arrived. In many parts of the continent, victors in war often enslaved the conquered. Throughout the Middle Ages, several African civilizations had traded in slaves. Mali, Songhai, and other African kingdoms had grown rich partly by selling slaves to Arab merchants from North Africa. This trans-Saharan slave trade eventually involved millions of Africans, many of them women and children, who were sold in Egypt, Persia, and the Ottoman Empire. Ambitious Muslim rulers, prosperous businessmen, and wealthy merchants all wanted slaves, sometimes as household servants, sometimes as agricultural workers.

But after the Portuguese encounter with Africa, the slave trade began to take on a new and horrifying dimension. Shortly after Portugal began trading with Benin, Columbus landed in the New World. As you've learned, the kings of Spain and Portugal claimed vast territories in the Americas. They conquered the native peoples and forced them to work in fields and mines. But millions of native people died, either in battle or from diseases brought by the Europeans. As the native people died, the supply of workers shrank. So the Spaniards and Portuguese had to look elsewhere for a labor supply. They found it in Africa, where the Portuguese were already trading in slaves.

Beginning in the 1520s, the Spanish hired Portuguese merchants to transport African slaves across the Atlantic to their New World colonies. Slaves were shackled, then crammed into the holds of overcrowded ships.

Benin Says "No More Men"

The ruler of Benin grew concerned about the number of able-bodied men being exported as slaves. In 1516, he restricted the export of male slaves and eventually stopped it altogether. The Portuguese and Spanish found other African suppliers.

Disease, filth, and stench below decks made the journey terrible and often deadly. This was the beginning of the transatlantic slave trade—a trade that went on for three hundred years.

The transatlantic slave trade accelerated in the sixteenth century, when the Portuguese began growing sugar on plantations in their own colony of Brazil. Vast fortunes could be made from sugar, which Europeans loved. It was backbreaking labor to cut the sugarcane and squeeze out the juice. The task required enormous numbers of workers. As the demand for sugar soared, so did the demand for slaves. To satisfy the sweet tooth of Europe, hundreds of thousands of Africans lost their freedom, and many lost their lives.

Portugal and Spain started the transatlantic slave trade. But soon other European nations—England, France, and the Netherlands—joined in the terrible commerce. Over the next three hundred years, African slavers captured as many as eleven million Africans to satisfy the demand for cheap labor in New World colonies. The majority never even made it across the Atlantic. Many were held in slavery in Africa, and others died on the brutal march from their points of capture to the slave ports on the coast. Another one to two million died of disease and mistreatment as they crossed the Atlantic, chained together in the filthy, overcrowded holds of slave ships.

The trans-Saharan slave trade continued, but by 1650 more Africans were being captured for the transatlantic trade than for Saharan trade to the Muslim world. The encounter between Portugal and Benin set the stage for a human catastrophe of tremendous proportions. You'll read more about this catastrophe in a later chapter.

African slaves work on a sugar plantation in the Americas. Slaves replaced the native peoples who died largely as a result of diseases brought from the Old World.

Why Is It the *Middle* Passage?

Slave-trading ships carried their tragic cargo across the Atlantic Ocean, from Africa to the Americas. This ghastly voyage came to be known as the Middle Passage. It got that name because of a three-legged trade route that developed between western Europe, Africa, and the Americas.

On the first leg of the journey, ships carried manufactured goods from Europe to Africa. European merchants sold their cargo on Africa's west coast, and bought slaves. In the second or "middle" leg of the journey, they transported the slaves across the Atlantic and sold them in the West Indies or elsewhere. Finally, the merchants purchased sugar or tobacco, and sailed back to Europe. Because the slave crossing represented the "middle" leg of the journey, it became known as the Middle Passage.

Queen Elizabeth I rides through London in an open litter carried by her courtiers. The reign of "Good Queen Bess" was a golden age in the history of England, a time of great achievement in the arts and exploration.

Elizabethan England and North American Initiatives

O n the morning of January 14, 1559, light snow fell from the gray London skies. Nothing, however, could dampen the enthusiasm of the people lining the streets, eagerly waiting to see the woman who

was about to become their queen— Elizabeth I.

As Elizabeth rode into sight, a great shout went up. She sat in an open litter lined with white satin and edged with gold brocade. On her left and her right marched her honor guard in crimson tunics, carrying gilded battle-axes. In front strode her trumpeters, and behind her walked dozens of ladies-in-waiting. A thousand mounted courtiers brought up the rear.

Words of encouragement greeted Elizabeth all along the way—prayers, good wishes, welcoming cheers. She acknowledged them all with a kind smile, a wave of her hand, a gentle reply.

The next day brought the coronation at Westminster Abbey, where

English monarchs had been crowned since the time of William the Conqueror, almost half a millennium earlier. Trumpets sounded as Elizabeth accepted a ring that symbolically wed her to her people. Then a bishop placed the crown of England on her red head.

Elizabeth was only the second woman in history to rule England as queen. The next half century came to be known as the Elizabethan Age.

Inheriting a Troubled Realm

Elizabeth's father, King Henry VIII, would have been very surprised to see his *daughter* on the throne. Let's look back at how things stood in England at the end of Henry's reign.

This chapter focuses on England in the sixteenth century.

Henry VIII, you recall, was the king who broke with the pope in Rome and established the Church of England. Henry had done everything in his power to make sure he had a *male* heir. Henry married six times in hopes of having sons. To his first wife, the Spanish princess Catherine of Aragon, a daughter was born, named Mary. His second wife, Anne Boleyn, gave birth to Elizabeth. Henry married four more times; his third wife, Jane Seymour, had a son named Edward.

When Henry VIII died in 1547, nine-year-old Edward became England's king. But he ruled England for only six years before he fell ill and died. When Edward died, something unprecedented happened— a woman ascended the English throne. England had never been ruled by a woman. Edward's half-sister Mary became the first queen to rule England on her own, with no king at her side.

Why So Few Queens?

Queens ruling in their own right were rare in Renaissance Europe. Men were thought to be reasonable beings endowed by God with authority. Women were believed to be impulsive, passionate, and inferior in intellect. But the early sixteenth century was a time of turmoil in England. The country had seen strife between Protestants and Catholics. People wondered if England might soon find itself at war with foreign powers such as France and Spain. In such troubled times, the English people thought it was important for the throne to pass peacefully to a rightful heir. They believed that an English queen was infinitely preferable to a French or Spanish king.

Mary, who had been raised by her Spanish mother, was Catholic. She wanted to bring England back to the Roman Catholic Church. When she announced her plan to marry King Philip II of Spain, a revolt broke out among Protestants. She married him anyway.

Queen Mary then revived laws against heresy and tried to outlaw the new Protestant churches. More than three hundred people were burned at the stake for heresy. Many Protestants fled the country.

Mary's reign marked hard times for England. In 1554, thousands of rebels marched on London in an unsuccessful effort to get rid of the woman they called "Bloody Mary."

When Mary died four years later, the crown passed to Elizabeth. England's first experience under the rule of a queen had not gone well. Many wondered whether 25-year-old Elizabeth was up to the task of governing—especially without a husband to guide her.

A New Queen for a New Age

Elizabeth was a woman of many talents. From an early age, she learned how to live with danger, change, and suspicion. For years she moved from one drafty palace to another. She even spent time locked up in the Tower of London when Queen Mary feared that her sister might lead a revolt against her.

Elizabeth was a brilliant student. While her father had desperately wanted a son to inherit the throne, he still made sure that his daughters received excellent educations. Elizabeth studied under the finest scholars

A portrait painted around 1592 depicts Queen Elizabeth as an all-powerful monarch. She stands with her feet planted on a map of England. Behind her, stormy skies give way to the sun—symbol of royal rule and the glory of Elizabeth's reign.

in the land. She learned Latin, Italian, Greek, and French.

The first problem the young queen faced was religious conflict. Unlike her half-sister Mary, Elizabeth was a Protestant. Her father, Henry VIII, had established the Church of England. Then Mary had tried to restore Catholicism as the nation's official religion. This caused angry protests.

Elizabeth tried to find a solution that would satisfy most of her subjects. She declared England a Protestant nation and restored the Church of England as the nation's official church. She made the English monarch head of the church. She replaced the Catholic bishops that Mary had appointed with Protestant ones.

For some time, Elizabeth did not punish Catholics for practicing their religion in private. She said she had no desire to "make windows into men's hearts." That is, she had no interest in dictating people's private beliefs. This tolerance did not last, but Elizabeth's policies helped quiet unrest at home early on.

Francis Drake, the first captain to sail around the world, rests his hand on a globe.

Catholicism in Elizabethan England

In 1571, Parliament declared it treason to question Elizabeth's title as head of the Church of England. That made the practice of Catholicism treasonous, since Catholics believed that the pope was the Church's true head. English authorities confiscated Catholic Church properties. They arrested and tortured those who showed any devotion to the old faith, and executed 183 Catholics between 1577 and 1603.

Meanwhile, however, another problem was looming on the European horizon—Spain.

Francis Drake Takes On Spain

Spain's powerful King Philip II saw himself as a defender of the Catholic Church against the rise of Protestantism. In this cause, he was supported by the pope, the Inquisition, and the Jesuits.

Philip also possessed the wealth of Spain's territories in the New World. In the early 1500s, Spain and its neighbor Portugal led Europe in the exploration of foreign lands. Their sailors and soldiers carved out empires and built trade networks that spanned the globe. Spices, gems, silver, gold, and slaves all crossed the Atlantic in Spanish vessels. Riches beyond imagination poured into the port cities of Spain.

The English saw this wealth and wanted some of it for their own. During Elizabeth's reign, English mariners set sail in a quest for treasure, glory, and overseas territories. English ships began to nose their way into the Caribbean, much to Spain's alarm.

The Englishman who caused the Spanish the most concern was a stocky, redheaded captain named Francis Drake. In 1572, Drake sailed to Panama, one of Spain's colonies. He led his men inland, seized 30 tons of Spanish silver, and slipped back aboard his ship before his enemies knew what had hit them.

Raiding Spanish settlements in the New World became Drake's favorite activity. On his journeys back and forth across the Atlantic,

he preyed on Spanish treasure ships transporting South American gold and silver. Vessel after vessel fell victim to Drake's guns.

The Spanish called Drake a pirate. Queen Elizabeth pretended to disapprove of Drake in public, but in private she thrilled at news of his latest exploits.

In December 1577, with Elizabeth's support, Drake set sail from Plymouth aboard the *Golden Hind*. His job was to seek out opportunities for English trade and settlement. But Drake, who was a superb navigator, had another aim as well—to sail around the world.

First, the *Golden Hind* voyaged down the west coast of Africa, targeting Spanish and Portuguese ships along the way, before crossing the Atlantic to South America. The ship survived a terrible gale in the Strait of Magellan, then sailed up the west side of the continent. There Drake plundered Spanish settlements and ships filled with Inca treasures.

Next, Drake struck out across the Pacific Ocean. For 68 days he saw no land. Finally, after sailing through the Philippines, he reached the Spice Islands of the Indies. Following the route of earlier Portuguese sailors, he crossed the Indian Ocean. The *Golden Hind* sailed around Africa's Cape of Good Hope and up the continent's west coast. By now the ship was leaking badly and riding low in the water, weighed down by tons of silver, gold, and precious jewels.

Drake and his crew finally returned to England three years after they had left. He was the first captain to sail around the world. (Years before, although one of Magellan's ships rounded the globe, the captain himself had died on the homeward journey.)

A royal barge carries Queen Elizabeth toward Drake's ship, the Golden Hind. *Drake's acts of "piracy" outraged the Spanish, but thrilled the queen.*

From Dragon to Golden Knight

The Spanish were outraged at Drake, whom they called "the Dragon." King Philip demanded his arrest. But at home Drake was hailed as a hero. He had single-handedly challenged the idea that Spain alone ruled the seas. He had proved that English mariners could be as bold as sailors from Spain or Portugal. Where Drake had led, other Englishmen were sure to follow.

No one took greater pleasure in Drake's exploits than Elizabeth herself. She invited him to the palace, where he arrived with packhorses carrying treasures for his grateful queen, including a crown set with five huge emeralds.

A short time later, the queen visited Drake aboard the *Golden Hind*. The ship was by then moored on the River Thames (temz), and a noisy crowd of well-wishers followed Elizabeth to the dock. So many people tried to follow her onto the ship that the plank gave way and dozens fell into the river.

Drake escorted the queen around the ship. At one point she told him that the Spanish had demanded his execution. Reaching for a sword, she joked that she should have Drake's head there and then. Instead, she handed the weapon to an ambassador who had accompanied her on her visit. At the queen's command, Drake knelt on the deck. She smiled as the ambassador knighted him by placing the blade on both of Drake's shoulders. When the mariner arose, he was Sir Francis, or as Elizabeth referred to him, "our golden knight."

Tall, handsome, and dashing, Sir Walter Raleigh became Queen Elizabeth's favorite courtier. He established the first English colony in North America.

Walter Raleigh's New World Initiatives

In Elizabethan England, Drake was one of many bold young men driven by dreams of gold, glory, and devotion to their queen. Another was the swashbuckling courtier Sir Walter Raleigh.

Raleigh was an accomplished soldier and sailor. Strikingly handsome, he stood more than six feet tall, at a time when most men were half a foot shorter. He had a dark beard, curly hair, and a reputation for bravado. Twice he had been imprisoned for brawling. On one occasion he had silenced a noisy bully in a tavern by filling the man's mouth with wax and tying his beard to his moustache.

Raleigh was also known for wearing bright colors, gaudy jewelry, and magnificent cloaks. One day, according to a famous legend, he and Elizabeth were walking together when they

This map fancifully depicts English ships approaching Roanoke Island off the coast of Virginia, in what is today the state of North Carolina. Although Raleigh's Roanoke colony did not survive, it inspired other adventurers to establish settlements. England's colonization of North America had begun.

came upon a puddle. With a flourish, Raleigh spread his cloak on the wet ground in order to keep the royal feet dry. The queen was impressed. The legend says that thanks to this act of gallantry, Raleigh became her favorite courtier. She awarded him huge estates in Ireland. Raleigh, however, was more intrigued with the idea of exploring North America.

The queen granted Walter Raleigh permission to establish a colony in North America. For a settlement site, he chose a tiny bit of land off the coast of what is now North Carolina, called Roanoke Island. He named the colony "Virginia," in honor of Elizabeth, who was known as the Virgin Queen since she had never married.

To Raleigh's great disappointment, however, Elizabeth decided she could not spare her favorite courtier. Although Elizabeth refused to let Raleigh go on the voyage to North America, she liked his idea. So Raleigh gave command of the venture to a relative. In April 1585,

six English ships set sail for the New World.

Several months later, the expedition's explorers returned to England. They brought back, among other things, tobacco. England soon learned that North American tobacco was almost as valuable as South American gold. Europeans paid enormous prices for the golden weed. They loved to smoke it and believed it

Why Didn't Elizabeth Marry?

We don't know for sure. Perhaps she never took a husband because she knew that if she did, it would mean giving up some of her power to him. Many suitors pursued Elizabeth over the years, including kings and princes from other countries. In order to gain alliances and keep the peace, she led suitors to believe that she *might* someday marry.

Perhaps the main reason Elizabeth never married was that she felt such a great responsibility to England—in effect, she was already "married" to the English people.

could cure almost any ailment. Raleigh himself liked to smoke tobacco in a silver pipe, much to the queen's amusement.

Raleigh dispatched a second expedition to found a settlement at Roanoke Island. The colony was a failure. The settlers soon disappeared with barely a trace. Although the "Lost Colony" of Roanoke Island did not succeed, Raleigh had laid the foundations for further English colonization of North America. As we'll soon see, many more English settlers crossed the Atlantic in the years to come.

The "Invincible" Spanish Armada

Raleigh's expeditions infuriated the Spanish. He had dared to send Englishmen to the New World, which the Spanish considered to be *their* domain.

Relations between England and Spain worsened. Then Elizabeth took a fateful step. She sent men and money to support Dutch Protestants fighting for independence from Catholic Spain. King Philip II viewed Elizabeth's action as a declaration of war. In the ports of Lisbon and Cádiz, he gathered a huge fleet to invade England.

The English prepared for war. They turned the whole south coast into an armed camp. They established a chain of beacons to provide an early warning of invasion. Containers sited on hilltops and filled with tar-soaked brushwood could be ignited at the first sign of danger. If the Spanish fleet approached the English coast, the warning signal could reach London within 20 minutes.

On July 29, 1588, some 130 enemy ships sailed into English waters. The Spanish Armada, as it was known, had arrived. The pope called it the Invincible Armada. (*Invincible* means undefeatable.) He saw it as part of a holy crusade, on a mission to crush the English, get rid of Elizabeth, and restore England to the Catholic faith.

The Spanish Armada sailed in a great crescent two miles wide as it entered the English Channel. Its towering warships looked like floating castles. And like castles, they were packed with soldiers—some 19,000 of them—armed with muskets, pikes, and grappling hooks, ready for battle. The Spanish plan was to get close enough to the English ships to board them.

But Sir Francis Drake and the other English commanders intended to stay well away from the enemy. Their small, light ships were more

English and French Claims to North America

Five years after Columbus planted Spain's flag in the New World, another Italian explorer reached North America. Giovanni Caboto (joh-VAHN-nee kah-BOH-toh)—whose name has been translated as John Cabot—sailed under the British flag. In 1497, he landed in Canada. England used Cabot's trip as the basis for claims to much of North America.

England's old rival, France, was not idle. Between 1534 and 1536, the French explorer Jacques Cartier (zhahk kahr-TYAY) sailed into the St. Lawrence River. He claimed much of eastern Canada for France. In the seventeenth century, both the French and the English continued to claim more land in North America.

maneuverable than the Spanish vessels. They also had more fire-power. Using their greater mobility and longer-range guns, the English planned to fire broadside after broadside from a safe distance.

As the chain of beacons flashed a warning to all corners of the kingdom, the ships of the Armada swept up the English Channel, their white sails snapping in the wind. Only when they had passed Portsmouth did Drake and his ships venture out. The English sailed around both flanks, keeping their distance.

For four hours the English raked the enemy with burst after burst of cannon fire, unleashing four shots for every one the Spanish let loose. Flames broke out on one Spanish warship, and its gunpowder exploded, killing about 200 crewmen. Another, the 52-gun *Rosario,* collided with its neighbor. It was so damaged it was unable to move. During the night, Drake pounced on the ship and seized the 55,000 gold ducats it carried.

Eventually, the Armada fled for the safety of the French coastline. But during the night of August 7, things got even worse for the Spanish. The English sent eight "hell burners" among the anchored vessels. These small, unmanned vessels were packed with tar, twigs, gunpowder, and loaded guns. The English set them on fire and floated them into the midst of the towering Spanish ships. As the gunpowder exploded, the guns began to fire. The confused Spanish captains sailed blindly in the darkness.

When morning dawned, English warships drove in close to fire their broadsides. The Armada took a terrible battering. When Drake spotted the Spanish flagship, he pounded shot after shot into its side. Amazingly, the vessel stayed afloat. Four ships around it did not. Perhaps 4,000 Spanish soldiers and sailors died that day before the English ran out of ammunition and the fighting ceased.

Where the English left off, nature took over. A fierce storm drove the remaining Spanish ships up the east coast of England toward Scotland. The English called it "the Protestant wind," taking it as a sign from God. More ships sank off the rocky

Distant English "hell burners" approach the anchored ships of the Spanish Armada. The small unmanned, gunpowder-packed vessels caused havoc in the midst of the enemy fleet. English warships closed in for the kill the next morning.

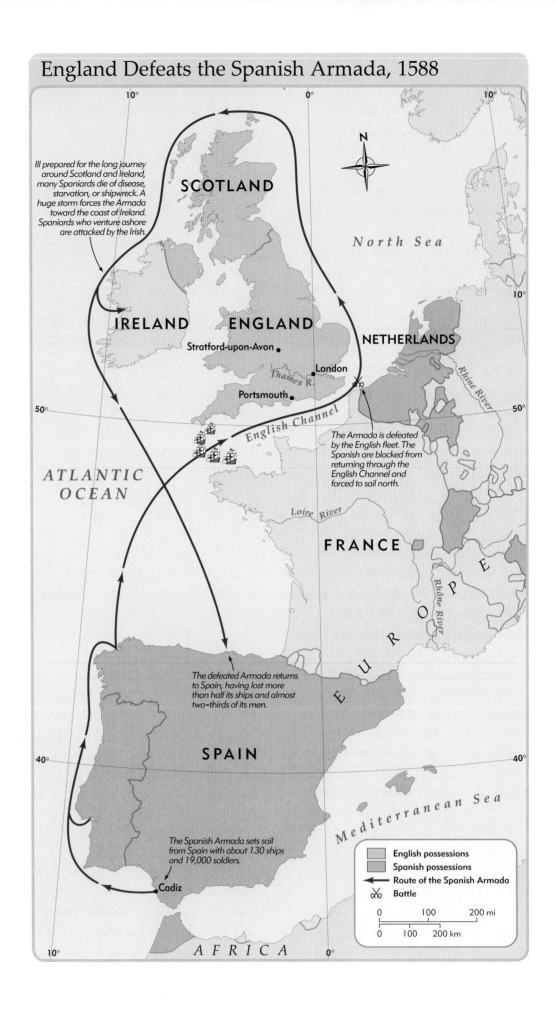

England Defeats the Spanish Armada, 1588

Ill prepared for the long journey around Scotland and Ireland, many Spaniards die of disease, starvation, or shipwreck. A huge storm forces the Armada toward the coast of Ireland. Spaniards who venture ashore are attacked by the Irish.

SCOTLAND

North Sea

IRELAND ENGLAND

NETHERLANDS

Stratford-upon-Avon

London

Thames R.

Portsmouth

The Armada is defeated by the English fleet. The Spanish are blocked from returning through the English Channel and forced to sail north.

English Channel

ATLANTIC OCEAN

Rhine River

Loire River

FRANCE

Rhône River

The defeated Armada returns to Spain, having lost more than half its ships and almost two-thirds of its men.

E U R O P E

SPAIN

Mediterranean Sea

The Spanish Armada sets sail from Spain with about 130 ships and 19,000 soldiers.

Cadiz

A F R I C A

	English possessions
	Spanish possessions
←	Route of the Spanish Armada
✗	Battle

| 0 | 100 | 200 mi |
| 0 | 100 | 200 km |

coasts of Scotland and Ireland, as the remains of the Spanish Armada made its long journey home.

The English had lost a hundred men and none of their ships. The Spanish had lost almost two-thirds of their men and well over half of their ships. The defeat of the Spanish Armada in 1588 cleared the way for England to build its own overseas empire.

A Golden Age

Hostilities with Spain dragged on until the end of Elizabeth's reign. But England was now emerging as a major European power. London became a prosperous city where merchants and shopkeepers thrived. Ships bearing fleece and wool sailed down the Thames and pointed their bows toward Asia, Africa, and the Americas. The island kingdom swelled with confidence and ambition.

Writers breathed new vitality into English poetry and drama. Sir Walter Raleigh himself was a poet, but he recognized superior talent when he saw it. He knew that his patriotic friend, Edmund Spenser, was a master of the craft. In 1590, Raleigh brought Spenser to the queen's attention. Spenser was writing an epic poem called *The Faerie Queene*. The "queen" mentioned in the title was none other than Elizabeth herself. Her majesty was charmed.

Spenser intended the poem to be twelve books long. In each book, a knight met adventure and faced a trial to master a virtue, such as temperance, holiness, or courage. Spenser had three books ready in 1590, and the queen was so pleased she gave

him a pension. He completed the next three books in 1596 but died before finishing the entire work. Spenser blended a strong knowledge of the classics, a love of the English language, and a deep familiarity with Italian writers. Of course, he wrote his epic poem in English.

A knight slays a dragon in this illustration from Edmund Spenser's The Faerie Queene. *The patriotic writer dedicated this epic poem to his real-life queen and patron, Elizabeth.*

A Dedication Fit for a Queen

In *The Faerie Queene*, Edmund Spenser wrote the following dedication to his patron, Elizabeth. (The spelling and punctuation have been modernized here.)

"To the most high, mighty, and magnificent Empress renowned for piety, virtue, and all gracious government—Elizabeth, by the grace of God, Queen of England ... and Ireland and of Virginia, Defender of the Faith, etc. Her most humble servant Edmund Spenser doth in all humility dedicate, present, and consecrate these his labors to live with the eternity of her fame."

It was theater, however, that drew Londoners like a magnet. Theatergoers came from every walk of life, from the humblest worker to lords and ladies. The queen herself delighted in the latest comedy, the most popular tragedy, the grandest historical drama of the day. A gifted generation of writers produced plays not matched since the days of ancient Athens.

William Shakespeare was the greatest playwright of Elizabethan England and perhaps of all time. His portrait appears on the title page of a book of his plays, published in 1623.

M\^R\. WILLIAM,
SHAKESPEARES
COMEDIES,
HISTORIES, and
TRAGEDIES.

Publiſhed according to the True Originall Copies.

LONDON
Printed by Iſaac Iaggard, and Ed. Blount. 1623.

The greatest playwright of them all was William Shakespeare. Shakespeare wrote dozens of plays, 38 of which survive today. His plays held something for everyone, from bawdy humor and hilarious farce to exciting swordfights and tender romance. Through it all, Shakespeare showed the keenest insights into human nature and an unrivaled command of the English language. "The Bard," as Shakespeare is known, drew his inspiration from Greek comedies and tragedies, Italian romances, and English history, as well as from street ballads and folk traditions.

As the seventeenth century approached, the queen who sparked England's golden age was growing old and frail. Elizabeth's thinning hair was now topped with a red wig, her once ruddy complexion enhanced by rouge. Her health was poor. The light that had illumined England for nearly half a century was beginning to lose its glow.

Elizabeth's Legacy

In 1603, Elizabeth died peacefully in her sleep. The remarkable queen had reigned for nearly half a century and transformed England.

When the young woman came to the throne, her realm was an inward-looking island perched on Europe's western reaches. But her shrewd insights and courageous leadership turned the island outward. Naval triumphs allowed the English to challenge Spain for control of the seas. English explorers and adventurers laid claim to previously unknown lands. In this time of growing national confidence, genius flowered in the arts and drama. English men and women—from the boldest of adventurers to the humblest of city-dwellers—felt a new national pride.

By the end of the Elizabethan Age, England was a formidable power with international reach, and the champion of Protestantism in Europe. The nation had successfully challenged its rivals on the seas. It was forging worldwide trading networks. And it had begun to establish colonies in North America. England was poised to influence the course of the human odyssey for centuries to come.

At the Globe with Shakespeare

Stratford-upon-Avon sits about 75 miles northwest of London beside a stream called the Avon. In the mid-sixteenth century, when Queen Elizabeth came to the throne, it counted only about 2,000 inhabitants. People all over the world now know the name of this little town because back in 1564, a Stratford couple named John and Mary Shakespeare gave birth to a son who grew up to become, in the eyes of many, the greatest writer of the English language.

Historical Close-up

Atrumpet blast broke through the edge of the woods. A drum rat-a-tat-tatted its way down the road. The word quickly spread. "The players are coming to town!"

A crowd gathered to watch the small group of traveling performers parade into Stratford-upon-Avon. Children tugged at their mothers' dresses and asked what kind of play they would see. A story about Saint George and the Dragon? The adventures of Robin Hood? The grinning actors unpacked their boxes and slipped into their costumes, and soon the magic began.

Young Will Shakespeare stood in the audience with eyes and ears wide open, soaking up tales. He picked up even more stories at school, which he and his fellow students attended for about nine hours a day. There they memorized Greek and Latin poems. Reading the great writers of ancient Athens and Rome fired Will's imagination, and he stored the ancient tales away in his memory. One day he would breathe new life into them, adding fresh and surprising twists of his own.

We don't know much about Shakespeare's life during these early years. His father practiced glove-making and other trades, with ups and downs in fortune, and Will may have helped in the family business. But by the late 1580s, Will seems to have made his way to London. It's possible he arrived in 1588, the year the Spanish Armada menaced England's coasts.

Nearly a quarter of a million people populated noisy, overcrowded London. Busy markets sold fish, meat, and vegetables. Carts clattered along narrow cobblestone streets filled with shoppers, pickpockets, and beggars. Sewage often filled the gutters, which attracted rats and spread diseases that led to frequent outbreaks of plague.

London Bridge spanned the city's great river, the Thames. Shops and houses crowded the length of the bridge, all the way to the river's south bank, where taverns, gambling dens, and theaters clustered. In those theaters Will Shakespeare found work.

Shakespeare began as an actor, but his real genius lay in writing. During the 1590s, he penned about 20 plays, packed with intrigue, romance, and adventure. In Shakespeare's dramas, scheming princes vie for England's throne. Mischievous fairies play tricks on lovesick youths. Clowns roam the stage spouting words of wisdom.

Most of his plays fall into one of three categories—histories, tragedies, and comedies. The histories, such as *Henry V* and *Richard III*, tell stirring tales of English kings, both good and bad, in times of war or rebellion. The tragedies feature some of the most complex and fascinating characters ever imagined, such as the ambitious Scottish general, Macbeth, or the thoughtful Prince Hamlet of Denmark. *Romeo and Juliet*, one of Shakespeare's most famous tragedies, tells the moving story of a pair of "star-crossed lovers."

THE GLOBE THEATRE.

A flag above the Globe Theatre (foreground) indicates a play will be performed that day.

Shakespeare's comedies, such as *A Midsummer Night's Dream*, are full of mistaken identities and silly complications, all happily resolved by the end of the play.

By 1598, Shakespeare was one of London's most popular playwrights. He and a handful of partners earned enough money to build their own theater on the Thames's south bank—the famous Globe Theatre.

The Globe—"this wooden O," as Shakespeare called it—was an

octagonal building with a courtyard in the middle. Much of the theater stood open to the sky, so the Globe staged plays only in summer. When it rained, no performances took place. And because it had no artificial lighting, performances began at two o'clock in the afternoon. In the morning, a man climbed up to the Globe's turret and raised a silk flag to announce that the actors planned to stage a play that day.

Londoners across the river saw the flag. Hundreds of them, rich and poor alike, began to head toward the Globe. They poured across London Bridge, eager to get there in time to find a good spot. Others crossed by boat, ferried by Thames watermen in small craft called wherries. Just before the play began, a trumpeter gave three blasts to hurry latecomers along.

As many as 2,500 people squeezed into the Globe to see a play—more than the entire population of Shakespeare's hometown of Stratford! The theatergoers passed through a gate in the 30-foot-high walls and dropped their money into a box held by the "gatherer." (That's where we get the term *box office*, which is what we call a ticket office in a theater.)

A penny allowed theatergoers to stand in the courtyard around the stage. These spectators were called the "groundlings." The groundlings often drank too much ale, and they could get rowdy if they didn't like the play. They brought nuts, apples, and pears to eat—or occasionally to throw at the actors. At other times, they sang along to the songs or even jumped onto the stage to join in the sword fights.

Gentlemen who paid two or three pence watched from one of the three galleries, where a thatched roof protected them from the sun. Or they could pay a little more and sit on the stage itself. These richer theatergoers could sometimes be a nuisance. If they lost interest in the play, they talked, smoked, and played cards. Some heckled the actors, while others got up and left, chattering on their way out.

Shakespeare relied on little scenery and few props. A table and chairs might represent a banquet hall, a potted bush the countryside. But the theater did have special effects. The roof of the stage—painted with stars and known as the heavens—held a trapdoor. If a play called for a god to descend from the sky, ropes lowered him through the trapdoor onto the stage. Characters could also appear or disappear through a trapdoor in the floor. Rolling a cannon-ball around offstage created the sound of thunder. And a cannon fired blanks for the battle scenes. An actor in a sword fight might hide a pouch of sheep's blood under his shirt. When stabbed, he pricked the pouch and spilled the blood, much to the pleasure of the groundlings.

About a dozen actors staged plays in the Globe. All were men, because people did not consider acting a fit profession for women. Boys with high voices and beardless faces played the female parts. Actors had to be swordsmen, acrobats, dancers, and musicians to perform their different roles.

Year after year, Shakespeare wrote plays that delighted all members of his audience, from the groundlings to Queen Elizabeth herself. His acting company regularly performed at one of the royal palaces. He even wrote one of his plays, *The Merry Wives of Windsor*, at the queen's request. (According to legend, he dashed it off in just 14 days.)

By 1599, Shakespeare towered over other English playwrights. For the opening of the Globe, he staged one of his most popular comedies, a high-spirited tale called *Twelfth Night*. He filled the play with many crowd-pleasing elements—disguises, mixed-up identities, fast-paced dialogue, and love at first sight. Like many of his comedies, *Twelfth Night* has plot twists that keep the

Queen Elizabeth watches a performance of The Merry Wives of Windsor *at the Globe.*

audience laughing and guessing until the last scene. And like everything written by this master of the English language, it sparkles with memorable lines.

In *Twelfth Night*, Shakespeare tells how a ship wrecks off the rocky coast of an unknown land. The survivors include a young woman named Viola (VIY-oh-luh). She's glad to be alive, but distraught that her beloved twin brother, Sebastian, has drowned in the waves. The ship's captain advises Viola to disguise herself as a young man and seek work at the court of the local ruler, Duke Orsino. Viola takes his advice and introduces herself to the duke as a young man named Cesario. The duke employs "him" as his page. (In other words, a boy actor plays a woman pretending to be a man!)

Soon Viola falls in love with the Duke, but alas, he loves a beauty named Lady Olivia. The Duke sends his page, Cesario—who is, you recall, Viola disguised as a boy—to tell Olivia of the Duke's love. Olivia spurns the Duke's love, but she falls in love with Cesario—that is, with the disguised Viola!

Meanwhile, it turns out that Viola's twin brother, Sebastian, did not drown, but was rescued and has landed safely on shore. When he chances upon the home of Lady Olivia, she promptly mistakes him for the page she loves. And Olivia's beauty dazzles Sebastian. Can you see why Shakespeare's comedies always leave the audience wondering what will happen next?

You'll have to read *Twelfth Night* to find out how the confusion finally clears. As in many Shakespearean comedies, the play ends with a song:

When that I was and a little tiny boy,
With hey, ho, the wind and the rain,
A foolish thing was but a toy,
For the rain it raineth every day.

. . . .

A great while ago the world begun,
With hey, ho, the wind and the rain.
But that's all one, our play is done,
And we'll strive to please you every day.

Please the audience, they did. The groundlings filed out of the theater, each a penny poorer but looking forward to Will Shakespeare's next play at the Globe.

A: Symbol of English monarchy—the crown used
for centuries in the coronation of England's kings
and queens

B: A seventeenth-century map of Virginia, England's
first colony in North America

England: Civil War and Empire

*E*ngland thrived under the rule of Queen Elizabeth. During her reign, England's navy came to rule the seas. English merchants prospered. The English theater produced drama for the ages. And the little island nation extended its reach across the Atlantic to North America.

Elizabeth came from the royal family known as the Tudors. When she died unmarried and childless, she left no Tudor heirs. Legend has it that on her deathbed Elizabeth whispered the name of her successor—her distant cousin, King James VI of Scotland, a member of the Stuart royal family. He became King James I of England.

When James was crowned in 1603, for the first time in history the kingdoms of England and Scotland were united under a single monarch. But James I did not unite much else. Under James and the Stuart kings that followed him, England was torn by struggles that led to civil war.

These troubles at home prompted some Englishmen to look abroad. For various reasons, many set sail for the English colonies in North America.

Let's focus our attention on England in the seventeenth century, first on the home front, and then on England's colonies overseas.

James Causes Strain

In 1603, the English people warmly welcomed their new king. Like Elizabeth, James was Protestant, so the people were confident that he would support the Church of England. He had two sons, one of whom could someday inherit the throne. And he brought the kingdoms of England and Scotland under one crown, promising peace between

James VI of Scotland became James I of England, uniting the two kingdoms. He was the first of the Stuart kings of England.

two nations that had often fought in the past.

- On a globe or world map, find the island known as Great Britain. Find England and Scotland.

What Is the Difference Between England and Great Britain?

Great Britain is the large island off the northwest coast of Europe. In 1603, England (which then included the western province of Wales) covered the southern two-thirds of this island, and Scotland covered the northern third. When James I came to the English throne that year to rule both England and Scotland, people began to refer to the inhabitants of this united realm as "British," and to the joined domains as "Great Britain."

Great Britain, c. 1603

The English people soon discovered that James was a proud man who had strong ideas about kingly power. He believed in the divine right of kings—the idea that kings received their power directly from God. He said kings were answerable to God alone, and not to Parliament.

England's Parliament was the body of bishops, nobles, and elected representatives who advised the English king and helped make laws. Some form of Parliament had existed in England since the Middle Ages. In the seventeenth century, Parliament consisted of two main bodies. The first, the House of Commons, was made of representatives elected by men who owned property. The second, the House of Lords, was made of nobles who inherited their titles or were appointed to Parliament by the king. Some high-ranking clergy of the Church of England also sat in the House of Lords.

As king, James I tirelessly lectured both houses of Parliament about his divine right. By this time, however, Parliament had acquired important rights for itself. Chief among them was the right to raise taxes. If the English king needed money, he had to go to Parliament to ask for new taxes. If Parliament said yes, the king got his new taxes; if they said no, he didn't.

King James needed money. He had inherited debts from England's long years of war against Spain. And he lived in luxury. In four years of peace, he practically doubled the debt left by Elizabeth. Yet James did not like to ask Parliament for money. So how could he pay his debts?

James tried to go around Parliament. He did not ask their permission for new taxes on the English people. Instead, he decided to raise money for his expenses by imposing import duties—taxes on goods entering English ports. Since import duties were not a direct tax on the people, and since they were a traditional way for English kings to raise money, James believed he did not need Parliament's permission. This angered many members of Parliament. More and more, James found himself at odds with Parliament.

King James and the Puritans

At this time, many members of England's Parliament were Puritans. Puritans followed the teachings of the Protestant reformer John Calvin. They wanted to "purify" many practices of the Church of England.

The Puritans claimed that the Church of England was too much like the Roman Catholic Church. Like the Catholic Church, the Church of England had bishops, ritual prayers, and elaborate ceremonies. And just as the Catholic Church was headed by the pope, the Church of England was headed by the king or queen.

The Puritans wanted to change the way the Church of England was governed. They wanted to do away with many ceremonies and simplify many practices. Because they dissented—which means "disagreed with"—many actions of the Church of England, the Puritans were sometimes called dissenters.

At a meeting in 1604, the Puritans presented their demands to reform the Church of England. They hoped that King James, who was himself a Calvinist, would support their cause. The king did agree to one of the Puritans' requests—he authorized a new English translation of the Bible. But James rejected all demands to change the government of the Church.

The King James Bible

In 1604, King James authorized a historic translation of the Bible into English. You may remember that during the Reformation, scholars had begun to translate the Bible into the vernacular—the native language of a place. Martin Luther had translated the Bible from Latin into German. In England, many critics said the English translations did not truly represent the original texts. James wanted a scholarly English translation that would closely follow the original Hebrew and Greek.

Forty-seven scholars undertook the task. They followed strict rules in order to make sure that no single translator would impose his individual beliefs or style on the text. The result was a literary masterpiece. First published in 1611, it is known as the King James version of the Bible. Its stories, rhythms, and language have had a profound and lasting effect on literature written in English.

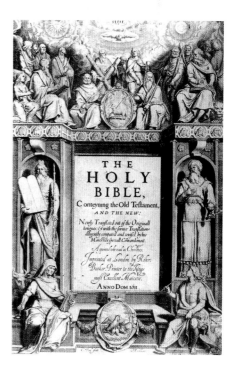

James's son, the foppish King Charles I, tried to rule England as an all-powerful monarch. His disagreements with Parliament pushed the country into civil war.

came to the throne in 1625, and things got even worse.

Like James before him, King Charles I insisted on the divine right of kings. For a time, he dissolved Parliament—that is, he sent its members home—and tried to rule on his own.

Charles's father, King James, had disappointed the Puritans. But Charles himself caused great alarm among the dissenters, particularly when he married. His bride, Henrietta Maria, sister of the king of France, was a devout Catholic. And the Puritans, of course, were opposed to all things Catholic.

In 1640, a war with rebellious Scots forced Charles to call Parliament back into session. Its members were in no mood to cooperate. Charles wanted money for the war. But the Puritan members wanted the king to accept limits on his power and admit Parliament's right to meet regularly.

Urged on by his queen, Charles decided to take action against the key troublemakers. On January 4, 1642, he did something no English king had ever done. At the head of a group of armed guards, he marched into the House of Commons and tried to arrest five members.

The public was outraged. Charles had gone too far. Thousands of soldiers rushed to defend Parliament against the king. Days later Charles fled from London.

In the end, the Puritans were disappointed in King James. He did not support their demands to change the government of the Church or simplify its ceremonies and rituals. And his luxurious habits offended the Puritans' preference for plain and simple ways.

Charles I Clashes with Parliament

During the reign of King James I, the king and Parliament often quarreled. After James died, his son Charles

The English Civil War: Cavaliers vs. Roundheads

By the summer of 1642, the English people were divided. On one side were those who supported the king. On the other side were those who supported Parliament. England was on the verge of a civil war.

Those who backed the king were known as Royalists. Because many of them were dashing horsemen, they also became known as Cavaliers. (The word *cavalier* comes from the Italian word *cavaliere* for "horseman.")

Parliament's Puritan supporters were called Roundheads. They obtained that nickname because some wore their hair cropped short and round against their faces.

Both sides were armed and ready. They had cavalrymen, musketeers, and gunners manning cannons.

When the fighting began, both sides had successes on the battlefield. But gradually the Roundheads began to forge a well-trained and dedicated army. It was led by one of Parliament's leaders, Oliver Cromwell. Cromwell had no previous military experience, but he soon proved to be a brilliant organizer and soldier.

The Roundheads fought the king's armies across England, especially in the north and west of the country, where the Royalists had most support. Thanks to Cromwell, they won great victories. Cromwell, a devout Puritan, said he saw "the hand of God" at work in the victories of the parliamentary forces.

By 1648, the Royalists were defeated. Many people blamed King Charles for continuing the war and causing so much bloodshed. They believed the king should no longer rule England. Some Puritans in Par-liament went further. They believed the king had committed crimes against the nation, and that for these crimes, he should pay with his life.

The Execution of Charles I

The Roundheads captured Charles and brought him to London for trial before a special court set up by Parliament. The court declared him "a tyrant, traitor, murderer, and public enemy to the good people of this nation." The court sentenced him to "death by the severing of his head from his body."

On January 30, 1649, Charles stepped onto a scaffold erected outside the royal palace of Whitehall. It

During England's civil war, Oliver Cromwell led the Roundhead army of Parliament to victory against the Royalist forces of the king. In this painting, the boy fastening Cromwell's sash is his son Richard.

A liuely Representation of the manner how his late Magesty was beheaded uppon the Scaffold Ian:30:1648:

King Charles (second from right) stands on a scaffold and addresses the crowd before being beheaded. After the Roundheads captured the king, a parliamentary court declared him a tyrant and sentenced him to death.

was a cold day, and he wore two shirts so that no one would think he shivered with fear. He prayed and lowered his head onto the block. The executioner swung his axe. The English had killed their king.

A few Royalists rallied to support the king's teenage son, Prince Charles. But Cromwell quickly put down the last remaining resistance. After a final defeat, Prince Charles managed to escape capture. Disguised as a lady's maid, the prince fled to the south coast. There he boarded a boat for France and sailed to safety.

Cromwell and the Commonwealth

After the execution of Charles I, Parliament declared the end of the monarchy. England, they said, would no longer be ruled by a king or queen. Instead, Parliament declared England a republic, to be governed by the people's representatives.

The period of the republic became known as the Commonwealth. Real power, however, was not held in common. It belonged to the army and to the man who had built that army into such a force, Oliver Cromwell.

The Parliamentary army drew up England's first written constitution, the Instrument of Government. This constitution placed a "lord protector" at the head of the government.

Oliver Cromwell became England's lord protector. According to the constitution, he would work with a new Parliament, which would make the country's laws. But, like James and Charles before him, Cromwell also had his problems with Parliament. In the end, Cromwell closed Parliament by force and decided to govern without it. The lord protector now ruled England as a military dictator.

During the Commonwealth, the lord protector exercised greater power than Charles or James ever had as king. Cromwell and his Puritan supporters closed theaters and other forms of entertainment that they saw as immoral or evil. They banned Christmas and Easter celebrations, which they claimed were based in pagan traditions. And they tried to force people to accept Puritan religious beliefs.

Cromwell's army invaded Ireland and Scotland, crushing all resistance and bringing both under his control. The lord protector also won a war against Spain, gaining new territory for England in the Americas.

1660: The Restoration

By the late 1650s, the English people had had enough of Cromwell's military dictatorship. Many longed for a return of the monarchy. They began to look back to the years under King Charles as the good old days.

When Oliver Cromwell died in 1658, Parliament met again. The body that had struggled for so long against two Stuart kings decided the country should invite a new Stuart to the throne. Parliament invited Prince Charles, who had fled England a decade earlier, to return from France.

On May 29, 1660, the son of the executed Charles I rode into London. Cheering crowds lined the streets to welcome him back. The 30-year-old prince remarked that he had never known he was so popular in England. He ascended the throne as King Charles II. The time of the Commonwealth was over. England was restored to monarchy.

The nation thrived during the Restoration, as this period of English history is known. Theaters reopened. Elegant buildings rose in the capital. Philosophers, architects, and scientists made great advances under the reign of Charles II.

Charles had learned some lessons from his father's death. He knew that any king who ignored the wishes of

Crowds of cheering Londoners welcome Charles II back to the English capital on May 29, 1660. The return of the Stuarts to the throne is known as the Restoration.

Parliament did so at his own risk. So he began his reign by doing his best to maintain good relations with Parliament, while Parliament kept the powers it had fought so hard to win.

In religious matters, Charles II formally supported the Church of England. But his mother, Henrietta Maria, had been French and Catholic. So Charles had Catholic sympathies. Both the king's official support of the Church of England and his suspected loyalty to Catholicism made Puritans unhappy.

Meanwhile, many Englishmen remembered how Cromwell and his Puritan supporters had closed theaters and banned Christmas during the days of the Commonwealth. They were tired of the Puritans' strict ways and in no mood to make them feel welcome. During the Restoration, a number of Puritans left England. Charles II was happy to help dissenters find ways to leave, sometimes by granting them gifts of land in North America.

Let's turn now to look across the Atlantic and find out what the British had been doing in North America since the reign of James I. Just as the power of Parliament grew during this time, so did the English empire overseas.

England Reaches Across the Sea

During the reign of Queen Elizabeth, England's first attempts to colonize the North American continent did not end well. As you learned, Sir Walter Raleigh sent out two groups of colonists, but the first group returned within a year, and the second simply disappeared.

These early failures did not dampen English interest in North America. Explorers told of thick forests, rich soil, and abundant wildlife. And as always, there was the lure of gold.

For decades, the English had watched jealously as Spain brought back shiploads of gold, silver, and other treasures from its empire in the New World. The English thought: If there was gold in South America, then why shouldn't there be gold in North America as well?

The first permanent English settlement in North America began as a quest for gold. In 1606, King James I granted a charter to a group of private investors to form the Virginia Company of London. The company's mission was to colonize Virginia and find gold on the eastern shore of North America.

The Virginia Company sent 104 men across the Atlantic in search of treasure. Just as the colony of Virginia had been named after Elizabeth, the Virgin Queen, these new colonists named their settlement Jamestown in honor of their king.

- On the map on page 305, locate Jamestown.

A Hard Start at Jamestown

Jamestown was a swampy spot alongside a broad waterway that the colonists named the James River. (They tried to flatter the king by naming everything after him.) The settlers, all male, were divided between upper-class gentlemen looking for adventure and poor vagrants from the streets of London. From the moment they landed in the spring of 1607, they were more interested in hunting for gold than building homes. When gold didn't appear, they still resisted the hard work of planting crops, building shelter, and finding fresh water. They preferred to play cards and argue over who was eating more than his share of the dwindling supplies.

The result was fatal. Hunger and disease killed most of the men. Within nine months, all but 38 of the original 104 colonists had died. It looked like Jamestown might turn into another "Lost Colony."

But the Virginia Company sent more settlers, and in 1608 a red-bearded man named Captain John Smith took charge. He forced every colonist to work six hours a day, planting in the fields and building a fort. Anyone who didn't work, he said, didn't eat.

The colonists grumbled about Captain Smith's rules. When an accident forced Smith to return to England in 1609, many colonists were relieved. But they suffered without his discipline, and the winter after his departure became known as "the starving time."

Left: Captain John Smith was one of the early leaders of Jamestown, the first permanent English settlement in North America. Smith forced the settlers to work in the fields and build a fort.

Below: Jamestown sits on the edge of the wilderness next to the James River, which, like the settlement itself, was named in honor of England's King James I. Inside the wooden palisades, the settlers constructed a church, a storehouse, and houses.

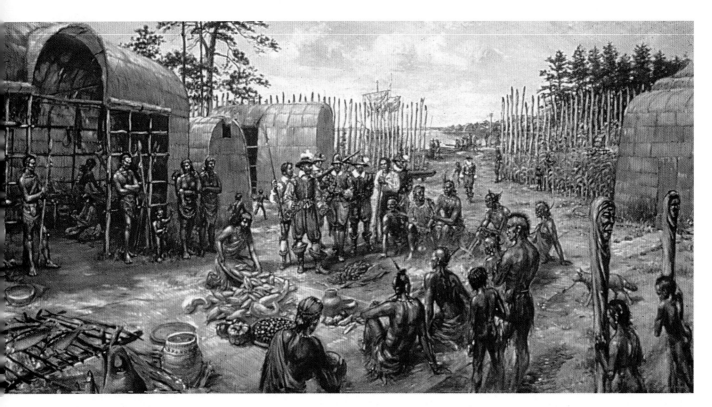

The English traded with the Indians at Jamestown. In order to survive, the Jamestown settlers had to depend on the local Powhatan Indians for corn and other food.

To survive, colonists bought, begged, and stole food from the Powhatan (pow-uh-TAN) Indians. Finally, the exhausted men decided to give up and return to England. They were just sailing into the Chesapeake Bay when they met three relief ships sent by the Virginia Company. One of the ships carried a new governor who ordered everyone back to Jamestown.

In all, the Virginia Company sent about 10,000 men and eventually women to Jamestown between 1607 and 1622. Only one out of every five colonists survived.

The Eastern Woodland Indians

The Powhatan were a small but important Eastern Woodland tribe who lived in the area that is now Virginia. They ruled a group of more than 30 tribes known as the Powhatan Confederacy. These people hunted, fished, farmed, and settled in small villages.

Unlike the Aztecs in Mexico or the Inca in South America, Eastern Woodland Indians were not city-builders. Nor were they as numerous. The densely forested wilderness of North America's eastern seaboard was sparsely populated. While the Aztec city of Tenochtitlán had 150,000 inhabitants, a large village on a river in North America might have just a thousand. Also, smallpox had spread rapidly north, and the disease devastated the Eastern Woodland tribes in the late 1500s, just before the arrival of the English.

Tobacco and Slavery

The Jamestown colony survived because of an idea pursued by one man, John Rolfe. As you might recall from your studies of American history, Rolfe was the Englishman who married Pocahontas, daughter of Powhatan, the Indian chief. Rolfe saw how well tobacco grew in Virginia's hot and humid summers. He watched how his wife's people cultivated their crops.

In 1612, under Rolfe's direction, the Jamestown colonists planted their first tobacco crop. They sent their harvest back to England, where tobacco sold for five to ten times as much as it cost to grow in Virginia. At last the colony had a "cash crop," a way of supporting itself and paying for supplies from England. In Virginia and elsewhere in the south, plantations sprang up to grow this "brown gold."

It was hard work to grow tobacco. Where would Virginia farmers get the labor they needed to cultivate their crops?

In 1619, a Dutch ship pulled into Jamestown. Aboard were the first abducted Africans to land in North America. Like the Spanish and Portuguese, who used slaves on their sugar plantations in the West Indies and Brazil, planters in Virginia saw African labor as the solution to their problems. (In a later chapter, we will examine slavery in more detail.)

Although the tobacco boom saved the colony, it came too late to keep the Virginia Company from bankruptcy. King James took control of Virginia as the first royal colony in the new English empire.

Seeking God in Plymouth

Before the Virginia Company dissolved, it granted a small part of the colony to some Englishmen living in the Netherlands, including two named William Bradford and William Brewster. Bradford and Brewster were leaders of a group of Separatists. Separatists were Puritans who had grown so discouraged with the Church of England that they separated from the Church and formed their own congregations.

Bradford and Brewster had led their Separatist group to the Netherlands, hoping to find a place where they could worship as they wished. But they decided they didn't want to raise their families in the Netherlands. These two Englishmen looked to North America as a land where they might worship God as they saw fit.

Only 35 Separatists were willing to make the first voyage, too few to start a colony. So Bradford and Brewster advertised for other colonists. Sixty-seven people who were not Separatists—"strangers," as the Separatists called them— volunteered. This group of Separatists and strangers eventually became known as the Pilgrims.

In 1620, the Pilgrims—who included men, women, and children —leased an old wine ship named the *Mayflower*. They loaded it with food, furniture, supplies, dogs, goats, sheep, and poultry. On the long, crowded voyage across the Atlantic, the Separatists and strangers got on each others' nerves.

The Pilgrims prepare to set sail from England aboard the Mayflower *in 1620. Many of the passengers were Separatists— Puritans who had broken with the Church of England. They traveled to the New World to find the freedom to worship God in their own way.*

The Mayflower carried the Pilgrims to Plymouth, far to the north of Virginia, in what is now the state of Massachusetts. Winters there were long and cold. To survive, the Pilgrims had to build shelter soon after they landed. They began work on Christmas Day, 1620.

Things became especially tense when they realized the *Mayflower* had gone far off course. The land they were approaching was far north of the land they had been granted in Virginia. Some of the strangers said this change canceled their original agreement to follow Separatist rules.

But the Pilgrims recognized that if they hoped to survive in this new land, they would have to work together. So before they went ashore, 41 men, the heads of every household, gathered in the ship's cabin and signed an agreement known as the Mayflower Compact. The Pilgrims said they joined together into a "civil body politic" and that they would meet from time to time to

The Mayflower Compact

When the Pilgrims signed the Mayflower Compact in November 1620, they pledged loyalty to King James. But the colonists went on to declare that they would meet from time to time to make laws for their colony. Thus the Mayflower Compact set an important precedent for later colonies: While the colonists were loyal to the British crown, they assumed from the start that mostly they would govern themselves.

pass "just and equal laws" for the general good of the colony. The signers all pledged to respect the laws enacted by their fellow colonists.

In late 1620, the *Mayflower* arrived at that part of the New World now called Massachusetts. After a few weeks of exploring the coast, the Pilgrims came ashore at a place they named Plymouth. They knew this wasn't Virginia and they had no permission to stay, but the biting wind was so cold that they could not bear to sail any farther. So they decided to remain on this rocky piece of land.

- On the map on page 305, locate Plymouth.

The next few months were brutally cold. Hunger and disease killed half of the Pilgrims. But in the spring, the survivors did not, as the Jamestown settlers had done, waste time playing cards, arguing over supplies, or searching for gold. The Pilgrims believed they honored God best when they worked hard. So, following the advice of a Patuxet Indian named Tisquantum (also known as Squanto), they planted crops, fished, hunted, and built houses. By the autumn of 1621, they had so much food that they were able to invite Squanto and other Indians to a three-day feast of thanksgiving.

Puritans in New England

While some Puritans remained in England to confront the king with their demands, others boarded ships for America. In 1629, one group of Puritans established themselves as the

Massachusetts Bay Company. They asked King Charles I for a royal charter to settle near Plymouth.

The king granted the company authority to "govern and rule all of His Majesty's subjects that reside within the limits of our plantation." (In the seventeenth century, the English sometimes used the word *plantation* to mean a new settlement in the Americas.) This remarkable charter made the Massachusetts Bay Company in most respects a self-governing community. Once in America, the company set up a representative form of government in which Puritan men elected their governor, their deputy governor, and a legislature known as the General Court.

Why did King Charles I allow so much self-government in Massachusetts and in other colonies? Perhaps he was coming to understand that England would not get gold, silver, and other treasures from North America, the way Spain had from South America. The most the king could hope for was that some settlements might send back timber and fur, and someday start paying taxes.

Also, Charles had plenty on his mind without having to worry about running the North American colonies. He needed fewer enemies and more friends. Why not use the land in America to reward friends or get rid of enemies? Charles, you remember, often clashed with the Puritans in Parliament. If more Puritans went to North America, then there would be fewer to trouble Charles at home.

So Charles was generous in his grants of North American land. Before Oliver Cromwell became lord protector, Puritans settled most of the region that came to be called New England.

Maryland: Another Gift from Charles I

One Englishman to whom Charles I granted North American land was Cecilius Calvert. Calvert's father had been a high official under King James. But when Calvert's father revealed he was a Roman Catholic, not a member of the Church of England, he had to leave the government. Nevertheless, the Calvert family remained loyal to the king. Their loyalty paid off. In 1632, Charles I awarded Cecilius Calvert, also known as Lord Baltimore, a charter for twelve million acres at the northern end of the Chesapeake Bay.

Lord Baltimore named the new colony Maryland. He said he was naming the colony after King Charles's wife, Henrietta Maria. But he probably had another motivation as well. Lord Baltimore wanted Maryland to be a safe haven for Catholics. So it's likely he intended the colony's name to honor not just the queen but also the Virgin Mary.

Because Lord Baltimore wanted to prove that Catholics and Protestants could live together peacefully, he opened the colony to any Christian. He appointed his younger brother, Leonard Calvert, governor of the colony, and sent him to America in 1634 with two shiploads of Catholics and Protestants.

To encourage settlement of the colony, the governor offered one

After four English warships sailed into New Amsterdam harbor, the Dutch governor, Peter Stuyvesant, surrendered the city and the colony of New Netherland. The English renamed the place New York in honor of the Duke of York, brother of King Charles II.

hundred acres, free, to every adult settler. Soon Lord Baltimore's original colonists were outnumbered by Puritans and another religious group called Quakers. These newcomers were fleeing the nearby colony of Virginia, where the Church of England still outlawed their religious beliefs. They were welcome in Maryland, which in 1649 had passed a law guaranteeing toleration for all religions.

Charles II Expands the Empire

King Charles I watched with dismay as other countries claimed portions of the continent that he believed belonged to England. For example, a Dutch company laid claim to an area it called New Netherland. The capital, New Amsterdam, quickly became a busy port on the island of Manhattan. King Charles was so

busy with civil war and unrest in England that he did little to resist the Dutch claim.

King Charles I did not live long enough to see the English take action against the Dutch. But in 1664, when Charles I's son, Charles II, was king, four English warships sailed into New Amsterdam harbor and aimed their guns at the homes of Dutch merchants. The commander of the warships demanded the surrender of the colony.

The Dutch governor, Peter Stuyvesant (STIY-vuh-suhnt), wanted to fight for his colony. But his soldiers did not have enough dry gunpowder, and the settlers of New Amsterdam begged him to surrender before their homes were destroyed. Angrily, but without a shot, Governor Stuyvesant handed over New Netherland. The English took control of the colony and changed its name to New York. The city of New Amsterdam was also renamed New York. The English named both the colony and the city in honor of the Duke of York, brother of King Charles II.

Charles II encouraged more colonization. He followed his

Quakers: The Society of Friends

Quakers are members of the Religious Society of Friends. When this Protestant denomination began in seventeenth-century England, its followers were dubbed "quakers" after their leader told an English judge that he should "tremble at the Word of the Lord."

England's North American Colonies, c. 1705

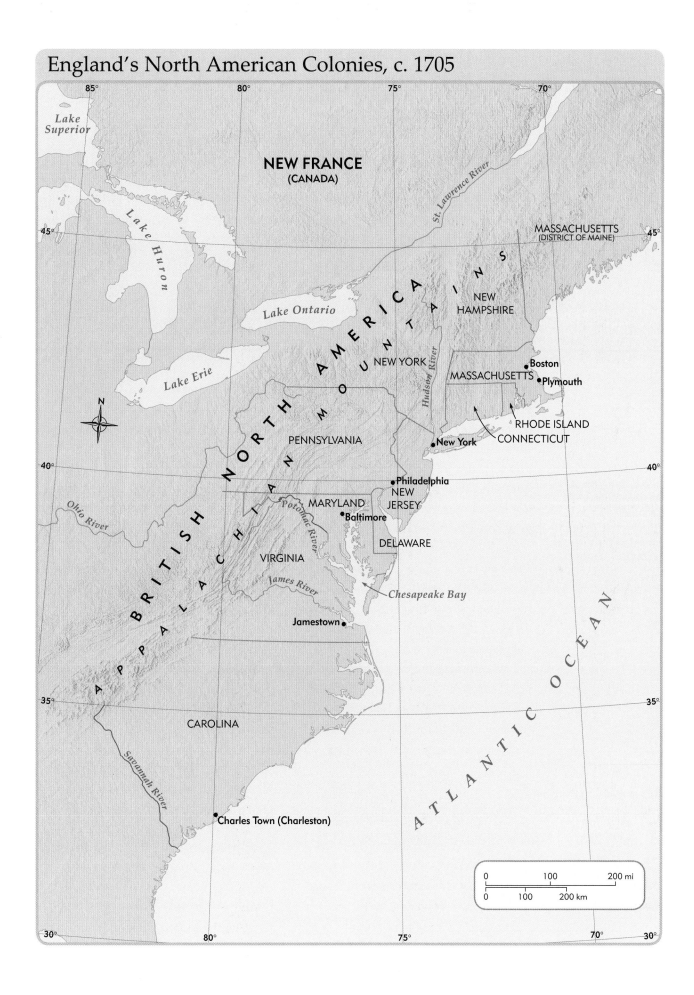

Lake Superior

Lake Huron

Lake Ontario

Lake Erie

NEW FRANCE
(CANADA)

St. Lawrence River

MASSACHUSETTS
(DISTRICT OF MAINE)

NEW
HAMPSHIRE

NEW YORK

Hudson River

MASSACHUSETTS

●Boston
●Plymouth

RHODE ISLAND
CONNECTICUT

B R I T I S H   N O R T H   A M E R I C A

A P P A L A C H I A N   M O U N T A I N S

PENNSYLVANIA

●New York

Ohio River

●Philadelphia
NEW
JERSEY

MARYLAND

Potomac River

●Baltimore

DELAWARE

VIRGINIA

James River

Chesapeake Bay

Jamestown●

CAROLINA

Savannah River

●Charles Town (Charleston)

A T L A N T I C   O C E A N

0   100   200 mi
0   100   200 km

N

William Penn, a Quaker, founded the colony of Pennsylvania. Penn tried to treat fairly the Indians who lived in Pennsylvania. He also welcomed people of other faiths to the colony. He named its largest settlement Philadelphia, "the city of brotherly love."

father's example of making land grants to reward friends and rid himself of enemies. A large tract of unsettled land lay between Virginia and Florida. In 1663, Charles II gave this land to eight English nobles. They sent settlers to their new colony of Carolina. With its rich soil and the fine harbor of Charles Town (now Charleston) in the south, the colony appeared to have a promising future. Tobacco grew well there, and rice and indigo also became important crops.

Another large English colony got its start because King Charles II owed sixteen thousand pounds to the powerful Penn family. The elder Penn, an admiral in the British navy and a friend of the king, had loaned the money when the king needed it. The admiral's son, William Penn, caused a scandal when he became a Quaker. During the Restoration, many Quakers, including young Penn, were thrown in jail for their beliefs.

When Penn was released from jail, he went to Charles II to remind the king of his debt to the Penn family. To pay the debt, the king gave William Penn the colony that he called Pennsylvania, which means "Penn's Woods." Penn was determined to create a colony where all religious faiths would be welcome.

Other Europeans, mainly Swedes and Dutch, were already living in the land granted to Penn. They were soon outnumbered by the English, who were attracted by Penn's promise of religious freedom and self-government. Philadelphia, Penn's "city of brotherly love," quickly grew into a thriving colonial city.

England's Diverse Colonies

By 1705, 11 English colonies had grown up along the eastern seaboard

Why Carolina?

Carolina took its name from *Carol,* which is Latin for Charles. The colony of Carolina was huge. It did not officially divide into North and South Carolina until 1712. A later king of England, King George, took back a piece of South Carolina. This piece became the colony called—you guessed it—Georgia.

of North America. Some were owned by individuals, such as Penn or Calvert. Some, like Virginia, were owned by the crown. Some, like Massachusetts Bay, were owned by companies. All were loyal to the English king.

In contrast to the Spanish colonies, England's North American colonists mostly governed themselves. The English colonies had not produced fabulous wealth in gold or silver, so the king had never demanded strong control.

Nearly every American colony had its own elected assembly that passed laws for the colonists. Colonists had to own property in order to vote for representatives to the assembly, but property was cheap, so many male colonists voted. Each colony also had its own governor. The governor was sometimes appointed by the king, but he was often paid by the colonial assembly—which made him especially responsive to the wishes of colonists.

As the English colonies became more settled and less dangerous places, more Europeans were willing to make their homes there. England's North American colonies, where labor was in demand and land was inexpensive, offered a ray of hope to many English peasants who were being forced off the land.

In England, many landowners had decided to enclose their fields and use them for grazing sheep. The European wool industry boomed, but peasants who had been farming the land now had to find new homes. Some decided to become indentured servants—they traded their freedom

for a voyage across the Atlantic and a commitment to four to seven years of labor in someone else's fields. Many of the immigrants who arrived in the colonies after the 1630s came as indentured servants. One English pamphlet written in the late seventeenth century called the colonies "the best poor man's country."

Meanwhile, British and Dutch merchants had become involved in the transatlantic slave trade. Starting in 1619, they brought African laborers to the shores of Virginia. These first Africans were considered indentured servants. But by the 1660s, Africans were coming to America as slaves with no prospect of freedom. The southern colonies, with their large tobacco and rice plantations, came to rely increasingly on slave labor.

By around 1700, England's diverse North American colonies were engaged in an active trade with the mother country. They were sending lumber, fur, rice, tobacco, and even iron ore to England. They were buying manufactured items like pins, fine cloth, thread, and guns from England. All seemed well—for the time being.

Colonists load a ship with Virginia's most valuable export— tobacco. England's North American colonies thrived by the end of the seventeenth century. They also exported lumber, fur, and rice back to the mother country.

For many centuries, since the time of the ancient Greeks and Romans, people believed that the Earth stood still at the center of the universe. But this seventeenth-century engraving shows the Earth and other planets circling the sun—a new insight achieved during the Scientific Revolution.

The Scientific Revolution

During the Renaissance and the Age of Exploration, Europe was charged with a new spirit of inquiry and adventure. Leonardo da Vinci pursued many paths of knowledge, while Michelangelo breathed life into stone. Columbus and Magellan sailed uncharted waters. Shakespeare dramatized both the folly and glory of the human spirit in some of the greatest plays ever written.

As you've learned, many artists and writers of the Renaissance fell in love with the literature, art, and architecture of ancient Greece and Rome. Inspired by classical models, they created bold new works. Curiously, however, while this high regard for classical works and ancient philosophy opened new worlds for Renaissance writers and artists, it discouraged original thinking about how the natural world works.

For many centuries, people assumed that ancient Greek and Roman ideas about the physical world were correct. For example, in the early 1500s, astrologers and alchemists studied classical texts as they tried to explore what they saw as mysterious, hidden forces in nature. Astrologers watched the stars move and tried to predict the future. Alchemists tried to discover ways to turn lead into gold.

Of course the stars cannot predict the future and lead cannot turn into gold. And yet, even though astrologers and alchemists were looking for knowledge in the wrong

Medieval astrologers tried to tell the future by observing the stars and other heavenly bodies.

places, they were looking—they were curious about nature. That curiosity, when combined with a willingness to question ancient ideas, opened the way to important new discoveries about the natural world and how it works.

During the 1600s, in a period known as the Scientific Revolution, scholars began to make great progress in understanding the workings of nature. They looked closely at the natural world and questioned explanations that had been accepted since ancient Greek and Roman times. We're about to meet some of the leading thinkers of the Scientific Revolution, including Galileo Galilei (gal-uh-LAY-oh gal-uh-LAY-ee) and Isaac Newton. But first we'll learn about two figures from the mid-1500s—the physician Vesalius (vuh-SAY-lee-us) and the astronomer Copernicus. Their work laid the foundations for big changes to come.

Vesalius Explores the Human Body

In the early 1500s, doctors had little real knowledge of how the human body functioned or what caused most diseases. Instead they relied on what they read in classical texts.

Through the Middle Ages and into the Renaissance, medical students learned human anatomy—the study of what's inside the body and how the parts function—by reading the works of Galen (GAY-luhn). Both students and teachers believed that this Greek physician knew just about everything there was to know about the human body.

Galen's methods were advanced for his time—the second century A.D. He learned much by dissecting the bodies of dogs, pigs, and monkeys. He wrote many volumes to explain his ideas about how the human body works.

For many hundreds of years, no one questioned Galen's authority. It seemed that he had said all there was to say about treating the human body. But in the 1500s, Vesalius, a physician from Flanders, began to question what Galen had written.

Vesalius taught anatomy at the University of Padua in Italy. He taught by cutting into dead human bodies and showing his students the different organs inside.

The more Vesalius peered into corpses, the more he noticed that Galen was often wrong. He finally figured out why. In Galen's day, dissecting human corpses was forbidden. Galen had probably never looked inside a human body. Instead he had cut into the bodies of dogs or pigs, and guessed about human anatomy based on what he saw there. But the organs of dogs and pigs are very different from human organs.

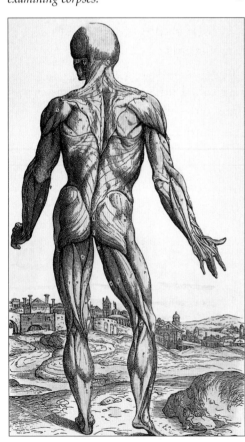

Vesalius's careful description of the human body changed the study of anatomy and the practice of medicine. The Flemish professor made breakthroughs by cutting into and carefully examining corpses.

In 1543, Vesalius published *On the Structure of the Human Body*, a book based on his own careful observations. Vesalius hired fine Renaissance artists to illustrate the book. This masterful work gave the first really accurate and detailed picture of human anatomy.

Copernicus Explores Heavenly Bodies

The year in which Vesalius published his study of the human body, 1543, also saw the publication of a book by the Polish astronomer Nicolaus Copernicus. In a way, this book—*On the Revolution of Heavenly Bodies*—turned the world on its head.

When Copernicus first studied the stars, he learned the ideas of Ptolemy (TAH-luh-mee), an astronomer and geographer of Greek descent who lived in ancient Egypt into the second century A.D. Just as Europeans in the early 1500s trusted Galen as the authority on medicine, they looked to Ptolemy as the authority on astronomy.

According to Ptolemy, the Earth stood still at the center of the universe, and the sun and the planets revolved in great spheres around the Earth. Most people accepted this idea. After all, they saw the sun "come up" in the morning and "go down" at night. So it made sense to think that the sun moved and the Earth stood still. It seemed obvious.

But Copernicus questioned the obvious. When he applied mathematics to the movements of the sun and the planets, he found that Ptolemy's ideas didn't add up. He came to the radical conclusion that the Ptolemaic (tah-luh-MAY-ik)

understanding of the universe was wrong. The sun didn't revolve around the Earth. Rather, said Copernicus, the Earth—along with the other planets of the solar system—revolves around the sun. Mathematically, that was the only conclusion that made sense.

For three decades Copernicus worked to put his ideas into writing. "When I considered how absurd my doctrine would appear," he wrote, "I long hesitated whether I should publish my book." Some friends did convince him to publish it. But by then Copernicus was old and sick. In fact, he barely lived to see his book published. Legend has it that his friends placed the first copy in his hands just before he died.

Observation, Experimentation, and Mathematics

At first, not many people accepted the discoveries of either Vesalius or Copernicus. But their work pointed the way toward the Scientific Revolution of the 1600s. They showed the importance of observation and experimentation—two central features of modern science.

Vesalius learned from Galen but he did not unquestioningly accept everything Galen had written.

The Polish astronomer Nicolaus Copernicus studies the night sky. His observations made him doubt the conclusions of Ptolemy, who had said that the sun and the planets revolve around the Earth.

Geo or Helio?

Ptolemy's theory that the Earth is the center of the universe is called the "geocentric" theory. *Geo* is the Latin root for "Earth." Copernicus's idea that the sun is in the center became known as the "heliocentric" theory. *Helio* is Latin for "sun."

Like Copernicus, René Descartes refused to accept without question the beliefs of ancient Greek and Roman thinkers. The inquiring Frenchman believed mathematics could unlock the secrets of the heavens.

Cartesian Coordinates

René Descartes had weak lungs, a condition that caused him to spend much time resting in bed. He got into the habit of doing much of his thinking in bed. In fact, he was lying in bed when he came up with one of his most famous ideas.

One morning Descartes saw a fly buzz through the air and settle on the ceiling. He began to think about the best way to describe its exact location. He imagined two lines on the ceiling, one vertical and the other horizontal, each passing through the fly. He realized that if he called the vertical line y and the horizontal line x, he could describe the fly's position as "where x meets y."

His idea of locating a point where two lines come together came to be called the Cartesian coordinate system, after Descartes himself (from the Latin spelling of his last name—Cartesius). Cartesian coordinates allow people to draw a graph to describe an object's position or size. Descartes is often called the father of modern mathematics because of his coordinate system and other mathematical insights.

Instead, as Vesalius learned about anatomy by examining human corpses, he tested the old understandings against his own observations of nature.

Copernicus also showed the way for future scientists. He demonstrated that while careful observation is important, observation alone can sometimes be deceptive. After all, observation seems to show that the sun goes around the Earth. To get at the truth, we often have to consider more than one kind of evidence. Copernicus tested his observations by applying the calculations of mathematics to the data he had collected.

The approaches of Vesalius and Copernicus were reinforced in the early 1600s by two other thinkers who helped initiate the Scientific Revolution. One was the Englishman Francis Bacon, the other the Frenchman René Descartes (ruh-NAY day-KAHRT).

Both Bacon and Descartes criticized the thinkers of their time for unquestioningly accepting the writings of ancient Greek and Roman philosophers. Both Bacon and Descartes wanted to develop a more reliable way to acquire knowledge about the physical world. But they had different ideas about how to do this.

Bacon reinforced the approach used by Vesalius in his studies of the human body. First and foremost, said Bacon, scientists should rely on what they can observe with their senses. His work reinforced the need for experimentation. Scientists, he said, should only accept ideas that have been proven through repeated observations and practical experiments.

Descartes, however, extended the approach used by Copernicus in his studies of the solar system. Descartes emphasized the use of mathematics. For the French thinker, no experiment could be as reliable as the logical proofs of mathematics.

These two approaches—the experimental and the mathematical—could work together, as demonstrated in the lives of the next two scientists we'll study, Galileo and Newton.

Galileo Reaches for the Stars

In 1581, a young Italian named Galileo Galilei entered the University of Pisa to study medicine. The short, stocky student had a fiery spirit. He constantly challenged his professors. He refused to believe that anything was so just because they said it was. He never accepted an idea unless he saw evidence that it was true. Galileo was so argumentative that his teachers gave him a nickname— "The Wrangler."

Although an outstanding student, Galileo soon lost interest in medicine. Instead he developed a passion for mathematics. He was such a brilliant mathematician that he became a professor of mathematics at the age of 25. He taught first at Pisa and then at the University of Padua, where Vesalius had taught a generation before.

While teaching at Padua, Galileo started designing scientific instruments. He came up with a new and improved kind of thermometer as well as an improved compass. Then, in the year 1609, Galileo heard about a remarkable new invention—a metal tube with glass lenses inside that you could look through to make far-off things seem closer. This invention, the telescope, was becoming popular all over Europe. But people considered it little more than a toy. The lenses in the tube were weak, so you couldn't see very far, and what you saw looked blurry.

Galileo recognized that if he could make a better telescope, it could become a powerful tool for scientific research. Within a few months, he managed to design a telescope 10 times more powerful than earlier models. Galileo's telescope had a power of 30—that is, it made something 30 miles away look as if it were only 1 mile away.

Galileo Galilei demonstrates his telescope to the leading citizens of Venice. His discoveries made him the best-known astronomer of his time.

One night, Galileo turned his telescope toward the sky. What he saw amazed him and changed the course of history. Ptolemy had taught—and many people still believed—that the moon had a smooth, polished surface. But peering at the magnified moon, Galileo saw that Ptolemy was wrong. He saw that the moon's surface was, as he later wrote, "rough and uneven" with "lofty mountains and deep valleys," similar to the surface of the Earth.

Thrilled by this "beautiful and delightful sight," Galileo kept studying the heavens, night after night. He discovered that the Milky Way—that large white blur stretching across the night sky—was really "a mass of innumerable stars planted together in clusters." He also discovered four moons orbiting the planet Jupiter.

Before making these discoveries, Galileo had never been greatly interested in astronomy. He had read about Copernicus's ideas, and had thought that they made more sense than Ptolemy's. But now Galileo had evidence that seemed to confirm Copernicus's ideas. Through his telescope, Galileo saw that Ptolemy was wrong to say that all heavenly bodies revolved in great spheres around the Earth. The moons revolving around Jupiter seemed to disprove that idea. The more Galileo observed the night sky, the more convinced he became that Copernicus had been right.

In 1610, Galileo published a book titled *The Starry Messenger*, which described the "great and marvelous sights" he had seen through his telescope. At the end of the book he showed that he agreed with Copernicus. The Earth, he wrote, does not sit at the center of the universe but instead "travels over a mighty orbit about the Sun."

Galileo's Celestial Observations

A Page from the Past

Galileo, who insisted on observation and experimentation, became known as the father of experimental science. In this selection from The Starry Messenger, *Galileo describes how he constructed a telescope and what he observed with it.*

A Fleming is a person from Flanders.

To *give credence* is to accept as true.

Refraction is the change in direction of light when it goes from one medium (such as air) into a different medium (such as glass).

A *convex* lens is curved outward. A *concave* lens is curved inward.

About ten months ago a report reached my ears that a certain Fleming had constructed a spyglass by means of which visible objects, though very distant from the eye of the observer, were distinctly seen as if nearby. Of this truly remarkable effect several experiences were related, to which some persons gave credence while others denied them. A few days later the report was confirmed to me in a letter from a noble Frenchman at Paris, Jacques Badovere, which caused me to apply myself wholeheartedly to inquire into the means by which I might arrive at the invention of a similar instrument. This I did shortly afterwards, my basis being the theory of refraction. First I prepared a tube of lead, at the ends of which I fitted two glass lenses, both plane on one side while on the other side one was spherically convex and the other concave. Then placing my eye near the concave lens I perceived objects satisfactorily large and near, for they appeared three times closer and nine times larger than when seen with the naked eye alone. Next I constructed another one, more accurate, which represented objects as enlarged more than sixty times. Finally, sparing neither labor nor expense, I succeeded in constructing for myself so excellent an instrument that objects seen by means of it appeared nearly one thousand times larger and over thirty times closer than when regarded with our natural vision.

It would be superfluous to enumerate the number and importance of the advantages of such an instrument at sea as well as on land. But forsaking terrestrial observations, I turned to celestial ones, and first I saw the moon from as near at hand as if it were scarcely two terrestrial radii away. After that I observed often with wondering delight both the planets and the fixed stars, and since I saw these latter to be very crowded, I began to seek (and eventually found) a method by which I might measure their distances apart….

Now let us review the observations made during the past two months…. Let us speak first of that surface of the moon which faces us. For greater clarity I distinguish two parts of this surface, a lighter and a darker; the lighter part seems to surround and to pervade the whole hemisphere, while the darker part discolors the moon's surface like a kind of cloud, and makes it appear covered with spots…. From observations of these spots repeated many times I have been led to the opinion and conviction that the surface of the moon is not smooth, uniform, and precisely spherical as a great number of philosophers believe it (and the other heavenly bodies) to be, but is uneven, rough, and full of cavities and prominences, being not unlike the face of the Earth, relieved by chains of mountains and deep valleys.

Galileo sketched the rough lunar surface as he saw it through his telescope. These drawings show the Earth's shadow on the moon.

Superfluous means unnecessary.

Terrestrial means relating to the Earth; *celestial* means relating to sky or the heavens.

The term *terrestrial radii* is an astronomical measure of distance.

Galileo Under Fire

Galileo based his writings on observation, experimentation, and mathematics. His discoveries made him the most famous astronomer of his time. One poet declared that Galileo was a greater explorer than Columbus, because he explored distant stars and planets without ever leaving home. The famous Medici family of Florence made Galileo their court mathematician.

But if some people found Galileo's discoveries exciting, others found them disturbing. Some officials of the Catholic Church argued that the ideas of Copernicus and Galileo went against the teachings of the Bible. According to the Bible, they said, God made Earth as a special home for man, so it was much more than just a planet among other planets. Besides, they said, some parts of the Bible clearly show that the sun moves while the Earth stays in one place. In the Book of Joshua, for example, God works a miracle by making the sun stand still.

Faced with these arguments, Galileo, as he always did, argued back. People should not always read Scripture literally, he said. True, the Bible writers talked about the sun standing still. But they were giving a poetic description, Galileo insisted, not stating a scientific fact. Galileo said that the Bible was not an astronomy textbook. "The Bible shows us how to go to heaven," he declared, "not how the heavens go."

Galileo failed to convince his religious opponents that Copernicus's view of the universe was accurate. In 1616, the Catholic Church called

the ideas of Copernicus foolish and absurd. It banned any books containing the new astronomical ideas. Threatened by the power of the Church, Galileo fell silent—but only for a time. After a few years he was challenging authority again, and more boldly than ever.

In 1632, Galileo published *Dialogue on the Great World Systems*, another book defending Copernicus's ideas. The leaders of the Church were furious. Galileo had defied the Church's law by writing the book. Even worse, he had written it not in Latin, the language of scholars, but in Italian, the language of the people. The book sold widely, and Galileo's ideas spread quickly.

Galileo was called to Rome to face the Inquisition—the dreaded court that punished people for going against the teachings of the Catholic Church. Galileo went on trial. He knew that he faced torture and execution unless he told the Inquisitors what they wanted to hear.

For the first time, Galileo backed down from a fight with authority. He signed a paper taking back his radical ideas. He claimed to agree with the Church that the sun revolved around the Earth.

Why did Galileo submit? Perhaps he was frightened. Perhaps he gave in because he was now old and tired of fighting. Or perhaps he wanted to stay alive in order to make more discoveries.

After his trial, Galileo continued to do important scientific work. When he died in 1642, many people mourned the passing of the man they honored as the greatest scientist in Europe.

Over the next few decades, scholars translated Galileo's *Dialogue* into many different languages. The printing press rapidly spread his ideas. People all over Europe began to embrace the new astronomy. The Church may have silenced Galileo, but it could do nothing to stop the spread of his ideas.

Isaac Newton Pulls It Together

In 1643, a year after Galileo died, a boy named Isaac Newton was born in England. Newton's father died before he was born. His mother hoped that when the boy grew up, he would take over her farm. But young Isaac had no interest in farming. When he was supposed to be watching the cows, he would sit under a tree and read.

One of Newton's teachers, who saw the boy's brilliance, convinced his mother to send him to Cambridge University. At Cambridge, Newton immersed himself in physics, mathematics, and astronomy. He devoured the writings of Copernicus and Galileo. At the same time he made his own astronomical observations, tracking comets as they flared across the night sky.

Newton earned one degree at Cambridge and started work on a higher degree. Then in 1665, disaster interrupted his studies. Bubonic plague broke out in London, killing thousands of people a week. When the plague spread to Cambridge, the university closed down. Newton went off to live in the countryside for two years.

Although he had to leave the university, the move helped Newton advance in his work. He always worked best in solitude. Now, in the quiet of the country, he came up with new and revolutionary ideas.

According to a well-known story, one day, while Newton was sitting in his garden, he watched an apple fall from a tree. This started him musing about gravity, the mysterious force that draws things toward the Earth. How far, Newton wondered, did gravity extend? Everyone knows that if you throw an apple from the top of a tall mountain, it will fall toward the Earth, just as if it were falling from a tree. So gravity must extend to the highest places on Earth.

Newton speculated further. Perhaps, he thought, when an apple falls, not only does the Earth exert a force on the apple, but the apple also exerts a force on the Earth. Perhaps gravity is the force that pulls all objects toward each other. Maybe, thought Newton, the moon is pulled toward the Earth just as the apple is pulled toward the ground. Maybe, in fact, it is the force of gravity that keeps the moon in its orbit around the Earth. If this is so, Newton reasoned, then it must be gravity that keeps the Earth and the other planets locked in their orbits around the sun. Newton had arrived at the theory of universal gravitation—a theory that revolutionized astronomy.

A popular legend says that an apple falling from a tree started Isaac Newton thinking about the force of gravity. His theory of universal gravitation revolutionized astronomy and physics.

During his two years in the countryside, Newton made breakthroughs in other fields. He invented a new branch of mathematics that could be used to calculate the speed, direction, and position of moving bodies like the planets. (Today we call this branch of mathematics "calculus.") He also performed important experiments on the nature of light. Aiming a ray of white light through a prism, Newton saw how it separated into rays of different colors. White light, he had discovered, was actually made up of the many different colors of the spectrum.

After the university reopened, Newton returned to Cambridge to continue his studies. He was so successful that within a couple of years the university made him a professor of mathematics.

Newton Ponders "The Great Ocean of Truth"

Newton was what people today call an "absentminded professor." Completely focused on his scientific work, he neglected his appearance, walking around with unbrushed hair and messy clothes. Sometimes he even forgot to eat. When Newton gave a lecture, the students often found his ideas so hard to understand that they got up and left. Lost in thought, Newton went on talking to the empty room.

But this odd and unsociable scholar was producing the most advanced scientific ideas of his time. Calculus, Newton's new mathematics, allowed him to describe the movements of the planets far more accurately than they had been described before. In a book called *Mathematical Principles of Natural Philosophy*, Newton laid out three laws of motion that are still the basis for studying how things move. Newton argued that all the objects in the universe— from moons and planets to balls and apples—obey these same laws.

It was no easy task to read Newton's book. One day a student pointed to the scientist and said, "There goes the man that wrote a book that neither he nor anyone else understands." But for those who could understand Newton's work, it implied something thrilling. Newton seemed to be saying that, through science and mathematics, human beings could come to understand the fundamental workings of the universe. Nothing seemed beyond the grasp of the human mind.

As Newton went on developing his ideas in astronomy, mathematics, and physics, he became the most admired and celebrated scientist of his time. In 1703, he was elected president of the Royal Society, the main scientific organization in Great Britain. In 1705, he was knighted. His fame spread far beyond his own country. The tsar of Russia even traveled to England to meet him.

In 1727, Newton came to the end of his long and brilliant life. Shortly before he died, he told a visitor that his discoveries had not really been very important. "To myself," said Newton, "I seem to have been only like a boy playing on the sea-shore and diverting myself in now and

Newton directs a ray of sunlight through a prism, splitting it into the colors of the rainbow. He proved that white light is made up of different colors.

The first telescope Newton made to observe the heavens was only six inches long and one inch in diameter—yet it magnified more than 30 times. His beloved telescope stands next to his book, Mathematical Principles of Natural Philosophy.

then finding a smoother pebble or a prettier shell than ordinary, while the great ocean of truth lay all undiscovered before me."

Almost no one else agreed with Newton's humble view. Most people recognized that Newton had opened vast new realms of knowledge. They would have agreed with the later words of the English poet Alexander Pope, who wrote:

> Nature and Nature's laws lay hid
> in night;
> God said, "Let Newton be," and
> all was light.

The Promise of Science

Galileo and Newton blazed a new path. In effect, they opened the way for modern science as we know it. Science became a distinct way of gaining knowledge about the

natural world through careful observation, experimentation, and mathematics. All over Europe, educated people talked about the latest scientific discoveries and inventions. Governments poured money into special organizations in which scientists could share the results of their research.

One such organization was England's Royal Society, which Newton had served as president. This society had a Latin motto, *Nullius in Verba*, which loosely translates as "On the words of no one"—meaning that none of its scientists automatically accepted the claims of past authorities such as Galen or Ptolemy. Instead, they pursued truth through observation, experimentation, and mathematics.

Vesalius, Copernicus, Bacon, Descartes, Galileo, Newton—these are some of the most brilliant minds that contributed to that great and gradual change in thinking that we now call the Scientific Revolution. Beginning in the mid-1500s and proceeding through and beyond the 1600s, the Scientific Revolution replaced old views of nature as the workings of mysterious, hidden forces. Instead, thinkers began to experiment and observe very carefully. They wrote down their observations, communicated their evidence to others, and used math in new ways. They began to understand much more about the workings of nature, from the flow of blood in the human body to the movements of the heavenly bodies. Science, the organized study of how nature

Newton's Three Laws of Motion

Newton published his *Mathematical Principles of Natural Philosophy* in 1687. Because its title was originally in Latin—*Philosophiae Naturalis Principia Mathematica*—it is often referred to as the *Principia* (prin-SIH-pee-uh). In the *Principia*, Newton acknowledged that the work of his scientific predecessors, such as Galileo and Descartes, enabled him to develop his ideas about motion.

Here, in simplified terms, are Newton's three laws of motion:

1. Inertia: A body in motion will stay in motion, and a body at rest will remain at rest, unless acted on by an unbalanced force.
2. The force of an object is equal to its mass times its acceleration.
3. For every action there is an equal and opposite reaction.

works, was born—and that, some would say, marked the birth of our modern world.

The Scientific Revolution disturbed some people. The discoveries of Copernicus and Galileo, they thought, made the universe seem like a more mechanical, less friendly place. The Earth was no longer the center of the universe, but instead only one of numberless planets in a dark void. The human inhabitants of this small planet were no longer the rulers of creation. The revolution in science, these people thought, lessened the dignity of man.

But many others disagreed. To them, the Scientific Revolution added to the store of human potential. It brought an end to the idea that ancient thinkers knew all there was to know. It helped give birth to our modern notions of progress—that people can increase their knowledge of the world by discovering principles of nature, and that they can create things to improve their lives. Newton had revealed that the universe followed certain laws, and that human beings could understand these laws. There seemed to be few if any limits to what the human mind might achieve.

Queen Elizabeth I of England watches as a scientist performs an experiment with electricity and magnetism. From the mid-1500s on, the Scientific Revolution changed people's views of the world.

The Enlightenment was a time of confidence in the power of reason and education to improve society. French Enlightenment philosophers tried to organize all knowledge into a huge encyclopedia.

The Enlightenment:
An Age of Reason

G alileo Galilei in Italy and Sir Isaac Newton in England helped launch the movement known as the Scientific Revolution. By observing, experimenting, and calculating, they made important new discoveries about the natural world and how it works. To them, nature seemed to operate in rational, orderly ways that could be explained by mathematical principles, such as the laws of motion that Newton formulated.

Galileo and Newton had focused on investigating the *physical* world. Now other thinkers began to ask: If there are laws that govern the physical world, might there also be laws or principles that apply to the *social* world, the world of human activity and government? If reason structured the physical world, then might reason also be found in the social world?

To that question, many thinkers confidently answered, Yes—and furthermore, they said, we can understand and explain these laws or principles by applying the power of human reason. As the seventeenth-century English philosopher John Locke affirmed, reason must be "our last judge and our guide in everything."

It was not the first time in history that people placed confidence in the power of reason. Ancient Greek philosophers and Renaissance humanists had looked to reason as their guide. But on the heels of the Scientific Revolution, many thinkers felt a new optimism. Scholars began to examine all aspects of human life, from the power of kings to the role of religion. They were sure that through reason, people could examine their

This chapter focuses on ideas that swept both sides of the Atlantic in the 1600s and 1700s.

world and improve it. Some boldly predicted they could even perfect human nature itself.

This period from the 1600s to the late 1700s became known as the Age of Reason. It has also been called the Enlightenment, because so many thinkers believed that reason could illuminate truth.

John Locke's Stormy Youth

According to John Locke, reason was "the candle of the Lord set up by Himself in men's minds." Locke's writings on how human beings learn and how they should govern themselves helped transform the world around him.

Born in 1632, Locke lived during a troubled period of English history. He once wrote, "I no sooner perceived myself in the world than I found myself in a storm." In part that storm was caused by the friction between King Charles I and the English Parliament. Charles insisted on his "divine right" to rule, while Parliament insisted on its own rights.

When John Locke was just 10, his Puritan father marched off to fight alongside fellow Roundheads in the English Civil War against Charles I. A few years later, when Locke was a student in London, the king faced execution on a scaffold near the boy's school. His schoolmaster refused to allow the boys to attend the execution.

Locke went on to attend Oxford University during the time that Oliver Cromwell ruled the country. At Oxford, Locke studied medicine and turned to the new experimental sciences. He became a physician. In

1668, he was invited to become a member of the Royal Society, the scientific organization that brought together some of the best minds of England. Soon, Locke turned his active mind from science to politics and philosophy.

Plotting Against the King

In 1660, Charles II, the son of the executed king, was restored to the English throne. For Locke, it seemed that now, after the stormy years of his youth, calm days might lie ahead. Indeed, things went well during the early years of King Charles II. But by the 1680s, the political storm clouds were gathering again.

Like his executed father, Charles II found Parliament troublesome, and tried to rule without it. Once again English nobles became angry when the king did not consult them. Many landowners had grown wealthy from the booming wool trade, and they resented having no voice. Similarly, English merchants

and cloth manufacturers thought they should be heard, but Charles did not listen.

Another thing troubled many of the English people: Charles II had no direct heir. His brother James was next in line for the British throne. This worried the mostly Protestant populace, because James was a Roman Catholic. English men and women still told tales of the country's last Catholic monarch, "Bloody Mary." They feared that if James became king, he would also persecute Protestants and try to return England to Catholicism.

Some people, including one of Locke's close friends, began to plot against Charles and James. In 1683, one group planned to assassinate the two royal brothers at the same time. But before they could strike, their plot was discovered. As arrests began, Locke fled England for the Netherlands.

Did John Locke take part in the assassination plot? Historians do not have enough evidence to know for sure. But apparently he worried that his safety was at risk. And his writings show that he did not approve of the way King Charles ruled.

Locke, Natural Law, and Natural Rights

From 1683 to 1688, Locke wrote and worked for change from his new home in the Netherlands. He came to believe that just as certain principles or "laws of nature" govern the physical world, there are also moral laws at work in the universe. Locke called this moral order "natural law." According to Locke, natural law has always existed. It is timeless. It existed before any king ever issued a command or any government ever exercised power.

Locke argued that people can discover this natural law by using reason. In Locke's view, reason tells us that murder is naturally wrong. So is stealing. Moreover, Locke argued, reason makes it apparent that even before any government existed, people had certain rights. Among the "natural rights" Locke specified are the rights of life, liberty, and the ownership of property. "No one," Locke declared, "ought to harm another in

Charles II rides through the city of London before his coronation. The restoration of the monarchy in England seemed to promise a time of peace and stability. But then the English people began to fear that Charles's successor, his Catholic brother James, would persecute Protestants if he came to the throne. Some began to plot against the two brothers.

John Locke believed that "natural law" governed the moral order of the universe.

his life, health, liberty, or posses-sions." The job of governments, he claimed, was to respect natural law and protect natural rights.

Locke said that even kings were subject to natural law, just like everyone else. Kings must exercise power for the good of the commu-nity, not for their own self-interest. Reason, said Locke, tells us that it is the obligation of kings to protect the natural rights of their subjects.

And what if a ruler failed the test of reason? What if he became a tyrant who, as Locke put it, "makes not the law, but his will, the rule"? In such circumstances, Locke con-cluded, "it is lawful for the people … to resist their King."

Back in England, Locke's native land, that is exactly what people were doing. English men and women were planning to resist their king.

1689: The Glorious Revolution

In 1685, about a year and a half after John Locke fled to the Neth-erlands, King Charles II died. His brother James became king. The fears of many Protestants were soon realized.

King James II began to appoint Catholics to high positions in the army, government, and universi-ties. When his subjects protested, he simply ignored them. Like Charles, he relied on royal power and ruled without Parliament.

English Protestant leaders decided that James had to go. They wanted the throne to go to James's daughter Mary, who was a Protestant, and to her Dutch husband, William of Orange, who ruled the Netherlands. So they asked William of Orange to come to England with his army.

In November 1688, William set sail from the Netherlands. With him traveled a Protestant army of Dutch, English, Scottish, and French troops. When he arrived in Devon in the south of England, William confidently ordered his transport ships back home. He was certain the English people would welcome him, and that James's soldiers would refuse to fight.

The Dutchman was right. Soon after William's army began to march on London, King James fled the capital for France. Perhaps he recalled what had happened to his grandfather, Charles I, less than a decade before.

With almost no bloodshed, the will of Parliament prevailed, and England rid itself of a troublesome monarch. The English people gave the overthrow of King James a splen-did name—the Glorious Revolution. Beginning with the Glorious Revolu-tion, Parliament claimed the right to have the final say about who could become king of England.

The English Bill of Rights

Now that the hated monarch was gone, Parliament was free to meet. In January 1689, Parliament declared the English throne vacant because James II had broken "the original contract between king and people." Members of Parliament then offered the throne to William and Mary. The offer came with an important string attached. The royal couple had to accept a Bill of Rights.

This Bill of Rights restricted the powers of the king and formally increased the power of Parliament. It said that a king needed Parliament's permission to set aside laws, maintain an army in peacetime, or tax people. It said that government had to be based on law, not on a king's desires. The Bill of Rights also settled a recurring quarrel by banning Roman Catholics from England's throne.

When William and Mary accepted the Bill of Rights and became England's rulers, John Locke felt safe to return to his homeland. He became a favorite at court.

In 1690, he published his essays called *Two Treatises of Government*, in which he explained his ideas about the relationship between the people and their government. Locke wrote that it is government's job to protect the natural rights of life, liberty, and property. If a government robs people of those rights, then, said Locke, the people have a right of revolution. That means they have a right to replace their government, just as the English people had replaced their king and given Parliament more power in the Glorious Revolution.

According to Locke's *Two Treatises of Government*, the Glorious Revolution represented great progress. It was a sign that people could design governments that protected their liberties and worked for the common good. Thinkers all over Europe read John Locke's essays. His writings became milestones of Enlightenment thought and influenced political ideas for centuries to come.

In the Glorious Revolution, William and Mary were invited by Parliament to replace James II. But the royal couple had to agree to a Bill of Rights that increased Parliament's power.

From John Locke's
Two Treatises of Government

In his Two Treatises of Government, *published in 1690, John Locke explained the principles of the Glorious Revolution. He argued that all people are naturally free and have a right to life, liberty, and property. According to Locke, people bring government into existence as a way to protect these rights. If a government tramples on those rights, the people can overthrow it.*

A Page from the Past

T o understand political power … we must consider what state all men are naturally in, and that is, a state of perfect freedom to order their actions, and dispose of their possessions and persons, as they think fit, within the bounds of the law of nature, without asking leave, or depending upon the will of any other man….

The state of nature has a law of nature to govern it, which obliges every one: and reason, which is that law, teaches all mankind … that being all equal and independent, no one ought to harm another in his life, health, liberty, or possessions….

Every man has a property in his own person: this nobody has any right to but himself. The labor of his body, and the work of his hands, we may say, are properly his….

Men being, as has been said, by nature, all free, equal, and independent, no one can be put out of this estate, and subjected to the political power of another, without his own consent. The only way whereby any one divests himself of his natural liberty, and puts on the bonds of civil society, is by agreeing with other men to join and unite into a community for their comfortable, safe, and peaceable living one amongst another, in a secure enjoyment of their properties….

The great and chief end, therefore, of men's uniting into commonwealths, and putting themselves under government, is the preservation of their property….

The great end of men's entering into society, being the enjoyment of their properties in peace and safety, and the great instrument and means of that being the laws established in that society; the first and fundamental … law of all commonwealths is the establishing of the legislative power….

Though the legislative … be the supreme power in every commonwealth, yet, it is not … absolutely arbitrary over the lives and fortunes of the people….

The supreme power cannot take from any man any part of his property without his own consent….

These are the bounds which … society, and the law of God and nature, have set to the legislative power of every commonwealth, in all forms of government:

First, they are to govern by … established laws, not to be varied in particular cases, but to have one rule for rich and poor, for the favorite at court, and the country man at plow.

Secondly, these laws also ought to be designed for no other end ultimately, but the good of the people….

Whenever the legislators … either by ambition, fear, folly or corruption, endeavor to grasp … an absolute power over the lives, liberties, and estates of the people, by this breach of trust they forfeit the power the people had put into their hands … and it devolves to the people, who have a right to resume their original liberty, and, by the establishment of a new legislative, (such as they shall think fit) provide for their own safety and security….

In the Realm of the Sun King

England took steps to limit the power of the king, and John Locke explained why it was reasonable to take such steps. By contrast, in England's neighbor to the south, France, there were few limits on royal power.

France at this time was ruled by Louis XIV. He called himself "the Sun King" because he considered himself as important as the sun itself. From 1643 to 1715, over the course of his 72-year reign, Louis dominated France. He is said to have boasted, *L'état, c'est moi*—"I am the state."

Louis saw himself as God's representative on earth. He fancied himself the center of the universe. And nowhere did he display this more than at Versailles (vuhr-SIY), a town about 15 miles outside of Paris.

In 1682, Louis moved his court from Paris to a fabulous palace at Versailles. At enormous expense, the top architects, decorators, and landscapers of the day transformed the town into Europe's most elegant seat of government. The finest tapestries, marble, and lace filled the palace, which had taken 36,000 workers five decades to complete. The 1,400 fountains that dotted the estate used more water than the entire city of Paris. When Louis strolled the grounds, gardeners replaced flowerbeds so the king would not have to look upon the same view twice.

At Versailles, Louis and his courtiers lived lives of splendor and excess. Noble lords and ladies tried to outdo each other in their fashions. Women wore their hair in coiffures so high that staircases had to be redesigned in order to accommodate

Left: Louis XIV of France is a figure of confidence and grandeur in this portrait of 1701. The self-styled "Sun King" believed he had received his authority from God and had to share power with no one.

Below: The Hall of Mirrors is the most famous room at Versailles, the palace to which Louis moved his royal court in 1682.

them. Some women even wore headdresses designed to look like mountains, forests, and sailing ships. While traveling in carriages, these French ladies often had to sit with their hair pointing out the window.

The world of the French monarchy under the Sun King was far removed from the everyday struggles of working people, or the

Poor peasant families made up most of the population of seventeenth- and eighteenth-century France. They lived in humble dwellings far removed from the splendors of Versailles.

unfairly. They ridiculed many religious beliefs and practices as mere superstitions that went against reason. Some philosophes disliked the Roman Catholic Church because they believed it discouraged freedom of thought. They also asked: Why should the Church possess so much wealth while so many people are so poor?

sufferings of the poor, or the trials of those persecuted for their religious beliefs. With good reason, French philosophers were beginning to question the way Louis ruled. After Louis died in 1715, they continued to criticize his successors.

Voltaire and the French Philosophes

The keenest thinkers of eighteenth-century France were known as *philosophes* (fee-luh-ZAWFS), a word that comes from the Greek for "friends of wisdom." The philosophes believed that wisdom, reason, and knowledge could bring the justice, equality, and freedom their country needed. They believed that by using reason, people could learn to live happier and better lives.

The philosophes often criticized France's government for its corruption and for treating people

But many of these thinkers discovered that it could be dangerous to criticize powerful institutions. One philosophe who learned this lesson was François-Marie Arouet, better known by his pen name, Voltaire (vohl-TAIR).

Voltaire's writings often got him in trouble with the law. The police burned some of Voltaire's works in which he questioned the teachings of the Church. His poems poking fun at the French government briefly landed him in jail.

Voltaire preferred to keep away from the suspicious eyes of the police in Paris. At various times he lived in London, Strasbourg, Berlin, and Geneva. He was, he liked to say, an old bird with no nest.

In London, Voltaire came to admire Isaac Newton, and he was also impressed by John Locke's ideas and the English system of government. In his *Letters Concerning the English Nation*, Voltaire praised England's laws, political liberty, and religious freedom. It is said that Voltaire traveled to England as a poet and left as a philosopher.

Late in life the "old bird with no nest" moved to an estate in eastern France. He chose the location partly because it was close to the Swiss frontier. In case of trouble with the authorities, he would be able to slip across the border to safety in the city of Geneva.

Voltaire continued to write against the injustices he saw around him. Few men ever wrote as much. He authored scores of plays, pamphlets, and letters—so many, in fact, that the king of Prussia at first believed that there must be more than one Voltaire.

In some of his writings, Voltaire examined the treatment of France's Protestant minority, called Huguenots. King Louis XIV had issued a royal decree ordering his Huguenot subjects to abandon their faith and accept the teachings of the Catholic Church. Voltaire thought it was impossible to force men and women to believe particular ideas. Rather, he said, people should be free to use their reason and make up their own minds about religion, politics, and philosophy.

Although Voltaire often disagreed with the way the king ruled France, he was no enemy of monarchy. Yes, he believed that the king had too much power. But he did not recommend that the French people

rid themselves of their king. Rather, he believed that enlightened advisers should guide the king in his policies and his laws. And the advisers, of course, should be guided by reason.

Montesquieu and *The Spirit of Laws*

What might reason tell us about how people should be governed? This question especially engaged one philosophe, the Baron de la Brede et de Montesquieu (mohn-tes-kyou). Montesquieu was a Frenchman who had lived in England. He admired the work of Locke. He praised English liberties. He mocked the French court and Parisian social life.

In his work called *The Spirit of Laws*, Montesquieu describes three kinds of government—monarchies, republics, and despotic governments. In a monarchy, Montesquieu explained, a king or queen holds limited powers. A republican government, he said, can take one of two forms. It can be an aristocracy, in which just a few people hold power.

The philosophe Voltaire was imprisoned for almost a year in Paris for criticizing France's rulers. He ridiculed the government's corruption and questioned the Church's teachings.

Religion in an Age of Reason

During the Enlightenment, the new emphasis on reason prompted some thinkers to question time-honored faiths, both Catholic and Protestant. By the late eighteenth century, some thinkers began to speak not only of natural law but also of "natural religion." These Enlightenment thinkers put forth a system of thought called Deism (DEE-ih-zuhm). Deists said that reason proved there was a God, and that God was the creator of an ordered universe. But God, said the Deists, does not actively take part in the workings of the world or in people's affairs. In the Deist view, God is sometimes imagined as a "Divine Watchmaker" who created a mechanism and then left it to run on its own.

Above: Montesquieu believed government powers should be divided among three different branches—a legislative branch, an executive branch, and a judicial branch.

Right: Among the subjects included in Diderot's 28-volume Encyclopédie *was an article on calligraphy.*

Below: Denis Diderot tried to organize all human knowledge in a collection of books called the Encyclopédie.

Or it can be a democracy, in which power is held by all the people. Finally, said Montesquieu, in a despotic government, a tyrant holds all the power.

Montesquieu was opposed to despotic governments. He thought that either monarchies or republics could be good forms of government, depending on the circumstances. He believed that the best way to protect liberty was to separate a government's powers into three branches: a legislative branch (the law-making part), an executive branch (the law-enforcing part), and a judicial branch (the courts). With power divided among the three branches, Montesquieu explained, no single part of the government could become too powerful.

Montesquieu's writings, published in 1748, influenced the creation of several constitutions in the eighteenth and nineteenth centuries, including the Constitution of the United States.

Diderot's Great Book of Knowledge

Just as the philosophes cherished reason, they also placed a high value on knowledge. In the mid-eighteenth century, one of the philosophes, the French writer Denis Diderot (duh-nee DEE-duh-roh), embarked on a monumental task. He decided to publish a massive collection that would organize all knowledge. He called this work the *Encyclopédie* (ahn-see-kloh-peh-DEE). Our word *encyclopedia* comes from the Greek words *enkyklios paideia*, meaning "general education."

Diderot knew he had set an ambitious goal. To accomplish it, he called on dozens of fellow philosophes to help. Both Voltaire and Montesquieu contributed entries.

In 1751, Diderot published his first volume. He published 27 more volumes over the next 20 years. The *Encyclopédie* included a diverse range of articles, not only on big ideas of philosophy and politics, but also on practical pursuits such as swordsmanship, farming, and calligraphy.

The *Encyclopédie* caused a stir. Diderot was an atheist—someone who does not believe in the existence of God. Some of his articles reflected his disbelief, so French religious and political leaders condemned his work. For a time the police banned the *Encyclopédie*. But the public loved it and bought every one of the 4,000 sets printed.

Condorcet's Belief in Progress

The philosophes believed in the power of reason and knowledge. They were optimistic about the future. They believed that wise people could improve just about everything, from medicine to government, for the benefit of mankind. Perhaps the most optimistic philosophe of all was a man named Marie Jean Antoine Nicolas de Caritat, better known as the Marquis de Condorcet (kawn-dor-SAY).

Condorcet was the son of a cavalry officer father and a deeply religious mother. It was said that his mother named him Marie in honor of the Virgin Mary. Religion was an important part of Condorcet's early life. Jesuit priests educated him, and he became a brilliant mathematician.

But as an adult he turned his back on the Church. Religion, Condorcet decided, was nothing more than a collection of superstitions, contrary to reason. However, if he could not find perfection, truth, and goodness in religious faith, he believed he could find them in the nature of man.

Condorcet's major work was his *Sketch for a Historical Picture of the Progress of the Human Mind*, published in 1795. In this book he argued that men and women could achieve perfection if only they could free themselves of unreasonable rules created by monarchs and religious leaders. With the right laws and with forms of government based on reason, said Condorcet, people could eliminate evil from the world.

Condorcet believed that history was on his side. He was convinced that throughout history, humanity had made slow but certain progress toward a state of enlightenment and reason. Condorcet said that obstacles such as kings and priests still stood in the way. But he believed that mankind would eventually overcome these obstacles and enjoy a future of equality, justice, and harmony.

The Marquis de Condorcet was a great optimist who believed that people could perfect themselves and their societies. The Age of Reason, he believed, would produce a better world for everyone.

Condorcet's faith in human progress represented a high point of Enlightenment optimism. Still, it was characteristic of his time. In this *siècle des lumières*—this "Age of the Enlightened," as the French called it—thinkers placed their faith in the power of reason to understand and improve the world.

The ideas of the Enlightenment did not end many problems in Europe, at least not right away. But the writings of Locke, Voltaire, Montesquieu, Condorcet, and others eventually helped bring about enormous changes.

In this Age of Reason, philosophers championed new ideas about natural law, natural rights, human dignity, and freedom. These ideas transformed the way people thought about governing themselves. Progress in mathematics and science made Enlightenment thinkers optimistic about similar progress in the social world. As we'll see in the next stage of our human odyssey, Enlightenment ideas triggered political earthquakes on both sides of the Atlantic Ocean.

Benjamin Franklin and the Spark of Reason

Historical Close-up

One of the most famous Enlightenment thinkers was an American—Benjamin Franklin. Few men of his time did so many things so well. During his long life, Franklin's activities ranged from investigating the nature of lightning to helping found the United States. Many Europeans such as Voltaire and Diderot admired his Enlightenment confidence in the human ability to understand the physical and social world. Let's follow Benjamin Franklin through his early career.

Ben Franklin had an idea. This was nothing new. The boys playing near Mill Pond in Boston knew Ben Franklin always had an idea.

Apprentice Ben at work in his brother's print shop in Boston

This time his idea was about swimming faster. He rigged a pair of hand paddles and wooden flippers for his feet, and sure enough, they made him whiz through the water. The other boys wanted flippers and paddles, too, so Ben showed them how to make them.

Then he had another idea. He put a kite in the air, held on to its string, and waded back into the water. When the soaring kite tugged him off his feet, he flipped over on his back and let the kite pull him across the pond. He made the trip, he later remembered, "without the least fatigue and with the greatest pleasure imaginable."

Ben attended school for only two years before he started working in his father's candle-making shop at the age of 10. With 13 children in the Franklin household, everyone had to work to put food on the table. Still, Ben kept on having good ideas.

In 1718, at the age of 12, Ben went to learn the printing business in the print shop of his brother, James. He signed papers agreeing to work as an unpaid apprentice for eight years, with one paid year after that.

Ben liked the printing business. He liked plucking letters from the type rack, lining them up to make words, and running the press that printed his brother's newspaper, the *New England Courant*. He also enjoyed proofreading articles and suggesting improvements. But he had to be careful about this, since his strict brother James didn't think apprentices should pretend to be editors. When Ben wrote articles, he did so anonymously.

Even though he wasn't paid for his work as an apprentice, Ben was granted a small food allowance, most of which he spent on books. There was so much to learn—about science, philosophy, history, mathematics—and Ben was curious about everything.

He was also eager to be on his own. In the autumn of 1723, four years before his apprenticeship was complete, Ben ran away from his brother's print shop in Boston. He sold some of his precious books to pay for his trip and arrived in a new home, Philadelphia, with just enough money to buy three bread rolls.

Ben found a job in a print shop. This time he was paid for his work, and he saved his money carefully. In 1728, when he was 22, he became part-owner of a print shop. Two years later, he was publishing his own newspaper, the *Pennsylvania Gazette*.

Franklin still had plenty of good ideas, and he wrote about them in the *Gazette*. For example, he wrote about better ways to deliver mail, put out fires, educate young people, care for the sick, and share books. Soon he was taking charge of the post office and setting up a volunteer fire department. He started a hospital, a library, and an academy that became the University of Pennsylvania.

Franklin's good ideas kept coming. On cold winter mornings, for instance, he noticed that most of the heat in a fireplace went straight up the chimney. So in the early 1740s, he designed an iron insert that fit into a fireplace and stuck out into the room, where it spread warmth. He called this new contraption a Pennsylvania Fireplace, but most people called it a Franklin stove.

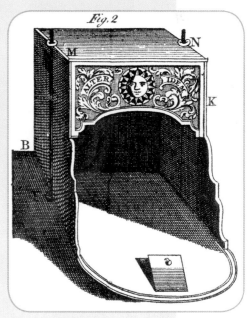

The Franklin stove warmed homes throughout the northern colonies.

Because Franklin stoves used less wood but produced more heat, they were soon warming homes and shops throughout the northern colonies. The governor of Pennsylvania was so grateful that he offered Franklin a patent. This patent would have required anyone who copied his design to pay Franklin a fee. The patent would have made Franklin rich, but he turned it down. "As we enjoy great advantages from the invention of others," he wrote, "we should be glad of an opportunity to serve others by any invention of ours, and this we should do freely and generously."

Franklin never applied for patents on any of his other inventions, such as bifocal glasses or storage batteries. But he kept coming up with bright ideas. Probably the most important scientific ideas he developed were those concerning electricity.

No one in the early 1700s knew much about electricity. If anything, people considered it a source of entertainment. Traveling "electricians" put on shows in which they made sparks fly.

After Franklin saw such a show on a visit to Boston in 1746, he returned home determined to unlock the mysteries of electricity. He set up a laboratory in his home where he experimented with static electricity stored in special containers called Leyden jars. He knew serious electrical experiments were being performed in Europe, but the news from Europe was so slow in reaching the American colonies that Franklin thought the European scientists must be ahead of him in their experimentation.

Franklin suspected that lightning might in fact be electricity. In 1752, he set out to prove this idea. How? By flying a kite, similar to the one that had once pulled him across Mill Pond. But this time he would fly the kite during a thunderstorm.

He wasn't sure what would happen. Would he receive a shock? Would he be killed?

Franklin normally enjoyed an audience, but for this experiment he didn't want a crowd watching him. He went out in a summer storm with only his son William as a witness.

Franklin attached a metal key near the end of the kite string, sent the kite up into the stormy sky, and waited to see what would happen.

At first nothing happened. Then Franklin saw the string stiffen. When he touched the key with his knuckle, he received a mild electrical shock. This proved Franklin's theory that lightning was really electricity charging across the sky.

Franklin kept careful notes of his experiments and corresponded with members of the Royal Society of London. A scientist-friend in Europe spread the news among other scientists, who marveled at Franklin's discovery.

Franklin believed that lightning was really electricity. He and his son William flew a kite in a summer storm to prove his theory.

In 1751, Franklin's papers were collected and published as *Experiments and Observations on Electricity*. The next year his works were translated into French. Franklin's fame grew. Meanwhile, the ever-practical Franklin designed lightning rods to protect buildings from fires started by lightning.

As lightning rods shot up across Europe and America, universities gave Franklin honorary degrees, and London's Royal Society honored him with their most prestigious medal. To the British, Franklin's achievement seemed all the more amazing because he lived in what they saw as the backwoods of colonial America.

In 1757, Franklin traveled to London. He spent most of the next 15 years in Britain as a spokesman for the American colonies. He began reading more political philosophy. Just as John Locke had turned from science to politics, so did Franklin. What natural laws could he discover there? Could reason explain the relationship between the mother country and its distant colonies? One of Franklin's first works written overseas was on this very topic.

With an impressive career as a printer, civic leader, scientist, and inventor behind him, Benjamin Franklin was now turning into a diplomat and a statesman. Some of his best ideas were yet to come—and they would help to found a new nation.

The Italian astronomer Galileo Galilei, shown here dictating to his assistant, lived at a time of great advances in our knowledge of the Earth and the natural world.

Expanding the Known World

The Age of Exploration. The Scientific Revolution. The Enlightenment. The names attest to a central theme in the years from about 1400 to 1750—the growth of knowledge. Between those years, human knowledge grew by leaps and bounds. Mariners charted unfamiliar oceans. Scientists unlocked many mysteries of the natural world. Philosophers explained ideas about natural law, natural rights, and human dignity. Many people began to hope that reason and knowledge held the key to better lives in a better world.

But during this same time, advances in knowledge and confidence in reason went hand-in-hand with brutality and conquest. As European colonizers imposed their will, millions of native people died of disease and abuse. Thousands, and in time millions, of Africans were sold into slavery.

Let's look back on this dramatic, often inspiring, and sometimes troubling part of our journey.

Mapping the Globe

Between 1400 and 1522, the known world expanded from nearby lands to pretty much the whole globe. Portugal's Prince Henry the Navigator wanted to know: How far south did Africa go? Was there any easy route to the East? He sent expeditions along the African coast. Small, fast-moving caravels sped sailors on their way. Instruments such as the astrolabe and quadrant helped them navigate.

The Portuguese and other European sailors did not venture into unknown waters in pursuit of knowledge alone. Their goal was trade with Asia. They wanted silk, spices, and gems from the

East. Muslim empires controlled the land route to the East, so European merchants took to the water.

In 1488, Bartolomeu Dias became the first European explorer to round Africa's southern tip, the Cape of Good Hope. Another Portuguese explorer, Vasco da Gama, passed the Cape and landed in India in 1498.

Troubled by these Portuguese successes, the Spanish launched expeditions of their own. In 1492, Spain's king and queen gambled that the Italian adventurer Christopher Columbus could do what he said—reach the East by sailing west. The risk paid off. When Columbus landed—not in the Indies, but in the Americas—he claimed vast lands for Spain.

On September 6, 1522, Magellan's surviving crew returned to Spain, the first to circle the globe. Their harrowing three-year journey had taken them across the Atlantic, through a narrow strait at the southern tip of South America, across the Pacific and Indian Oceans, and back again to Europe.

In all of history, never before had humans traveled so far. Never before had they collected so much information about so many parts of the world. For the first time in history, people had an idea of how big their world was, and where its various oceans and landmasses lay. For the first time, they could draw a reasonably accurate map of the world. For those who yearned for knowledge, it was an exciting time.

Portraits of four explorers of the "New World" surround this 1596 Dutch map of the Americas. Columbus stands in the upper left, Vespucci in the upper right, Magellan in the lower left, and Pizarro in the lower right.

An Age of Colonization

When Europeans encountered new civilizations, they were often amazed, enchanted, delighted—and then they proceeded without hesitation to conquer them. The Age of Exploration was also an age of colonization. Spain, Portugal, England, France, and Holland all staked claims in the "New World."

In the lands claimed by Spain, the Aztec and Inca had built thriving cities. Both the walls of the temples and the necks of rulers were adorned with exquisite works of gold, silver, and turquoise.

The Spaniards were determined to have these riches. They wasted no time in sending conquistadors, with their guns, cannons, and horses. In 1521, Hernán Cortés defeated the Aztecs. In 1533, Pizarro vanquished the Inca.

In the end, disease proved the deadliest killer. The Aztec and Inca had no immunities to European diseases. Millions died of smallpox.

In the 1500s, the Spanish and Portuguese built colonial empires in the New World. They tore down old cities and built new ones. Both Spain and Portugal governed their colonies strictly and reaped enormous

From their magnificent capital city of Tenochtitlán, the Aztecs ruled a vast empire in central Mexico.

One Artist Admires Another

In 1520, the year before Cortés conquered the Aztecs, the German Renaissance artist Albrecht Dürer saw some of the first Aztec art to reach Europe. "In all my life," he wrote, "I have never seen anything that gladdened my heart so much as these things ... more beautiful to me than miracles."

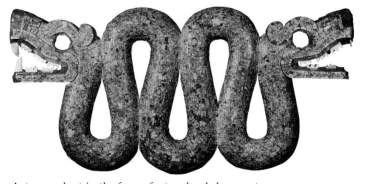

Aztec pendant in the form of a two-headed serpent

Spanish conquistadors overthrew the Aztec empire in 1521. Twelve years later, other Spanish colonists conquered the Inca empire of South America.

What Happened to Portugal?

Portugal, the early leader in the Age of Exploration, hoped to extend its colonial empire in the 1700s. But its ambitions were thwarted by a powerful foe—nature. On November 1, 1755, a devastating earthquake rocked Lisbon, ripping chasms 15 feet wide in the Earth's surface. Survivors raced to the docks, where they thought they would be safe. But within half an hour a giant tsunami crashed down on the harbor. Areas unharmed by the tsunami were engulfed in flames that burned for five days.

The earthquake, tsunami, and fires killed nearly a hundred thousand people. Portugal's royal palace, library, and archives were destroyed. All the records and journals of Vasco da Gama and other early navigators were lost. The once great imperial power suffered a devastating blow.

The Lisbon earthquake reminds us that, as we learn about what happened, we should keep in mind that things could have happened differently. What if no earthquake had struck? Would Portugal have remained a great colonial power, perhaps challenging the claims of England and Spain? History is full of fascinating "What if's...."

wealth. While Spanish missionaries converted the Indians to Christianity, colonial merchants shipped gold, silver, and precious stones back to the Iberian Peninsula.

In time, Catholic Spain was challenged by Protestant England and its ruler, Elizabeth I. In 1588, the queen's navy defeated the Spanish Armada. By the time James I ascended the throne, the English were determined to establish some colonies of their own.

In the early 1600s, the English were disappointed in their new North American colonies, like Jamestown in Virginia. Where were the gold and silver that Spain had found in abundance in Mexico and in South and Central America? Instead, England's North American colonies seemed capable of providing only tobacco, lumber, and fur. Since the riches were limited, English rulers let the colonies proceed with only limited supervision. Unlike Spain, England did not try to rule its colonies with a firm hand. It let individuals or private companies establish the rules. Many colonies started electing their own assemblies to pass laws.

Sometimes English rulers granted huge stretches of land to friends or to troublesome religious dissenters. Thus Pilgrims, Puritans, Quakers, and Catholics found lands waiting for them in the New World. By 1750, a diverse and sometimes quarrelsome group of English colonies was established on North America's Atlantic coast.

The lands settled by the English were already inhabited by various Native American peoples. Sometimes they helped the English, and sometimes the English treated them decently. More often one side attacked the other. As the English population grew, they pushed the Indians farther into the forest.

These native people were devastated by the same diseases that had wiped out the Aztec and Inca.

Forced Labor and Slavery

In the early years of colonization, Bartolomé de Las Casas—one of the missionaries trying to convert conquered natives to Christianity—bitterly noted the contradiction between Christian ideals of charity

Above: England's Queen Elizabeth I challenged the power of Spain. In 1588, her navy defeated the Spanish Armada, which was sent to invade England.

Below: English explorers and adventurers eventually set up colonies in North America. Here, Native Americans watch as English colonists build a settlement in Virginia.

and the Europeans' brutal treatment of Indians. The Spanish and Portuguese forced the conquered natives to work in mines and on farms. As gold, silver, and sugar flowed back to Spain and Portugal, Indians by the thousands died from overwork, abuse, and disease. As the Indians died out, who would labor in the mines and fields?

African slaves. Europeans already traded with African civilizations for gold, ivory, and pepper. By about 1520, European merchants began buying slaves from African rulers and transporting them across the Atlantic.

The transatlantic slave trade boomed because of the demand for labor on sugar plantations in the West Indies and Brazil. In the 1600s, as British colonists settled North America, southern planters also wanted slaves to work on tobacco and rice plantations.

Many British vessels became slave ships. During the Middle Passage across the Atlantic, slaves were shackled and crammed below

The brutal transatlantic trade in African slaves provided labor for the plantations of North and South America. Slaves were often shackled with iron collars like these, which date from around 1790.

deck, suffering weeks of hunger, thirst, stench, and disease. Those who survived were destined to lives of hard labor in the West Indies, Central and South America, and British North America.

Forced labor and slavery left wounds in the social order that, even to this day, have yet to heal.

The Light of Science

The sixteenth and seventeenth centuries gave birth to the organized study of how nature works—in other words, to modern science.

Think about Copernicus and Galileo. In 1543, a book by Copernicus, *On the Revolution of Heavenly Bodies*, set forth views that would shake the world. Copernicus used mathematics to conclude that the sun does not revolve around the Earth, as everyone thought. Instead, he showed that the Earth and the other planets revolve around the sun. Seventy years later, Galileo used a telescope to confirm that Copernicus had been right. When Galileo published his findings, a commotion followed. The Church even put him on trial for his findings.

In 1643, a year after Galileo died in Italy, Isaac Newton was born in England. Newton discovered laws of planetary motion and explained how gravity works. He separated rays of light into the colors of the spectrum. He invented calculus,

a new branch of mathematics that proved invaluable to modern scientists and mathematicians. At his life's end, he said that he felt just like "a boy playing on the seashore … whilst the great ocean of truth lay all undiscovered before me." But in truth, Newton helped chart the vast sea of knowledge.

Copernicus, Galileo, Newton, and others introduced the world to modern science. They understood that mathematics, observation, and careful experimentation could help people figure out the workings of nature. Their work vastly enlarged the scope of the known world.

Enlightenment Thinkers Place Their Confidence in Reason

If human reason could reveal so much about how the natural world works, could it also shine a light on the social world? Could reason reveal "natural laws" about government and society? If people discovered those laws,

might that lead to greater happiness and progress? In the eighteenth century, many European thinkers said "yes." Their confidence in the power of reason to illuminate a brighter future led many to call this age the Enlightenment.

The English philosopher John Locke said that there was a natural law, a moral order in society that could be understood through reason. Reason revealed that human beings had natural rights, including, said Locke, the rights to life, liberty, and property. Locke boldly asserted that kings had no right to violate their subjects' natural rights. If they did, he said, then they should be overthrown. As you'll soon see, Locke's idea of the "right of revolution" would play out in a great drama in England's North American colonies.

French *philosophes*, such as Voltaire, Montesquieu, Diderot, and Condorcet, believed reason and knowledge alone should order human affairs. They criticized the monarchy and the Church. They hoped for the dawn of liberty in France.

Many eighteenth-century thinkers shared high hopes for an age when reason and reasonable people might solve most problems and improve the world in which they lived. In the next part of this book, you'll see how these ideas would bring revolutionary change.

Left: Galileo Galilei studies the heavens through one of his telescopes. Galileo confirmed Copernicus's theory that the Earth and the other planets revolve around the sun.

Below: The French philosophe Voltaire ridiculed intolerance and tyranny. The philosophes insisted that people could use reason to advance science and solve many of society's problems.

Time Line (1400–1800)

1400

1500

1492
Columbus sails from Spain across the Atlantic to the Americas.

c. 1440
The Inca begin building Machu Picchu high in the Andes.

c. 1520
The transatlantic slave trade begins between Africa and the New World.

1558
Elizabeth I begins her reign as queen of England.

c. 1500
Emperor Askia Muhammad expands the Songhai empire and rebuilds Timbuktu.

1543
Nicholas Copernicus publishes *On the Revolution of Heavenly Bodies*, demonstrating that the Earth revolves around the sun.

1519
Hernán Cortés begins his conquest of the Aztec capital, Tenochtitlán.

1522
Ferdinand Magellan's expedition completes the first round-the-world voyage.

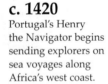

c. 1420
Portugal's Henry the Navigator begins sending explorers on sea voyages along Africa's west coast.

1588
England's navy defeats the Spanish Armada.

1690

After the Glorious Revolution, John Locke returns to England and publishes his *Two Treatises of Government*.

1607

English settlers arrive at Jamestown, Virginia.

1687

Newton publishes his *Mathematical Principles of Natural Philosophy*, including his laws of motion and theory of gravitation.

1609

Galileo Galilei builds his first telescope.

1751

Denis Diderot publishes the first volume of his *Encyclopédie*.

Top: Parisians storm the Bastille, a hated symbol of royal power, at the outset of the French Revolution in 1789. During the eighteenth and nineteenth centuries, millions of people in Europe and the Americas rebelled against the rule of kings.

Bottom: An 1876 lithograph illustrates some of the many examples of technological progress in the nineteenth century—the steam press, the telegraph, the locomotive, and the steamboat.

An Age of Democratic and Industrial Revolution

Our studies have brought us to within about two and a half centuries of the present. If you read Volume 1 of *The Human Odyssey*, you've traveled more than ten thousand years on the time line. During all those millennia, much about people's daily lives changed. And much did not change.

For example, for thousands of years, the way people labored stayed pretty much the same. If they needed to turn the earth in a field, they hooked horses or oxen to a plow. If they needed to dig a ditch, they took a shovel in hand. Sometimes people used water or wind power to help do work. But for the most part, they relied on human muscle or animal strength.

Most people lived in the country or small villages. Over time, cities dotted the Earth, such as Babylon, Rome, Timbuktu, and Tenochtitlán. But the majority of humanity lived outside such cities. They farmed the land, made most things they needed, and bartered for the rest.

People rarely strayed more than a few miles from home. When they traveled, they might ride a horse or camel, or perhaps go by carriage or wagon. Mostly they walked. If they traveled by water, they paddled or sailed. As you've seen, in the fifteenth century the Portuguese and others made great advances in sailing. Still, winds and currents determined where they could go.

Messages traveled no faster than the swiftest horse or ship. Occasionally people used fires or other signals for quicker communications. But in 1750, most messages traveled no faster than they did in the days of ancient Rome.

Until about two and a half centuries ago, few people had the basic political freedoms that we take for granted today. For a while, ancient Athenians had enjoyed democracy, and the Romans lived in a republic. A few other civilizations, including the English, experimented with representative government. But even in these cases, citizenship was limited and few had the right to vote. Since the time of the first civilizations, the vast majority of humanity lived under the rule of kings, emperors, lords, or rulers who said, in effect: "I will tell you how you may live, what you may say, and what you must do for me. If you don't do as I say, I can imprison you, exile you, or kill you. You are mine to command."

Big Changes in a Short Time

Our account of the human odyssey now takes us to the eighteenth and nineteenth centuries, a time of extraordinary change for millions of people. In many respects, the way people live and work changed more in the last 250 years than in all previous history.

During the Industrial Revolution, people began to rely on machines to do work for them. At right, workers operate a steam-powered press to print a newspaper.

People began to invent amazing machines to do their work. They turned to new sources of power to run those machines. They found new ways to speed people across oceans, mountains, plains, and continents. They invented ways to send messages hundreds of miles in seconds.

For millions of people, daily labor changed from producing by hand to producing by machine. A flood of humanity poured out of the countryside and into cities. These were profound changes—and not always for the better.

No less remarkable, millions of people began to take a stand against the rule of kings. They insisted on basic rights and freedoms. They tried to form governments run by the people's representatives. The seed of democracy planted in ancient Athens flowered in the modern world.

These big changes in the eighteenth and nineteenth centuries were partly a result of the Scientific Revolution, which gave people the knowledge to invent new machines and solve age-old problems. The works of Enlightenment thinkers, such as John Locke, inspired new awareness of rights and new hope for political progress. New knowledge and new confidence led to an age of democratic and industrial revolution.

Surrendering British soldiers march next to a mounted American officer after the battle of Yorktown, Virginia. The victorious Americans assemble under the Stars and Stripes on the right, their French allies under the royal flag of France on the left.

The World Turned Upside Down: The American Revolution

Just before the dawn of the eighteenth century, John Locke looked with pleasure on his native land. England had enjoyed a peaceful transition in leadership—King James II had stepped aside to be replaced by William and Mary, and William and Mary had agreed to accept a Bill of Rights that limited their royal power.

These events were in keeping with the ideas Locke put forth in his *Two Treatises of Government*. All people, Locke wrote, have the natural rights of life, liberty, and property. Government, said Locke, is obligated to protect these rights. If a government injures those rights, then it is the right of the people to replace the government, just as the English people had peacefully replaced the king in the Glorious Revolution.

Decades later, those ideas helped spark another revolution—and this time, not a peaceful one. Once again, people living under British rule rose up to demand their rights and overthrow their government. This time, however, it was not people in England who rebelled. Rather, it was those subjects of the crown who lived across the Atlantic in England's North American colonies.

Let's look back at the ideas and events that led to this remarkable turn of events.

Proud to Be British

In the year 1763, Britain's colonists in North America were celebrating. They were proud to be part of the British Empire, which now ruled much of the North American continent. At this moment, they were especially proud to be British. Why? Because

This chapter focuses on the American Revolution of the late eighteenth century.

they had just helped defeat Britain's longtime rival, France.

This war with France, known as the French and Indian War, had taken place not in Europe but in North America. For seven years, the French and the British had been struggling for control of North America. On one side were the French and their Indian allies. Opposing them were British troops, aided by colonists who had signed up to fight in the colonial militias. One of the militia commanders—who took part in the very first battle of the war—was a young officer from Virginia named George Washington.

A *militia* is a group of citizens who are not full-time soldiers but who fight as part of the army during wartime or emergencies.

A young George Washington of Virginia fought for Britain during the French and Indian War, and later led the American colonies to independence.

Thirteen Colonies

By 1763, there were thirteen British colonies along the eastern seaboard in North America. Georgia became a colony in 1733, and Carolina had been divided into North and South Carolina. The thirteen colonies were Massachusetts, New Hampshire, Connecticut, Rhode Island, New York, New Jersey, Pennsylvania, Delaware, Virginia, Maryland, North Carolina, South Carolina, and Georgia.

In the war, the British had won neighboring Canada from the French, as well as territory to the west of the Appalachian Mountains. More land meant more prosperous farms, more bustling towns, more opportunity. People in all thirteen colonies had high hopes for their future.

It's important to keep in mind that most colonists thought of themselves as British. Of course this doesn't include the many colonists who had come from other European lands, such as Germany or the Netherlands. And nearly one-fifth of the population consisted of African slaves. Still, the great majority of North American colonists were of English descent. They referred to Britain as "the mother country." They liked the young king, George III, who had come to the throne in 1760.

The Colonists Enjoy Their Freedoms

The colonists took pride in their English heritage not only because of Britain's power, but also because of their rights and freedoms as Englishmen. In many European countries, the king held almost all political power. But in England, since the time of the Magna Carta, limits had been placed on the power of the king. And for centuries Englishmen had enjoyed certain basic rights—such as the right to trial by jury—that no government had the power to take away. Indeed, it was the purpose of government to protect such liberty and rights—so stated John Locke, whose writings were widely read in the colonies.

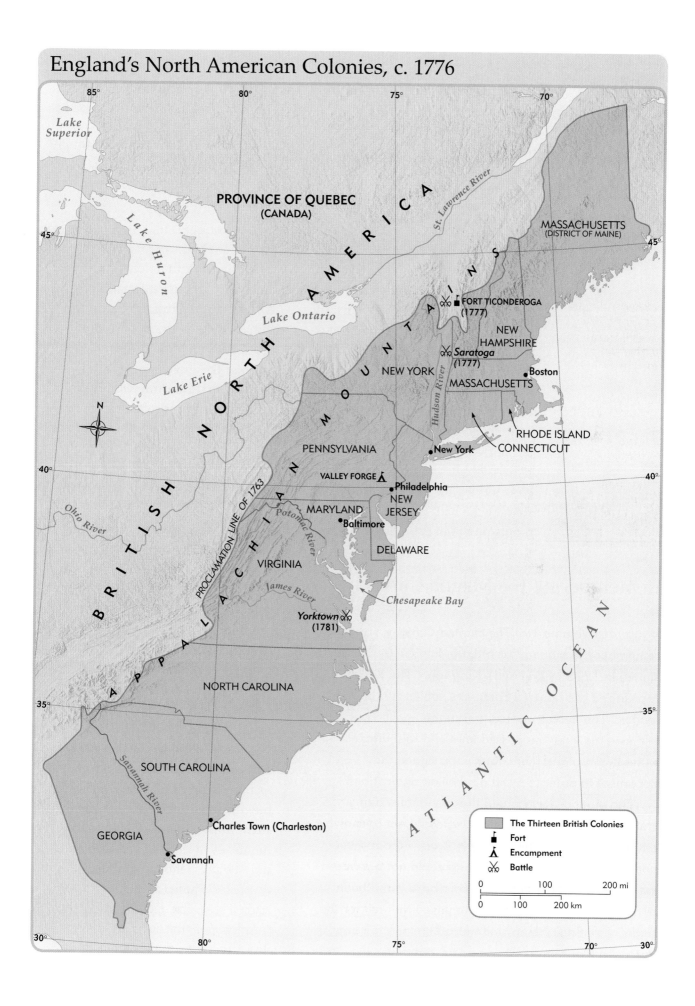

England's North American Colonies, c. 1776

PROVINCE OF QUEBEC
(CANADA)

Lake Superior

Lake Huron

Lake Ontario

Lake Erie

B R I T I S H   N O R T H   A M E R I C A

St. Lawrence River

MASSACHUSETTS
(DISTRICT OF MAINE)

A P P A L A C H I A N   M O U N T A I N S

⚔️ ◼ FORT TICONDEROGA
(1777)

NEW HAMPSHIRE

⚔️ *Saratoga*
(1777)

NEW YORK

• Boston

MASSACHUSETTS

RHODE ISLAND
CONNECTICUT

Hudson River

PENNSYLVANIA

• New York

VALLEY FORGE ⛺
• Philadelphia

Ohio River

PROCLAMATION LINE OF 1763

MARYLAND

NEW JERSEY

• Baltimore

Potomac River

DELAWARE

VIRGINIA

James River

Chesapeake Bay

Yorktown ⚔️
(1781)

NORTH CAROLINA

SOUTH CAROLINA

Savannah River

• Charles Town (Charleston)

GEORGIA

• Savannah

A T L A N T I C   O C E A N

	The Thirteen British Colonies
◼	Fort
⛺	Encampment
⚔️	Battle

0   100   200 mi
0   100   200 km

While the colonists were proud to be part of the British Empire, they were also pleased that the government in far-off London largely let the colonies govern themselves. Most colonies had a governor appointed by the king. But the governor generally had less power than the colonial assembly. Also, most colonial assemblies paid the governor, which made him consider their wishes carefully. These colonial assemblies were elected by colonists who had the right to vote. The assemblies passed the laws that affected the day-to-day lives of the colonists.

Most of the colonial assemblies held the all-important "power of the purse"—only the representative assemblies could pass taxes to raise money for the government. John Locke had said that governments must not raise taxes "without the consent of the people," and the American colonists heartily agreed.

"No taxation without representation!"

In 1763, King George III could not have been more popular in North America. But this popularity would not last long.

Britain had fought the long and expensive war to defeat France and defend the colonies. It had debts. And it still had thousands of troops stationed in America, partly to protect colonists against Indian attacks. The government in London decided that the American colonists needed to pay more to support the troops in the colonies. So Parliament passed laws requiring the colonists to pay new taxes.

The colonists reacted angrily. They argued that Parliament had not taxed them before. Instead, the colonial assemblies had always passed their own taxes. For a century, Englishmen had insisted that before they could be taxed, their representatives in Parliament must give their consent. But the colonists pointed out that they had no representatives in Parliament. Thus, the colonists argued, they were being taxed without their consent.

Above all, the colonists hated a new tax passed in 1765, known as the Stamp Act. This law said that most printed material—newspapers, pamphlets, almanacs, legal documents, even playing cards—could only be published on paper bearing an official stamp, which the colonists had to buy. The act stirred up so much anger that riots broke out in some towns and cities. Mobs

Remembering the Magna Carta

If you read Volume 1 of *The Human Odyssey*, you may remember the Magna Carta (Latin for "Great Charter"), signed in 1215 by England's King John. The document recognized the rights of England's nobles and church leaders. The nobles wanted their rights spelled out because the king had passed laws and raised taxes without consulting them. King John signed the document in order to avoid a rebellion against him.

The Magna Carta stated that the nobles and church leaders had rights the king could not take away, and that the king could not raise taxes without their approval. It also said that the king could not put free men in jail unless they had broken the law and been tried by a jury. The Magna Carta paved the way for the rights of all Englishmen, and helped change the English people's ideas about justice and government.

An Emblem of the Effects of the STAMP

O! the fatal Stamp

of colonists forced tax officials to hand over the hated stamps. Sometimes they burned down the officials' houses.

John Locke had calmly argued that governments must not raise taxes "without the consent of the people." Now the colonists turned that idea into the angry cry, "No taxation without representation!"

The colonists' violent reaction to the Stamp Act stunned the British government. Parliament repealed the act, but then British lawmakers went on to pass new taxes on goods the colonists imported from Britain. (To *repeal* a law is to cancel it.) Many defiant colonial merchants declared that they would no longer buy goods imported from Britain. Once again, Parliament gave in and repealed the hated taxes, except for a small tax on tea. Parliament and the king left that tax in place to show that they could tax Americans if they wanted to.

The Path to Revolution

By this time, many colonists had grown openly rebellious. Groups called the Sons of Liberty sprang up in several colonies, declaring their opposition to what they called "tyranny." Montesquieu, the Enlightenment author of *The Spirit of Laws*, had defined tyranny as "the exercise of power beyond right." Many American colonists thought Parliament and the king were exercising their power well "beyond right."

Boston, in the colony of Massachusetts, was a hotbed of agitation. So in 1768, the British government sent troops to occupy the city and keep the peace. Bostonians bitterly resented the occupation. One night in 1770, an angry crowd confronted a small group of soldiers. Yelling insults, the crowd pelted the soldiers with chunks of ice, oyster shells, and pieces of garbage. The soldiers opened fire, killing five people. This

Left: "O! the fatal Stamp," declares this cartoon in the Pennsylvania Journal. *The skull and crossbones image is a symbol of death. Colonists worried that the Stamp Act, which taxed them without their consent, meant death to their liberty.*

Below: Paul Revere, a patriot and silversmith, created this engraving of the Boston Massacre. Newspapers throughout the colonies reprinted it, helping to turn many colonists against Britain.

event, which became known as the Boston Massacre, shocked people throughout the colonies. For the first time British troops had opened fire on colonists. Anger against the mother country grew.

Meanwhile, colonists still resented the tax that Parliament had left on tea. They feared that if they paid this duty, other taxes might follow. You might already know what the colonists did about the tea tax. One icy December night in 1773, a group of colonists disguised as Indians made their way to Boston Harbor, where they silently boarded three British ships carrying cargoes of tea. The disguised colonists quietly split open 342 crates of tea and tossed them into the harbor. Afterwards, colonists joked about the "Boston Tea Party."

The British government was not amused. It sent more troops across the Atlantic to control the rebellious colonists. The colonists started organizing themselves into militias to resist the British troops.

On April 19, 1775, British soldiers confronted colonial militiamen on a field in Lexington, a town outside Boston. The British commander cried, "Lay down your arms, you damned rebels, and disperse!" When the militiamen refused, the British troops fired, killing eight colonists. The colonists retreated, but the next day they attacked the British soldiers, driving them back toward Boston. The militiamen, a poet later wrote, had "fired the shot heard 'round the world." The American Revolution had begun.

A duty *is a tax, especially on imported goods.*

American colonists and British soldiers fight at Lexington, Massachusetts, in the first battle of the American Revolution. The fighting at Lexington and nearby Concord was later called "the shot heard 'round the world" because it began the American Revolution, and set off a series of wars for democratic rule.

Thomas Paine's *Common Sense*

Soon representatives from all the colonies met to set up a Continental Army to fight the British troops. The representatives chose George Washington of Virginia to serve as the commanding general. Washington accepted command graciously but grimly. He knew that he was in for a long, tough fight against one of the world's strongest armies.

The colonists had a general to lead them. But what exactly were they fighting for? Did they just want Britain to withdraw its soldiers and pledge to respect the rights of the colonial assemblies? Or did they want to make a complete break with the mother country?

Up to this time, most colonists had not imagined anything so drastic. After all, they admired their home country. Was there really any reason to commit themselves to the radical goal of *independence*?

In early 1776, many colonists made up their minds for independence when they read a remarkable pamphlet called *Common Sense*. The author, Thomas Paine, had little formal education, but he had thoroughly absorbed the Enlightenment confidence in human reason. Institutions of government, Paine insisted, should be reasonable. Was it reasonable, he asked, for a king to rule colonies far away?

Paine argued that it went against common sense for a small island like Great Britain to rule a gigantic continent like North America. Once, when the colonies were small and weak, it might have made sense to think of them as children and

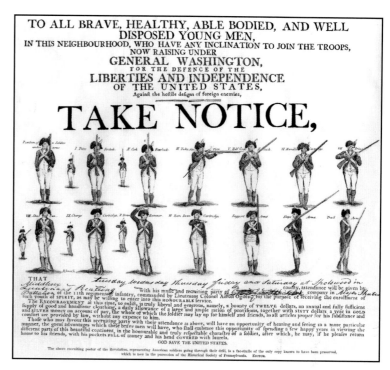

A recruiting poster calls upon young men to enlist in the army being formed under General Washington. The colonists who joined had to fight against one of the best-trained armies in the world.

England as their "mother." But the time had come, Paine argued, for the colonies to go their own way, just as grown children move out of their parents' house. "'Tis time to part," Paine boldly declared.

After arguing that it defied common sense for the American colonies to remain subjects of a distant king, Paine took his argument one step further: Why, he asked, should *anyone* ever

Reviving Classical Ideals of Liberty

Between 1763 and 1776, American newspapers published thousands of columns by angry colonists denouncing the "tyranny" of the mother country. In an age before people signed their own names to articles, writers used pen names. The angry colonists chose names from ancient Greece and Rome, such as Lycurgus, Solon, Demosthenes, and Brutus. Why? Because they saw themselves defending ideals of liberty handed down from classical times.

In his pamphlet Common Sense, *Thomas Paine urged his fellow colonists to break their links with Great Britain. Paine argued that Americans had a right to declare their independence from a tyrannical king and govern themselves.*

COMMON SENSE;

ADDRESSED TO THE

INHABITANTS

O F

AMERICA,

On the following interesting

SUBJECTS.

I. Of the Origin and Design of Government in general, with concise Remarks on the English Constitution.

II. Of Monarchy and Hereditary Succession.

III. Thoughts on the present State of American Affairs.

IV. Of the present Ability of America, with some miscellaneous Reflections.

Man knows no Master save creating HEAVEN,
Or those whom choice and common good ordain.
                                        THOMSON.

PHILADELPHIA;
Printed, and Sold, by R. BELL, in Third-Street.

MDCCLXXVI.

obey a king? This was a startlingly radical idea. Paine was questioning the wisdom of monarchy itself—a system of government that had been in place for centuries.

Look at it in the light of common sense, Paine said: What was a king, anyway, but someone whose ancestors had taken other people's land by force? "Of more worth is one honest man to society … than all the crowned ruffians that ever lived," he insisted. America, Paine argued, should become a country without a king, where the people ruled themselves. Then, all over the world, people would follow its example and fight for their own freedom. "The birthday of a new world is at hand," Paine wrote.

In little more than a decade, many Americans had changed from proud British subjects to agitators for independence. The colonists, who had been conveniently ignoring the distant British government for quite a while, had become accustomed to governing themselves. Paine's pamphlet pushed them to think the unthinkable: Why shouldn't these colonies be *independent*?

More than 200,000 copies of *Common Sense* were sold. Paine's bold, forcefully stated ideas helped convince people in every colony of the need for a complete break from Britain.

Paine Offers Common Sense

Here is an excerpt from Thomas Paine's Common Sense, *published in January 1776.*

A Page from the Past

Volumes have been written on the subject of the struggle between England and America. Men of all ranks have embarked in the controversy….

The sun never shined on a cause of greater worth. 'Tis not the affair of a city, a county, a province, or a kingdom, but of a continent—of at least one eighth part of the habitable globe…. Now is the seed-time of continental union, faith and honor.

But Britain is the parent country, say some. Then the more shame upon her conduct. Even brutes do not devour their young, nor savages make war upon their families…. Europe, and not England, is the parent country of America. This new world hath been the asylum for the persecuted lovers of civil and religious liberty from *every part* of Europe. Hither have they fled, not from the tender embraces of the mother, but from the cruelty of the monster; and it is so far true of England, that the same tyranny which drove the first emigrants from home, pursues their descendants still….

> An *asylum* is a place of safety and protection.

Every thing that is right or natural pleads for separation. The blood of the slain, the weeping voice of nature cries, *'Tis time to part*….

It is repugnant to reason, to the universal order of things, to all examples from former ages, to suppose, that this continent can longer remain subject to any external power…. Small islands not capable of protecting themselves are the proper objects for kingdoms to take under their care; but there is something very absurd, in supposing a continent to be perpetually governed by an island. In no instance hath nature made the satellite larger than its primary planet….

> *Repugnant* means strongly opposed to, completely at odds with.

The powers of governing still remaining in the hands of the king, he will have a negative over the whole legislation of this continent…. He hath shewn himself … an inveterate enemy to liberty…. We may be as effectually enslaved by the want of laws in America, as by submitting to laws made for us in England….

> *Inveterate* means firmly established by long habit or repetition.

To bring the matter to one point: Is the power who is jealous of our prosperity, a proper power to govern us? Whoever says *No* to this question, is an *independent*, for independency means no more, than, whether we shall make our own laws, or whether the king, the greatest enemy this continent hath, or can have, shall tell us *"There shall be no laws but such as I like."*

Declaring Independence

In the summer of 1776, representatives from the colonies met in Philadelphia to debate independence. On July 4, they adopted a Declaration of Independence, which had been drafted by a brilliant young representative from Virginia, Thomas Jefferson.

Jefferson wrote with elegance and clarity. He built on the work of John Locke and other Enlightenment thinkers. With Enlightenment concern for careful rational argument, Jefferson began by acknowledging that Americans were about to take a momentous step. It was therefore necessary for Americans

Colonial representatives meeting in Philadelphia in 1776 issued the Declaration of Independence. From left to right, John Adams, Roger Sherman, Robert Livingston, Thomas Jefferson, and Ben Franklin present the Declaration to John Hancock (seated), president of the Continental Congress.

to explain "the causes that impel them to separation."

The Declaration of Independence went on to insist that governments exist for the benefit of those ruled, and not for the rulers. Governments get their power, Jefferson wrote, "from the consent of the governed."

John Locke had argued that people have certain rights, including the rights of life, liberty, and the ownership of property. In the Declaration of Independence, Jefferson built on Locke's thinking but added a new, democratic dimension. It is "self-evident," wrote Jefferson, "that all men are created equal, that they are endowed by their Creator with certain unalienable rights, that among these are life, liberty, and the pursuit of happiness." While Locke had spoken of property, Jefferson referred to "the pursuit of happiness." Jefferson offered a broader concept. The "pursuit of happiness" includes not only the right to own property and have it protected, but also the right to strive for the common good, in addition to one's personal happiness.

Like Locke, Jefferson believed that people have a right to resist and replace a ruler who has become a tyrant. When a government "becomes destructive of" the people's "unalienable rights," then, said Jefferson, "it is the right of the people to alter or to abolish it, and to institute new Government."

Jefferson argued that "the history of the present King of Great Britain is a history of repeated injuries and usurpations, all having in direct object the establishment of an absolute tyranny over these states." He went on to describe in detail how the British government had trampled on American rights. He closed by boldly declaring:

> We, therefore, the representatives of the United States of America, … do, in the name, and by authority of the good people of these colonies, solemnly publish and declare, that these united colonies are, and of right ought to be free and independent states; that they are absolved from all allegiance to the British Crown, and that all political connection between them and the State of Great Britain, is and ought to be totally dissolved….

Fighting a Revolution

To win independence, rather than just declare it, the Americans had to beat the British on the battlefield. This was a daunting task. British forces outnumbered those of the Americans. At the beginning of the war, the British had almost twice as many troops in the field, including a large number of German mercenaries. (*Mercenaries* are paid soldiers hired to fight for a country other than their own.)

Moreover, the British army was a professional fighting force, superbly trained and disciplined. By contrast, the American army was made mostly of ordinary men—farmers, merchants, fishermen—who had volunteered to fight for freedom. Some didn't think they should be forced to take orders, even from their own officers. Soldiers from one colony often quarreled with those from another.

At first it seemed as if the British army would easily defeat the rebels. But George Washington's leadership proved invaluable. Steady, deliberate, and determined, he led American troops through a grueling winter at Valley Forge and then on to important victories. Americans proved they could stand up to the British on the battlefield.

Still, as the war ground on, the British continued to win more battles than they lost. In the summer of 1777, a large British force swept down from Canada in an attempt to cut New England off from the rest of the states. The British swiftly captured an important American stronghold, Fort Ticonderoga in New York. When King George III heard about the fall of Ticonderoga, he rushed to the queen's bedroom, clapping his hands and shouting, "I have beaten the Americans!"

The king had spoken too soon. A few months later, the Americans stopped the advancing British army at the Battle of Saratoga in New York. The victory at Saratoga encouraged the French to send troops to help the Americans.

The French Lend a Hand, and the World Turns Upside Down

In the spring of 1778, Americans got news that revived their hopes. A powerful ally was coming to their aid.

Since 1763, the French had longed to avenge their defeat in the French and Indian War and the loss of their colonies in North America. When revolution broke out in America, they saw their chance to get back at the British. At first, not wanting to risk open warfare with Britain, the French secretly sent money, arms, and gunpowder to the Americans.

American soldiers accept the surrender of the British army after the Battle of Saratoga. The Americans' victory at Saratoga encouraged France to join the war as a United States ally.

But after the American victory at Saratoga, they decided that the Americans stood a good chance of defeating the British.

The French government, led by King Louis XVI, signed a treaty with the Americans, pledging to fight beside them until the United States won its independence. When news of the treaty reached America, the entire Continental Army mustered to celebrate, cheering "Long live the King of France!"

When this treaty was signed, one young French nobleman, the Marquis de Lafayette (mahr-KEE duh lah-fee-ET), had already been fighting alongside the Americans for many months. Like Thomas Paine, Lafayette believed that the Americans were fighting not just for their own independence but for "the happiness of humanity." Lafayette was eager to advance the goals of Enlightenment thinkers. He had read the writings of French philosophes such as Voltaire and Condorcet, who celebrated the cause of liberty

The Marquis de Lafayette was among the first Frenchmen to fight for the American cause. Washington made him a general in the Continental Army.

against tyranny. Shortly before his twentieth birthday, Lafayette had left a life of wealth and ease in France and sailed off to America to join the fight for freedom. Washington was so impressed by Lafayette that, despite his youth, he made him a general in the Continental Army.

French help was especially important because the French had a powerful navy. The French government sent ships to protect the ports of the northern American states from British attack. At the same time, the British army was encountering fierce resistance from rebels in New England and the mid-Atlantic states. In 1779, the British generals decided to carry the war to the South. They hoped that South Carolina and Georgia, where many people remained loyal to Britain, would be easier to subdue.

At first the British won major victories in the South. They captured important cities, including Charleston and Savannah. But the colonists in the South fought back. Ragtag American troops ambushed British soldiers, disrupted their supply lines, and even beat the king's men in the field.

In 1781, the main British army withdrew to the village of Yorktown in Virginia. There, American and French forces surrounded the British troops and pounded them with cannon fire, while a French fleet cut off escape by sea. On October 19, 1781, the British commander surrendered.

As British soldiers marched away to become prisoners of war, their band played an old song called "The World Turned Upside Down." When people back in Britain heard the news, it must

England Looks for Help from the Tories

Not everyone in the American colonies wanted independence from Britain. Some people disagreed with the decision to declare independence. They remained loyal to King George. These colonists were known as Royalists or Tories.

Many Tories lived in the southern colonies, and British military leaders hoped large numbers would join the king's army and help fight rebellious colonists. But the British were disappointed. Fewer Tories than they expected took up arms to fight for the king.

General Washington fires a cannon during the siege of Yorktown in Virginia. The Battle of Yorktown brought an end to the American Revolution.

have seemed to them that everything had indeed gone topsy-turvy. A colonial army of farmers and craftsmen—with help from Britain's old enemy, France—had beaten one of the most powerful militaries in the world.

The Constitutional Convention

From the battlefield at Yorktown, Lafayette wrote joyfully to a friend in Paris: "The play, sir, is over." The revolutionaries had won. A few months after Yorktown, the British Parliament voted to end the war. In 1783, the British signed a peace treaty acknowledging the independence of the new United States of America.

One great question remained: What form of government was the new nation to have? In 1781, the states had agreed to come together into a loose union governed by a document called the Articles of Confederation. Under this system, the states sent representatives to a federal legislature called the Congress of the Confederation. But this Congress had very little power. It could not collect taxes. It could pass laws, but the states didn't have to obey them

unless they wanted to. The Congress had no power to force states to meet their obligations.

Consequently the thirteen states acted almost like thirteen separate nations. They passed their own regulations about commerce with foreign countries. They ignored treaties that didn't suit them. They decided whether or not to fight the Indians on the frontier. They built their own navies. They even printed their own money.

It soon became clear that such a weak central government was creating confusion and leaving the nation defenseless against its enemies. Many American leaders, including George Washington, argued that the Articles of Confederation should be replaced.

In the summer of 1787, delegates from 12 states met in Philadelphia and drew up a new constitution for the United States. (Little Rhode Island refused to participate.) This meeting, the Constitutional Convention, was an amazing event. For the past century, Enlightenment thinkers in England and France had written of their hope that human beings could

Under the watchful eye of George Washington, delegates to the Constitutional Convention prepare to sign the U.S. Constitution in Philadelphia in the summer of 1787.

establish a new kind of government—a government based not on a king who had by chance inherited a crown or commanded a powerful army, but on the reason and experience of people who governed themselves. Now the Americans seemed to have that opportunity.

One of the delegates to the Constitutional Convention, Alexander Hamilton of New York, reflected on the importance of their work. "It seems to have been reserved to the people of this country," Hamilton wrote, "to decide the important question, whether societies of men are really capable or not of establishing good government from reflection and choice, or whether they are forever destined to depend for their political constitutions on accident and force."

In Philadelphia in 1787, the framers of the United States Constitution attempted to ignore the sticky summer heat and to use reason and experience as their guide. Experience had taught them the weakness of the Articles of Confederation, so in the Constitution they gave much more authority to the central, or federal, government. At the same time they protected the rights of the people and the states by dividing the power of the federal government among three different branches. They were well aware of Montesquieu's arguments for the separation of powers, and they carefully considered the words of one

A Lasting Constitution

The Constitution of the United States was written in a time of crisis, and attempted to solve difficult problems that plagued the new nation. After the document was written, one delegate asked George Washington how long he thought the Constitution would last. Perhaps a generation, Washington replied. But the framers of the Constitution did their work so well that their plan has lasted far beyond Washington's expectations. Now moving into its third century, the U.S. Constitution is the oldest functioning written constitution in the world.

of their own, John Adams, who had written much about the importance of balancing power among the branches.

The framers of the Constitution decided that the executive branch was to be headed by an elected president. The judicial branch was to consist of judges appointed for life so that they could apply the law honestly and fairly without fear of losing their jobs. The legislative branch, or Congress, was to consist of a House of Representatives elected by the people and a Senate selected by the state legislatures. Today the U.S. Senate, like the House of Representatives, is directly elected by the people; otherwise the basic structure of the federal government has changed very little since the Constitution was adopted.

Europe Watches the American Experiment

Meanwhile, many people in Europe were closely watching America's experiment in republican government. Especially in France, writers and thinkers were excited by the idea that a government could be based on a constitution that reflected the will of the people. In 1789, a French poet wrote about America:

> This vast Continent, surrounded
>   by the sea,
> Will shortly change Europe and
>   the Universe.

The poet was right. In fact, the political universe had already changed in 1789. Britain's former colonists now ruled themselves—the United States was an independent nation. Americans were no longer subjects but citizens. They spoke proudly of their liberty, their republic, and the freedoms they were guaranteed by their Constitution.

The Americans saw themselves as a new Greece or Rome, as modern bearers of the classical democratic tradition. Such exciting ideas would prove contagious. Democratic revolution was about to spread to France and beyond.

The preamble to the U.S. Constitution boldly declares that "we the people" are the source of the basic law of the land. To protect the rights of the people and the states, the Constitution divided federal power among three branches of government— an executive, a legislature, and a judiciary.

Parisians storm the Bastille, the hated symbol of royal power in Paris. The fall of the fortress marked the beginning of the French Revolution.

Liberty, Equality, Fraternity: The French Revolution

*I*n the American Revolution, French forces fought alongside Americans against the British. Even some French nobles joined the fight. A few fought because they wanted to vanquish France's historic enemy, England. Others, including the Marquis de Lafayette, fought for the cause of liberty and people's rights.

When Lafayette returned to France in 1782, he came home to a land where some people had grown impatient with their king and hopeful for a different future. Enlightenment ideas about natural rights, representative governments, and written constitutions were taking root in French soil. Voltaire had mocked the excesses of France's monarchy. Montesquieu had argued that the power of government should be divided among separate branches. Articles in Diderot's *Encyclopédie* looked skeptically at certain French traditions.

All these Enlightenment ideas began to make some people in France challenge the idea of absolute monarchy—the idea that a king should rule with almost unlimited power.

Absolute Monarchs in France

At the time of Lafayette's return to France, Louis XVI reigned as king. Louis XVI came from a long line of all-powerful French kings. You've met his ancestor, Louis XIV, the Sun King who built Versailles and demanded that his every whim be obeyed.

Louis XIV liked to declare, *"L'état, c'est moi"*—"I am the state." During his 72-year-reign, the Sun King behaved as if he *were* indeed the sole power in the state. He ruled as an absolute monarch— he held almost all the power in the French government. He said it was

This chapter focuses on France during its revolution in the late eighteenth century.

Like his ancestor Louis XIV (the Sun King), Louis XVI, pictured at right, saw himself as an absolute monarch. He lived in luxury while millions of his subjects suffered in poverty.

his "divine right" to rule. In other words, he claimed that his authority to rule came from God alone. No one could challenge his decrees.

Louis XIV built the lavish palace for himself at Versailles. There was no Parliament to object to his spending. He lured rebellious French nobles to reside at Versailles so that he could keep an eye on them. All who visited were overawed by the power of the Sun King.

During the Sun King's reign, France became the most powerful and most populous nation in Europe. Wealthy people all over the continent wore French clothes, ate French food, read French books, and spoke the French language.

On his deathbed in 1715, Louis XIV began to question the way he had governed. He warned his

successor to spend less money and to stop taxing the people so heavily. Unfortunately, his actions spoke louder than his words, and later kings failed to follow his advice.

France's next king, Louis XV, was not a wise ruler. This great-grandson of the Sun King fought a number of expensive wars and seemed more interested in pleasure than governing. When he died in 1774, many of his subjects despised him. His grandson, Louis XVI, became king.

Like the Sun King, Louis XVI ruled as an absolute monarch. But unlike the Sun King, Louis XVI had little talent for the details of governing. He preferred to enjoy his favorite pastimes at Versailles—eating, hunting, reading, and repairing locks and watches. When one of his government ministers decided to leave office, Louis remarked, "Why can't I resign, too?"

At the age of 15, Louis married a lively and willful princess, Marie Antoinette, the 14-year-old daughter of the Austrian emperor. The royal couple spent their days at Versailles, surrounded by fawning courtiers and privileged nobles. They lived

"Let them eat cake."

Many people in France disliked Marie Antoinette because she amused herself with fancy balls and plays while ordinary people went hungry. According to one story, the queen once asked an official why Parisians were so resentful. When told that they had run out of bread, she replied, "Then let them eat cake." The story might not have been true, but Parisians believed it and spread the tale.

Marie Antoinette

lives of luxury that the ordinary people of France could barely imagine. Yet ordinary people—some of whom could spend half their daily wages on bread—had always been expected to pay for the privileges of royalty and the nobility.

The Three Estates

Most people in France at this time were over-taxed peasants. They paid taxes to the crown. They paid feudal dues to local lords. And they paid tithes (usually a thirteenth of their harvest) to the Catholic Church, an immensely rich institution that was the largest landowner in France. A political cartoon of the day summed up France's system of taxes. It showed an elderly peasant, bent almost double, carrying on his back a nobleman and a clergyman.

The three individuals in the cartoon represented the three major groupings, or "estates," in French

society. The clergy—about 130,000 individuals—made up the First Estate. The Second Estate included some 400,000 nobles, or aristocrats. The rest of the people of France comprised the Third Estate. The "commoners" of the Third Estate ranged from prosperous merchants

Above: Louis spent most of his time at the palace of Versailles, where he devoted little attention to the business of government.

Left: The poor of eighteenth-century France, who paid many taxes to support both the Church and wealthy nobles, were bent low with economic burdens. Here, a cartoon depicts a peasant carrying a gray-clad clergyman and a nobleman with a plumed hat.

The three major groupings in French society were the clergy of the First Estate (above, left), the nobles of the Second Estate (above, middle), and the commoners of the Third Estate (above, right). Representatives of each estate met in Versailles in the spring of 1789 after King Louis called for a meeting of the Estates-General.

to poor rural peasants and laborers in cities—about 26 million people in all.

The king could summon delegates of the three estates to come together in a representative body known as the Estates-General. But the Estates-General had not met in 175 years. In 1789, ever so reluctantly, Louis XVI once again convened the Estates-General.

The king had one simple reason for doing so. He desperately needed money. France had paid dearly for its wars against Britain, and the nation was almost bankrupt. Louis XVI wanted to get money by creating new taxes. Even though the king held most of the power in France, in 1789 he could not impose new taxes without convening the Estates-General. Many nobles, clergy, and rich merchants insisted that it was about time.

The Estates-General Meet

In the spring of 1789, deputies representing all three estates arrived at Versailles. The event caused great enthusiasm throughout the land, especially among members of the Third Estate. The poor hoped the meeting would improve their lives and ease their burdens, while the richer commoners saw it as a chance to gain political power.

Louis received the deputies of the first two estates in the magnificent Hall of Mirrors in his palace at Versailles. The clergy entered first—bishops in their official velvet robes, parish priests in their simple garb. Next came the nobles, strutting like peacocks in satin suits and gold cloaks, with great plumed hats perched on their heads.

But the 600 deputies of the Third Estate had to wait. Dressed in plain suits of black cloth, they stood for more than three hours to meet the king. He finally received them in one of the palace's more modest rooms.

Three days later the royal couple presided over the first session of the Estates-General. The king sat on his velvet-covered throne in a suit of gold cloth. In an armchair next to him sat the queen, wearing a silver-spangled dress and a heron plume in her hair.

The deputies of the Third Estate soon grew frustrated with events. These merchants, laborers, and farmers produced most of the wealth in France, and paid most of the taxes. They also had more deputies in the Estates-General than the First Estate and Second Estate combined. But the members of the clergy (the First Estate) and nobility (the Second Estate) planned for the Estates-General to make decisions by giving each estate one vote. So if the First and Second Estates stuck together, they could always outvote the Third Estate by a two-to-one margin. They could force higher taxes on France's commoners, and the Third Estate could not stop them.

The deputies of the Third Estate wanted change. And if they didn't get it, they were prepared to claim it in the name of the French nation. "What is the Third Estate?" asked one of its deputies. "Everything. What has it been thus far in the political order? Nothing. What does it demand? To become something."

Determined to "become something," the deputies of the Third Estate gave themselves a new name—the National Assembly. And they declared themselves capable of acting on behalf of the whole kingdom.

These actions angered the king. He threatened to dissolve the Estates-General and use force against the National Assembly. When the members of the National Assembly tried to meet on the morning of June 20,

they found the door of their hall locked against them. Rain was falling. The dripping deputies wandered around, looking for a place to gather. A huge crowd of people thronged around, chanting *Vive l'Assemblée!* (veev lah-sahm-blay)—"Long live the Assembly!"

Finally the deputies found an indoor tennis court and filed inside. There, one young deputy declared that they must swear an oath never to disband until they had drafted a new constitution for the French government. One by one, arms raised in salute, the deputies came forward to take the oath, now known as the Tennis Court Oath. King Louis sent word that the National Assembly should disband, but the deputies refused. "The assembled

Deputies of the Third Estate raise their arms to take the so-called Tennis Court Oath. By this act, they swore not to disband until France had a new constitution.

nation cannot be given orders," they declared. It was a bold—indeed, a revolutionary—assertion.

Storming the Bastille and Starting a Revolution

All this time, people throughout France were growing restless and bitter. The harvest of 1788 had been poor, and the price of bread soared. Many people could not find work. Angry crowds thronged the roads between Paris and Versailles, just 12 miles apart.

King Louis saw all this unrest and took no action. He watched as the National Assembly continued to meet for several days after the Tennis Court Oath. Then the king began to gather his troops for a showdown with the Assembly. By now, however, many French soldiers had gone over to the side of the people. Still, Louis had many troops who would obey his commands. He ordered thousands of these troops to France's capital city, Paris.

Rumors flew through the city. Any day now, people said, the king's soldiers would march into the city and slit their throats. The people began to arm themselves. On July 14, 1789, the shout arose, "To the Bastille (ba-STEEL)!" Some 8,000 Parisians swarmed to the armory in the east of the city. They hoped they would find arms and ammunition there.

The Bastille, a fortress built in the fourteenth century, had eight round towers linked by 100-foot-high walls. From those walls cannons pointed down over the city. The Bastille also served as a prison. Many celebrated prisoners had spent time there, among them the great *philosophe* Voltaire. But now it contained just seven prisoners.

Above all, the Bastille was a hated symbol of royal power. The crowd demanded its surrender. The fortress's governor, backed by about a hundred soldiers, refused. As the two sides confronted each other, a musket shot rang out. No one knows who fired it. Then one of the cannons roared. Three hours of bitter fighting followed, in which 98 of the attackers were killed. (See the image on page 368.)

When the attackers found five cannons of their own and aimed them at the main gate, the governor surrendered. He opened the gate and the enraged crowd rushed in to take revenge on the defenders. They killed the Bastille's governor, cut off his head, and hoisted it on a pike.

That same day the king had been out hunting. He received word of the fall of the Bastille late in the evening. "Why, this is a revolt," he exclaimed to one of his courtiers, the Grand Master of the Wardrobe. "No, sire," the man replied. "It is a revolution."

Indeed—the French Revolution had begun.

Power to the People

When the Bastille fell, the National Assembly became in effect the governing body of France. No one was yet calling for a government without a king. But the National Assembly was determined to create a constitutional monarchy—a government in which written rules define the powers of the king and set forth the rights of the people.

The National Assembly issued a document called the Declaration of the Rights of Man and of the Citizen. Like the American Declaration of Independence, the French declaration drew on the "natural law" philosophy of the English philosopher John Locke, as well as the writings of the French philosophes. "Men are born and remain free and equal in rights," proclaimed the Assembly. Those rights included the right to "liberty, property, security, and resistance to oppression."

The Declaration of the Rights of Man and of the Citizen was printed in thousands of pamphlets and spread throughout France. People everywhere read and repeated its words. The National Assembly also decreed sweeping changes for France. It abolished the old feudal taxes that peasants paid to their landlords. It decreed that clergy, nobles, and local lords would have no special tax privileges—they, too, would be taxed. The Assembly took away all titles of nobility. And it made more than half the adult male population eligible to vote.

"Men are born and remain free," declared the Declaration of the Rights of Man and of the Citizen.

The Declaration of the Rights of Man and of the Citizen

The National Assembly drew up the Declaration of the Rights of Man and of the Citizen in August 1789. Like the American Declaration of Independence, issued 13 years earlier, it expressed many ideals of the Enlightenment. Here are 12 of the 17 rights stated in the French Declaration.

The National Assembly recognizes and proclaims in the presence and under the auspices of the Supreme Being the following rights of man and of the citizen:

A Page from the Past

1. Men are born and remain free and equal in rights. Social distinctions can only be founded upon the general good.

2. The aim of all political association is the preservation of the natural ... rights of man. These rights are liberty, property, security, and resistance to oppression.

4. Liberty consists of being able to do everything which injures no one else; hence the exercise of the natural rights of each man has no limits except those which assure to the other members of the society the enjoyment of the same rights. These limits can only be determined by law.

6. Law is the expression of the general will. Every citizen has a right to participate personally or through his representative in its formation. It must be the same for all, whether it protects or punishes. All citizens, being equal in the eyes of the law, are equally eligible to all dignities and to all public positions and occupations according to their abilities, and without distinction except that of their virtues and talents.

7. No person shall be accused, arrested, or imprisoned except in the cases and according to the forms prescribed by law....

Disquieted means disturbed.

10. No one shall be disquieted on account of his opinions, including his religious views....

11. The free communication of ideas and opinions is one of the most precious of the rights of man. Every citizen may, accordingly, speak, write, and print with freedom, being responsible, however, for such abuses of this freedom as shall be defined by law.

12. The security of the rights of man and of the citizen requires public military force. These forces are, therefore, established for the good of all and not for the personal advantage of those to whom they shall be entrusted.

14. All the citizens have a right to decide either personally or by their representatives as to the necessity of the public contribution [taxation], to grant this freely, to know to what uses it is put, and to fix the proportion, the mode of assessment and of collection, and the duration of the taxes.

15. Society has the right to require of every public agent an account of his administration.

16. A society in which the observance of the law is not assured nor the separation of powers defined has no constitution at all.

17. Property being an inviolable and sacred right, no one shall be deprived thereof except where public necessity, legally determined, shall clearly demand it, and then only on condition that the owner shall have been previously and equitably indemnified. ⌇

> To be *equitably indemnified* is to be fairly compensated or paid back for one's losses.

Louis Plans and Plots

For a while it seemed as though King Louis might accept the changes taking place. But he refused to give them his approval. Instead, he stalled for time while he tried to figure out how to regain control of the government. Many people did not trust him. In October 1789, a crowd of revolutionaries marched on Versailles and forced Louis, Marie Antoinette, and their four-year-old son to move to Paris. There the people could keep an eye on the royal family.

Publicly, Louis pretended to cooperate with the Assembly. When the Assembly drafted a constitution with a one-house legislature and a limited monarchy, he indicated that he would support it. But privately,

Accompanied by sympathetic guardsmen, Parisian women march on Versailles to bring the royal family back to the capital. The people no longer believed that the king and queen supported the Revolution.

he seethed and wondered what his brother-in-law, the emperor of Austria, could do to help.

The National Assembly pressed ahead. Soon it seized the immense landholdings of the Roman Catholic Church. Church properties were sold to pay some of the nation's large debt. The National Assembly also decreed religious toleration for both Protestants and Jews.

There was little Louis could do, but still he plotted to stop the Revolution. Royal courtiers secretly urged Marie Antoinette's brother, the Austrian emperor, to march his army into France and restore the king's power. One June night in 1791, the royal family disguised themselves as peasants and tried to slip out of the country to join the Austrians on the eastern frontier. They never made it. Watchful citizens blocked their escape and hauled them back to Paris.

The king's attempted flight provoked fear and anger among the French people. They said he had betrayed the Revolution—he had said he would support the constitution, and then had treacherously tried to sneak away to Austria. No one doubted that, once at the border, he planned to lead an army back into France to crush the Revolution by force.

From Monarchy to Republic

The French people faced a momentous decision. What should they do with their king?

At first the Assembly assumed that Louis would cooperate, so they restored him to the throne. But Louis continued to plot against the Revolution. In August 1792, an armed, well-organized group of Parisians took matters into their own hands. They stormed the palace where the king was living, imprisoned the royal family, and held them prisoner. A new body called the National Convention was elected.

The National Convention decided that the country no longer needed a king. In September 1792, it declared France a republic. The streets rang with the cry of the nation's official slogan: *"Liberté, Egalité, Fraternité"* (lee-behr-TAY, ay-gah-lee-TAY, fra-tehr-nee-TAY)—"Liberty, Equality, Fraternity." (*Fraternity* means comradeship, brotherly affection.)

With the National Convention, the French Revolution entered a new phase—the most violent and also the most democratic phase to

Taking On the Church

For decades Voltaire and other French philosophes had ridiculed the Roman Catholic Church. They disliked the Catholic Church's wealth and power. Many philosophes discouraged religious beliefs because, they said, religion ran contrary to reason.

The French revolutionaries openly challenged the Roman Catholic Church. In 1789, the National Assembly took control of lands owned by the Church. The next year, the Assembly passed a law requiring the election of priests and bishops by voters. When the pope rejected this idea, the National Assembly closed Church monasteries and convents. In 1793, the revolutionary government even outlawed religion and officially renamed the Cathedral of Notre Dame the "Temple of Reason." Tension between revolutionaries and Church supporters continued throughout the French Revolution.

Crowds gather in the Place de la Révolution in Paris to watch the guillotine claim its latest victim. Thousands of priests, aristocrats, and commoners were executed here—as was King Louis XVI.

date. The Convention decided to punish Louis. It put him on trial for treason and found him guilty. Louis XVI, descendant of the Sun King, was sentenced to death—decapitation by the guillotine (GIH-luh-teen or GHEE-yuh-teen).

In Paris, the guillotine stood in the center of a huge public square. There, on the morning of January 21, 1793, King Louis XVI prepared to pay for his "crimes against the Revolution." With dignity, the king mounted the scaffold. He addressed the crowd and pardoned his enemies, but a drum roll drowned out his final words.

The executioner pushed the king down onto the guillotine and placed his head inside the wooden clamp. The blade fell. An era ended. A few shouts rang out from the onlookers: *"Vive la République!"* (veev lah ray-poo-bleek)—"Long live the republic!"

When news of the execution of Louis XVI spread, the rulers of neighboring countries, many of them relatives of Marie Antoinette, were outraged. They feared that the violence of the French Revolution might spread to their own lands. So Europe's kings and nobles agreed to attack the French republic and put down the Revolution. As the armies

The Guillotine

In France before the Revolution, ordinary people who were condemned to death faced execution by hanging. Only nobles had the right to a quicker execution—having their heads chopped off by an axe. However, a mild-mannered doctor named Joseph-Ignace Guillotin believed that in this new era of equality, all citizens should share this "right."

Guillotin invented a machine that would make the process of decapitation as painless as possible. It used a razor-sharp blade dropped between two wooden supports. The guillotine was intended to be a fast and merciful form of execution.

The man most responsible for plunging France into the bloody Reign of Terror was an immaculately dressed lawyer named Maximilien Robespierre. Everywhere he turned, Robespierre saw enemies of the Revolution.

of Western Europe gathered along the frontiers of France, thousands of Frenchmen volunteered to join the army. To the cry of "Liberty, Equality, Fraternity," they marched off to defend their Revolution.

Terror and Equality

As neighboring countries prepared to attack France, the country faced internal threats as well. In the provinces, royalists—supporters of the king—launched uprisings. All over the country, people struggled with each other for power. All this disorder and conflict threatened the success of the Revolution.

Some leaders decided they must use any means to keep the Revolution alive. They told themselves that the goals of the Revolution— "Liberty, Equality, Fraternity"—were so noble that they justified extreme means, even violence and terror. Leading the way was a man named

Maximilien Robespierre (mahk-see-meel-yan ROHBZ-pyehr).

Robespierre had won election to the Estates-General of 1789. He was a lawyer in his early thirties, a small, thin man with carefully powdered hair and a pale complexion. He always seemed nervous and rarely looked anyone in the eye. But as a lawyer Robespierre was willing to take the cases of poor clients that other lawyers refused to accept. He brilliantly defended clients who could not pay him. Parisians admired him for this, as well for his honesty. They called him Robespierre the Incorruptible.

Since 1789, Robespierre had risen through the ranks to become a leading figure of the Revolution. Although he supported the king's execution, he probably didn't watch it. The sight of blood sickened him, and he never attended executions. Yet in 1793 and 1794, under Robespierre's leadership, the Revolution plunged into its bloodiest phase, both at home and abroad.

What Did the Americans Think?

In the young United States, news of Louis XVI's execution was greeted with dismay. Louis XVI was the king who had sent troops to aid the Americans in their Revolutionary War against the British. George Washington had a bust of the king in his home. Americans had named a town after him (Louisville, Kentucky). Washington worried that the French were "rushing so fast to swallow the cup of liberty, that they will drink its dregs and scald their throats." Thomas Jefferson held a different view. Although he had once called Louis XVI "a good man," he also believed that sometimes blood must be shed in order for people to gain their rights and liberty. He pointed out that kings should be "amenable to punishment like other criminals."

At home, Robespierre and his supporters saw enemies of the Revolution everywhere. They persuaded the other deputies to pass a Law of Suspects. This law allowed the police to arrest any citizen who had shown himself to be a "supporter of tyranny" or an "enemy of liberty." This could mean anyone who had not demonstrated constant support for the Revolution.

Soon no citizen, however innocent, could feel safe from the threat of arrest. If a man spoke of some happy event in years past, a police spy might accuse him of being a supporter of the old monarchy. If he complained about food shortages or about the war, he risked arrest. Many prisoners did not even know the reason for their arrest.

Every day, carts rumbled through the streets of Paris, carrying victims to the guillotine. Crowds followed, each spectator pushing to get a better view of the execution. Some even made a day out of it, bringing along their knitting or their lunch.

The "Lost" Dauphin

King Louis XVI and Marie Antoinette had a son named Louis-Charles. When the Revolution began in 1789, the boy was four years old. Louis-Charles was the *dauphin* (DAW-fuhn or doh-FAN), the heir to the French throne. But in 1792, revolutionaries threw him into prison with the rest of his family. The next year, guards tore him from his mother's arms and took him to a small, windowless room, where they forced him to live alone. The French government reported that ten-year-old Louis-Charles died in prison in 1795, and that he was buried in an unmarked grave.

Soon rumors began to fly through Europe that the young dauphin had escaped and was still alive, waiting to reclaim his throne. But where was he? Some people believed that he had been smuggled to the United States for safekeeping. It was said that the famous American naturalist John James Audubon was really Louis-Charles. A missionary in Wisconsin and a German clockmaker both claimed to be the dauphin. Over the decades, hundreds of would-be royal heirs popped up.

The mystery of the "Lost Dauphin" lasted for more than 200 years. In 2000, scientists compared the heart of the boy who died in prison with a lock of Marie Antoinette's hair. The boy and the queen were clearly related. So it seems that the "Lost Dauphin" died in prison after all.

Louis-Charles, the young dauphin, is taken away from his mother. Two years later he died in prison and was buried in an unmarked grave.

Marie Antoinette followed her husband to the guillotine. Thousands of others perished in the same way. Some were aristocrats. Some were nuns and priests. Others were ordinary citizens of France, workers and peasants.

Month after month the slaughter continued. Up to 40,000 perished under the swift-falling blade. This phase of the Revolution, marked by bloodshed and fear, became known as the Reign of Terror.

But Frenchmen put up with the bloodshed, partly because the National Convention was taking bold strides toward *egalité*, or equality. The Convention established free primary schooling for all boys and girls. It passed laws that required equal inheritance for both sons and daughters. (Prior to this, only first-born sons could inherit estates.) It pioneered universal male suffrage—for the first time, all French men could vote. Before the Revolution, men had to own property and pay taxes in order to vote. The National Convention also declared slavery illegal, even in France's colonies.

Finally, the Convention undertook another reform designed to make France strong. It instituted a military draft in order to fight France's revolutionary wars. Serving in the military, the Convention proclaimed, was the duty of every French citizen. If a man had the right to vote, he had the duty to defend the republic. With the draft in place, France could marshal huge armies in the field.

As we'll see, not all of these changes would last. But the Convention's push for equal rights would make the French Revolution a force for change in Europe for the next two centuries.

Marie Antoinette is led to her execution on October 16, 1793, nine months after her husband met his doom on the guillotine. Louis XVI's Austrian-born wife had never been popular with Parisians. Thousands of them turned out to watch her execution.

Saving the Revolution?

By the spring of 1793, Robespierre was acting more and more like a tyrant. He and his supporters held onto power by killing off many of their opponents. He talked of plots and intrigues. Rivals who disagreed with him were branded traitors to the Revolution.

Eventually the Convention turned on Robespierre. His rivals decided to stick together, stand up to the tyrant, and hope that they could convince most of the deputies to stand with them. The plan worked. On July 28, 1794, the guillotine brought an end to Robespierre's life and reign of terror.

After Robespierre's death, a five-man body known as the Directory came to power in France. The five Directors faced many enemies. On one side, Robespierre's allies plotted a return to power. On the other side, royalists schemed to restore the monarchy. And foreign armies menaced the borders. France was still a republic, but a republic holding on by just a thread.

The desperate Directors turned to the army for help. They came to place their trust in one successful young officer who had won great victories for France on foreign fields of battle. His name was Napoleon Bonaparte (nuh-POHL-yuhn BOH-nuh-pahrt). The directors believed they could control this general and guide him to do their will. But in 1799 Napoleon seized power from the government, and soon he wielded as much power as a king.

Ten years had passed since Parisians had stormed the Bastille and launched their Revolution against Louis XVI's absolute rule. The French Revolution was coming to an end, but not before it had brought remarkable and far-reaching changes.

The last victims of the Reign of Terror await execution in a Parisian jail in July 1794. Days later, Robespierre himself would share their fate.

Napoleon Bonaparte—shown here crossing the Alps into northern Italy—forged an empire and spread revolution across Europe.

Napoleon: Revolution and Empire

Revolution changed France from top to bottom. It toppled an absolute monarchy—both king and queen met their fate on the guillotine. It ended the privileges of the upper classes and gave new rights to workers and peasants. A new republic replaced the old monarchy and proclaimed "Liberty, Equality, and Fraternity" for all.

But in 1799, a mere 10 years after the fall of the Bastille, the army general named Napoleon Bonaparte seized control of the French government. Soon he was as powerful as any European monarch. Indeed, Napoleon might well have echoed the words of France's own Sun King, Louis XIV: "I am the state."

So, had the French people rid themselves of one absolute monarch only to get a new all-powerful ruler? Had the Revolution really come to this? Napoleon had a simple answer: "I am the Revolution."

Let's begin our examination of Napoleon's extraordinary career by looking back at how he came to power.

Napoleon: Soldier of the Revolution

Napoleon Bonaparte was born in 1769 to a family of minor nobility on the Mediterranean island of Corsica. When he was nine years old his father sent him to military school in France. The boy was an average student in most subjects, although he excelled in geography and math. He went on to attend a military college in Paris, from which he graduated in the bottom third of the class. Fellow students remembered him as a loner with a strange accent.

After the Revolution began, Napoleon rose quickly in the French

This chapter focuses on Napoleonic Europe during the late eighteenth and early nineteenth centuries.

army. In 1792, he became captain of an artillery unit and fought well in battles against the Revolution's enemies. He soon won promotion to the rank of brigadier general. He was just 24 years old.

Like many young officers of the day, Napoleon welcomed the French Revolution. Indeed, he called himself a "soldier of the Revolution." In 1795, he helped put down a royalist uprising in Paris. Within a year he was in command of a new French army in Italy.

Northern Italy formed part of the empire of Austria, France's enemy. There Napoleon fought brilliantly and won the devotion of his troops. During one battle in Italy, he surprised his men by personally aiming a cannon at the Austrian positions. Normally only

Napoleon Rallies His Troops

A Page from the Past

Napoleon Bonaparte was a military genius who knew how to inspire his troops. You get a glimpse of his ability in this proclamation to his troops in Italy, issued in 1796.

Soldiers:

In a fortnight you have won six victories, taken twenty-one standards, fifty-five pieces of artillery, several strong positions, and conquered the richest part of Piedmont [in northern Italy]; you have captured 15,000 prisoners and killed or wounded more than 10,000 men....You have won battles without cannon, crossed rivers without bridges, made forced marches without shoes, camped without brandy and often without bread. Soldiers of liberty, only republican troops could have endured what you have endured. Soldiers, you have our thanks! The grateful *Patrie* (pah-tree) will owe its prosperity to you....

The two armies which but recently attacked you with audacity are fleeing before you in terror; the wicked men who laughed at your misery and rejoiced at the thought of the triumphs of your enemies are confounded and trembling.

But, soldiers, as yet you have done nothing compared with what remains to be done.... Undoubtedly the greatest obstacles have been overcome; but you still have battles to fight, cities to capture, rivers to cross. Is there one among you whose courage is abating? No.... All of you are consumed with a desire to extend the glory of the French people; all of you long to humiliate those arrogant kings who dare to contemplate placing us in fetters; all of you lowly corporals performed such risky tasks. From that day on, the men affectionately referred to their commander—who was of average height for his day but shorter than most French army officers—as "the little corporal."

From "Little Corporal" to Emperor

After driving the enemy out of Italy and advancing to within 75 miles of Vienna, Napoleon negotiated a treaty with the Austrians. He returned to Paris in glory, as adored by the public as he was by his troops. In 1799, he joined a coup (koo) that overthrew the Directory, as the government of France was then known.

In place of the Directory, three men called consuls took over as the highest officials in France.

A *coup* is an unexpected move or act, in this case, a sudden takeover of a government.

desire to dictate a glorious peace, one which will indemnify the Patrie for the immense sacrifices it has made; all of you wish to be able to say with pride as you return to your villages, "I was with the victorious army in Italy!"

To *indemnify* is to compensate or pay back for losses.

Napoleon's victorious army in northern Italy, 1797

Each consul was supposed to possess an equal share of power. But it soon became clear who held the real power—the First Consul, General Bonaparte.

Each consul was supposed to hold office for 10 years, but Napoleon managed to have himself made consul for life. He became so powerful that in effect he ruled France as a dictator. Then, in December 1804, he took one final step to replace representative government with one-man rule. He had his collaborators proclaim him emperor.

Consuls: Harking Back to Rome

After overthrowing the Directory, Napoleon and two other men ruled France as consuls. They took the term *consul* **from ancient Rome. The ancient Roman republic had been ruled by two elected officials called consuls. Near the end of the republic, the great Roman general Julius Caesar became consul, and later Dictator for Life. Napoleon saw himself as a new Caesar, and even hoped to surpass Caesar in power and influence.**

Julius Caesar inspired Napoleon to dream of empire and greatness.

From near and far, 8,000 dignitaries came to see Napoleon crowned as emperor. They squeezed into the Cathedral of Notre Dame in Paris to witness his coronation. An orchestra and a choir stood ready. Napoleon rose before them, dressed in elaborate robes. He carried a scepter said to belong to the great medieval ruler of France, Charlemagne.

The pope, who had come from Rome for the great occasion, approached and anointed Napoleon with sacred oil. Then, to the astonishment of the audience, Napoleon took the crown from the pope's hand and placed it firmly on his own head. With this act, he seemed to proclaim that he did not receive his authority to rule from a higher power such as the Catholic Church. Napoleon intended to answer to no one.

"Vive l'Empereur!"—"Long live the Emperor!"—the people cried. Hundreds of church bells pealed, and cannons roared. The man once known as the "little corporal" now stood before his people as Napoleon I, Emperor of the French.

"Stabilizing" the Revolution

You've seen how Napoleon rose like a shooting star from "little corporal" to emperor. Let's turn now to examine some of his major actions during the various phases of his rule of France.

The French Revolution had been a bloody, chaotic time. As the Revolution drew to a close, Napoleon knew that France needed order. As he put it, the time had come to "stabilize" the Revolution.

Napoleon stands in his coronation robes after being crowned Emperor of the French in Notre Dame Cathedral. During the ceremony, Napoleon took the crown out of the pope's hands and put it on his own head.

He set about this task by reforming the French government. He enlarged the Ministry of Police and gave it new powers to keep order. He set up a civil service system, in which citizens could be promoted based on their talent and hard work, not their family background.

Paris became the center of authority for government throughout France. Napoleon modernized the capital city. He improved Paris's sidewalks, sewers, and water supply. He built new markets and quays (keez) along the Seine (sen) River. Throughout the country he built a new system

On a waterway, a *quay* is a wharf or other structure where boats can load and unload.

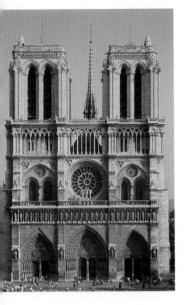

Above: Napoleon saved Notre Dame from demolition. He also made religion legal again in France.

Right: Napoleon commissioned this grand monument—the Arc de Triomphe in Paris—to commemorate his military victories. Centuries before, Roman emperors had built triumphal arches to celebrate their accomplishments.

of roads. He also created new theaters, established an efficient postal service, and worked to improve schools.

During the Revolution, religion had been officially outlawed in France. Napoleon made religion legal again. He also saved the Cathedral of Notre Dame. In 1795, the Directory had sold the Cathedral to a man who was going to demolish it for its stones. Fortunately, he did not act quickly. In 1802, Napoleon stepped in. He saved Notre Dame from destruction and reintroduced Catholicism with a solemn ceremony on Easter Sunday. (And, as you've read, he was pleased to crown himself in Notre Dame in 1804.)

Napoleon did not return property that the French government had seized from the Catholic Church. He kept much of the Church in France under the control of the state.

The Napoleonic Code

Most important among the many reforms he instituted, Napoleon reformed France's legal system. Traditionally, northern France used one type of law, while southern France used another. The result was legal chaos—a country divided between two legal systems.

Napoleon decided to give France a single set of laws that would apply

Napoleon's wife Josephine favored loose high-waisted gowns, imitating those worn by Greek women. This style became known as an "Empire" gown.

to all citizens without distinction, no matter who they were or where they lived. His system became known as the Napoleonic Code.

The Napoleonic Code preserved most of the gains of the Revolution. It protected freedom of speech and worship, and the right to trial by jury. The Code affirmed equality before the law, although men still had greater rights than women. It permitted individuals to choose their own professions. And it assured that feudalism was over.

Feudal dues had been abolished at the beginning of the Revolution in 1789. The Napoleonic Code brought a definite end to medieval practices that had reduced peasants to little more than servants of lords who held the lion's share of legal rights.

Napoleon took great pride in his Code. He claimed that establishing the Code gave him greater satisfaction than all of his 40 battles. This

was high praise indeed, for few men excelled on the field of battle as decisively as Napoleon.

Napoleon Expands His Empire

Without doubt, Napoleon was one of the greatest generals of all time. He amassed a Grand Army, as it was called, second to none. Where did he get the troops? For the most part from the French people themselves—citizen-soldiers, as they became known.

In 1793, Robespierre and the National Convention had decreed mandatory military service as the obligation of male citizens between ages 18 to 25. Napoleon continued the practice. He knew that many French people did not like this obligation, but he called on them to make the sacrifice. He was popular and managed to mobilize enormous forces. These forces were needed

Napoleon's Empire, c. 1812

because when Napoleon became consul in 1799, France was at war with its neighbors. The fighting continued, with only the briefest of interruptions, for the next 16 years.

At the head of his Grand Army, Napoleon won a string of spectacular victories across the continent. One by one, the allied armies of Austria, Prussia, and Russia fell before him. Napoleon seemed unstoppable. Only Great Britain stood in his way, defiant and undefeated across the English Channel.

The Continental System

Napoleon quickly drew up plans for invading Britain. But he had to get past the Royal Navy. In 1805, Admiral Horatio Nelson, Britain's great naval hero, defeated a combined French and Spanish fleet off the southwest coast of Spain. Nelson lost his own life at the Battle of Trafalgar. But his victory put an end to Napoleon's plans to invade Britain by crossing the English Channel.

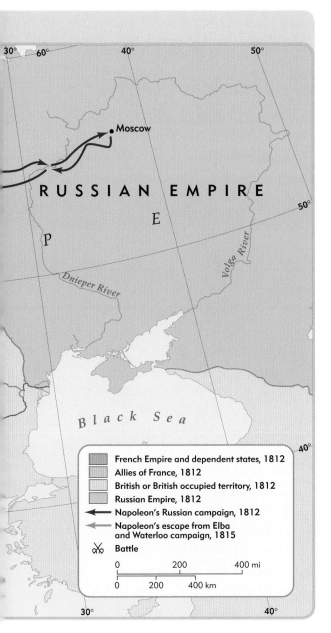

All the countries on the European continent had to keep British ships out of their ports. There could be no exceptions. But on the Iberian Peninsula, the British found ports willing to welcome their ships. The Portuguese continued to trade with Britain. So did the Spanish, who were supposedly allies of the French.

Britain's Royal Navy captured 20 French and Spanish ships at the Battle of Trafalgar, without losing a ship of its own. The French defeat ended Napoleon's hopes of sailing across the English Channel and invading Britain.

- On the map above, locate the Battle of Trafalgar.

Napoleon decided on another way to defeat the British. He tried to stop the nations he had conquered from trading with Britain. Since Britain depended on buying and selling with its neighbors on the continent, this plan could ruin the island nation's finances. Napoleon called his trade blockade the Continental System.

To be effective, the Continental System had to be truly *continental*.

Selling Louisiana to Pay for War

Wars are expensive. How did Napoleon pay for his? Partly through the sale of land. France claimed vast expanses of land in North America west of the Mississippi River. Americans were eager to own the French city of New Orleans, at the mouth of the Mississippi. In 1803, President Thomas Jefferson sent Americans to Paris to strike a deal. The Americans were shocked when Napoleon offered to sell the young United States the whole of the Louisiana Territory, from the Mississippi River to the Rocky Mountains, from the Canadian border to the Gulf of Mexico. The Americans gladly paid the price. The Louisiana Purchase, as it is called, doubled the size of the United States.

In 1807, to enforce his Continental System and cut off all trade with the British, Napoleon invaded the Iberian Peninsula. He toppled the Spanish king and placed his brother Joseph on the Spanish throne. But the peninsular war dragged on for another five years. With the help of the British, Spanish forces kept 300,000 French troops engaged in a long series of battles. This weakened Napoleon by depriving him of soldiers he could have used elsewhere.

Catastrophe in Russia

Napoleon found that other countries were not willing to continue cutting off all trade with Britain. In late 1810, the Russian ruler Tsar Alexander I pulled out of the Continental System. Napoleon prepared to punish the Russians. He built up his Grand Army, adding soldiers from regions he had conquered—Germans, Dutch, Swiss, Italians, Poles, and Lithuanians. The Grand Army represented the largest military force ever assembled in Europe to that date. In June 1812, Napoleon launched his most ambitious campaign. He invaded Russia with more than 600,000 troops.

Triggering Faraway Revolutions

Napoleon's invasion of Spain provoked a wave of democratic revolutions on a continent three thousand miles away. In Central and South America, Spanish colonists rejected the idea of being subject to a French emperor. In 1810, many Spanish-American colonies declared their independence, as much from France as from Spain. (You'll read more about these revolutions in the next chapter.)

The emperor hoped for a quick victory against the Russians. "My forces are three times greater than yours," Napoleon wrote to Alexander. "At this time, with the whole of Europe behind me, how do you expect to be able to stop me?"

But the tsar had a plan. He refused to meet Napoleon in battle. Instead, his troops pulled back before the Grand Army. As they withdrew, they burned their own villages and fields, preventing the invaders from finding food and supplies. Tens of thousands of Napoleon's soldiers died from starvation, heat, and disease. When Napoleon did meet the Russians in battle, he lost many men.

The Grand Army marched on until it reached Moscow, an important Russian city. But Napoleon got small pleasure from the prize. He found it almost deserted. And the next day a fire—perhaps started by the Russians themselves—destroyed two-thirds of the city. Worse, the Russians refused to surrender. Instead they continued to strengthen their army.

Lacking supplies, Napoleon realized that he could not stay in Moscow through the long, hard Russian winter. So on October 18 he ordered a retreat westward. Along the way his army suffered terribly in the bitter cold. Poorly supplied and weak from hunger, the troops were barely able to march. Men and horses froze in the snow or died of starvation. Soldiers deserted by the hundreds. The Russians killed or captured those who fell behind. The Grand Army turned into a ragtag mob.

Napoleon had entered Russia with more than 600,000 troops. By the time his army returned to Paris, there were barely 40,000 left.

A Showdown at Waterloo

Several European powers—Austria, Britain, Russia, Prussia, and Sweden—formed an alliance and rushed to defeat Napoleon while he was weakened. In 1813, the allies drove Napoleon's troops out of Germany. The following year they invaded France itself and marched into Paris. The once mighty Napoleon had no choice but to surrender his throne.

The victorious allies exiled Napoleon from France. But they allowed him to keep the title of emperor, and even gave him a new territory to rule—the tiny island of Elba, 86 square miles of mountainous scrubland off the northwest coast of Italy.

Napoleon quickly grew bored on Elba. After just 10 months, he slipped back to France, landing on the southern coast with about a thousand followers. Soon he met a regiment dispatched to halt and arrest him. For several tense minutes it seemed as if fighting were about to break out between the two sides. But Napoleon's ability to connect with common soldiers came to his rescue. Opening his coat, he spoke to them. "Soldiers of the fifth regiment! I am your emperor…. If there is a man among you who would kill his emperor, here I am!"

Napoleon waited. No one raised a musket. Shouting *"Vive l'Empereur!"* the troops went over to his side. On March 20, 1815, Paris welcomed back the Emperor of the French.

Above: The defeated Grand Army struggles through the Russian countryside on its retreat to France. Only a fraction of Napoleon's army survived the disastrous Russian campaign.

Below: Napoleon wins over troops sent to arrest him after his escape from Elba. Soon he was back in power in Paris, ready to raise another army and wage another war.

Napoleon and his troops flee the field at Waterloo after meeting their match in the Duke of Wellington and an allied army of British and Prussians. Waterloo was the final battle in the Napoleonic Wars.

To the allies, however, Napoleon was nothing more than an outlaw. They prepared to invade France again. While they made their plans, Napoleon raised another army and struck first. His targets were two allied armies—one British, one Prussian—encamped near a small town called Waterloo, in the country now called Belgium.

"Meeting Your Waterloo"

The Duke of Wellington and his Prussian allies dealt Napoleon a crippling defeat at Waterloo. Today, when someone suffers a complete defeat, we sometimes say he has "met his Waterloo."

He intended to defeat the allies before the British and Prussian troops could unite.

- On the map on pages 392–93, locate Waterloo.

But Napoleon met his match in the Duke of Wellington, commander of the British troops. Wellington had fought the French in Spain and never lost. He did not intend to start losing now. On June 18, 1815, his troops turned back the attacking French troops. When Prussian reinforcements arrived on the field of battle, Napoleon realized the end had come. The Battle of Waterloo marked the emperor's final defeat.

Napoleon fled west, to the Atlantic coast of France, where he surrendered to the British. He hoped that he would be able to retire to the United States. But his enemies did not want to take the chance that he might raise another army. They exiled the one-time master of Europe to St. Helena, a tiny island in the South Atlantic, 1,200 miles off the coast of Africa.

On St. Helena, Napoleon spent the last six years of his life fighting yet another battle—the battle for his reputation. By dictating his memoirs, he tried to shape the way he would be remembered—as a man of reason, genius, and action. He was such a man, but history also remembers him as a man of extreme ambition who wanted to dominate a continent.

Napoleon's Legacy

Napoleon Bonaparte had dreamed grand dreams. The self-styled Emperor of the French imagined ruling all of Europe from Paris, just as Caesar had ruled from Rome. He came close. In fact, his European empire was comparable to that of Caesar and larger than that of Napoleon's other great hero, Charlemagne. At its height, Napoleon's domain stretched from Spain in the west to the borders of Russia in the east.

Wherever his Grand Army marched, Napoleon took the message of the French Revolution.

No longer master of Europe, Napoleon stands aboard a Royal Navy ship and broods over his imminent exile on the South Atlantic island of St. Helena. The one-time commander of the Grand Army was allowed just five friends to accompany him to his new home.

"The peoples of Germany, the peoples of France, of Italy, of Spain all desire equality," he declared. In countries across Europe he swept away old governments ruled by dukes, princes, and other nobles. In their place, he introduced constitutions and legal systems in which all were equal in the eyes of the law.

Napoleon defended the idea that people's abilities, not their families' titles, should determine how far they rise in the world. After all, this "little corporal" from a Mediterranean island rose to become emperor of France.

Napoleon's most important legacy is the Napoleonic Code, which is regarded as one of the most important codes of law in history. Napoleon saw it as a universal standard for all. After his death, the Code lived on in France. It also continued to influence the legal systems of Belgium, the Netherlands, Germany, Switzerland, and Italy. Even faraway lands in the Americas adopted modified versions of the Code.

Napoleon's conquests changed the map of Europe. He did away with old boundaries from feudal times. He sometimes united people who shared a common language, religion, and culture. For example, in Germany, he formed the Rhine Confederation, which brought together some 300 small German states.

Napoleon unintentionally united people who disliked his rule. He saw himself as a liberator who freed Europe from its old feudal ways in which a privileged few had ruled the masses. But many of his new subjects in Spain, Germany, Italy, and elsewhere regarded him as a tyrant and foreign conqueror. They

The Napoleonic Code is Napoleon's enduring legacy, not just to France but also to much of Europe and beyond. The emperor himself claimed that establishing his law code gave him greater satisfaction than all of his 40 battles.

CODE CIVIL

DES

FRANÇAIS.

ÉDITION ORIGINALE ET SEULE OFFICIELLE.

À PARIS,
DE L'IMPRIMERIE DE LA RÉPUBLIQUE.
An XII. 1804.

also hated the fact that he often put his relatives in charge of the various parts of his ever-growing empire.

Three of his brothers sat on royal thrones—the kingdom of Holland, the kingdom of Spain, and the newly created German kingdom of Westphalia. In Italy, he made one of his sisters the duchess of Tuscany, and another became queen of Naples. He took the title of King of Italy for himself and made his stepson Italy's viceroy.

Across the continent, the presence of French rulers and French soldiers stirred a wave of nationalism—a strong sense of attachment or belonging to one's own country. With the French foreigners in charge, people in various countries began to take great pride in their own countries and traditions. People in Italy, Germany, and other lands conquered by Napoleon began to think: We'd better stick together to make sure we're never conquered by outsiders again. After all, we share the same language and customs. Instead of squabbling among ourselves, we should think about the things that unite us.

After Napoleon

With Napoleon in exile, representatives from Britain, Prussia, Russia, Austria, and other lands met in the city of Vienna. In this meeting, called the Congress of Vienna, the representatives of the major European powers planned how to create a stable continent on the ruins of the Napoleonic empire.

They understood all too well the forces that the French Revolution and French emperor had unleashed. They regarded Napoleon as the "Enemy and Disturber of the Tranquility of the World." They wanted to make sure that no one else tried to upset their royal power. They were disgusted with the idea of republics. And they wanted no more wars that raged across the continent.

At the Congress of Vienna, the allies who had defeated Napoleon agreed that France should once more be ruled by a king. So they asked the brother of the executed Louis XVI to take the throne. Then the monarchs of Prussia, Russia, and Austria divided some of Napoleon's empire among themselves. In those kingdoms, secret police worked tirelessly to stamp out "liberty, equality, and fraternity," the ideals that had fueled the French Revolution.

After Napoleon's defeat, Europe returned to some of its old ways. Kings were again on their thrones, more than ever convinced that the people really did need monarchs to rule them.

Still, the ideas that started the French Revolution—including the idea that people have rights and can govern themselves—refused to die in Europe and elsewhere. As we'll see in the next chapter, across the ocean in South America, people were using words such as "liberty" and "equality," and asking themselves why they should have to be ruled by distant monarchs.

Simón Bolívar leads his troops against Spanish soldiers. Bolívar, who was born in Venezuela, was one of the great heroes of the South American independence movements.

Latin American Independence Movements

After the revolutions in the United States and France, anything seemed possible. As Thomas Jefferson wrote in 1795, "The ball of liberty is now so well in motion that it will roll around the globe." It soon reached the Spanish and Portuguese colonies in the region known as Latin America.

In 1800, the king of Spain still ruled his colonies in the Americas with a tight grip. The Spanish-born officials known as peninsulares carried out the king's will. They made sure that much of the New World's wealth flowed to Spain.

Some Spanish colonists began to grumble, especially the Creoles—those of Spanish descent but born and raised in the Americas. Why should the king tell them what they could grow on their farms? Why should he tell them where they could trade their goods? And why should they have to take orders from people born in Spain?

As the eighteenth century drew to a close, more and more Spanish colonists dared to speak of a revolution of their own.

Latin America

Latin America is a term used to describe a vast area in the Western Hemisphere south of the United States. It includes Mexico, Central America, South America, and islands in the West Indies. As you've learned, beginning in the late fifteenth century, many European colonists from Spain and Portugal settled in this part of the world. Today the majority of people in Latin America speak Spanish or Portuguese. Those languages developed from Latin, which is why the area is called Latin America.

By the late eighteenth century, Spain had divided its lands in the Americas into four large viceroyalties, each ruled by a viceroy.

The Viceroyalty of New Spain included what is now Mexico and most of Central America. It also included some Caribbean islands and portions of what is now the western United States.

The Viceroyalty of New Granada included what is now Colombia, Venezuela, Ecuador, and Panama.

The Viceroyalty of Río de la Plata included what is now Argentina, Bolivia, Paraguay, and Uruguay.

The Viceroyalty of Peru included what is now Peru and Chile.

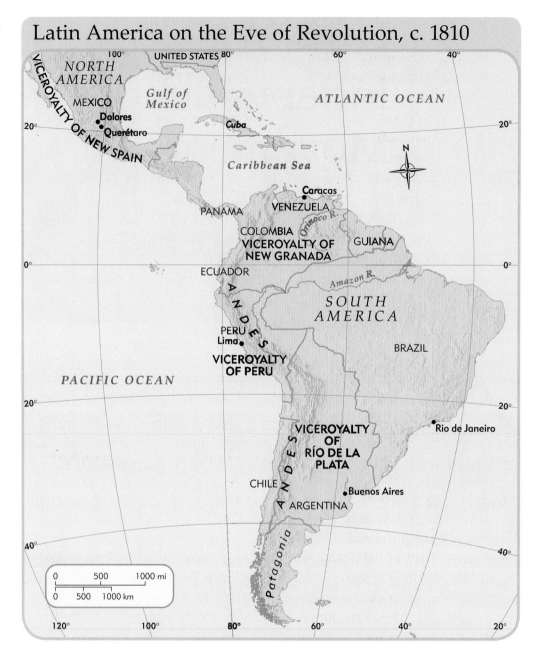

Latin America on the Eve of Revolution, c. 1810

Miranda: Dreamer of Independence

One of the first Spanish-American colonists to dream of independence was Francisco de Miranda (mee-RAHN-duh). He was born in 1750 in the province of Venezuela, near where Columbus had first set foot on the South American continent.

• On the map above, locate Venezuela.

Miranda was the son of a wealthy merchant. At the age of 20 he left home for Spain, where his father's money bought him a post as captain in the royal army. Miranda fought bravely, but his superior officers accused the proud young Creole of disobedience. One colonel complained that Miranda spent too little time following orders and too much time reading. And what did he read? Histories that criticized the conquest of the New World, and philosophies that talked of freedom for all as a natural right.

In 1780, in the midst of the American Revolution, Miranda traveled to Cuba with a Spanish military force. Spain had lost Florida to Britain and wanted it back, and was eager to make trouble for the British. Three years later, Miranda deserted the Spanish army and embarked on a tour of the new United States.

Handsome, charming, and well spoken, the Venezuelan soon made himself popular. He spent hours talking with Thomas Jefferson, James Madison, and Thomas Paine. He even met General Washington, soon to become the new nation's first president.

The freedoms of the United States dazzled Miranda. After attending a gathering in South Carolina, he wrote in his journal: "The very first magistrates and people of note ate and drank with the common folk, passing the plate around, and drinking out of the same glass. A more purely democratic assembly could not be imagined."

The more Miranda saw of the United States, the more determined he became to launch a revolution against Spain. He wanted not only to free Venezuela but also to win "the liberty and independence of the entire Spanish-American continent."

For 20 years, Miranda traveled from one country to the next, telling everyone he met about his vision of an independent nation reaching from the Mississippi River to the southern tip of South America. He traveled to Russia, France, and Britain, and asked for help to free Spain's colonies, but all said no.

Finally he decided to launch his own revolutionary expedition. In 1806, with a tiny volunteer army of Americans and Spanish Americans, he sailed off to liberate Venezuela.

The expedition failed. Spies had warned Spanish authorities about Miranda's plans. And Miranda could not convince the colonists in Venezuela to join him in rebellion against Spanish rule. Instead of liberating the colony, he ended up fleeing to England in 1807. The frustrated revolutionary must have wondered if his native land would ever be free of Spain.

But the very next year, in 1808, events took a dramatic turn when Napoleon invaded Spain. Napoleon took the king of Spain back to France as a prisoner. Then he placed his own brother, Joseph, on the Spanish throne.

Above: Francisco de Miranda became one of the first leaders of the South American independence movement.

Below: The Spanish artist Francisco Goya depicted the people of Madrid rebelling against the French soldiers occupying the Spanish capital during the Napoleonic Wars. The French conquest of Spain inspired South American colonists to rebel against Spanish rule.

Spain's colonists in the New World were used to obeying a faraway Spanish king. It was what they had always done. But now the king of Spain was a Frenchman! This was too much for most Spanish-American colonists. In 1810, they began to declare independence.

Bolívar Vows to Break the Chains

Spain ruled an almost unimaginably vast empire in the Americas. It took weeks to sail from one end to the other. There was no quick means of communication between cities thousands of miles apart. Despite all this, in 1810 groups of colonists across the continent arose to overthrow their colonial Spanish governments.

The first rebellion took place in Venezuela. Weeks later, the colonists expelled the Spanish viceroy from Buenos Aires in Argentina. Revolution soon broke out in Mexico and Chile. Other uprisings followed.

- On the map on page 402, locate Caracas in Venezuela, and Buenos Aires in Argentina. Locate Mexico and Chile.

Among the revolutionaries in Caracas was a fiery young Venezuelan with curly hair and intense dark eyes, Simón Bolívar (see-MOHN buh-LEE-vahr). Bolívar

was born in 1783, the last year of the American Revolution. His family was aristocratic, respected, and very wealthy. His parents died when he was just a boy, but his share of the family fortune made him one of the richest people in Venezuela.

When he was 15, Bolívar went to Spain. There, in the city of Madrid, he devoted himself to the study of literature. He eagerly read the classics as well as Enlightenment writers such as Locke, Voltaire, and Montesquieu.

The proud young Creole bristled when Spanish nobles looked down on him for being born in a colony. As he traveled in Europe, his thoughts turned toward the future of his beloved homeland. On a hill in Rome, the historic home of republican government, he made a solemn vow: "I will not rest, not in body or soul, till I have broken the chains of Spain."

When Napoleon invaded Spain, Bolívar rushed back to Venezuela to join the revolution in Caracas. Then he sailed for London, hoping to persuade the British government to help Venezuela's cause. The British were not much help. But while he was in London, Bolívar met Francisco de Miranda.

Miranda, now 60 years old, was an experienced soldier. He had devoted his life to the cause of

Venezuelan independence. Who better, thought Bolívar, to lead Venezuelans to victory?

The Fate of Miranda

At Bolívar's urging, Miranda returned to Venezuela to command the rebel army. But everything seemed to go wrong. The Venezuelan soldiers were poorly trained and ill equipped. Many of the officers disliked Miranda, who had been away so many years that he seemed a stranger to their country.

And then a terrible earthquake hit. It destroyed Caracas and other cities in rebellion, but left cities loyal to Spain with only minor damage. Some said it was a sign from God. Bolívar was undaunted. "If nature opposes us," he cried, "we shall fight against her and make her obey us."

But there was yet more bad news to come. General Miranda had surrendered.

Bolívar was furious. With a group of fellow revolutionaries, he arrested Miranda as a traitor and handed him over to the Spaniards. Francisco de Miranda went back to Spain in chains and spent his last years in a dungeon.

After one short year of independence, Venezuela once again lay under Spanish rule. Bolívar, his lands seized by the Spaniards, found himself penniless.

Bolívar: "The Liberator"

Bolívar traveled to Colombia, where people were also struggling for independence from Spain. He joined the Colombian revolutionaries and quickly made a name for

himself as a bold, decisive leader, known for daring moves and surprise attacks.

- On the map on page 402, locate Colombia.

Under Bolívar's command, Colombian forces crossed the border into Venezuela in 1813 and fought their way across the country. Four months later, to the sound of pealing bells and booming cannons, the victorious rebel army marched into Caracas. Flowers

The aging Miranda led a Venezuelan rebel army against Spanish forces. But he infuriated Bolívar by surrendering. Bolívar had him handed over to the Spanish, who shipped Miranda off to a Spanish prison.

rained down from the balconies, and cheering Venezuelans hailed Bolívar as *El Libertador*—The Liberator.

The celebration did not last long. In 1814, troops loyal to Spain attacked and once again regained control. Over the next several years, Bolívar launched repeated assaults on the coast of Venezuela, but without success.

Despite these defeats, many people in Venezuela still wanted to be free of Spanish control. Bolívar found allies in frontiersmen who were good riders and fighters. He also welcomed people of African descent into the revolutionary army, and promised freedom to slaves willing to fight for independence.

Bolívar came up with a daring plan. Instead of attacking the coast, he sailed up the Orinoco River into the remote, swampy plains of southern Venezuela. Bolívar and his men

hacked their way through jungles crawling with poisonous spiders. Holding their guns and packs above their heads, they slogged through waist-deep mud and forded raging rivers. Rain poured down in sheets, day and night. They slept in their wet clothes on the hard ground, no campfire to warm them, no food to eat but cold, raw meat.

At last, in August 1819, the ragged army crossed into Colombia and met the enemy. Bolívar's daring strategy paid off. The rebels crushed the Spaniards. Once again, Bolívar was The Liberator.

San Martín: Hero of the South

Meanwhile, in another part of South America, in Argentina, a very different liberator emerged—José de San Martín (hoh-SAY day sahn mahr-TEEN).

• On the map on page 402, locate Argentina.

Few who knew San Martín as a boy could have imagined that he would grow up to become a revolutionary and the greatest hero of Argentina. Both his parents were peninsulares. His mother came from Spanish nobility. His father was a high-ranking colonial official. When José was only seven, his family left Argentina and returned to Spain.

San Martín entered the Spanish army at the age of 11. He was 13 when he fought in his first battle. By the time Napoleon invaded Spain in 1808, José de San Martín had served as a Spanish army officer for 20 years.

He fought heroically against the French invaders. But when the cause

Astride his white horse, Simón Bolívar presents a flag of liberation to his victorious troops after they freed Venezuela from Spanish control. For his achievements, Bolívar was known as El Libertador— *The Liberator.*

was lost, San Martín made a life-changing decision. He resigned his army post, traveled to London, and then returned to the land of his birth to join the struggle for independence. Now he would fight for Argentina against Spanish royalists!

Why did he do it? All those years he had been loyal to Spain. Argentina could have been no more than a distant memory. Perhaps his experience in the Spanish army changed him. San Martín had served nearly two decades, and he might have been fed up by Spanish prejudice against anyone born in the colonies. San Martín was also a man who did what he thought was right. He spent long weeks in London discussing the revolutions in South America. After much thought, he came to believe that Spain's tight control of Latin America was wrong, and that his rightful place lay with the rebels.

Soon after San Martín arrived in Argentina, he became a general and helped lead the fight against Spain. In 1816, at his urging, Argentines officially declared their independence. Argentina was free—but not yet secure from Spain.

San Martín knew that as long as Spanish forces remained on the continent, there could be no safety for an independent Argentina. And like Miranda and Bolívar, he wanted to see all of Latin America completely free from Spain. San Martín therefore set his sights on liberating Chile and Peru.

San Martín's plan was bold: Cross the Andes mountains into Chile, which the Spaniards had reconquered after revolution there; defeat the Spaniards; then, sail up the coast to free Peru.

- On the map on page 402, locate the Andes mountains, Chile, and Peru.

His plan, while bold, seemed impossible. The peaks of the Andes soared to nearly 23,000 feet. Snow and ice blocked the few passes most of the year. In the height of summer—January—experienced traders leading pack mules might make the 300-mile journey over perilous, winding trails cut into the steep mountainsides. But how could an entire army get over such mountains?

Across the Towering Andes

Unlike the quick and fiery Bolívar, San Martín was a patient and highly disciplined man who took his time to plan and organize. For three years, he prepared his Army of the Andes for the mountain crossing. His closest advisor was an exiled patriot commander from Chile, a Creole of Irish descent named Bernardo O'Higgins.

San Martín and O'Higgins did not neglect a single detail. They packed lanterns, drinking water, and an entire carriage full of maps. They brought a wagonload of wheat and a baker to turn it into bread. Their equipment included sleds to haul the cannons, along with slings, blocks, and tackles for the steepest cliffs. They even packed garlic and onions for the men to chew to help guard against the dreaded nausea and dizziness of altitude sickness.

Bernardo O'Higgins is remembered as the father of Chilean independence. He and San Martín led the effort to force Spanish troops out of Chile.

José de San Martín watches as the patriot Army of the Andes makes its way from Argentina to Chile through the towering Andes mountains. His army defeated Spanish forces in Chile, and Bernardo O'Higgins became the head of the newly liberated nation.

In January 1817, the Army of the Andes set off on its march with more than 5,000 men. They took with them 10,600 mules, 1,600 horses, 700 head of cattle, 13,000 rounds of ammunition, and thousands of sabers.

As San Martín later recalled, "The difficulties that had to be overcome in the crossing of the mountains can only be imagined by those who have actually gone through it." By day, the Army of the Andes roasted under the sun. By night, they froze. Blizzards buried them, and hailstorms rained chunks of ice as sharp as knives. They clung to the mountainsides, knowing that at any moment a powerful gust of wind might sweep them into the void below. As the air grew thinner at high altitudes, the soldiers gasped for breath. Many did not survive.

Finally, one moonlit night, after 21 days of marching, the Army of the Andes reached its destination on the other side of the mountains—Chile. With San Martín and O'Higgins in the lead, the exhausted but determined soldiers charged down on the panicked Spaniards.

The rebels fought ferociously. Soon many of the Spanish forces lay wounded or dead. The others fled. The Army of the Andes had struck a blow for independence.

San Martín and Bolívar Close on Peru

After a second major battle, the liberation of Chile was complete. The grateful citizens asked San Martín to be the head of their new government, but he refused, passing that honor on to Bernardo O'Higgins. San Martín remained focused on his final goal—freeing Peru.

As San Martín prepared to move north, Simón Bolívar was moving south, piling victory on victory. Bolívar drove the Spaniards from Colombia and then Venezuela. Later Panama and Ecuador threw off Spanish rule. Then a separate state, Bolivia, was named for The Liberator himself.

The rebel armies of Bolívar and San Martín squeezed Peru in their grip. San Martín seized the capital, Lima, in 1821. He declared Peru independent, and he was named its Protector. But forces loyal to the king of Spain kept fighting back.

For over a year, San Martín acted as Protector of Peru. He abolished slavery and tried to improve conditions for the Indians.

But after so many years of tight royal control, he still did not believe the people of Peru were ready to rule themselves. He favored a constitutional monarchy—a government headed by a king but following a written constitution.

Bolívar shared San Martín's concerns about republican government. In 1815, Bolívar had written that Spanish domination "has not only deprived us of our rights but has kept us in a sort of permanent infancy with regard to public affairs." Not only did the colonists have no experience at all in governing themselves, he complained, but they were "dominated by the vices that one learns under the rule of a nation like Spain, which has only distinguished itself in ferocity, ambition, vindictiveness, and greed."

Bolívar's wartime experiences convinced him that Latin American nations needed strong leadership. When he wrote the constitution for Bolivia, he gave the president a lifetime term. Yet he stopped short of supporting a monarchy. He was unwilling to give up his dream of free, republican government in South America. He wanted South Americans to learn to rule themselves.

Caudillos: Military Dictators Take Charge

Bolívar led the final victory over the Spaniards in Peru in 1824. San Martín, meanwhile, grew discouraged over disputes among Latin American leaders, who often plotted against each other for power. He returned to Europe, where he spent the rest of his life.

Bolívar also went on to experience bitter disappointment. Once adored as The Liberator, his zeal to impose his will on South America made him more and more unpopular. He hoped to form a large nation covering much of South America,

From a Lima balcony, San Martín proclaims the independence of Peru. For more than a year, San Martín served as protector of Peru, defending the country from Spanish royalist forces.

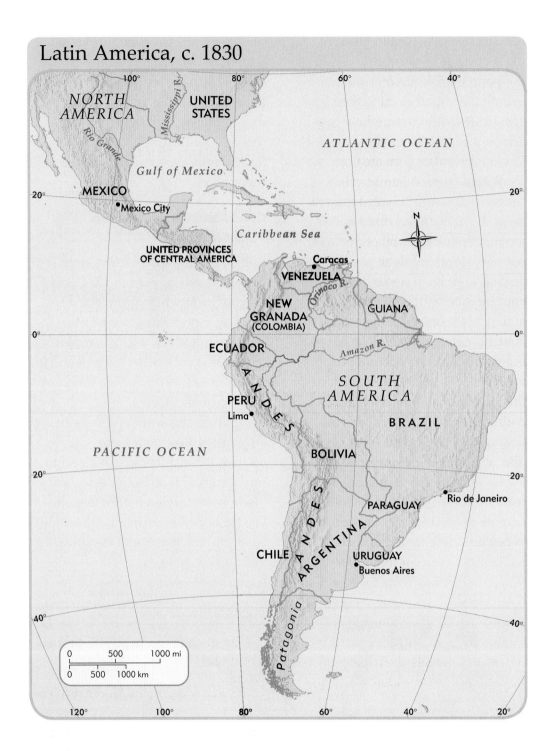

Latin America, c. 1830

NORTH AMERICA
UNITED STATES
Mississippi R.
Rio Grande
ATLANTIC OCEAN
Gulf of Mexico
MEXICO
• Mexico City
Caribbean Sea
N
UNITED PROVINCES OF CENTRAL AMERICA
• Caracas
VENEZUELA
Orinoco R.
NEW GRANADA (COLOMBIA)
GUIANA
ECUADOR
Amazon R.
A N D E S
SOUTH AMERICA
PERU
Lima •
BRAZIL
PACIFIC OCEAN
BOLIVIA
A N D E S
ARGENTINA
PARAGUAY
• Rio de Janeiro
CHILE
URUGUAY
• Buenos Aires
Patagonia

0   500   1000 mi
0   500   1000 km

but by the time he died in 1830, Spain's old territories had split into several different countries.

- On the map above, note the nations that emerged in Latin America after the revolutions against Spain.

In the end, what both Bolívar and San Martín feared came to pass—political chaos. For three hundred years, the Spanish monarch had exercised strict control over the colonies. When this royal control was gone, no one was sure how to create governments that would work in

Latin America. Republics are not easy to create or sustain. The people of these new Latin American nations had no history of electing their own representatives, passing laws, or charting their own future.

This uncertainty created an opening for military strongmen called caudillos (kaw-DEEL-yohs) to seize control. The caudillos commanded armies held together by personal loyalties and a desire for loot. Most caudillos were not interested in liberty and equality. They cared only for power, and they were not willing to share it.

Competing caudillos often fought each other for years on end. Governments kept changing hands until one caudillo or another gained complete victory. The victorious caudillo would then make himself a dictator and rely on force to maintain control.

Unfortunately, independence from Spain did not lead to enlightened republican government in Latin America. The grip of the caudillos proved tighter than that of the distant king. Through the first half of the nineteenth century, many governments in Latin America became military dictatorships. Citizens of the new nations had exchanged one kind of tyranny for another.

Brazilian Independence from Portugal

About the same time that other South American nations gained independence from Spain, Brazil gained independence from Portugal. But Brazil did not go through a long, bloody revolution. Instead, events in Europe led to Brazil's independence.

- On the map on page 402, locate Brazil.

When Napoleon invaded Portugal in 1807, the Portuguese royal family quickly boarded a ship and sailed for their South American colony. They settled in Rio de Janeiro (REE-oh day zhuh-NERH-oh). They made that beautiful Brazilian city the new capital of their Portuguese Empire.

When Napoleon was defeated in 1815, the Portuguese royal family declared Brazil a separate kingdom under their power. A few years later the king returned to Portugal, leaving his son Pedro to rule Brazil.

In 1822, Pedro declared his kingdom of Brazil independent of Portugal. He drew up a constitution and had himself crowned emperor. The new nation was not a republic, but was legally independent of Portugal.

Independence for Mexico

We've seen how colonies in South America broke away from Spain and Portugal. But what about Spain's largest colony, Mexico?

- On the map on page 402, locate Mexico.

At the beginning of the nineteenth century, colonists in Mexico, like others in Latin America, were whispering explosive words—independence, liberty, rebellion. The stage for revolution was set. It needed only a spark to set it off.

That spark came in 1810 from the father of Mexican independence, a Creole priest named Miguel Hidalgo y Costilla (mee-GEHL ee-DAHL-goh ee kahs-TEE-yah). Here is his story.

Father Hidalgo's Cry for Freedom

Historical Close-up

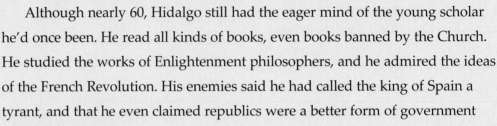

Father Hidalgo was an unlikely-looking revolutionary. A gaunt, stooped man with a fringe of white hair around his balding head, he wore the long black cloak and round sombrero of a simple village priest.

Although nearly 60, Hidalgo still had the eager mind of the young scholar he'd once been. He read all kinds of books, even books banned by the Church. He studied the works of Enlightenment philosophers, and he admired the ideas of the French Revolution. His enemies said he had called the king of Spain a tyrant, and that he even claimed republics were a better form of government than monarchies.

Such behavior in a Creole priest did not please his Spanish-born superiors. As a punishment, they sent Father Hidalgo to the dusty little Mexican parish of Dolores (doh-LOH-res), far from the culture and learning he adored.

Dolores means "sorrows." For the Indians and mestizos struggling to survive on the scraps of land left by their Spanish masters, the town lived up to its name.

Like the friar Bartolomé de Las Casas three hundred years before, Hidalgo saw the suffering of his parishioners. He considered it his duty to do all he could to offer help and comfort in this life, not just the next.

In Dolores, he set up shops for teaching carpentry, blacksmithing, and weaving. He showed the people how to turn clay into sturdy pottery and bricks. He taught them to tan the hides of cows instead of buying leather at high prices from Spanish merchants. He labored alongside the Indians and mestizos, digging ditches, growing grapes to make wine, and planting mulberry trees to feed the worms that made silk.

The poor people of Dolores loved this Creole priest who spoke to them in their own language and gave all his energy to helping them create a better life. But his actions angered the peninsulares. They believed that Mexicans were supposed to work to make the Spaniards rich. They were not supposed to make their own leather and silk and wine!

Father Hidalgo gradually came to see that his Indian and mestizo parishioners needed more than just new skills. They needed a whole new government.

Hidalgo had a friend that he confided in, a captain stationed in a town not far from Dolores. His name was Ignacio Allende (uh-YEN-day).

Captain Allende was a wealthy Creole landowner. As a younger man, his main hobbies had been gambling, flirting, and cheering the bullfights. But his experiences in the army turned his thoughts to rebellion.

Captain Allende had money, talent, and education. He came from a respected family. He was a fine soldier and an excellent horseman. Why, then, should he have to put up with the sneers and insults of Spanish-born officers who thought a Creole unfit to be even a captain? Why should he give up all hope of becoming a general, simply because he'd been born in Mexico?

Allende was not alone. All over Mexico, groups of Creoles were gathering to discuss their troubles. To keep Spanish officials from suspecting their purpose, they called themselves "literary clubs." What they really talked about, though, was how they could win their country's independence.

Father Hidalgo told Allende how he felt about the Spanish government. Allende confided that he belonged to a literary club that met in the city of Querétaro (kay-RAY-tah-roh), fifty miles from Dolores. Would Hidalgo like to join?

It was a long horseback ride over bad roads to Querétaro. But Hidalgo didn't mind. Here was a chance to talk about exciting new ideas of liberty and equality—and, perhaps, do more than talk.

Mexico for the Mexicans! That was the slogan of the growing movement against Spanish rule. But who, exactly, were these Mexicans?

To Captain Allende and the other members of the Querétaro club, Mexicans meant Creoles only. They had no interest in getting rid of Mexico's class system. They just wanted to be at the top, along with the peninsulares—or, better yet, to send the peninsulares back to Spain and take their place.

Hidalgo, however, had his own ideas. To him, "Mexico for the Mexicans" meant all Mexicans, whatever their background—Spanish, Indian, African, or mixed.

The Creole priest Miguel Hidalgo y Costilla believed that Mexico should belong to all Mexicans— whether Spanish, Indian, African, or of mixed race.

The little group of revolutionaries made their plans. In December 1810, a great fair was to be held nearby. People would be coming from all over. What better time to raise the banner and proclaim Mexico's independence?

Quietly, they began to spread the word, recruiting other Creoles to their cause. They gathered guns and ammunition and hid them in the house of one of their members.

Unfortunately, they were not quiet enough. Rumors of the conspiracy reached Mexico City, and officials came to Querétaro to investigate. They searched and uncovered the stash of weapons. Then they ordered the local governor to have the leaders of the group arrested.

But the Spaniards did not know that the governor's wife was in on the plot. On the night of September 15, 1810, she sent a messenger to warn Father Hidalgo and Allende, who was in Dolores visiting the priest.

At 2 a.m., Father Hidalgo woke to a loud pounding on his door. When he went to answer it, the messenger burst in and announced the danger. All seemed lost. Allende told his friend that they must flee immediately and go into hiding.

Hidalgo put on his boots and stuck a pistol in his belt. He would not flee. The revolution, he said, must begin today.

As dawn broke over the parish of Dolores on September 16, the aging priest climbed the stairs to the bell tower of his little church. With all his strength, he pulled the rope. The bell pealed out across the countryside, summoning the people.

When they reached the church, they found Father Hidalgo standing on the steps. "My children!" he called out to them. "This new day brings us a new way of life. Are you ready to receive it? Will you free yourselves? Will you recover from the hated Spaniards the land stolen from your forefathers three hundred years ago?"

As he spoke, the crowd's enthusiasm grew. At last, the priest cried, "Long live true religion! … Death to bad government!"

His parishioners roared back, "Death to the Spaniards!"

Hastily, they armed themselves with any weapons they could find—knives and axes, miner's picks, machetes used for chopping sugarcane, even bows and arrows like the ones their Aztec ancestors had wielded against the guns of the conquistadors. With Hidalgo at their head, the ragged little band set out on the road.

Word of Father Hidalgo's plea for independence swept the countryside. His stirring speech on the church steps eventually became known as the *Grito de Dolores*— the Cry of Dolores. His words stirred the people to revolt. Hidalgo's army swelled from a few hundred to a thousand, and eventually up to eighty thousand.

But this was not the orderly revolutionary army that Captain Allende had imagined. It was a bloodthirsty mob bent on revenge for generations of Spanish cruelty and oppression.

Wealthy Creoles quickly realized that the Indian and mestizo rebels could see little difference between them and the peninsulares. Fearing for their lives and property, many joined forces with Spain. The two sides clashed in an all-out civil war.

Six months after the Grito de Dolores, the Spaniards captured and executed Father Hidalgo and his friend Allende. But the fighting did not end. Thousands of Mexicans kept up the battle for freedom. After 11 years of bloodshed, the revolutionaries finally prevailed. In 1821, Mexico declared its independence from Spain.

The declaration would have pleased Father Hidalgo. It said that all the people of Mexico were independent citizens, and that anyone could hold any position based on merit, not on birth.

But the new nation did not date its independence to the signing of this declaration. Instead, Mexico chose September 16 as its independence day—the day on which Father Hidalgo rang the bell and gave the cry that sparked a revolution.

Father Hidalgo rallies his band of followers to fight the Spanish. The priest was eventually captured and executed, but Mexicans continued to fight for their freedom. For his bravery, Hidalgo is revered as the father of Mexican independence.

In the 1820s, Mexico, like many South American countries, fell prey to caudillos and ambitious military dictators. In 1822, one such military chieftain even proclaimed himself Emperor of Mexico. His reign lasted only 10 months. Mexico soon declared itself a republic, but for 50 years the new nation was torn by continuing political conflicts.

The double-headed eagle was the crest of Russia's Romanov rulers. Like the country itself, the eagle looks both west to Europe and east to Asia.

The Russia of the Romanovs

A cross the Americas and Europe, several countries were marching on the road to democratic revolution. But to the east, Russia pursued a different path. This vast nation remained in the grip of iron-fisted tsars.

In the fifteenth century, Ivan the Great had united Russia. He hired Italian engineers to help him build the Kremlin, a symbol of his power. His grandson, Ivan the Terrible, built St. Basil's Cathedral, which he intended to rival any cathedral in western Europe. In general, however, during the Renaissance and the Age of Exploration, Russian rulers turned their backs on western Europe.

Russians of the 1600s sent few expeditions to explore distant lands or open new trade routes. They rarely embraced technological advances or new political ideas. Russians did not even use the same calendar as western Europeans; instead of using the birth of Christ

as their starting point, they dated their calendar from the time they believed the world was created.

Russia's geography set it apart from much of Europe. The land of the tsars straddled Europe and Asia. Under the early tsars, Russia had few outlets to the sea and no ice-free seaports. This made trade and communication with western Europe difficult.

In the seventeenth century, Russia was also set apart by serfdom. Serfs were peasants who were bound by law to the land on which they worked. In most of Europe, the practice of serfdom had declined at the end of the Middle Ages. In Russia, however, the number of serfs increased under the rule of

This chapter focuses on imperial Russia, which once stretched from Europe across northern Asia to Alaska.

Russia, 1689–1825

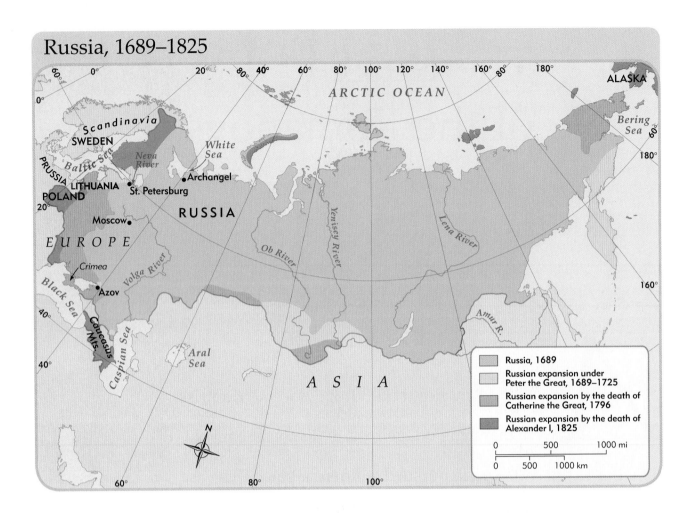

ARCTIC OCEAN

ALASKA

Scandinavia
SWEDEN
White Sea
Neva River
PRUSSIA
Baltic Sea
LITHUANIA
Archangel
St. Petersburg
POLAND
Moscow
RUSSIA
EUROPE
Crimea
Volga River
Azov
Black Sea
Caucasus Mts
Caspian Sea
Aral Sea
Ob River
Yenisey River
Lena River
Amur R.
Bering Sea

A S I A

N

	Russia, 1689
	Russian expansion under Peter the Great, 1689–1725
	Russian expansion by the death of Catherine the Great, 1796
	Russian expansion by the death of Alexander I, 1825

0   500   1000 mi
0   500   1000 km

the tsars. Russian serfs had as few rights as slaves. In fact, on official records serfs were listed as the property of the nobleman whose fields they tilled.

For these reasons, as the eighteenth century approached, Russia seemed a remote and even backward place to many Europeans. But much would change when one tsar decided to look to western Europe.

Peter the Great Looks West

In the early seventeenth century, a family called the Romanovs came to power in Russia. The Romanovs produced a long line of tsars who reigned into the twentieth century. One Romanov, Peter I, took power in 1689. (That was the year William and Mary signed the English Bill of Rights.) Peter was intrigued by events overseas, and he used his power to pull Russia into the modern world. For his efforts and achievements, history remembers him as Peter the Great.

Peter was unlike any tsar his people had known. Standing more than six and a half feet tall, he possessed immense strength and boundless energy. He rose at four o'clock every morning. Still in his bedclothes, he would call for his government ministers and plunge into a workday that often lasted 14 hours.

Peter's curiosity matched his energy. He looked west, beyond the boundaries of his native Russia, to more technologically advanced lands. He knew that western

Europeans were skilled in navigation and making tools. They did things differently. Just how differently, Peter wanted to find out for himself.

In 1697, Peter set off on an 18-month tour of western Europe—the first Russian ruler to venture abroad during times of peace. He wanted to see how people in the West built ships, forged tools, and tackled problems. At first he traveled in disguise as an ordinary citizen, so that he could observe people and avoid attention. "Carpenter Peter," as he liked to be known, took a job as a shipbuilder in Holland. In the England of Isaac Newton and John Locke, he studied navigation, surgery, and printing. And in Germany, he practiced marksmanship with a unit of artillery gunners.

Peter returned to Russia excited about his newfound skills. After his experiences in London, he considered himself a qualified surgeon. Fortunately for his subjects, he limited himself to dentistry, practicing on courtiers and servants, and keeping their extracted teeth in a bag. After seeing fashions in western Europe, he also decided that his nobles' long whiskers were adornments that belonged to the past. The morning after his return, he took a barber's razor and cut off a few beards.

Peter recruited more than 800 European experts to follow him back to Russia. They included shipwrights, naval officers, navigators, doctors, mathematicians, engineers, and architects. The tsar had big plans. He wanted these experts to help him turn Russia into a modern country.

Tsar Peter I (shown here overseeing a construction project) was a great builder and modernizer of Russia. He traveled to other countries in Europe to learn about Western ways and practices. For his accomplishments he is remembered as Peter the Great.

Reforming Russia

Peter launched a crusade to reform Russia in almost every way. First, he organized his government. When Peter first came to power, the boyars—Russia's nobles—were powerful and his government was disorganized. It had more than eighty departments, each operating by its own rules or no rules at all. Peter reduced the departments to nine, all of which reported to him

Traveling in Disguise

Peter the Great stood more than six and a half feet tall—very tall for his time—and spoke other languages with a distinctive Russian accent. So although he sometimes dressed as a carpenter during his European tour, he didn't exactly go unnoticed. Still his European hosts let him enjoy his disguise.

and had to follow clear regulations. Peter also abolished the boyar council, a group that had helped the tsar run the government and given the nobles a great deal of influence.

In later years, Peter took other steps to limit the power of the boyars. For example, he wanted men in his country to advance because of merit, not merely because they had been born into noble families. He set up a Table of Ranks that made social status depend on service in the government or the army. All who worked for the government, whether they came from families of rich landowners or humble peasants, had to start at the bottom of the table, at the fourteenth rank, and work their way up to higher social status.

Peter reorganized the Russian Orthodox Church. He believed that the head of the Church, the patriarch of Moscow, had grown too powerful, so he eliminated that office. He found men who would obey him and put them in charge of overseeing Church activities.

Peter also set out to modernize daily life. He insisted that his boyars and government officials dress like western Europeans. In 1700, he did away with the old Russian calendar and adopted the one used in England. He opened secular schools for children of nobility, soldiers, and government officials. He ordered the construction of roads and canals, and opened factories that produced all kinds of new goods for the people. He introduced an official state currency for Russia.

Peter the Great pushed his people as hard as he pushed himself. He

Secular means not related to religious matters.

built up the army, training and equipping it to fight more like the armies of western Europe. Infantrymen shouldered modern muskets, and gunners fired the most up-to-date artillery. In the space of six months, Peter ordered one-quarter of all the church bells in Russia melted down and recast as cannons for his army.

Soon that army was at war with Russia's neighbors. Victories on the field of battle expanded the country's borders. Peter wanted his armies to win an even more valuable prize— a warm-water outlet to the sea.

Winning Ports and Building a City

At the beginning of Peter's reign, Russia had only one major port, called Archangel. Since this port lay in the north, on the shores of the White Sea, it was frozen solid for six months of every year.

Peter decided that one way or another, including military force, he would gain more ports for Russia. He sent his army to fight the Turks and captured the port of Azov, which gave Russia access to the Black Sea. Russian armies also seized part of the Baltic coastline from the Swedes. On the edge of a wilderness prowled by wild bears and wolves, Peter decided to build a new harbor for his ships. He also built a new city there, one that would be a new capital for the Russian empire. He named the city St. Petersburg.

- On the map on page 418, locate Azov, the Black Sea, the Baltic Sea, and St. Petersburg.

On the swampy deltas of the Neva River, an army of workers

Elegant government buildings line the banks of the Neva River in the port city of St. Petersburg. Founded by Peter the Great, St. Petersburg opened up trade through the Baltic Sea and became Russia's "window on the West."

toiled to construct St. Petersburg. They endured frigid cold in winter and flooding in summer. Without enough picks and shovels, they sometimes dug the foundations with their bare hands. Thousands of men lost their lives.

The Russians called St. Petersburg a "city built on bones." It also turned out to be one of the loveliest cities in the world—a glittering new capital where waterborne traffic sailed past graceful buildings. Along the banks of the Neva River spread a new palace for the tsar, gardens modeled after parks in western Europe, dockyards to build ships for the Russian navy, and a fortress to protect the new city from attacks by sea. Because of its many islands and the bridges that linked them to the shore, St. Petersburg was dubbed the "Venice of the North." But for Peter, the city's access to the Baltic Sea made it his "window on the West."

By the time he died in 1725, Peter had succeeded in introducing Russia to many new ideas and technological

advances from the West. He had made Russia an important European power.

Yet for all his efforts, this reforming, modernizing tsar did little to improve life for the vast majority of his subjects—Russia's serfs. In fact, in order to finance his wars and building projects, Peter imposed new taxes and regulations on Russia's poor. He also spread serfdom to the lands he conquered. Though he admired both Holland and England, he imported none of their ideas about natural rights or liberty.

When Peter died, Russia was still a feudal nation led by an all-powerful tsar, and still dependent on serfdom.

Poor peasants, most of them serfs, made up most of the population of imperial Russia. They benefited little from Tsar Peter's modernizations.

Catherine the Great

The tsars who followed Peter lacked his skill and energy. Not until 1762 did the country once again have a strong, ambitious ruler. This time it was a woman, Catherine II.

Catherine was a princess from a tiny German state who married into the Romanov family. Her husband, a grandson of Peter the Great, became tsar in 1761. Within six months, he had made himself so generally hated that Catherine was able to gain the support of the nobles and the army to force her husband to give up the throne. Soon after, Catherine was crowned empress of Russia. She, too, eventually came to be called "the Great."

Catherine the Great had much in common with Peter. She was full of energy. She rose early each morning, rubbed her face with ice, drank several cups of coffee, and went on to work long days, talking with advisors, studying reports, and issuing decrees. Like Peter, she wanted Russia to be an outward-looking, powerful, and prosperous state.

Catherine tried to get Russians to adopt new farming methods used in England. She encouraged industry and trade with her European neighbors. She ordered the rebuilding of more than 200 towns across the country, as well as the construction of new roads to connect them.

Like Peter, Catherine succeeded in enlarging her realm. In the south, her armies won territory in the Crimea (kriy-MEE-uh), a large peninsula on the Black Sea. She also expanded her empire past the Caucasus (KAW-kuh-suhs) Mountains. To the west, Russian troops won territories in Poland and Lithuania. In the east, Russia expanded across the Bering Sea as far as Alaska. (The Russians would hold on to Alaska for almost a century before selling it to the United States.) Under Catherine, the Russian empire stretched some 6,000 miles from east to west.

- On the map on page 418, note the territories added to Russia by the end of Catherine the Great's reign.

Catherine the Great continued Peter I's efforts to turn Russia into a modern nation. She encouraged industry, rebuilt towns, constructed new roads, and enlarged the empire.

Catherine Promotes Culture and Education

Catherine extended Peter's efforts to promote European ways in Russia. But while Peter was most interested in technical matters, such as shipbuilding and medicine, Catherine was very interested in European philosophy, writing, and education.

She became fascinated with the Enlightenment philosophes. She regularly corresponded with Voltaire.

Potemkin Villages

In 1787, Catherine the Great set off on a tour of her newly won lands in the Crimea. Some accounts tell how the new Russian governor of the Crimea, Grigory Potemkin, went to great lengths to make the impoverished lands appear prosperous to the empress. Potemkin reportedly built fake, one-street villages and arranged for crowds of happy-looking villagers to cheer Catherine along the way.

While Potemkin did spruce up the area along Catherine's route, many historians think he did not go so far as to construct sham villages. Nevertheless, the term "Potemkin village" has come to mean false or showy evidence intended to hide a bad situation.

Denis Diderot, whose *Encylopédie* ranked among her favorite works, spent time at her court. During her reign she supported writers and intellectuals, poets and playwrights. She founded a literary magazine and encouraged the publication of a wide range of books. Many works of Western literature were translated into Russian for the first time. Catherine herself helped adapt Shakespeare's *Merry Wives of Windsor* to Russian.

Catherine transformed the Hermitage—her private residence within her palace at St. Petersburg—into a center of culture. In the Hermitage, she displayed paintings by Dutch and Flemish masters. The Hermitage eventually became one of the world's great museums of art.

Catherine also built her own theater in the Hermitage, where she enjoyed plays, ballet, and opera. Theater admission was free to courtiers, officers, and even to servants, as long as they were appropriately dressed. Catherine loved Shakespeare, and her keen interest in drama spurred her to write plays of her own, including several comedies and historical dramas.

In keeping with the ideas of the Enlightenment, Catherine believed in the power of education to reform and improve individuals. She believed that by bettering individuals through education, she could improve Russian society as a whole. The empress set up boarding schools to help produce model citizens. She started the first girl's school in Russia, intended for the education of noble women. A newly established college helped train Russian teachers.

Catherine supported the arts in Russia. She displayed the work of Europe's great painters in the Hermitage, her palatial private residence in St. Petersburg. The Hermitage later became a major museum of art.

When Catherine came to power, she envisioned a more humane society shaped by Enlightenment ideas of reason and progress. She dreamed of introducing liberal ideas to Russia. In eighteenth-century Europe, *liberal* was the word used to describe ideas intended to liberate people from ignorance and backwardness. People who supported liberal ideas believed in the power of reason and education to reform society.

While Catherine initially promoted many liberal programs, her ideas eventually collided with her times and with the reality that continued to blight her country—the hard lives of the serfs.

Serfdom Endures and Expands

Huddled in single-room cabins made of logs or clay, the peasants of Catherine's Russia lived lives that had changed little since the days of Ivan the Terrible. Serfs made up more than three-quarters of the population. They owned no land and possessed few rights. They paid high taxes. Some "escaped" but to lives of almost equal hardship—serving in the army, working in factories, or toiling in one of the country's great construction projects.

Before she became empress, Catherine dreamed of freeing the serfs. But once she came to power, she changed her mind. The mostly agricultural Russian economy was built on the backs of the serfs. The landowning nobles—on whose support Catherine relied—would not tolerate losing their labor force.

Well into the nineteenth century, Russian peasants remained serfs, tied to the land of the lords they served.

So Catherine made no attempt to pass laws to free the serfs or protect them from their owners. In fact, under Catherine the number of serfs increased. As her realm expanded, millions of formerly free peasants became serfs.

In 1773, all hopes of easing the plight of the serfs faded when a peasant rebellion erupted. Serfs rampaged throughout southeastern Russia, demanding their freedom. They slaughtered nobles and looted their estates. They even threatened to march on Moscow. Their actions horrified the empress, who quickly lost any sympathy with their cause. Catherine sent her imperial troops to put down the revolt.

Catherine, like other European monarchs, felt threatened by the French Revolution. She grew suspicious of "new" ideas, which she blamed for the violence racking much of Europe. As time went on, she sometimes arrested thinkers who called for reforms that might threaten her power. In 1790, when a Russian author wrote a book condemning serfdom, Catherine exiled him to Siberia, a frozen land in northern Russia.

During the thirty-three and a half years of her rule, Catherine the Great brought new ideas about art, literature, philosophy, theater, and education to Russia. In the end, however, Catherine did nothing to help Russia's millions of serfs gain basic rights. Under Catherine, for the vast majority of the people of Russia, most of whom were serfs, life had only grown worse.

Serfs for Sale

In Catherine's time, advertisements such as the following often appeared in Moscow's newspaper: "For sale, two plump coachmen; two girls eighteen and fifteen years, quick at manual work. Two barbers: one twenty-one, knows how to read and write and play a musical instrument; the other can do ladies' and gentlemen's hair."

Catherine Proposes a New Code of Laws

In 1767, early in her reign, Catherine the Great called for a new code of laws for Russia. Catherine had no commitment to democracy or equality, but she wanted to apply reason and the rule of law to her empire. She prepared a document, known as Catherine's Instruction, to guide officials as they considered new laws for Russia. Unfortunately, the officials considered Catherine's ideas too liberal, and they did nothing.

Here are some passages from Catherine's Instruction.

A Page
from the Past

What is the true end of monarchy? Not to deprive people of their natural liberty, but to correct their actions, in order to attain the supreme good.

The laws ought to be so framed, as to secure the safety of every citizen as much as possible.… The equality of citizens consists in this: that they should all be subject to the same laws.

Liberty is the right of doing whatsoever the laws allow. And if any one citizen could do what the laws forbid, there would be no more liberty, because others would have an equal power of doing the same.

Catherine the Great

The usage of torture is contrary to all the dictates of nature and reason; even mankind itself cries out against it and demands loudly the total abolition of it.

That law … is highly beneficial … which ordains that every man shall be judged by his peers and equals. For when the fate of a citizen is in question, all prejudices arising from the difference of rank or fortune should be stifled, because they ought to have no influence between the judges and the parties accused.

No man ought to be looked upon as guilty before he has received his judicial sentence.… What right therefore can power give to any to inflict punishment upon a citizen at a time when it is yet dubious whether he is innocent or guilty?

It is highly necessary that the law should prescribe a rule to the lords for a more judicious method of raising their revenues, and oblige them to levy such a tax as tends least to separate the peasant from his house and family.

"Monsieur Alexander" Takes Charge

When Catherine the Great died in 1796, her son Paul became tsar. Paul was a tyrannical ruler. For four years he terrorized the Russian people, until he was killed by a group of assassins. In 1801, Catherine's grandson, Alexander I, ascended the throne.

Catherine had always doted on "Monsieur Alexander," as she called him, and had always considered him her true heir. She had herself taken responsibility for his upbringing. Determined to get things just right, she studied advice on child-rearing in writings by French and English philosophers. No more than two candles lit the boy's room, so as not to pollute the air. He was always to sleep with the windows open. And each morning he took a bath in a room where the temperature did not exceed 59 degrees.

Catherine found an English nanny for her grandson. When he was older, she hired a tutor. When Diderot turned down the job, she selected a Swiss scholar who taught Monsieur Alexander not only the French language, but also French ideas—including the revolutionary principles of liberty, equality, and fraternity.

Alexander's first actions as tsar delighted Russian liberals. His father had forbidden foreign books and closed private publishing houses. Alexander reversed those decisions. He freed prisoners jailed for their political beliefs and lifted a ban on travel abroad. He took steps to improve the country's education system. Above all, he hoped to deal with the thorny question of serfdom.

By 1805, however, Alexander found himself at war with Napoleon Bonaparte, who had seized control of revolutionary France and launched his armies across Europe. After several French victories, Alexander agreed to terms of peace in 1807. The peace did not endure. Five years later, Napoleon's Grand Army invaded Russia and captured Moscow.

To help save their country, the Russians sacrificed their old capital.

Tsar Alexander I was Catherine's grandson and her great hope for the future of Russia. As a young man, Alexander sympathized with the revolutionary ideas coming out of France. However, the tsar soon found himself at war with the new emperor of France, Napoleon I.

A fire burned down most of the city, and the French grew desperate for supplies. Unable to spend the winter in Moscow, Napoleon's army retraced its steps across Russia, with the tsar's army in hot pursuit.

As you learned, Napoleon was forced to surrender when allied troops from Prussia, Austria, Britain, and Russia overwhelmed France. On March 31, 1814, Alexander led the allied forces into Paris. Parisian crowds hailed the tsar as a liberator. They applauded his regiment of mounted Cossacks— wild-looking cavalrymen with exotic beards and tanned, high cheekbones, wearing flowing cloaks and wide pantaloons. Alexander described the day as the happiest of his life.

Russia's old capital, Moscow, burns in September 1812 after its capture by the French.

Russia's "National Disgrace"

Upon his return to Russia, Alexander continued to talk about freeing the serfs. But his talk resulted in little action. In 1816, he ordered a study of the gradual abolition of serfdom in Russia. When the report was complete, he read it and then filed it away with other papers.

Alexander did free some serfs in his empire's Baltic and Polish regions. But he did not require the serfs' former owners to give them any land to farm. The peasants, though technically "free," still depended on landowners, and they remained dirt poor.

Like Russian rulers before him, Alexander would not risk losing the support of the boyars by siding with the serfs. Also, Napoleon's invasion of Russia had changed Alexander's views. If Napoleon's attempt to spread the French Revolution was what came of "enlightened" ideas,

then Alexander wanted little to do with such ideas. After Napoleon's defeat, Alexander viewed himself as the leader of an alliance of European monarchs against revolutionary change.

But some Russians believed that revolutionary change was long overdue. A group of army officers who had fought in France came back to Russia with revolutionary notions about liberty, equality, and fraternity. They asked: Have the Russian peasants in Alexander's army fought to free Europe only to remain in near-slavery?

When Alexander died suddenly in late 1825, the army officers staged a rebellion against the new tsar, Nicholas I. They gathered nearly 3,000 supporters in a St. Petersburg square. The rebels demanded a constitutional government and an end to

Russian peasants continued to endure many hardships. After the defeat of Napoleon, Tsar Alexander rejected revolutionary ideas and took little action to end serfdom, Russia's enduring "national disgrace."

serfdom, which they called Russia's "national disgrace."

Imperial troops moved in to put down the uprising. Mounted guards charged the rebels, but their horses slipped on icy cobblestones, and they had to retreat under fire. An artillery unit came to their help, and the cannons began to roar. Just over an hour later, 60 to 70 rebels lay dead or dying on the frozen ground. The revolt, known as the Decembrist Uprising, was over. Russia's attempted revolution ended in failure.

Much had changed in Russia since 1689, when Peter the Great took power. Peter had thrown open a "window on the West." He and

Catherine the Great had brought western European technology and education, as well as some Enlightenment ideas, to Russia. They also turned east and expanded the empire. Later, Alexander I helped liberate Europe from Napoleonic domination.

By the 1800s, Russia had stepped from the shadows of isolation and was becoming one of the world's great powers. Yet iron-fisted tsars continued to rule with enormous power. The majority of Russia's people remained enslaved as serfs, untouched by the ideas of liberty, equality, and natural rights that were changing the Americas and western Europe.

Imperial troops crushed the Decembrist Uprising in 1825. Russia remained a state that gave all power to the tsar and few freedoms to the people.

The painting Wanderer Above a Sea of Fog, *by Caspar David Friedrich, depicts a wild, untamed landscape. The natural world inspired painters, writers, and composers during the Romantic era, when a new cultural movement challenged Enlightenment ideas.*

Romantic Art in an Age of Revolution

When the French Revolution broke out in 1789, the people of Europe sensed the coming of tremendous change. All over the continent, young artists and intellectuals hoped that the principles that had inspired the French Revolution—"Liberty, Equality, and Fraternity"—would prevail in their own countries. Remembering the excitement of those times, the English poet William Wordsworth would later write:

> *Bliss was it in that dawn to be alive,*
> *But to be young was very Heaven!*

If the dawn was bliss, the day brought disappointment. The dream of liberty and equality turned into the nightmare of the Reign of Terror. Napoleon emerged to restore order, but then went on to become a dictator who led the French into a series of destructive wars. After Napoleon's final defeat in 1815, kings came back to the throne of France. Throughout most of Europe, kings and aristocrats held the reins of power more firmly than ever.

Despite the disappointments of the French Revolution, the excitement of the time helped inspire another kind of revolution—a revolution in literature and the arts. Poets, painters, and composers took part in this creative revolution, which gave rise to a new cultural movement called Romanticism.

A revolution rejects the existing order. What did Romanticism reject? In part, it rejected the thinking and values of the Enlightenment. During the Enlightenment, eighteenth-century thinkers valued logic and reason. They admired the scientific method. As practiced by geniuses like Isaac Newton, science had brought about a new understanding of the natural world.

Neoclassical Painting: Jacques-Louis David

Romantic artists developed their style in part as a reaction against the Neoclassical style. The leading Neoclassical painter in France was Jacques-Louis David (zhahk LOO-ee dah-veed). He lived during the French Revolution and the reign of Napoleon.

For the *Oath of the Horatii* (huh-RAY-shee-iy), David, like other Neoclassical artists, chose a subject from the classical world. The painting depicts a moment in a war between ancient Rome and a rival city-state. The enemies agreed to settle the war by sending three warriors from each side to fight to the death. The three sons of Horace (the Horatii) fought for Rome. In the painting, Horace holds his sons' swords high as the young men pledge allegiance to Rome.

David's painting embodies the Neoclassical traits of order and balance. The men stand in rigid poses like ancient statues. The sons on the left are balanced by the women and children on the right, who grieve for the losses to come. The figures are posed against an orderly background of massive columns and arches.

Some Enlightenment thinkers thought that if they applied reason and scientific thinking to human affairs, then they could solve most of the problems of human society.

If the Enlightenment was an "Age of Reason," it was also an age of reasonable art. Throughout most of the 1700s, the dominant style in the arts of Europe was *neoclassicism*. The name means "new classicism." Neoclassical artists admired certain qualities of Greek and Roman art and literature, such as harmony, order, and balance. Neoclassical poets translated and imitated the epics of Homer and Virgil. Architects designed stately buildings with Greek columns and Roman domes. Painters and sculptors copied the forms of ancient Roman statues.

The neoclassicists created art and literature that appealed to reason and the intellect—in other words, art for the Enlightenment. But in the turbulent times of the French Revolution, writers and artists began to attack the principles of neoclassicism and of the Enlightenment itself.

Writers and artists who shared such views would come to be known as Romantics. They insisted that the deepest truths lay not in reason but in the appreciation of nature and in the expression of individual emotion. In the early 1800s, this new perspective produced a great outpouring of daring and imaginative work in poetry, painting, and music.

Before we encounter some of these Romantic writers and artists, let's step back a few decades to meet a French philosopher of the mid-1700s, Jean-Jacques Rousseau (zhahn-zhahk roo-SOH). While Rousseau was one of the most important thinkers of the Enlightenment, many of his ideas paved the way for the coming of Romanticism.

Rousseau: Forerunner of Romanticism

In Paris, Rousseau was an active member of the lively group of thinkers known as the *philosophes*. He wrote articles on music for Denis Diderot's ambitious *Encyclopédie*. He argued against the most respected French composers of the time. Their music, he said, was too bound up in following formal rules. Rousseau argued for more freedom in music. This idea—that creative freedom in art is more important than following

traditional rules—became one of the central beliefs of Romanticism.

From music, Rousseau turned to philosophy and politics. He remained a champion of freedom. "Man is born free, and everywhere he is in chains," Rousseau wrote. In celebrating liberty and condemning tyranny, Rousseau agreed with many other thinkers of the Enlightenment. But in other ways, he disagreed with his fellow philosophes.

Most Enlightenment thinkers believed in the power of reason to solve human problems. But Rousseau thought that reason made people cold and unsympathetic to others. He declared that we should follow our emotions rather than our reason. Rousseau himself was a hugely emotional person. Once, when he came up with an especially good idea for an essay, he was so moved that he cried until his shirt was drenched with tears.

Rousseau also stressed the importance of following nature. He hated cities, which he called

Why "Romantics"?

The popular meaning of the word *romance* brings to mind roses, Valentines, and people in love. But there is a historical meaning as well. During the Middle Ages, people wrote down rambling stories that were often full of adventure, magic, and high emotion. These stories came to be known as medieval romances.

In the late eighteenth century and first half of the nineteenth century, some artists revived interest in the medieval romances. Many writers, painters, and composers went on to embrace ideas well beyond the medieval stories, but it was from those old stories that their movement got its name—Romanticism.

The French philosopher Jean-Jacques Rousseau loved the countryside. He believed that nature had many valuable lessons to teach people. His writings paved the way for Romanticism.

"the abyss of the human species." He loved the countryside, and spent many of his years living in rural homes. (He *had* to go live in the country when his writings angered Parisian officials who called for his arrest.)

Rousseau disliked the schools of his time, which kept children cooped up indoors. In a novel called *Émile* (ay-MEEL), he offered his ideas on education. Students, Rousseau said, should be taught in a rural setting, where they could learn about the natural world around them. Teachers should not burden their students with tiresome lessons, but should appeal to their natural interests. Young students, said Rousseau, should be allowed to run around outside, enjoying the beauty of nature and exercising their inborn curiosity. In such circumstances, Rousseau believed, students would blossom like wild flowers.

Rousseau's ideas about education flowed from his fundamental beliefs about human nature. Human beings, Rousseau believed, are naturally good. By nature, said Rousseau, people are free, happy, and innocent—but then we are corrupted by society.

Many of Rousseau's ideas influenced the writers and artists who came after him. His beliefs about the goodness of human nature and the evil of society became a central assumption of Romanticism. And, like Rousseau, many of the great Romantic poets and artists celebrated nature and called for people to follow their hearts rather than their heads.

Goethe's Werther: A Hero of Feeling

In 1774, a novel was published that introduced readers to a hero who completely followed his heart rather than his head. The novel is called *The Sorrows of Young Werther* (VEHR-tuh). Werther's tale is told mainly through a series of letters. In these letters he often describes what he is thinking—or, more precisely, what he is feeling:

> *A wonderful serenity has taken possession of my entire soul, like these sweet mornings of spring which I enjoy with my whole heart. I am alone, and feel the charm of existence in this spot, which was created for the bliss of souls like mine. I am so happy, my dear friend….*
>
> *Oh, would I could describe these conceptions, could impress upon paper all that is living so full and warm within me, that it might be the mirror of my soul….*

In many of his letters, Werther writes about his love for a young woman named Lotte. Unfortunately, Lotte is already engaged to another man—a man as unimaginative and practical as Werther is fanciful and artistic. In the end, Werther's intense emotions lead to tragic consequences.

Werther was a new kind of hero—a hero of strong feelings rather than bold actions. While his story was controversial—some people wanted to censor the novel—it was also wildly popular. (Napoleon is reported to have read the book seven times!) For a while, a kind of "Werther fever" gripped much of Europe, as young men imitated the sensitive hero, even dressing like Werther in a blue coat and yellow vest.

The novel brought widespread fame to its author, Johann Wolfgang von Goethe (GUR-tuh). At this time, Goethe, along with other young German writers, was part of a movement called *Sturm und Drang* (shturm oont DRAHNG), or Storm and Stress. Rousseau was one of the strong influences on this movement.

In contrast to the Enlightenment emphasis on reason and order, Sturm und Drang writers stressed the importance of emotion and the inspiring power of nature. They celebrated the creative individual who opposes accepted norms and standards. In many ways, *The Sorrows of Young Werther* is the most representative expression of the Sturm und Drang movement.

While Goethe based parts of *The Sorrows of Young Werther* on incidents from his own life, Goethe was not Werther. Unlike his fictional hero, Goethe mastered his feelings through his extraordinary intellect and will. He was a "Renaissance man" of his times—not only a novelist but also a poet, playwright, critic, and even a scientist. Goethe went on to become widely acknowledged as the greatest figure in German

Johann Wolfgang von Goethe was a leading member of the Sturm und Drang *(Storm and Stress) movement of German writers. The movement celebrated literary heroes who followed their emotions and challenged society's accepted standards.*

literature. Indeed, the Romantic period in Germany is sometimes known as "the age of Goethe."

William Wordsworth: Poet of Nature

In the early days of the French Revolution, when he was a young man, the poet William Wordsworth traveled from England to France to support the revolutionary cause. Disillusioned by what he saw, Wordsworth returned home. He spent the rest of his life in the mountainous Lake District in northern England. The beauty of that region's landscape—and its effect on his emotions—became a central subject of his poems.

Wordsworth believed that by immersing ourselves in nature, we connect ourselves to something larger and purer. "My heart leaps up," said Wordsworth, "when I behold / A rainbow in the sky."

William Wordsworth was one of the founders of the Romantic movement in English poetry.

William Wordsworth roamed England's Lake District for inspiration.

And the round ocean and the
    living air,
And the blue sky, and in the
    mind of man....

For Romantics like Wordsworth, nature conveyed "a sense sublime"—a feeling of something lofty, grand, and awe-inspiring. Nature communicated a spiritual truth. The Romantics believed that experiencing this truth makes us better and more complete human beings.

Wordsworth rejected the Enlightenment's emphasis on reason, which he saw as "meddling intellect." At the same time, he attacked the principles of neoclassical literature. The neoclassical poets had composed their poems according to strict rules. Wordsworth wanted poets to write in a much freer, more individual, and more emotional style. Poetry, he asserted, should be "the spontaneous overflow of powerful feelings."

In such moments, he wrote:

... I have felt
A presence that disturbs me
    with the joy
Of elevated thoughts; a sense
    sublime
Of something far more deeply
    interfused,
Whose dwelling is the light of
    setting suns,

The Romantic View of Science

For some Romantic writers, science was less a way of understanding nature than of destroying its wonder and beauty. Newton had used a prism to break light into the colors of the spectrum—an act that the English poet John Keats saw as "unweav[ing] a rainbow." When Keats's fellow poet, Wordsworth, considered how scientists analyze the natural world, he did not admire their powers of reason. Instead, he wrote:

Sweet is the lore which nature brings;
Our meddling intellect
Misshapes the beauteous forms of things—
We murder to dissect.

Byron: The Poet Who Broke the Rules

Soon other English poets, such as John Keats and Percy Shelley, joined Wordsworth's literary revolution. They celebrated nature as a source of truth. They valued emotion over reason. And they rejoiced in their ability to break the old forms and rules.

The poet George Gordon Byron, who at age 10 inherited the title Lord Byron, became a hero of Romanticism partly because he broke so many rules—not just artistic rules but also social ones. When the young aristocrat went off to Cambridge University, he found that a college rule prevented him from bringing his dog with him.

So he brought a tame bear instead. He even jokingly asked college officials to give the bear a scholarship.

Despite his aristocratic background, Byron became known as a political radical. (A *radical* is someone who wants to make extreme changes in existing views, conditions, or institutions.) He fought in Parliament for the rights of oppressed workers. Summing up his rebellious spirit, Byron declared, "I was born for opposition."

In long poems, Byron created the "Byronic hero"—a solitary, brooding figure who defies society's standards and rules. These characters—and their resemblance to the poet himself—fascinated readers so much that Byron became the most celebrated poet of his time.

Byron's life ended in a way that fit his freedom-loving nature. In the early 1820s, the people of Greece, a land Byron loved, rose up in revolt against their Ottoman Turkish rulers. Inspired by their struggle, Byron sailed off to Greece to join in the fight. But shortly after his arrival he came down with a fever and died. He was only 36. All over Europe people mourned Byron's death.

Byron had lived a very different life from Wordsworth. While Wordsworth chose to stay in northern England, writing about the calm beauty of his native landscape, Byron traveled widely, seeking adventure in exotic lands. The poets represent two different sides of Romanticism. Some Romantic artists, like Wordsworth, sought to show the beauty and depth of everyday life. Others, like Byron, tried to convey the

Arm raised, Lord Byron declares his readiness to help the Greeks win independence from the Ottoman Turks. In his poetry as in his life, Byron was a rebel "born for opposition."

excitement of new and sometimes dangerous experiences.

But both kinds of Romanticism valued emotion over reason. And both looked to nature for inspiration and spiritual renewal, as you can see in these famous lines that Byron wrote about the ocean:

Mary Shelley's *Frankenstein*

Young Mary Shelley penned the novel Frankenstein.

In 1816, Mary Wollstonecraft Shelley, the wife of the Romantic poet Percy Shelley, and just shy of 19 years old, started writing a remarkable novel called *Frankenstein.* In this chilling book, a scientist named Victor Frankenstein creates a monster by sewing together parts of dead bodies. The creature comes to life and escapes from Frankenstein's laboratory. At first the monster is gentle, but people treat him cruelly because of his frightening appearance. (Shelley describes him as eight feet tall, with black lips and shriveled skin.) In revenge, the monster goes on a murderous rampage.

Frankenstein became one of the most famous horror stories of all time. But it is also a powerful work of Romantic literature, full of intense emotion. Victor Frankenstein seems almost like a Romantic artist in his determination to break the rules—in his case, the rule of nature that says you can't create life out of death.

In our own time, *Frankenstein* has become the subject of many movies, and people often mistake the name of the scientist, Frankenstein, for the name of the monster he created.

*There is a pleasure in the
  pathless woods;
There is a rapture on the
  lonely shore;
There is society, where
  none intrudes,
By the deep sea, and music
  in its roar:
I love not man the less,
  but Nature more.*

John Constable: Painter of Gentle Landscapes

In the early nineteenth century, Romantic ideas spread swiftly across Europe, inspiring visual artists as well as poets. Like the Romantic poets, Romantic painters celebrated the beauty and power of nature. Back in the 1700s, many artists had looked down on landscape painting—paintings that show forests, lakes, mountains, or other scenes from nature as their main subject. Instead, artists preferred to paint famous scenes from history. (David, you recall, painted a scene from Roman history in his *Oath of the Horatii;* see page 432.) But during the Romantic period, some of the most talented artists devoted themselves to landscape painting.

One such artist was the English painter John Constable. Earlier painters, said Constable, merely copied the landscapes they had seen in other people's paintings. Instead, Constable urged artists to get out into nature and paint exactly what they saw. He took his easel out of his studio and set it up in the grass, working in the open air—an unusual practice at the time. In this way he produced vivid and dramatic pictures of the English countryside.

Constable has been called "the Wordsworth of painters." Like Wordsworth, he had no interest in exotic foreign places. He concentrated on capturing the scenery of the region where he grew up, around the River Stour in southern England. Constable wrote, "The sound of water escaping from mill dams, willows, old rotten planks, slimy posts and brickwork, I love such things. These scenes made me a painter."

Eugene Delacroix: Painter of Color and Feeling

If Constable was the Wordsworth of painting, then the French painter Eugene Delacroix (del-uh-KWAH) was its Byron. In fact, Delacroix was a devoted admirer of Byron's poetry, and even made illustrations for some of the poet's works.

Like Byron, Delacroix was inspired by traveling to exotic lands. On a journey to Morocco in northern Africa, he was delighted by exotic sights. His artist's eye was enchanted by the people's flowing, brightly colored clothes, so unlike the drab, tight-fitting clothes worn by Europeans. For years after his return to France, Delacroix painted dramatic North African scenes, such as Moroccan warriors on a lion hunt.

Like Byron, Delacroix was inspired by the struggle of the Greeks against their Ottoman rulers. Also like Byron, Delacroix

Like the Romantic poets, Romantic painters were inspired by nature. The English landscape painter John Constable loved to depict the countryside where he grew up, as in this 1821 painting called The Hay Wain.

Eugene Delacroix, pictured here in a self-portrait, was the leading painter of the Romantic movement in France.

supported freedom at home as well as abroad. He grew up during the years in which Napoleon set aside the revolutionary ideals of "liberty, fraternity, and equality" and instead proclaimed himself dictator. After Napoleon, kings once again ruled France—and not always well. In July of 1830, a revolution broke out against the oppressive policies of King Charles X. For a few days, Paris once again filled with barricades and clouds of rifle-smoke, and then the king gave up his throne.

To celebrate this short, successful revolution, Delacroix painted his most famous work, *Liberty Leading the People*. It depicts the symbolic female figure of Liberty leading a charge over a barricade. To her left, brandishing two pistols, is a young street urchin in tattered clothes. To her right, holding a rifle, is a well-dressed man in a top hat.

Caspar David Friedrich's Man and Woman Contemplating the Moon *captures a couple's sense of wonder as they gaze at the night sky. Friedrich's work often depicted the power of nature in dark forests, rocky coastlines, and wild landscapes.*

In *Liberty Leading the People*, Delacroix conveys his belief that a true revolution can bring people of very different classes and backgrounds together in a struggle against tyranny. To further show his sympathy with the rebels, Delacroix gave the man in the top hat a familiar face—his own.

Caspar David Friedrich: Painter of Untamed Landscapes

The Romantic movement in the visual arts extended beyond France and England. In Germany, a Romantic painter named Caspar David Friedrich (FREE-drihk) painted almost nothing but landscapes, like England's John Constable. But Friedrich's landscapes greatly differ from those of Constable.

While the English artist loved the gentle scenery of green fields and quiet rivers, Friedrich was drawn to rocky seacoasts and dark forests. He often clambered fearlessly over cliffs that towered high above the sea. He stood outside in thunderstorms, soaked to the skin but rejoicing in the violent power of nature. Once, when he saw a tall tree split by lightning, he murmured, "How great, how mighty, how wonderful."

Friedrich wrote, "The artist should paint not only what he sees before him, but also what he sees within him." Deep and powerful emotions must have stirred in Friedrich. His paintings depict wild, untamed landscapes, often showing a human figure posed against the vastness of an ocean, a mountain range, or the sky. (See page 430.) In Friedrich's eyes, nature possesses an awe-inspiring, sometimes frightening, power.

Beethoven: Musical Revolutionary

Beginning in the mid-1700s, the greatest composers—such as Franz Joseph Haydn (HIY-dn) and Wolfgang Amadeus Mozart (MOHT-sahrt)—wrote music in what is called the Classical style. Like neoclassical art and literature, most music of the Classical period emphasized the values of order, balance, and clarity. But in the early 1800s, the ideas of Romantic writers and painters began to influence music as well. One of the leaders of this new Romantic movement in music was the German composer Ludwig van Beethoven (BAY-toh-vuhn).

Beethoven began as a composer in the Classical style. But as his career progressed, he was increasingly influenced by Romanticism. Like the Romantic artists, he declared his profound love of the natural world. "No one can love the country as much as I do," he wrote. "For surely woods, trees, and rocks produce the echo which man desires to hear." He worked hard to get the "echo" of nature into some of his compositions. For example, his Sixth Symphony, known as the Pastoral Symphony, evokes a day in the country by using instruments to imitate the sounds of birdsong and thunder.

Like the Romantic poets and painters, Beethoven was willing to break the old rules of composition: "What is in my heart must come out and so I must write it down," he said. Beethoven's symphonies amazed people because they were longer, more complex, and more passionate than any musical pieces they had heard before. Some critics attacked them as "too long" and "much too noisy."

Like Mozart and the other composers, Beethoven depended on aristocratic patrons to help support his work. But, fully aware of his own genius, Beethoven refused to bow and scrape before any patron. Quarrelling with one of his patrons, a prince, he declared, "Prince, you are what you are through accident of birth; what I am, I am through myself. There have been and will be thousands of princes; there is only one Beethoven." Perhaps even more than Byron, Beethoven embodies the defiantly independent spirit of the Romantic artist.

By 1802, Beethoven had published many of his first important piano sonatas and string quartets, as well as two symphonies. He was well on his way to a successful career. Then, tragedy struck.

For some time Beethoven had been noticing symptoms of hearing loss. He anxiously consulted doctors and tried various treatments. But soon he could not avoid the terrible fact—he was going deaf.

Classical Music: General and Specific

The term *classical music* has both a broad, general meaning and a specific, historical meaning. In a general sense, classical music (often contrasted with "popular music") includes music written for orchestras, choirs, string quartets, pianists, and other performers. In this broad usage, classical music includes composers from before Johann Sebastian Bach (1685–1750) to the present day. Within this category of music, however, there is a specific period known as the Classical period, from the mid-1700s to the early 1800s.

As each day passed, Beethoven —whose very existence was made up of sound, melody, harmony— could hear less and less of the music he wrote. Somehow he found the determination to continue. His music changed. Some works began to express the emotions of a hero struggling against overwhelming challenges and emerging victorious. This sense of struggle and triumph is perhaps nowhere more dramatic than in his Fifth Symphony. The opening notes of the Fifth Symphony have become possibly the best-known passage in all of classical music.

By 1816, Beethoven's hearing was almost completely gone. His style changed again. His last works are deeply personal and highly spiritual. The crowning achievement of this time was his massive Ninth Symphony.

The Ninth, Beethoven's last symphony, takes more than an hour to perform. In the fourth and final movement, Beethoven—as though the vast resources of an orchestra were not enough to express the deep feelings within him—included a full chorus and vocal soloists. After a brief and stormy introduction, the music stops short, and a soloist sings these words:

O friends, no more these sounds!
Let us sing more cheerful songs,
More full of joy!

The soloists and chorus go on to sing a poem known as the "Ode to Joy," by the German poet Friedrich von Schiller (SHIL-uhr). Their voices rise to express a hope that motivated many Romantic artists—the dream of universal

Ludwig van Beethoven's music straddled the Classical and Romantic eras. He was inspired by writers like Goethe and by the ideals of the French Revolution. Passionate and forceful, Beethoven once declared, "What is in my heart, I must write down."

brotherhood. "All men become brothers / Under the sway of [Joy's] gentle wings," they sing. In this final movement, one critic has written, Beethoven was "reaching out for that quality of joy which will unite all creation in ecstatic song."

Beethoven conducted the first performance of his Ninth Symphony in 1824. (Since Beethoven could not hear, an assistant conductor stood near him, keeping time for the orchestra to follow.) When the symphony ended, the audience burst into cheers and applause.

Beethoven, however, could hear nothing—not the playing of his own music or the enthusiasm of the crowd. At last one of the singers prompted him to turn around. As this singer later recalled, Beethoven was greeted by "a volcanic explosion of sympathy and admiration ... which was repeated again and again, and seemed as if it would never end."

In this 1792 painting, a steam pump drains water from a British coal mine. During the Industrial Revolution, steam engines began to perform work previously done by humans and by animals—and quickly changed life for millions.

Britain Begins the Industrial Revolution

*I*n 1776, Great Britain tried without success to crush the American Revolution. Almost four decades later, the British successfully defeated Napoleon when he tried to export the French Revolution.

While all this was going on, the British launched a revolution of their own. It wasn't a democratic revolution. No one stormed a castle or got rid of a king. But this revolution was just as dramatic and far-reaching. In fact, it changed civilization throughout western Europe, and eventually, throughout the world. This upheaval, sparked in Great Britain, is known as the Industrial Revolution.

It was a revolution in the way people worked and lived. In 1750, most people in Europe lived and worked on farms and in small villages. They raised wheat and grew vegetables. When growing conditions were good, they ate; when conditions were bad, they starved. Weavers, spinners, and craftsmen worked in their cottages or homes. But over the next hundred years, during the Industrial Revolution, machines began to do the work of thousands of craftsmen. People moved from the country to cities, and factories replaced homes as the centers of production.

Why did the Industrial Revolution start in England? In part because the land had certain natural advantages. As an island nation, separated from the rest of Europe by the English Channel, England managed to avoid the destruction of the wars racking the European continent. Also, because England's fields were fertile, British farmers produced more and more food. The

This chapter focuses on the Industrial Revolution, which started in Great Britain.

nation's population grew, and so did its prosperity. A bigger population and a richer nation meant that more people could buy more products.

Fertile fields were not England's only natural resource. In its rolling hills lay large deposits of coal and iron. Coal and iron made it possible to power the new factories and build new machinery as never before.

Perhaps Britain's greatest advantage lay in the minds of its inventive people. The spirit of Isaac Newton, who probed the physical universe to discover how it operated, lived on in England. The British always seemed to be looking for ways to understand how things worked and how to make things work better. In the late eighteenth and early nineteenth centuries, British inventors learned how to use power-driven machines in place of human muscles. Other British thinkers made huge strides in figuring out how their economy worked.

Let's turn now to meet an important British thinker, Adam Smith. He challenged the way people thought about wealth and provided the philosophy for an economic system that still affects us today.

Adam Smith Rethinks Wealth

At the University of Glasgow in Scotland, students told many tales of their absent-minded professor of philosophy, Adam Smith. They often saw him ambling down the street, nodding his head and mumbling to himself. Occasionally he bumped into lampposts or buildings. Once he left his house in a bathrobe and walked 15 miles, lost in thought.

Smith failed to notice the everyday world because his head was so full of big ideas. He liked to think about how nations grew and prospered. He was especially interested in trying to understand why some nations were richer than others. He knew that most people believed that a nation's wealth consisted of its gold and silver. European kings thought that if a nation sold more goods than it bought, it was sure to pile up gold. So governments passed laws aimed at making sure their citizens sold more to other countries than they bought.

For example, the British government placed special taxes, called duties, on cloth, wine, and other products bought from France.

Workers perform separate tasks in a pin-making workshop. In The Wealth of Nations, *Adam Smith concluded that such division of labor results in a more efficient manufacturing process. This illustration appeared in Denis Diderot's* Encyclopédie.

Because these taxes made French products more expensive, the British were encouraged to buy cloth and wine made in England. Meanwhile the French government made it illegal to import printed calico, a cloth made in India, because the government wanted French citizens to buy cloth made in France. The French government even executed people for selling illegal cloth in France.

Adam Smith spent many years thinking about the proper role of government in creating wealth. He concluded that all these duties and punishments helped no one. In 1776, while the Americans were declaring their independence, Smith set forth his conclusions in a book called *The Wealth of Nations*. It was a pathbreaking work that laid the foundation for the modern science of economics—the study of how goods and services are produced, distributed, and consumed. Smith, in fact, is often called the father of modern economics.

Smith began *The Wealth of Nations* by looking at the "division of labor" and how it increased people's ability to produce things. As an example, Smith described how the production of a single pin could be broken into many separate steps, such as forming a thin wire, straightening it, cutting the wire into pieces, sharpening each piece, and so forth. If one inexperienced man did the whole job, he could probably make no more than one pin a day. But Smith told of a pin-making workshop in which ten men divided the job so that each man performed just two or three steps. Each man did his task so well that the ten men together could make about 48,000 pins a day.

Smith explained how the division of labor worked throughout society. Even a product as humble as a workman's woolen coat was really the result of many different tasks performed by many different people—shepherds, weavers, cloth dyers, button-makers, tailors, and others. Most of these people never met each other, yet their work fit together to produce the coat.

In fact, Smith realized, all people were connected through their work, forming one big network. Somehow, everyone cooperated to produce exactly the goods and services society needed. How could such a

Britain was an island nation, and its economy depended on trade with overseas nations and colonies. Adam Smith's theories helped that trade flourish, turning Britain into an economic powerhouse.

complicated system work without any planning? Just as John Locke had pondered the "natural laws" that explain how governments should work, Smith wondered whether there might be similar laws to explain how economies operated.

The Market's "Invisible Hand"

Smith found his answer in the market. By "the market," he meant the whole system of buying and selling. People, he said, have an inborn tendency to bargain. If people want something, Smith said, they will pay good money for it and the price will go up, encouraging others to go into the business of making it. If too much of a product comes into the market, the price will drop, so people will stop producing it.

Smith wrote that the market is almost like an "invisible hand" that guides the business decisions people make. This invisible hand makes sure that people produce the things and provide the services that society needs, usually at reasonable prices. Anyone who overcharges loses business to competitors. Anyone who undercharges goes broke.

What makes the market work, Smith said, is self-interest. That is, people are naturally very interested in getting the things they need to have happy, comfortable lives. This self-interest causes them to work for money, and to produce and trade different things. Smith wrote, "It is not from the benevolence of the butcher … or the baker that we expect our dinner, but from their regard to their own interest."

Finally, Smith noted, those who make money are often motivated to save it and turn it into capital—money used to start or enlarge a business. Then, as Smith noted, more and bigger businesses can create more and cheaper products.

The wealth of a nation, Smith concluded, lies in the prosperity of all its citizens. That is, it lies in their ability to produce and consume goods. To make this wealth grow, Smith recommended an economic system in which businesses produce goods and services in order to make money. This economic system is now known as capitalism.

Smith said that government should not interfere with most business decisions. It should let the invisible hand, or the natural laws of the economy, take over. Smith argued that competition would keep prices low. After all, why would you buy a rake from the Green Rake Company for 50 dollars when you can buy just as good a rake from the Red Rake Company for 15 dollars? As Smith saw it, businesses that made bad decisions would go out of business.

After Adam Smith died in 1790, the prestige of his book continued to grow. Powerful people in the British government began to follow his advice. Over the next few decades, the government lifted duties to let trade flow freely in and out of the country. People could try most business schemes without government permission. The government allowed banks to loan money as they saw fit. Ambitious businessmen willing to take risks could now use borrowed money to tackle big projects.

Adam Smith's work was not the only reason these things happened. While he was writing about the wealth of nations, his countrymen were hard at work creating wealth. They were experimenting with new ways to make things faster, especially in the important textile industry.

Smith Calls for Competition

Adam Smith believed that competition among businesses was important. Competition, he said, causes the most efficient businesses to survive. And it helps purchasers get the best price. But Smith said that competition is hard to ensure because "people of the same trade seldom meet together, even for merriment and diversion" without the conversation ending in "some contrivance to raise prices." In other words, without some regulation and control, businessmen might plot together to fix prices at a high level. Because he believed in the need for competition among businesses, Smith insisted that there should be no monopolies, no industries in which a single group controls all the production and prices.

From Adam Smith's
The Wealth of Nations

*A Page
from the Past*

A *maxim* is a
fundamental truth
or principle.

To be *prudent* is
to be wise and
careful in managing
one's affairs.

In these excerpts from An Inquiry into the Nature and Causes of the Wealth of Nations, *published in 1776, Adam Smith discusses the division of labor and the power of self-interest.*

The greatest improvements in the productive powers of labor … seem to have been the effects of the division of labor…. It is the maxim of every prudent master of a family, never to attempt to make at home what it will cost him more to make than to buy. The tailor does not attempt to make his own shoes, but buys them of the shoemaker. The shoemaker does not attempt to make his own clothes, but employs a tailor…. [They] find it for their interest to employ their whole industry in a way in which they have some advantage over their neighbors, and to purchase … whatever else they have occasion for….

Man has almost constant occasion for the help of his brethren, and it is in vain for him to expect it from their benevolence only. He will be more likely to prevail if he can interest their self-love in his favor, and show them that it is for their own advantage to do for him what he requires of them. Whoever offers to another a bargain of any kind proposes to do this….

It is only for the sake of profit that any man employs capital in the support of industry…. He generally, indeed, neither intends to promote the public interest, nor knows how much he is promoting it…. He intends only his own gain; and he is in this, as in many other cases, led by an invisible hand to promote an end which was no part of his intention. Nor is it always the worse for the society that it was no part of it. By pursuing his own interest, he frequently promotes that of the society more effectually than when he really intends to promote it.

Adam Smith

From Handmade to Machine-made

The Industrial Revolution began in England's textile industry. For centuries, weavers had made cloth by throwing thread-bearing wooden shuttles back and forth on their looms. (A loom is a machine that weaves threads together to make cloth. A shuttle is a device used to carry a thread between other threads on a loom.) This method worked, but it was exhausting to throw the shuttle back and forth, and a single weaver could not make material wider than his outstretched arms. To make wider cloth, two weavers had to work side-by-side and pass the shuttle between them.

In the 1730s, a weaver named John Kay came up with a way for one weaver to make wide cloth by himself. He mounted a shuttle on wheels in a track so a weaver could shoot the shuttle from side to side by pulling a cord. This "flying shuttle" made it possible for weavers to make wider cloth, and make it much faster.

But Kay's invention also created a problem. Looms could now make cloth so fast that spinners—those who made thread—could not keep up with the demand for thread. They continued to twist fibers together on spinning wheels that made thread just one strand at a time.

John Kay's flying shuttle loom was one of the new machines that revolutionized the textile industry in Britain. The loom allowed weavers to make wider pieces of cloth—and make them at much faster speeds.

A woman operates a spinning jenny, a machine invented by James Hargreaves to increase the production of thread.

For years a number of inventors worked on this problem. The man generally credited with solving it was a poor weaver named James Hargreaves. James and his wife, Elizabeth, had 13 children, and the whole family pitched in to spin thread for his loom. But even with everyone working, they couldn't produce as much thread as the flying shuttle could use.

Hargreaves tried to think of a way to speed up the production of thread. In the 1760s, he came up with a contraption called a "spinning jenny." The spinning jenny could spin 16 strands of thread at once.

Together, the flying shuttle and the spinning jenny made it possible to make fabric much faster and cheaper.

Why "Jenny"?

For years people said that James Hargreaves named the spinning jenny after one of his daughters, Jenny. But some historians say that "jenny" came from "gin," short for "engine."

These inventions moved the textile industry from handmade to machine-made. Many weavers and spinners hated the new machines, which they feared would put them out of work. Crowds were so hostile to John Kay that he had to flee one city hidden in a sack. An angry mob broke into James Hargreaves's home, put a hammer in his hand, and forced him to destroy his own machinery.

Amateurs at Work: Arkwright and Cartwright

As fast as flying shuttles and spinning jennies were, they required human muscles to power them. That meant they were limited by the strength of the people operating them. But other inventors continued to tinker their way toward the next big advances in the British textile industry.

In the 1760s, a barber and wig-maker named Richard Arkwright built a machine called a water frame. The water frame used a flowing river as a source of power. Waterpower made it possible to spin as many as 80 strands of thread at once.

Arkwright found investors to help him build a mill, where he employed 300 men who used his water frame to spin thread around the clock. He soon expanded to 10 mills and made so much money that he never had to cut hair again.

Now even the looms with flying shuttles could not keep up with the amount of thread being produced. When a clergyman named Edmund Cartwright heard about this problem, he came up with a solution.

Even though he had never used a loom or watched a weaver at work,

Richard Arkwright's water frame was capable of making stronger thread than Hargreaves's jenny, and it could make 80 strands of thread at once. The water frame used a flowing river as its source of power.

The Rise of the Iron Industry

The iron industry developed alongside the textile industry. In several parts of England there were mines with plentiful supplies of iron ore. In the early 1700s, English iron makers improved the process of smelting (separating the iron from the ore). They went on to develop ways to melt the iron and, while it was still white-hot, shape it into tools and parts for looms, jennies, and other machines.

In the late eighteenth century, iron masters honed their skills in building Ironbridge, the world's first large structure made of iron. The bridge spanned the River Severn in Shropshire, England, with a 100-foot arch. Ironmasters first figured out how to produce large quantities of iron while working on this project. The bridge was completed in 1779 and is still used for pedestrian traffic. Because of its historic role in the Industrial Revolution, Ironbridge is a British national monument.

Ironbridge in Shropshire, England

Reverend Cartwright devised a mechanical loom that could be powered by either a horse or a waterwheel. One person operating this power loom could produce as much fabric as 15 old-style weavers working at their traditional looms. Cartwright's new power looms were so simple that even children could use them—and many did.

Back then few people worried about children working all day. After all, they reasoned, youngsters had been working on farms for years. When businessmen realized that children could operate the new power looms, they did not hesitate to sign them up. The work led to very hard lives for the youngsters, but in the late eighteenth century inventors were not focusing on those children. They were thinking about producing more cloth. (In a later chapter, we'll learn more about child labor and other problems caused by the Industrial Revolution.)

James Watt and Steam Power

While inventions like the spinning jenny and the power loom kicked the Industrial Revolution into gear, there was still one big limit to productivity. That limit was power—the energy needed to make machines work. Horses and waterwheels could provide only so much power. If machines were to do more, they would need more power behind them.

One obvious source of power for machines was fire, but what could be used for fuel? Many of England's trees had already been chopped down for fuel and building. The country was running short on wood, as well as charcoal, which is made of wood.

The wood shortage proved the truth of the old saying, "Necessity is the mother of invention." As the supply of wood in England's forests dwindled, England turned to its rich coal deposits in the central and northern hills. Coal began to fuel the fires that powered Britain's new machines.

As men and boys went underground to mine coal, they often found themselves knee-deep in water. Underground springs flooded the mines, and even when flooding wasn't a problem, the springs themselves often kept miners from reaching new seams of coal.

Since the early 1700s, some mines had been using pumps, known as the Miner's Friend, to clear water out of the mines. These pumps were powered by crude steam engines, but the engines were very inefficient and often broke down.

In 1763, a student at Scotland's University of Glasgow was asked to repair one of these broken-down engines. James Watt, the clever son of a Scottish shopkeeper, was

James Watt studies the operation of an early piston-driven pump. The young Scottish student was fascinated by the workings of such steam engines.

studying to be a mathematical instrument-maker, but he didn't mind taking on this job.

Watt was fascinated by how the engine worked. In those days steam engines were powered by the up-and-down motion of a device called a piston. Heat from a boiler caused the piston to rise inside a cylinder. When it reached the top, a spray of cold water pushed the piston back down to the bottom of the cylinder, where the piston had to be reheated so it would rise again.

As Watt worked on the engine, he realized that the cycle of heating, cooling, and reheating the piston was very inefficient. Wouldn't it be better, he thought, to keep the whole cylinder hot and divert the used steam to a separate chamber where it could cool down?

It took Watt several years to build a working engine. He spent much of that time looking for a financial backer. He also needed craftsmen who could make the valves and other complicated parts his new engine would need. He found an ally and friend in Matthew Boulton, an Englishman who ran a factory near Birmingham, England.

Boulton was interested in power for his factory, which turned out silver buckles, gold buttons, and brass candlesticks. He employed many craftsmen, and he had money. So in 1775, Boulton and Watt formed a partnership. Finally Watt was able to produce engines with pistons that moved more efficiently.

The new engines were fine for pumping water out of flooded mines. But Watt wanted his engines to do more. He wanted them to power the gears, belts, and pulleys in looms, jennies, and other machines. By the end of the 1780s, Watt was building steam engines that could power all kinds of machines.

After years of effort, Watt produced his own piston-driven steam engine, a reconstruction of which is shown above. Watt's steam engines, which were more efficient than earlier versions, gave a huge boost to Britain's Industrial Revolution.

Row upon row of workers bend over their machines in a nineteenth-century ammunition factory. The owners of this factory have made full use of two great breakthroughs of the Industrial Revolution—Adam Smith's division of labor and James Watt's steam technology.

These steam engines changed the world. The strength of a person's muscles no longer limited what he or she could do. Mills no longer had to sit by flowing rivers and use water for power. Ships no longer had to depend on the wind. Machines could churn out fabric, thread, pins, ammunition, and much more, and at rates far faster than human power ever allowed.

Watt's steam engine made all of these things possible. As Boulton once told a visitor to Watt's engine factory, "I sell here, Sir, what all the world desires to have—POWER."

How Many Watts?

Have you ever noticed that light bulbs carry a stamp that tells how many watts they use? So do many electric appliances. The unit of power called the *watt* is named in honor of James Watt, whose steam engine helped power the Industrial Revolution.

The Industrial Revolution Spreads

With James Watt's engines powering their machines and Adam Smith's ideas churning in their heads, British businessmen built factories to manufacture everything from children's toys to iron coffins. Men, women, and children spent twelve to sixteen hours a day, six days a week, tending the clattering machines. In the past, one gunsmith might have made two or three finely crafted guns a year. In factories that followed Adam Smith's principle of the division of labor, there might be hundreds of workers, each performing just one or two tasks over and over. One British gun factory produced 100,000 weapons in one year.

At first British businessmen tried to keep to themselves their knowledge of how to make the new machines and how to operate factories. The British government passed

Left: The British
government made
it illegal to export
textile machinery
like these cotton-
spinning machines.
Even so, the new
technologies were
soon spreading to
North America and
other countries in
western Europe.

Below: When Samuel
Slater emigrated
from England to the
United States, he
took with him a
thorough knowledge
of textile machinery,
including Richard
Arkwright's water
frame. In 1793 in
Rhode Island, Slater
built America's first
successful cotton mill.

laws that made it illegal to export textile machinery. The government even said that anyone who knew how to design a textile machine could not leave the country.

But in 1789, a young Englishman named Samuel Slater disguised himself and immigrated to America with something precious—experience working in English cotton mills. He had carefully stored in his head everything he needed to know to start his own mill.

It wasn't long before Slater established a mill in Rhode Island. His venture was a success, and within a few years he also had mills in Massachusetts, Connecticut, and New Hampshire. New England cotton mills spun thread and wove cloth yarn from bales of southern cotton. Soon other factories sprang up in the United States, making iron, guns, tools, and other goods. America would prove to be one of England's biggest industrial competitors.

As the Industrial Revolution spread to North America and western Europe, people marveled at the improvements and abundance it brought. Machines could produce more goods at a lower cost than ever before. But as men and women struggled to endure fourteen-hour days in the mills, and small children trudged off to work in factories six days a week, many began to ask: What is the price of all of this progress?

We'll soon examine that question, but first let's explore another important revolution—a revolution in transportation and communication.

Smoke billows as a steam locomotive emerges from a tunnel on the railroad between London and Bristol. Steam power revolutionized transportation in the nineteenth century.

A Revolution in Transportation and Communication

The Industrial Revolution began in Great Britain, and its first big success was in the textile industry. Inventions such as the flying shuttle, spinning jenny, and steam engine helped speed up production. But the Industrial Revolution would not have brought such huge changes to the world without a simultaneous revolution in transportation and communication.

Let's look at transportation first. In the late eighteenth century, the British could mine coal and smelt iron, but how could they haul cargo to faraway ports and cities? It wasn't until people found ways to move heavy goods quickly over long distances that the Industrial Revolution could gain momentum.

Improving Roads

The revolution in transportation started with roads. In ancient times, the Romans had built splendid roads, but those crumbled during the Middle Ages. In Britain, the responsibility for road repair passed to church parishes. Local volunteers did the work. They didn't care if the roads were bumpy since they rarely traveled far from home.

In the late 1700s, for most people travel over land was travail, which means toil, agony, hardship. (The words *travel* and *travail* both come from the old French word *travaillier*, which means to torture or to labor very hard at something.) Travelers suffered bone-jarring journeys over muddy, rutted roads. Passengers in horse-drawn coaches often got out to walk alongside the coach for stretches, because walking hurt less.

Eventually a few big landowners began pooling their money and hiring workers to build private

A carriage enters an English turnpike. Travelers who wanted to use turnpikes had to pay a toll before they could pass through the gates. The turnpike above led from London to northwest England.

roads called turnpikes. The word *turnpike* came from medieval times, when revolving gates tipped with sharp pikes were used to block certain roads. Eighteenth-century turnpikes didn't necessarily have pikes, but they did have gates and guards. Those who wanted to use the roads had to pay a toll, and the tolls paid for construction and road repair. Some turnpikes even made a profit, which motivated business-minded groups to build more.

Macadam for Your Driveway?

John McAdam's process for road surfacing is with us still. In fact, his name has become a word—*macadam*—used for roadways built by the principles McAdam developed. Macadam roads or driveways employ layers of small stones or finely ground rock over well-drained soil.

In 1815, a Scotsman named John McAdam started putting into practice some scientific principles he'd been working on for road-building. He laid a foundation of crushed rock that raised a roadbed a few inches above the surrounding ground. Such roads drained well and held up to heavy traffic. Other road builders began to use McAdam's system. On these better roads, merchants could haul heavier loads with fewer horses. Trade increased, prices fell, and over the course of a century, passenger traffic between British cities multiplied more than 10 times over.

Building Canals

It had always been easier to move heavy cargo over water than land. But rivers did not go everywhere, and many streams were too shallow for big boats. In the late eighteenth century, however, the British Parliament passed laws directing that rivers be dug deeper and made wider. Private firms cut canals at key points. They hired gangs of workers who used picks, shovels, and gunpowder to connect rivers and create new waterways. Now boats could get to towns they had never reached before.

Francis Egerton, the Duke of Bridgewater, led the building of the first important canal in Britain. As a young man, while on a tour of Europe, he became fascinated by the workings of a canal in France. Back in England, where the duke owned lands with plenty of coal, he needed a way to get the coal from the mines to the manufacturing towns. So he spent much of his fortune cutting a waterway from his estates to the city of Manchester. No river ran nearby, so he filled his canal with water drained out of Bridgewater's coal mines. As soon as it opened in 1761, the Bridgewater Canal attracted toll-paying traffic, which made the duke a very rich man.

In the next 15 years, Parliament authorized many more canal projects. Soon a web of waterways laced the English countryside.

Not to be outdone, Americans also started digging canals. In 1825, workers in New York completed the Erie Canal. This waterway ran from the Hudson River to Lake Erie, connecting the Atlantic Coast to lands hundreds of miles inland. It was the longest canal in the western world at that time—40 feet wide, 4 feet deep, and 363 miles long. It had paths on

The Duke of Bridgewater built the first important canal in Britain. At left, the duke gestures toward his canal, which crosses a river by means of an aqueduct.

either side for mules to walk as they pulled boats. New York Governor DeWitt Clinton put his career on the line when he poured taxpayer money into this expensive project. The Erie Canal paid for itself many times over, and Clinton ended up a hero.

Steam Engines Take to the Water

In 1787, a young American named Robert Fulton went to England. The son of a failed farmer, Fulton was eager to prove himself to the world. He went to England to study art, and hoped to make his name as a painter. In that field, his talent may not have taken him far. But all the excitement about canals in England sparked Fulton's imagination. He decided to drop painting and try his hand at inventing and engineering.

Fulton went to France to sell Napoleon an idea for a submarine. The busy conqueror turned him down, but Fulton met inventors who

were trying to build boats powered by steam. One Frenchman actually built such a boat. It worked for 15 minutes. Then the heavy engine broke through the floor and the boat sank.

Returning to the United States, Fulton found scores of would-be inventors with ideas for steamboats. At the time, several American mining companies were using steam engines to pump water out of mines. Benjamin Franklin had toyed with mounting a steam pump to a boat. He pictured it sucking water from the front of the boat and blowing it out the back, thus forcing the boat forward. Another inventor, Colonel John Stevens, made a steam-driven paddle boat, but the engine shook the boat to pieces.

Still another man, John Fitch, invented a boat with steam-powered oars. His invention worked so well that in 1790 he was able to offer steamboat rides between Burlington,

New Jersey, and Philadelphia, Pennsylvania. But many people were reluctant to board his steamboat, even for free. They knew that steam engines sometimes exploded and often caused dangerous fires. Besides, Fitch's boat belched black smoke and made a horrid shrieking noise.

Robert Fulton smelled opportunity. He teamed up with a well-connected politician named Robert Livingston. Using Livingston's money, Fulton built a 133-foot paddleboat powered by a steam engine imported from Scotland. The newspapers called his boat the *Clermont*, after Livingston's estate.

In August 1807, Fulton attracted a huge crowd to the banks of the Hudson River to watch him launch his boat. Most expected to see a grand explosion. Instead, Fulton lit the boilers and the boat went chugging up the river at four miles per hour—against the current!

Fulton and Livingston were better businessmen than most steamboat inventors. They got a regular steamboat service going between Albany and New York City. Fulton achieved all the success he had dreamed of. He even got popular credit for "inventing the steamboat," though he built on other people's ideas and made them work as a business.

A few years later, a steamboat designed by Fulton began traveling the Mississippi River between New Orleans, Louisiana, and Natchez, Mississippi. Soon steamboats were chugging up and down rivers and around the Great Lakes. Most of the steamboats carried freight such as cotton and lumber. Some were grand passenger vessels—floating hotels where travelers danced on the decks, ate in luxurious dining rooms, and slept in cozy staterooms.

Oceangoing steamships took longer to develop because crossing the Atlantic presented special problems. Steamships had to burn wood or coal. On a river they could pick up fuel along the way. On ocean crossings, they had to start out with all the fuel they would need. Carrying so much fuel left little room for cargo or passengers.

Gradually, however, inventors designed more powerful and efficient steam engines. Propellers replaced paddle wheels. Shipbuilders began to build ships out of iron instead of

In 1863, the Cunard steamship *Scotia* crossed the Atlantic in eight days and three hours. The *Scotia* was the most magnificent passenger ship of her day.

wood. By 1860, the British-owned Cunard Steamship Company was offering regular service across the Atlantic, with ships departing frequently in each direction.

George Stephenson: "Father of the Railroad"

While some inventors were hard at work trying to move people and goods over water, others tackled new ways to speed transportation over land. In the development of railroads, one Englishman played a leading role—George Stephenson.

Stephenson was the son of a poor coal miner. In the small village where he grew up, he often saw horses pulling wagonloads of coal from the mines to the riverfront docks. These wagons moved on a tramway.

A tramway had two strips of wood along each edge and crossbars between them to keep the planks evenly spaced. In fact, tramways were what we now call railroads, except that they were made of wood, and the carts that moved on them were pulled by mules, horses, or people. The carts' wheels rested on the wooden tracks. Most mines in Europe and America had tramways for moving material to the nearest shipping docks.

When he was nine, George got a job keeping cows off the tramway. Machines fascinated the boy. He studied the tramway and wondered if some machine could be built to pull the wagons. Later, he was put in charge of the mine's steam pump. He spent many hours taking that machine apart to see how it worked.

Eventually, George Stephenson rose to be head engineer of a mining operation. Now, at last, he could set to work on the project he had been pondering since childhood. He built a steam-powered locomotive, a vehicle for moving railroad cars. In 1814, he tested his first locomotive—the *Blücher*, as he named it—on the tramway from the mine to the shipping dock. It managed to pull eight wagons loaded with thirty tons of coal at about four miles per hour.

Over the next five years, Stephenson built several more locomotives, each one stronger and safer than the last. Other inventors were also at work. They built steam locomotives that they called by names such as *Puffing Billy* and *Comet*.

In those years, a number of English companies built tramways between cities, and these tramways came to be known as railroads. Some railroads carried passengers as well as freight. At first horses or mules pulled the cars. In 1829, the new Liverpool & Manchester Railway decided to use locomotives instead of animals. But whose locomotive would the company use?

To make its choice, the company decided to stage a locomotive race at a place called Rainhill. Three locomotives were entered in the race: the *Novelty*, the *Sanspareil* (which means "incomparable" in French), and George Stephenson's masterpiece, the *Rocket*. A huge crowd gathered to watch the contest, just as they would a horse race.

Stephenson's *Rocket* blew the competition away. It reached a then-unheard-of speed of 24 miles per hour pulling passengers, and 12.5 miles per hour pulling freight. Overnight, Stephenson's victory made the *Rocket* the world's most famous locomotive.

Railroad companies fought to hire Stephenson as their chief engineer. From a childhood of poverty, Stephenson rose to great wealth. He died in 1848, respected around the world as the "Father of the Railroad."

Railroads in America

The Rainhill race made headlines in the United States. By this time, America also had several railroads, but they still used animals to pull the cars. John Stevens, who had built some of the first steamboats, insisted that steam-powered locomotives could replace animals. But he had trouble finding financial backers. Most people felt locomotives were not practical because they were so

George Stephenson's Rocket *could travel at 24 miles per hour while pulling passengers, an amazing speed for its era. The* Rocket *became the most famous locomotive in the world.*

On August 28, 1830, Peter Cooper's Tom Thumb *pulled a load of 40 passengers on the Baltimore & Ohio Railroad. Its speeds varied from 5 to 18 miles per hour.*

The Pony Express Speeds Up the Mail

In 1860, there were no railroads stretching across the western part of the United States. But people still wanted a quick way to move their mail across the continent. So in that year, a group of Missouri businessmen decided to start their own speedy private mail service, using a relay system. They called it the Pony Express.

With 400 fast ponies or horses, 80 young riders, and more than 150 stations, the Pony Express could deliver mail between St. Joseph, Missouri, and Sacramento, California (nearly 2,000 miles apart), in 8 days. The service lasted only about a year and a half. It could not compete with the much speedier telegraph (which you'll read about later in this chapter). In 1861, Americans finished building a telegraph line across the continent, and the Pony Express went out of business.

heavy. They said that railroad tracks would have to be made of iron to carry the locomotives, and that would make railroads too expensive to compete with steamships. Just to show that it could be done, Stevens set up a circular track in Albany, New York, and built a "steam wagon" to run on it.

By 1829, when the *Rocket* won its race in England, more American inventors turned their attention to railroads. In 1830, Peter Cooper of New York built a small locomotive called the *Tom Thumb*. It ran on a track laid between Baltimore, Maryland, and a town 13 miles away. It worked so well that railroad companies took a chance on ordering full-sized steam locomotives.

As it turned out, railroad tracks did have to be made of iron. But steam-powered trains proved so profitable that railroad companies could pay for such tracks. State and local governments helped by giving railroad companies loans and free land on which to lay their tracks.

Of course, there were problems at first. Early railroad tracks were wooden beams covered with iron. Sometimes these broke loose, curled up, and poked up into the cars. Sparks from the boilers could set trains on fire. In 1835, railroad companies were building or planning dozens of new railroad lines in the United States, but they were not all the same gauge—that is, the space between the rails differed. This meant a steam locomotive could not always travel from one set of tracks to another.

In time, iron tracks replaced wooden ones. Railroad companies agreed to use the same gauge. Improved steam engines made trains safer. By 1840, more than 3,000 miles of track ran up, down, and across the eastern part of the United States. In the next decade the amount of track almost tripled. By 1860, people were even talking of building a railroad all the way to the Pacific Ocean.

Railroad Development in the United States, 1840–1860

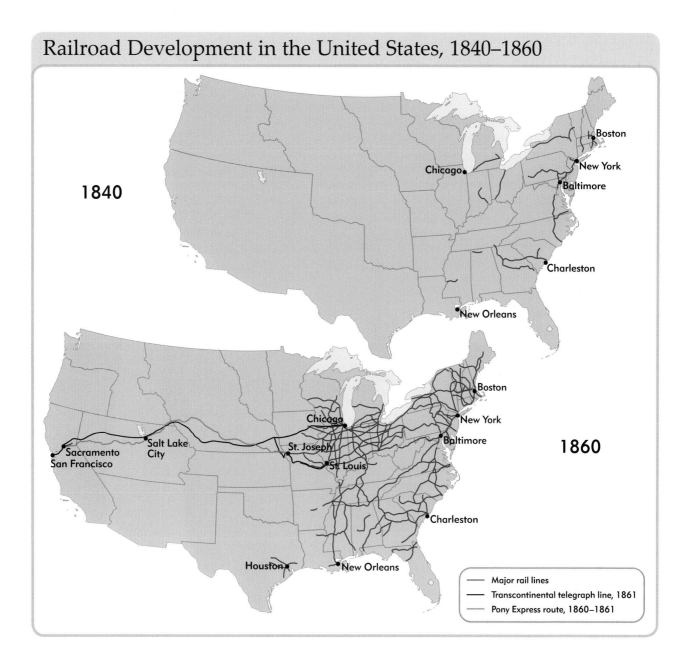

1840

Boston
Chicago
New York
Baltimore
Charleston
New Orleans

1860

Sacramento
San Francisco
Salt Lake City
St. Joseph
Chicago
St. Louis
Boston
New York
Baltimore
Charleston
Houston
New Orleans

—— Major rail lines
—— Transcontinental telegraph line, 1861
—— Pony Express route, 1860–1861

On the Move

In the space of a mere half-century, a revolution in transportation had occurred. Goods and people could now move much more easily between many towns in the United States or Great Britain. Trains could transport products to seaports, and steamers could carry them across the ocean for distribution through the ever-growing network of roads, waterways, and railroad tracks.

Before these busy networks formed, almost all the ordinary items people needed had to be made locally. A small town in Britain or the United States that had only 500 inhabitants might have dozens of workshops making everything from candles to soap to hats. Someone who needed a hat went to a hat maker, who made a hat to fit that particular customer. And people made countless goods for themselves, in their own homes or on their own farms—everything from brooms to nails to tables.

After the revolution in transportation and manufacturing, all that changed. Towns began to specialize in producing goods that they shipped to other markets for sale. Now people who needed new hats did not go to the local hat maker but instead to a store that carried hats made in a distant factory. Inside that store, they could try on different sizes and find one that fit.

Steam-driven boats and trains could easily bring materials such as coal and iron to factories. That made bigger factories possible. Out of these ever-bigger factories poured ever-bigger steamships and locomotives in ever-growing numbers. Thus the transportation revolution fed the industrial revolution, which in turn fed the transportation revolution. Round and round the changes went, with people and goods—and life in general—moving faster and faster.

Around the World—In How Long?

In 1873, the French novelist Jules Verne published *Around the World in Eighty Days.* In that novel, a man named Phileas Fogg makes a bet that he can travel around the world in eighty days or less. Today, that seems very slow. Two centuries ago, it would have been impossible except on a magic carpet. But by the time Verne wrote his book, people were beginning to wonder if it would be possible to make such a long trip in such a short time. In 1889, a New York reporter named Nellie Bly set out to duplicate the fictional feat in real life. After her journey, Bly was able to write her own bestseller, a work of nonfiction called *Nellie Bly's Book: Around the World in Seventy-two Days.*

Author Nellie Bly

Samuel Morse Invents the Telegraph

While a revolution in transportation was taking place in the nineteenth century, a revolution in communication was occurring as well. One of the people who made the communication revolution possible was an American inventor named Samuel Morse. You might have heard of Morse code. Let's learn about Morse's life and his important invention.

Historical Close-up

From the window of his rented room, the young American looked down on the streets of London's artist quarter. The year was 1811. His heart beat with excitement, but he also felt a stab of homesickness. His parents might be worrying about him at this very moment, wondering how he had fared during his 22-day ocean voyage.

Pen in hand, the young man sat down at his desk to write a letter to his parents back in Massachusetts, telling them he had arrived safely. He added:

I wish that in an instant I could communicate the information: but three thousand miles are not passed over in an instant, and we must wait four long weeks before we can hear from each other.

Little did Samuel Morse know that one day messages would travel almost instantly between America and England—and that he would make it possible!

Morse was not a scientist. He was an artist who had come to London to study painting. He loved to look at Renaissance artwork. His ambition as an artist was, as he put it, "to be among those who shall revive the splendor of the fifteenth century, to rival the genius of a Raphael, a Michelangelo or a Titian."

But this was the nineteenth century, and Morse was as fascinated by electricity as everyone else. He had been nine years old in 1800, when Alessandro Volta demonstrated the first electric battery and made it possible to store electric current for use in experiments. It wasn't just scientists who were intrigued by electricity. So were ordinary people. Crowds jammed into lecture halls for public demonstrations of this seemingly magical force.

When Morse was in college at Yale, in Connecticut, he had enjoyed attending science lectures, especially about electricity. One professor had his students hold hands in a circle, and then he passed an electric shock through the human circuit.

After college, Morse studied art at the Royal Academy in London. Returning home to the United States, he earned a reputation as a promising young artist. After he painted an official portrait of President James Monroe, he found himself in great demand. He often had to travel for his work, spending months at a time away from his wife and children in Connecticut.

In 1825, Morse went to Washington, D.C., to paint the Marquis de Lafayette. He was thrilled to meet this legendary hero of the American Revolution. But while he was gone, his wife died suddenly. A message couldn't travel any faster than a horse could run, so by the time Morse learned the tragic news, his wife had already been buried.

Other blows followed. Morse's father died soon afterwards, then his mother. Devastated, he went back to Europe, where he spent the next three years studying and painting.

In France, he had the chance to see a signal system that linked Paris to smaller towns and military posts. Flags were attached to long wooden arms on top of a high tower. By changing the position of the arms, people could send messages to the next tower, five or ten miles away. In this way, news could travel hundreds of miles a day.

This way of sending messages was known as the semaphore system. It was also known by another name—the telegraph. The word *telegraph* came from Greek words for "writing at a distance."

Compared to sending messages by horse or ship, this signaling system was rapid communication. But it had many drawbacks. It took four or five people to move the arms to which the flags were attached. Each position stood for just one letter or number. It was a complicated task to spell out an entire message. It didn't work at night or in bad weather. And if people in one tower misread the flags in another, a message could be garbled.

As Morse crossed the ocean yet again, returning home aboard a ship called the *Sully*, the problem of communicating over long distances was still on his mind. One day at lunch, he joined a group of passengers gathered around a young doctor who was enthusiastically describing the latest electrical experiments he'd seen in Europe.

One of the passengers asked whether the electric current took a long time to move through a wire. No, said the doctor. No matter how long the wire— even if it stretched for miles—electricity seemed to pass instantly from one end to the other.

Morse was intrigued. If this were true, he pointed out, "I see no reason why intelligence might not be transmitted instantaneously by the electricity."

For the others, the discussion may have simply been a pleasant way to pass time on board ship. But not for Morse. He rushed back to his cabin, dug out a notebook, and started planning an electric telegraph.

As used here by Morse, *intelligence* means information, news.

Morse's understanding of electricity was limited, and he knew nothing of recent advances in the field. Oddly enough, his ignorance kept him from giving up. As far as Morse knew, his idea was original. He didn't realize that others were already working on similar systems. And he had no clue as to how many difficulties he would face.

Back in the United States, he took a job teaching art at a college in New York City. He spent his free time building a working model of his telegraph. He used cheap materials— works from an old clock, an artist's canvas stretcher, a homemade battery. The most important part of his invention, however, required no materials at all. It was the code he created for sending messages over the wire.

In Morse's system, when an operator pressed a key, an electrical circuit closed and current flowed down the wire. A short push of the key was a "dot," and a long push was a "dash." Morse gave each letter and number its own combination of dots and dashes. Letters that were used most often had the simplest pattern. For example, in Morse code

Samuel Morse, inventor of the electric telegraph and Morse code

the letter *e* is represented by a single dot, while *q* is two dashes, then a dot, then a dash.

Morse's first telegraph was crude and complicated, but it was good enough to raise the interest of several men who had the scientific and mechanical skills he lacked. With their help, he prepared his device for its first public demonstration.

Six years after his burst of inspiration on the *Sully*, Morse unveiled his telegraph in a packed lecture hall. Ten miles of wire were coiled between the sender and receiver. Using his code, Morse astonished the crowd by transmitting a message at the breakneck speed of ten words per minute.

Morse never imagined the telegraph being used for everyday communication. But he thought that the government might use it to send urgent official messages. So he applied to the government for $30,000 to run the first telegraph line from Baltimore, Maryland, to Washington, D.C.

Congress considered Morse's invention an amusing novelty—what practical value could it have? Still, the government agreed to give him money to set up his telegraph line.

Morse set to work. At first he tried to lay the wire underground, but that failed. Undaunted, he changed his plan and strung the wire on poles alongside the track of the Baltimore & Ohio Railroad.

At last, construction was completed. On May 24, 1844, onlookers crowded into the Supreme Court chambers in Washington to watch Morse send the first official telegraph message over the wire to Baltimore, 35 miles away. In Morse code, he tapped out a brief quotation from the Bible: "What hath God wrought!"

Nervously, everyone waited. Then a response came back—the same words, in dots and dashes. The telegraph was a success.

At first, no one was sure exactly what use to make of Morse's "Lightning Line," as it was called. Messages were rare, and telegraph operators spent their days playing chess over the wire.

Soon, though, people realized its usefulness. Storekeepers and suppliers traded up-to-the-minute information. News of a death in the family reached distant relatives in time for them to travel to the funeral. Police in one town could send out descriptions of criminals, so police in other towns could be on the lookout and ready to capture the outlaws.

The telegraph spread—slowly at first, to Philadelphia, New York, and Boston. Then, following the railroad tracks in their westward expansion, wires spread all across the continent. Within 10 years of Morse's first demonstration, 23,000 miles of wire crackled with messages.

This web of telegraph lines tied the young nation together, linking remote frontier settlements with cities back East. Hearing the news as it happened made Americans feel connected with distant events. Newspapers could get information by telegraph and quickly publish it for their readers. Railroads used the telegraph to find out where their trains were, and whether they were running on time. Quicker communications helped banking and business to boom. Companies in one state could communicate by telegraph with companies in other states.

Soon telegraph wires began to link countries around the world. Companies set up telegraph lines in England, Germany, Russia, and other nations. In 1850, an underwater telegraph cable was laid across the English Channel, connecting Great Britain with the rest of Europe. Sixteen years later, a British steamship succeeded in laying a telegraph cable across the bottom of the Atlantic Ocean, between Ireland and Newfoundland, Canada.

By the time Samuel Morse died in 1872, more than 650,000 miles of wire had been strung, including 30,000 miles of underwater cable. A person in California could telegraph a message to someone in India. A London newspaper called the *Daily Telegraph* boldly declared, "Time itself is telegraphed out of existence."

Telegraph wires on the Great Plains followed the railroad tracks westward.

*A London street scene captures the poverty
and hardship that many people endured
during the Industrial Revolution.*

Strife and Struggle: Hard Times and New Ideas During the Industrial Revolution

The wonders of the Industrial Revolution! Railroads and steamships carried goods and people faster and farther. Messages crackled across miles of telegraph lines. Great Britain, where factories turned out everything from shirts to shoes to chairs, became known as the "workshop of the world."

In 1851, a giant fair drew more than six million people to London. The fair featured the amazing tools and machines the British produced—a steam hammer, a knife with 80 blades, the latest locomotive engines, and much more.

All these marvels were displayed in a building that seemed to belong to a future age. The Crystal Palace, as it was called, was a huge cast-iron skeleton sheathed in a million square feet of glass. Tourists from around the world came to visit the Crystal Palace. The mood was jubilant and triumphant.

But these industrial wonders had come at a high price. While factories produced many marvelous products, they also produced misery. Through the first half of the century, men, women, and children spent long days laboring in London's dark, dangerous factories. By night, they trudged home to filthy, overcrowded apartment buildings. London grew faster than ever before, doubling its population from one to two million

The Crystal Palace celebrated industrial progress in nineteenth-century Britain. Here, beneath a million square feet of glass, British manufacturers displayed their achievements and inventions.

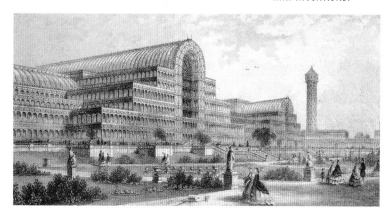

Right: Workers tend fires and shovel coal in a smoke-filled London factory that produced gas for lighting streets and homes.

Below: Operating machines like these printing presses could be dangerous. Workers sometimes caught fingers and hands in the machinery.

between 1800 and 1840. Many of its neighborhoods were grimy places ravaged by crime and disease. In the poorest section of town, deaths often outnumbered births.

And yet London, like other industrial cities, kept growing. Why did people keep coming? Why did so many leave their farms and villages for cities? They came to work—and the work was in the factories.

Working in Factories

"Places of work," as factories were called in the early nineteenth century, were usually dirty, dark, and poorly ventilated. For twelve to sixteen hours per day, six days a week, men, women, and children tended noisy machines in stifling heat. Factory owners didn't want their expensive machines to stand idle, so workers had to keep working, with only a half-hour break for dinner.

Factory workers had to arrive at a certain time, eat dinner at a certain time, and leave at a certain time. In between, they performed the same tasks, over and over.

To keep everyone on task and on schedule, factory owners imposed unbending rules and stiff penalties for breaking them. A worker who arrived two minutes late could lose half a day's pay. Conversations between workers were not allowed; all questions had to concern work itself, and be directed to a supervisor. Supervisors could fire workers on the spot any time they wanted, even for unfair reasons.

Factories were dangerous places to work. The foul air made people sick. Exhausted after long hours, a worker might let his attention lapse for a second, only to find his hand mangled by the clanking, grinding machines.

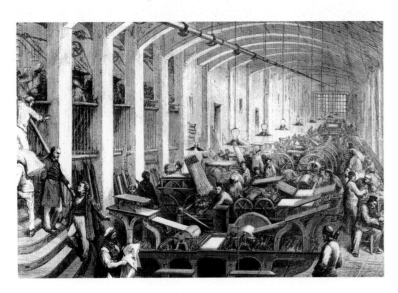

No matter how miserable they were, workers usually did not quit. Why? Because they had nowhere else to earn a living. Some of the poorest people were forced to work. They lived in workhouses, where they were locked up for the night, often in the company of criminals or the insane. In the mornings, these workhouses sent cartloads of people to factories and coal mines. At the end of a grueling day, the carts carried the people back to the filthy workhouses. For these people, life was little more than an endless cycle of toil and degradation.

Children at Work

By 1830, two-thirds of the workers in the cotton industry were children and women. They earned just a fraction of what men were paid for the same hours of work. Not that the men were paid well—factory owners kept everyone's wages low so their own profits would be higher.

Many factory owners preferred hiring children, some as young as six. In the eyes of the owners, the children had not yet developed "bad habits" and could be molded to work on a factory schedule.

It was not uncommon for children to work from five o'clock in the morning to eight or nine o'clock at night. If a child looked drowsy, his supervisor might wake him up by dunking him headfirst into a cistern of water.

Sometimes punishments were more severe. When young Sarah Carpenter's machine stopped (through no fault of her own) in an English textile mill, her boss

In some factories, women and children made up most of the workforce. Below, young workers make twine in a dusty mill.

beat her with a stick. When she threatened to tell her mother, Sarah reported that her boss "then went out and fetched the master in to me. The master started beating me with a stick over the head till it was full of lumps and bled."

Living in the Cities

After spending twelve to sixteen hours in a hot, noisy factory, workers went home to overcrowded row houses and tenements. Families of eight or nine people often lived in a single room just seven feet square. In 1838, one government inspector reported visiting a tenement in England with five or six people packed in each bed. In 1847, inspectors reported more than thirty people per home in one neighborhood of London. The overcrowding in such poor neighborhoods spread misery and death.

Bad as these homes were, life was even worse for the many homeless people living in the streets, begging and stealing. Hordes of dirty, hungry children, mostly orphans, roamed the streets, sleeping in outhouses and doorways at night.

Factory towns didn't concern themselves with health or sanitation. The smoke from thousands of mills and furnaces hung like a gray shroud over cities. It showered tons of fine soot that caused lung disease for many of the inhabitants.

City streets were often used as open sewers and drains. Garbage, along with human and animal waste, gave off a horrible stench as it flowed through open gutters. A government report in 1842 stated that "the annual loss of life from filth and bad ventilation is greater than the loss from death of wounds in any wars in which the country has been engaged."

One summer the stench from the River Thames became overpowering. The "Great Stink" closed the law courts and threatened to shut down Parliament itself. Most Londoners drank water siphoned from the Thames. Back in 1800 the river had been clean enough for Londoners to catch salmon in it. But 30 years later, the city's sewers regularly polluted the Thames. In 1831, a waterborne disease called cholera struck the capital. In poor districts, diseases and unsanitary conditions led to the deaths of one in three children before their first birthday.

A *tenement* is an apartment building where poor people live.

Working conditions for the poor were bad, and their living conditions were not much better. Many lived in overcrowded row houses and tenements.

In the city markets, food sellers often tried to cheat their poor customers. Some merchants watered down beer and milk. Some even sold poisonous red lead as a substitute for pepper. At first, the government refused to do anything about these problems. A British parliamentary committee, callously interpreting the principles of Adam Smith, said that "more benefit is likely to result from the effects of a free competition … than can be expected to result from any regulations."

Factory life and urban squalor took a terrible toll on the poor. Young factory workers were much shorter, skinnier, and more subject to disease than the sons and daughters of middle-class families. Typhus, yellow fever, cholera, and smallpox killed many people. The death rates rose dramatically in industrial cities.

Hard Times in Industrial England

If you know A Christmas Carol*—the tale of Ebenezer Scrooge and the ghosts of Christmas Past, Present, and Future—then you know of Charles Dickens, the great mid-nineteenth-century English novelist. Through his writing, Dickens achieved worldwide fame and great wealth—a far cry from his childhood years of humiliation and poverty.*

A Page from the Past

Dickens grew up struggling. His father went to prison because he could not pay his debts. At the age of 12, young Charles started working in a London factory, where he pasted labels on bottles of shoe polish. Dickens managed to leave the factory and attend school. Eventually he became a newspaper reporter.

At first, he wrote articles about debates in Parliament and other London events. Then he began to write fiction. He wrote about children starving in workhouses, street urchins picking pockets, widows taking in laundry, debtors serving time in prison, families struggling to get by. Dickens's stories about the hard lives of the urban poor touched

Charles Dickens

many readers' hearts. His books, such as Oliver Twist, Little Dorrit, *and* Bleak House, *awakened middle-class readers to the need for reform.*

Dickens paints his harshest picture of the effects of the Industrial Revolution in his 1854 novel, Hard Times. *In the following passages from* Hard Times, *Dickens introduces us to the industrial city of Coketown, and to one of the workers, Stephen Blackpool.*

It was a town of red brick, or of brick that would have been red if the smoke and ashes had allowed it; but as matters stood, it was a town of unnatural red and black…. It was a town of machinery and tall chimneys, out of which interminable serpents of smoke trailed themselves for ever and ever, and never got uncoiled. It had a black canal in it, and a river that ran purple with ill-smelling dye, and vast piles of buildings full of windows where there was a rattling and a trembling all day long, and where the piston of the steam-engine worked monotonously up and down like the head of an elephant in a state of melancholy madness. It contained several large streets all very like one another, and many small streets still more like one another, inhabited by people equally like one another, who all went in and out at the same hours, with the same sound upon the same pavements, to do the same work, and to whom every day was the same as yesterday and tomorrow, and every year the counterpart of the last and the next….

Smokestacks of Sheffield, England

Among the multitude of Coketown, generically called "the Hands,"—a race who would have found more favor with some people, if Providence had seen fit to make them only hands, or, like the lower creatures of the seashore, only hands and stomachs—lived a certain Stephen Blackpool, forty years of age.

Stephen looked older, but he had had a hard life. It is said that every life has its roses and thorns; there seemed, however, to have been a misadventure or mistake in Stephen's case, whereby somebody else had become possessed of his roses, and he had become possessed of the same somebody else's thorns in addition to his own. He had known, to use his words, a peck of trouble....

Pale morning showed the monstrous serpents of smoke trailing themselves over Coketown. A clattering of clogs upon the pavement; a rapid ringing of bells; and all the melancholy mad elephants, polished and oiled up for the day's monotony, were at their heavy exercise again.

Stephen bent over his loom, quiet, watchful, and steady. A special contrast, as every man was in the forest of looms where Stephen worked, to the crashing, smashing, tearing piece of mechanism at which he labored....

The day grew strong, and showed itself outside, even against the flaming lights within. The lights were turned out, and the work went on. The rain fell, and the Smoke-serpents ... trailed themselves upon the earth. In the waste-yard outside, the steam from the escape pipe, the litter of barrels and old iron, the shining heaps of coals, the ashes everywhere, were shrouded in a veil of mist and rain.

Taking Action in Victorian England

Faced with such terrible conditions, many voices demanded reform. Londoners took the lead. Reformers investigated the living and working conditions of what they called "the lower classes" or the "deserving poor." They were especially horrified at the working conditions of children in textile mills, where some youngsters worked 96 hours a week.

During the early part of the nineteenth century, Parliament had passed a series of Factory Acts. These laws limited the workday for children in textile mills to twelve hours. They also outlawed employing children younger than nine years old. The factories, however, often ignored such laws.

During the 1830s and 1840s, new laws limited children's work in the textile mills to nine hours a day, and women to ten hours. The laws required factory owners to put fences around dangerous machinery,

The new London police force patrolled city streets on the lookout for pickpockets and robbers. The policemen were known as "bobbies" after Sir Robert Peel, who persuaded Parliament they were needed.

keep workplaces clean, and help educate child laborers. Conditions in the factories began to improve, but progress was slow. Most factories remained grim places.

Londoners also took steps to deal with crime. Pickpockets, robbers, and muggers roamed the streets, but London had no citywide police department. In 1829, Sir Robert Peel urged Parliament to pass laws establishing London's first metropolitan police force. Because of Sir Robert's

leadership, the new police officers were nicknamed "Bobby's boys," and later known simply as "bobbies."

Although the bobbies helped make London a safer city, it was still not safe enough to convince England's Queen Victoria and her husband Prince Albert to live in London. In the 1840s, she and Albert built two castle homes far from London, while British officials pressed for more laws to improve conditions in the city.

One reformer, Sir Edwin Chadwick, worked tirelessly as commissioner of the Board of Health. He got London's leaders to take charge of the capital's sewage system, which was pouring waste into the River Thames. In the 1850s, the Metropolitan Board of Public Works built new sewers, which discharged their contents farther downstream, away from the city, to help in the fight against disease.

The Board of Public Works also tried to clear away many of the capital's slums and run new roads

Victorian England

In 1837, 18-year-old Victoria became queen of England. She was strong-willed and determined to make her mark. Victoria ruled for more than 60 years and greatly influenced the values and culture of her day. The time of her reign (1837–1901) is known as Victorian England.

As queen, Victoria emphasized duty, hard work, and proper behavior. Her name has become an adjective—*Victorian*—that sums up the values she emphasized. Sometimes *Victorian* also implies a certain stiffness and stuffiness.

Britain's Queen Victoria

through some of the worst neighborhoods. These efforts had mixed results. Crime-ridden streets disappeared, but so did the homes of the people who once lived along those streets. Not enough new homes were built, so tens of thousands of poor people jammed into existing quarters, making overcrowding worse.

The poor in British cities were not alone in their misery. Soon Paris, Berlin, and New York faced similar problems.

In 1850, an American statistician named Lemuel Shattuck compiled a report that showed the death rates from disease in Boston were rising, and that people were dying at younger ages than they had been 50 years earlier. The Industrial Revolution was taking its toll throughout the western world.

Karl Marx Criticizes Capitalism

Many reformers blamed capitalism for bringing misery and squalor. These reformers said that in a capitalist economic system, business owners were motivated only by a desire to make money. In such a system, owners would not care about the workers' safety or living conditions. Some reformers believed that if government controlled businesses, then workers would not be mistreated or live such wretched lives. These reformers, called socialists, wanted governments to step in, make some rules, and plan key aspects of the economy.

The most famous socialist was a German named Karl Marx. Marx was born in 1818 to middle-class parents. His family was Jewish, but his

New York's poor suffered problems similar to those in London. Above, New Yorkers sleep in the street outside their tenement buildings on a hot summer night.

father, a successful lawyer, converted to Christianity. As young Karl grew older and became interested in socialist ideas, he rejected both his Jewish roots and his father's Christianity. As far as he could tell, religion did nothing to make poor people's lives better.

Marx became a journalist. He wrote articles criticizing the government, condemning the powerful, and calling for the overthrow of the capitalists and business owners. Marx overwhelmed almost everyone he met with the force of his personality and his convictions. He read widely and argued hotly. He made many friends, but most of these friendships ended because of disagreements over ideas.

One friend he never lost was Friedrich Engels, a writer whose

Karl Marx urged the poor to rise up and overthrow capitalists. "Let the ruling classes tremble," he wrote in The Communist Manifesto. *"The proletarians have nothing to lose but their chains." Marx and other communists believed that a society's wealth should be shared by all.*

wealthy family owned a textile mill. When Marx and Engels got to know each other in Paris in 1843, they fell into a conversation that lasted 10 days. It was the beginning of a life-long bond. The two worked together for 40 years.

Marx and Engels together wrote a pamphlet called *The Communist Manifesto. The Communist Manifesto* said that every aspect of a society is shaped by its economic system—its way of producing and distributing food, clothing, shelter, medical care, and other needed goods and services. Communists dreamed of an economic system in which the wealth of a society would be shared by all—quite a contrast to capitalism, in which individuals and businesses can own wealth and compete for more of it.

Every economic system, said Marx and Engels, divides people into

classes. Moreover, these classes are always struggling with one another for a bigger share of economic resources. Indeed, Marx and Engels asserted, "The history of all hitherto existing society is the history of class struggles."

If we look at past times, said Marx and Engels, then "we find almost everywhere a complicated arrangement of society into various orders…. In ancient Rome we have patricians, knights, plebeians, slaves; in the Middle Ages, feudal lords, vassals, guild-masters, journeymen, apprentices, serfs." Modern society, they said, "has not done away with class antagonisms. It has but estab-lished new classes, new conditions of oppression, new forms of struggle in place of the old ones." As Marx and Engels saw it, "Society as a whole is more and more splitting up into two great hostile camps, into two great classes directly facing each other—bourgeoisie (bourzh-wah-ZEE) and proletariat (PROH-luh-TEHR-ee-uht)…."

The term *bourgeoisie* is often used to refer to middle class people in general, but Marx and Engels mainly had in mind people who make their living through doing business, such as factory owners, bankers, and mer-chants. Opposed to the bourgeoisie was the proletariat—those who, like factory laborers, work for wages.

Marx and Engels went on to explain that the group that owns the "means of production" becomes the ruling class. In an economic system based on farming, the people who own the land make the rules—thus, landowners were the ruling class in

Revolutionaries man the barricades in Berlin during the uprising of 1848. In that year, similar revolts broke out against monarchies across western Europe.

feudal Europe. Now that the economic system was based on manufacturing, the wealthy owners of industry had replaced feudal land barons as rulers, and the proletarians had replaced the feudal serfs.

The Communist Manifesto said that no class can rule forever. Eventually changes in the economic system will lead to changes in society, including a new ruling class. Marx and Engels declared that the Industrial Revolution had caused just such a change by making manufacturing more important than farming and capital more important than land.

The Communist Manifesto predicted that proletarians would soon overthrow the capitalists: "Let the ruling classes tremble…. The proletarians have nothing to lose but their chains…. Working men of all countries, unite!"

In 1848, the year *The Communist Manifesto* appeared, uprisings broke out across western Europe, and Marx and Engels had to flee France. Marx found safety in London, the heart of capitalist England.

Marx's *Das Kapital*

After 1849, Marx lived in London in poor health and grinding poverty. He had a wife and six children, but he never sought a job besides writing. Engels occasionally sent him money, but for long periods, Marx and his family could afford only a two-room apartment. Once he pawned his coat

1848: Year of Revolutions

Since the defeat of Napoleon at Waterloo in 1815, kings had tried to stamp out ideas about liberty, equality, and self-rule in Europe. But in 1830 and even more in 1848, those ideas flared to life in a series of revolutionary uprisings.

In 1848, revolution broke out in France, Germany, and the Austrian Empire (which then included parts of Italy). Workers rioted for better wages and conditions. Rebel armies tried to drive foreign rulers from their thrones. People demanded new freedoms and constitutions to guarantee their political rights.

At first, it looked like some of the revolutions might succeed. Then the rulers turned their armies against the people and soon managed to crush the uprisings. But, as you'll read in later chapters, these democratic stirrings refused to die.

to buy paper. One year, his children could not go to school because they had no shoes. Still, Marx refused to take employment that was not intellectual.

Marx spent his days—often 10 hours at a time—in the British Museum, thinking and studying. There, over the course of 18 years, he wrote a 2,500-page work called *Das Kapital* (dahs kahp-ee-TAHL), a title that means "Capital." *Das Kapital* fleshed out the ideas of *The Communist Manifesto*.

Das Kapital predicted the end of capitalism. Marx, who considered himself a scientist, believed he had discovered the laws of history, just as Newton had discovered the laws of motion. So when he said that capitalism was doomed, he meant it would collapse as surely as water runs downhill.

Marx explained that in a capitalist economy, factories and other businesses compete against each other as they try to sell their products. In order to survive this ruthless competition, Marx said, capitalists would have to produce goods ever more cheaply—which means they would have to cut wages, replace workers with machinery, or do both.

Eventually, Marx said, society would divide into two classes: a shrinking number of wealthy capitalists and a growing number of poverty-stricken proletarians. Finally, the workers would revolt, overthrow the owners, and take over the factories. Private property—property owned by individuals—would no longer exist. In this new communist society, there would be only one class—the working class.

Capitalism did not collapse as Marx predicted. Industries continued to boom in Europe and America. Many people dismissed Marx as a man with crazy ideas. When he died in 1883, only 11 people came to his funeral. But four decades after Marx's death, his ideas turned out to be very meaningful for revolutionaries in Russia. That is another story, but one that made a large difference in the course of the twentieth century.

Since Marx's time, "communism" has come to refer to an economic system that calls for government ownership of land, factories, and resources. Under communism, the government controls the economy and there is a minimum of private property. Marx's hope was that a communist system would provide equality and security for all, but the reality of communism in the twentieth century turned out very differently.

Darwin Sees Competition in Nature

Karl Marx saw society as a fierce competitive struggle. At about the

Smith vs. Marx

In Adam Smith and Karl Marx, the Industrial Revolution produced two thinkers with very different ideas about how the economy and society work. In 1776, Smith predicted that free competition would lead to increased wealth and productivity. Marx, who lived to see the consequences of the Industrial Revolution, said that competition would lead to much misery. He predicted that workers would someday unite in revolution against the ruling class and eventually win equality. Smith and Marx are still studied by economists today.

same time, an English scientist, Charles Darwin, began to take a similar view of nature. His ideas would change modern science and rock the foundations of late nineteenth-century society.

On a blustery December day in 1831, the HMS *Beagle* set sail from Devonport, England, on a survey expedition around the southernmost tip of South America. Among the 74 people who squeezed aboard the tiny ship was Charles Darwin, at this time a fledgling scientist only 22 years old.

In South America, Darwin hacked his way through jungles and paddled up rivers, always with a notebook close at hand. All around him he saw things he could not explain. Why did the fossils he found look so similar to the bones of modern animals living in the same place? What were seashells doing high in the peaks of the Andes mountains? How did plants growing on one side of a mountain come to be different from plants on the other side?

His most striking discoveries came in the Galápagos (guh-LAH-puh-guhs) Islands off the coast of what is now Ecuador. Compared to the lush rain forests of South America, these islands at first appeared dry and barren. But Darwin soon found that they were home to a fascinating variety of life. Every island, for example, had its own species of finch. One species might have a long, slender beak, another a small beak, and a third a big, strong beak. Why?

Over the course of the voyage of the *Beagle*, Darwin sent thousands of specimens to scientists back in England. He sent fossils, insects, minerals, animal skins, pickled fish, and plants. In 1836, the *Beagle* finally returned home. Darwin brought back thousands of pages of notes. He also brought many unanswered questions.

Two years after his return, Darwin read an essay that had been written in 1798 by the British economist Robert Malthus. Malthus had argued that human population grows at a rate far beyond the growth of the available food supply.

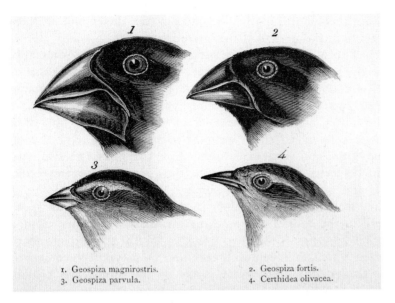

1. Geospiza magnirostris.
2. Geospiza fortis.
3. Geospiza parvula.
4. Certhidea olivacea.

In the Galápagos Islands, Darwin observed differences in finches' beaks. Darwin concluded that "natural selection" had ensured that each island had its own species of finch, with traits suited to local conditions.

Population, said Malthus, expands to the limits of the food supply, and when those limits are reached, then famine, war, and disease work to limit further population growth.

Malthus painted a bleak picture of society. While some predicted ever-greater human progress, Malthus saw ever-greater struggle for limited resources.

It was this central idea in Malthus's writings—the idea of struggle for limited resources—that helped Darwin answer his many questions. Darwin and other scientists had often observed that living things produced more offspring than could

survive. They noticed that the offspring differed slightly from each other. For example, in a brood of finches, one chick might be born with a longer, thinner beak than others. In a struggle for scarce resources, such a difference could prove to be an advantage or disadvantage.

If the finches happened to live on an island where a short, strong beak was needed to crack seeds with hard shells, then finches with the long, thin beaks would get less food. Thus the long-beaked finches would be less likely to survive, and so produce fewer offspring. But on another island, a long, thin beak might be well suited to picking out bugs from a cactus. Here the finches with long, thin beaks would be more likely to live and reproduce, passing the trait to their offspring. Eventually, after many generations, each island would have its own species, with traits suited to local conditions—exactly as Darwin had found in the Galápagos.

Darwin called this process "natural selection." As Darwin saw it, in the overpopulated realm of nature, creatures are born with different traits, and they compete for limited resources. The creatures most likely to survive—and thus most likely to reproduce and pass on their traits— are those whose traits make them best suited to win the struggle for limited resources. A later writer and admirer of Darwin summarized this principle as "survival of the fittest."

Darwin's *Origin of Species*

Charles Darwin didn't publish his ideas right away. In fact, he tried hard to keep his thoughts secret as he

Scrooge Echoes Malthus

Malthus's ideas about population growth exceeding the food supply made their way into political debates, the press, and even literature. In Charles Dickens's popular tale, *A Christmas Carol*, a gentleman asks the miserly Scrooge to make a donation to help the poor. When Scrooge points out that there are workhouses for the poor, the gentleman responds that many would rather die than go to the workhouses. To which Scrooge icily responds: "If they would rather die, they had better do it, and decrease the surplus population."

slowly and carefully assembled more evidence to prove that natural selection occurs. He knew that his ideas would upset many people. Indeed, it sometimes made Darwin sick to his stomach just to think about the response his ideas would provoke.

Twenty years went by before the cautious Darwin was ready to go public. In 1859, he published *On the Origin of Species by Means of Natural Selection or the Preservation of Favoured Races in the Struggle for Life*. Despite its long title, the book was a bestseller.

When the book came out, some scientists disagreed with Darwin—one scorned natural selection as the "law of higgledy-piggledy." Many of Darwin's fellow scientists, however, agreed with his arguments about evolution—the idea that living things have changed over time. (Darwin referred to evolution as "descent"—it was not until the sixth and last edition of *The Origin of Species*, published in 1872, that he used the term *evolution* in his book.)

While many scientists supported Darwin, *The Origin of Species* sparked strong opposition from many religious leaders. If a natural process could explain how species became suited to their environment, what role did that leave for God? And how could God be perceived as kind and loving if thousands died so that the "fittest" could survive?

Darwin's theories brought up another possibility that some found even more disturbing. Darwin had shown how similarities between different species suggest that these species evolved from a common ancestor. But, his critics asked, could

After Charles Darwin published The Origin of Species, *newspapers ridiculed him for claiming that humans were descended from apes. This cartoon depicts an elderly Darwin as a monkey swinging from a tree.*

this idea apply to humans as well? The newspapers were quick to run sensational stories that ridiculed Darwin for claiming that humans had descended from apes.

While the arguments raged on, Darwin's ideas became the basis for a new science, evolutionary biology. Today most scientists accept Darwin's theory of evolution and the idea of natural selection as the basic mechanism in the process of evolution. And today, just as in Darwin's time, people continue to argue about the implications of Darwin's theories.

When Darwin died, he was buried near his fellow scientist, Isaac Newton, in London's Westminster Abbey.

"Survival of the Fittest"

Many people associate Darwin's ideas with the phrase, "survival of the fittest." It was not Darwin, however, but Herbert Spencer, an English philosopher and sociologist, who coined the phrase in a book he published in 1864.

During the eighteenth and nineteenth centuries, millions of Africans were sold into slavery worldwide. Many were taken to the Americas, where they labored at tasks such as cutting cane on sugar plantations.

Slavery in a Changing World

From the late seventeenth to the eighteenth centuries, many new ideas emerged about liberty, natural rights, and human dignity. In England in 1690, John Locke wrote that "all men are naturally in … a state of perfect freedom to order their actions." Locke went on to explain that "every man has a property in his own person: this nobody has any right to but himself. The labor of his body, and the work of his hands, we may say, are properly his…."

Building on Locke's ideas, Thomas Jefferson wrote in 1776 that "all men are created equal, that they are endowed by their Creator with certain unalienable rights, that among these are life, liberty, and the pursuit of happiness." Little more than a decade later, the citizens of revolutionary France vigorously championed "liberty, fraternity, and equality."

Those are bold and inspiring ideas. In their time, however, those ideas were a far cry from the reality of most people's everyday lives. The reality was this: By the end of the eighteenth century, three-quarters of the world's population lived in bondage of some sort, as slaves or serfs.

Think about that—*three-quarters* of the world's population knew nothing of liberty or equality. To adapt Locke's words, the "labor of their bodies and the work of their hands" were not their own, but owned and controlled by others.

Tens of millions of farm laborers in Asia toiled in outright slavery. The vast majority of Russians labored as serfs. Millions of Africans were enslaved on their own continent. The Aztecs and many other Native American peoples enslaved people they captured in war. The Ottomans did the same. And, as you've seen, the Europeans practiced slavery on a massive scale in their American colonies.

Slavery was an evil that wouldn't quit. For many centuries, in many parts of the world, people were bought and sold like oxen or tools. They could be ordered to do any task, no matter how degrading or dangerous. Most slaves had no freedom and few if any rights. Masters often treated slaves as objects to be used, sometimes abused, and replaced when no longer useful.

In this chapter, we'll examine two parts of the world that, by the eighteenth century, had come to depend heavily on slave labor. We'll focus mainly on Europe's colonies in the Americas, which were supplied by the transatlantic slave trade. We'll also look at slavery in the Muslim world of North Africa, the Middle East, and central Asia.

Members of a family are separated at a slave market on the coast of West Africa. In the distance, a ship waits to transport captives across the Atlantic to the Americas.

Both Europeans and Muslims at this time turned to one continent for a large and inexpensive supply of slaves—Africa.

The Slave Trade in Africa

By 1700, the African continent was home to hundreds of peoples with different languages and ways of life. For many centuries slavery had existed in Africa. When wars occurred, the victors often enslaved the defeated. Sometimes raiders from one village would kidnap and enslave people from another village. Torn from their families, the captives were often taken to faraway communities where they could not even speak the language. They had to obey their masters, who looked down on them as inferiors.

But the grimmest fate awaited slaves who were sent to the Americas or to Muslim lands. In order to ship their captives across the sea, African slave traders first marched them to

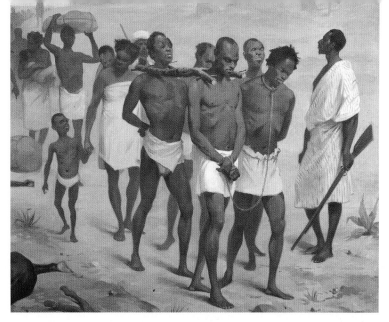

the coast. Lashed together by ropes around their necks, the slaves were forced to walk in the searing heat, sometimes for hundreds of miles, weighed down with loads of supplies. The traders gave the slaves just enough water and food to keep them alive. Still, more than one-third of the captives perished before reaching the coast, struck down by thirst, disease, or exhaustion.

Some slaves were marched to the Indian Ocean on the east coast of Africa. From there, ships carried them to the island of Zanzibar, or to Persia or one of the Arab lands of the Middle East. Other slaves were marched to the Atlantic Ocean on Africa's west coast. They were transported across the ocean to labor in the Americas.

The Transatlantic Trade

You've learned that in the 1500s, Portugal and Spain launched the Age of Exploration. Europeans began sailing across uncharted seas in search of spices, gold, and other riches. The Portuguese and Spanish started a transatlantic slave trade, in which they brought slaves from Africa to work on sugar plantations in the West Indies and Brazil. Slaves also worked in the gold and silver mines of Peru and Mexico.

Over the next two hundred years, other Europeans, including the British, the French, and the Dutch, claimed colonies in the West Indies. In short order they too joined this terrible human commerce.

By the middle of the eighteenth century, when Great Britain ruled the seas with the world's most powerful navy, British merchants transported more slaves than any other European nation. Most of those slaves were taken to work on sugar plantations in Britain's island colonies in the Caribbean Sea. The rest were taken to the British colonies in North America.

Slaves sent to the Caribbean and to South America often did not live long. A harsh climate, diseases, and terrible living conditions led to a high mortality rate among these mostly male slaves. As they died, plantation owners bought new slaves to replace them.

In North America, life expectancy for slaves was longer. Because many

Captives were often marched hundreds of miles from Africa's interior to the coast, where they were loaded onto slave ships and carried to foreign lands.

Where Were Transatlantic Slaves Taken?

By 1750, the Spanish, Portuguese, French, Dutch, and British all participated in the transatlantic slave trade. About 45 percent of slaves who crossed the Atlantic were sold to work in the sugar fields of the West Indies. About 40 percent were sent to the Portuguese colony of Brazil. Another 10 percent were taken elsewhere in the Caribbean and Spanish-American colonies of Central and South America. About 5 percent went to the North American colonies that later became the United States.

The Transatlantic Slave Trade in the Eighteenth Century

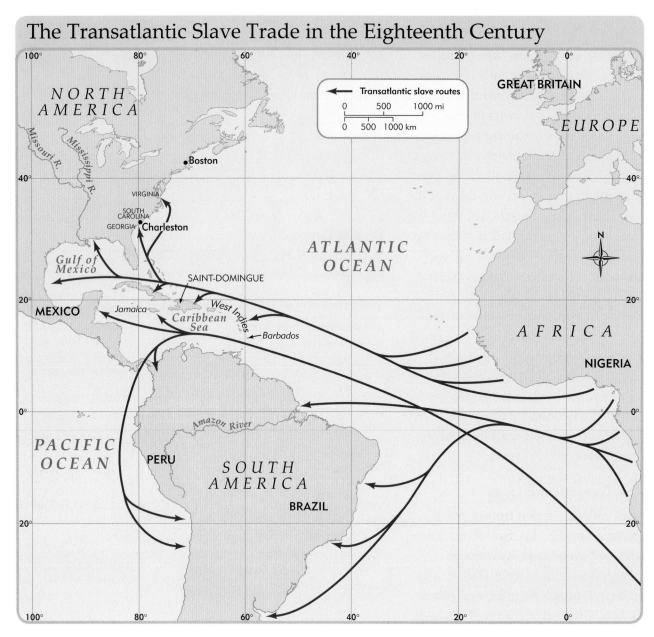

On the map above, you can find the major destinations of slaves taken from Africa to the Americas— the West Indies, Brazil, the Spanish-American colonies (including Mexico and Peru), and the American South.

of these slaves were women, more North American slaves had children, who also became slaves. Thus, the North American slave population grew. By the middle of the nineteenth century, one-third of the New World's slaves lived in the United States.

A Slave's Journey: Olaudah Equiano Tells His Story

What was life like for Africans who were sold into transatlantic slavery? Historians have answered this

question in part by turning to accounts written or told by slaves.

One such account is *The Interesting Narrative of the Life of Olaudah Equiano* (oh-LOW-duh ek-wee-AHN-oh), published in 1789. Equiano spent several years as the slave of a British naval officer. When he was about 21, his owner allowed him to buy his freedom. Equiano had learned to read and write English. He became a sailor, fought in naval battles, and traveled all over the world.

In writing his life story, Equiano began by describing his life in Africa before he was kidnapped. He recalled the time when, as an 11-year-old boy, he was captured by slave raiders from a nearby village and taken to what is today the nation of Nigeria. At first, he was sold to a series of African families. His last African master sold him for 172 cowrie shells to a dealer who supplied slaves to Atlantic coast ships. Equiano later recalled, "The first object which saluted my eyes when I arrived on the coast was the sea, and a slave ship … waiting for its cargo. These filled me with astonishment, which was soon converted into terror when I was carried on board."

Suddenly men with white faces surrounded him. They poked and prodded him to see if he was healthy. Then Equiano saw something that terrified him. Lined up in front of a big, boiling pot, he saw "a multitude of black people of every description chained together, every one of their countenances expressing dejection and sorrow." He was sure that he would be "eaten by those white men with horrible looks, red faces, and loose hair." He fainted at the thought.

When Equiano revived, some of the other slaves reassured him that their captors were not cannibals. But, as Equiano soon found out, they were very cruel. They chained Equiano and the other slaves in a suffocating space below the decks. At mealtime, the boy felt sick to his stomach and refused to eat. Angered by his refusal, two of the white men tied him to the deck and beat him savagely with a whip.

After his beating, Equiano felt such despair that he thought of jumping into the sea. But then he noticed the big net strung around the ship to keep the slaves from jumping overboard. The slave traders wanted to keep the slaves from killing themselves—not because they cared about them as human beings, but because they didn't want to lose their valuable property.

Equiano traveled on a British vessel typical of the slavers' ships. During most of the voyage, the slaves were chained together in spaces so small they could not even stand. The tight quarters meant that if one slave became sick, many did. During the Middle Passage—the voyage across the

During the voyage across the Atlantic, slaves were packed below decks. British reformers who wanted to end slavery drew these diagrams of the slave ship Brooks *for a poster to help people see the horror of the slave trade.*

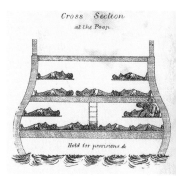

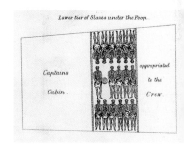

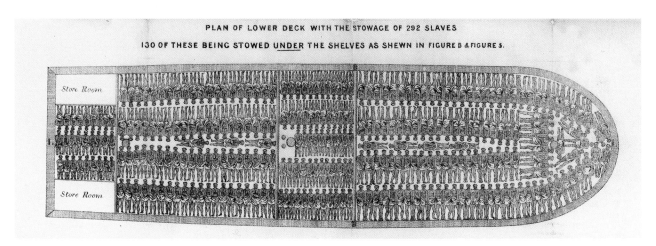

PLAN OF LOWER DECK WITH THE STOWAGE OF 292 SLAVES
130 OF THESE BEING STOWED UNDER THE SHELVES AS SHEWN IN FIGURE B & FIGURE 5.

Atlantic to the New World—many slaves died of disease. Between the brutal march to the African coast and the cruel journey across the Atlantic Ocean, only a little more than half of the slaves captured in Africa arrived in the New World alive.

Eleven-year-old Olaudah Equiano survived the voyage across the Atlantic. He was sold to a Virginia plantation owner.

Aboard a Slave Ship

In this excerpt from The Interesting Narrative of the Life of Olaudah Equiano, *the former slave describes incidents in the terrible voyage across the Atlantic Ocean aboard a slave ship.*

A Page from the Past

Loathsome means disgusting, sickening, extremely offensive.

Pestilential means deadly, tending to cause disease.

Copious means plentiful.

At last, when the ship we were in had got in all her cargo, they made ready with many fearful noises, and we were all put under deck, so that we could not see how they managed the vessel. But this disappointment was the least of my sorrow. The stench of the hold while we were on the coast was so intolerably loathsome, that it was dangerous to remain there for any time, and some of us had been permitted to stay on the deck for the fresh air; but now that the whole ship's cargo were confined together, it became absolutely pestilential. The closeness of the place, and the heat of the climate, added to the number in the ship, which was so crowded that each had scarcely room to turn himself, almost suffocated us. This produced copious perspirations, so that the air soon became unfit for respiration, from a variety of loathsome smells, and brought on a sickness among the slaves, of which many died…. The shrieks of the women, and the groans of the dying, rendered the whole a scene of horror almost inconceivable.

Happily perhaps for myself, I was soon reduced so low here that it was thought necessary to keep me almost always on deck…. One day they had taken a number of fishes; and when they had killed and satisfied themselves

Olaudah Equiano

with as many as they thought fit, to our astonishment who were on the deck, rather than give any of them to us to eat as we expected, they tossed the remaining fish into the sea again, although we begged and prayed for some as well as we could, but in vain; and some of my countrymen, being pressed by hunger, took an opportunity, when they thought no one saw them, of trying to get a little privately; but they were discovered, and the attempt procured them some very severe floggings.

One day, when we had a smooth sea and moderate wind, two of my wearied countrymen who were chained together (I was near them at the time), preferring death to such a life of misery, somehow made through the nettings and jumped into the sea: immediately another quite dejected fellow, who, on account of his illness, was suffered to be out of irons, also followed their example…. Two of the wretches were drowned, but they got the other, and afterwards flogged him unmercifully for thus attempting to prefer death to slavery. In this manner we continued to undergo more hardships than I can now relate, hardships which are inseparable from this accursed trade.

> *Floggings* are beatings with a whip.

Slavery in the Caribbean

Europeans of the 1700s craved sugar. As the continent grew more prosperous, drinks that were once luxuries—coffee, tea, and cocoa—became popular among ordinary people. Most people wanted to sweeten their hot drinks with sugar.

Where did most of Europe's sugar come from? It came from the Portuguese colony of Brazil. It came from Caribbean islands such as Jamaica and Barbados, which were ruled by Britain, and from Saint-Domingue (sehn-daw-MEHNG), a colony ruled by France. (Saint-Domingue is now known as Haiti.)

In these colonies, where did the sugar growers get the vast new supply of labor they needed to work on the plantations? From Africa. Most of the slaves shipped across the Atlantic wound up in one of the sugar colonies.

It was terrible toil to grow and harvest sugarcane. At harvesttime

African slaves cut sugarcane on a plantation in the West Indies.

the slaves worked all day in the tropical heat, chopping and lifting the heavy cane stalks. They kept working into the night, crushing the juice out of the stalks and standing over boiling cauldrons for up to 12 hours to make the sugar. Many planters forced their slaves to work 15 or 18 hours a day. Those who couldn't keep up were whipped or put in the stocks. All were poorly fed. Tens of thousands died from overwork or abuse.

Harsh laws governed every aspect of slave life in Brazil and the Caribbean colonies. Slaves could not own property or bring cases to court. They could not set foot off their masters' plantations without permission. Many were branded to discourage flight. Runaway slaves were flogged. Some were sentenced to death by being burned alive.

Slavery in North America

In the early seventeenth century, the British began importing slaves into their North American colonies. There, as in the Caribbean and South America, most slaves were agricultural workers. In North America, however, the important crops were not sugar but rice, tobacco, and indigo.

These crops were grown in the southern colonies. Therefore many more slaves lived in the South than in the North. Some Northerners did use slaves on their farms and as household servants. In the middle of the eighteenth century, slaves made up 12 percent of the population of New York City.

In South Carolina, so many slaves were needed to harvest the rice crop that they became the majority of the population. With huge numbers of slaves to control, whites

The First Black Republic

In the late eighteenth century, Saint-Domingue, now called Haiti, was a French-ruled colony in the Caribbean Sea. Of the 570,000 people living on the island, about 500,000 were slaves. During the French Revolution, slaves on Haiti heard talk of equality and liberty. In 1791, inspired by the Revolution, they rebelled against their French masters.

A former slave, Toussaint L'Ouverture (too-SEHN loo-vair-tyour), emerged as leader of the black revolutionaries. He inspired thousands of slaves and won many battles against the French. Toussaint's battlefield triumphs encouraged the French to abolish slavery in the colony. Within a few years, after conflicts with various rivals, Toussaint emerged as the colony's ruler.

Toussaint's victory was short-lived. In 1802, Napoleon regained control of the colony and brought back slavery. Toussaint was captured and deported to a French jail. He died in a French prison in 1803, but the following year France gave up the colony. The island, renamed Haiti, became the world's first black republic.

Toussaint L'Ouverture

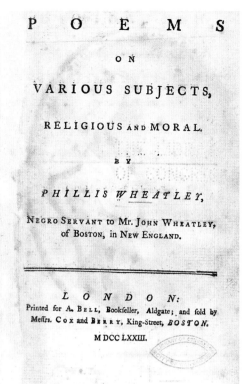

When she was just nine, Phillis Wheatley was taken as a slave from Africa to Boston. A few years later, she began to write poetry. She published her first poem when she was seventeen, thus becoming America's first published black poet. Three years later, in 1773, a book of her poems was published in London.

in the southern colonies began to grow nervous, especially after the rebellions in Saint-Domingue. So they passed laws as harsh as those in the Caribbean colonies. Slaves could be branded for running away. In Charleston, South Carolina, a slave found on the streets late at night without a pass could be shot.

By 1776, when the American Revolution broke out, one in every five Americans was a slave. Many of them hoped that the Revolution would bring an end to slavery. Phillis Wheatley, a Boston slave who became a noted poet, wrote, "In every human breast, God has implanted a principle, which we call Love of Freedom…. I will assert that same principle lives in us."

When the American colonies won their independence, only the northern states passed laws to abolish slavery. Even then, some people in the North continued to keep slaves. In the South, the

agricultural economy depended on slave labor. Southern states did not change their laws.

How an Invention Increased the Demand for Slaves

Many Americans were troubled by slavery. How, they asked, can this nation be dedicated to liberty while allowing some men to keep others as slaves? Some who felt this way

Slavery at the Constitutional Convention

During the Constitutional Convention of 1787, Americans were divided about the issue of slavery. Some wanted to stop the transatlantic slave trade. But most knew that the southern states would never approve the new Constitution if it ended the slave trade. The American founders compromised by including a clause that said the government could not stop the slave trade for 20 years after the Constitution went into effect. The importation of slaves became illegal after 1808.

believed the South would gradually phase out slavery since it was becoming expensive to keep large numbers of slaves. But then an unexpected invention made the institution of slavery even stronger.

You've already learned about some inventions that changed society. For example, in England during the Industrial Revolution, the flying shuttle, the spinning jenny, the power loom, and the steam engine greatly expanded the textile industry. They made it possible to make fabric quickly and cheaply. And they increased the demand for cotton fiber to turn into cloth.

American cotton growers couldn't keep up with the increased demand from English manufacturers. The cotton growers faced a problem. The seeds must be removed from cotton fiber before it can be turned into cloth. But it was a slow process to pick out the seeds by hand.

In 1793, a young teacher from Massachusetts, Eli Whitney, was visiting a friend in the South. He heard about the problem of removing seeds from cotton. Whitney, who had already invented a nail-making machine, invented a device called the cotton gin (*gin*, you recall, is short for "engine"). In the cotton gin, thin wire hooks mounted on a rotating drum pulled the fibers through a screen. The slots in the screen were big enough to accept the cotton fibers but too small for seeds to get through.

By using Whitney's machine, a worker could clean 50 times more cotton in a day than he could by hand. The cotton gin turned cotton farming into a profitable business. Farmers across the South

In an image that probably makes the reality seem more pleasant than it was, slaves operate one of the early cotton gins invented by Eli Whitney. The cotton gin allowed the American South to meet English manufacturers' demand for cotton.

rushed to plant more cotton. Cotton production soared—and so did the need for labor to harvest the cotton. That labor came in the form of slaves.

Thus it was that an invention changed society—the cotton gin made Southern farmers more committed to growing cotton, and more dependent than ever on slave labor.

Slavery and Racism

In the late eighteenth and early nineteenth centuries, one idea helped strengthen the acceptance of slavery. This idea was racism—the belief that some races of people are morally, culturally, or physically superior to others. In Europe and America, some argued that people of European origin were superior to people of African descent. They claimed that dark-skinned people were inferior to light-skinned people, and thus didn't deserve the same rights or privileges.

Racism wasn't invented in the nineteenth century. Egyptians, Greeks, and Romans enslaved those they thought were inferior. The Chinese viewed most foreigners as barbarians and locked them out. The Japanese held similar views. But in the late eighteenth and nineteenth centuries, the concept of "race"—the idea that the human species is divided into separate biological groups with different traits—became a key justification for slavery. Racism, like a cancer, began to grow in the industrializing world.

Why did racism grow at this time? Partly because two realities collided. One was the need for cheap labor. The other was the growth of ideas about natural rights. How could people believe in natural rights but also justify the cheapest form of labor, slavery? Only by believing that some people are less human than others. Racism allowed people to see some races as biologically inferior and not entitled to basic human rights.

Thomas Jefferson, an advocate of liberty and the author of the Declaration of Independence, wrestled with these ideas. In the Declaration, he wrote that "all men are created equal." Did that mean all races deserved equal rights, including the right to liberty? If so, then how could Jefferson justify owning slaves? Did he think that some races were inferior and not entitled to the right to liberty?

Jefferson concluded that liberty is an undeniable and universal right. But he also saw that the United States in his day depended so much on slave labor that it would be difficult for Americans to abolish slavery anytime soon. He expressed his hope that slavery would eventually disappear in the United States. But he did not free his own slaves.

While Jefferson struggled with questions about slavery, many others confidently accepted and defended the practice. For them, racism became a way of justifying enslavement. Many of slavery's defenders said that people of African descent were "primitive" or "childlike." They even argued that Africans benefited from the institution of slavery. These racist ideas, along with a booming cotton economy, kept slavery alive.

In 1808, the United States kept its commitment to ban the importation of slaves

In the mid-nine-teenth century, the cotton picked by African slaves made up half of America's total exports.

Above: Slave families could be auctioned off, as in this slave market in Virginia. Slaves born in Virginia were often sold to work on cotton plantations in the deep South.

Right: A slave family picks cotton in fields near Savannah, Georgia, around 1860. By this time, the Southern economy was so dependent on slavery that many planters believed they could not do without their slaves.

from Africa. But this did not end slavery in the United States—far from it. Instead, it put new pressures on American slave owners to build up their own supply of slaves.

Most of the cotton plantations were in the deep South—in Georgia, South Carolina, Louisiana, and Alabama. Planters from those states, seeking more slave labor, looked to the states of the upper South, like Virginia, which had more slaves than they could use. Some Virginia planters began to breed slaves so they could sell the children. They auctioned off slaves and shipped them hundreds of miles from their homes.

By the middle of the nineteenth century, it seemed that American slavery had become harder than ever to abolish. The cotton picked by slaves had become America's major cash crop, making up half of the nation's total exports. Many Southerners argued that the prosperity of the United States depended on slavery.

These southern defenders of slavery were opposed by northern abolitionists—people who wanted to

end the practice of slavery. The abolitionists said that nothing could justify the evil of slavery. They rejected arguments that justified the enslavement of so-called "inferior" races.

As you'll learn in a later chapter, it took a bloody civil war to settle the issue of slavery in the United States, and racism remained a challenge for more than a century thereafter.

Abolitionism in Britain

In the 1700s, Great Britain was more heavily involved in the transatlantic slave trade than any other nation. Yet in the next century, the British took

the lead in attempting to end the slave trade and abolish slavery completely.

Why did the British people have such a change of heart? Britain had profitable sugar and coffee plantations overseas, and its economy depended on the slave trade. But people began to speak out against the cruelties of the slave trade. At first it was a few brave voices, then more joined in, until at last their message was too strong to ignore.

Some of the most committed opponents of slavery were British Quakers on both sides of the Atlantic. Throughout the 1700s, they had worked to abolish slavery. They argued that slavery was un-Christian—every man, they said, is equal in the eyes of God. But most British people regarded Quakers as extremists, and paid little attention to their arguments.

Not until the 1780s did a strong abolitionist movement emerge in Great Britain. It was sparked by a young Anglican clergyman named Thomas Clarkson.

While studying at the University of Cambridge, Clarkson entered a contest. Students were challenged to write an essay in Latin on this topic: "Is it lawful to make slaves of others against their will?" Clarkson wasn't very interested in slavery, but he was good at Latin, and he wanted to win the award. So he plunged into research to prepare for his essay. The more he found out, the more outraged he became. In Latin, he wrote a powerful essay against the practice of enslavement. And he won the contest.

After his graduation, Clarkson resolved that he would spend his life working to abolish slavery. He began to look for others who shared his views. In 1786, he met a Quaker printer in London, who agreed to publish his essay in English. The two men discovered their common passion to end slavery.

They formed a committee with the daring goal of abolishing an evil that had existed for centuries. Nine Quakers and three Anglicans formed The Society for Effecting the Abolition of the Slave Trade.

Clarkson was a born organizer. He rode from town to town collecting as much evidence as he could about brutal practices in the slave trade. He spoke with doctors, seamen, and captains of slave ships. Wherever he went, he carefully copied records. As he traveled, he formed new abolitionist committees in many towns.

In London, Clarkson and his fellow committee members gave out antislavery pamphlets. They drew posters showing the awful conditions on slave ships. They made antislavery

Thomas Clarkson was an Anglican clergyman who began the abolitionist movement in Britain. He spent much of his life writing about the evils of slavery.

medallions, took horrifying cases to court, and stirred people to action. Their goal was to compel Parliament to change the nation's laws and end slavery once and for all.

The End of the British Slave Trade

To help move Parliament to action, Clarkson enlisted the assistance of William Wilberforce, a frail but determined young man with a mighty voice and a reputation for integrity.

Born to a wealthy family, Wilberforce had become a member of the British Parliament at the young age of twenty-one. In his mid-twenties, he went through a religious conversion. He was Anglican—a member of the Church of England. After his conversion, he gained a new enthusiasm for living a life faithful to the gospels. This earned him and others the label "evangelical." (*Evangel* is another word for "gospel.") These Evangelical Anglicans became a key force in the British antislavery movement.

Wilberforce wanted to improve life for the people of England, especially the poor and powerless. But the cause closest to his heart was the abolition of the slave trade. He was shocked by the brutalities of slavery and ashamed that his countrymen traded in slaves. After reading accounts of the cruelty of the slave trade, Wilberforce said, "I … determined that I would never rest until I had effected its abolition."

Wilberforce called for Parliamentary hearings to investigate the slave trade. Clarkson helped provide the evidence. He and his colleagues brought forth witness after witness to testify to brutal floggings, inhumane crowding in the ships, and horrifyingly unsanitary conditions.

In public meetings and in Parliament, Wilberforce spoke passionately against slavery. In one speech he declared that "this most detestable and guilty practice, the Slave Trade, hold[s] in bondage, in darkness and in blood, one-third of the habitable globe; … it erects a barrier along more than 3,000 miles of the shores of that vast continent [Africa], which shuts out light and truth, humanity and kindness."

Wilberforce, Clarkson, and their fellow abolitionists faced tough opposition. The wealthy sugar planters of the Caribbean colonies had a strong voice in Parliament. They argued that because sugar was such an important crop, the British economy would be ruined if the slave trade were ended.

Despite such arguments, the ranks of the abolitionists grew steadily as the British public learned more about the evils of slavery. Clarkson's group gathered thousands of signatures on antislavery petitions. Newspapers reprinted some of these petitions. They also published Olaudah Equiano's account of his life as a slave. Equiano published his work as a book and it became a bestseller. Slowly but steadily, British public opinion mounted against slavery.

The British abolitionists reached every major town with their accounts of the cruel treatment of slaves. They flooded Parliament with more petitions calling for an end to the slave trade. British women took up the cause. They tried a new strategy that had been practiced years before by Americans against British tea—the boycott. (To *boycott* is to refuse to do business with a group, often in order to compel them to reform in some way.) In one year, nearly 300,000 Britons boycotted slave-grown sugar.

In 1807, the British Parliament responded to the popular outcry and abolished the slave trade.

In Britain as in America, the end of the slave trade did not mean an immediate end to slavery itself. Change came slowly. Slaves continued to work on the sugar plantations in Britain's colonies. Even when Parliament voted to outlaw slavery in all of its colonies in 1833, British sugar planters still forced the "freed" slaves to work on their plantations.

Nevertheless, Britain became the nation most opposed to slavery. It became the center of abolitionist activity worldwide. International conferences in London focused on the evils of slavery. The British navy stopped slave ships at sea and liberated the captured slaves. The British government encouraged or pressured other countries to end their involvement in slavery.

Slavery in the Muslim World

In the first half of the nineteenth century, most European countries followed Great Britain's example and stopped participating in the slave trade. But the Muslim lands of northern Africa and the Middle East continued an active slave trade for nearly another century. In fact, during the nineteenth century, Muslim traders enslaved more Africans than they had in any other century.

Since the founding of Islam in the 600s, slavery had been practiced in Muslim societies. From the Middle

An Unexpected Result: The Women's Movement

In 1840, a group of women tried to attend an anti-slavery conference in London, but they were barred from taking part. Instead, the ladies were escorted to an upstairs gallery where they were told they could watch and listen to men discussing ideas about freedom.

Two of these women were Americans who had crossed the Atlantic for the conference. Lucretia Mott and Elizabeth Cady Stanton began to wonder about their own freedom. They returned to America and helped organize the world's first conference on women's rights, which took place in 1848 at Seneca Falls, New York. The conference issued a document modeled after the U.S. Declaration of Independence. It included this statement: "We hold these truths to be self-evident: that all men and women are created equal."

Elizabeth Cady Stanton addresses the first conference on women's rights in Seneca Falls, New York.

As the transatlantic slave trade drew to an end, trade in slaves to the Islamic world continued to grow. At right, enslaved African women await transportation to the Middle East.

Ages on, Muslim traders had transported slaves from sub-Saharan Africa to such Islamic lands as Egypt, Arabia, Persia, and the Ottoman Empire. During the Middle Ages, Muslim raiders enslaved not only captive Africans but also conquered Europeans. The Muslim Tatars, for example, enslaved most of the Slavic population they conquered in the Crimea between the sixteenth and eighteenth centuries.

As European countries grew powerful, fewer Europeans were taken into slavery. Muslim slave traders turned more and more to Africa. In the nineteenth century, improved methods of transportation, like the steamship, made it possible to ship large numbers of slaves from Africa to the lands of the Middle East. Thus, while the transatlantic slave trade was coming to an end, the Islamic slave trade continued to grow.

About a third of the Africans enslaved by Muslim traders were men, and they became agricultural workers or soldiers. Slaves taken to Zanzibar, for example, often labored on plantations that produced cloves, a valuable spice. Slaves taken to Egypt served in the army.

Most African slaves transported to the Muslim world were women and children. Historians estimate that as many as two-thirds were women. They did not work in fields. They worked as household slaves, and had no choice but to do whatever their masters commanded.

Those captured in western Africa were sent to work in North African countries such as Morocco or Egypt. Slave traders marched them for 60 or 70 days across the Sahara. This vast, empty desert was broiling hot by day, freezing cold at night. Many died on the way from exhaustion, exposure, or thirst. Some were killed by slave dealers who thought them too slow.

Slaves captured in eastern Africa were marched to the Indian Ocean. Those who survived the march were crowded onto boats bound

The Islamic Slave Trade in the 18th and 19th Centuries

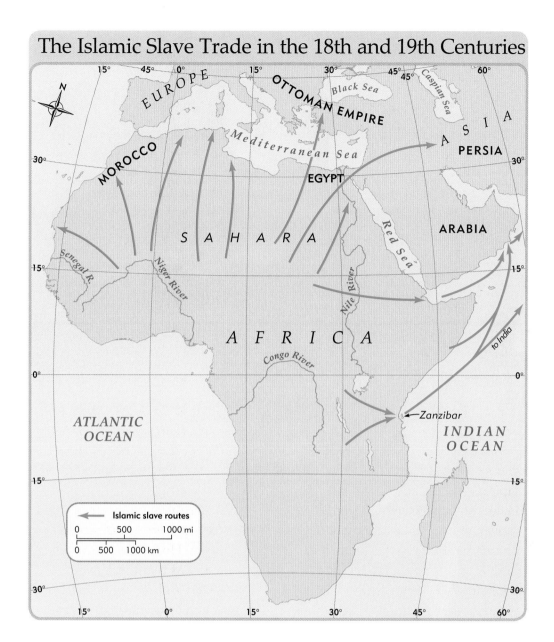

for the island of Zanzibar or for the Middle East.

- On the map above, locate the routes of the Islamic slave trade. Also locate the Sahara and Zanzibar.

An End in Sight

Throughout the nineteenth century, European nations, with Britain in the lead, pressured Asian and African countries to abolish slavery. In 1877, the government of Egypt signed an agreement with Britain restricting the slave trade. In 1889, the Sultan of the Ottoman Empire, which controlled most Muslim countries in the Middle East, issued a similar law. Although these laws helped to end the slave trade, it would take even longer to abolish slavery in the Muslim world.

Still, by the beginning of the twentieth century, the painful story of human slavery was coming to an end. The final chapter remains to be written. Though slavery is no longer common, it still exists in some parts of the world today.

A: During the Industrial Revolution, printing presses powered by steam made newspapers available to more people than ever before.

B: The American Revolution helped set off a wave of democratic rebellions against kings in the eighteenth and nineteenth centuries.

C: In the nineteenth century, railroads spread across Europe and North America, allowing people and goods to travel long distances quickly.

Revolutions Change the World

*I*n many ways, our modern world was shaped during the late eighteenth and early nineteenth centuries by two kinds of revolution. The first was a wave of democratic revolutions. On both sides of the Atlantic, people spoke of natural rights. They questioned monarchy, wrote new constitutions, and experimented with representative government.

The second kind of revolution was a massive change in technology and economics. The Industrial Revolution changed the way people lived, worked, and got around. It created new jobs, new wealth, and new problems.

The Rights of Man and the Flame of Revolution

Ideas can be powerful things. When they inspire people to action, ideas can change everything.

Many people were inspired by John Locke's ideas about natural rights and liberty. In 1776, those ideas helped spark a revolution by English colonists in North America.

Prior to this revolution, Britain's North American colonists thought of themselves as proudly British. An ocean away from the mother country, the colonies mostly governed themselves. Most colonies elected their own assemblies and set their own taxes. But then King George III and the British Parliament tried to tax the colonists to help pay for the expenses of a war that had been fought partly on American soil. Americans had no representation in Parliament; they said there should be "no taxation without representation."

The split between colonies and mother country widened. As Parliament and king passed laws

Early American flags took different shapes and sizes. This one, which dates to about 1776, bears 13 stars and 13 stripes to symbolize the 13 colonies that declared independence from British rule.

tightening royal control, colonists cried, "Tyranny!"

On July 4, 1776, the thirteen colonies decided to exercise what John Locke had called the "right of revolution." They launched a war for independence and republican government. They insisted, in Thomas Jefferson's words, "that all men are created equal; that they are endowed by their creator with certain unalienable rights, and that among these are ... life, liberty, and the pursuit of happiness."

The Americans won their independence. They went on to produce a Constitution that established republican government for the whole nation—a first for modern times.

From North America, the flame of revolution spread. In Europe, the people of France were ruled by an all-powerful king. But France had been home to *philosophes* like Voltaire and Montesquieu, who celebrated reason and the power of educated people to chart their future. Many Frenchmen had fought in the American Revolution, and they were inspired by ideas about the rights of man.

When King Louis XVI tried to collect more taxes from people whose pockets were already near empty, many asked: Why should we submit? Why should we pay for the privileges of the royalty, nobility, and clergy? Why should we let others have all the power and wealth? Ideas of "liberty, equality, and fraternity"—along with years of seething resentment and anger—inspired the people to take up arms and fight for their rights. On July 14, 1789, angry men and women stormed the Bastille. The French Revolution had begun.

In three years, France changed from an absolute monarchy to a republic. The French sent shock waves through Europe when they beheaded their king, eliminated privileges of the nobility and clergy, and gave all French men the vote.

What began as a democratic revolution turned into a very bloody affair. During the Reign of Terror, the guillotine claimed the lives of thousands of people who were declared "enemies of the Revolution."

No sooner had the French beheaded their king than they found themselves at war with royal families throughout nearly all of Europe. Napoleon rose from the military ranks to lead France. He said that he believed in the Revolution, and yet he crowned himself emperor of the French.

Napoleon and his troops spread the revolution abroad. People in other lands resented the French invasions, but they did not forget the ideas Napoleon said he stood for—liberty, equality, and rule by law.

When the European allies defeated Napoleon at Waterloo in 1815, the flame of revolution seemed extinguished in France. But elsewhere it continued to flare.

Across the Atlantic, Spain's colonists resented strict Spanish control. Inspired by events in North America and Europe, they talked eagerly about being free from the rule of kings. In 1810, many Latin American colonies declared their independence. By 1824, the struggles were largely over. The revolutionaries had won. Many declared new, independent republics. But these former colonies had little experience with representative government.

Military strong men, called *caudillos*, often seized power.

Back in Europe, in 1830 and 1848, democratic uprisings flared again. In France, Germany, Italy, and Austria, protesters demanded greater liberties. They called for constitutions to define and defend their rights. Monarchs resisted, but they took a few grudging steps toward meeting those demands. In some lands, they allowed people to form representative bodies and write constitutions.

Slowly, and often violently, Europe moved toward a more democratic future. The idea of the rights of man was an idea with a fuse, which, once lit, ignited a burning desire for liberty and independence.

French revolutionaries in Paris proclaim a republic after overthrowing their king in 1848. The revolt was soon crushed, but such uprisings proved that democratic ideas were very much alive in Europe.

Right: The Comet, *the first commercial steam paddler in Europe, began carrying passengers in Scotland in 1812. Steamboats revolutionized water travel.*

Below: This late nineteenth-century diagram illustrates Samuel Morse's telegraph system. In 1844, Morse sent the first long-distance telegraph message from Washington, D.C., to Baltimore, Maryland. Thirty years later, telegraph wires linked countries around the world.

The Transforming Power of Machines

If our modern world was shaped by these democratic revolutions, it was also shaped as much if not more by the Industrial Revolution.

The West moved quickly toward an industrial future. Adam Smith's ideas about free trade and competition made England a catalyst for change. Investors and inventors took advantage of England's booming capitalist economy.

Just as powerful ideas can change society, so can certain inventions. In the eighteenth century, the flying shuttle, spinning jenny, and mechanical loom speeded up production in the textile industry. When James Watt invented a practical steam engine, the Industrial Revolution took off. The steam engine powered all sorts of machines, from pumps that could remove water from coal mines to mechanical looms in textile mills. Soon more steam-powered factories sprang up, producing cloth, guns, ironware, and more.

The steam engine powered the revolution in transportation. In 1807, Robert Fulton's steamboat started speeding goods up and down rivers. Within about three decades, steamships were carrying people and goods across the Atlantic. And steam-powered trains chugged along in Europe and North America.

Steamships and railroads hurried letters on their way. But Samuel Morse's telegraph made it possible to communicate in an instant. Telegraph wires linked cities and even continents.

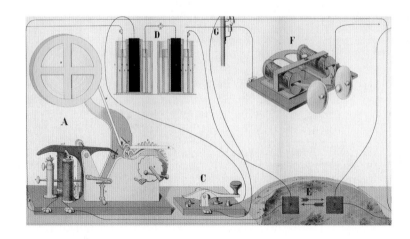

By 1860, the hum of machinery was transforming the West. Romantic artists questioned whether this transformation was all for the best. They celebrated nature and personal freedom. They questioned what they perceived as coldly rational scientific thinking. Such thinking might lead to industrial innovations, but was this really progress? When we think scientifically, the English poet William Wordsworth charged, we "murder to dissect."

The Plight of Labor

In Europe and America, new jobs in the cities drew workers from the countryside to the new urban factories. These early factories were often dark, dirty, dangerous places. Women and children worked 12 or 14 hour days, and men 16 hours. Drowsy children were beaten. Late workers were severely fined.

The growing cities where most industrial workers lived turned into filthy, overcrowded, unhealthy places. Workers went home to tenements in crime-ridden slums. In England, Charles Dickens wrote novels about the plight of London's laboring poor. Karl Marx predicted a revolution of workers, whom he said suffered under a system of "wage slavery."

In other parts of the world, real slavery was on the rise. Advances in technology increased the demand for slaves. Now that British textile

Workers sift coal mined in eastern France in this scene from about 1860. The air in this room, filled with coal dust, was harmful to breathe. The Industrial Revolution brought many marvels, but all too often it also brought hazardous, unhealthy work conditions.

mills could weave faster, merchants needed more cotton to supply the mills. The American South had ideal growing conditions for cotton. In the late 1790s, the cotton gin made large-scale cotton production possible. Plantation owners needed a large labor force to pick cotton—they used slaves.

Since the early days of tobacco, rice, and sugar cultivation, plantation owners had been importing slaves from Africa. From the shores of Africa, millions of slaves were transported to the West Indies, Latin America, and the American South.

Slavery and Serfdom Worldwide

Europeans and Americans were not the only ones to use African slaves or forced labor. Slave traders from the Islamic world—Egypt, Arabia, Persia, and the Ottoman Empire—bought millions of African slaves, mostly women and children. Russian tsars and nobles relied on the forced labor of Russian peasants. In 1850, the vast majority of Russian people were serfs, workers who were bound to the land and could be bought and sold as property.

Slave traders march their captives across central Africa for sale in the Islamic world.

The slaves suffered floggings and malnutrition. Many died at a young age, only to be replaced by newly imported slaves.

In the United States, Congress prohibited the importing of slaves after 1808. Southern planters knew their livelihood depended on a large slave population. So they encouraged slaves to marry and have children. But slave families were often torn apart since slaves could be bought and sold by their masters at will.

By 1860, one thing was clear—the world's growing labor force desperately needed change. Workers endured exhausting schedules, repetitive tasks, and hazardous conditions. Slaves were often beaten and flogged, and many were ripped from their families when bought or sold. What hope could they have for a better future?

The Hope for Change

It takes time for ideas to reshape reality. In the West, the Enlightenment ideals of natural rights, equality, liberty, and human dignity led to great changes in government. Even after these changes, however, there were still glaring contradictions between those ideals and the conditions in which many people lived and worked. In the 1800s, reformers asked: If natural rights and human dignity are important, why are workers enduring such harsh conditions? Why does slavery continue to exist?

In part the Industrial Revolution had grown out of the Enlightenment's confidence in reason and in our ability to understand the physical universe. Many reformers said: If we are capable of great technological progress, then surely we can figure out ways to solve the hard new problems of urban, industrial life. Surely we can figure out how to make safer, cleaner, and healthier places for people to live and work.

These calls for reform slowly prompted change. Governments began to limit the number of hours worked by women and children in factories. They imposed modest new requirements for safety in the workplace.

The greatest changes were prompted by the tireless efforts of abolitionists to end slavery. How could governments say "all men are created equal" while enslaving millions? Some people tried to justify slavery by saying that some races were inferior to others. But the abolitionists refused to accept such arguments. The antislavery movement on both sides of the Atlantic condemned a system that depended on denying the humanity of others. The abolitionists at last succeeded in ending the transatlantic slave trade.

The democratic and industrial revolutions of the eighteenth and nineteenth centuries had mixed results, creating both new opportunities and new problems. Still, by 1860, more people began to look to the future with new hope. Investors and inventors hoped new technologies would speed up production and communication. Artists and thinkers

hoped for greater creative freedom. Reformers hoped their work would improve millions of lives in significant ways.

Was such progress possible? It would require people to think big and reach higher than ever before.

Abolitionists used this image of a shackled slave to remind the public that all human beings have natural rights. They put it on posters, medallions (see page 504), snuff boxes, and even hair ornaments. "Am I Not a Man & a Brother" became a motto of the abolitionist movement.

Time Line (1750–1860)

1750	1760	1770	1780	1790	1800

1776
Adam Smith, "the father of modern economics," publishes *The Wealth of Nations*.

1776
Delegates from thirteen British colonies adopt the Declaration of Independence, rejecting British rule and creating the United States of America.

1807
Britain outlaws the slave trade.

1793
King Louis XVI of France is executed; the Reign of Terror begins.

1789
The Bastille falls, marking the beginning of the French Revolution.

1762
Catherine the Great becomes empress of Russia.

1800
Napoleon leads French troops into Italy.

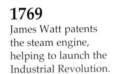

1769
James Watt patents the steam engine, helping to launch the Industrial Revolution.

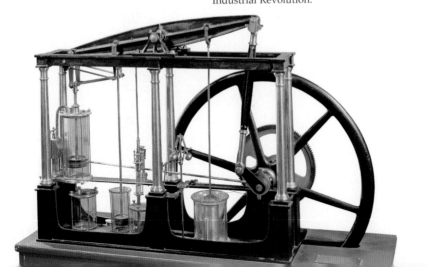

| 1810 | 1820 | 1830 | 1840 | 1850 | 1860 |

1848
Marx and Engels publish *The Communist Manifesto*; revolutions break out across Europe.

1815
Napoleon is defeated at the Battle of Waterloo.

1837
Eighteen-year-old Victoria becomes queen of England; she reigns until 1901.

1814
George Stephenson invents the first practical steam locomotive.

1844
Samuel Morse sends a telegraph message from Washington, D.C., to Baltimore, Maryland.

1859
Charles Darwin publishes *The Origin of Species*.

1810
Revolutions break out across Latin America; Simón Bolívar and others begin to fight for independence.

A: An 1892 cartoon shows Cecil Rhodes's ambition to extend the reach of the British Empire across Africa.

B: Otto Lilienthal makes one of his pioneering flights in Germany.

C: The Brooklyn Bridge spans the East River in New York City.

An Age of Outreach and Overreach

*H*istory shows over and over that people want to accomplish big things. Something in human nature causes people to want to reach a little farther, build a little higher, learn a little more, create something that's never been made before.

Since the earliest civilizations, people have poured massive amounts of energy into huge projects. Ziggurats in ancient Mesopotamia. Pyramids in Egypt. The Great Wall of China. Miles of roads and aqueducts in the Roman Empire. Grand mosques and towering Gothic cathedrals during the Middle Ages.

Time and again, we've watched people push the boundaries of knowledge. Think of Leonardo scribbling in his notebooks about everything from new ways of painting to flying machines to human anatomy. Remember Galileo training his telescope on the night sky and discovering unknown moons orbiting Jupiter, or Columbus heading west into uncharted waters.

We've seen people working hard to give the world new achievements and inventions. Think of Brunelleschi building his marvelous dome for Florence's cathedral, or James Watt perfecting his steam engine.

Rulers are almost always driven to do big things—not necessarily good things, but certainly big things. We've seen many a king or general try to control as many lands, people, and resources as possible. In ancient times, Alexander the Great, barely 30 years old, having conquered an empire of more than a million square miles—the largest the world had known to that time—is said to have wept because there were "no worlds left to conquer." In the early nineteenth century, Napoleon gathered enormous armies and overran much of Europe.

In the following chapters, as we move into the late nineteenth and early twentieth centuries, you'll see these same human urges and ambitions still at work. Particularly in Europe and the United States, a feeling of confidence was in the air— a feeling that sometimes turned into overconfidence and arrogance.

This confidence and ambition partly grew out of the Scientific Revolution and Industrial Revolution. Inventions such as the steam engine, railroad, and telegraph gave people the ability to do more, make more, go faster. Beginning in the late nineteenth century, many people sensed that they were living in a

The Eiffel Tower was built to mark the hundredth anniversary of the French Revolution. The modern tower that rose above the Paris skyline seemed to sum up the spirit of the times—high hopes and dreams of unlimited progress.

time when they could use new scientific knowledge to solve one problem after another. They believed they could build or do just about anything they set their minds to.

This burst of confidence created much of the world we know today, especially the technology we take for granted. Electric power, telephones, radios, automobiles, airplanes—all of these came out of the time near the turn of the twentieth century.

As late as the 1800s, people died by the thousands when diseases struck their town or city. In the late nineteenth century, scientists discovered new ways to fight diseases. Reformers and government officials found ways to make cities safer and healthier places, with planned neighborhoods and effective water systems. One result is that most people today can expect to live significantly longer lives.

While builders of the ancient world erected pyramids and cathedrals, modern engineers figured out how to make buildings rise higher than ever before. The skyscrapers that define our urban landscapes are the result of their efforts.

This period helped shape the way billions of people entertain themselves today. Have you been to a movie lately? Visited an amusement park? Or crowded into a stadium to watch your favorite professional sports team? Those pastimes all came out of the late nineteenth century.

During the late 1800s and early 1900s, people with grand visions founded modern nations. The boundaries of several countries were established during this time. It was a

In New York City, skyscrapers began to climb ever higher. Above, two men work on the beams of the Metropolitan Tower, which was the world's tallest building until 1913.

time when some people resolved to fight for liberty and self-rule. It was also a time when industrialized powers set out to claim gigantic empires. This frenzied grab for land and resources left long-lasting anger and resentment among many peoples, especially in Africa and Asia.

Never before had the world seen a period when humans were reaching, and sometimes overreaching, to accomplish so much. The period between the late nineteenth century and 1914 leads right to the doorstep of our contemporary world.

Giuseppe Garibaldi leads his army of liberation ashore in Sicily in 1860. He holds aloft the banner that became the first flag of Italy.

Italy and Germany: Nationalism and the New Map of Europe

How many countries can you name in Europe? If you need to refresh your memory, take a look at the map of Europe in the atlas at the back of this book. Among the European nations you'll see Italy and Germany. Italy is the boot-shaped nation that juts into the Mediterranean Sea. Look north and you'll find Germany.

In the scale of historical time, you don't have to go back very far—only a couple hundred years—to reach a time when Italy and Germany did not exist, at least not as the countries we recognize on a map today. Of course the lands existed, but it wasn't until the mid-nineteenth century that Italy and Germany emerged as independent nations.

For many centuries, the lands that make up Italy and Germany were like jigsaw puzzles, an array of interlocking pieces, with each piece representing a different city-state or kingdom with a different ruler.

As time passed, wars changed the arrangement of the pieces. But the pieces remained.

In this chapter we're going to see what caused those pieces to come together as the unified nations we now know as Italy and Germany. One cause was the revival of democratic revolutions. In the early 1800s, when Napoleon toppled old governments ruled by dukes and princes, he also spread the ideas of the French Revolution. After Napoleon met his Waterloo in 1815, his enemies tried to put everything back the way it was before the French Revolution. They tried to freeze the map of Europe, restore royal families to

This chapter focuses on Italy and Germany in the nineteenth century.

The modern flag of Italy dates from the time of Napoleonic rule, when tricolor flags with vertical bars became popular. By 1848, revolutionaries used the green, white, and red flag as a symbol of Italian unity. When Italy became a republic in 1946, the royal crest that once adorned the middle of the flag was dropped.

their thrones, and stamp out revolutionary ideas.

For a few years, Europe seemed calm on the surface. But by 1830, European streets and coffeehouses buzzed with talk of constitutions and republics. There were occasional uprisings, but in 1848, these stirrings turned into upheaval across Europe. Students and workers took to the streets. Revolutionaries announced that they would no longer be ruled by foreign kings or emperors.

These revolutionary stirrings were accompanied by waves of *nationalism*, the strong sense of attachment or belonging to one's own country. In this chapter, we'll meet the people whose fervent nationalistic beliefs helped create two modern nations—Italy and Germany.

Italy and Dreams of Former Glory

Near the middle of the Italian peninsula sits the great city of Rome. Once all roads led to Rome—or so said proud citizens of the ancient Roman Empire back in the first and second centuries A.D. At that time, the Italian peninsula was the nerve center of a mighty empire. But Rome fell, and

you've learned that by the time of the Renaissance, the Italian peninsula had become a jigsaw puzzle of small city-states. Each city-state had its own government and its own army.

Some people, like Dante and Machiavelli, hoped for a day when all Italy would be united. But most did not. They did not think of themselves as "Italians." Rather, they thought of themselves as citizens of, for example, Florence, Genoa, or Venice. Often these city-states went to war against each other. Often foreign monarchs sent armies to invade the peninsula.

In 1797, Napoleon and his troops conquered northern Italy. The French ruler imposed reforms that in some ways united the long-divided people. For the first time since ancient Rome, Italians were using the same currency and fighting in the same army. Napoleon's conquest stirred feelings of nationalism—people began to experience a new sense of unity in their shared dislike of being under the rule of French outsiders. They began to dream of an Italy that would be both unified and free from foreign rule.

But following Napoleon's defeat, the Italian peninsula once again broke into a jumble of separate states ruled by foreign powers. Austria dominated most of the north. In central Italy, the pope ruled the Papal States, though he relied on help from Austria. Members of the Spanish royal family ruled southern Italy.

Only one major state was not dominated by a foreign power—the Kingdom of Sardinia. That kingdom included the island of Sardinia and a region near the Alps in northwestern Italy. This region was known as *Piedmont*, a word meaning "at the foot of the mountains." Since the capital city was located there, the entire Kingdom of Sardinia was often called simply "Piedmont."

- On the map on page 528, locate the Kingdom of Sardinia, including both the island of Sardinia and the region called Piedmont. Locate Rome, the Papal States, and the Austrian Empire.

Mazzini and Young Italy

Around 1830, in the various states of Italy, students and other young people often staged protests in the streets. They denounced their rulers. They demanded constitutions to protect their rights. They called for a free press. They called for elections so they could choose their own leaders.

To show they belonged to a new generation eager for change, these protesters wore long hair and sported full beards. The police arrested them, sometimes shaved them, and often beat them and threw them into prison. Some of the protesters formed secret societies to fight for their causes.

Among these protesters, Giuseppe Mazzini (joo-ZEP-pay maht-SEE-nee) emerged as a powerful voice for freedom and Italian unity. Mazzini had hoped to become a playwright or historical novelist, but instead he became a leading revolutionary. Even as a teenager, he dedicated himself to the idea that, as he put it, "we Italians *could* and therefore *ought* to struggle for the liberty of our country." He joined a secret revolutionary society that worked to overthrow Italy's foreign rulers.

In 1831, Mazzini started an organization called Young Italy. The Young Italy movement combined nationalist and democratic ideals. Mazzini's nationalist goal was to free the Italian states from their foreign rulers and unify them as an independent republic. Mazzini passionately argued that people of the same nationality—people who share a language, culture, and history—have a common destiny to live in freedom as a single nation.

Mazzini's democratic goal was to achieve a freely elected government in a united Italy. He wanted more power for the people: "Neither pope nor king," said Mazzini; "Only God and the people will open the way of the future to us."

The Young Italy movement spread rapidly. Young people across Italy started branches of

The patriot Giuseppe Mazzini formed Young Italy to unite his fellow countrymen and free Italy from foreign rule. He believed that people who shared the Italian language, culture, and history should live in a single nation.

the organization. They tried to organize uprisings against foreign rule, but their efforts failed. In one attempt, the rebels were arrested before their revolt even began. Twelve were executed. Mazzini was not captured but a death sentence was put on his head.

The Oath of Young Italy

*A Page
from the Past*

In 1832, Giuseppe Mazzini formed a secret society called Young Italy to organize uprisings against foreign rule of Italy. The uprisings failed, but Mazzini's work helped persuade many Italians that Italy should be a united country, free of foreign control.

When new members were initiated into Young Italy, they pledged the following oath:

In the name of God and of Italy—
In the name of all the martyrs of the holy Italian cause who have fallen beneath foreign and domestic tyranny—

By the duties which bind me to the land wherein God has placed me and to the brothers whom God has given me—

By the love, innate in all men, I bear to the country that gave my mother birth and will be the home of my children—

By the hatred, innate in all men, I bear to evil, injustice, usurpation, and arbitrary rule—

By the blush that rises to my brow when I stand before the citizens of other lands, to know that I have no rights of citizenship, no country, and no national flag—

By the aspiration that thrills my soul toward that liberty for which it was created and is impotent to exert; toward the good it was created to strive after and is impotent to achieve in the silence and isolation of slavery—

By the memory of our former greatness and sense of our present degradation—

By the tears of Italian mothers for their sons dead on the scaffold, in prison, or in exile—

By the sufferings of the millions—

I, _____, believing in the mission entrusted by God to Italy and the duty of every Italian to strive to attempt its fulfillment—

Innate means existing within an individual from birth.

Usurpation means the seizing of power or office without right.

Aspiration means the strong desire for something great.

Impotent means lacking power or strength.

A **scaffold** is a platform, often a platform on which a criminal is executed.

Convinced that where God has ordained that a nation shall be, he has given the requisite power to create it; that the people are the depositories of that power, and that in its right direction for the people and by the people lies the secret of victory—

Convinced that virtue consists in action and sacrifice, and strength in union and constancy of purpose—

I give my name to Young Italy, an association of men holding the same faith, and swear to dedicate myself wholly and forever to endeavor with them to constitute Italy one free, independent, republican nation.

> *Requisite* means necessary.
>
> A *depository* is a place where something is put for safekeeping.
>
> A *republican nation* is one in which citizens elect leaders who govern on behalf of the people.

Garibaldi and the Redshirts

Although the Young Italy movement did not change things right away, its ideals inspired many Italians. One was a dashing young revolutionary from Sardinia named Giuseppe Garibaldi (gair-uh-BAHL-dee).

Garibaldi craved action. At the age of 15, he went to sea as an apprentice seaman and ended up fighting pirates. By age 26, he was the captain of his own little ship. He sailed to ports all around the Mediterranean, and in taverns along the waterfronts he met other Italians, some from Sardinia, some from the Papal States, others from Austrian-ruled lands. They spoke of their resentment at the way foreign rulers had divided Italy. They talked of a day when the peninsula might become a strong and united country. Sometimes they spoke of Mazzini and his secret society, Young Italy.

In 1833, Garibaldi joined Young Italy. The next year he participated in a plot to overthrow the king of Sardinia. But the plot failed at the last minute, and Garibaldi found himself in the port of Genoa surrounded by the king's troops. A woman who ran a fruit stall hid him and gave him some peasant clothes, and he managed to slip away. He fled west toward France, walking country roads and using the stars as his guide. French officials arrested him

Giuseppe Garibaldi was a man of action as well as ideas. He took part in revolutions in South America before returning to his homeland to fight for Italian unity.

Italy, c. 1848

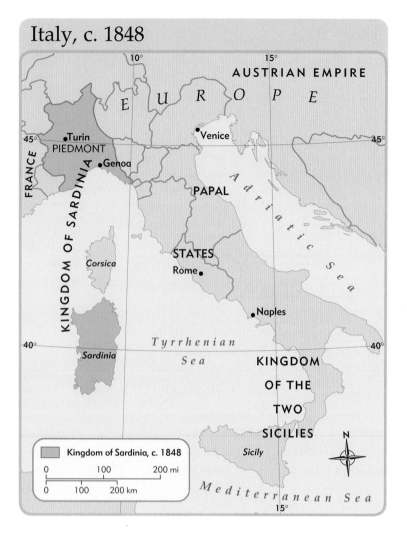

Kingdom of Sardinia, c. 1848

0   100   200 mi

0   100   200 km

daring fighters, a reputation that traveled across the ocean to Italy.

During the years he lived and fought for freedom in South America, Garibaldi never forgot his dream of a united Italy. He began to receive urgent letters from Mazzini: "Your country will soon need you." In 1848, Garibaldi sailed home with his Redshirts. When they stepped ashore in northern Italy, a crowd swarmed around them roaring, "*Evviva Garibaldi!* Long live Garibaldi!"

In 1848, the year of Garibaldi's return, revolutions were breaking out across Europe, including Italy. The people of Rome revolted against the pope's rule and declared their city-state the Roman Republic. Garibaldi hurried his Redshirts to help the uprising. Rome, he later wrote, "seemed to represent to me the united will of the Italian people to live as one people, content and free under a government of their own choosing."

In Rome, the Redshirts fought hard but lost against French troops that had come to the pope's aid. Garibaldi survived and escaped to the United States. In 1854, however, he returned once more to his homeland, the Kingdom of Sardinia.

Uniting Italy

The Kingdom of Sardinia—also known as Piedmont—was, you recall, the only major state on the Italian peninsula not ruled by a foreign power. Its young king, Victor Emmanuel II, was a fiery patriot who longed to unite Italy under his rule. For help in running

and made plans to send him back to Sardinia, but the rebel managed to jump out of a window and disappear into the night. Soon he was on board a ship, bound for South America.

In South America, Garibaldi plunged back into revolutionary action. The people of Uruguay were fighting for independence from Argentina. Garibaldi organized a group of Italian exiles to help them fight. His men wore the cheapest uniforms they could get—red robes that butchers had thrown away. These garments were red to keep bloodstains from showing. Garibaldi's troops thus came to be known as the "Redshirts." They earned a reputation as fierce and his kingdom, Victor Emmanuel turned to a cunning politician, the Count di Cavour (kuh-VUR). In 1852, the king made Cavour his prime minister. (A prime minister is the leader of a parliamentary government.)

Cavour wanted Piedmont to be the most powerful state in northern Italy. He wanted a popular hero like Garibaldi on his side. So Cavour arranged a number of secret conversations between Victor Emmanuel and Garibaldi. After all, the king and the rebel had something in common—they both wanted foreign rulers out of Italy.

Meanwhile, Cavour schemed to enlist the aid of France against Austria. He persuaded the French to help Piedmont if it came under attack. Then he deliberately provoked disagreements with Austria. When these disagreements erupted into war, French troops arrived to help defend Piedmont. They were joined by Garibaldi, who took to the field again at the head of a Piedmontese army. Throughout northern Italy, a cry flew from village to village: "Garibaldi is back! Long live Italy!" The rebel leader passed through villages with his troops and addressed the crowds: "Come! He who stays at home is a coward! I promise you weariness, hardship, and battles. But we will conquer or die."

The French and Piedmontese clashed with the Austrians in 1859. When the fighting ended, the Austrians had lost their hold on all the northern Italian states except Venice.

But then something happened that the French did not expect. The newly liberated states in northern

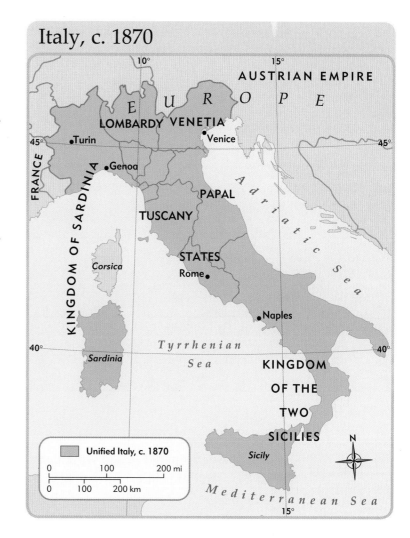

Italy, c. 1870

Unified Italy, c. 1870

Italy decided to join the Kingdom of Sardinia. Even parts of the Papal States decided to join Victor Emmanuel's kingdom. The French were alarmed to find that a united and sizable Italian kingdom had suddenly taken shape on France's southern border.

By this time, in the Kingdom of the Two Sicilies to the south, many people were rebelling against their

Hero of Two Worlds

Early in his career, Giuseppe Garibaldi fought with both Brazilian and Uruguayan revolutionaries. He then led campaigns for Italian independence from foreign rule. For his revolutionary successes in both South America and Europe, Garibaldi became known as the Hero of Two Worlds.

Garibaldi's Redshirts rout royalist forces in Sicily in 1860. Next, they crossed to the Italian mainland and captured Naples, capital of the Kingdom of the Two Sicilies.

rulers, who were members of the Spanish royal family. From Piedmont, Garibaldi prepared to sail with about a thousand of his Redshirts to help the rebels.

"Garibaldi's Thousand" had only rusty flintlock rifles and very little

The State of Vatican City

In 1929, the Roman Catholic Church and the Italian government finally negotiated a treaty. The pope recognized Italy as a nation with its capital at Rome, and Italy recognized Vatican City as an independent state. Vatican City, a 109-acre territory in the city of Rome, is the world's smallest nation.

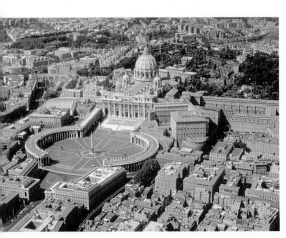

St. Peter's Basilica and the Vatican

ammunition. Cavour tried to talk them out of a scheme he considered dangerous, but Garibaldi would not listen.

- On the map on page 528, locate the Kingdom of the Two Sicilies.

In 1860, Garibaldi and his band landed in Sicily and astonished the world by swiftly defeating the kingdom's forces. That victory lit a fire. Thousands rushed to join Garibaldi's army of patriots. Garibaldi then marched on Naples, the capital of the Kingdom of the Two Sicilies. The king fled without a fight. Just like that, Garibaldi controlled all of southern Italy.

Garibaldi's success made Cavour nervous. The prime minister worried that Garibaldi would establish a republic, an act that might cause European monarchs to invade Italy. Cavour sent Piedmontese troops south. Italy braced for another clash.

But no clash came. Garibaldi sincerely wanted Italy to become one nation. He handed over the newly freed territories to Victor Emmanuel, who became king of a united Italy. Garibaldi and the king rode through Naples in an open carriage, cheered by thousands.

Only the cities of Venice and Rome remained in foreign hands. In 1866, Venice broke away from Austria and joined Italy. Four years later, Victor Emmanuel marched into Rome and declared it his capital. The pope refused to accept the Italian government. He retired indignantly to a small section of Rome called Vatican City and vowed never to come out. Indeed, no pope set foot outside Vatican City again until 1929.

Garibaldi was disappointed that the nation he helped create turned out to be a monarchy rather than a republic. But he was overjoyed that Italy was at last one nation. He retired to his farm, where he continued to support democracy and workers' movements everywhere. When he died in 1882, he was buried under a simple granite tombstone, revered by his countrymen as the man who had made their nation.

- On the map on page 529, note the borders of Italy after unification.

Growing Nationalism in German Lands

Meanwhile, to the north of Italy, feelings of nationalism had also been growing among German-speaking people.

Until about 1800, the German-speaking people had never been united under one government. For centuries, most had lived within the borders of the Holy Roman Empire. That empire, however, was little more than a loose collection of separate states. People within the empire felt loyal chiefly to their own smaller kingdom or duchy. (A *duchy*, you recall, is a small territory ruled by a duke.)

Before Napoleon, the German-speaking people in the Holy Roman Empire did not feel a great sense of unity. They shared a language and some customs but did not think of themselves as belonging to one nation. But when Napoleon and his armies swept in, the Germans felt a new sense of unity in their opposition

Garibaldi rides through Naples in an open carriage alongside Victor Emmanuel, who would be crowned king of a united Italy. Even though Garibaldi longed for a republic, he accepted a monarchy for the sake of Italian unity.

Germany, c. 1848

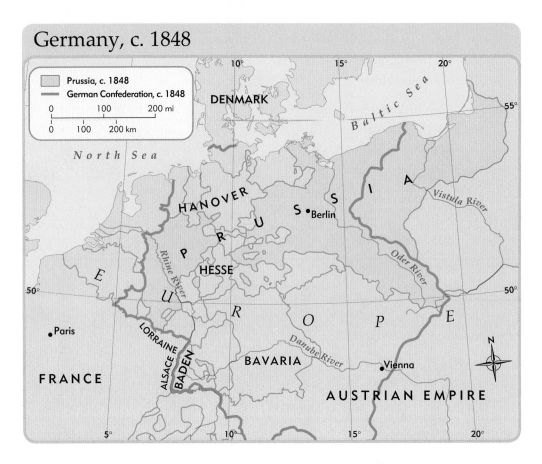

to the French. Napoleon's domination sparked a sense of German nationalism. Many people began to take pride in their German heritage and spirit.

Some Germans began to build on an idea proposed by German philosophers. These thinkers wrote

The Holy Roman Empire and Austria's Habsburgs

The Holy Roman Empire was a loosely organized group of territories in central and eastern Europe. Many people in the empire spoke German. Since 1438, the Holy Roman Emperor had been a member of the Habsburg family. In 1453, the Habsburgs made Austria the archduchy—the chief state—of the Holy Roman Empire. After that, Austria's importance grew. People began to speak of the "Austrian emperor" rather than the Holy Roman Emperor. Vienna, the capital of Austria and home of the emperor, became an important city.

that each nation has its own unique spirit, which they called the *volksgeist* (FOLKS-giyst)—the soul of the people. German nationalists argued that in a time when Napoleon and the French ruled German lands, it was more important than ever for the German people to tap into their volksgeist and express their unique national identity.

Even after Germans succeeded in driving Napoleon's troops from their soil, they were still divided. In 1815, the German-speaking people lived in 39 states ruled by various kings, princes, and dukes. The most powerful state was Austria. It was ruled by the Habsburg family, whose huge empire also included many non-Germans. The next most powerful state was Prussia. Other Germans lived in kingdoms such as Bavaria and Hanover, or duchies such as Baden (BAH-dn) or Hesse.

- On the map on page 532, note the numerous German-speaking states after the fall of Napoleon. Locate the Austrian Empire and Prussia.

Although the German-speaking people remained divided, their battles to oust Napoleon had done much to encourage nationalism. New feelings of German unity and patriotism lasted into peacetime and, like a great wave, began to sweep over the land. People began to take pride in being German, not just Prussian or Bavarian or Hessian.

Otto von Bismarck: Prussia's Iron Man

By the middle of the nineteenth century, a strong-willed, masterful politician from Prussia realized that he could forge the German states

into one nation. His name was Otto von Bismarck.

In 1862, the king of Prussia, Wilhelm I, appointed Bismarck as

Prussia's Otto von Bismarck wanted to unite several German states into a single German nation.

Folktales and the German *Volksgeist*

Two brothers, Jakob and Wilhelm Grimm, went looking for the German *volksgeist* among the people. The brothers were librarians and scholars who had written a German dictionary. They began collecting folktales to show that Germans had their own deeply rooted stories, myths, and wisdom.

The Grimms published their first book of folktales in 1812. Among the stories they collected are tales that we know by such titles as *Sleeping Beauty, Rapunzel,* and *Snow White.* They evoked a world of giants, dwarves, and wolves, and of strange sorcery unfolding in deep, dark woods. The stories reminded Germans of the land, literature, and spirit they shared. The tales of the Brothers Grimm have been translated into many languages and have enchanted children all over the world.

Title page of the Grimm fairy tale Snow White

his chancellor. (A chancellor is like a prime minister.) Pictures of Bismarck show a huge, square-shouldered man in a greatcoat. A gigantic moustache covers his grim mouth, and bushy eyebrows hang over stern eyes. It's hard to imagine him laughing. Bismarck once said, "Not by speeches and majority votes are the great questions of the day decided … but by blood and iron."

Bismarck presented himself as a simple country squire, gruff and bluff and honest. But he was every bit as cunning as Cavour. And he commanded a far more powerful state.

At the start of his career, Bismarck had no interest in unifying German lands. He only wanted to build a powerful Prussia. But Austria, the most powerful German-speaking state, stood between him and his goal.

Bismarck knew that Germans were talking of a unified German nation. He also saw that the smaller states might decide to join Austria instead of Prussia. The new Austrian emperor, Franz Josef, would be pleased to have the smaller German states on his side. If that happened, Prussia would be weakened. So Bismarck decided to act first.

Bismarck Unites the Germans

Bismarck laid his plans. He knew that he would have to work carefully to overcome Prussia's powerful rival, Austria. He strengthened the Prussian army and built up Prussia's industries. Under Bismarck, Prussia began producing more iron and building more railroads.

By 1866, Bismarck was ready. That year, he purposefully started a quarrel with Austria. Tension mounted until war broke out—exactly as Bismarck had planned. The Austrians didn't mind. They still saw Prussia as a weaker power that had been demolished by Napoleon. They intended to teach Bismarck a lesson.

But the Prussian army struck like lightning. Its troops had a new weapon, the needle gun, which could fire five times a minute. Prussian generals used railroads to move their troops rapidly into position. Prussia won the fight, known as the Seven Week War, before most of Europe realized it had begun.

This victory made Prussia the leading German state. Bismarck used his new prestige to form a confederation of German states. Twenty-two states joined, but Prussia had the most power.

Bismarck disliked democracy, but he knew that the German people wanted a voice in their government. He won them over by allowing their leaders to write a constitution and

Bismarck's Remarks

Bismarck was famous for his pointed remarks. Here are a few that reveal his personality and aims:

- "Better pointed bullets than pointed words."

- "People never lie so much as after a hunt, during a war, or before an election."

- "Laws are like sausages. It's better not to see them being made."

- "We Germans fear God, but nothing else."

- "The main thing is to make history, not to write it."

Prussian soldiers assemble during the Franco-Prussian War. Bismarck had picked this fight with France. He knew he had to defeat the French in order to unify Germany.

form a parliament. He let all male citizens vote for representatives to the lower house of this new parliament, called the *Reichstag* (RIYKS-tahk). Even in Great Britain at this time, less than half of all males were allowed to vote.

Although Bismarck gave all male citizens the right to vote, he made sure the Reichstag had little power. The king of Prussia—or more often, Bismarck acting in the king's name—could overrule all decisions made by the Reichstag.

A big question remained: How was Bismarck going to draw the remaining German states away from Austria? He decided that he needed another war. In 1870, he looked to France for a fight.

Defeating the French and Decreeing Germany

When Bismarck defeated Austria, Napoleon's nephew, Napoleon III, sat on the French throne. He kept a watchful eye on Prussia's maneuvers. He worried that unified German states would weaken France's power in Europe.

Napoleon III sent an ambassador to the town of Ems, where the Prussian king was on vacation. The ambassador and the king discussed certain issues between their countries. The king then sent Bismarck a telegram about their talks. Bismarck rewrote the telegram to make it sound as if the French ambassador and the Prussian king had insulted each other. He then published his version of what has become known as "the Ems telegram," sparking outrage among both French and Germans.

Napoleon III fell into the trap. On July 19, 1870, he declared war on Prussia. Nationalist feelings drew the many small German states to Prussia's side—after all, Germans still cursed the memory of Napoleon Bonaparte. This war took even less than seven weeks. On September 2, the main French army surrendered, handing over Napoleon III himself. The Prussians poured over France's border and laid siege to Paris.

Germany, c. 1871

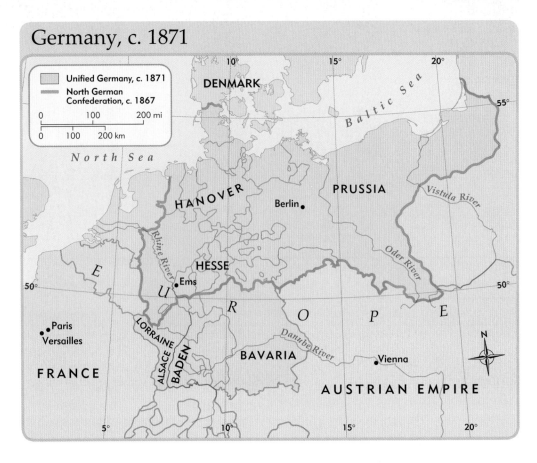

Legend:
- Unified Germany, c. 1871
- North German Confederation, c. 1867

0   100   200 mi
0   100   200 km

DENMARK

Baltic Sea

North Sea

HANOVER

PRUSSIA

Berlin

Vistula River

Rhine River

HESSE

Ems

Oder River

EUROPE

Paris
Versailles

LORRAINE

Danube River

ALSACE

BADEN

BAVARIA

Vienna

FRANCE

AUSTRIAN EMPIRE

Napoleon III surrenders his sword to the Prussian king, Wilhelm I. By this act, he acknowledged Prussia's victory in the Franco-Prussian War.

The German grip on the city was relentless. Inside Paris, food and supplies dwindled. Weeks passed, and the Parisians were reduced to eating rats. After four months, they surrendered their capital.

Meanwhile, at nearby Versailles, once the palace home of Louis XIV, Bismarck declared the birth of the German Empire. This nation included every German state except Austria. At last, German lands were united in a single country that could be called "Germany." Prussia led the new nation.

- On the map above, note the borders of Germany after unification.

Bismarck required France to pay Germany five billion gold francs. He also demanded that France turn over Alsace (al-SAS) and Lorraine (luh-RAYN), two mostly German-speaking provinces rich in coal and iron, which Bismarck wanted for German industries.

Bismarck's strategy quickly placed Germany at the center of

the European stage. Prussia's king became an emperor, or, as he called himself, the Kaiser. (*Kaiser* means "Caesar" in German.) He was Kaiser Wilhelm I.

For several more years, Bismarck continued to dominate Germany and the European scene. But in 1888, Wilhelm I died. The new Kaiser, Wilhelm II, wanted to rule without Bismarck's guidance. He pushed the chancellor to resign. "I am the big shadow that stands between him and the sun of fame," said Bismarck. He retired, leaving the country in the hands of Wilhelm II.

A New Map of Europe

The births of Italy and Germany changed the map of Europe. These new nations wiped away many little kingdoms, duchies, and city-states that European rulers had arranged after the fall of Napoleon. Little states that had covered much of the continent like jigsaw puzzle pieces were gone. Large, unified nations stood in their place.

Growing feelings of nationalism—strong attachment to one's own country—caused much of this change. Democratic revolutions also helped. People declared that they were tired of being ruled by dukes, princes, and nobles. And they were tired of being ruled by distant monarchs and royal families, such as the Habsburgs of Austria.

Europe was not the only place to be changed by these forces. Nationalism and democratic movements would continue to reshape the world in the century to come.

Bismarck (center, dressed in white) watches as Wilhelm I is crowned emperor, or kaiser, of Germany. In a final humiliation for France, the ceremony took place in the Hall of Mirrors at Versailles, once the palace of the kings of France.

Union soldiers (left) fight Confederates at Franklin, Tennessee. The American Civil War settled the question of whether the United States would remain one nation.

Civil War in the United States: A House Divided and Reunited

While Garibaldi and Bismarck struggled to unite new nations in Europe, another nation struggled for unity across the Atlantic Ocean.

Less than one hundred years earlier, thirteen colonies in North America had declared their independence from Britain and fought to become the United States of America. The young United States grew quickly. In 1803, Napoleon sold Americans a chunk of territory that stretched from the Mississippi River in the east to the Rocky Mountains in the west—in one stroke, the Louisiana Purchase more than doubled the country's size. Land-hungry pioneers pressed westward across the Appalachian Mountains. They clashed with Native American peoples. They cleared brush, felled trees, planted crops, and built towns.

Not long after the Louisiana Purchase, the United States wrested Florida away from Spain. Then, in the 1840s, the United States battled Mexico. When the fighting ended, the United States owned everything from Texas to California. After another purchase from Mexico and a treaty with Great Britain, the United States stretched from the Atlantic Ocean to the Pacific—in the words of the familiar song, "from sea to shining sea."

- On the map on page 540, note the growth of the United States between the nation's founding and 1853.

By the mid-1800s, Americans had settled half the continent and were still pushing west. No republic had ever been so large. But, as history has repeatedly shown, at least

This chapter focuses on the American Civil War in the nineteenth century.

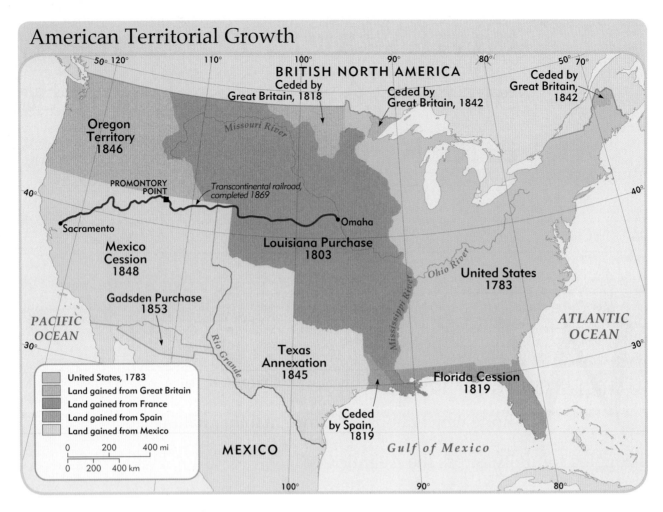

American Territorial Growth

BRITISH NORTH AMERICA
Ceded by Great Britain, 1818
Ceded by Great Britain, 1842
Ceded by Great Britain, 1842

Oregon Territory 1846

Missouri River

PROMONTORY POINT

Transcontinental railroad, completed 1869

Sacramento

Omaha

Mexico Cession 1848

Louisiana Purchase 1803

Ohio River

United States 1783

Gadsden Purchase 1853

PACIFIC OCEAN

Rio Grande

Mississippi River

ATLANTIC OCEAN

Texas Annexation 1845

Florida Cession 1819

Ceded by Spain, 1819

MEXICO

Gulf of Mexico

United States, 1783
Land gained from Great Britain
Land gained from France
Land gained from Spain
Land gained from Mexico

0   200   400 mi
0   200   400 km

since the times of ancient Rome, size brings its own challenges. The United States faced a challenge that threatened to undermine its unity as a nation.

One Nation or Two?

This huge new republic had a glaring flaw. Although founded on the principles of equality, liberty, and natural rights, it continued to allow slavery. The British had abolished the slave trade in 1807 and made slavery illegal in 1833. Many Latin American nations had outlawed slavery in the 1810s and 1820s. But in parts of the United States, the terrible practice persisted.

Since the early 1800s, abolitionists in the northern United States had worked to end slavery. By the mid-1800s, most northern states had made it illegal. Their economies did not depend on slavery.

The Industrial Revolution was changing the North. Businessmen were building textile mills and other factories that churned out machine-made goods. Most Northerners still lived on small farms, but immigrants were flooding into northern cities to take factory jobs or dig canals. By 1860, New York had more than a million people. Philadelphia had more than half a million. In and around these northern cities, smokestacks, railroad tracks, and the clatter of machinery abounded.

But in America's South, with its tobacco and cotton plantations, slavery remained in place. In 1860, there were 15 slave states in the American

Northern cities were centers of industry in the years before the Civil War. Pittsburgh, Pennsylvania (left), was known as "Iron City" because it produced a great deal of iron.

republic. In those states, millions of black people were the legal property of their owners.

The South remained largely rooted in agriculture. Its largest city, New Orleans, had fewer than 170,000 people. Its second-largest city, Charleston, had fewer than 40,000. Plantations covered much of the South. On large plantations, hundreds of slaves did the work. The wealthiest plantation-owning families owned much of the land in the South.

In colonial days, southern plantations first grew tobacco, rice, and indigo. When the Industrial Revolution produced a booming textile industry in Great Britain, southern plantation owners turned to growing cotton. British factory owners wanted to buy all the American cotton they could get. Southern plantation owners were happy to oblige, especially (as you've seen) after the invention of the cotton gin made cotton farming a very profitable business.

Agriculture was the basis of the economy in the South. Plantation owners used slave labor to grow cotton, which they shipped to textile mills in northern states and Great Britain.

With slaves to do the difficult work of planting and picking, the South could send shipload after shipload of cotton to British factories. Southerners liked to say, "Cotton is king!" Indeed, cotton brought more money into the United States than all other exports combined.

Two Leaders, Two Paths

In the United States in the mid-1800s, the careers of two men illustrate the growing split between northern and southern ways of life. Abraham Lincoln and Jefferson Davis were both born in Kentucky, about a hundred miles from each other. From this common starting point, their paths diverged.

Davis's parents moved south to Mississippi when he was a boy. There his father and uncle bought land and slaves and went into farming. Davis's uncle built his holdings into a plantation, and Jefferson Davis grew up as a southern gentleman.

When Davis came of age, he joined the army. He was known as a determined, honorable man. Once, he entered a contest of wills with an army colonel who considered Davis too lowly to court his daughter. Davis married the daughter anyway, and the colonel—Zachary Taylor—went on to become the twelfth President of the United States. Later in life, Davis was elected to the United States Senate. By that time, many people in the North wanted to stop the spread of slavery to new territories.

Davis and others spoke out against such demands. Instead of defending slavery, however, they talked about states' rights. They insisted that the federal government could not force its laws onto the states. They said that each state had the right to decide which federal laws to obey, and which not. Davis and others claimed that the states were independent powers. As they saw it, the United States was united only as a kind of confederation, a grouping to which all the states belonged by their own choice.

Uncle Tom's Cabin

Harriet Beecher Stowe hoped to see an end to slavery in her lifetime. Stowe was the daughter of a New England minister and lived for 18 years in the border state of Ohio, where she met fugitive slaves and grew to hate slavery. In 1852, she published her antislavery novel, *Uncle Tom's Cabin.* The book quickly became a best-seller in the United States and Great Britain.

Harriet Beecher Stowe

The novel shows the trials of a dignified, elderly slave named Tom, who is bought and sold to three different masters. Tom dies after his third master has him beaten for refusing to tell where runaway slaves are hiding. The tale of Tom's sufferings moved many people to oppose slavery.

Stowe believed slavery was America's "national sin." She hoped that by showing the evils of slavery, her novel would help bring about a peaceful end to slavery in the United States. In fact, the book increased anger and suspicion between North and South. The book was celebrated in the North, but harshly criticized by Southerners as an unjust and inaccurate portrayal of slave life.

In contrast to Davis, Abraham Lincoln was born to parents who had little besides their ability to work and the land they tilled. When he was young, they moved north to Illinois. Lincoln grew up in the backwoods. There, he taught himself to read and write. As a young man, he impressed crowds by winning wood-chopping contests and other feats of strength. He joined a debating society and gained a reputation for his quick mind, sharp tongue, and dry sense of humor. He ran for the state legislature and won four terms.

In 1858, Lincoln ran for the U.S. Senate from Illinois. In a series of public meetings, he and his opponent Stephen Douglas debated the issues of slavery and states' rights. Lincoln bluntly called slavery "a moral, social, and political evil." The United States, he said, was one country, and final power on the issue of slavery belonged not to the states but to the national government. Quoting the Bible, he said that "a house divided against itself cannot stand." He predicted that the United States would become either a nation in which slavery was legal in all states, or a nation in which slavery was illegal in all states.

Lincoln lost the Senate race, but the campaign brought him national attention. In 1860, he was elected president of the United States. Lincoln's election alarmed southern leaders. One by one, southern states seceded—that is, they withdrew from the United States.

Jefferson Davis explained why, in an emotional speech to his fellow senators. Davis said he loved the United States but owed his first loyalty to his state, Mississippi. The people of Mississippi, he said, wanted only what the colonists had fought for in the American Revolution—self-rule.

A few weeks later, Davis received a message. The breakaway states had formed a new country, the Confederate States of America. They wanted Davis to be president of the Confederacy.

Abraham Lincoln debates Stephen Douglas during his race for the U.S. Senate in 1858. Lincoln called slavery "a moral, social, and political evil." When he won the U.S. presidency two years later, southern states seceded from the Union.

The United States During the Civil War

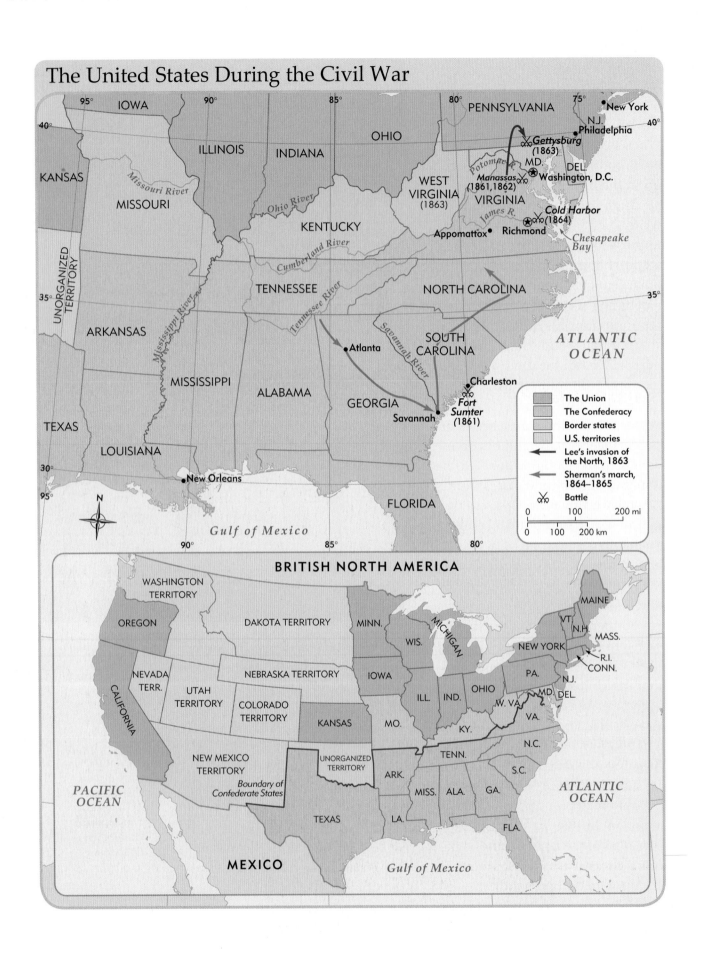

IOWA 95° 90° 85° 80° 75° **New York**

PENNSYLVANIA

40° N.J.

ILLINOIS **INDIANA** **OHIO** Philadelphia

KANSAS

Gettysburg (1863)

Missouri River

MISSOURI **WEST** MD. DEL.

VIRGINIA Potomac R. Manassas Washington, D.C.

Ohio River (1863) (1861,1862)

KENTUCKY **VIRGINIA** James R. Cold Harbor (1864)

Cumberland River Appomattox Richmond Chesapeake Bay

35° UNORGANIZED TERRITORY 35°

TENNESSEE **NORTH CAROLINA**

Tennessee River

ARKANSAS Savannah River

SOUTH **ATLANTIC OCEAN**

CAROLINA

Atlanta

MISSISSIPPI Charleston

ALABAMA

TEXAS **GEORGIA** Fort Sumter (1861)

Savannah

LOUISIANA

30°

New Orleans

95° **FLORIDA**

N

Gulf of Mexico 90° 85° 80°

	The Union
	The Confederacy
	Border states
	U.S. territories
←	Lee's invasion of the North, 1863
→	Sherman's march, 1864–1865
✗	Battle

0 100 200 mi

0 100 200 km

BRITISH NORTH AMERICA

WASHINGTON TERRITORY **MAINE**

OREGON **DAKOTA TERRITORY** **MINN.** MICHIGAN VT. N.H. MASS.

WIS. **NEW YORK** R.I.

NEVADA **NEBRASKA TERRITORY** IOWA PA. CONN.

TERR. **UTAH** N.J.

CALIFORNIA **TERRITORY** **COLORADO** ILL. IND. OHIO MD. DEL.

TERRITORY **KANSAS** MO. W. VA. VA.

KY.

N.C.

NEW MEXICO **UNORGANIZED** TENN.

TERRITORY **TERRITORY** ARK. S.C.

Boundary of MISS. ALA. GA.

PACIFIC Confederate States **ATLANTIC**

OCEAN TEXAS LA. **OCEAN**

FLA.

MEXICO Gulf of Mexico

The American Civil War began in April 1861 when Confederate forces bombarded Fort Sumter in Charleston, South Carolina.

The Civil War Begins

By the time Abraham Lincoln was sworn into office as president, seven southern states had seceded. Some people said Lincoln should let them go and just try to hold the remaining states together. Lincoln never considered that course. He declared the secession a rebellion. He dedicated himself to preserving the Union—to keeping the United States united as one nation. (People who opposed the southern states' secession often referred to the United States as "the Union.")

On April 12, 1861, Confederate troops fired on Fort Sumter, a federal post in Charleston, South Carolina. With those shots, the war began. Four more southern states seceded, bringing the total of Confederate states to eleven.

Twenty-three states fought for the Union. Four of them—Delaware, Maryland, Kentucky, and Missouri—were states that bordered the Confederacy. In those states, slavery remained legal.

• On the map on page 544, locate the Confederate states and the states that remained in the Union. Also locate the border slave states that remained loyal to the Union.

Both sides quickly formed armies. Both sides believed the war would be short. The North had good reason for confidence. It had more than five times as many factories as the South. It had more money. It had over twenty-two million people. Only nine million people lived in the South and of those, three and a half million were slaves. Confident Northerners thought: How can we lose?

Yet the South felt confident, too. The North would have to invade the South to impose its will. Confederate soldiers would be fighting on familiar ground. Moreover, the South had many fine generals, including Robert E. Lee, the brilliant commander who took charge of Confederate forces.

General Robert E. Lee became commander of the Confederate forces.

The Confederates chose Richmond, Virginia, as their capital. It lay only 100 miles from Washington, D.C. In late July 1861, a large Union army marched out of Washington to Virginia. A southern force met it near the town of Manassas, Virginia.

Black Troops Fight for the Union

Early in the Civil War, thousands of black men wanted to join the Union army. But they couldn't—the Union army would not accept blacks. The eloquent black abolitionist, Frederick Douglass, expressed his disbelief that Union leaders would "refuse to receive the very class of men which has a deeper interest in the defeat and humiliation of the rebels than all others.... Such is the pride, the stupid prejudice and folly that rules the hour."

In 1863, after the Emancipation Proclamation, the northern army allowed black soldiers to join the fight. In all, 180,000 black soldiers served in army combat regiments, and another 20,000 served in the navy. There were 166 black regiments in the army. By war's end, those regiments had fought in nearly five hundred battles, and many became renowned for their heroism.

African American soldiers on duty at a Union fort defending Washington, D.C.

On that Sunday, fashionable folks from Washington rode into the countryside with picnic lunches to watch the battle, as if it were a sporting event. They expected to see the South crushed and the rebellion ended. Instead, they saw Confederate soldiers rout the Union army. Close to five thousand men were killed or wounded. The Battle of Manassas drove home a shocking truth—this war would not be quick or easy. Something terrible had begun.

The War Takes On New Meaning

Over the next two years, Lincoln kept replacing his generals, who could not seem to win decisive victories. Meanwhile, General Lee and his Confederate officers kept winning battle after bloody battle.

European nations began to consider taking sides. Great Britain—which had abolished both slavery and the slave trade—leaned toward aiding the South. Why? Because the South supplied its cotton. The British public opposed slavery, but for the moment economic interests outweighed all other arguments.

In January 1863, Lincoln signed the Emancipation Proclamation. This order proclaimed that all slaves in rebellious states were now free and invited them to join the Union army. Prior to this time, Lincoln had insisted that his main goal was not to end slavery but to preserve the Union. With the Emancipation Proclamation, however, Lincoln was in effect declaring that the war was not only about keeping the United States together, but also about ending slavery.

After the Emancipation Proclamation, European nations, including Great Britain, hesitated to aid the South. Few nations wanted to be seen as siding with states that were fighting to preserve slavery. The South would have to win the war without foreign assistance.

Lincoln's Vision at Gettysburg

After the start of the Civil War, the North's navy began a blockade of southern ports. No cotton could get out; no supplies could get in. Lee saw himself in a race against time. A long war would wear down the South. So he took a daring gamble. He decided to invade the North. If he could defeat the Union army on northern soil, then perhaps Lincoln would be forced to call an end to the war.

Lee made it into Pennsylvania, but there, near the town of Gettysburg, a northern army met him. A great battle raged for three days. Both sides suffered staggering losses—some fifty thousand men were killed or wounded. Lee was forced to retreat; the tide of the war had turned.

Later that year, Abraham Lincoln attended a ceremony at Gettysburg to honor the Union soldiers who had died there. A former senator and secretary of state, Edward Everett, opened the ceremonies. He gave a two-hour speech.

Then President Lincoln took the podium. He spoke for about two minutes. Lincoln's speech was over before many in the crowd realized it had begun. They went away disappointed. The next morning, however, the Gettysburg Address, as it has

A French newspaper published this engraving of blacks celebrating the Emancipation Proclamation. Once the North made the Civil War a fight against slavery, European nations were unwilling to support the South.

become known, was printed in a newspaper. Then it was reprinted in many other newspapers. Slowly the nation came to realize that the president had expressed something of immense significance. In less than 300 words, not only had Lincoln explained the war, but he had also set forth a powerful vision of the meaning of the United States.

European nationalists, such as Italy's Mazzini, had said that a nation is held together by things its people share—their language, their spirit, their common history and culture. Lincoln declared that this nation, the United States, was bound together by a powerful idea— "the proposition," as he put it, "that all men are created equal." Slavery had no place in this land. The United States embodied a dream that a government "of the people, by the people, and for the people" could really work. That dream, Lincoln firmly resolved, "shall not perish from the earth."

The Gettysburg Address

Abraham Lincoln's Gettysburg Address, delivered November 19, 1863, envisions the United States as a nation dedicated to the principle that "all men are created equal."

A Page from the Past

Four score and seven years ago, our fathers brought forth on this continent, a new nation, conceived in liberty, and dedicated to the proposition that all men are created equal.

Now we are engaged in a great civil war, testing whether that nation, or any nation so conceived and so dedicated, can long endure. We are met on a great battlefield of that war. We have come to dedicate a portion of that field, as a final resting place for those who here gave their lives that that nation might live. It is altogether fitting and proper that we should do this.

President Lincoln delivers a speech in honor of Union troops killed at the battle of Gettysburg. The Gettysburg Address lasted only two minutes.

But in a larger sense we can not dedicate, we can not consecrate, we can not hallow this ground. The brave men, living and dead, who struggled here, have consecrated it far above our poor power to add or detract. The world will little note, nor long remember, what we say here, but it can never forget what they did here. It is for us the living, rather, to be dedicated here to the unfinished work which they who fought here have thus far so nobly advanced. It is rather for us to be here dedicated to the great task remaining before us—that from these honored dead we take increased devotion to that cause for which they gave the last full measure of devotion—that we here highly resolve that these dead shall not have died in vain—that this nation, under God, shall have a new birth of freedom—and that government of the people, by the people, for the people, shall not perish from the earth.

Grant Takes Charge

After Gettysburg, the bloodshed continued for almost two more years. But Lincoln had finally found his general—Ulysses S. Grant.

In Grant, the North had a general as gifted as Lee—but how different the two men were. The dignified Lee dressed elegantly, spoke eloquently, and impressed all with his fine manners. Grant could not be bothered with refinement. He groomed his horse better than he did himself. He said little and when he spoke, he kept it short. When asked about his philosophy of war, he said, "Find out where your enemy is … strike him as hard as you can, and keep moving on."

Grant sent General William Tecumseh Sherman into Georgia and the Carolinas. Sherman burned the city of Atlanta, marched east to Savannah, then turned north, destroying everything in his path.

Meanwhile, Grant captured Petersburg and then Richmond. Confident of victory, Abraham Lincoln visited the vanquished Confederate capital, escorted by an all-black Union cavalry. Then Grant trapped Lee near Appomattox, Virginia.

Outnumbered five to one, Lee knew there was no point in fighting on. On April 9, 1865, he put on his finest dress uniform, a silk sash, and a jeweled sword. Then he surrendered to a grim, mud-spattered Grant. The war had ended.

The First Modern War

The American Civil War was in many ways the world's first modern war. The death toll was staggering. The factories and inventions of the Industrial Revolution had made it possible. They produced a new kind of war, and that war spurred still more industrial growth.

Factories mass-produced uniforms, shoes, and bullets. They also made lethal new weapons—exploding artillery shells, guns that soldiers could load and fire quickly, cannons that shot farther than ever before. During the Civil War, ironmasters turned to new tasks: producing ironclad warships, land and water mines, and a submarine that could sink a warship.

This new modern warfare also relied on advances in transportation. Trains moved massive armies and their equipment to and from battlefields. Lincoln pushed Congress to complete a transcontinental railroad as soon as possible. The North even experimented with conducting war from the air when it sent balloons aloft to spy on enemy terrain.

Above: Ulysses S. Grant realized that if he kept hurling troops against the Confederate armies, he would eventually wear them down.

Below: Union forces under General William Tecumseh Sherman burned Atlanta, Georgia.

Both North and South used huge, deadly guns like this Confederate cannon captured by Sherman near Savannah, Georgia.

fighting left more than 620,000 people dead of wounds or disease, and many more disabled for life.

By comparison, earlier European warfare seemed to resemble a chess game fought by well-drilled armies moving in precise formations. The Civil War ended all that. It gave birth to the concept of "total war." From now on, clashing nations would go all out to defeat the enemy. Armies would bomb cities, destroy farms, and uproot railroads. War would pit whole societies against each other, not just their armies.

The Civil War was the first modern war in another way—it was the first war that reporters widely covered. Newspapers in both the North and South were eager to give their readers information about the fighting. Thanks to the telegraph, reporters could quickly get news to their papers.

The Civil War brought something else new to wartime—photographs from the front. In the 1830s, a Frenchman named Louis J.M. Daguerre (dah-GAIR) had developed the first practical form of photography. His camera was bulky and his subjects had to sit perfectly still, at first for 20 to 30 minutes! These images, called daguerreotypes (duh-GEH-roh-tiyps), became very popular in the United States.

New weapons and new ways to transport troops gave armies the ability to inflict terrible damage on each other. The Battle of Gettysburg, where 165,000 soldiers clashed on a single field, was the biggest battle the Western Hemisphere had ever seen. In 1864, at Cold Harbor, Virginia, 8,500 men were killed in eight bloody minutes. The four years of

By the time of the Civil War, photography had become more advanced, but journalists still had to haul big, clumsy cameras to the front. They took pictures of soldiers in camps or of battlefield carnage. This new technology made it possible for people far from the fighting to see what war looked like.

Bismarck Learns a Lesson

In Prussia, Otto von Bismarck studied tactics used in the American Civil War. He eagerly read reports about how the North and the South used railroads to move their armies quickly into position. He later used this lesson to beat Austria and crush France. By encouraging the construction of railroads and rapidly mobilizing Prussian troops by rail, he was able to defeat foreign foes and achieve German unification.

Looking to the Future

The United States came out of the war dramatically transformed and, considering the extent of the carnage, strangely renewed. Much of the South had been devastated— crops burned, railroads torn up, towns destroyed. Yet the United States was still a country with lots of land and resources. For four years, factories had concentrated on making guns, ammunition, uniforms, and other goods for war. Americans had grown very adept at making things. Now, with war behind them, they could turn to producing new railroads, bridges, ships, buildings— all the things the country needed to grow. The United States was becoming a great economic power in the Industrial Revolution.

The war settled the issue of whether the United States would be one nation or two. The Union had survived. The war also answered the important question of whether slavery had a place in this republic. In December 1865, Americans added the 13th Amendment to the Constitution. It said that slavery was illegal in the United States. The nation committed itself to upholding the idea that all men—not just propertied men or white men—were born with basic rights, including the right to life and liberty. Five years later another amendment to the Constitution gave black men the right to vote.

During the Civil War, photography brought the horrors of the battlefield home to the public. Above, a photograph shows some of the dead at Gettysburg.

Clara Barton, who later founded the American Red Cross, served as a volunteer nurse for Union forces. She was called the Angel of the Battlefield.

The Civil War also changed the roles of women in American society. During the war, some women served as battlefield nurses and hospital volunteers. Others organized fund-raising fairs and formed local soldier aid societies that sewed uniforms and gathered medical supplies. More women entered the work force. They labored as government clerks, visitors to military camps, and even as spies. Northern women were among the leaders of the abolitionist movement, too. Lincoln issued the Emancipation Proclamation partly in response to the urging of that movement.

Just as many Americans came to appreciate the heroism of black soldiers, many also came to recognize the valuable wartime contributions of women. For their sacrifices and efforts, some said, women had earned a political voice. Many women began to develop new ideas about liberty and equal rights for the female half of the nation's population. But while black men won the vote in 1865, American women would have to wait until 1920.

It took a long time for the wounds of the Civil War to heal, especially in the South, where the fighting had caused so much destruction. The southern way of life—with its plantations, aristocracy, and slaves—was gone. Once-wealthy landowners now had to rethink and rebuild. Four million former slaves faced the challenge of making new lives for themselves. In the South, the land of their former captivity, they would face racial prejudice and the economic hardship of scratching out a living in a region devastated by war.

A Railroad Links the Land

Gradually the bitterness left by the Civil War began to fade. The 11 southern states that had seceded were readmitted to the Union. Congress passed laws that attempted to protect the rights of former slaves and guarantee them the right to vote. (It would take many years for some of those

Slavery and Serfdom Worldwide

Americans amended their Constitution in 1865 to make slavery illegal. By 1860, most western European nations had outlawed slavery. The exception was Russia, where most of the people were enslaved as serfs. In 1861, however, Russia's Tsar Alexander II realized that if his country was ever going to catch up with the West, it had to end serfdom. So he freed Russia's serfs. It would take years for Russia's peasants to achieve true freedom, but at least the institution of serfdom had officially ended.

In South America, most nations made slavery illegal by 1860. The exception was Brazil, where slavery was legal until the 1880s.

In much of the Muslim world, the slave trade continued through the nineteenth century. In China, slavery became illegal in 1906.

laws to be put into practice.) Farms and factories in the North prospered. The railroad industry boomed.

In 1869, something happened that connected the people of the United States as never before. The country built a railroad across the Rocky Mountains to the Pacific coast. Americans could say with pride that this transcontinental railroad was the first to link a continent. Suddenly citizens of the United States could ride the rails from one side of their vast nation to the other.

Let's take a closer look at this remarkable feat of engineering that helped pull the United States together in the wake of the Civil War.

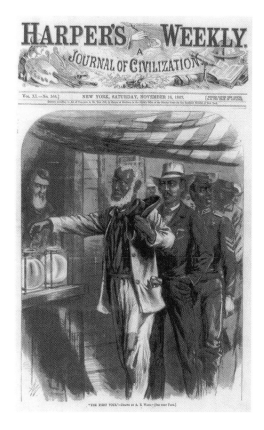

After the Civil War, former slaves were able to vote in elections for the first time. Harper's Weekly *was a popular magazine during the nineteenth century. This issue appeared in 1867.*

A Big Day at Promontory Point

Promontory Point, Utah, was a high, dry, desolate little town, its one street lined by a handful of rough wooden shacks and tents, with nothing much else besides sagebrush and scrubby cedars. It was an unlikely spot for a grand celebration.

But on May 10, 1869, a boisterous crowd gathered at Promontory Point for what the *New York Times* called "the completion of the greatest enterprise ever yet undertaken"—the building of a railroad across the United States— a *transcontinental* railroad.

Two locomotives faced each other on the track—one looking east, the other looking west. The Stars and Stripes waved in the breeze, and a brass band struck up a tune as the last two rails were carried forward. One was carried by a crew of Chinese workmen from the Central Pacific Railroad Company, the other by Irish laborers from the Union Pacific. Executives of the two rival railroads stood by, looking out of place in their silk hats and formal suits.

A final spike sat ready to be hammered into the last tie—not an ordinary iron spike, but one made of California gold. Leland Stanford, president of the Central Pacific, raised a silver-headed sledgehammer.

Historical Close-up

The crowd pressed forward. Newspaper reporters elbowed each other out of the way. And all across the nation, so recently ripped apart by war, Americans waited eagerly for the telegraph signal to tell them they were now linked from east to west by rail.

Before the transcontinental railroad, a journey from coast to coast took months. Travelers rattled west in stagecoaches or covered wagons. Some rode mules on the rough trails, or even trudged on foot across icy mountain passes and endless plains. Ruthless bandits, hostile Indians, stampeding herds of wild buffalo—danger came from all directions, and many who started the trek did not survive.

In the 1830s, when railroads were still new in the United States, a few visionaries dreamed of running trains from San Francisco to New York. Most people thought they were crazy. Lay tracks across thousands of miles of empty prairie, over mountain ranges, through unknown territory? Who could possibly accomplish such a feat? As one member of Congress said, they might as well try to build a railroad to the moon.

But over the next couple of decades, a great deal changed. Trains turned out to be a quick, cheap, easy way of moving goods and people. Soon a web of railroad lines spread across the industrial East, reaching as far as the Missouri River. Then, in 1849, the discovery of gold in California set off the Gold Rush. With hordes of frenzied treasure seekers heading west, the notion of building a transcontinental railroad didn't sound so crazy anymore.

But what route would it take? Northern politicians wanted the railroad to run through northern states. Southern politicians wanted it to take a southern route. For years, Congress couldn't make up its mind.

Then came the Civil War. When the southern states seceded, their representatives and senators resigned from Congress. No one was left to oppose a northern route. And the need to keep the distant state of California loyal to the Union gave the project a new urgency. On July 1, 1862, President Lincoln signed into law the Pacific Railroad Act—"An Act to aid in the Construction of a Railroad and Telegraph Line from the Missouri River to the Pacific Ocean, and to secure to the Government the Use of the same for Postal, Military, and Other Purposes."

The Pacific Railroad Act said that two companies would build at the same time. The Union Pacific Company would start where the current railroad stopped at the Missouri River, and work west. The Central Pacific Company would start in California and work east.

In fact, the Central Pacific had already started. But it hadn't gotten very far. A massive obstacle stood in the way, like a wall of granite shutting California off from the rest of the continent—the Sierra Nevada. The mountain range's glacier-wrapped peaks were too steep and treacherous for any railroad track. The builders would have to cut into the mountainside and blast tunnels through the granite. No one had ever tried anything like it before.

Two thousand workers signed on and rode the Central Pacific train to the Sierra. Most just wanted a free ride to the Nevada silver mines, where they hoped to strike it rich. After one week on the job, fewer than a hundred men remained.

Who would build the railroad? One of the company directors had a suggestion. Many Chinese immigrants had recently arrived in California. Why not hire them to work on the Central Pacific?

At first, Irish railroad bosses doubted these small, slender men could do the job. But the Chinese soon proved to be steady workers who did just as much, or more, than any other crew.

Workers building the Central Pacific Railroad blast their way through rugged terrain. Many of the railroad workers in the West were immigrants from China.

Their skill and courage met a challenge in the three-mile stretch of sheer cliff nicknamed Cape Horn. For the railroad to continue, somehow a track must be blasted into the side of the cliff. Experienced engineers said it could not be done.

Yes, it could, said the Chinese workers—but they would need some reeds from San Francisco. When the reeds arrived, they wove them into baskets. They tied ropes to the baskets and lowered each other down.

Dangling 2,200 feet above the American River, the fearless workers drilled holes in the cliff, pushed in black explosive powder (invented in China), lit the fuse, and signaled to be hauled back up. Usually, they made it up before the explosion. Sometimes, they didn't.

The Pacific Railway Act gave the Central Pacific the right to build only as far as the California-Nevada border. The company protested: If they conquered the Sierra before their competitors reached California, why should they stop there? Why not keep on laying tracks—and winning huge amounts of land and money from the government—until the two railroads met?

Congress amended the Pacific Railway Act. Each company was now allowed to build as far and as fast as it could. The race was on.

The Union Pacific had the advantage of laying its first tracks along the flat, open prairie. Still, if their route lacked obstacles, it also lacked everything else the workers needed—lumber for the railroad ties, iron for the rails, tools and supplies of all kinds, and most of all, water.

How could they transport huge quantities of heavy items over such a distance? The construction boss, a former Civil War general named Jack Casement, came up with an ingenious solution. They could use the very tracks the men were building. The first car of his "Casement train" was a sturdy platform loaded with 700-pound iron rails to build the track. More cars followed—one for tools, one for spikes and bolts, and so on. There was a dining car with tables and a kitchen, and a car with built-in bunks where the men could sleep in rough weather.

General Casement ran his operation like an army. Fortunately, many of his men—who included immigrants from Ireland, Sweden, and Germany, as well as former slaves—had also fought in the war, so they were used to taking orders and working as a team. Sadly, they also needed their military skills for skirmishes against the Sioux and Cheyenne, whose hunting grounds were being destroyed by the advance of the railroad.

As the space between the two competing railroads shrank, the companies pushed their crews to work harder and faster. The Central Pacific set a record when its workers laid five miles of track in one day. Not to be outdone, the Union Pacific laid six, then seven and a half, then eight and a half. Finally, a crew of "iron men" from the Central Pacific laid a full ten miles in a single day, even stopping an hour for lunch.

The Union Pacific couldn't break the record of the "Ten Mile Day" because by this time the two sets of tracks were less than nine miles apart. Twelve days later, the railroads met at Promontory Point for the great celebration.

As the golden spike slipped into place, a telegraph operator tapped out the one-word message that sped to distant cities and towns: "Done." The facing locomotives inched closer and closer, until the drivers could reach out to shake hands. From the Atlantic coast to the Pacific coast, the American people were now linked by the transcontinental railroad.

Americans went wild. New York, Chicago, San Francisco—all over the nation, church bells pealed and cannons boomed. Throngs of people filled the streets, shouting and singing. For the first time ever, railroad tracks spanned a continent, and seemed to promise new unity for a war-torn nation.

The meeting of the Central Pacific and Union Pacific Railroads in 1869 helped Americans feel more united during the years following the Civil War.

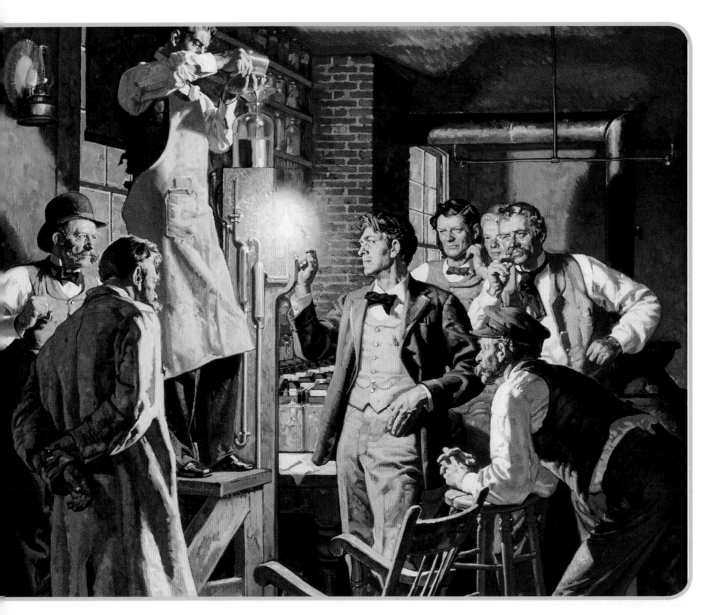

Thomas Edison (center) and his associates test a new lamp at the "invention factory" in Menlo Park, New Jersey. Edison was the greatest inventor in the Age of Innovation.

An Age of Innovation

During the late nineteenth century, many people in Europe and the United States looked to the future with optimism. They hoped that they had put war and turmoil behind them. Germany and Italy had gone through struggles to unify their nations. The United States had endured its bloody Civil War. After so many struggles, people looked forward to times of peace and prosperity.

Hopes for a better future were fueled in part by advances in technology. By the late nineteenth century, the marvels of the Industrial Revolution—steam power, railroads, the telegraph—had become part of everyday life, taken for granted. But all across Europe and the United States, people were tinkering in workshops and laboratories, paving the way for what would amount to a second industrial revolution.

The late 1800s gave us many of the advances that are part of the world we know today—electric lights, telephones, automobiles. Historians sometimes call this period the Age of Innovation.

A Second Industrial Revolution: From Iron to Steel

The first Industrial Revolution was built largely on iron. Steam engines, machine parts, railroad tracks, pipes, bridges—all were made of iron. While iron was strong, it was not an ideal material for building. It was often difficult to shape precisely. High winds and heavy loads could crack bridges made of iron. So inventors began to look to another material—steel.

Steel is made mostly of iron, but it's lighter, stronger, and more flexible than iron. It was not a new invention in the nineteenth century.

Completed in 1890, the Forth Bridge, a railway bridge in Scotland, was the first bridge in Britain to be built of steel.

Steel-making was known in ancient Egypt, India, and China. For centuries, Japanese and Middle Eastern smiths had made swords of steel. Medieval Europeans tried to use it in their knights' armor. But steel was hard to produce, and therefore very expensive.

In 1856, an Englishman named Henry Bessemer invented a special furnace that could cheaply turn iron into steel. In 1861, a German-born inventor named Charles William Siemens pioneered a process for making steel in a gas furnace. Now steel could be made in large quantities.

Soon railroads began using steel for their tracks. In Scotland, after the disastrous collapse of a railway bridge made of wrought iron, engineers building another bridge decided instead to use steel. The Forth Bridge, just west of Edinburgh, Scotland's capital city, was completed in 1890. An engineering marvel, it was the first bridge in Britain to be made of steel.

With steel, industrial nations experienced a second industrial revolution. They could build bigger factories with more powerful machines to make more goods than ever before. Steel could be formed into exact

shapes much more easily than iron. That made it perfect for complicated machinery and fine tools with sharp edges, such as saws.

German companies proved especially good at using steel to build precision machinery. Steel helped Germany catch up to Britain as an industrial power. Soon, however, both Britain and Germany were surpassed in steel production by another country—the United States, largely because of the efforts of a business genius named Andrew Carnegie (KAHR-nuh-gee).

Andrew Carnegie: Man of Steel

Andrew Carnegie was born in Scotland into desperate poverty. His father was a weaver, but the mechanized loom did away with his job. Seeing his father beg for work, the boy vowed never to end up the same.

After his family moved to the United States in 1848, Andrew found a job working in a cotton factory. Later he became a messenger boy in a telegraph office. Eventually he worked his way up to supervisor on the Pennsylvania Railroad. During the Civil War, he helped the Union army organize railroad and telegraph operations.

When the war ended, Carnegie went into business making iron bridges. But he realized that steel was the building material of the future. He invested everything he owned into forming a steel company.

Carnegie wanted to make and sell lots of steel easily. So he bought not only steel mills but also iron ore deposits that supplied the raw materials for making steel. He also bought railroads and ships to transport those materials.

By 1900, his company, Carnegie Steel, was outproducing all of the steel mills in Great Britain. Carnegie Steel helped turn the United States into an economic power during the second industrial revolution. (In a later chapter, you'll read more about how Carnegie treated workers and how he spent his fortune.)

New Sources of Energy: Petroleum and Electricity

As steel replaced iron, people also began looking for new fuels. They wanted new sources of energy to run the increasing numbers of factories and machines, and to provide heat for homes in growing cities.

They saw promise in petroleum, a liquid mineral found beneath the ground. Petroleum could be processed into flammable liquids such as gasoline and kerosene. These fuels were easier to transport than coal, wood, and other solid fuels, and they burned far more readily. In the late nineteenth century, kerosene lamps became a popular source of lighting.

Gasoline burned almost too easily—it could explode if not handled carefully. Some people used small amounts in cooking stoves, but most had no practical use for it. Nevertheless, gasoline fascinated inventors, and they tried to figure out how to make good use of it. As we'll see later in this chapter, gasoline soon became an important fuel.

Electricity sparked the most widespread interest as a source of energy. While scientists were trying to explain how electricity worked, inventors were finding uses for it. For example, Samuel Morse's telegraph used electricity to send messages across a continent at lightning speed. By the 1870s, telegraph offices had opened in towns all over the United States.

Some inventors believed that electricity could be put to even more dramatic uses. One such man was Alexander Graham Bell.

Above: A Carnegie plant in Braddock, Pennsylvania, produces steel for the rapidly expanding Pennsylvania Railroad. Carnegie Steel helped transform the United States into a major industrial power.

Below: Women in many countries learned Morse code so they could work as telegraphers.

Alexander Graham Bell: Speech by Wire

Like Andrew Carnegie, Alexander Graham Bell was born in Scotland and later moved to the United States. He grew up steeped in the science of sound and voice. His grandfather specialized in treating people with speech difficulties, such as lisping. His father taught deaf people to speak and gained fame for inventing Visible Speech, an alphabet that provided a written symbol for almost every sound a human voice can make.

Young Alexander had a knack for inventing, too. At the age of 11, he invented a device for taking the tough outer husk off grains of wheat, a task that took hours of hard work if done by hand. Four years later, Bell and his brother invented a machine that made a crying sound—very useful for playing practical jokes on their busy mother.

As Bell grew older, he was driven by two passions—to do some good in the world and to invent. He fed his first passion by moving to Boston, Massachusetts, where he opened a school to train teachers of the deaf.

Word of his good work spread. Visitors came to Bell's school to learn about his work.

Once Bell was visited by the emperor of Brazil, Pedro II. (Brazil's ruler at this time held the title of "emperor.") The emperor was very interested in learning about innovations he could bring to his country. As you'll soon see,

Alexander Graham Bell operates the "Centennial phone" that he demonstrated at the Philadelphia Centennial Exposition in 1876. He set up the Bell Telephone Company a year later.

this visit turned out to be lucky for the young inventor.

Bell, meanwhile, had other things on his mind. He fell in love with one of his students, a young woman named Mabel Hubbard. Mabel did not seem very interested in Bell. She protested that she was too young for marriage. But Mabel's father admired the young man's passion for inventing. Gardiner Hubbard, a patent attorney, talked Bell into forming a partnership with him. He believed that Bell could make a fortune by inventing some improvement on the telegraph.

Bell was not content with the dots and dashes of Morse code. He wanted to use electricity to send the human voice through a wire. Bell did not know much about electricity, but he hired someone who did, a mechanic named Thomas Watson.

Month after month, Bell and Watson tinkered with currents and switches, reeds and strings. One night Watson plucked a reed-like part on a device he was handling. The same tone twanged out of the box near Bell. The inventors pondered the apparatus, and suddenly Bell understood how to make a telephone.

It took months to build what Bell envisioned, but on March 10, 1876, he was ready. Sending Watson to another room, Bell prepared to test his transmitter. Suddenly he spilled some battery acid on his clothes and cried out, "Mr. Watson, come here—I want you!" Those turned out to be the first words spoken by telephone. Watson rushed to tell his boss that he had heard every word clearly.

That June, Bell took his device to the Philadelphia Centennial Exposition, a giant celebration of America's one-hundredth birthday, where visitors could see the latest inventions and products. Ten million people attended the exposition. At first few of them visited Bell's little booth. It looked as though his invention would go unnoticed.

Then into Bell's exhibit walked a familiar face—Pedro II, the emperor of Brazil. He remembered his visit with Bell in Boston, and he stopped to chat with the inventor. Big crowds followed the emperor wherever he went. So with hordes of people (including reporters) watching, Bell demonstrated his invention to the emperor, who could only stammer, "I hear, I hear…!" Suddenly word began to spread about Bell's remarkable device.

Bell and his partner, Gardiner Hubbard, started the Bell Telephone Company in 1877. By this time, Bell had married Mabel Hubbard. The couple boarded a ship and traveled to England to introduce the telephone there.

The Bell Telephone Company and others like it began stringing lines and installing telephones in offices and homes. By 1891, a phone line ran between London and Paris. The next year, phone service began between New York City and Chicago. For the first time in history, people could use the power of electricity to talk with each other across vast distances.

Bell went on to other interests. He started an organization to benefit the deaf and worked to gain women the right to vote. He never gave up inventing. He worked on methods to record sounds, detect icebergs using echoes, and make fresh water out of vapor in the air. He experimented with kites that could carry people.

Alexander Graham Bell possessed one of the most inventive minds of his day. But another ingenious fellow proved even more inventive—Thomas Edison.

Telephone, telegraph, and electricity wires crisscross above a New York City street.

Thomas Edison: The Wizard of Menlo Park

From the time he was a boy in the little town of Milan, Ohio, Thomas Alva Edison was always asking questions.

He drove his first teacher crazy with questions, so she sent him home after three months, thus ending his formal schooling. Edison's mother then tried to teach him, but she could not keep up with the boy. His parents finally gave him a library card and let him teach himself.

At the age of 12, Edison got a job on a commuter train selling snacks as well as a newspaper he published himself. He used his earnings to set up a secret laboratory in one of the baggage cars, where he experimented with different chemicals. When he accidentally started a fire, the conductor slapped his ear.

That incident might have made Edison's hearing even worse. He had suffered hearing problems since early childhood. Eventually, he went mostly deaf. He took it in stride, however. Years later, he refused an operation that might have restored his hearing. In a noisier world, he said, he might not be able to think.

Edison got his first patent for an electric voting machine. The politicians rejected it. They liked the slow process of counting votes by hand. It gave them time to make deals that might change the outcome. Edison made a vow—from then on, he would only invent things that people wanted. (Twenty-four years after Edison invented his

electric voting machine, some states finally began to use it.)

In 1869, Edison borrowed money to move to New York City. He applied for a job at a stockbroker's office. He was told there were no openings, but he could get acquainted with the equipment. One day he was in the office when the stock ticker—a machine that gave information about stock market prices—broke down. The brokers panicked. Without that machine, they couldn't work. Edison pushed to the front, examined the device, and calmly fixed it. The firm hired him on the spot. Later that year, Edison invented an improved stock ticker, which he sold to the company for $40,000. He was on his way.

Edison set up a laboratory in Menlo Park, New Jersey. He called it his "invention factory." With a staff of assistants, he began inventing things. He used the money from each invention to finance more inventions. Eventually he built an even bigger laboratory in the town of West Orange, New Jersey. Edison's "invention factory" was itself a sort of invention—a research and development lab. Today, many corporations have such facilities where they develop new products.

One of Edison's new projects was figuring out

Thomas Edison's filament lamp had a single loop of carbon that glowed when a current flowed through it. The glass bulb contained a partial vacuum that allowed the filament to get very hot without catching fire.

A *patent* is an official document from the government stating that an inventor owns his or her invention and has the right to make, use, or sell it.

how to use electricity to make light. Many other inventors were after the same thing.

Edison and his rivals all knew that they could make filament—a threadlike conductor—glow by passing electric current through it. What if the filament could be made to glow so brightly that it could light a room? It sounded like a good idea, but no one had yet discovered how to make it work. The problem was, as the filament began to shine brightly, it grew so hot that it burned to cinders.

In 1879, Edison solved this problem. He and his colleagues managed to get improved results by pumping all the air out of a glass bulb. When sealed in the vacuum within the bulb, the filament could still glow, but without oxygen it was less likely to burn up. As for the filament itself, Edison finally succeeded in finding the right material. He found that a bulb with a carbon filament would stay lit for more than 40 hours. Although Edison did not invent the first incandescent light—or the light bulb, as we usually call it—he figured out how to make a light bulb that really worked.

Of course, what good are light bulbs without electricity to power them? Edison set up a power station in New York City to generate electricity. He invented wiring systems and switches to carry the current to homes and businesses. He invented devices that could measure the flow of electricity, so that people could be charged for what they used. In short, he created an electric company. Other cities soon copied Edison's system.

Unlike Alexander Graham Bell, Edison had only one real interest—inventing. He worked at it all hours of the day. He went on to invent a phonograph to record sound and play it back. He invented one of the first movie cameras. Over a forty-year career, he and his employees invented something new about once every two weeks. When he died at the age of 84, he held 1,093 patents. No other inventor holds so many.

Edison spent many long hours in his laboratory in West Orange, New Jersey. "Genius," he said, "is one percent inspiration and ninety-nine percent perspiration."

Getting There: From Velocipede to Bicycle

One of the greatest advances in this age of innovation emerged over a number of years—the bicycle, which developed, strangely enough, out of a children's toy called the hobby horse.

The hobby horse was an animal-shaped toy with wheels. Children sat on it and pushed it along with their feet. In 1816, a German engineer made an adult-sized two-wheeled version of this toy. He replaced the animal shape with a light frame of metal tubes. The "swiftwalker" was born.

Eventually, mechanics started making the front wheel bigger. Then someone attached pedals to this wheel. A rider sitting above the wheel could move the device forward by working the pedals. The swiftwalker had turned into a "velocipede."

The bigger a velocipede's front wheel, the faster it could travel. But the oversize wheel made velocipedes difficult to ride.

The bigger the front wheel, the faster it went, so velocipedes eventually had front wheels more than five feet high. Riders had to mount from a platform, and getting off was quite a challenge. A velocipede that hit a stone could flip over and send the rider flying. People were hurt and even killed on these things. The danger appealed to some young men, among whom velocipedes became all the rage.

By the 1880s, velocipedes largely gave way to "safety bicycles." These looked much like modern bicycles, with two wheels of equal size, handlebars for steering, pedals connected to the rear wheel by a chain, and inflatable rubber tires.

Velocipede riders scoffed and said that safeties were for sissies. Nonetheless, bicycles began to sell wildly. Only the very rich could afford to keep horses in a city, but almost anyone could own a bicycle. They were easy to store—and they needed no hay!

By the late 1880s, millions of bicycles filled the streets of major cities in Europe and America. City officials started to make smoother, firmer roads just for bicycle traffic. In this way, bicycles literally paved the way for the next big thing— automobiles.

Getting There Faster: From Bicycle to Automobile

In 1859, a Belgian mechanic named Étienne Lenoir invented an alternative to the steam engine. Steam engines have a separate part called a boiler, in which burning wood or coal brings water to a boil. As the water turns into steam, it expands and pushes into the engine, making the parts turn. Lenoir's engine had no boiler. It used no steam. Instead, explosions of coal gas deep inside the engine made the parts turn. The burning of fuel in the presence of oxygen is called combustion. In Lenoir's invention, the combustion took place inside the engine itself, not in a separate boiler, so the device was called an internal combustion engine.

Engines powered by exploding fuel were dangerous. They could not

"Safety bicycles" replaced velocipedes during the 1880s. At right, riders practice at a cycling school in Berlin.

safely be made of iron, because iron breaks too easily. But with the invention of steel, the internal combustion engine became practical.

In 1885, two German mechanics, Gottlieb Daimler (GAHT-leeb DIYM-lur) and Wilhelm Maybach (MIY-bahk), made a small, safe internal combustion engine that ran on gasoline. They mounted it to a bicycle frame and thus invented the motorcycle. They could never have made such a device with a steam engine that needed to be fed hundreds of pounds of wood or coal.

Meanwhile, another German, Karl Benz, made a gas-powered three-wheeled vehicle with a steering wheel and brakes. Was this the first true automobile? Many people think so.

At first, people would not buy Benz's machine because they didn't trust it. So Benz's wife, Bertha, decided to show how safe and reliable her husband's invention really was. She climbed into his machine with her two sons and drove on rough roads to a town 60 miles away. No one had heard of a woman making such a journey. She made her husband's invention famous and got his business started.

Not to be outdone, Maybach and Daimler mounted a more powerful engine to a bigger frame. This vehicle had four wheels. Was this the first true automobile? Many say yes, but the argument will never be settled. One thing we do know—in the period from 1880 to 1900, the bicycle, through a series of improvements, turned into an automobile.

The companies founded by Daimler and Benz eventually merged into one company. It made an

automobile named after the daughter of a friend of Daimler. Her name was Mercedes. The company still uses the name: Mercedes-Benz.

In France, in England, and especially in the United States, mechanics kept creating bigger and better vehicles powered by internal combustion engines. In a later chapter, you'll read about how an American, Henry Ford, brought the automobile to millions of people.

Gottlieb Daimler sits in the rear of his—and perhaps the world's—first automobile. One of his later cars was named the Mercedes-Benz. Both were made possible by the internal combustion engine.

From Bird Cages to Automobiles

During this age of innovation, companies had to adapt quickly to keep up with the times. For example, during the late nineteenth century, George N. Pierce & Company, a manufacturing firm in Buffalo, New York, made household items such as wire birdcages. When the bicycle craze came along, the company used its experience making wire products to manufacture bicycles. Later it turned to making motorcycles. At the beginning of the twentieth century, part of the company merged with another firm and became the Pierce-Arrow Motor Car Company, which manufactured automobiles. For nearly three decades, the Pierce-Arrows were considered some of the finest cars on American roads.

Guglielmo Marconi: Father of Radio

Advances in technology made many people excited about the future. If people could speak by telephone to distant friends, light their homes with electricity, and ride in carriages that didn't need horses to move, then what could possibly be impossible? As the twentieth century dawned, an Italian named Guglielmo Marconi (gool-YEL-moh mahr-KOH-nee) gave the world yet another amazing invention—a way to send messages through the air without wires.

Historical
Close-up

Guglielmo Marconi was just 10 years old when he first became fascinated by electricity. He spent many hours in the library of his family's house in Italy, reading about the experiments of his heroes: the British scientist Michael Faraday, inventor of the first electric generator, and the American inventor, Benjamin Franklin.

Once, imitating Franklin, Marconi and a friend climbed onto the roof to set up a lightning conductor. From it, they ran wires to a bell inside the house and waited for a storm. When it came, the two boys found to their delight that every flash of lightning made the bell ring.

Marconi's mother, a young woman from a wealthy Irish family, encouraged his experiments. His older, sterner father, an Italian businessman, thought they were a waste of time. Still, he bought his teenage son subscriptions to scientific journals, which allowed the boy to keep up on all the new advances being made in Europe and America.

In 1894, when Marconi was 20, the German scientist Heinrich Hertz (HIYN-rik hurts) died. Hertz was famous for proving the existence of electromagnetic waves. (Radio waves are one kind of electromagnetic wave.) After his death, journals were full of articles about Hertz's work. They described how he had built a transmitter to spark a wave and send it to a receiver on the other side of his laboratory.

Why, Marconi wondered, couldn't equipment like Hertz's be used to send waves as telegraphic signals? A wireless telegraph! The idea gripped him. Imagine if a signal could be sent straight through the air, without having to string a wire between the two points. Messages could travel anywhere—even to or from a moving ship!

There was just one problem. Hertz had sent his waves only a short distance, across a room. Could the waves be made to travel many miles?

Marconi was determined to find out. That summer, he cleared out a space in the attic and began building a transmitter and receiver. Hardly noticing the stifling heat, he worked morning till night, day after day, week after week. At last, he was able to send a signal from one end of the room to the other. Success!

But it was only the first step. Marconi moved his work outdoors into the fields. The stronger the spark, he found, the farther a wave would travel. Then he made another discovery. Raising a wire in the air from the transmitter also added power to the signal. The higher the wire, the farther away the receiver could pick up the signal. Marconi had invented the aerial radio antenna, capable of both sending and receiving signals.

One day, Marconi had a helper carry the receiver a mile away to the other side of a hill. The man took a gun with him. Marconi told him to fire the gun into the air if he received a signal.

Marconi sent a signal with his transmitter. Then he listened as he peered into the distance.

Bang!

Now, even his hardheaded father was impressed. This wireless telegraph had real potential. But Marconi knew his parents had supported his work long enough. It was time to find a wider audience.

British post office officials examine the apparatus Guglielmo Marconi used to send a wireless message over a distance of eight miles in 1897. Two years later, Marconi broadcast a message across the English Channel.

In 1896, he sailed for England, where he demonstrated his invention to the public on the platform of a London lecture hall. Marconi and his "magic box" were a sensation. The British government gave him a patent, and he set up Marconi's Wireless Telegraph Company.

Marconi never missed an opportunity to show off the advantages of his system. When a blizzard brought down telegraph wires, cutting off communication in the country, Marconi used his new wireless stations to relay messages in Morse code to London. And when Edward, Prince of Wales, was laid up with a broken leg on board his royal yacht, Marconi rigged an antenna to the mast so Edward could send ship-to-shore messages to his worried mother, Queen Victoria.

In 1899, Marconi amazed Europe when he set up one wireless station in England and another in France. Some scientists said he would never be able to send a signal that far. The young Italian soon proved them wrong. He sent Morse code signals back and forth across the English Channel— a distance of 31 miles.

Most people thought Marconi had pushed wireless to its absolute limit. But as the twentieth century dawned, he had a secret ambition. He wanted to build a wireless transmitter powerful enough to send messages all the way across the Atlantic Ocean, to America.

Again many scientists said it was impossible. Because the earth was curved, they theorized, the waves would simply head straight into outer space.

Marconi didn't know if they were right or wrong, but he knew there was only one way to find out. In 1901, he began to build antennas in Cornwall, England, and Cape Cod, Massachusetts.

Disaster seemed to haunt the project from the first. The giant sparks and terrifying thunderclaps of the transmitters caused workers to run and horses to stampede. Marconi's men struggled to keep the towering antennas from blowing apart in high winds. The antenna in Cornwall collapsed in September. Two months later, the one on Cape Cod crashed to the ground.

Marconi pushed on. He found a new spot in North America, in Newfoundland, Canada. Where he couldn't build a structure, he sent up his wires on balloons; when balloons failed, he used kites. Curious reporters found Marconi cool and confident as always. Years later, however, the inventor revealed his real feelings: "The mere memory of it makes me shudder," he said. "It may seem a simple story to the world, but to me it was a question of the life and death of my future."

On December 12, 1901, Marconi huddled in the half-built Canadian station, pressing a receiver to his ear as icy winds howled outside. The situation seemed hopeless. Then he heard it: *dot-dot-dot*. Had he imagined it? He listened, and heard it again: *dot-dot-dot*. It was a signal from Cornwall. A wireless message had made it across the Atlantic.

Guglielmo Marconi spent the rest of his life working on improvements to his wireless telegraph. He was awarded the Nobel Prize in Physics for his efforts.

Soon the world began to see how useful his wireless telegraph messages could be. In 1909, an ocean liner and a freighter collided at sea, but 1,700 people were saved because the radio operator signaled for help. The next year, a notorious English murderer named Dr. Crippen boarded a ship and tried to escape to America. The captain recognized the murderer and sent a wireless message back to England notifying authorities. A detective boarded a faster vessel, steamed to Montreal, Canada, and arrested Crippen when his ship docked.

The Father of Radio, Guglielmo Marconi

The ultimate effects of Marconi's invention went beyond sending the dots and dashes of Morse code. Other scientists and inventors built on his work. They helped figure out how to send voices and music through the air. By the 1920s, radio broadcasts were bringing sound, from symphonies to sportscasts, into homes across America and Europe. Today Guglielmo Marconi is remembered as the Father of Radio.

Figures representing Germany, Russia, and Britain grab territory in Africa and Asia in this 1885 cartoon. During the late 1800s, European powers scrambled for colonies around the world.

The New Imperialism

Think back to the 1500s and 1600s, to the Age of Exploration. During this time, European powers explored and colonized distant lands, not only in the Americas, but in Africa and Asia as well. In the 1400s, the Portuguese set up trading posts on Africa's west coast. In the 1500s, Spain claimed the Philippines in the Pacific Ocean. In the 1600s, British companies pushed to open markets in India. The Dutch colonized the Spice Islands (now part of Indonesia). The French claimed parts of North Africa.

In the late nineteenth century, European nations grew even more interested in overseas colonies. This growing interest was partly a result of the Industrial Revolution. European nations were producing more cloth, steel, tools, and weapons than ever before. And they were building large, modern navies, mostly to protect themselves from each other.

Where would these industrial nations get the vast amounts of coal, iron, and rubber they needed to continue their relentless growth? Where would they get diamonds they used in their cutting tools? Where would they fuel their naval vessels and merchant ships on long voyages? Where would they find markets to sell their products?

In the late 1800s, European nations answered those questions by looking abroad. In an attempt to ensure their prosperity and spread what they saw as their superior civilization, many nations set out to build empires. Great Britain, France, Belgium, Russia, and the new nation-states of Germany and Italy reached for colonies in Asia and Africa.

Beyond Europe, other nations—including Japan and, to a lesser extent, the United States—also began to practice this empire building, or *imperialism*. Imperialism is the policy or action by which one country controls another country or territory. Imperialism may involve political or economic control.

This grab for empire from the 1870s to about 1910 is called the New Imperialism. It's called "New" to distinguish it from the earlier empire-building activities of the sixteenth and seventeenth centuries.

The number of imperialist initiatives during the late nineteenth and early twentieth centuries staggers the imagination. It would require a separate book, and a long one at that, to tell the story in detail. Here, we'll focus on the empire-building activities of the leading power of that time, Great Britain. Then, we'll look at what happened in Africa in the nineteenth century, because Africa's story tells a lot about how industrialized nations approached empire building. Finally,

we'll take a brief look at how the New Imperialism changed the map of Asia.

"The Sun Never Sets on the British Empire"

In 1897, England's Queen Victoria celebrated the anniversary of her sixtieth year as queen with a spectacular parade. Marching before her were Scots Guards with feathered caps and Australian cavalrymen in spiked helmets. Close behind came blue-coated "hussars" from Canada, straight-backed riflemen from southern Africa, and turbaned riders on camelback from northwest India and Egypt. Seventeen princes from India paraded in the ranks. Troops from Hong Kong, Jamaica, Cyprus, Niger, and Africa's Gold Coast saluted the queen as well.

The participants in this colorful pageant were all Victoria's subjects, all part of the enormous British Empire. At that time people said, "The sun never sets on the British empire"—which meant the empire was so vast that some part of it was

In 1897, Queen Victoria celebrated 60 years on the British throne with a grand parade through London. Victoria reigned over a huge, world-wide empire, one upon which "the sun never set."

always in daylight. By 1897, the British Empire stretched from the Atlantic to the Indian and Pacific Oceans. Its many territories included Ireland, Canada, Australia, New Zealand, India, Malaya, Hong Kong, and large parts of Africa.

How did the little island of Great Britain come to rule so vast an empire? It started hundreds of years back. You've learned that in the sixteenth century, English merchants formed the Virginia Company to establish colonies in North America. At about the same time, another British business, the East India Company, set up trading posts in India.

In 1763, the British won Canada from the French. The American Revolution briefly shrank the empire, but the British soon claimed Australia and New Zealand as colonies. After the defeat of Napoleon, Britain claimed a few more West Indian colonies in the Caribbean, along with the Asian island of Ceylon (now known as Sri Lanka). In the early nineteenth century, the British gained the Asian ports of Singapore and Hong Kong.

Until the nineteenth century, the British Empire grew haphazardly. Private companies took the lead. But in the mid-nineteenth century, the British government stepped in and started to exercise more control. By the 1870s, British officials were actively directing an enormous empire.

India: "The Jewel in the Imperial Crown"

Events in India pushed the British government to take more direct control of its colonies. Here is how it happened.

The British East India Company, a private company, started out by establishing trading posts in India in the 1600s. For many years, company officials made arrangements with Mughal princes to get the goods the British wanted—spices, silk, sugar, indigo, cotton cloth. But some company officials preferred to control the Mughal leaders rather than cooperate with them. Occasional conflicts followed, and in 1757, the troops employed by the British East India Company defeated India's Mughal princes. The company continued to expand its rule over the Indian subcontinent. It collected taxes, redistributed land, and organized Indian troops, outfitting them with uniforms and guns.

Some of those troops, called Sepoys, rebelled in 1857. To understand what started this Sepoy Mutiny, keep in mind that most Indians were either Hindus or Muslims. A year before the rebellion, the East India Company supplied its Hindu and Muslim soldiers with new rifles. These rifles used greased cartridges as ammunition. To load the gun, a rifleman had to bite off the end of the greased cartridge. The grease was partly made from the fat of cows and hogs. Many Hindus do not eat beef, and Muslims are not supposed to eat pork. Thus the Hindu and Muslim soldiers saw this new requirement as a religious insult and a sin, and they rebelled.

When the Sepoys mutinied, the rebellion spread quickly, because many other Indians resented the East

The *Sepoy Mutiny* is sometimes called the Indian Mutiny.

India Company. For years, tension had been building up as the British tried to impose their ways on the Indian population. The mutiny allowed for the violent release of these pent-up tensions.

A bloody conflict followed. It took two years for the British to restore order, often through cruel means. When the conflict ended, the British government shut down the East India Company and decided to rule India directly.

The British set about building railroads across India. They built telegraph and telephone systems. They expanded irrigation networks and established universities.

British colonial officials ride atop magnificently adorned elephants during a celebration of British rule in India. The British government took control of India from the East India Company in 1858.

In 1876, Queen Victoria took the title "Empress of India." The queen proudly proclaimed India as the brightest "jewel in the imperial crown." But while the resources of India enriched the British, most Indians lived in poverty.

Rethinking Empire

About the time of the Sepoy Mutiny, the British were beginning to worry about competition from their European neighbors. The French, Germans, and Russians were catching up to British factories and industry. In 1871, a newly united Germany mobilized a huge

army and defeated England's long-time rival, France.

Other European nations were starting to build strong navies and establish colonies. The British already had many colonies and a great navy. But in the face of this new competition, the British began to think of their far-flung empire in a new way—as a resource and a big advantage for the future. They saw that they could use their colonies to raise more troops and get more resources if necessary.

In 1872, a British statesman, Benjamin Disraeli (diz-RAY-lee), challenged the British people to decide "whether you will be content to be a comfortable England … or whether you will be a great country, an Imperial country." To many Britons, being an "imperial country" seemed both a great honor and a noble duty. They thought of themselves, as one British schoolmaster put it, as "citizens of the greatest empire under heaven." The British even declared a new holiday, "Empire Day," to be celebrated on Queen Victoria's birthday.

Newspapers and the nation's schools took up the call. They spoke of the need for "faith in the divinely ordered mission of their country." They praised the superiority of "the British race." They spoke of British duties to "the lesser breeds." They looked forward to Britain's eventual triumph over "inferior races" such as the Teutons (Germans) or Slavs (Russians).

Does this sound familiar? You learned from your study of slavery that racism was growing in the western world in the nineteenth century. Prior to the early 1800s, most educated westerners had thought of one big "human race" and not of separate races. But after Charles Darwin published *The Origin of Species*, new ideas were in the air.

Some new "social scientists" applied Darwin's ideas about different species to differences between races.

Kipling: Champion and Critic of Empire

You may know Rudyard Kipling as the author of *The Jungle Book*, a beloved collection of children's tales set mostly in India. Kipling, the son of British missionaries, was born in India. After being educated in England, he returned in 1882 to the land of his youth to work as a reporter.

Rudyard Kipling was both a booster and critic of empire building.

Kipling saw empire building as a noble if thankless task. It was, as he put it in a famous poem, "the white man's burden" to spread what he and his countrymen saw as the benefits of civilization.

While Kipling's writings often boosted British patriotism and pride, he sometimes criticized British colonial actions. In one poem, he mocked the idea that the British could bring "civilization" to its colonies by using cruel and unnecessary violence against native peoples. He wrote with irony: "So shall we teach by death and dearth, / Goodwill to men and peace on earth."

They claimed that certain races had characteristics that made them naturally superior to others. The British had no doubt about the superiority of the "British race." They looked upon the Scots, Welsh, and Irish Celts—all of whom the British had colonized centuries before—as inferior. And while Americans and Canadians might be descended from the British, the British still perceived them as inferior. In British eyes, Asians and Africans were at the bottom of the racial pyramid.

Pseudo- (SOO-doh) is a prefix that means false, fake.

This new, pseudo-scientific view of race affected the way the British treated their different colonies. In the late nineteenth century, the Office of Colonial Affairs concluded that Canada, Australia, and New Zealand were capable of some self-government because many colonists there were of English descent. But the British believed that India, Africa, and other colonies populated by people of different races required strong imperial rule.

In the nineteenth century, the British were busy expanding their influence in Africa. But, as you will see, they were not alone. Let's look at how the various European powers approached African colonization in this age of the New Imperialism.

Livingstone Explores Africa

In the mid- to late-1800s, one man more than any other shaped the way that Europeans thought about Africa—a Scottish missionary, physician, and explorer named David Livingstone. Livingstone had wanted to be a medical missionary since his youth. He was enormously curious about other lands. At first, he hoped to go to China, but another missionary persuaded him to think about Africa.

Livingstone agreed, in part because he hoped to help stop the continuing trade in African slaves. Although Britain had abolished slavery in its colonies in 1833, slavery and the slave trade still existed in Africa. Arab merchants continued to buy large numbers of Africans and sell them in Muslim lands such as the Sudan and Arabia.

In 1841, Dr. Livingstone traveled to the southern part of Africa. Within months of his arrival, he became fascinated by the vast continent before him. He made plans to explore parts that no outsider had ever seen.

Traveling by foot, donkey, ox, and canoe, he covered thousands of miles. He suffered fevers, malaria, and dysentery. Once he was attacked and severely injured by a lion. Still he persisted. In 1853, he declared, "I shall open up a path to the interior or perish." In May 1856, he became the first European to travel the width of the continent, from coast to coast.

During his African travels, Livingstone tried to convert the people he met to Christianity. He also tried to help them find profitable businesses to replace the slave trade.

Livingstone kept careful records of his explorations and geographic findings. On one trek he pressed along the Zambezi River. In a spot between what is now Zimbabwe and Zambia, he came upon the thundering waters of a spectacular waterfall. In a patriotic gesture, he named it Victoria Falls.

When Livingstone returned to Britain, he was greeted as a hero. He toured the country, making speeches about the evils of the slave trade, the beauty of Africa, and the great economic potential of Africa. The Christian faith and Western commerce, he declared, could spread across the continent as "the pioneers of civilization."

Like other Europeans of his time, Livingstone saw Africa as a "dark continent" in need of the "light" of European civilization. Like many missionaries, he worked to provide medical care and to end the evils of the slave trade. But not for a moment did Livingstone doubt that he had a duty to bring his "superior" civilization to Africa. Livingstone himself was hailed in Britain as the "light of Africa."

In 1857, David Livingstone wrote about his explorations and adventures in *Missionary Travels and Researches in South Africa*. Not since Marco Polo published his book had Europeans been so fascinated by a single traveler's account of unknown lands. Livingstone's book sold 70,000 copies. His writing evoked an Africa few Europeans had ever imagined.

"Dr. Livingstone, I presume."

Livingstone's fame spread until he became the most celebrated explorer of his day. He undertook a second expedition to Africa between 1858 and 1864, and wrote another book packed with new geographic and scientific information. The Royal Geographic Society then persuaded him to take up a new challenge — to find the source of the Nile, the longest river in the world.

Livingstone agreed to the challenge, but he said he would take no European colleagues with him. He claimed that the Europeans who had accompanied him on his previous expedition had bickered too much. So, with Asian and African assistants, Livingstone again set forth into Africa.

For several years no one heard from him. The European public grew anxious. At one time rumors spread that he had been killed. Finally, the *New York Herald* sent a young reporter, Henry Morton Stanley, to Africa. His employers gave him a simple instruction: "Find Livingstone."

In November 1871, after 200 exhausting days, Stanley found the missing explorer. He discovered the Scotsman at an Arab slaving station on the eastern shore of Lake Tanganyika, deep in Africa's interior. There Stanley greeted him with the now-famous words, "Dr. Livingstone, I presume."

Christian Missionaries in Africa and Asia

In the early to mid-nineteenth century, a wave of missionary fervor swept England and North America. Christians, many of whom had been working to abolish the slave trade, began to send missionaries to India, China, and Africa. They often set up hospitals and schools while they tried to make converts to Christianity. But many native people resented these attempts to turn them away from their traditional faiths. The missionaries' work sometimes became a source of conflict in India, China, and parts of Africa.

"Dr. Livingstone, I presume," declares Henry Stanley (above, left) upon finding the Scottish missionary in Africa in 1871. Livingstone and Stanley both explored huge areas of what Europeans called the "dark continent."

channels, introduced the planting of cotton, and helped train the Egyptian army.

Even as the French settled in Africa, they puzzled over how to get around it. That's because the African continent presented a huge geographic obstacle to French and other European merchants and navies. To reach their outposts in Asia, European ships had to sail all the way around Africa—a long, dangerous, and expensive voyage. The French wondered: How can we shorten this journey?

An eager French diplomat, Ferdinand de Lesseps (lay-SEPS), pondered a solution. While Livingstone explored southern Africa, Lesseps had big ideas for the north. Full of the confidence of this new age of innovation, Lesseps wanted to build a canal across the Isthmus of Suez to link the Mediterranean and Red Seas.

- On the map on page 587, locate Egypt, the Mediterranean Sea, the Red Sea, and the Isthmus of Suez.

Lesseps's thinking harmonized with the ambitions of the *khedive* (kuh-DEEV)—the ruler of Egypt— at this time, Sa'id Pasha (sah-EED PAH-shah). Sa'id Pasha believed that a canal linking his nation's two great seas would transform Egypt and restore it to its former glory. In 1856, he turned to Lesseps for help. Lesseps, who was eager to increase French trade with Asia, formed a company and gladly accepted the task of building the canal. In return, Lesseps's French firm and its partners would have

Livingstone refused to abandon his quest for the source of the Nile, and eventually Stanley returned to England without him. Fourteen months later, in a remote village in what is now the country of Zambia, the explorer died on the continent to which he had devoted 30 years of his life. Livingstone's African servants found him dead, kneeling on the ground as if in one final act of prayer. Livingstone's body was taken back to London and he was honored with a burial at Westminster Abbey.

East Meets West: Building the Suez Canal

Even before Livingstone's explorations, other Europeans had made inroads into Africa. The French longed to extend their empire into Egypt. Napoleon had marched his armies there. After Napoleon's fall, the French still had settlements in Egypt. They built irrigation

the right to operate the canal for 99 years.

In April 1859, Lesseps and his colleagues met on the Mediterranean coast to begin building the Suez Canal. They planted the Egyptian flag, and Lesseps himself struck the first blow with a pickax.

It was a huge undertaking to dig a hundred-mile-long channel across the Isthmus of Suez. No one had ever tried to construct a canal of this size. Skeptics doubted it could be done. The London *Times* newspaper declared that Lesseps was about to spend a fortune "digging holes in the sand."

To build the Suez Canal, Lesseps's company forced thousands of men into what amounted to slave labor. The workers used tools that people had used for centuries—picks, shovels, and baskets. Conditions in the hot, dusty desert were brutal. Other European nations began to criticize the treatment of the workers at Suez. So Lesseps decided to try a new approach. He turned to machines.

Soon the roar of hundreds of motors drowned out the sound of picks and shovels. Machines powered by coal and steam carved tunnels and removed debris. Dredgers scooped sand and mud from the canal bottom, which had to be at least 26 feet deep to permit passage of the latest steamships. A rail line alongside the canal helped move men and equipment.

After 10 years of effort, the Suez Canal was finished. On August 15, 1869, the Mediterranean and Red Seas flowed quietly together in the canal. By this time Egypt had

A dredging machine deepens a partially completed section of the Suez Canal. Machines carried out much of the work on the hundred-mile-long canal.

a new khedive. He declared the Suez "the meeting point of Europe and the Orient."

The Canal Opens and Britain Takes Over

Several weeks later, dignitaries from far and near arrived for a grand party to celebrate the opening of the canal. Some 6,000 guests, including many of the crowned heads of Europe, joined the festivities. There were banquets, concerts, plays, horse races, and fireworks.

On November 17, 1869, a fleet of ships gathered at the northern end of the Suez Canal. Led by a French

What Is the "Orient"?

Orient is an old term for "east." From the Middle Ages to the nineteenth century, westerners referred to all lands east of Jerusalem as "the Orient." The Suez stands on the western edge of that east-west divide.

vessel, the fleet proceeded slowly down the canal, making the journey from the Mediterranean to the Red Sea in three days. Lesseps and his firm had completed one of the greatest engineering feats of the nineteenth century. The canal was hailed as "a monument as durable as the Pyramids."

The once-skeptical London *Times* celebrated the "waterway between two great seas—a shortcut from the Western to the Eastern world." The British had good reason to be enthusiastic. Ships traveling from London to the British colony of India faced a three-month voyage when sailing around the southern tip of Africa. Now, by sailing through the Suez Canal, they could get to India in three weeks.

Soon after the Suez Canal opened, three-quarters of the ships using it were British. The British came to depend on this route to their growing empire in the East, including India, Hong Kong, Singapore, and Australia. One English newspaper wrote that the canal "should have been constructed with English capital and by English energy."

Though they did not build it, the British quickly moved to take control of the canal. In 1875, the khedive of Egypt, desperate for money, sold Queen Victoria his shares of stock in the project. A few years later, when an anti-European riot erupted in Egypt, the Royal Navy bombarded Alexandria, the country's major port. A British army stormed ashore and seized the canal zone.

Britain soon dominated Egypt's capital, Cairo, and the rest of the

Crowds watch as the ships of many nations make their way through the Suez Canal on its opening day. The canal linked the Mediterranean and Red Seas, providing a quick route between East and West.

country. Egypt was not formally a British colony, but British officials had a strong hand in running Egyptian affairs.

King Leopold and the "Magnificent African Cake"

North of France and west of Germany sits the small European nation of Belgium. In the late nineteenth century, Belgium's King Leopold II was fascinated by the writings of David Livingstone. He read Livingstone's arguments about Africa's need for "civilization." And King Leopold decided to provide it.

The king described his mission in Africa as a crusade "to open to civilization the only part of our globe where it has not yet penetrated, to pierce the darkness which envelops whole populations." But Leopold also had economic motives. He saw in Africa a continent rich in raw materials. In bringing "civilization" to Africa, he meant to bring riches to Europe, and to himself. In 1877, he summed up the way many Europeans felt about overseas colonies: "We must," he declared, "obtain a slice of this *magnifique gateau africain*"—this magnificent African cake.

The slice Leopold cut for himself was the Congo River basin in the middle of the continent. There he set up his own private kingdom, financed by his personal fortune. Leopold considered what title to adopt. First he thought of calling himself Emperor of the Congo. Eventually he decided on the title King-Sovereign of the Congo Free State.

- On the map on page 587, locate the Congo (later called Belgian Congo).

Meanwhile, several European nations—including Portugal, France, Germany, and Britain—were scrambling to gain control of African land and resources. As each nation moved to colonize parts of Africa, it looked at the other nations with suspicion.

To prevent disputes among themselves, the Europeans decided they should meet and talk. In 1884 and 1885, representatives of the major European powers met in Germany. They agreed to various guidelines for colonizing Africa, and one result was that Leopold was allowed to set up his Congo Free State.

The decisions made at the conference affected the lives of millions of people in Africa. No Africans were invited to the meeting.

The Human Cost in the Congo

Leopold's Congo Free State had many resources that Europeans wanted. It had ivory, palm oil, timber, and copper. And most of all, the Congo had rubber.

Europe wanted rubber, and lots of it, especially for tires. In the 1880s, a Scottish veterinarian named John Boyd Dunlop invented pneumatic tires—rubber tires inflated with air. These tires made bicycles much more comfortable. Millions of Europeans and Americans took to riding bikes. Soon, factories began making pneumatic tires for the new "horseless carriages," or automobiles. As new industries found more and more uses for rubber, demand soared.

In the equatorial forests of central Africa, thick vines grew around the trees. Leopold set up a company in the Congo to collect a milky fluid from these vines, which was used to make rubber. But who would do the work for the king?

There weren't enough Europeans in the region. Leopold had a simple solution. Because he had declared himself King-Sovereign of the Congo Free State, he considered the local people to be his subjects. And because they were his subjects, then, Leopold reasoned, they owed their king taxes. Leopold decided that they would pay these taxes by collecting rubber for the king's company. Leopold never doubted that he had the right to require such work of his "subjects."

By 1900, Leopold's company had set up rubber collection posts throughout the Congo. To improve transportation of raw materials, it also built a railroad. Tens of thousands of Africans worked on its construction. Their bosses were brutal—the workers died at the rate of 150 a month.

Each local village was assigned a quota—a required amount—of rubber to tap from the vines. Armed African guards directed by Belgian officials made sure the villagers met their quotas. They flogged and imprisoned those who fell behind. Sometimes they cut off their hands, or simply shot them. Women and children joined the workforce in a desperate attempt to meet quotas. Company officers burned villages, killed uncooperative chiefs, and slaughtered people who refused to collect rubber. The Congolese died at a horrifying rate.

At first, these barbaric methods got results. In 1890, the Congo had exported just 100 tons of rubber. In 1898, exports rose to 2,000 tons, then again to 6,000 tons in 1901.

Colonial bosses oversee the weighing of rubber collected by Africans in King Leopold's colony in the Congo. Leopold claimed he was bringing "civilization" to Africa. But his demands for rubber resulted in terrible brutality and massive death.

But soon the company exhausted the supply of rubber. The efforts to get more and more rubber had killed the vines.

Far worse, the savage treatment of African workers killed *millions*. Eight to ten million people died from the forced labor, mass murder, disease, and starvation that occurred under King Leopold's reign. Leopold, who claimed to bring "civilization" to Africa, was responsible for one of the worst slaughters in history.

When news of the horrors in the Congo got out, other countries, especially Britain and the United States, responded with outrage. In 1908, the Belgian Parliament acted. It removed the Congo Free State from King Leopold's direct rule, made it a Belgian territory, and put an end to the worst practices.

Cecil Rhodes, Empire Builder

King Leopold was not the only European with ambitions in Africa. The English business-man Cecil Rhodes had his own imperialist visions.

Rhodes first arrived in southern Africa in 1870, about thirty years after David Livingstone's explora-tions, and one year after the open-ing of the Suez Canal. Rhodes, who sometimes suffered from poor health, followed his doctor's advice to live in a warm climate. He decided to go and live with his brother in southern Africa.

Rhodes was a self-confident man of enormous ambition. Within twenty years, he controlled Africa's diamond industry and had made his first investments in gold mining.

Cecil Rhodes bestrides the African continent in this 1892 cartoon. Rhodes dreamed of a British empire that would extend the length of Africa. He even carved out a new country, Rhodesia, which he named after himself.

Though Rhodes was a mil-lionaire before he reached 30, he didn't just want to make money. He devoted himself to expanding the British Empire. Like his late-nineteenth-century countrymen, Rhodes believed in the superiority of the English people. He believed it was the right—indeed, the obligation—of the British to spread their way of life around the globe.

"I contend," said Rhodes, "that we are the finest race in the world, and that the more of the world we inhabit, the better it is for the human race." Maps of the time often showed British possessions in red. Thus, said Rhodes, "If there be a God, I think what he would like me to do is to paint as much of Africa British red as possible." With this arrogant attitude, he moved ahead with his plans.

Missionaries, hunters, and traders came to southern Africa with reports of lands to the north. Rhodes believed that the British should claim this territory. "Africa is still lying ready for us," he proclaimed. "It is our duty to take it." Rhodes meant: *Take it before our European competitors get it first.*

So Rhodes pushed north. Using his personal fortune, he raised troops to conquer a vast region. By 1889, he added nearly a million square miles to Britain's African empire. He eventually carved out a new country that he named after himself—Rhodesia.

Rhodes Scholars

Cecil Rhodes left a very generous will—so generous that today, when people hear the name "Rhodes," they think less of imperialism and more of academic excellence. That's because Rhodes left most of his fortune to be used as scholarships for young men from the British colonies and the United States to study at Oxford University in England. He wanted to promote unity among English-speaking peoples. Rhodes did not allow scholarship discrimination on the basis of race, so people from many backgrounds benefited.

Today, about ninety Rhodes Scholarships are awarded yearly to young men—and now women as well—with high scholastic achievement and good qualities of character and leadership. Because the British Empire once extended far and wide, Rhodes Scholars come from around the world.

- On the map on page 587, locate Rhodesia (later divided as Northern and Southern Rhodesia).

"From the Cape to Cairo"

Cecil Rhodes wanted still more colonies. He once remarked, "I would annex the planets if I could." He envisioned an unbroken line of African colonies for Britain, each linked by a railroad running the length of the continent. He dreamed of a British empire that would sprawl, as he put it, "from the Cape to Cairo." By that he meant from the Cape of Good Hope, at the continent's southern end, to Cairo, Egypt, in the north.

But in this age of the New Imperialism, other European powers didn't just stand by and watch Rhodes claim all of Africa for Britain. To the north of Rhodesia lay King Leopold's Congo Free State. To the east the Portuguese had carved out a colony along the coast. Under Bismarck, Germany was also establishing colonies in the east. And in South Africa, the Dutch and their descendants, known as Boers, emerged as strong rivals.

In 1895, Rhodes made the mistake of authorizing a badly planned attack on Boer territories. Later a full-scale war broke out. The British won those wars, but by that time, Rhodes's health was very poor. When he died in 1902, Britain's African empire was firmly established, but it did not stretch "from the Cape to Cairo." On his deathbed, Rhodes is said to have uttered these words: "So little done. So much to do."

The New Imperialism in Africa, c. 1914

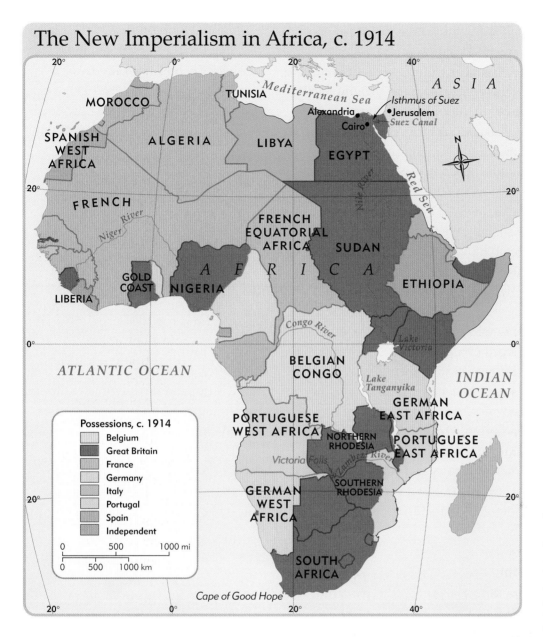

Possessions, c. 1914
- Belgium
- Great Britain
- France
- Germany
- Italy
- Portugal
- Spain
- Independent

French forces capture the capital of Algeria in 1830. By the end of the nineteenth century, France had created a large empire in northern and western Africa.

Carving Up the Continent

As the nineteenth century drew to a close, various European powers had colonized much of Africa.

In the early 1800s, France conquered and colonized Algeria. By 1900, the French empire also included the huge area of French West Africa and Tunisia. France soon controlled most of Morocco.

The Spanish took pieces of northwest Africa. The Germans

set up colonies on Africa's eastern and western coasts.

Not to be outdone, Italy tried to occupy Ethiopia in the mid-1880s. But the Ethiopians—equipped with modern European weapons and trained by European military advisors—fought back ferociously. In 1896, the Ethiopians defeated a 17,000-man Italian army. The Italians gave up their attempts to grab Ethiopia, but held on to other areas in Africa.

By the dawn of the twentieth century, the European powers had carved up nearly the entire African continent. In part, this new imperialism was made possible by the "second industrial revolution." Western powers had technologies that overpowered African peoples. They had advanced weaponry, such as machine guns and repeating rifles. They had railroads and steamships that could quickly transport troops and raw materials. The telegraph, and eventually the telephone, allowed European armies to communicate rapidly. By 1900, the only African lands free of European control were Liberia in the west and Ethiopia in the east.

• On the map on page 587, note the colonies controlled by Britain, France, Spain, Portugal, Belgium, Germany, and Italy.

African raw materials—cotton from north Africa, copper and diamonds from Rhodesia, rubber and ivory from the Congo—flowed to Europe. European factories turned the cotton into cloth, and rubber into tires. European businessmen shipped manufactured goods back to Africa for sale in the colonies.

The New Imperialism put millions of Africans under the control of colonial rulers. New canals, roads, railroads, bridges, irrigation systems,

One reason for the New Imperialism was Europe's appetite for Africa's raw materials. Colonials often treated native laborers harshly, as at this diamond mine in South Africa.

The New Imperialism in Asia, c. 1914

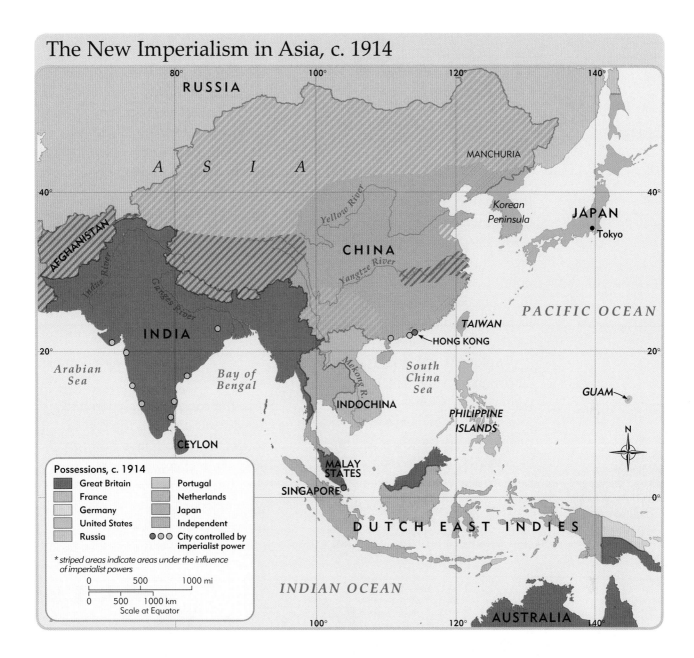

Possessions, c. 1914
- Great Britain
- France
- Germany
- United States
- Russia
- Portugal
- Netherlands
- Japan
- Independent
- ○○○ City controlled by imperialist power

* striped areas indicate areas under the influence of imperialist powers

0   500   1000 mi
0   500   1000 km
Scale at Equator

---

schools, hospitals, and telegraph and telephone lines dotted the land. But a legacy of racism endured, along with deep bitterness and resentment against the colonial rulers.

The New Imperialism and the Map of Asia

Africa was not the only continent transformed by the New Imperialism of the late nineteenth and early twentieth centuries. Asia, the world's largest continent, saw an even greater scramble for colonies.

The story of the New Imperialism in Asia goes far beyond what we can tell here. The very brief overview that follows is meant to help you get a sense of the extent of imperialist activity in Asia.

Imperial Powers in China

During the nineteenth century, industrial powers competed for trade in China. British warships steamed up to coastal cities and demanded trading rights. Other western nations began to do the same.

- On the map on page 589, locate China.

The Chinese tried to resist. But they could not withstand foreign troops equipped with advanced weapons. Britain, France, Germany, Russia, the United States, and Japan each claimed parts of China.

In 1899, most of the colonizing countries worked out an "open door" policy. This policy guaranteed that one country would not close its piece of China to trade with the other colonizing countries.

Diplomats, soldiers, traders, and Christian missionaries flooded into China. Many Chinese people came to resent the new ways of these people, whom they saw as "foreign devils." In 1900, some Chinese, called Boxers by westerners, decided to fight back. The Boxers were members of a secret society that practiced a form of martial arts

that they believed would protect them against bullets.

The Boxer Rebellion spread from the countryside to the cities. The rebels killed westerners and Chinese Christians. They burned schools, churches, and homes.

Finally eight industrial nations sent soldiers to China. Like other colonized peoples, the Boxers fell before the firepower of modern guns. The international troops crushed the rebellion. Once again, China was under the control of outsiders.

The Americans Open Japan

Since the early 1600s, Japan had closed itself off from the rest of the world. That changed on July 8, 1853, when Commodore Matthew Perry boldly sailed into Tokyo Bay with four U.S. warships. The Japanese knew they could not defeat such powerful vessels, so

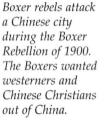

Boxer rebels attack a Chinese city during the Boxer Rebellion of 1900. The Boxers wanted westerners and Chinese Christians out of China.

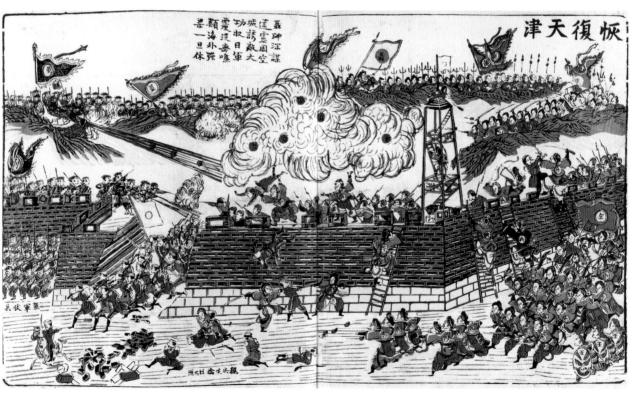

they agreed to open their country to trade with the outside world.

- On the map on page 589, locate Japan.

The Japanese in China and Korea

During the 1870s, the Japanese began to modernize their country. They built up their army and navy. Soon they also turned to empire building. In 1895, the Japanese invaded China. They set up a colony on the Chinese island of Taiwan, which they used for rice and sugar production. In 1905, the Japanese surprised the world by defeating Russia. The Japanese seized Russian-controlled land on the mainland of China, as well as the Korean peninsula.

- On the map on page 589, locate Taiwan, the Korean peninsula, and Japanese-controlled territory in China.

The Russians in Central Asia and Manchuria

The tsars had steadily enlarged the Russian empire. In the nineteenth century, they acquired territory in central Asia, which brought them closer to India, part of Britain's empire. To avoid conflict, Russia and Britain marked off Afghanistan as a land to separate their competing empires. The Russians turned east and occupied Manchuria, but this led to a clash with Japan's growing empire. In 1905, a disastrous war with the Japanese ended Russian expansion in Asia.

- On the map on page 589, locate Afghanistan and Manchuria.

The French in Indochina

During the 1800s, French missionaries worked to convert people in Southeast Asia to Catholicism. But local rulers sometimes killed the missionaries and their converts. In the mid-nineteenth century, the French sent troops to protect the missionaries—and to get their hands on the region's natural resources. Eventually, much of Southeast Asia became part of the French empire. The French called this region Indochina. Their rule extended over what are now Vietnam, Cambodia, and Laos, where they established large rubber, sugar, and rice plantations.

- On the map on page 589, locate the region the French called Indochina.

The United States in the Pacific

About a hundred years after the United States freed itself from British rule, some Americans had their own dreams of empire. In 1898, the United States fought the Spanish-American War to help liberate Cuba from rule by Spain. The United States won the war and gained two Spanish possessions in Asia—Guam and the Philippine Islands. In 1899, the Filipinos revolted against their new colonial rulers. The Americans sent tens of thousands of troops to enforce U.S. control. The Philippines did not gain complete independence until 1946.

- On the map on page 589, locate the Philippine Islands and Guam.

Immigrants poured into New York City in the late nineteenth century, making it one of the world's most densely populated places.

Organizing for Change: Cities, Workers, and Women

A s industrialized nations reached for colonies overseas, they faced new challenges at home. The second industrial revolution brought more factories, steel mills, and machine shops. Millions of people headed to the cities for jobs. In 1800, Berlin had about 150,000 inhabitants; in 1900, it struggled to cope with two million. London was bulging with six and a half million people. As cities in Europe and the United States faced overcrowding, disease, filth, and crime, people began to ask: How can we make our cities healthier, better places to live?

Many people who had moved to the cities to find jobs began to demand better working conditions. Since the earliest textile mills of the Industrial Revolution, most workers had endured long hours, low wages, and miserable conditions in dark, stifling factories. Workers began to ask: How can we improve our workplaces and our lives?

Another big group—women—also began to think hard about improving their lives. For decades, ideas about basic rights and liberties had been circulating in Europe and America. Yet nowhere did women enjoy the same rights as men. As they saw change sweeping the world, many women began to ask: Why shouldn't things change for us, too?

As the twentieth century approached, many people in the industrial world were organizing for change.

The Emperor and the Baron Plan Paris

London, Berlin, Vienna, New York— on both sides of the Atlantic, cities faced similar challenges as their

An 1866 cartoon shows the figure of death pumping polluted water for London's poor. Outbreaks of cholera—a disease that could be spread by contaminated water from public pumps—were common among the poor.

populations exploded. One city took the lead in meeting the new challenges. Determined leaders in Paris figured out that one of the best ways to solve problems is to plan to avoid them. Before we look at how Paris solved some of its problems, let's step back to see how it got in such a mess.

In 1789, the year the Bastille fell and the French Revolution began, half a million people crowded inside the city's medieval walls. In less than a hundred years, the population more than doubled—by the mid-nineteenth century, more than a million people called Paris home. And the numbers kept growing.

Another *Emperor* Napoleon?

It didn't start that way. The 1848 revolution led to a "Second Republic" for France. The people elected Louis Napoleon, the 40-year-old nephew of Napoleon Bonaparte, as their president. He was elected by a huge majority. He took an oath to defend the republic. But like his uncle, this Napoleon preferred having all the power in his own hands. So in 1852, he abolished the republic and declared himself Emperor Napoleon III.

Tens of thousands of newcomers packed into rat-infested housing. Mud oozed in the city's winding, narrow streets. Garbage clotted every path. The odor of horse manure competed with the stench of sewage that flowed directly into the River Seine. Diseases such as cholera and tuberculosis killed many thousands. Criminals lurked in the shadows of this city from which, as the great French writer Victor Hugo put it, "a forest of steeples, of turrets, of chimneys" blocked the light.

In 1852, when Napoleon Bonaparte's nephew, Louis Napoleon, became Napoleon III, Emperor of France, he decided to transform Paris. He wanted to make the city the envy of the world. He envisioned an elegant city with impressive government buildings, museums, monuments, and parks. But who could transform a city of filth and shadows into one of grandeur and light?

When Napoleon III met Georges-Eugène Haussmann (ohs-MAHN), he found the man to make it happen. Haussmann, who had held several administrative posts in the provinces, believed that Paris should be "the head and heart of France." He urged the emperor to tear things down and start over. Eliminate the tangled web of medieval streets. Get rid of the slums. Open up space and let in light. An enthusiastic Napoleon III appointed Baron Haussmann "prefect of the Seine"—in other words, the chief administrator of Paris. (The ambitious Haussmann claimed the title of "Baron," a rank of nobility, from his mother's family.)

The emperor and the baron embarked on a project unlike any

since Pericles rebuilt Athens in the fifth century B.C. They wanted to avoid the fate of a city like London, which had grown higgledy-piggledy without a plan. Napoleon III presented Haussmann with a color-coded map of the city and his priorities. Haussmann added ideas of his own. Between 1852 and 1869, the baron and the emperor met almost every day. Together they reinvented Paris.

Untangling Paris

The old Paris was a tangled knot of narrow, winding streets. Haussmann and Napoleon III set out to untangle the knot.

Haussmann proposed many grand boulevards—broad, straight avenues, each at least 60 feet wide, running east to west and north to south, and lined by more than 100,000 trees. The majestic boulevards met in grand, green circular plazas. The wide streets allowed Parisians to gaze from afar at their historic monuments—the cathedral of Notre Dame, the Louvre museum, the imposing Arc de Triomphe.

In his 17 years of work, Haussmann built 85 miles of new boulevards; he broadened and paved hundreds of miles of old roads. Elegant lamps and wrought iron benches lined many of the broad new avenues. Haussmann and Napoleon insisted that buildings along the new boulevards be built at the same height with the same warm, yellow-white limestone. Sunlight glowed from its surface by day and gas lights shone on the stone by night, with dazzling effect.

The boulevards made it possible for Parisians to move about more easily. By the end of the century, electric trams, trolleys, and even an underground rail system—the Metro—moved Parisians quickly

In the 1850s and 1860s, Baron Haussmann planned wide boulevards flanked by lovely buildings for Parisian neighborhoods. Later, the broad avenues allowed for automobiles, as this 1905 postcard shows.

to their destinations. By about 1900, the gracious boulevards proved useful for something that neither Napoleon nor Haussmann had imagined—automobile traffic.

Tearing Down to Build Anew

Paris needed not just fine boulevards, but also the basics. Haussmann planned new aqueducts to bring fresh water from the countryside. By 1871, aqueducts reached the capital from hundreds of miles away. Haussmann also cleaned up the city's underbelly with its miles of aging, stinking sewers. He expanded the underground system, building huge tunnels for new sewer lines. In the 1860s, visitors to Paris lined up for tours of the new sewer system.

As Haussmann tore down and rebuilt Paris, Europe watched warily. Down came many historic neighborhoods, homes, and slums. Was all

this modernizing good? One writer lamented that Paris was becoming a "city without a past." He went on to ask: "Who will live in his father's house? Who will pray in the church where he was baptized? My house has been torn down and the earth has swallowed it up."

Haussmann was unmoved. He even tore down the house where he had been born. He and Napoleon III demolished more than 117,000 dwellings. In their place, they built 273,000 new ones.

Wealthy people and a growing middle class began to move back to the city. They occupied the fashionable new apartments and bought lovely things in lovely shops. They visited museums, dined in cafes, and attended performances at the new opera house.

But for the poor of Paris, the benefits were not so obvious. They were squeezed into buildings that had been spruced up on the outside but

Out in the Suburbs

During the late 1800s, trains, trolleys, and electric trams began to connect big cities with outlying areas called suburbs. A *suburb* is a community lying just outside a larger city. The word comes from the Latin words *sub*, meaning "under" or "near," and *urbs*, meaning "city."

As part of its planning, Paris pushed factories out of the beautiful central part of the city and into the new suburbs. Many factory workers began to live and work there.

In other growing cities, like London, Vienna, and Berlin, it was not factory workers but wealthy merchants and a growing middle class that moved to the new suburbs to escape the crowded city centers. Trains and trolley cars carried them between their suburban homes and their jobs in city shops, banks, and offices.

remained wretched within. Many poor Parisians were forced to leave the old part of the city and live farther from the center of town.

Still, Haussmann's changes made Paris a safer place. The grand boulevards and broadened streets made it easier to get around. The new sewers and fresh water systems reduced diseases. New gas lights (and later, electric lights) brightened streets at night and helped reduce crime.

City dwellers around the world took note of the great changes in Paris. In 1913, an article in a U.S. journal, *Engineering News*, claimed, "We want a Baron Haussmann in many of our cities of early origin; and while we fortunately have few of the huddles of old houses and labyrinthine streets that the third Napoleon caused to be removed from Paris, the example he set is well worthy of imitation." (*Labyrinthine*

means like a maze, full of twisting and turning passages.)

The reconstruction of Paris marked the beginning of modern "urban planning"—the designing and organizing of all aspects of city life, as opposed to hit-or-miss reform or simply letting things take their random course. The efforts of Haussmann and Napoleon III would have delighted the *philosophes* of Enlightenment France. Through reason, careful consideration, and large-scale planning, the baron and the emperor took Paris out of the Middle Ages and into modern times. They made Paris, as later writers called it, "the capital of the nineteenth century."

New York Grows Up—and Up

If Paris was the "capital of the nineteenth century," New York City became the capital of the twentieth. It had the world's busiest ports, the

A family of Italian immigrants arrives at the port of New York around 1900. New arrivals from Europe made New York one of the fastest growing cities in the world.

children made up 80 percent or more of New York City's population. New York had more Italians than the Italian cities of Florence, Genoa, and Venice put together. It was home to more Irish than Dublin, Ireland's capital city, and to more Germans than Hamburg in Germany. By 1900, the city was home to three million people.

How could the city handle its rapidly growing population? Geography posed a challenge. The heart of New York City is Manhattan, a small island only thirteen miles long and just over two miles wide. How could millions of people work and live in such a tight space?

The answer was for New York to grow up—literally. Until the 1860s, it was not possible to erect a building higher than four or five stories. Any higher than that and the building would collapse under its own weight. But steel made it possible to build tall buildings. And another innovation—a safe, efficient elevator invented by Elisha Otis—made tall buildings practical places in which to work and live.

busiest banks, the busiest industries, and the fastest growing population.

Job seekers, including hundreds of thousands of immigrants from Europe, flooded into New York. By the 1890s, immigrants and their

The Brooklyn Bridge

The island of Manhattan needed a connection to parts of New York that lay across the river. Engineers embarked on one of the most ambitious feats of the day—building the majestic 1,600-foot-long Brooklyn Bridge across the East River. The Brooklyn Bridge, completed in 1883, was the longest suspension bridge in the world, supported by thick twisted steel cables that hung from massive 275-foot towers.

The Brooklyn Bridge under construction in 1877

Ten and twelve-story buildings began to rise in New York City. Each year, these skyscrapers, as they were called, seemed to soar higher and higher. When the Woolworth Building was completed in 1913, it rose an incredible 55 stories, or nearly 800 feet high. It was nicknamed the Cathedral of Commerce. New York became the site of more tall buildings than any city in the world.

Bringing the Country to the City

Some New Yorkers wanted places with no buildings at all, where they could enjoy the beauty of nature. Other cities had built parks on their outskirts. But New York decided to place a huge park right in the heart of the city.

Central Park opened in 1876. Its chief designer was Frederick Law Olmsted. Instead of the formal parks common in European cities, Olmsted created a space that seemed to be entirely natural. Yet almost every square inch of it was carefully planned.

Workers hauled millions of loads of dirt to reshape the landscape. They planted almost five million trees and shrubs. They built bridges and footpaths. And they left many areas as wide-open spaces.

New Yorkers stroll and ride through Central Park, the huge open space at the heart of their city. The park's designer, Frederick Law Olmsted, wanted Central Park to look as much like the countryside as possible.

Central Park was designed to look as little like the city as possible. Olmsted wanted the park to be a place of calm and harmony, a place that would restore the spirits of city-dwellers. "The enjoyment of scenery," Olmsted wrote, "employs the mind without fatigue and yet exercises it, tranquilizes it and yet enlivens it; and thus, through the influence of the mind over the body, gives the effect of refreshing rest and reinvigoration of the whole system." Olmsted went on to apply this philosophy in his designs for parks in many other cities.

Louis Pasteur: Fighting Disease

Historical Close-up

One of the greatest challenges facing growing cities such as Paris and New York was public health. In the great urban centers, diseases often spread quickly, killing thousands. Governments began to take an interest in finding ways to stop epidemics. Some built laboratories and paid scientists to find ways to identify, treat, and control diseases. A French chemist made world-changing breakthroughs. His name was Louis Pasteur (LOO-ee pas-TUR).

Louis Pasteur was used to spending long hours in his university laboratory in Paris. It was an honor to work there, he told himself. After all, wasn't the École Normale Supérieure one of the most famous institutions of learning in the world? And hadn't his great supporter, Emperor Napoleon III himself, paid for this fine new lab in 1867?

Pasteur worked hard to repay the honor. He worked so hard that sometimes his health suffered. Still, now and then, in a quiet moment, he would relax and let his thoughts return to his childhood days, happy times spent in his small hometown in eastern France.

As a boy, he hadn't shown any signs of scientific genius. (For "genius" is what people were calling him now.) His real talent back then was in art. He sketched fine pastel drawings of his family and friends, and painted lovely landscapes of the surrounding countryside. He hoped that one day he would become an artist. But that was not to be.

Now, when Professor Pasteur drew, it would likely be a chain of small circles on a blackboard—representations of the tiny microbes he spent so much time studying.

Microbes, or microorganisms, are tiny living things too small to be seen with the naked eye.

Pasteur had already made a name for himself by studying how these organisms affected French wines. He discovered that during the process of fermentation, when grape juice turns into wine, certain microbes can spoil the juice and turn it bitter. He then proved that heat can kill these harmful microbes and keep the wine from going bad. Later, scientists used his ideas to eliminate microorganisms that cause milk and other food products to spoil. The process used to keep such products from spoiling came to be known as *pasteurization*.

The more Pasteur studied, the more he became convinced that there was a strong link between microbes and contagious diseases that made humans and animals sick. In 1878, he was studying a poultry disease called chicken cholera. It had recently killed a tenth of the chickens in France. Pasteur grew some disease-causing microbes in chicken broth. When he injected the broth culture into chickens, they fell ill and died within days.

In a laboratory, scientists can produce a *culture*, a sample of living material, such as cells or microorganisms, grown in a nutrient-rich substance.

One summer when Pasteur went on vacation, a culture of chicken cholera microbes was put to one side and forgotten. When he returned to his lab, Pasteur was about to throw it away. But he changed his mind and decided to inject it into a hen.

The bird became mildly sick but recovered quickly. Pasteur was intrigued. He injected more hens with the old culture. Each time he got the same result. He then injected the

The French chemist Louis Pasteur worked tirelessly in the fight against disease.

same birds with a fresh culture, one that should have been strong enough to kill them. But the hens were unaffected.

Pasteur injected the fresh culture into another batch of hens that had not been treated with the old culture. All of these birds died.

Pasteur realized that the microbes in the old culture must have weakened over time. They had given the hens a very mild case of cholera—not enough to harm them, but enough to cause their bodies to build up a resistance to the disease and protect them from it. The birds had been *vaccinated* against the disease.

Pasteur became convinced that vaccines were the best hope of conquering disease. In 1877, he and a team of fellow researchers started working on a disease called anthrax.

Anthrax was a disease that killed cattle and sheep. People could also die from anthrax. Even a pinprick was enough to pass on the deadly microbe.

Pasteur decided to make a vaccine for anthrax. He gave shots of weak anthrax microbes to healthy sheep. Just like the hens, the sheep grew only mildly sick and then recovered. Pasteur began to make more anthrax vaccine. His assistants traveled all over France. They vaccinated hundreds of thousands of sheep and cattle.

Next, Pasteur turned his attention to another disease—rabies. Rabies is an inflammation of the brain that destroys nerve cells and almost always causes death. The disease affects foxes, wolves, dogs, cats, and other carnivores. A bite from a rabid animal can infect and kill a human.

Pasteur and his colleagues reasoned that they could find the disease-causing microbe in the brain and spinal cord of an infected animal. So they took samples from the spinal cord of a dog that had died from rabies and injected them into a rabbit. Two weeks later the rabbit had rabies. When it died, Pasteur and his fellow scientists took some of its spinal cord and injected it into another rabbit. They did this over and over again, weakening the microbes with each transfer. Eventually Pasteur succeeded in vaccinating dogs to make them immune to rabies.

Pasteur still hadn't tested the rabies vaccine on any humans.

What Are Vaccines?

A *vaccine* is a preparation of microorganisms (usually weakened or killed) given to patients to build up their resistance to a specific disease. A British doctor, Edward Jenner, developed the first vaccinations. In 1796, he used the virus from cowpox—a cattle disease generally not harmful to humans—as a vaccine to protect against a related virus often deadly to humans, smallpox.

But on the morning of July 6, 1885, a frantic mother rushed into Pasteur's laboratory with her nine-year-old son, Joseph Meister. Two days earlier, a rabid dog had bitten Joseph. The mother begged Pasteur to save her son.

Pasteur faced a terrible dilemma. He was not yet ready to try his rabies vaccine on humans—he did not know the risks or whether it would work. But if he did nothing, then Joseph would likely die. Pasteur decided the vaccine was the boy's only hope.

That evening, Pasteur supervised a doctor who injected the vaccine into young Joseph. Over the next 10 days, they gave more injections, each day a stronger one. The bites healed. Joseph never contracted rabies. The vaccine worked.

News of the cure flashed all around Europe. Victims of bites from rabid animals rushed to Paris to receive Pasteur's treatment. He treated hundreds of patients, and almost all lived.

To support Pasteur in his work, the French Academy of Sciences set up an institute for the treatment of rabies and the development of other vaccines. Money to support the research poured in from all over the word. In 1888, when Pasteur was 65 years old, the Pasteur Institute opened its doors in Paris. Pasteur's former patient, Joseph Meister, took a job as gatekeeper at the Institute.

Pasteur himself did not work much longer. He died on September 28, 1895, at the age of 72. He was buried in a chapel at the Pasteur Institute. Joseph Meister took on the task of caring for the tomb of the man who had saved his life.

Other researchers continued the work Pasteur had begun. All over the industrialized world, scientists hunted for the microbes that caused deadly urban diseases such as tuberculosis and cholera. By the end of the century, they had identified many germs behind the most common diseases. Over time, they were able to develop vaccines. In the early years of the twentieth century, physicians and governments launched mass vaccination campaigns to protect people. Thanks to Louis Pasteur, the world had become a safer place. ✒

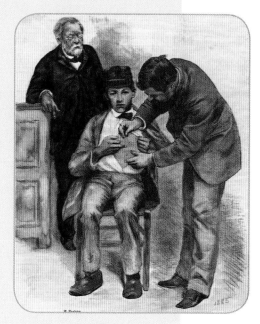

Louis Pasteur watches as an assistant vaccinates a patient.

Two "spindle boys" operate machinery in a cotton mill in Georgia around 1909. During the late nineteenth and early twentieth centuries, governments began to limit, but not eliminate, child labor.

Labor Organizes for Change

You've learned that in the early 1800s, when the Industrial Revolution began, many men, women, and children worked in miserable and dangerous conditions. Charles Dickens described factories "where there was a rattling and a trembling all day long, and where the piston of the steam-engine worked monotonously up and down," and every day streams of workers "went in and out at the same hours … to do the same work, and … every day was the same as yesterday and tomorrow…."

By the mid-nineteenth century, some governments began to limit the number of hours that women and children could work. But governments were slow to do much more. They didn't think they should tell industry owners how to run their businesses.

Workers in steel mills, gas refineries, and ironworks often faced 14-hour days in dark factories filled with dangerous fumes. Other laborers worked in "sweatshops," makeshift factories in the crowded tenements where they lived. In New York City, poor immigrants were jammed into overcrowded, unhealthy sweatshops to roll cigars or sew clothing.

There seemed to be little that workers could do to improve their situation. If an employee complained, he could be fired. But, as the saying goes, there's strength in numbers. Workers realized that if they joined together, they could speak as a group—and perhaps be heard.

Workers in various trades—such as the ironworkers or coal miners—began to organize. They formed trade unions. Each union bargained with its employers for better hours, higher wages, and improved working conditions. This bargaining as a group, known as collective bargaining, gave workers strength that they lacked individually.

Going on Strike

Even when they joined together in unions, what power did workers have? Employers had the money. Often they had the government on their side. But the workers had their labor, the power of their minds, hands, and bodies. If collective bargaining failed—if an employer refused to offer better conditions or higher pay—then, as a last resort, the workers could withhold their labor. They could refuse to work—in other words, they could go on strike.

When hundreds of workers walked off the job, factories ground to a halt. In the large factories, mines, and steel mills of the second industrial revolution, a strike could cost an employer millions of dollars. Of course a strike was hard on the workers as well, because they had to go without pay. Still, trade unions learned they could use the threat of a strike to put pressure on the employers. Even the stingiest employer might agree to raise pay rather than see his factories idle and losing money.

By 1871, trade unions and strikes were legal in Great Britain and elsewhere. Blacksmiths, shoemakers, printers, cotton spinners, ironworkers, dockworkers, and steelworkers began to form unions to fight for better conditions.

Sometimes the unions succeeded, as in the case of England's Bryant & May match factory, where the employees were mostly women who worked 14 hours a day for little pay. The company imposed

Young women at the Bryant & May match factory went on strike in 1888. The Matchgirls' Union won a victory that not only improved conditions for its members, but also encouraged other trade unions in Britain.

fines for offenses such as talking, dropping matches, or visiting the restroom without permission. When some employees protested these rules, they were fired. So in 1888, fourteen hundred workers at Bryant & May went on strike and formed the Matchgirls' Union. After three weeks, the owners gave in. They hired back the fired workers and ended the system of fines. It was a victory not just for the Matchgirls but for unions in general.

The Tolpuddle Martyrs

Trade unions began as early as the 1830s in Great Britain. In 1834, six English farm laborers from the village of Tolpuddle agreed they would accept no less than 10 shillings a week for their work. They pledged loyalty to a newly formed union, the Friendly Society of Agricultural Laborers. The six were promptly arrested and sentenced to seven years of labor in Britain's penal colony of Australia. But the story of the Tolpuddle Martyrs, as they came to be known, spread quickly. Their efforts inspired others to speak out for the rights of laborers.

Sometimes disputes between workers and factory owners turned violent. The 1892 strike by steelworkers at the Carnegie mill in Homestead, Pennsylvania, led to bloodshed.

Employers Strike Back

Of course the employers hated unions and strikes. They sometimes circulated blacklists, which named union organizers. People named on blacklists were often fired or refused employment. Employers also used lockouts to fight union demands. In a lockout, an employer barred the factory doors to keep out union members. The employer might suffer some losses while the factory was closed, but he figured that the workers would suffer even more when they received no pay. The employer calculated that when the workers grew desperate, they would return to work on the employer's terms. During a lockout, some employers even replaced union members with nonunion workers.

Some employers went beyond blacklists and lockouts and took violent action against unions. For example, in 1892, when Andrew Carnegie's steel mill in Homestead, Pennsylvania, announced that it was cutting wages, the angry steelworkers called for a strike. The company began a lockout and hired new non-union laborers and armed guards to protect the mill. But the locked-out workers took up arms as well. Violence erupted, and 10 men died in the fighting.

The governor of Pennsylvania sent in the National Guard. The union was crushed. The company slashed wages, imposed a 12-hour minimum workday, and eliminated 500 jobs. The company's owner, Andrew Carnegie, was vacationing in Scotland at the time. Although he had said he supported unions, he remained silent and did nothing to stop the confrontation.

Despite such setbacks, organized labor grew in numbers and influence. Union membership in Britain rose from 1.5 million in 1894 to 4.1 million in 1914. Some 3.7 million workers in Germany had joined unions by 1912. In the United States, a British immigrant and cigar-maker named Samuel Gompers organized the American Federation of Labor. In 1898, the AFL had more than 250,000 members. Two years later, it had more than a million.

Women in the Workforce

Since the earliest days of the Industrial Revolution, when the first textile mills opened, women had been part of the industrial workforce. Throughout the nineteenth century, many women continued to work in factories.

We can get a glimpse of what factory life was like for women in the novel *Sister Carrie*, by the American writer Theodore Dreiser. Dreiser tells the story of young Carrie Meeber, who found work in a Chicago shoe factory in 1889. Carrie spends all day at a clacking machine that punches holes in pieces of leather. As Dreiser wrote:

> The pieces of leather came from the girl at the machine to her right, and were passed on to the girl at her left. Carrie saw at once that an average speed was necessary or the work would pile up on her and all those below would be delayed. She had no time to look about, and bent anxiously to her task….
>
> Once, when she was fumbling at the little clamp, having made a slight error in setting in the leather, a great hand appeared before her eyes and fastened the clamp for her. It was the foreman. Her heart thumped so that she could scarcely see to go on.
>
> "Start your machine," he said, "start your machine. Don't keep the line waiting."

Throughout the industrialized world, thousands of women like Carrie Meeber bent over machines and performed the same task again and again, anxious not to "keep the line waiting." But in the second half of the nineteenth century, some women found jobs that were more pleasant and paid more than factory

Women operate a switchboard in a Paris telephone exchange.

work. Growing businesses needed employees to keep records, so women worked as file clerks, typists, and secretaries. With the invention of the telephone, women went to work in large numbers as switchboard operators.

While many women found jobs in business and industry, even more took jobs as domestic servants— for example, as maids, nannies, or cooks. No matter what work they did, women almost always earned less than men, even for the same job.

"Deeds Not Words": Women Seek the Vote

As some women joined the workforce, others began to campaign for new rights. Many focused on a fundamental right they did not yet have—the right to vote.

In 1848, women in the antislavery movement held the first conference for women's rights in Seneca Falls, New York. In 1872, Susan B. Anthony

Emmeline Pankhurst makes a speech in 1908 in favor of suffrage for women. British women campaigned, protested, and went to jail for 20 more years before Parliament finally granted them full voting rights.

tried to cast a vote in the U.S. presidential election. She was arrested and fined for casting an illegal ballot. Anthony gave a stirring speech, quoting words that Thomas Jefferson had kept on his desk: "Resistance to tyranny is obedience to God!"

By the late 1800s, many educated women on both sides of the Atlantic were working for suffrage, the right to vote. The suffrage movement sparked both ridicule and anger.

Too Busy to Join the Campaign

The woman's suffrage movement was led by a growing number of well-educated and well-to-do women. Poor and working-class women were notably absent from the campaign. Women working as domestic servants or in factories were too busy trying to earn a living to go out and fight for the right to vote.

Some people said that giving women the right to vote would destroy the family. Others said women lacked the intelligence to vote.

In Britain, Emmeline Goulden Pankhurst had plenty of intelligence and a strong belief in women's rights. She had been raised to value natural rights and freedom. As a girl, she had listened to her mother reading aloud *Uncle Tom's Cabin*. "Young as I was," Emmeline recalled, "I knew perfectly well the meaning of the words *slavery* and *emancipation*."

Emmeline saw special significance in her birthday, July 14, Bastille Day. On that day in 1789, French revolutionaries had stormed the old fortress and ignited the French Revolution. As Emmeline pointed out, "it was women who gave the signal to spur on the crowd, and led to the final taking of that monument of tyranny, the Bastille, in Paris."

Emmeline, too, was destined to spur on crowds. In 1872, the year of Susan B. Anthony's arrest, 14-year-old Emmeline attended her first woman suffrage meeting in Manchester, England. There she found her life's work. She later married a Manchester lawyer named Richard Pankhurst. She and her husband successfully campaigned for the right of married women to vote in local elections. When her husband died in 1898, Emmeline kept pressing for the right of women to vote in national elections.

In 1903, Pankhurst founded the Women's Social and Political Union, or WSPU. The WSPU made woman suffrage its chief goal. Its motto was "Deeds not Words." Many deeds followed.

At a political rally in 1905, WSPU members demanded that the organizers of the rally support the idea of votes for women. They were thrown out of the meeting. When confronted by police on the street, they protested vigorously. The women were arrested but refused to pay their fines. Eventually they were released from jail, but they were more determined than ever to press for their cause.

WSPU members interrupted meetings of officials in Parliament. They pelted politicians with eggs. Once they tried to storm the House of Commons in Parliament. They faced jail for their protests.

Pankhurst herself often went to jail, where she would go on hunger strikes—that is, she refused to eat as a way to call attention to her cause. Sometimes officials ordered her release so she could recover her health. Sometimes they ordered the jailers to force-feed her. Once free, Pankhurst would go back to agitating, and sooner or later back to jail.

In 1912, Pankhurst's daughter, Christabel, organized activities in which WSPU members smashed windows and set fire to churches. They thought these churches encouraged the idea that women should stay at home and let their husbands vote for them. This violence was too much for most people. Emmeline Pankhurst was arrested 12 times that year, and served about 30 days in jail.

Pankhurst eventually condemned the WSPU's violent tactics. But confrontations continued to flare over women's right to vote. In most of the industrialized world, women waited decades for results. Emmeline Pankhurst worked tirelessly for the cause and lived to see the British Parliament enact full voting rights for women a month before she died in 1928.

Pankhurst was not alone in her struggles. Across the western world, woman suffragists campaigned for the right to vote. Their efforts challenged governments to live up to the promise of their ideals, and eventually led to change that affected millions of lives.

Woman Suffrage When?

In 1893, New Zealand became the first nation to give women full voting rights. Australia followed in 1902. Finland approved woman suffrage in 1906. In 1920, the United States ratified the 19th Amendment to the Constitution, giving women the right to vote. Britain extended full voting equality to women in 1928. French women had to wait until 1945 to cast their ballots.

American women celebrate ratification of the 19th Amendment.

*Crowds flock to a public park in Vienna,
Austria, at the turn of the twentieth century,
a time when goods, services, and entertainment
began to reach millions of people.*

Reaching Millions

*P*icture in your mind western Europe in 1800. It's a rural world in which most people are peasants, scratching a living from the soil.

Now move ahead a hundred years—barely a tick of the watch in the grand scale of historical time. But in this short time, the world has been transformed. Yes, many people still live on farms and villages. But now there are crowded cities with busy streets, well-lit at night. Electric street cars clatter along. Telephone wires stretch overhead. Factories produce all sorts of goods, from bicycles to sewing machines to typewriters.

In these big cities, handsome mansions fill a few rich neighborhoods. In other areas, the poor live in slums. But in much of the city, there are well-kept apartment buildings and little houses. These belong to a large group of people who aren't rich or poor but somewhere in between— a group known as the middle class.

By 1900, millions of middle-class families lived in Europe and America, and their numbers were growing. Members of the middle class worked in offices, stores, factories, and other businesses. While much less wealthy than the factory owners, middle-class workers far outnumbered the rich. As a group, the middle class possessed a large chunk of spending money.

In the cities, more businesses began to cater to this growing middle class. Its members needed shirts, dresses, coats, hats, and household goods. Sometimes they liked to buy small luxuries, such as pocket watches or jewelry. They wanted newspapers to read. In their spare time, they wanted entertainment, such as plays or music.

As the twentieth century approached, a growing middle class had more money to spend. In Paris, shoppers could spend their money at Aristide Boucicaut's enormous new department store.

In 1800, only the rich could afford many of these things. But by 1900, new products, inventions, and entertainments were available to many more people. This period witnessed the birth of what has been called "mass society."

In "mass society," the word *mass* means "a large quantity or amount." It's a good word to apply to the beginning of the twentieth century. By 1900, factories were producing masses of goods. We call that mass production. Masses of people were buying those goods—that's mass consumerism. More and more people were finding ways to amuse themselves—that's mass entertainment. Mass education made it possible for more people to read and write. Mass communication, such as the telephone and wireless telegraph, enabled more people to get in touch with each other.

In this time of the beginnings of mass society, the goods and services created by the Industrial Revolution were beginning to reach millions of people.

Marketing the New Abundance

In 1829, a traveling salesman named Aristide Boucicaut (ah-ree-steed BOO-sih-koh) decided to settle down in Paris. A few years later he married a local deli owner, and together the couple bought a little dry goods store, which sold ready-to-wear clothes, small household items, and the like. The Boucicauts called their store the *Bon Marché* (bohn mar-SHAY), which means "good buy" in French.

Paris was growing, and the Boucicauts did well. They expanded their store so much that to keep track of everything, they had to sort their goods into separate categories, or departments. The Boucicauts created one of the first department stores.

In 1869, Aristide Boucicaut borrowed some money and built an enormous new store in the heart of Paris. It wasn't just big. It changed the whole idea of shopping.

In the past, when customers walked into a fashionable store, they didn't see much on the shelves. Most of the items for sale were kept in storage. The customers discussed what they wanted with a salesclerk and then haggled over the price. The new Bon Marché did away with haggling. Boucicaut set fixed prices, marked them on the products, and put the products on display.

And what display! By 1870, Boucicaut showed his merchandise in themed settings. One aisle might be a Moroccan alleyway, another an Egyptian temple, and beyond, a Japanese garden. By day, sunlight shone through plate glass windows on the rows and rows of goods. Later, when electric lights became affordable, the store gleamed at night as well.

Boucicaut astounded Paris with new marketing ideas. He lured shoppers by holding sales. He placed advertisements in newspapers. He allowed people to return items they had bought if they decided they did not need them after all. He let people buy things on credit and pay for them over time. He introduced many practices that consumers now take for granted.

Boucicaut kept his prices low by selling mass-produced goods at great volume. But his gorgeous displays made the customers feel as though they were buying luxuries. Best of all, no one had to buy a thing at the Bon Marché. Shoppers could simply roam and browse.

Department stores like the Bon Marché turned shopping into a sort of entertainment. Men and women could stroll down the street and gaze through store windows at the displays. Today we call it "window-shopping." Women went out with their women friends to go window-shopping on their own. This was something new. Until this time, middle-class women were supposed to leave the home only in the company of men.

Department stores similar to the Bon Marché sprang up all over Europe and the United States. They became the marketplaces of choice for many thousands of urban, middle-class consumers.

Richard Warren Sears: Selling to Millions

In the United States and other industrial nations, many people still lived on farms outside the crowded cities. Many of these farmers had extra cash to spend, because modern machinery had helped make their farms productive and profitable. Because these people lived far from the big cities, they didn't shop in the new department stores. Instead they relied on traveling salesmen and peddlers for their purchases. They paid high prices and often had little variety to choose from.

A business genius named Richard Warren Sears realized that if he mailed people a catalog offering goods for sale, they might order products from him rather than buy from traveling salesmen. So he bought bargain items in the city—such as watches, jewelry, and silverware—and listed them in an appealing 14-page catalog. He sent the catalog to people living in the country. Now these farmers and other rural people had the opportunity to shop by mail.

Sears had a genius for writing and designing catalogs. Soon he was selling his watches and jewelry almost as fast as he could put his catalogs in the mail. He began to add more products to his catalog. Then he discovered his other great talent—sensing what the masses wanted. Sears had an uncanny knack for knowing what to add to his catalog and when to drop an item.

In 1887, he took on a business partner, Alvah Curtis Roebuck. By that time, the U.S. rail and postal networks were so well-developed that almost anything could be shipped almost anywhere. Sears and Roebuck turned their catalog into a nationwide mail-order business that gave rural families the chance to buy the same goods as city folk.

By 1895, the company was producing a hefty 507-page catalog, every line of which was written by Sears—except for the 50 pages of letters from satisfied customers. The company sold thousands of products—sewing machines, bicycles, furniture, ready-made clothing, vacuum cleaners, books, cured meats, coffee, medicines, and even farm equipment.

Success breeds imitators. Other catalog companies sprang up in America and in Europe. With all the buying and selling through catalogs and department stores, businesses on both sides of the Atlantic grew.

Leisure for the Many

Before the Industrial Revolution, when most people lived on farms, the weather and the seasons set the rhythms of work and play. After the Industrial Revolution, the clock began to control people's schedules.

When workers first started toiling in factories, they had little if any spare time. They labored twelve hours a day, six days a week, every week of the year. Those who got time off on Sunday often spent it in church.

But over the course of the nineteenth century, workers formed unions and pushed for shorter hours and higher wages. By 1900, the typical workday had shrunk to ten hours. Most people got half of Saturday off as well as Sunday. This

Catalogs as Historical Tools

The Sears, Roebuck catalog was often called "The Nation's Wish Book." Old catalogs give a detailed picture of American life during the late nineteenth and early twentieth centuries. Through them, you can track when gadgets such as toasters were invented, because as soon as inventors came up with a useful product, it showed up in the catalog. The Sears, Roebuck catalog also reveals the strong and growing appetite of the new middle class, which was hungry to buy an amazing assortment of products by mail, from books to stoves to prefabricated houses.

Sears, Roebuck catalog, 1899

was the beginning of the idea of "the weekend"—a regular weekly interval set aside for leisure.

Millions of people in the middle class enjoyed a growing supply of leisure time. They didn't have to spend all weekend at home doing chores because of innovations such as piped water, electric power, gas stoves, and washing machines. So, with their free time and spare money, they sought entertainment in the evenings, on weekends, and eventually during summer vacations.

For a long time, only the wealthy could afford a vacation at a seaside resort, but now thousands of ordinary "day-trippers" flocked to beach towns on weekends. Trains took them there for the day. Outside the cities at the ends of the trolley lines, streetcar companies built "trolley parks." These parks offered dance halls, picnic tables, and carnival rides such as the Ferris wheel, invented by George Ferris. Some trolley parks grew into huge amusement parks. New York had its Coney Island, while Blackpool Pleasure Beach drew crowds of Londoners on weekends. Vienna had its new amusement park with the *Riesenrad*, a giant Ferris wheel. (See page 610.)

More leisure time meant time for travel. In Great Britain, Thomas Cook created the first travel agency. Cook had once worked for a religious group, making travel arrangements for members who were going to conferences to discuss the evils of drinking. Cook realized he could sell the same services—booking tickets, making hotel reservations, hunting up travel bargains—to middle-class

English families who wanted enjoyable vacation trips. In the 1860s, Cook began offering tours to Paris. Tourism soon grew into a big business. By the 1890s, Cook's firm offered trips to countries all over the world, from Switzerland to Egypt to Australia.

Sports as Entertainment

New businesses developed to feed the hunger for entertainment. People had always enjoyed playing sports, but now they could pay money to *watch* professional athletes play. Professional rugby and soccer leagues formed in Britain. Stadiums were built to accommodate the games. In 1872, 2,000 fans attended the British Soccer Cup finals. By 1885, the crowd had swelled to 10,000. By 1901, some 100,000 flocked to the games.

In the United States, baseball became a favorite sport. American baseball had developed from an English game called "rounders," in which players used a bat to hit a ball

A labor-saving washing machine made in 1897

In Britain and many other lands, soccer is called *football*.

New Yorkers crowd the beach at Coney Island.

and then ran around bases. New England colonists played the game, modified the rules, and eventually came up with the American game of baseball. During the Civil War, the game's popularity spread as Union soldiers taught it to each other and to Confederate prisoners. After the war, many towns organized baseball clubs, and in 1869 a Cincinnati club decided to pay all its players. The first professional baseball team in the United States, the Cincinnati Red Stockings, was born. Soon other American cities began paying their players and forming professional leagues.

The growing interest in sports gave birth to the modern Olympic Games. A French nobleman named Baron Pierre de Coubertin (koo-behr-tan) proposed to revive the games that had been held every four years in ancient Greece. The first modern Olympics were held in Athens in 1896. Amateur athletes from Greece, France, Britain, the United States, and many other countries competed in sports such as cycling, gymnastics, and wrestling. The 1900 Olympics were held in Paris, and the 1904 games in St. Louis, Missouri.

Improved transportation enabled athletes and spectators to travel across oceans and continents to attend the international games. Telegraph reports allowed newspapers to print news about how the athletes were faring in the contests. By 1908, when the games were held in London, the modern Olympics had fans all over the world.

A Night on the Town

The upper classes had long enjoyed an evening at the theater, watching a play or opera. Most people could not afford such entertainments. A new type of theater, the variety show, provided affordable mass entertainment. In the United States of the 1890s, these variety shows were called vaudeville (VAWD-vil), a word that probably came from *Vau-de-Vire*, a valley in France where for centuries people had composed entertaining, comic songs. In Europe, similar shows were staged at so-called music halls.

Vaudeville and music hall theaters opened in the morning and ran long into the night. Tickets were cheap, and people could stay as long as they liked. The shows featured many performers in a series of short acts, one after the other. People could arrive any time, whenever they finished work. It didn't matter what they'd missed — something else would start soon.

In a single visit, a customer might see a trained monkey, a singer,

International interest in watching sports led to a revival of ancient Greece's Olympic Games. The first modern Olympics were held in Athens in 1896.

a juggler, a comedian, a two-headed goat, the survivor of a shipwreck, or a 15-minute version of Shakespeare's *Hamlet*. Some music halls offered burlesque, bawdy entertainment unfit for children. Other theaters stuck to acts that would appeal to families.

New Technologies: Phonographs and Motion Pictures

The age of invention spawned new forms of mass entertainment to compete with vaudeville and music halls. The invention of the phonograph brought music out of the concert hall and, eventually, into the home. Thomas Edison invented the phonograph in 1877. He made his first recording on a cylinder covered with tin foil. A stylus etched grooves in the foil, capturing the sounds of Edison's voice as he spoke: "Mary had a little lamb...."

These early recordings on cylinders proved difficult to mass produce. Recording technology took a step forward when a German-born immigrant to the United States, Emile Berliner, successfully captured sound on flat discs. Berliner's gramophone, as he called it, still suffered a problem—it was hard to get the disc to rotate at a steady speed. An engineer named Eldridge Johnson solved this problem by designing a phonograph with a new kind of motor.

In 1901, Berliner and Johnson teamed up to start the Victor Talking Machine Company. They produced affordable phonographs, called Victrolas, and recordings of famous singers. Some of the most popular recordings were made by an Italian tenor, Enrico Caruso, who sang with the Metropolitan Opera in New York City. The phonograph helped turn Caruso into one of the first examples of what we would today call a "pop star."

Another invention from Thomas Edison and his staff of engineers helped bring entertainment to millions in the form of "moving pictures" or, as you know them, movies. Edison showed his first

Performer W.C. Fields juggles top hats in a vaudeville show. Such entertainment was popular among people who could not afford to attend plays or operas.

Left: A dog named Nipper was the trademark, or symbol, of the Victor Talking Machine Company, which manufactured phonographs. This painting of Nipper, called His Master's Voice, *became one of the most recognized images in the world.*

On the Radio

In 1910, in honor of Guglielmo Marconi, radio's Italian inventor, the first radio program broadcast to the public featured the Italian tenor Enrico Caruso singing live from the Metropolitan Opera House in New York City. By the 1920s, millions of people were listening to regularly scheduled radio broadcasts of music, news, and sports.

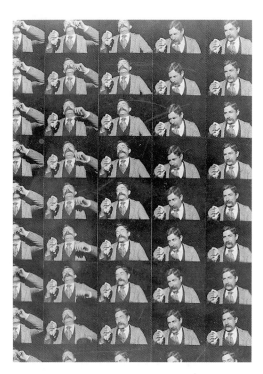

Thomas Edison's first movie, The Sneeze, *was played on a device called a Kinetoscope. Such moving pictures seemed miraculous to late nineteenth-century viewers, and people lined up to see them.*

movies on a device called the Kinetoscope, from the Greek words *kineto* (movement) and *scopos* (to watch). These movies were very short, and their images flickered with jerky movements. Edison's first effort was a movie called *The Sneeze.* It showed a man sneezing—nothing more.

In 1894, a Kinetoscope parlor opened in New York City. For a quarter, customers could peer, one at a time, into a row of five Kinetoscopes

News at the Movies

Early moviegoers in the United States were drawn to theaters to see accounts of news in the making. For example, in 1898, Edison hired a filmmaker to record events surrounding the Spanish-American War. No actual battles were filmed, but the producers did use members of the New Jersey National Guard to film simulations of key battles. In 1901, movies showed scenes from the funeral of President William McKinley, who had been assassinated. Americans started *seeing* the news, instead of just reading or hearing about it.

and see moving pictures of vaudeville dancers or boxing matches.

Most of the earliest motion pictures showed scenes from life, such as vaudeville performers, moving railway trains, or firemen at work. Then in 1903, one of Edison's employees, Edwin Porter, made an eight-minute movie that told a story. *The Great Train Robbery* ended with a man pointing a gun straight at the audience. People shrieked with delighted terror. Other filmmakers made story films with titles such as *Trailed by the Bloodhounds,* which promised audiences thrills and scares.

Movies became more popular when they moved from booths for individual viewers to rooms in which the pictures were projected onto a large screen. The first movie theaters—called nickelodeons because the price of admission was a nickel—opened in 1905. They showed a variety of movies all day long, including fare that appealed to women and children. The early movies were silent, with no words or sounds, although sometimes a piano player, organist, or small band played music to go along with a film's story. By 1908, there were more than 8,000 nickelodeons in the United States.

Nickelodeons declined as businessmen built larger theaters and producers made longer movies. By 1910, the United States had 10,000 movie theaters drawing an estimated five million people a day. Theaters sprang up across Europe as well. In large studios in France and Italy, filmmakers produced movies about everything from

ancient Rome to imaginary flights to the moon.

Mass Publishing: Pulp Fiction and Yellow Journalism

In the second half of the nineteenth century, people in industrialized nations had more and more books to read. New high-speed printing presses gave rise to mass publishing. Millions of middle-class readers bought books called "dime novels" in the United States and "penny dreadfuls" in Britain. For just a few cents, anyone could spend an afternoon reading a detective story, an outlaw tale, or a breathless romance.

In the late nineteenth century, magazines called *pulps* became popular in Europe and the United States. Their name came from the fact that they were printed on cheap wood-pulp paper. The magazines specialized in short, exciting "pulp fiction" stories that included science fiction and tales about cowboys in the American West.

In the United States, two publishers, Joseph Pulitzer and William Randolph Hearst, transformed the daily newspaper into a form of entertainment. Their

newspapers still carried news, but they favored sensational stories about murders, scandals, and the like. The stories often stretched the truth to entertain people.

The newspapers of Pulitzer and Hearst also contained whole sections devoted to sports and other entertainments, as well as illustrated stories called comics. The first comic strip featured a wildly popular character called The Yellow Kid. And so the sensational news reporting in the Hearst and Pulitzer papers came to be called "yellow journalism."

The Ideal of Universal Education

In the late 1800s and early 1900s, technology helped make possible mass publications such as newspapers and pulp fiction magazines. But such publications were in demand only because by this time many people could read.

As recently as the late eighteenth century in Europe, only children with wealthy parents could get a good education. While they were young, children usually studied at home with tutors. When boys reached their teenage years, they might go off to private schools, and after that to universities where they learned Greek and Latin and studied the classics. Girls usually received much less formal schooling than boys. And poor children usually got no schooling. Those who did attended church schools where they learned not just reading, writing, and arithmetic, but also obedience and religious lessons.

During the French Revolution, some thinkers had made grand

Left: A scene from the 1902 film A Trip to the Moon *shows the man in the moon with a rocket in his eye.*

Above: The sensational reporting in some U.S. newspapers came to be called "yellow journalism." The name came from The Yellow Kid, a character in a popular comic strip in the Sunday World, *a newspaper published in New York.*

speeches urging education for all the people. In that chaotic time, however, little came of such talk. Later, Napoleon did manage to set up some government-funded schools and universities. Still, relatively few people got much schooling.

In Britain, public education lagged further behind. In 1807, as part of a bill called the Poor Laws, a politician named Samuel Whitbread suggested that penniless British children should receive at least two years of church schooling. Many people protested that so much education would make the lower classes rebellious.

In 1870, the British Parliament passed a law stating that the government *should* provide an elementary education for all children, including the poorest of the poor. Turning "should" into "would," however, took another 20 years. During those 20 years, Germany moved ahead of Britain as an industrial power.

The English poet Matthew Arnold, who worked as a school inspector for a time, toured Europe. He was impressed that German children received at least eight years of schooling in state-supported schools. Arnold and other critics suggested that better-educated citizens might be giving Germany an economic edge over Britain. Economic competition from the United States—where, by 1890, most young children had access to free public schooling—provided a further spur to change in Britain. In 1891, Britain passed a law funding universal public education.

As the twentieth century dawned, much of western Europe had laws forbidding children to go to work and requiring them to go to school. By funding public schools, governments weakened the role of churches in education. The new public schools generally emphasized reading, writing, and arithmetic, as well as science, national history, and the literature of each country's national language.

Public education ensured that the majority of adults in western Europe and the United States could read. In eastern Europe, by contrast, where universal public education had not taken hold, fewer adults could read. As a result, the western part of the continent moved even further ahead of the eastern regions.

More for More

How was the western world different in 1900 from 1800? One word sums it up—*more*.

More people were connected with each other in more ways. Millions of people were wearing the same mass-produced hats or gloves, reading the same mass-produced

Public Schooling in the United States

In the 1830s, two American educators, Horace Mann and Henry Barnard, argued for "common schools" that would help educate all children, rich or poor. They believed state governments should set up elementary schools and require all children to attend them. In 1852, Massachusetts became the first state to pass a law requiring children to go to school. During the next few decades, the other states followed. Public high schools in the United States began to multiply after 1900.

books and magazines, or listening to the same music on mass-produced phonograph records. Among the rapidly growing middle class, more people owned more goods and had more choices. Mass communication made this vast public more aware of itself and its opinions.

With so much for so many, did people have everything they needed? Did the abundance of material goods and entertainment opportunities also bring more meaning to people's lives? We'll consider that question in the next chapter.

By the time this photo was taken in London in 1910, millions of children in western Europe and the United States were attending public schools.

Henry Ford: Motor Cars for the Multitudes

The new abundance of material goods available to consumers in the early twentieth century included a technological marvel once available only to the few—the automobile. Let's meet the man who made owning automobiles a reality for millions of people—Henry Ford, who in many ways invented the automobile industry.

Historical Close-up

Young Henry Ford was fascinated by anything with moving parts. Growing up on a Michigan farm, he stayed up late at night, taking things apart and figuring out how they worked. He tinkered with everything from pocket watches to farm equipment.

His family learned to be careful around Henry. "When we had mechanical or wind-up toys given to us at Christmas," his younger sister later remembered, "we always said, 'Don't let Henry see them! He'll take them apart!'"

In the summer of 1876, when he was 12 years old, Henry was riding in his father's horse-drawn wagon when he saw a machine that fascinated him—a "road engine" that literally ran on its own steam. A steam engine and a boiler were mounted on wheels, carrying a man who stood on a platform shoveling coal to keep the engine running.

Henry hopped off his father's wagon so he could inspect the machine. It was an awkward-looking contraption, with a water tank and coal cart trailing behind it. Nearly 50 years later, Henry Ford vividly recalled that machine. It was, he wrote, "as though I had seen it only yesterday, for it was the first vehicle other than horse-drawn that I had ever seen."

Young Henry decided, right then and there, that he would spend his life, as he put it, "making a machine that would travel the roads."

His father wanted Henry to stay and work on the family farm, but Henry had no interest in being a farmer. "My earliest recollection," he wrote years later, "is that, considering the results, there was too much work on the place.... Even when very young, I suspected that much might somehow be done in a better way."

Henry left home at the age of 16 to find a job that would allow him to continue tinkering with machines. He moved to Detroit, Michigan, where he eventually became a mechanical engineer at the Edison Illuminating Company. While working at Edison, he spent most of his free time trying to build a road machine, or, as it was sometimes called, a "horseless carriage."

In the mid-1880s, the German inventors Gottlieb Daimler and Karl Benz had built the first gasoline-powered automobiles. By the end of the decade, many other people were trying to build them as well. Ford wanted to make a car that was lighter, faster, and cheaper than anyone else's. He rented a shed and enlisted friends to help him build what he called a quadricycle, a small chassis with four bicycle wheels and a simple gasoline engine.

Work on the quadricycle took over Ford's life. He skipped meals and lost sleep. Finally, the quadricycle was ready for a test drive. At four o'clock in the morning of June 4, 1896, Ford climbed aboard his quadricycle and prepared to take it for a spin.

Then he realized the machine wouldn't fit through the shed door. Not to be stopped at this point, he picked up an axe, knocked a hole through the wall, and wheeled out his quadricycle.

Ford started the engine and drove down Grand River Avenue. A friend rode ahead of him on a bicycle to warn off any horse-drawn carriages that might be on the street at that hour.

Ford was soon driving around Detroit at all hours, with his wife and son sitting on a board next to him. His "gasoline buggy," he later wrote, was "considered to be something of a nuisance, for it made a racket and it scared horses." But it fascinated

Henry Ford sits in his first gasoline buggy— also called the quadricycle—which he built in a shed in 1896.

people. So many wanted to try driving the quadricycle that Ford had to chain it to a lamppost whenever he left it on the street.

Finally, after he had driven the machine about a thousand miles, Ford sold it and built two more cars, each one lighter and better than the last. Then he left his job at the Edison power company to join some investors in starting the Detroit Automobile Company.

Many people thought he was crazy. "At first," as Ford later recalled, "the 'horseless carriage' was considered merely a freak notion, and many wise people explained with particularity why it could never be more than a toy" for rich people.

One thing was sure: Only the rich could afford a car or truck made by the Detroit Automobile Company. The vehicles were built one at a time, in a painfully slow process that allowed each customer to specify what he or she wanted in a vehicle.

One visitor to the Detroit company watched Ford test-drive a car that had taken five men a full week to assemble. Everyone else thought the car was running fine, but not Henry Ford. "Come on, boys," he said, "we'll have to pull this to pieces." So they tore the car apart and started over again.

The Detroit Automobile Company closed shop in November 1900. But Ford kept designing cars and joined another partner in starting a new automobile company. That company failed, too. Then, in 1903, Ford rented a one-room brick shed and started the Ford Motor Company.

"I will build a motor car for the great multitude," he said. "It will be so low in price that no man making a good salary will be unable to own one." His idea was to mass-produce a simple, sturdy car. "The less complex an article, the easier it is to make, the cheaper it may be sold, and therefore the greater number may be sold," he explained.

Ford and his engineers experimented with several models. They named them after letters of the alphabet. Ford was at last satisfied with the Model T. At first he offered the car in different colors, but by 1914 he'd cut back on options. "Any customer can have a car painted any color that he wants," Ford said, "so long as it is black."

But even Model Ts were expensive, costing $825 at a time when the average worker earned $2.50 a day. The problem, Ford realized, was that production still took too long.

A Model T had about five thousand parts, and Ford followed the common practice of buying the parts from other companies. The parts were kept in a central location, with many of the larger parts in piles on the floor. Each worker came to the piles, found the part he needed at the moment, and took it back to the car he was working on.

Henry Ford designed the Model T to be an automobile that millions could afford.

This meant each worker spent most of his day walking through the shop and digging through piles—not an efficient use of anyone's time. There must be a better way, Ford thought.

He soon came up with the better way. He reorganized the factory to create an assembly line of workers. Conveyor belts delivered automobile parts to the workers, each of whom performed one particular task, such as adding a clamp or tightening a series of bolts.

Performing the same task over and over bored many workers, but it also speeded up production. The assembly line allowed Ford to reduce the amount of time it took to build a car from twelve and a half hours in 1912 to one and a half hours in 1914.

Ford's assembly lines transformed automobile manufacturing.

Ford also saved time and money by having his workers build uniform parts for Ford cars, so he didn't have to buy them from other manufacturers. Ford passed most of his savings on to customers. The cost of a Model T dropped to $550 in 1913, to $440 in 1915, and to $290 in 1924. Millions of Americans could afford to buy Model Ts—or Tin Lizzies, as they were affectionately called—and head out to the open road, where they could travel at the astonishing speed of 25 miles per hour.

Ford sold so many Tin Lizzies that he became one of the richest men in the world. He shared his profits by doubling the minimum wage for Ford workers to five dollars a day and reducing the workday from nine hours to eight. So many workers flocked to Ford factories that he had the luxury of choosing the best and brightest workers for his assembly lines.

Even more important, his Tin Lizzies were changing America. Dirt roads became paved highways. People no longer needed to live within walking distance of the places where they worked, shopped, or went to school. Henry Ford's cars eventually led to suburbs, shopping malls, and long commutes to homes with two-car garages. Indeed, Ford had succeeded in bringing motor cars to the multitudes.

Vincent van Gogh used vivid colors and bold, swirling brushstrokes in The Starry Night. *Toward the end of the nineteenth century, artists, writers, and philosophers looked at reality in new ways, and their works often shocked the public.*

Culture Shocks: Questioning Reason and Reality

*I*n the year 1889, to celebrate the one hundredth anniversary of the French Revolution, the French hosted a World's Fair in Paris. The capital gleamed for the occasion. Its broad, tree-lined boulevards and parks welcomed visitors.

Illuminated department store windows showed off fine clothing, gloves, and footwear. At the fair's opening ceremony, the president of France declared, "Today we contemplate, in its brilliancy and its splendor, the work born of this century of labor and of progress."

For many, the most breathtaking sight was the brand-new Eiffel Tower—the tallest man-made structure on earth at the time. A French engineer, Gustave Eiffel (IY-ful), designed the tower, made of wrought iron, to help celebrate the one hundredth birthday of the French Revolution. It required extraordinary confidence and vision even to imagine such a structure, a graceful spire soaring nearly a thousand feet into the sky.

Visitors could take an elevator to the top of the tower and peer down at the sprawling city—an astonishing experience in a time before air travel. For many visitors to the fair, the Eiffel Tower stood as the visible symbol of what the French president called

The Eiffel Tower rises above the 1889 World's Fair in Paris. At the time, it was highest man-made structure in the world. The tower symbolized the confidence of the era.

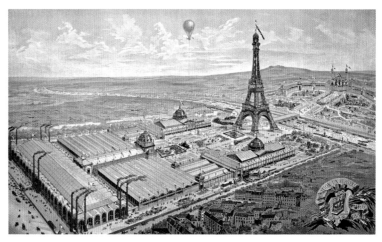

"this … century of progress," with all its advances in science, technology, education, and human rights. Europe was powerful, prosperous, and at peace—indeed, later generations would recall the late 1800s and early 1900s as Europe's *Belle Epoque*—the "Beautiful Time."

Yet beneath the surface of this prosperous, confident age were signs of doubt. In the wake of the Scientific Revolution and the Industrial Revolution, many people grew anxious as they wondered how long this time of progress could go on. Some asked whether all this material progress was making people any happier or life any more meaningful.

Philosophers, psychologists, and novelists wrote about an irrational and dark side of human nature. Artists rejected the new mass culture and challenged long-held assumptions about the relationship of art to reality. The works of these thinkers, writers, and artists sent shock waves through western culture, raising new questions about human nature and changing the way many people viewed their world.

Sigmund Freud: Probing the Unconscious Mind

You've learned that back in the eighteenth century, Enlightenment thinkers put forth an optimistic view of human nature. They believed that through reason, people could examine the world and make steady progress, perhaps even leading to the perfection of humanity. In one form or another, this basic confidence in reason and progress persisted into the nineteenth century.

In the late 1800s, some people began to challenge these ideas about human nature. Some of the most disquieting challenges were posed by a doctor named Sigmund Freud (froyd).

In the 1890s, Freud was a young physician living in Vienna, Austria. At the time, no one really knew why people became mentally ill. Some doctors theorized that mental illness was caused by injury to the body or the brain. Others speculated that it could be brought about by emotionally painful events, such as the death of a loved one. But Freud noticed that with many of his patients, neither of those explanations made sense. Gradually Freud came up with his own theory of mental illness—a theory that revolutionized our understanding of the human mind.

According to Freud, the mind has different parts. We think and solve problems with the *conscious* mind, the reasonable and reasoning part. But, said Freud, another part

Psychology is the study of the mind and behavior. *Psychologists* observe how people relate to each other and to their environment, and try to explain and predict behavior.

Sigmund Freud wrote about the workings of the human mind. He said unconscious motives often determine human behavior. Freud's work dramatically reshaped modern understanding of why people act as they do.

of the mind—the *unconscious*—is filled with powerful instincts and strong desires.

In stark contrast to the Enlightenment idea of humans as rational beings, Freud theorized that we are often driven by powerful *irrational* forces within us. We all have these unconscious feelings that influence our actions, he said, even though we are not aware of their influence. If disturbing thoughts, memories, or wishes threaten to come into our consciousness, then we try to *repress* them—we push them back into the unconscious. In some people, Freud theorized, the struggle to repress these feelings leads to mental illness.

Freud thought that mentally ill patients would get better only when they could understand their unconscious desires. To help his patients tap into the unconscious part of their minds, Freud developed a process called psychoanalysis.

In psychoanalysis, Freud tried different methods with his patients. In one method, patients described their dreams. Freud thought that our dreams contain symbols of hidden wishes and desires. The interpretation of dreams, said Freud, is "the royal road to the knowledge of the unconscious."

After 1900, Freud's ideas spread rapidly. They appealed not only to psychologists but also to some artists and writers who embraced the idea of exploring the dark, hidden places of the mind.

But many people found Freud's ideas troubling. Freud's theory of the unconscious mind implied that human beings are not the mainly rational creatures that Enlightenment thinkers described. Instead, in Freud's view, people are driven by desires and instincts that they cannot always understand or control. If human beings could not entirely control the way they acted, then the hope for unlimited progress seemed shaky at best.

Zola and Literary Naturalism

In the late 1800s, many writers also questioned whether human beings could really control their actions or fate. Some writers known as Naturalists, who were influenced by the ideas of Charles Darwin, wrote novels to show that human beings are mainly shaped by the environment in which they live. They set out to depict human life with the same objectivity that scientists bring to their observations of nature.

One of the greatest Naturalists was Émile Zola (ay-meel ZOH-luh) of France. Of himself and his fellow Naturalists, Zola wrote: "We believe that man cannot be separated from his milieu, that he is determined by his clothing, by his house, by his city, [and] by his region."

Milieu (mil-YUHR) means environment or setting.

Freudian Slips

Have you ever meant one thing but said another? Freud theorized that such slips of the tongue might reveal our repressed thoughts or feelings. These errors have come to be called "Freudian slips." For example, suppose you need to study for a test, but instead you spend the afternoon playing basketball with friends. After a while you need a break, and you start to say, "I have to take a rest." But instead, without meaning to, you say, "I have to take a test." That's a Freudian slip.

Zola's 1877 novel *L'Assommoir*
(lah-sohm-wahr) shows how the
social environment, or milieu,
determines the fate of the book's
characters. Zola depicts the
degrading effect of the slums of
Paris. (*L'Assommoir* roughly means
"slum bar" or "gin joint.") Zola
thought that earlier novelists had not
been realistic in depicting the lives of
the poor. *L'Assommoir*, by contrast, is
brutally realistic. Zola later boasted
that he had written the first novel
"that doesn't lie and that smells
of the people."

L'Assommoir tells the story of
Gervaise (jehr-vehz), a poor young

woman who works in a laundry
and lives in an ugly, prison-like
apartment building next to a
slaughterhouse. Despite her dirty,
depressing surroundings, Gervaise
is hardworking and ambitious. She
dreams of someday owning her
own laundry. She marries a worker,
Coupeau (coo-poh), who installs
gutters on the rooftops of the city.
At first they live together happily,
and Gervaise gives birth to their
daughter. Then one day Coupeau
falls from a roof and badly injures
himself. Because the couple is too
poor to afford a doctor, Gervaise
must care for her husband.

Coupeau slowly recovers, but
his injury makes him bitter. He begins
drinking constantly and hardly working at all. As Coupeau slips deeper
into alcoholism, the family gets poorer
and poorer, and often goes without
food. Eventually Coupeau drinks
himself to death, and Gervaise must
beg in the streets to survive.

Zola's novel suggested that if
poor people living in the slums often

seemed lazy, it was because they were crushed by the hopelessness of their surroundings. If they often became drunkards, it was because they turned to drink to escape their misery.

Zola said he wanted his novel to be "a frightful painting that will convey its own moral." But many of those who read Zola and the other Naturalists found this "moral" disturbing. If people's fates were determined by their surroundings, then how could one believe that human beings could always improve their lives through reason? The Naturalists seemed deeply pessimistic about the prospects for human progress.

Émile Zola Depicts Life in the Slums

This excerpt from Émile Zola's L'Assommoir is from a chapter entitled "Poverty and Degradation."(Degradation means being brought low or being dragged down.) At this point (near the novel's end), life has taken many turns for the worse for Gervaise and her husband, Coupeau. Here, Gervaise waits for her husband to come home as she thinks about how desperate her life has become.

A Page from the Past

The weather was intensely cold about the middle of January. Gervaise had not been able to pay her rent, due on the first. She had little or no work and consequently no food to speak of. The sky was dark and gloomy and the air heavy with the coming of a storm. Gervaise thought it barely possible that her husband might come in with a little money. After all, everything is possible, and he had said that he would work. Gervaise after a little, by dint of dwelling on this thought, had come to consider it a certainty. Yes, Coupeau would bring home some money, and they would have a good, hot, comfortable dinner....

As to herself, she had given up trying to get work, for no one would have her. This did not much trouble her, however, for she had arrived at that point when the mere exertion of moving had become intolerable to her. She now lay stretched on the bed, for she was warmer there.

Gervaise called it a bed. In reality it was only a pile of straw in the corner, for she had sold her bed and all her furniture. She occasionally swept the straw together with a broom, and, after all, it was neither dustier nor dirtier than everything else in the place. On this straw, therefore, Gervaise now lay with her eyes wide open. How long, she wondered, could people live without eating? She was not hungry, but there was a strange weight at the pit of her stomach. Her haggard eyes wandered about the room in search of anything she could sell. She vaguely wished someone would buy the spider webs which hung in all the corners. She knew them to be very good for cuts, but she doubted if they had any market value.

People used to apply spider webs to cuts to help stop bleeding.

Tired of this contemplation, she got up and took her one chair to the window and looked out into the dingy courtyard.

Her landlord had been there that day and declared he would wait only one week for his money, and if it were not forthcoming he would turn them into the street. It drove her wild to see him stand in his heavy overcoat and tell her so coldly that he would pack her off at once. She hated him with a vindictive hatred, as she did her fool of a husband…. In fact, she hated everyone on that especial day.

Vindictive means wanting to get revenge, to get even with someone.

A *fastidious* person is very picky, demanding, and hard to please.

A *bullock* is a young bull.

A *panada* is paste made of flour or of bread crumbs and water.

Unfortunately people can't live without eating, and before the woman's famished eyes floated visions of food. Not of dainty little dishes. She had long since ceased to care for those and ate all she could get without being in the least fastidious in regard to its quality. When she had a little money she bought a bullock's heart or a bit of cheese or some beans, and sometimes she begged from a restaurant and made a sort of panada of the crusts they gave her, which she cooked on a neighbor's stove…. She was quite willing to dispute with a dog for a bone. Once the thought of such things would have disgusted her, but at that time she did not—for three days in succession—

Conrad's *Heart of Darkness*

In 1899, a London journal published a short novel, *Heart of Darkness*, by Joseph Conrad, a Polish-born writer who had become a British citizen. The novel was based in part on Conrad's own experiences when he made a journey to King Leopold's Congo in 1890.

In *Heart of Darkness*, a character named Marlow sets out to find Kurtz, the manager of a trading station in the Congo. Kurtz had come to the Congo as "an emissary [agent] of science and progress." But when Marlow finally reaches Kurtz's trading station, he finds human heads—"black, dried, sunken, with closed eyelids"—stuck on pikes. Kurtz, Marlow learns, has engaged in acts of horrible cruelty and violence. When Kurtz dies, his last words are, "The horror! The horror!"

Conrad shows that despite their claims to be "civilizing" Africa, agents of "progress" in fact engaged in acts of barbaric savagery. Beneath the rational surface of civilization, Conrad suggests, there beats a "heart of darkness."

go without a morsel of food. She remembered how last week Coupeau had stolen a half loaf of bread and sold it, or rather exchanged it, for liquor.

She sat at the window, looking at the pale sky, and finally fell asleep. She dreamed that she was out in a snowstorm and could not find her way home. She awoke with a start and saw that night was coming on. How long the days are when one's stomach is empty! ✦

New Artistic Visions: Impressionism and After

In the late nineteenth century, while psychologists explored the irrational, and authors like Zola showed the dark side of human life, some artists began to ask: What is artistic truth? These artists, in their own way, also tried to find hidden meanings beneath surface appearances.

For painters, the question of artistic truth was complicated by the invention of photography. By the end of the nineteenth century, photography had become so cheap and popular that most European homes were full of family photographs. Before this time, if you wanted a family portrait or a picture of a landscape, you had to go to a painter. Now painters faced a challenge: How could their art compete with the true-to-life accuracy of a photograph?

Beginning in France in the 1860s, one group of painters decided that truth in art was not a matter of trying to make their paintings depict reality with photographic accuracy. Instead, they set out to capture the changing effects of light, or the many colors of water, or the shifting shades of the evening air. Critics said these artists simply gave their "impression" of a scene. And the name stuck. Thus this group of painters was called the Impressionists.

The major Impressionist painters included Edgar Degas (duh-GAH), Edouard Manet (ma-NAY), Claude Monet (moh-NAY), Pierre-Auguste Renoir (ruhn-wahr), and the American artist Mary Cassatt. Their technique was marked by short brushstrokes and vivid dabs of color, as though attempting to capture the fleeting light of a passing moment. As Claude Monet wrote, "Other painters paint a bridge, a house, a boat…. I want to paint the air in which the bridge, the house,

Like other Impressionists, the American painter Mary Cassatt tried to capture the movement of light and color on water. She painted Summertime *in 1894.*

the boat are to be found—the beauty of the atmosphere around them." In Monet's paintings, the outlines of things dissolve, and we see their shapes through a haze of flickering, shimmering light.

The Impressionists changed the way artists used color. They often painted in the open air and tried to capture the color of light on sea and sky. Artists like Monet and Renoir abandoned the muted greens, grays, and browns that many artists were then using. They turned to brighter and sunnier hues. In rose, peach, and blue, they captured lively outdoor gatherings and tranquil water scenes.

Beginning in the 1880s, some French painters grew dissatisfied with the Impressionist style. These artists are sometimes known as the Postimpressionists (*post* is a prefix that means "after"). The Postimpressionists included the brilliant Dutch painter Vincent van Gogh (van GOH).

Van Gogh admired the Impressionists but thought that their method did not leave the artist enough freedom to express his emotions. Van Gogh himself suffered from a mental illness that caused great surges of emotion—anger, depression, love—to come and go unpredictably. He felt driven

Claude Monet's Impression: Sunrise *depicts a harbor under a morning fog. When painting a landscape or seascape, Monet advised, "Paint it just as it looks to you, the exact color and shape, until it gives your own naive impression of the scene before you."*

Vincent van Gogh painted this unsettling Self-Portrait while in a mental hospital in 1889. His expression and the whirling chaos of the background suggest a mind in turmoil. Van Gogh killed himself the following year.

to get these emotions on canvas. He wrote, "I paint as a means to make life bearable."

Van Gogh painted some of the most vividly emotional pictures in the history of art. The swirling brushstrokes and blazing colors reflect his bouts of joy and anguish. When Van Gogh paints the night sky, the stars become whirlpools of light. (See page 626.) In his famous *Self-Portrait*, a man with fiery red hair glares out at us with disturbing intensity, while the swirling background suggests a mind in turmoil.

As Van Gogh grew older, he was in and out of mental hospitals. Once, distraught over a fight with a friend, he mutilated himself by cutting off part of his ear. At the age of 37, Van Gogh committed suicide. Today the tragic story of his life is almost as well-known as his magnificent paintings.

Spanish-born Pablo Picasso completed the cubist work Portrait of Daniel-Henry Kahnweiler *in 1910. Cubism is only one of the many styles in which Picasso was both an innovator and a master.*

New Artistic Visions: Cubism and Abstract Art

In the early twentieth century, more artists began to reject the idea that art should offer a realistic copy of nature. Indeed, some artists departed from techniques that had been practiced since the Renaissance. Renaissance artists, you recall, had discovered perspective—how to render the illusion of three-dimensional space on a flat canvas. They also learned how to paint human figures that appeared rounded and lifelike. These techniques had guided painters at least since the sixteenth century.

But around 1907, a young Spanish artist named Pablo Picasso started painting pictures that violated the old rules of perspective. As for depicting the human form in a lifelike way— well, take a look at Picasso's *Portrait of Daniel-Henry Kahnweiler*.

Gone is the illusion of space. A human form is recognizable, but barely. Look closely—can you see the nose and eyes, or the hands with crossed fingers? Picasso was perfectly capable of painting a lifelike portrait, but he chose a new path. He turned his subject into an array of geometric forms on a flat surface.

An older artist, looking at the shapes in Picasso's paintings of this time, complained, "But they're only little cubes!" Afterwards, people referred to the new style as Cubism.

The Cubist style—which Picasso developed with his friend, the French artist Georges Braque (brahk)—transformed modern art. Cubists broke away from the idea that art had to copy the textures, colors, and shapes of real objects. In Cubism, the artist's inner vision— breaking down objects and imaginatively reassembling them—takes precedence over external reality.

While Cubists broke down and imaginatively reassembled the objects they painted, the Russian painter Wassily Kandinsky (VAH-si-lee kan-DIN-skee) went further. He banished recognizable objects from his paintings. Kandinsky painted pictures full of strange, melting shapes with no particular resemblance to anything existing in reality.

Because Kandinsky's pictures are not pictures *of* anything, he is called an abstract artist. Abstract art does not try to depict recognizable subject matter. It does not try to recreate the physical world as we see it. Instead, abstract artists make art out of the elements of art itself—line, color, shapes, light, texture.

Look at Kandinsky's 1913 *Painting with White Border*. Kandinsky said this painting conveyed the "extremely powerful impressions [he] had experienced in Moscow—or more correctly, of Moscow itself."

Clearly, the painting does not offer a traditional view of the great Russian city. You can try to identify realistic objects in the painting—perhaps those dark lines at the upper left are horses?—but that misses the point. The key to this abstract painting lies in the title—*Painting with White Border*—which refuses to refer to any reality outside the painting itself. Perhaps the best description of the painting comes from the artist, who wrote that in this painting he aimed "to let … [himself] go and scatter a heap of small pleasures upon the canvas."

Modern Music: Stravinsky's *Rite of Spring*

Some say that in 1913, the year of Kandinsky's *Painting with White Border*, modern music was born. Of course it's impossible to date modern music to any single moment or work. Like Romanticism, modernism in music is more of an attitude than a single event. Still, one composer more than any other is associated with the beginning of modern

Painting with White Border *by the Russian painter Wassily Kandinsky is an example of abstract art. Abstract art does not try to depict recognizable subject matter.*

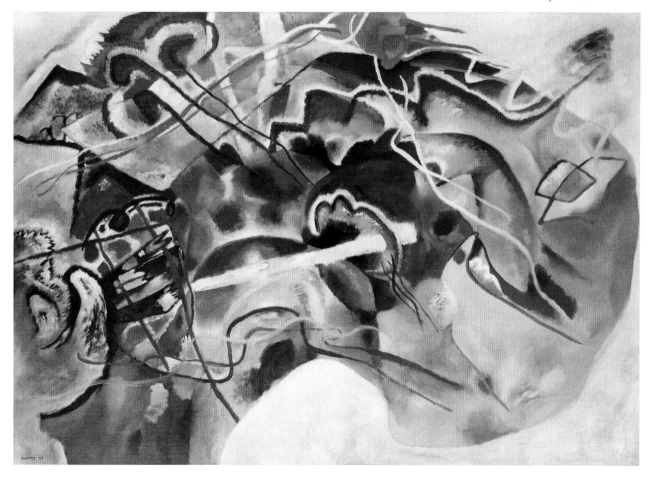

music—Igor Stravinsky (EE-gor struh-VIN-skee), who was born in Russia in 1882.

Stravinsky's first successes came with his scores for two ballets performed by the famed dance company, Ballets Russes (ba-lay roos). But it was the score for his third ballet, *The Rite of Spring*, that shocked the music world when it premiered in 1913.

On that May evening in Paris, the show opened with a traditional ballet. The theater filled with the sounds of lovely melodies as the dancers moved gracefully on stage. So far, the audience was getting just what they expected.

Next on the bill was the first performance of Stravinsky's *The Rite of Spring*. The title sounded inviting. Perhaps many in the audience expected bright and lively music to suggest the idea of rebirth in spring,

while the dancers swayed pleasantly to the melodies.

The music began—a single bassoon played in an unusually high range. The melody was eerie, ominous, unpredictable. Some members of the audience began to mutter.

Other instruments joined in—but instead of harmonizing, the instruments almost seemed to be struggling with each other. The sounds were harsh and dissonant. Some audience members hissed and booed. A few walked out in a huff.

Then the music stopped. But after a charged second of silence, it started again, this time with no melody but only a fierce, heavy, pounding beat.

The curtain rose to reveal the dancers. They moved in deliberately ugly ways, in response to the music's violent rhythms. As one dancer later recalled, "With every leap we landed heavily enough to jar every organ in us." Their harsh and jerky movements enacted the story of an ancient pagan ritual in which a young woman dances herself to death as a sacrifice to the god of spring.

This was not what the audience expected. They hissed, shouted, and whistled so loud that the dancers could not hear the orchestra. At one point, the choreographer stood backstage shouting directions to the confused dancers. In the meantime, fistfights had broken out in the crowd. Stravinsky's music, with its wild harmonies and unpredictable rhythms, along with the pagan rituals enacted onstage, sparked a near riot.

Although Stravinsky's first audiences failed to understand him, his work went on to have enormous influence on modern music. Like philosophers, psychologists, and writers, modern composers had also begun to explore the dark, irrational forces of the human mind.

On the Edge?

By the early 1900s, the western world was mostly at peace. People enjoyed the fruits of technological progress, symbolized by such inventions as the telephone and automobile, and by achievements like the Eiffel Tower. New vaccines had disease on the run. People lived in more sanitary cities, where they enjoyed electric light and running water. This progress seemed to promise a future of ever-greater prosperity and comfort.

Yet science and technological progress had created their own troubling doubts. Psychologists and philosophers explored an irrational side of human nature. Novelists wrote of people whose fate seemed shaped, often for the worse, by their environment. Painters created scenes that seemed to bend and question reality, while musicians composed pieces that broke all the old rules.

As the twentieth century dawned, artists, writers, and thinkers questioned the old certainties and looked uneasily toward an ill-defined future.

Stravinsky's *Rite* Animated

Pathbreaking music, like Stravinsky's *The Rite of Spring*, sometimes disturbs its first audiences. Over time, however, it can reshape listeners' expectations and become not just accepted but even celebrated. Such was the fate of *The Rite of Spring*. In 1940, the American filmmaker Walt Disney chose *The Rite of Spring* as one of eight selections for his ambitious film, *Fantasia*, which married stunning animated sequences to works of classical music. Against the backdrop of Stravinsky's music, Disney's animators depicted their vision of the Earth in primeval times, including erupting volcanoes and rampaging dinosaurs.

Stravinsky's The Rite of Spring *was one of the pieces of classical music that accompanied Walt Disney's animated film,* Fantasia. *(On the poster, the name "Stokowski" refers to the famous conductor.)*

A: Franz Josef, Habsburg emperor

B: Sun Yat-sen, Chinese revolutionary leader

C: India's Mohandas Gandhi, champion of freedom and natural rights

D: Queen Victoria, ruler of the British Empire

Rising Expectations in Waning Empires

Our last chapter was about changes in people's thinking in the late nineteenth and early twentieth centuries, and about developments in western literature, art, and music—in other words, about *culture*. Now we are going to turn to look again at the global picture—at empires expanding and crumbling, at leaders grasping for power, and people struggling for freedom. We are turning from cultural history back to political history.

Do you remember reading about Mazzini, Garibaldi, and the birth of the nation of Italy? Mazzini and Garibaldi united Italy by channeling two great historical forces. One was nationalism, the strong sense of attachment or belonging to one's own country. The other was freedom, the desire to be rid of kings or tyrants and put power instead in the hands of the people or their representatives.

At the beginning of the twentieth century, these two forces—nationalism and the desire for freedom—

posed challenges to the world's great empires. The nationalism that had swept western Europe since the mid-1800s was spreading to other lands. Some of these lands formed parts of the great empires. The people there took pride in their native culture, history, and traditions. And they embraced the new ideas about equality, natural rights, and self-rule. In short, they wanted freedom from their imperial rulers.

The Aging Ottoman Empire

One of those imperial powers was quite old. For hundreds of years, the Ottoman Turks had ruled one of the world's most powerful empires. This Islamic empire rolled out across Asia Minor,

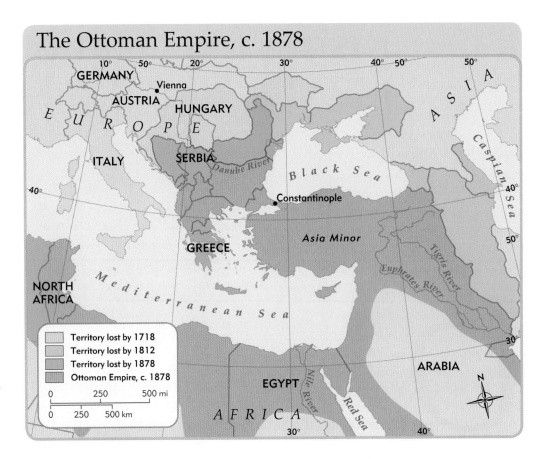

The Ottoman Empire, c. 1878

GERMANY
Vienna
AUSTRIA
HUNGARY
EUROPE
ITALY
SERBIA
Danube River
ASIA
Caspian Sea
Black Sea
Constantinople
GREECE
Asia Minor
Tigris River
Euphrates River
Mediterranean Sea
NORTH AFRICA
Territory lost by 1718
Territory lost by 1812
Territory lost by 1878
Ottoman Empire, c. 1878
0   250   500 mi
0   250   500 km
ARABIA
EGYPT
Nile River
Red Sea
AFRICA
N

Serb patriots revolt against their Ottoman rulers. At its height, the Ottoman Empire included parts of southeastern Europe as well as Asia Minor and much of North Africa and the Middle East.

Who Are the Slavs?

Slavic peoples, or Slavs, live mainly in eastern Europe and partly in Asia, in countries such as the Czech Republic, Poland, Slovakia, Slovenia, Bulgaria, Croatia, Serbia, Ukraine, and Russia. Their various languages and cultures, which are related, descend from a people that have lived in eastern Europe for thousands of years. Today there are some 275 million Slavs.

North Africa, much of the Middle East, and southeastern Europe.

You've learned that in 1683, Ottoman soldiers marched to the very gates of the Austrian capital, Vienna. But the Ottomans suffered defeat at the hands of the Austrians. And since that time, their empire slowly but surely started to shrink. In the 1700s, various peoples ruled by the Ottomans began to struggle for their independence. In the 1800s, feelings of nationalism grew even stronger.

One group of people that fought unceasingly for their freedom was the Serbs. The Serbs were a Slavic people from the Balkan Peninsula of southeastern Europe. Their land, known as Serbia, had formed part of the Ottoman Empire since 1389, when the Ottoman Turks had conquered it.

- On the map on page 642, locate the Ottoman Empire. Locate Serbia.

Even when they lived under the rule of the Ottoman Turks, the Serbs never lost their national pride. They continued to hope and agitate for an independent Serb state. The Serbs weren't the only challenge the Ottoman Empire faced, but their desire for independence is an example of what was happening worldwide.

In 1876, the Serbs launched a war of national liberation against the Ottomans. The Serbs lost. But in 1878, after the Ottomans lost a war to the Russians, Serbia finally won its independence. And yet the small nation soon fell under the shadow of another great imperial power—the Habsburg empire of Austria.

Franz Josef Governs the Habsburg Empire

The *Habsburg* in "Habsburg empire" refers to the ruling family of Austria. From the fifteenth century, the Habsburgs had ruled a huge realm at the heart of Europe. In the mid-nineteenth century, the Habsburg empire sprawled south and east from its Austrian heartland. It was the largest realm in Europe after Russia.

- On the map on page 644, locate the Habsburg empire.

The Habsburg empire was multiethnic, made up of many different peoples and cultures. The empire's fifty million subjects included Germans, Hungarians, and Slavs. Each of these groups was fiercely proud of its own customs and languages. Each distrusted its neighbors.

Over time, these groups began to demand special rights within the Habsburg empire. Some even dreamed of a future outside the empire, a future in which they would form their own independent countries. One man's dreams, however, can be another man's nightmares. And one whose sleep was particularly troubled during these years was the Emperor Franz Josef.

Franz Josef had become emperor in 1848, when he was only 18 years old. That year, you remember, was a time of unrest in western Europe, when many people rose up to demand democratic reforms. Within

Carriages wait outside the Hofburg, the imperial palace in Vienna. From here, the Habsburgs ruled their vast empire, a great multiethnic realm that included Germans, Hungarians, and Slavs. Today the palace is a popular tourist attraction.

the Habsburg empire, revolutionaries and nationalists in the city of Budapest insisted on a constitutional government for Hungary. They demanded greater freedom and more rights for Hungarians within the empire.

Franz Josef, though he had barely ascended the throne, acted swiftly and harshly. His imperial army, with Russian help, drove the Hungarian rebels out of Budapest. Most of the revolution's leaders fled abroad. But the young emperor decided to make an example of those he could lay his hands on. He ordered the execution of the 114 Hungarians he held most responsible for the uprising.

Emperor Franz Josef then dealt with the growing demands of the people. Many of his subjects called for a written constitution. They wanted clear statements of their rights and freedoms as imperial subjects. They wanted guarantees of the rights of the various peoples within the empire. Franz Josef listened to the demands of the people—or appeared to listen. In 1849, he delivered a constitution that dashed their hopes. The constitution mainly confirmed the power of the emperor and his government in Vienna.

Despite this disappointment, over the years many of Franz Josef's subjects came to love him. His portrait hung on the walls of countless homes. With his bushy moustache and sideburns, he looked like a kindly grandfather. But above the moustache peered eyes that seemed to reflect the

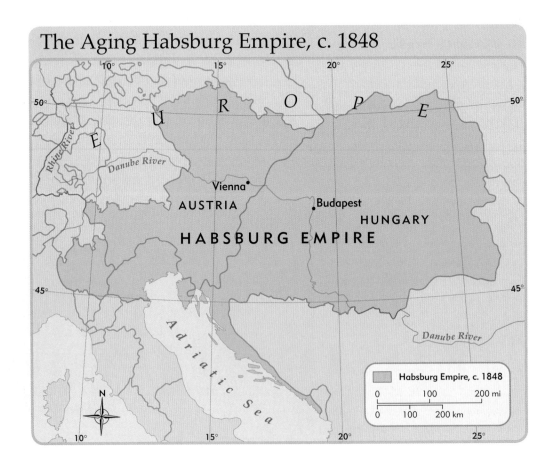

The Aging Habsburg Empire, c. 1848

tragedies of the emperor's long reign. Franz Josef's wife was assassinated in 1898, and the next year his only son, the crown prince, committed suicide. Franz Josef lived in constant dread that his empire would fare as badly as his family.

Indeed, things did not look good. By the second half of the nineteenth century, the Habsburgs had lost many German states they had once controlled. These states united under Bismarck and Kaiser Wilhelm to become part of the new German nation. The Habsburg's Italian provinces broke away to join the new nation of Italy. And Franz Josef feared that other areas would soon revolt. The strains of rising nationalism threatened to splinter his empire into pieces.

The Dual Monarchy of Austria-Hungary

The Hungarians were proving especially troublesome to Franz Josef. Again they were demanding special rights for Hungary, as they had in 1848. And again the emperor faced a dilemma. He still believed his empire needed firm rule from the imperial capital, Vienna. But 20 years as an emperor had taught him something. He knew that he needed the loyalty of his Hungarian subjects.

This time he did not send his imperial army to Budapest. Instead, in 1867, he accepted a compromise known as the Dual Monarchy of Austria-Hungary.

- On the map on page 647, locate the Dual Monarchy of Austria-Hungary, also called the Austro-Hungarian Empire.

Vienna's Golden Age

The capital of the Habsburg empire was Vienna. Like London, Paris, and Berlin in the mid-nineteenth century, Vienna grew enormously and underwent major renovation. In 1857, Franz Josef, impressed by Louis Napoleon's work in Paris, ordered the demolition of Vienna's old city walls and the construction of a wide avenue ringing the city. This boulevard, called the *Ringstrasse*, opened in 1865. Soon it encircled stately public buildings and lovely parks, including one park with a monument to the great composer Ludwig van Beethoven. Always famous for their music, the Viennese of the late 1800s listened to the symphonies of Johannes Brahms and danced to the music of "The Waltz King," Johann Strauss the Younger.

Lying on the eastern border of Austria, the city of Vienna was a great melting pot of Austrians, Germans, Slavs, Hungarians, and Jews. In the late nineteenth century, Vienna was like Renaissance Florence, alive with artistic creativity and intellectual activity. The Viennese eagerly discussed the work of the city's leading thinker, Sigmund Freud. Over drinks at their favorite coffeehouses, they caught up on the latest in politics, philosophy, art, and literature.

Viennese stroll on the Ringstrasse *in 1890.*

Crowds gather in Budapest in 1867 to watch the coronation of Franz Josef as king of Hungary. On horseback at far right, the new king raises his sword, a gesture symbolizing his protection of Hungary. Franz Josef allowed Hungarians to have their own constitution and parliament. He hoped that this arrangement would help hold together his vast empire.

The Dual Monarchy represented one of Franz Josef's greatest successes. The Hungarians got their own parliament and constitution. Franz Josef continued to lead. But now he reigned over the Hungarians not as Austrian emperor but as king of Hungary. Franz Josef hoped that this arrangement would help the Hungarians feel as though they had equal status with Austrians.

Franz Josef proved less successful in dealing with the Slavic peoples within his empire. They included Czechs (cheks), Slovaks (SLOH-vahks), Croats (CROH-ats), and Slovenes (SLOH-veens). They made up the majority of the empire's population. Most Slavs looked at Vienna and Budapest with envy. They resented having no Parliament of their own, and having no say over their

Musical Nationalism

The various peoples of Austria-Hungary not only enjoyed their own languages and customs, but also their own musical traditions. During the second part of the nineteenth century, the Czech

composer Antonín Dvořák (AHN-toh-neen DVOHR-zhawk) blended Slavic folk songs, polka rhythms, and traditional melodies with his classical compositions. His *Slavonic Dances, Gypsy Songs*, and nine symphonies delighted his countrymen and encouraged feelings of nationalistic pride among the Czech people. His musical fame spread far and wide, even to the United States, where he lived and taught for a while. is nicknamed "From the New World.")

A scene from an opera by Czech composer Antonín Dvořák

The Dual Monarchy of Austria-Hungary, c. 1867

Legend:
- Austria, c. 1867
- Hungary, c. 1867
- Austro-Hungarian Empire (Dual Monarchy of Austria-Hungary)

laws. If the Hungarians were entitled to these rights, why weren't Croats?

In the end, however, it was another Slavic people, the Serbs, who posed the greatest threat to the Habsburgs. In 1878, the Austrians occupied the province of Bosnia, which was home to many Serbs. This infuriated the new kingdom of Serbia. The Serbs had cast their eyes on Bosnia. They had hoped to make it part of a greater Serbia. Some of them decided to strike back at the Habsburg empire. As you'll soon see, their actions triggered a war that would shake the world to its core.

India's Mohandas Gandhi

Unlike the Ottoman and Habsburg empires, Britain's empire in the late nineteenth century seemed at the peak of its power. It was the largest empire in the world—the one upon which "the sun never set."

Red-coated British soldiers had battled many people in many lands to maintain this empire. They had fought in Africa, in south Asia, and in the Far East. But in the end, the greatest threat to the empire was not tribesmen armed with guns. It was a single man whose weapons were the strength of his will and the force of his ideas.

Mohandas Gandhi (GAHN-dee) was born in India in 1869. India was then part of the British Empire. British overlords made the laws for India, ran its government, and controlled the country's natural resources.

- On a globe or world map, locate India.

Gandhi was a follower of India's major religion, Hinduism. His family raised him in the traditions of his native land. Yet, like many wealthy Indians of his time, Gandhi traveled to England to continue his university education. In 1888, the 19-year-old scholar set out to study law in London, the heart of the British Empire.

At first Gandhi was shy in his new surroundings. But soon he began to enjoy British life. He had his hair cut in the Western style, learned English manners, and dressed like a fashionable London gentleman. Gandhi wore expensive, well-tailored suits with stiff-collared shirts, flashy ties, polished shoes, and a silk top hat. He took violin and dancing lessons. He attended parties carrying a silver-headed walking stick.

But young Gandhi picked up more than European styles. He also adopted British liberal ideals of liberty and natural rights. With these ideals he returned to India in 1891, by then a fully qualified lawyer. Two years later, Gandhi received a job offer from a law firm in South Africa. He decided to accept it.

- On a globe or world map, locate South Africa.

Gandhi in South Africa

Like India, South Africa at this time was part of the British Empire. About 100,000 Indians had traveled to South Africa for work. Many took jobs that no one else would do, especially working on farms and growing sugarcane. White South Africans, descendants of the British and Dutch, looked down on the Indians and treated them badly. And, as Gandhi quickly found out, it did not matter that he was a lawyer. White people scorned him as much as they did the poorest Indian laborer.

Soon after he arrived in South Africa, Gandhi purchased a first-class ticket and boarded a train for the city of Pretoria to start his new job. During the journey, a white passenger objected to sharing his compartment with a brown-skinned Indian. He complained to a policeman, who threw Gandhi off the train. Shivering on an empty station platform all night, Gandhi considered his future. He could ignore the insults and get on with his job. Or he could fight for the rights of Indians in South Africa. That night, he decided to fight.

Gandhi resolved to fight not with guns but with words and ideas. He wrote to the railway authorities and pointed out that even under their own regulations, he should not have suffered such treatment. He got a letter in return saying that first-class tickets would be issued to Indians "who were properly dressed." It was a small victory, but it was a start.

Indians faced many other harsh laws in South Africa. They could not vote. They were forced to pay three pounds (about six months' salary) just to be allowed to work in South Africa. They could be arrested for walking on the same sidewalk as white people. And, unless they were Christian, their marriages were not recognized.

Gandhi vigorously took up the Indian cause. He organized rallies, held protests, and wrote letters to newspapers. He challenged unjust laws in court. Laws that could not be changed, he declared, should be disobeyed, but peacefully.

Sometimes the authorities used force against the protesters. But Gandhi and his supporters met violence with nonviolence. Their

Mohandas Gandhi studied law in England and worked as a lawyer in South Africa. He struggled against injustice in white South Africa, particularly on behalf of Indians who came there to work.

strategy became known as passive resistance or civil disobedience. They refused to obey the unjust laws, but even when facing guns and bayonets, they did not fight back or take up weapons. They would go to jail if necessary, but they would not fight. Nonviolence, Gandhi preached, was not a weapon for the weak, but a weapon for the brave.

Mohandas Gandhi struggled against injustice in South Africa for 20 years. Many Indians followed his example. They started refusing to submit to unjust laws. They suffered imprisonment, beatings, and the loss of employment. But still they kept protesting the laws they knew to be wrong, and thousands joined the protests. By 1914, the government gave in—at least in part. It agreed to put an end to some of those laws. Gandhi had won a great victory for civil rights and human dignity.

The following year, Gandhi returned to India. The people greeted him as a hero and nicknamed him *Mahatma*, which means "Great Soul." By now, he had abandoned his

By the time he left South Africa to return to his native India, Gandhi had stopped wearing European clothes. Instead, he dressed like a Hindu peasant. His clothes became a statement. He believed that India belonged to the people of India, not British rulers.

European-style clothing in favor of the plain cotton robes and sandals worn by many poor Indians. He cared deeply for the future of his nation, which was still a part of the British Empire. In his homeland, he continued the struggle against injustice. Now he had a new cause that would occupy him for almost all of his life— gaining independence for India.

Gandhi's Nonviolent Resistance

Mohandas Gandhi believed that the best way to change unjust laws was to disobey them, but peacefully. He knew that those who disobeyed an unjust law would probably suffer. They might be thrown in jail, beaten, or even killed. But Gandhi insisted upon nonviolence. If enough people peacefully resisted, he said, others would see their suffering and eventually be moved to correct the injustice. "Real suffering bravely borne melts even a heart of stone," he wrote.

Gandhi spent much time in jail and risked his life many times while refusing to obey unjust laws, both in South Africa and, later, in his homeland of India. But his

A Page from the Past

tactics helped bring about much-needed reforms. Thanks to Gandhi's efforts, in 1947 India became an independent, self-governing nation.

Here are some of Gandhi's thoughts about the power of nonviolent resistance.

[Nonviolence] calls for the strength and courage to suffer without retaliation, to receive blows without returning any.

In the composition of the truly brave there should be no malice, no anger, no distrust, no fear of death or physical hurt. Nonviolence is certainly not for those who lack these essential qualities.

In nonviolence the masses have a weapon which enables a child, a woman, or even a decrepit old man to resist the mightiest government successfully. If your spirit is strong, mere lack of physical strength ceases to be a handicap.

The virtues of mercy, nonviolence, love, and truth in any man can be truly tested only when they are pitted against ruthlessness, violence, hate, and untruth.

If freedom has got to come, it must be obtained by our own internal strength, by our closing our ranks, by unity between all sections of the community.

Gandhi leads a prayer meeting while fasting to protest violence in India.

I know that the progress of nonviolence is seemingly a terribly slow progress. But experience has taught me it is the surest way to the common goal.

My optimism rests on my belief in the infinite possibilities of the individual to develop nonviolence. The more you develop it in your own being, the more infectious it becomes till it overwhelms your surroundings and by and by might oversweep the world. ⁓

China's Struggle

While Mohandas Gandhi was struggling for the rights of his fellow Indians in South Africa, revolutionaries in China were seeking the same rights for the people of their country.

- On a globe or world map, locate China.

Since ancient times, China had been home to one of the world's great civilizations. It had long been ruled by a succession of proud families that had turned their backs on the West.

Beginning in the seventeenth century, however, foreigners overpowered China. The glorious Ming dynasty fell to China's longtime enemies, the Mongols. The conquerors established the Manchu dynasty to rule China. The Manchus were often corrupt and incompetent. They brought ruin on the empire. Over the years the Chinese people tried to drive them out.

The Manchus desperately clung to power. They did so with the help of money and troops provided by European nations. In return, China's Manchu rulers agreed to sign treaties ensuring trade and commerce with their European backers. These treaties were a source of humiliation to many Chinese people.

The Manchus handed over the port of Hong Kong to the British. And they opened dozens of coastal cities to foreign ships. In these "treaty ports," foreigners lived in their own settlements and conducted business beyond the reach of Chinese law. They built railroads, worked mines, and operated textile mills and other factories.

The port of Shanghai (shang-HIY) became an almost European city. It boasted fine boulevards, a golf course, and a racetrack. Its waterfront avenue was lined with European banks and trading houses. European and American gunboats patrolled the waters of the Yangtze River.

In this photograph from the early part of the twentieth century, European architecture fills Shanghai's commercial center. European banks and trading houses dominated Shanghai, the first Chinese port to be opened to Western commerce.

This 1898 French cartoon shows imperialist rulers dividing China among themselves as a Chinese man watches in horror. Queen Victoria, Kaiser Wilhelm, Tsar Nicholas, and Japan's Emperor Meiji are joined by "Marianne," a symbol of the French republic. Like many political cartoons, this one exaggerates characters' features to draw attention to the situation.

Patriotic Chinese burned with indignation as they saw their country overwhelmed by foreign powers. They resented the foreigners, and they hated the Mongol Manchus for letting the foreigners in. In the words of one revolutionary, China was becoming "not the colony of one nation, but of all."

Sun Yat-sen Works for Change

The man who spoke those angry words was Sun Yat-sen (soun yaht-sen). He grew up in the south of China, near the ports of Macao and Canton, where foreign influence was strong.

Sun came from a humble peasant family but he managed to obtain a good education. His elder brother had immigrated to Hawaii as a laborer, and Sun followed him there. Later, Sun went to Hong Kong. In each place, he attended schools set up by Christian missionaries. Eventually he became a physician. He also became a convert to Christianity and picked up many Western political ideas. He returned to China and urged that his country catch up with Europe and North America by adopting nationalism and democracy "without delay."

Like other patriots, Sun felt humiliated by the presence of the treaty ports and by the feebleness of the Manchus. In 1894, he formed the Revive China Society. Members of the society shared three goals. They swore to expel the Manchus, to restore China, and to establish a republic.

Sun Yat-sen recognized, however, that the hated treaty ports were thriving communities. They contained much that a modern China needed—stability, wealth, and industry. This made him something of a reluctant revolutionary.

In 1895, Sun fled abroad after organizing an unsuccessful revolt against the Manchus. For the next 16 years he traveled the world, seeking support for the cause of Chinese nationalism.

"The Father of the Chinese Revolution"

In 1911, while having breakfast in a Denver, Colorado, restaurant, Sun Yat-sen read a newspaper account of recent events in China. An uprising by the imperial army had finally toppled the Manchu dynasty. Sun ended his fundraising tour of the United States and made his way home.

On Christmas Day, Sun Yat-sen sailed into Shanghai harbor. The people greeted him as a great leader of the revolution. Four days later, he was chosen temporary president of the new Chinese republic.

The reluctant revolutionary took care to protect the lives and property of foreigners living in China. And he proclaimed that the revolution had achieved the aims of nationalism and democracy.

But the new republic quickly ran into trouble. Sun's hold on power was short-lived. The army soon took control of the country.

Still, the work of Sun Yat-sen and his supporters had ended foreign rule and set China on the path to independence and self-government. He succeeded in blending one of the world's oldest cultures with much that was valuable from the West. As he put it, he tried to "choose the good fruit" of modern civilization and "reject the bad."

For his achievements, Americans called him "The Father of the Chinese Revolution." The President of the United States, Calvin Coolidge, later compared him to two great American heroes. Sun, he declared, was a "combined Benjamin Franklin and George Washington of China."

Nationalism: A Rising Tide

In the early part of the nineteenth century, Napoleon had helped provoke stirrings of nationalism in western Europe and in the Americas.

Sun Yat-sen not only dressed like a Western gentleman but was educated in Western schools and adopted Western ideas of natural rights, nationalism, and self-rule. He became the first president of the new Chinese republic.

Those stirrings led to the formation of new nations, first in South America and then in Europe.

In the late nineteenth and early twentieth century, nationalism was still a powerful force in Britain, Germany, France, and Italy. As you've seen in this chapter, nationalist dreams were shared by eastern Europeans, Slavs, Indians, and Chinese. They were shared by other peoples as well. Ideas about equal rights and freedom from foreign rule continued to spread. In the East as well as the West, "self-determination of nations" was becoming an important goal.

As the twentieth century dawned, such dreams and ideas began to rock once-powerful empires. By 1914, nationalism was becoming a force that would shake both western and non-western lands. In that year, nationalism in Europe helped ignite a terrible war that ravaged much of the world. You'll learn more about that war in the conclusion to this book, and in your future studies.

Above: Orville Wright flies a glider at Kitty Hawk, North Carolina, in 1902.

Right: Construction of a section of the Panama Canal in 1910

Linking the Seas and Reaching for the Skies

Throughout the nineteenth century, the world seemed to grow a little smaller. Not literally, of course. But advances in technology shrank once daunting distances. Steamships skimmed oceans, while railroads crossed wide plains and prairies. Telegraphs, telephones, and radio made it possible to communicate in an instant.

As the twentieth century opened, work began on two new projects that would shrink the world even more. The first was a canal connecting two oceans. The Panama Canal, one of the greatest engineering feats in history, dramatically shortened the sailing time between the Atlantic and Pacific.

The second great project was a machine to give humankind the freedom of birds—a flying machine. Many scoffed at the idea as a silly fantasy. But two brothers working in a small shop in Ohio made the dream of flight come true. The airplane transformed a transatlantic voyage—a five-week journey in the ships of Columbus, and even by steamship a trip of five days—to a matter of hours.

Before we reach for the skies, let's turn to the world-changing achievement that linked the seas, the Panama Canal.

They Built One in Egypt, So Why Not in Panama?

Ever since 1513, Europeans had dreamed of cutting through the narrowest part of Central America to connect the Atlantic and Pacific Oceans. In that year, a Spaniard named Vasco Núñez de Balboa led a group of conquistadors across a strip of land now known as the Isthmus of

Panama. Standing on a mountain top, Balboa saw a distant body of water. Thus he became the first European to gaze on the eastern shore of the Pacific Ocean.

- An isthmus is a narrow strip of land connecting two larger land areas. On a globe or world map, find the Isthmus of Panama. The modern-day country of Panama is located on this isthmus.

While the Isthmus of Panama is only 30 miles wide at its narrowest point, the land discouraged hopes of building a canal across it. First there was the Chagres (CHAH-grais) River. It looped through a hot, suffocating jungle. During the eight-month rainy season, it turned into a raging torrent.

But the biggest problem was the rocky mountain ranges that divided the country like a central spine. As early as 1625, a Jesuit scholar said that in Panama, God had made "strong and impenetrable mountains … to withstand the fury of two seas." Anyone who tried to break through those mountains, the priest warned, "should fear punishment from heaven."

Despite the river and the mountains, people kept thinking about cutting across the isthmus. Nations with big navies, merchant fleets, and interests in faraway colonies were eager to find a quicker way to travel between the Atlantic and Pacific.

The United States had a special interest in a canal that would link the oceans. Ships steaming from New York to San Francisco had to go all the way around South America's Cape Horn. A canal across Panama would save at least 8,000 miles and several weeks in travel time.

- On a globe or world map, trace your finger from New York City down the eastern coast of South America, around Cape Horn, and up the Americas' western coasts to San Francisco. Then trace your finger from New York City to Panama, across the Isthmus of Panama, and up North America's western coast to San Francisco.

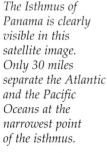

The Isthmus of Panama is clearly visible in this satellite image. Only 30 miles separate the Atlantic and the Pacific Oceans at the narrowest point of the isthmus.

Costa Rica

Panamá

Colombia

If engineers could build the 100-mile Suez Canal across the desert, shouldn't they be able to cut a much shorter canal across the Isthmus of Panama? Ferdinand de Lesseps thought so. He was the daring Frenchman who had become a national hero after building the Suez Canal in Egypt.

At the age of 74, Lesseps was young in spirit and ready for one last adventure. He planned to build a sea-level canal in Panama, just like the one at Suez. That is, he wanted to dig a deep channel all the way across the isthmus, so that water could flow at sea level from one end to the other. As he saw it, the canal would follow the path of a railroad across the isthmus.

That railroad had been built during the Gold Rush of the 1850s. In 1848, gold was discovered in California, and the next year, thousands of Americans in the eastern part of the United States began to head west with dreams of striking it rich. The transcontinental railroad had not yet been built, and traveling overland across the continent was a rough, dangerous journey. Some people reached California by sailing all the way around South America's Cape Horn. Others sailed to the Isthmus of Panama, crossed it by mule and on foot, and then boarded another ship for California.

A group of New York businessmen became interested in building a railroad to shorten the travel time over the isthmus. In 1850, Colombia (which at that time controlled the isthmus) gave them permission to build a track. By 1855, the Panama Railroad was carrying passengers and freight between ports on the Atlantic and Pacific Oceans. Ferdinand de Lesseps's canal company later bought the railroad in order to build his canal.

In 1879, Lesseps took his young wife and three of their children to Panama. They were welcomed with fireworks, ceremonial banquets, music, and dancing.

Nightmare in Panama

Lesseps and his party were so busy celebrating that they failed to pay enough attention to conditions in Panama. No one grasped the importance of sea tides, which rose and fell with unforgiving regularity. When the Lesseps family arrived late at a ceremony to mark the beginning of construction on the canal, they found the site flooded by the rising tide.

Lesseps waved off the inconvenience. He had a champagne box filled with sand and brought to the deck of his ship. There his seven-year-old daughter swung a shiny pickax to symbolize the beginning of construction.

When Lesseps returned to France, he raised money for his canal company by selling stock to investors. As he described it, the canal would not cost too much to build, and it would bring in nice profits. He truthfully told investors about Panama's exotic flowers and birds. Less truthfully, or perhaps just ignorantly, he described Panama as "an exceedingly healthy country."

Panama's tropical climate was far from healthy for those who went there to work on the canal. Malaria,

Tropical jungle and swamplands made it hard to build a canal in Panama. Here, an engineer surveys the canal's future route.

typhoid, cholera, smallpox, and dysentery killed workers by the hundreds. But the disease that struck down more people than any other was yellow fever. The symptoms began with fever and uncontrollable shivering, then moved on to horrible back pain, thirst, and yellow skin. Finally, victims coughed up black blood until they died.

As the French pressed ahead with their project, dozens of canal workers died every month. Funeral trains made daily runs to the cemetery on Monkey Hill. A cartoon in New York's *Harper's Weekly* magazine asked, "Is M. de Lesseps a Canal Digger or a Grave Digger?"

Those who escaped disease faced discouraging days of grueling work in the stifling heat. The French

Selling Stock

Imagine that you own a business, and that the business needs some money—perhaps to construct a new factory, or even to build a canal. How can the business raise money? It can sell stock.

When a company sells stock, it is selling a piece of ownership in the company. Each piece of stock is called a share. People who buy shares of stock are called stockholders or shareholders. They own a piece of the company, along with many other people who also own shares of the stock.

After the company sells stock, it can use the money from the sale to operate the business and launch new projects. If the company does well, it may pay each shareholder a part of the profits. Or shareholders can make money by selling their stock for more than they paid for it. But if the company does poorly, the value of its stock may go down, which means that shareholders may lose money.

painter Paul Gauguin (goh-GAN)—who had come to Panama because he needed money—wrote to his wife, "I have to dig … from five-thirty in the morning to six in the evening, under tropical sun and rain. At night I am devoured by mosquitoes." He left within a couple of weeks.

In 1886, Lesseps visited Panama again, hoping to raise morale. Once again he was welcomed warmly, but even his optimistic eyes could see the funeral trains. The work on his sea-level canal was constantly being undone by rains, floods, and mudslides. Yet few dared challenge Lesseps's basic strategies. His ideas had worked in Egypt, so why shouldn't they work in Panama? But they didn't work because the conditions were very different. And so Lesseps's great scheme continued to lose lives and money.

Stock in Lesseps's company fell until the company itself went out of business. Some 800,000 investors lost their money, many their life's savings. In 1889, work on the canal stopped, and jungle grew over the French equipment.

The United States Takes Over

From the moment that Lesseps had started work, many Americans objected. Why, they asked, are the French building this canal? When Lesseps failed, people in the United States were not terribly disappointed. They wanted a canal, but they wanted to be the ones to build it.

The Spanish-American War of 1898 made the United States even more eager for a canal. During the

IS M. DE LESSEPS A CANAL DIGGER OR A GRAVE DIGGER?

Thousands died working on Ferdinand de Lesseps's Panama Canal project, many from yellow fever or malaria. At left, an 1881 cartoon asks if Lesseps is "a Canal Digger or a Grave Digger."

when the Americans thought they had an agreement, Colombian government officials changed the terms.

Roosevelt was fed up. Many Panamanians were also irritated by the slow pace of negotiations. They worried the Americans would decide to build the canal in Nicaragua. The French worried that they would lose the sale of their company. The Americans just wanted to start work on a canal. All three of these groups started to think that an independent Panama, free of Colombian control, would be a very good idea.

On November 3, 1903, a group of Panamanian revolutionaries, encouraged by foreign businessmen, declared independence. American warships landed almost immediately. The Americans said they were there to protect American railroads in a land threatened by revolution. In fact, the Americans' main purpose was to prevent Colombian troops from marching to Panama City. Three days later, the United States formally recognized the new nation of Panama. The French also quickly recognized Panama's independence.

Less than two weeks after Panama became independent, it signed a treaty with the United States. The treaty gave

war, it took too long for American warships to steam between the Atlantic and Pacific Oceans. After the war, Congress set up a commission to study possible canal routes. One was through Panama, and another through Nicaragua.

The commission was still studying its options when young Theodore Roosevelt became President of the United States in 1901. Eager to establish the United States as a world power, he made building the canal a top priority.

In 1902, Roosevelt tried to arrange for the United States to buy the canal company from the French for $40 million. He also tried to strike a deal with Colombia, the South American country that governed Panama. Roosevelt wanted Colombia to allow the United States to begin building a canal. But Colombia was in no hurry to do business. The negotiations dragged on and on. Just

the United States exclusive use and control of a 10-mile zone around the proposed canal. The United States completed its purchase of the French canal company. The Americans finally had their canal site. Roosevelt sent engineers to Panama with instructions to "make dirt fly."

The new U.S. president, Theodore Roosevelt, promised to "make dirt fly" in the Panama Canal. This 1903 cartoon shows Roosevelt dumping a shovelful of dirt on Bogota, the capital of Colombia.

The Fight Against Yellow Fever

President Roosevelt learned from the misfortunes of Lesseps. He understood how crucial it was to fight the diseases that had killed so many workers. "I feel that sanitary and hygienic problems ... on the Isthmus are those which are literally of first importance," he said, "coming even before the engineering."

An army doctor who specialized in tropical diseases, Colonel William Crawford Gorgas, was placed in charge of the fight against yellow fever. He had been in the Spanish-American War, when vast numbers of U.S. troops stationed in Cuba contracted the yellow fever. Doctors had learned that mosquitoes transmitted the disease, first by biting an infected person and then a healthy one.

When Gorgas arrived in Panama, he found mosquitoes everywhere. Yet most people considered the flying insects little more than an annoyance. They believed yellow fever came from the fumes rising from the swamps.

Gorgas found no screens on windows and no mosquito nets over yellow fever patients. Everywhere he looked, he saw pools of standing water—the perfect breeding ground for mosquitoes. During their time in Panama, the French, in trying to discourage ants, had placed stone rings filled with water around plants in their lush gardens. They had even rested the legs of hospital beds in water. "If the French had been trying to propagate yellow fever," Gorgas observed, "they could not have provided conditions better adapted for this purpose."

Gorgas set out to eliminate standing water, install screens, and cover beds with mosquito netting. It was exhausting work. Every drop of standing water in this rainy climate had to be dumped or covered.

Back in the United States, some politicians dismissed the campaign to eliminate mosquitoes as "balderdash." But Gorgas pressed on. He and his men fumigated countless homes. They filled in every ditch they could find, and sprayed every open pool with a sealing oil. Pipes were installed so every community would have running water, which meant they

A system of locks made construction of the Panama Canal possible. Like giant steps, they raised the canal up to the level of the lake in the middle of Panama. Other locks lowered the canal back down to sea level on the far side.

had no reason to store water where mosquitoes could breed.

In two years, Gorgas brought yellow fever under control. One day he gathered hospital staff members around a corpse and told them to "take a good look" because this was likely to be the last victim of yellow fever they would see. It was.

Holding Back the Sea

The chief engineer of the canal project, John Stevens, let no obstacle get in his way. In 1905, he said, "There are three diseases in Panama. They are yellow fever, malaria, and cold feet; and the greatest of these is cold feet." With healthier workers, Stevens charged forward. By 1906, about 24,000 men from all over the world were digging. Trains hauled away dirt around the clock.

Floods and mudslides soon convinced Stevens that a sea-level canal, like the Suez in Egypt, would not work in Panama. He came up with a new plan. He proposed turning the trainloads of dirt into a large dam that would keep the Chagres River from flooding. The dam would form a huge man-made lake, 85 feet above sea level, at the center of the canal.

Ships entering the canal from the Atlantic Ocean would be raised up to the level of the lake—later named Gatún (gah-TOON) Lake—through a series of water-filled chambers, called locks. Ships would then travel 23 miles across the lake and through a nine-mile cut in the mountains. Another set of locks would lower ships to the level of the Pacific Ocean.

Many people, including President Roosevelt, worried about the

Engineers use dynamite to blast their way through the mountains of Panama and carve out the canal's route. The work was dangerous and accidents frequent. One explosion killed 23 men.

months later, however, the president was surprised and disappointed when Stevens resigned his post and left Panama. (The engineer gave no reason, though he was probably just exhausted.)

Now the president had to find someone else to complete the canal. He decided to give the job to "men who will stay on the job until I get tired of having them there, or till I say they may abandon it. I shall turn it over to the Army."

Roosevelt put a military engineer, Lieutenant Colonel George Goethals (GOH-thuhlz), in charge of the project. While soldiers joined civilians in the hot, muddy work of digging, Goethals made plans to build an efficient, well-equipped canal. In his design, the locks would be operated by 1,500 electric motors. These motors—as well as switches, lights, wiring, and generating equipment—would be manufactured in the United States by a new company, General Electric.

By 1910, nearly 40,000 men were at work on the canal. They used dynamite to blast away mountain rocks. There were frequent accidents. One explosion killed 23 men and wounded 60 others.

Mudslides plagued the construction. One mudslide in 1907 lasted 10 days. Always, the damage had to be repaired. "No one could say when the sun went down at night what the condition of the cut would be when the sun arose the next morning," wrote one of Goethals's advisors. "The work of months and years might be blotted out by an avalanche of earth."

safety of damming so much water. They remembered only too well the 1889 collapse of an earth dam in Johnstown, Pennsylvania, that had washed away more than two thousand lives. But Stevens used his knowledge of engineering to ease their doubts. He invited Roosevelt to visit Panama during the rainy season, so the president could better understand the need to dam the Chagres.

Roosevelt made the trip. Sloshing through mud and water convinced him that Stevens knew what he was doing. Just three

At last, however, the Panama Canal neared completion. In the fall of 1913, after the canal withstood a nearby earthquake without damage, world leaders began to make plans to attend the canal's official opening. Everyone looked forward to that glorious moment when the Atlantic and Pacific would come together, and the world would shrink a bit more.

You'll read about the canal's opening in this book's conclusion. But first, let's learn about another world-changing effort at the dawn of the twentieth century.

Reaching for the Sky

While thousands of men dug a path to link the oceans, others were reaching for the sky.

For centuries dreamers had toyed with the idea of flying. The ancient Greeks told a myth about a master craftsman, Daedalus, and his son Icarus, who flew with wings made of feathers and wax, until poor Icarus flew too close to the sun, which melted the wax and sent the boy plummeting into the sea.

The Chinese may have been the first adventurers to take a ride in the sky. Marco Polo reported seeing man-carrying kites when he visited China in the fourteenth century. Around 1500 in Italy, Leonardo da Vinci tried to design a flying machine with wings that were supposed to flap, but apparently it never got off the ground.

Near the end of the eighteenth century, two Frenchmen devised a large linen-and-paper balloon that allowed them to float over Paris. Hot-air balloons continued to fascinate people (and still do), but the difficulty of controlling their direction kept inventors searching for another way to fly.

In 1891, Otto Lilienthal (LIL-yuhn-tahl) of Germany made the first of some 2,000 flights in gliders, heavier-than-air aircraft with no engines. Around the world, other inventors read about his flights and tried to design their own gliders. Samuel P. Langley, secretary of the Smithsonian Institution in Washington, D.C., even built steam-driven aircraft, but they kept crashing into the Potomac River.

Otto Lilienthal's experiments with gliders in Germany inspired other inventors around the world. Below, he prepares to make a glider flight near Berlin in 1896. Lilienthal died later that year when one of his gliders crashed.

The Wright Brothers: From Bicycles to Gliders

Two American brothers, Wilbur and Orville Wright, eagerly read about these adventures. They had been tinkering with machines most of their lives. In the 1890s, they owned a bicycle shop in Dayton, Ohio. Building and fixing bicycles meant they had to know what causes a machine to turn left or right, and what causes it to stay balanced—all of which would be important in their later attempts to build a flying machine.

As they worked together, Wilbur and Orville found that some of their best ideas came when they argued with each other. Neighbors grew used to hearing the brothers' long, loud arguments, during which the two often switched sides. In the end, though, they usually came up with a solution that neither man would have thought of on his own. "I love to scrap with Orv," Wilbur once said. "He's such a good scrapper."

In the late 1890s, the brothers scrapped most often about the best design for a glider. They ordered books from the Smithsonian Institution and read everything they could about gliders. They studied Lilienthal's calculations about air pressure to learn how much to curve the wings. Then they began building a glider of their own.

When they were ready to test their glider, Wilbur wrote the U.S. Weather Bureau and asked where they could find a strong, steady wind. The Weather Bureau recommended the Outer Banks of North Carolina, on the Atlantic Ocean. So in September 1900, when the bicycle business was slowing for the winter, the Wright brothers went to the small village of Kitty Hawk.

- On a United States map, locate the Outer Banks of North Carolina—a chain of islands off the state's coast. Kitty Hawk lies on the northern section of the Outer Banks.

On the wide, sandy beaches near Kitty Hawk, the Wright brothers tested their glider. Wilbur even tried flying in it while Orville and a friend held its lines. But the glider bobbed up and down so dangerously that Wilbur cried, "Let me down!" The brothers decided to stick with unmanned flights until they could make them safer.

They usually flew their glider off a 90-foot sand dune known as Kill Devil Hill. Each time they launched the glider, they watched it carefully, took notes, and then made

What Is the Smithsonian?

In 1829, an English scientist named James Smithson died and left behind a curious will. Even though he had never visited the United States, he left his fortune to that country, with instructions that it be used "for the increase and diffusion of knowledge."

In 1846, the U.S. Congress used the generous gift to establish a museum, library, and research office called the Smithsonian Institution. Its first building, designed to look like a castle, stands near the U.S. Capitol in Washington, D.C. Today, the Smithsonian consists of 18 museums devoted to art, history, science, and culture, as well as several research centers and the National Zoo. The Smithsonian's National Air and Space Museum celebrates the history of flight.

a small adjustment, such as changing the angle of a wing, before trying again. Wilbur called this process "scientific kite flying."

Gradually, the brothers developed a glider that could fly and land smoothly. Then they began adding weight. Finally, they put a friend's nephew, 10-year-old Tom Tate, in the glider while they held on to control lines. The glider flew and landed smoothly.

The following summer, the Wright brothers built a larger glider, large enough to hold a grown man. But they could not get it to fly. What was wrong?

Discouraged, the brothers returned to Dayton. Over the next few months, they began to suspect that Lilienthal's calculations about the effect of air pressure on curved surfaces were wrong.

They used an old wash tub, a fan, and a large rectangular box to build a small wind tunnel—a chamber through which air is blown to study the effects of wind on an object, such as an airplane wing. The wind tunnel allowed them to watch how air flowed around wings of different shapes. The brothers soon realized that the calculations they had been using were indeed wrong. For example, they (and everyone else designing gliders) had figured that wings needed sharp front edges to cut through the air. But their experiments showed that blunt, rounded front edges worked best.

With this knowledge, the Wright brothers rebuilt their man-sized glider. The next summer, they took it to Kitty Hawk. It flew just fine. Over the winter of 1902–1903, they built propellers and a lightweight motor for their next project—an engine-powered flying machine.

The Flyer's First Flight

In the fall of 1903, the Wright brothers shipped the pieces of their new machine, nicknamed the *Flyer*, to Kitty Hawk. They were eager to test it.

On December 14, they put the *Flyer* on top of a long wooden rail that would guide the machine as it gained speed on its way (they hoped) to lifting off the ground. The brothers tossed a coin to see who would be the first pilot. Wilbur won the toss. He climbed on the *Flyer* and lay on his stomach between two cloth-covered wings, where he could handle the controls.

The *Flyer* lifted off the ground and stayed in the air three and a half seconds. Then it fell to the sand below.

Wilbur wasn't hurt, but several sticks and braces on the *Flyer* snapped. On December 17, 1903, with the *Flyer* repaired, the brothers were ready to try again. The freezing wind was almost too strong to be safe, but the brothers wanted to be home in Dayton for Christmas. They cranked the

Orville and Wilbur Wright built a small wind tunnel out of an old wash tub, a fan, and a large rectangular box. The wind tunnel allowed them to watch how air flows around wings of different shapes.

Wilbur Wright watches as the Flyer *lifts his brother Orville off the ground at Kitty Hawk, North Carolina, on December 17, 1903. The age of flight had begun.*

propeller and shook hands. Then Orville climbed onto the *Flyer*.

This time the *Flyer* stayed in the air 12 seconds. It landed 120 feet away from where it had started.

The brothers flew three more times that day. The longest flight, piloted by Wilbur, covered 852 feet and lasted 59 seconds. This flight, while brief, was the beginning of a new era—the age of flight.

The Age of Flight

The Wright brothers made it home for Christmas. Their family sent news of the flights to newspapers, but most ignored the story. Some editors thought it couldn't be true. Others thought a 59-second flight wasn't long enough to be important.

The editor of a Dayton newspaper later remembered that he liked the Wright brothers, but "sort of felt sorry for them. They seemed like well-meaning, decent enough young men. Yet there they were, neglecting their business to waste their time day after day on that ridiculous flying machine."

Others around the world were "wasting their time" in similar fashion. In 1906, Alberto Santos-Dumont, a Brazilian living in France, became the third person to fly an airplane successfully. Several French pilots made successful flights, and one, Louis Blériot (BLER-ee-oh), flew almost 24 miles across the English Channel from France to England.

Meanwhile, the Wright brothers kept working on new designs. In 1908, Wilbur took a ship to Paris to demonstrate what their latest airplane could do. As pilot, he swooped, turned, and drew figure eights in the sky. On the other side of the Atlantic, Orville performed similar demonstrations for the U.S. Army.

Orville was flying with an army officer when one of the plane's two propellers broke. The plane crashed, killing the officer and injuring Orville. But the tragic accident did not discourage the Wright brothers or the Army, which ordered the world's first military airplane from the brothers.

Other countries also began buying airplanes for military use. But an increasing number of pilots were flying just for fun, or for profit. In Europe and North America, stunt pilots flew from town to town, holding races and air circuses in which they showed off their tricks in the air. These tests of skill gave pilots valuable flying experience and caused some of them to suggest improvements in the design of their airplanes.

In 1914, the world's first scheduled commercial airline—a small seaplane that carried one passenger, along with freight, across Tampa Bay—began in Florida. The airline lost money and lasted only a few months.

But in the future there would be more airlines, more flights, and more people traveling in these fantastic machines that freed mankind from the grip of gravity.

Frenchman Louis Blériot flies over the white cliffs of Dover after crossing the English Channel in 1909. The flight covered almost 24 miles.

Bessie Coleman, Stunt Pilot

Only 10 years old when the Wright brothers made their first flight, Bessie Coleman dreamed of someday flying an airplane. A black female pilot in the early twentieth century? That seemed an impossible dream. But Coleman was determined. She spent years working and saving for flying lessons, only to learn that no U.S. flying school would teach a black woman. So she made her way to France, convinced a school to accept her, and spent more than a year in training. She returned to the United States in 1921, the world's first licensed black woman pilot. She spent the next few years performing acrobatic flights all over the country, dazzling audiences with her loop-the-loops, rolls, and tailspins.

Being a stunt pilot was a dangerous business. In 1926, Coleman lost her life in a flying accident. But her story reminds us of the daring and determination of those early pilots who helped lead the world into the age of flight.

A: A pilot flies an early airplane over the French countryside about 1910.

B: European immigrants arrive in New York in the late nineteenth century.

C: A Cook's travel poster shows that by 1900, the world had become a much smaller place.

Big Ambitions in a Shrinking World

*I*n early 1912, newspaper headlines filled people with a sense of pride, excitement, and optimism. A French aviator had flown faster than 100 miles per hour. A Norwegian explorer, Roald Amundsen, announced that his team

had reached the South Pole. The Chinese were celebrating their newly formed republic led by Sun Yat-sen. Mohandas Gandhi was marching for the rights of Indians in South Africa. And from the port of Southampton, in England, a huge and luxurious ocean liner, the *Titanic*, set out on its maiden voyage.

The very name, *Titanic*—which means having great force or power, or enormous in size or strength— suggests the spirit of the times, a time of big projects, high hopes, and dreams of unlimited progress. People around the world were thinking big, and the world seemed to be getting smaller.

Let's look back at these rising expectations in the shrinking world

of the late nineteenth and early twentieth centuries.

Nationalism and Imperialism on the Rise

Back in the late 1400s, proud citizens of Renaissance Florence felt loyal to their great city-state. But their loyalty stopped at the city walls. By the late nineteenth century, people's loyalties and hopes expanded to embrace larger political communities, moving beyond the local to the national.

Napoleon began this process in the early 1800s, when he exported the French Revolution and occupied many European lands. People in those lands were united by their shared dreams of being free from rule by outsiders. In 1861, Mazzini and

Garibaldi turned nationalist dreams into a united Italy. Ten years later Otto von Bismarck channeled nationalist feelings, military might, and political savvy into the formation of Germany as a single, united nation.

Waves of nationalism also swept England and France. The British proudly celebrated their long-lived monarch, Queen Victoria. The French rallied behind Emperor Napoleon III.

Across the Atlantic, the question of whether the United States would remain a single nation was answered by a bloody civil war. The Civil War ended slavery in the United States and set the stage for enormous industrial growth.

By the 1870s, nationalism in industrialized nations turned into imperialism. Many European leaders thought they could guarantee future prosperity for their countries by colonizing remote lands. Steamships and the shortcut afforded by the Suez Canal made it possible for industrial nations to reach distant lands more easily.

All These "-isms"

When we describe historical developments, we use words like *nationalism*, *imperialism*, or *racism*. These "-isms" describe big ideas and trends. The terms help us organize and understand history; they help give focus to a blurry multitude of events. But these "-isms" were not the real actors on the stage of history. Keep in mind that these ideas and movements all took shape in the minds and actions of real people. History books like this one can describe only a few of the major actors, but the stage of human history is populated by countless individuals who make real choices with real consequences.

The British took an early lead in empire building. It was said that "the sun never set on the British Empire," which at its height included large parts of Africa, Asia, North America, and Australia. Other industrial nations joined in the furious landgrab, swallowing nearly the entire continent of Africa and much of Asia.

Part of what drove the new imperialism was racism. The colonizing powers saw themselves as a superior race. They justified their actions as "survival of the fittest." They imagined they were bringing "civilization" and "progress" to people they saw as their inferiors.

But in colonizing distant lands, Western nations spread the very ideas that would lead to revolt. Their ideas of nationalism, natural rights, and self-rule stirred conquered peoples to action. By the early twentieth century, nationalism was not simply a Western idea. Nationalist movements emerged in India, China, and parts of the Ottoman and Austro-Hungarian Empires. Leaders like Gandhi in India and Sun Yat-sen in China struggled for an independent future for their countries.

Technological Progress and Bright Ideas

The burst of technological progress in the late nineteenth century made the future look bright indeed. By the early twentieth century, electric lights glowed in streets and many homes. Electricity powered many factories. New telephone and telegraph wires linked nations. The radio brought wireless communication. News traveled instantly from one land to the next.

In technology, "thinking big" brought big changes. Strong, light-weight steel made it possible to build towering skyscrapers. Twisted steel cables allowed the construction of massive suspension bridges, like New York's Brooklyn Bridge.

Technology turned industrialized societies into societies on the move. Electric trolleys and underground trains connected cities with growing suburbs. Henry Ford's assembly line made it possible to produce automobiles cheaply and efficiently so working people could afford them. Trains and steamships transported people and goods across vast distances, making the world seem to grow a little smaller.

Immigrants could buy passage aboard a steamship in Europe and transplant themselves to the Americas. Merchants could use the Suez Canal to speed goods from the Mediterranean Sea to the Indian Ocean. Americans anticipated the day when their ships would sail between the Atlantic and Pacific via the Panama Canal.

Steamships connected the world by water, but the airplane promised even quicker travel. By 1914, a few companies in America and Europe were producing commercial planes for sale. Progress was literally in the air.

An Age of Social Change: More, but Better?

As industrialization spread, new factories created more goods and more jobs. More businesses, stores, and offices opened. People flocked to cities for work. Women joined the workforce in larger numbers than

Streetcars, elevated trains, and electric light brought many big cities to life day and night.

ever before. A growing middle class had more money to spend. Some spent their money in the new department stores like the Bon Marché in Paris or Macy's in New York.

Cities in Europe moved out of the Middle Ages and into modern times as they tore down medieval walls and made improvements to meet the needs of larger populations.

The Wild West in Europe?

In the late nineteenth century, people began to enjoy new pastimes and entertainments, including extravagant shows that, because of the steamship, could travel from one continent to another. For example, the American cowboy Buffalo Bill took his Wild West show abroad. He loaded horses, buffalo, sharpshooters, Indians, and cowboys on a steamship and transported them to Europe. "Little Sure Shot" Annie Oakley performed for many European monarchs, including Queen Victoria and Germany's Crown Prince Wilhelm. At a performance in Berlin, Prince Wilhelm stepped down from the stands and dared Annie Oakley to shoot a cigarette out of his mouth. She hesitated about one second, lifted her rifle, and blew the cigarette away.

In the early 1900s, many cities improved their water supplies, sewers, and transportation systems. City-dwellers could visit museums, opera houses, theaters, parks, and plazas. Advances in medicine made it possible to vaccinate against diseases once easily spread by crowds.

But the problems of the industrial age lingered. Many workers and immigrants still lived in wretched tenements. Workers in the new steel mills, ironworks, gas refineries, and dockyards still labored long hours in awful conditions. In many sweatshops on both sides of the Atlantic, the poor labored to produce clothing or cigars in prison-like settings.

Women were paid less than men for whatever they did.

Laborers organized for change. Union members used collective bargaining and strikes to try to improve their wages and working conditions. To avoid the losses of a strike, some companies met the workers' demands. Other companies resisted the workers, and sometimes fighting broke out.

Suffragists also organized and insisted that women should have the right to vote. They were met with scorn and fury, but they persisted. And slowly but surely, one nation after another began to give women the vote.

The Good Life?

Technological progress and social change seemed to hold out the promise of "the good life" for many people—though certainly not for all. Millions of people in Africa and Asia did not control their own destinies. Western nations built railroads, strung telegraph lines, and constructed canals on their soil, but the colonized peoples rarely enjoyed the fruits of such progress. They saw their own natural resources, such as rubber and diamonds, hauled away, making westerners rich but leaving them poor. While these colonized peoples

Spreading the Word with New Tools

City-dwellers, laborers, and suffragists seeking change all benefited from new technology that spread their message—in words *and* pictures—to the public. Speedy presses made it possible to mass-produce powerful photographs. In 1890, for example, the journalist Jacob Riis (rees) published a book called *How the Other Half Lives*, about life in the tenements of New York City. It contained, as the title page announced, "illustrations chiefly from photographs taken by the author." Riis's vivid photographs aroused public indignation and concern about the terrible conditions in New York's slums.

In this Jacob Riis photo, three youngsters huddle for warmth in a slum area of New York.

hoped someday to live "the good life" of material progress, they longed most for independence from foreign rule.

Back in the western world, some thinkers, writers, and artists questioned whether "the good life" was more a deception than a dream. Was all this scientific and technological progress really leading to a better future?

Sigmund Freud suggested that humans are driven by irrational impulses and subconscious fears. Novelists like Émile Zola insisted that people's surroundings, not their reason and planning, determined their destinies. In their paintings, artists like Picasso and Kandinsky questioned the very nature of reality.

To a society rushing confidently, ambitiously, even arrogantly, headlong into the future, the works of these thinkers and artists seemed to say, "Stop. What are you racing toward and why? Does this sort of progress bring happiness?"

On the Edge: 1914

As the twentieth century entered its second decade, various events began to shake the western world's confidence in progress.

Only a few days into its first voyage, late on the evening of April 14, 1912, the *Titanic* struck an iceberg. Within hours, the huge ship, which its builders had described as "unsinkable," sank beneath the freezing waters. The overconfident owners had installed only enough lifeboats to carry half the passengers. Some 1,500 people died.

By early 1914, Mohandas Gandhi had been arrested for leading protests of Indian miners in South Africa. Sun Yat-sen had fled China as revolutionaries turned against him.

The "unsinkable" Titanic plunges beneath the waters of the Atlantic after hitting an iceberg on April 14, 1912.

Sigmund Freud on Modern Life

Sigmund Freud doubted whether new technologies could bring happiness. In his book called *Civilization and Its Discontents*, he wrote, "If there had been no railway to conquer distances, my child would never have left his native town and I should need no telephone to hear his voice; if traveling across the ocean by ship had not been introduced, my friend would not have embarked on his sea-voyage and I should not need a cable to relieve my anxiety about him.... And finally, what good to us is a long life if it is difficult and barren of joys?"

Former President Theodore Roosevelt was particularly scathing about this Armory Show painting, "Nude Descending a Staircase" by Marcel Duchamp. He compared it to a rug in his bathroom and said it might just as easily be called "A well-dressed man going up a ladder."

In the United States, American suffragists marched on Washington but without success. In New York City, the Armory Show, an exhibition of modern art, provoked former President Teddy Roosevelt to sputter that these new paintings were no better than the crude images etched on cave walls in prehistoric times.

In 1914, the Panama Canal withstood an earthquake. Its proud builders eagerly made plans for August 15, when they expected world leaders to gather in Panama for a festive celebration of the canal's opening. But there was no grand celebration. Instead, a shocking series of events unfolded that would change the world.

In June 1914, Archduke Franz Ferdinand, the nephew of Austria's Emperor Franz Josef, paid an official visit to Sarajevo (sar-uh-YAY-voh), the capital of Bosnia. Archduke Ferdinand was heir to the Habsburg throne in Austria. At that time, Bosnia was ruled by Austria. Many Serbs in Bosnia wanted to be free from Austrian control. They wanted Bosnia to become part of the kingdom of Serbia.

The archduke was warned that there might be trouble from Serb nationalists who were angry at Austria. But he went to Sarajevo anyway. On the morning of June 28, as the archduke's open car drove down a street in the city, a Serb gunman leaped aboard and shot both Franz Ferdinand and his wife.

The telegraph and telephone instantly spread the shocking news. Nations reacted quickly. In Austria, Emperor Franz Josef held the kingdom of Serbia responsible and declared war. Russia, encouraged by France, leaped to Serbia's defense. Germany declared war on Russia, and used the opportunity to storm west across Belgium to invade France. Britain rushed to defend France.

By August 1914, Europe's most powerful nations had chosen sides. World War I had begun. Many leaders expected a short, decisive, and glorious war, from which they would emerge victorious and enriched. They did not foresee ten million dead in a war that would ravage two continents.

On August 15, 1914, the Panama Canal opened in a quiet ceremony attended by few. The age of "thinking big"—the age of nationalism, imperialism, industrial power, rapid transportation, and instant communication—had led to something bigger and more terrible than anyone anticipated.

Left: Two tugboats pull an ocean-going vessel through the Panama Canal.

Below: British soldiers pour out of their trench and into battle during World War I.

Time Line (1860–1914)

1860

1870

1880

1860
Garibaldi and his Redshirts win victories that will soon lead to the creation of a united Italy.

1871
Bismarck forms a united German Empire after Prussia wins the Franco-Prussian War.

1869
In Egypt, the Suez Canal is completed, linking the Mediterranean and Red Seas.

1885
Gottlieb Daimler and Karl Benz build the first gasoline-powered automobiles; Louis Pasteur performs his first human vaccination.

1889
The 984-foot-tall Eiffel Tower is completed, at that time the tallest man-made structure in the world.

1865
Lee surrenders to Grant at Appomattox, ending the Civil War in the United States.

1879
Thomas Edison invents the first practical lightbulb.

In the United States, the transcontinental railroad is finished, linking the East and West Coasts.

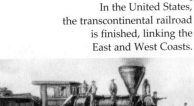

1890

1900

1910

c. 1905
The Women's Social and Political Union, led by Emmeline Goulden Pankhurst, works for woman suffrage in Britain.

1911
Sun Yat-sen becomes the first president of the new Chinese Republic.

c. 1900
Millions of African workers die under brutal conditions as they are forced to collect rubber in the Congo.

1893
Mohandas Gandhi begins his struggle for equal rights in South Africa.

c. 1907
Pablo Picasso fragments reality in his Cubist paintings.

1914
The First World War begins.

1895
Sigmund Freud writes and lectures on his theories about the role of the unconscious in human behavior.

1903
The Wright brothers record a 59-second manned flight at Kitty Hawk, North Carolina.

The Panama Canal is completed, linking the Atlantic and Pacific Oceans.

1897
Britain's Queen Victoria celebrates her sixtieth anniversary on the throne, ruling an empire that stretches around the globe.

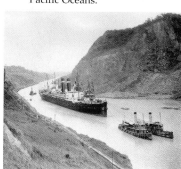

A: *The port of Venice during the Renaissance*

B: *An immigrant neighborhood in New York City about 1900*

C: *The modern skyline of Hong Kong*

Looking Back, Looking Forward

Some thoughtful people have said "world history" did not begin until the sixteenth century, meaning that even though important things were happening around the globe before 1500, those events did not form a connected story. There was no "world story" because people in different parts of the world were unaware of each other's existence. That began to change in the late fifteenth century. And by 1900, world history was being written at a furious pace.

World War I is the start of what historians often call the "contemporary era," the age in which we now live. The decades between that war and the present have been among the bloodiest in human history. They have also been the years of greatest opportunity, freedom, and advances in knowledge.

You will go on to learn more about contemporary history. When you do, you will be prepared, because the contemporary era is part of the modern world that you have been studying.

The roots of our time run deep. Our modern world is planted in the soil of the Renaissance, with that period's renewed confidence in human potential and keen interest in the here and now. We owe much to the creativity of the artists of that age, the courage of its explorers, and the curiosity of its scholars.

Our modern world still pins many of its hopes on the eighteenth-century ideal of reason, and the democratic ideals of natural rights and freedom. Our world is still a community of nations, many of which were born between the

An astronomer examines a celestial globe in this 1668 painting by Johannes Vermeer. Our modern world owes much to the curiosity of scholars from earlier ages.

lively city-states, where people exchanged goods and ideas. In the eighteenth and nineteenth centuries, the Industrial Revolution drew millions to cities. This urban explosion led to problems—disease, overcrowding, filth, crime. Reformers and planners worked—and continue to work—to solve these problems.

Our world is still filled with people who seek meaning in religion and philosophy, and who express their highest hopes and deepest fears in painting, sculpture, literature, and music. Our modern world still struggles with historic evils—the brutality of conquerors, the ugliness of racism, the scars of rapid technological change. We still grapple with how to use the powerful tools we create.

In 1914, doubt about the future mingled with nearly boundless hope. Some writers warned of overconfidence and impending doom. Others insisted the best years lay ahead.

Who was right? They both were.

In the twentieth century, we continued to make great strides in science and technology. As terrible diseases were eliminated and food production soared, people started to live longer, healthier lives. Just as mariners in the Age of Exploration set forth into uncharted waters, astronauts in the twentieth century explored the new frontier of outer space. In 1969, the first men set foot on the moon. Since then, many men and women have traveled into space, while unmanned probes, such as the *Mars Odyssey*, have begun to steer the human odyssey toward distant planets.

fifteenth and nineteenth centuries. We are still trying to figure out how nations can live together peacefully.

Much of our world was forged by the ideas and inventions of the Scientific and Industrial Revolutions. We are bound ever more closely by always-accelerating technology, which has taken us from railroads to space shuttles, from the telegraph to the Internet.

Much of the modern world's creative energy still pulses from cities. The Renaissance began in

Left: Eleanor Roosevelt, widow of U.S. President Franklin D. Roosevelt, examines a copy of the Universal Declaration of Human Rights, which she helped draft after World War II.

Below: In the twentieth century, astronauts began traveling into unknown realms much as adventurers from the Age of Exploration crossed uncharted waters.

While technology brought knowledge of other worlds, it might have led to the end of our own world. In the twentieth century, we fought two world wars. Millions died at the hands of evil tyrants. We invented nuclear weapons with the power to destroy the planet, and engaged in a frightening nuclear arms race. Weapons of vast destructive power remain a threat to civilization.

At the same time, in the twentieth century, more people have come to enjoy more political freedom than ever before. In 1948, shortly after the end of World War II, many nations of the world approved a Universal Declaration of Human Rights that declared, "All human beings are born free and equal in dignity and rights. They are endowed with reason and conscience and should act towards one another in a spirit of brotherhood." Those words reveal an unbroken thread from 1689 (the year of England's Glorious Revolution) to 1776 (when America declared its independence) to 1789 (when the French Revolution began) to our own time.

The human odyssey goes on. Where will it lead?

Appendix: Geographic Terms and Concepts

The word *geography* comes from the Greek terms for "description of the Earth." *Physical geography* concerns the natural features of the Earth such as landforms and climates. *Human geography* focuses on people and how they interact with their environments.

To understand historical events, we often need to understand the related geography. Historians want to know what a place was like long ago. They look for the influence the environment had on the people who lived there. They want to know the significance of location. They make connections between where events took place and why things happened as they did.

Throughout this book, we treat historical and geographic issues hand in hand. Here we offer a brief overview of some specific geographic terms and concepts.

The World in Spatial Terms
Globes, Maps, and Map Projections

Globes and *maps* represent the Earth. They are the geographer's most important tools. Since the Earth is roughly sphere-shaped, globes are the most accurate way to show it. However, flat maps are more practical. Try putting a globe in your pocket or on the page of a book!

While flat maps are practical, they all share one disadvantage. It's impossible to represent a sphere on a flat surface with complete accuracy. Thus all flat maps distort the Earth when they try to show it. Common distortions include distances, direction, and the shapes and sizes of landmasses.

Cartographers, or mapmakers, have developed various *map projections* as a way to minimize inaccuracies. One kind of projection might minimize distortions in the shape of landmasses, while another projection might minimize distortions in distance.

See pages 706–707 for examples of different map projections.

Types of Maps

Different kinds of maps provide different kinds of information.

Physical maps use symbols and colors to indicate natural features like mountains and rivers. For example, see pages 690–691. *Political maps* show man-made features such as national boundaries, cities, and roads. For example, see pages 692–693.

Some *general purpose maps* show both political features (such as national boundaries and cities) and physical features (such as rivers and mountains). The maps on pages 694–705 show both physical and political features.

Special purpose maps focus on one type of information such as climate or population. Historical maps might show trade routes or settlements. For examples of special purpose maps, see pages 708–711.

Today, Earth Resources Technology Satellites (ERTS) allow us to make maps from photographs of energy waves. Scientists and geographers use these *Landsat* maps, as they're called, to study the Earth's features and resources in greater detail than ever before.

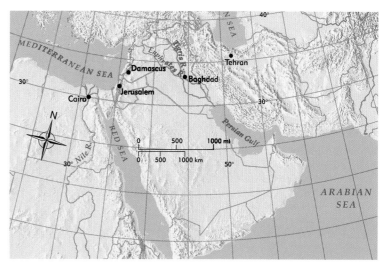

Map Symbols

A *map key* tells you what the symbols on a map mean. For example, a road map might use red lines for two-lane roads and blue lines for highways. Political maps often use a dot to represent cities, and sometimes a circled dot for the capital city.

See the Climates Zones map on page 708. At the bottom right is a map key that explains which color stands for which climate.

Many maps identify the *cardinal directions*—north, south, east, and west—with an arrow pointing north, or in a *compass rose* that shows all four directions.

Scale tells us the ratio between what is on the map and what is in the real world. A large-scale map of the Egyptian city of Cairo might use one inch on the map to represent 1,000 feet in the real world. A small-scale map of Africa might use one inch to represent 500 miles.

Locating Ourselves
Latitude and Longitude

Mapmakers use a grid of imaginary lines to divide the world into sections. This grid lets us locate places on a map or globe.

Running around the middle of the globe is an imaginary line called the *equator*. The equator is halfway between the North Pole and the South Pole.

On a globe you'll see lines running around the globe parallel to the equator. We call these lines of *latitude*, or *parallels*. Latitude lets us identify a location north or south of the equator, measured in units called *degrees*. The latitude of the equator is 0° (zero degrees). Lines of latitude are numbered from 0° (the equator) to 90° north (the North Pole), and 0° (the equator) to 90° south (the South Pole).

On a globe, the lines that run north and south, from pole to pole, are called lines of *longitude*, or *meridians*. You'll notice that meridians are not parallel since they come together at the poles. Meridians are also measured in degrees. An imaginary line called the *prime meridian* is 0°.

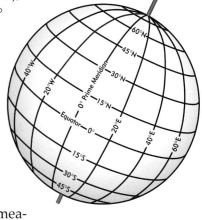

Lines of latitude and longitude

The prime meridian runs through Greenwich, England, at the original site of the Royal Greenwich Observatory. There are 180 degrees east of the prime meridian, and 180 degrees west.

Hemispheres

The equator and the prime meridian let us divide the Earth into halves, called *hemispheres*. North of the equator is the *Northern Hemisphere*, while south of the equator is the *Southern Hemisphere*. To the west of the prime meridian is the *Western Hemisphere*, while to the east of the prime meridian is the *Eastern Hemisphere*.

Every place on Earth is in two hemispheres at once. For example, the city of Chicago, Illinois, is in the Northern and Western Hemispheres. The city of Bombay in India is in the Southern and Eastern Hemispheres.

Absolute and Relative Location

The grid system allows us to identify any place on Earth by its specific position, or what geographers call its *absolute location*. Often, however, we use *relative location*—that is, the location of a place compared to another place. For example, if you're driving, knowing that Baltimore is about 35 miles (56 kilometers) northeast of Washington, D.C., can be more useful than knowing that it is at 39° N and 77° W.

Places, Regions, and Landforms

Geographers use concepts of *place* and *region*. One way to describe *place* is to look at natural physical features, including land, water, and climate.

Geographers group places that have similar characteristics into *regions*. Regions may be defined by various characteristics—for example, by a physical characteristic such as climate, or by a cultural characteristic such as language. In the United States, the Pacific Northwest is a mountainous, rainy region. Latin America—which includes Mexico, Central America, South America, and islands in the West Indies—is a vast region where most people speak Spanish or Portuguese, languages that developed from Latin.

Continents

About 30 percent of the Earth's surface is land. The largest land-masses are *continents*. Most

Degrees, Minutes, Seconds

Lines of latitude and longitude are spaced in units called *degrees*. The distance between one parallel and the next (one degree of latitude) is approximately 69 miles, or 111 kilometers. The distance between one meridian and the next (one degree of longitude) varies from about 69 miles at the equator to zero at the poles.

To help pinpoint locations more precisely, each degree is divided into smaller units called *minutes* and *seconds*. These minutes and seconds are measures of distance, not time. There are 60 minutes in a degree, and 60 seconds in a minute.

You can identify a location by its coordinates—that is, by the intersection of the parallel (latitude) and the meridian (longitude). For example, the coordinates of the Emperor's Palace in Tokyo, Japan, are 35°40′45″ N, 139°46′14″ E. You say that as "35 degrees, 40 minutes, 45 seconds north; 139 degrees, 46 minutes, 14 seconds east."

geographers identify seven continents—Asia, Africa, North America, South America, Antarctica, Europe, and Australia. Europe and Asia are part of the same landmass, called Eurasia, but are usually considered separate continents. On the map on pages 690–691, locate each of the seven continents.

Major Landforms

Landforms are natural land features. Major landforms include mountains, plateaus, and plains. We identify landforms by their *relief*, or shape, and their *elevation*, or height above sea level.

Mountains, sometimes called *highlands*, stand well above the surrounding landscape and have distinct relief, including steep slopes and peaks. They range from 2,000 feet (roughly 600 meters) above sea level, like parts of the Appalachians in eastern North America, to a high of about 29,000 feet (8,850 meters). The Himalaya in Asia are the highest mountains in the world.

Plateaus are areas of moderate or high elevation with little relief. They are sometimes called tablelands. The surface of a plateau may be flat or have small, rolling hills.

Plains are large areas of flat or almost flat land, usually at low elevations. *Coastal plains* lie near the shore at sea level.

Canyons and *valleys* are much lower than the land around them. *Islands* are landmasses surrounded by water. A *peninsula* is a landmass almost surrounded by water.

While those are some of the common landforms, there are others as well.

Top: Mountain peaks in the Himalaya, the highest mountain range in the world

Center: Canyonlands National Park in Utah

Bottom: One of the Maldive Islands in the Indian Ocean

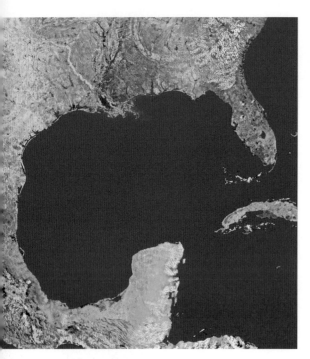

The Atlantic Ocean extends into the Gulf of Mexico. The Gulf is bounded by the coastline of the United States to the north and Mexico to the west.

Bodies of Water

Most of the Earth is covered by water. Water continually cycles from ocean to air to ground and back to ocean. Geographers identify bodies of water by their size, shape, and content.

Oceans and Seas

The enormous body of salt water that surrounds the continents and makes up more than 95 percent of the world's water is divided into four *oceans*—Arctic, Atlantic, Indian, and Pacific. All of the Earth's land could fit in the Pacific Ocean alone. If the highest mountain, Mount Everest, were placed in the Pacific at its deepest spot, Everest's peak would lie a mile beneath the ocean's surface.

Seas are smaller bodies of salt water, almost surrounded by land. Where portions of seas or oceans extend into coastlines, we find *gulfs* or *bays*.

Lakes and Rivers

Lakes are bodies of water completely surrounded by land. Most lakes hold fresh water. Many lakes were formed by glaciers that carved deep valleys in the Earth where rain and melting ice collected. The largest fresh water lake in the world is Lake Superior, one of the Great Lakes of North America.

Rivers are waterways that flow through land and into larger bodies of water. Rivers usually begin as *streams* at high elevation. The streams join one another to form a river. These rivers often combine to form larger rivers. A *tributary* is a stream or river that feeds into a larger stream, river, or lake. For example, the Ohio River is a tributary of the Mississippi River.

The longest river in the world is the Nile in Africa, which begins as several smaller rivers in the East African Highlands and flows more than 4,100 miles (6,650 kilometers) north to the Mediterranean Sea.

Climate

Weather refers to atmospheric conditions in a particular time and place—"We're having stormy weather today." *Climate* is the general weather pattern that occurs in an area over a long time—"We live in a dry climate." Climate is determined by many factors, including distance from the equator (latitude), elevation, and proximity to water or mountains. Geographers divide the Earth's many climates into four major zones. (See page 708 for a detailed climate map.)

A River Delta

A delta is a triangular piece of land at the mouth of a river. It's usually laden with rich deposits of alluvial soil (that is, soil deposited by flowing water). The term *delta* comes from the fourth letter of the Greek alphabet, which looks like this: Δ.

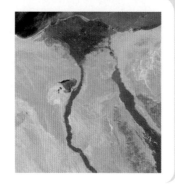

Tropical Climates

Near the equator there are two types of climate—tropical rain forest and tropical savanna. Because the sun's rays shine directly on the tropics year-round, temperatures there are always warm.

A *tropical rain forest* gets rain almost daily, totaling more than 80 inches (2,000 millimeters) per year. The result is dense vegetation and a remarkable variety of plant and animal life. Tropical rain forests are home to millions of species of plants and animals, more than anywhere else on Earth.

Tropical savannas extend farther from the equator than rain forests, but still in latitudes that are warm year-round. They experience dry and wet seasons. Savannas are grasslands with few trees.

Mid-latitude Climates

Farther from the equator are several climate zones grouped as *mid-latitude climates*. While they vary in their temperatures and precipitation, they are all moderate climates, and have distinct seasons.

These moderate climates are home to most people. See the map on page 708 to locate some of these mid-latitude climates, including Mediterranean, humid subtropical, humid continental, and marine west coast.

High-latitude Climates

In the polar regions farthest from the equator, climates are so cold that little vegetation can survive. High-latitude climates include the tundra, which supports short grasses during brief summers, and the ice sheet, where nothing grows. High-latitude conditions can also occur at very high elevations, regardless of latitude. For example, mountain peaks at high elevations are snow-capped even in the tropics.

Dry Climates

Dry climates are those with little or no precipitation. They can be hot year-round, or have bitterly cold winters. Because the air in these regions is so dry, temperatures tend to fall dramatically at night. *Deserts* typically receive less than 10 inches (250 millimeters) of rain per year. *Steppes* get 10 to 20 inches (250 to 500 millimeters) of rain annually.

Physical Systems: Our Changing Earth

The Earth's surface is constantly changing. Forces within the Earth and on the surface cause much of this change. But human activity also changes Earth's physical systems.

Internal Forces

The part of the Earth on which we walk and on which the oceans rest is called the *crust*. The crust varies in thickness, but generally extends about 25 miles (40 kilometers) beneath land surface. Below the

Above, top: Rain forest in northeastern Australia

Above: Dunes in the Sahara, the world's largest desert

Below: Elephants on an African savanna with Mount Kilimanjaro in the background

A river of lava flows from an erupting volcano in Hawaii. Lava is melted rock. Beneath the Earth's surface, it is called magma.

crust are the *mantle*, an *outer core*, and an *inner core*.

The crust is made up of *plates*, huge masses of rock that float on the semiliquid material in the mantle. These plates can shift position and bump or rub against each other, causing earthquakes. Earthquakes beneath the ocean cause tidal waves or tsunamis. Plates pushing against each other can also build mountains. When plates pull apart, they can form gorges and valleys.

Deep in the Earth flows melted rock called *magma*. When a volcano erupts, magma comes to the surface, where it is called lava. Volcanoes can dramatically change the Earth's surface.

External Forces

Some changes to the Earth's surface come from external forces such as wind and water. *Weathering* occurs when water breaks down the chemicals in rocks and they disintegrate. When water freezes and melts, it can split rocks apart.

Flowing water, wind, and the movement of glaciers are some of the causes of *erosion*, the wearing away of the Earth's surface.

Ecosystems and Human Systems
Ecosystems

An *ecosystem* is a group of living things and the environment in which they live. Ecosystems can be as small as a tiny pond and the living things it supports, or as large as the tundra.

Small changes in factors such as climate or air quality can alter or even destroy an ecosystem. Humans can change ecosystems when they alter some element of the environment around them. Some human activity, such as digging mines or clearing a forest, can have dramatic effects on the environment.

Human Systems

Historians and geographers ask questions about individuals and about groups of people. They study human settlements around the world and across time, and observe the distribution of population. They pay attention to patterns of *migration*— why people move from one place to another, and the results of those moves. They want to know about *culture*—the traditions and customs of a group of people, their ways of life and thought, and how those ways differ from the ways of other groups. Historians and geographers also look for patterns in the way groups of people trade and interact with each other, sometimes peacefully, sometimes not.

See pages 710–711 for maps that show cultural regions and population density.

Environment and Society
Resources

Geographers examine the resources available in different areas. *Renewable resources* can be replenished by the Earth's own processes or in some cases by human activity as they are used. These include water, forests, and solar power. *Nonrenewable resources* cannot be replenished once they are used. Minerals and fossil fuels like coal and oil are examples of nonrenewable resources. Because nonrenewable resources are limited, their use and distribution affects human interaction.

The specific resources that people use and value vary by place and have changed over time. For example, petroleum was not valued before the combustion engine was invented.

Human-Environmental Interaction

Humans adapt to their environments and change them. When we put on a winter coat, or jump into the surf to cool off, we are adapting to our environment. We change the environment every time we build a house or fertilize a lawn.

One dramatic historical example of humans adapting to and changing the environment occurred in the early 1500s, soon after Christopher Columbus came in contact with the Americas. The exchange of hundreds of species of plants and animals among continents in the years following his voyages resulted in profound changes in populations, ways of life, and ecosystems.

The geography of an area, in turn, has a huge impact on human activity in that area. People build differently in earthquake or hurricane zones than in the Amazon. Historians look at geography to explain, for example, why people in one part of the world developed farming communities while people elsewhere remained nomads. Geography affects economic, social, and political activity.

Wind turbines convert wind energy into electricity—a clean and renewable source of energy.

World Physical

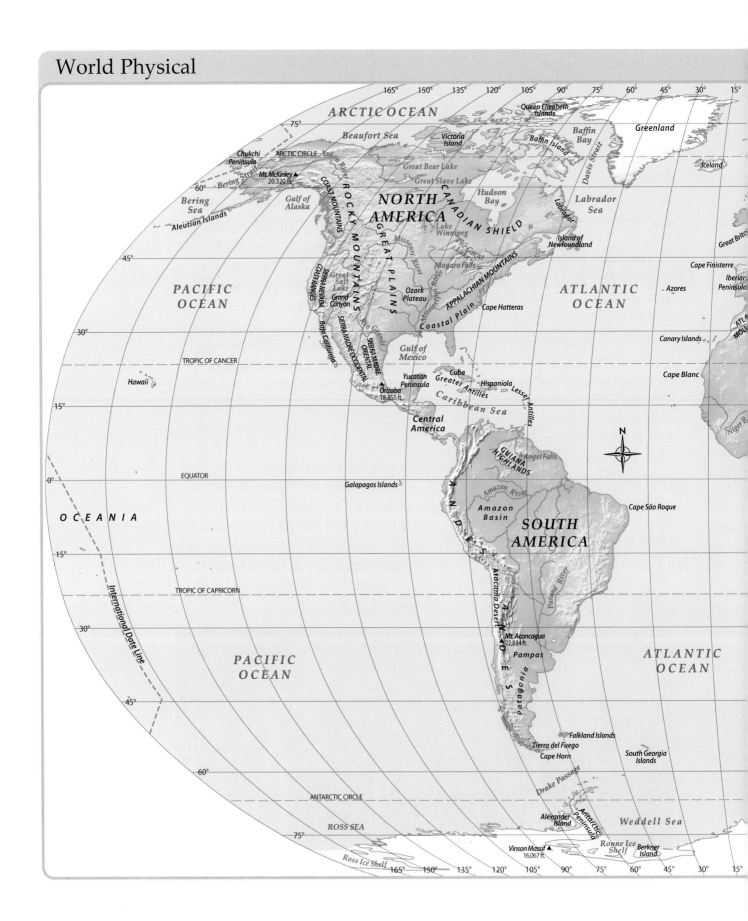

15° 30° 45° 60° 75° 90° 105° 120° 135° 150° 165°

Svalbard

Norwegian Sea

Barents Sea

Novaya Zemlya

Kara Sea

North Land

ARCTIC OCEAN

Laptev Sea

East Siberian Sea

75°

ARCTIC CIRCLE

Chukchi Peninsula

Scandinavia

Kola Peninsula

Northern European Plain

URAL MOUNTAINS

Yenisey River

Ob River

S I B E R I A

Central Siberian Plateau

Lena River

60°

Sea of Okhotsk

Kamchatka Peninsula

Bering Sea

Date Line

45°

EUROPE

Volga River

West Siberian Plain

A S I A

Sakhalin

Rhine R. Danube R.

CARPATHIAN MOUNTAINS

The Steppes

Mongolian Plateau

Hokkaido

ALPS

Balkan Peninsula

Black Sea

Elbrus 18,510 ft.

CAUCASUS MOUNTAINS

Caspian Sea

Aral Sea

TIAN SHAN

Gobi

Hwang He River

Sea of Japan

Shikoku

Honshu

PACIFIC OCEAN

Anatolia

Mt. Ararat 16,854 ft.

Taklimakan Desert

KUNLUN MOUNTAINS

Kyushu

30°

Mediterranean Sea

Syrian Desert

ZAGROS MOUNTAINS

Tigris River

K2 28,251 ft.

Plateau of Tibet

Yangtze River

East China Sea

Libyan Desert

Nile River

Sinai Peninsula An Nafûd

Red Sea

Euphrates River

HIMALAYA

Mt. Everest 29,035 ft.

TROPIC OF CANCER

S A H A R A

Arabian Peninsula

Arabian Sea

Great Indian Desert

Ganges River

Deccan Plateau

Indochina Peninsula

South China Sea

Taiwan

Philippine Sea

15°

S u d a n

AFRICA

ETHIOPIAN HIGHLANDS

Somali Peninsula

Cape Gwardafuy

Cape Comorin

Bay of Bengal

Malay Peninsula

Philippine Islands

Congo River

Congo Basin

Lake Victoria

Kilimanjaro 19,340 ft.

Lake Tanganyika

Sumatra

Borneo

New Guinea

EQUATOR

INDIAN OCEAN

Celebes

Katanga Plateau

Lake Malawi

Java

Arafura Sea

OCEANIA

15°

Victoria Falls

Mozambique Channel

Madagascar

Great Sandy Desert

Coral Sea

Namib Desert

Kalahari Desert

Réunion

TROPIC OF CAPRICORN

Western Plateau

AUSTRALIA

Great Victoria Desert

GREAT DIVIDING RANGE

Darling River

30°

Cape of Good Hope

Murray R.

Tasman Sea

North Island

New Zealand

Tasmania

South Island

45°

Kerguélen Is.

0   1000   2000 mi

0   1000   2000 km

Scale at equator

60°

ANTARCTIC CIRCLE

ANTARCTICA

TRANSANTARCTIC MOUNTAINS

75°

Ross Ice Shelf

15° 30° 45° 60° 75° 90° 105° 120° 135° 150° 165°

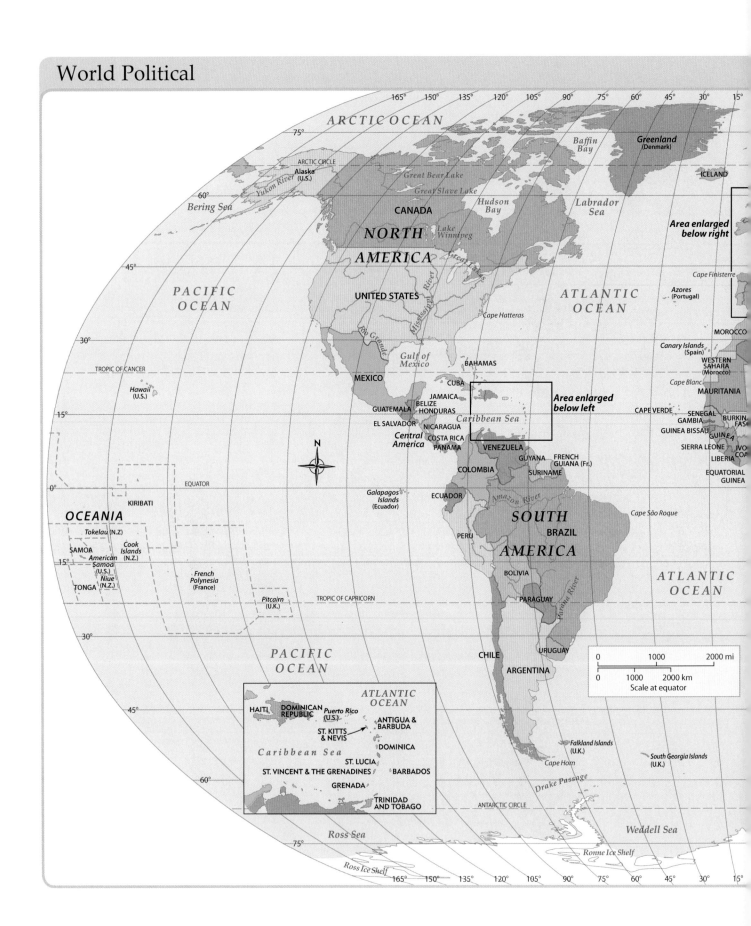

ARCTIC OCEAN

75°

ARCTIC CIRCLE

Alaska
(U.S.)

Yukon River

Bering Sea

60°

Great Bear Lake

Great Slave Lake

CANADA

NORTH
AMERICA

Lake
Winnipeg

Hudson
Bay

Baffin
Bay

Greenland
(Denmark)

ICELAND

Labrador
Sea

Area enlarged
below right

Cape Finisterre

45°

PACIFIC
OCEAN

UNITED STATES

Mississippi River

Cape Hatteras

ATLANTIC
OCEAN

Azores
(Portugal)

MOROCCO

30°

Rio Grande

Gulf of
Mexico

BAHAMAS

Canary Islands
(Spain)

WESTERN
SAHARA
(Morocco)

TROPIC OF CANCER

Hawaii
(U.S.)

MEXICO

CUBA

Cape Blanc

MAURITANIA

15°

GUATEMALA
EL SALVADOR
Central
America

JAMAICA
BELIZE
HONDURAS
NICARAGUA
COSTA RICA
PANAMA

Caribbean Sea

Area enlarged
below left

CAPE VERDE

SENEGAL
GAMBIA
GUINEA BISSAU
SIERRA LEONE
LIBERIA

BURKINA
FASO
GUINEA
IVORY
COAST
EQUATORIAL
GUINEA

VENEZUELA

GUYANA

FRENCH
GUIANA (Fr.)

EQUATOR

KIRIBATI

OCEANIA

Tokelau (N.Z)

SAMOA
American
Samoa
(U.S.)
TONGA

Cook
Islands
(N.Z.)
Niue
(N.Z.)

French
Polynesia
(France)

Galapagos
Islands
(Ecuador)

ECUADOR

COLOMBIA

SURINAME

Amazon River

SOUTH
AMERICA

BRAZIL

Cape São Roque

PERU

15°

Pitcairn
(U.K.)

TROPIC OF CAPRICORN

BOLIVIA

PARAGUAY

Paraná River

ATLANTIC
OCEAN

30°

PACIFIC
OCEAN

CHILE

URUGUAY

ARGENTINA

0   1000   2000 mi

0   1000   2000 km
Scale at equator

45°

HAITI

DOMINICAN
REPUBLIC

Puerto Rico
(U.S.)

ATLANTIC
OCEAN

ANTIGUA &
BARBUDA

ST. KITTS
& NEVIS

DOMINICA

Caribbean Sea

ST. LUCIA

ST. VINCENT & THE GRENADINES

BARBADOS

GRENADA

TRINIDAD
AND TOBAGO

Falkland Islands
(U.K.)

Cape Horn

South Georgia Islands
(U.K.)

Drake Passage

60°

ANTARCTIC CIRCLE

Weddell Sea

Ross Sea

75°

Ronne Ice Shelf

Ross Ice Shelf

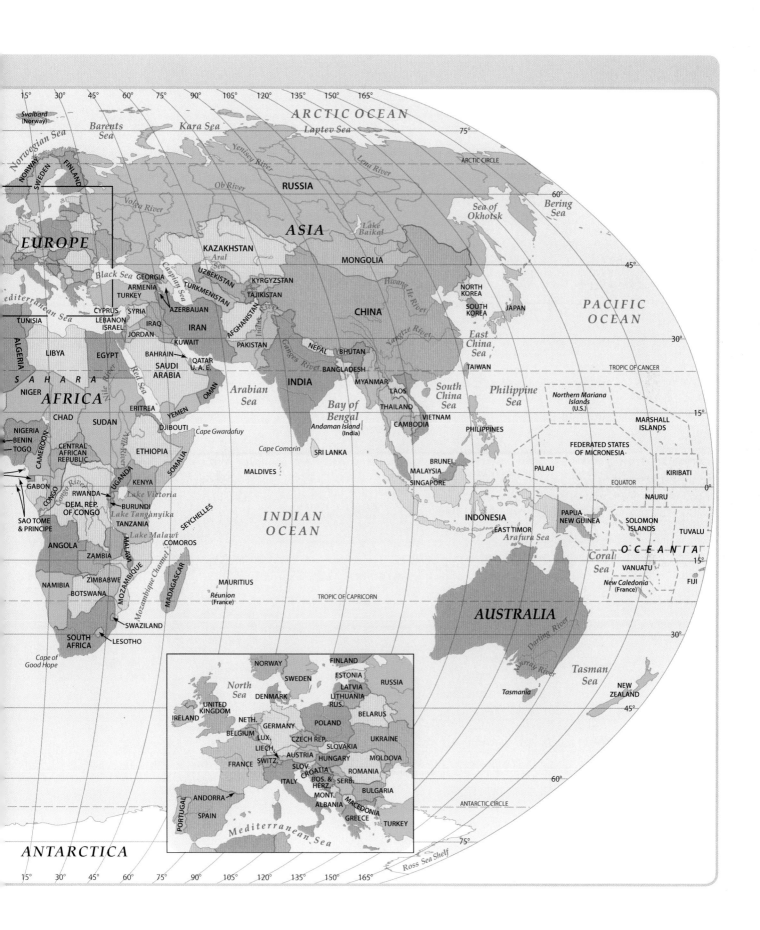

ARCTIC OCEAN

Svalbard
(Norway)

Barents
Sea

Kara Sea

Laptev Sea

75°

ARCTIC CIRCLE

Norwegian Sea

Yenisey River

Lena River

NORWAY
SWEDEN
FINLAND

RUSSIA

60°

Bering
Sea

Volga River

Ob River

Sea of
Okhotsk

EUROPE

ASIA

Lake
Baikal

KAZAKHSTAN

Aral
Sea

45°

Black Sea

GEORGIA

UZBEKISTAN

MONGOLIA

NORTH
KOREA

PACIFIC
OCEAN

ARMENIA
TURKEY

TURKMENISTAN

KYRGYZSTAN

Caspian Sea

TAJIKISTAN

SOUTH
KOREA

JAPAN

Mediterranean Sea

CYPRUS
LEBANON
ISRAEL

SYRIA

AZERBAIJAN

CHINA

East
China
Sea

TUNISIA

IRAQ

IRAN

AFGHANISTAN

JORDAN

30°

TAIWAN

TROPIC OF CANCER

ALGERIA

LIBYA

EGYPT

KUWAIT

BAHRAIN

PAKISTAN

NEPAL

BHUTAN

Hwang He River

Yangtze River

SAUDI
ARABIA

QATAR
U.A.E.

Ganges River

BANGLADESH

South
China
Sea

Philippine
Sea

Northern Mariana
Islands
(U.S.)

SAHARA

NIGER

AFRICA

Red Sea

OMAN

Arabian
Sea

INDIA

MYANMAR

LAOS

MARSHALL
ISLANDS

Nile River

ERITREA

YEMEN

Bay of
Bengal

THAILAND

15°

CHAD

SUDAN

DJIBOUTI

Cape Gwardafuy

Andaman Island
(India)

CAMBODIA

VIETNAM

FEDERATED STATES
OF MICRONESIA

NIGERIA
BENIN
TOGO

CENTRAL
AFRICAN
REPUBLIC

ETHIOPIA

Cape Comorin

SRI LANKA

PHILIPPINES

PALAU

KIRIBATI

CAMEROON

SOMALIA

MALDIVES

BRUNEI

EQUATOR

0°

GABON

Congo River

UGANDA

KENYA

MALAYSIA

NAURU

CONGO

RWANDA

Lake Victoria

SINGAPORE

SAO TOME
& PRINCIPE

DEM. REP.
OF CONGO

BURUNDI

Lake Tanganyika

SEYCHELLES

INDIAN
OCEAN

INDONESIA

PAPUA
NEW GUINEA

SOLOMON
ISLANDS

TANZANIA

Lake Malawi

EAST TIMOR

OCEANIA

TUVALU

ANGOLA

MALAWI

COMOROS

Arafura Sea

15°

ZAMBIA

MADAGASCAR

Coral
Sea

VANUATU

NAMIBIA

ZIMBABWE

Mozambique Channel

MAURITIUS

New Caledonia
(France)

FIJI

BOTSWANA

MOZAMBIQUE

Réunion
(France)

TROPIC OF CAPRICORN

AUSTRALIA

Darling River

30°

SWAZILAND

SOUTH
AFRICA

LESOTHO

Murray River

Tasman
Sea

NEW
ZEALAND

Cape of
Good Hope

NORWAY

FINLAND

Tasmania

North
Sea

SWEDEN

ESTONIA

RUSSIA

45°

UNITED
KINGDOM

DENMARK

LATVIA
LITHUANIA
RUS.

IRELAND

NETH.

GERMANY

POLAND

BELARUS

BELGIUM

LUX.
LIECH.

CZECH REP.

UKRAINE

FRANCE

SWITZ.

AUSTRIA

SLOVAKIA

HUNGARY

MOLDOVA

SLOV.

CROATIA

ROMANIA

ITALY

BOS. &
HERZ.

SERB.

ANDORRA

MONT.

BULGARIA

60°

PORTUGAL

SPAIN

ALBANIA

MACEDONIA

ANTARCTIC CIRCLE

GREECE

TURKEY

Mediterranean Sea

75°

ANTARCTICA

Ross Sea Shelf

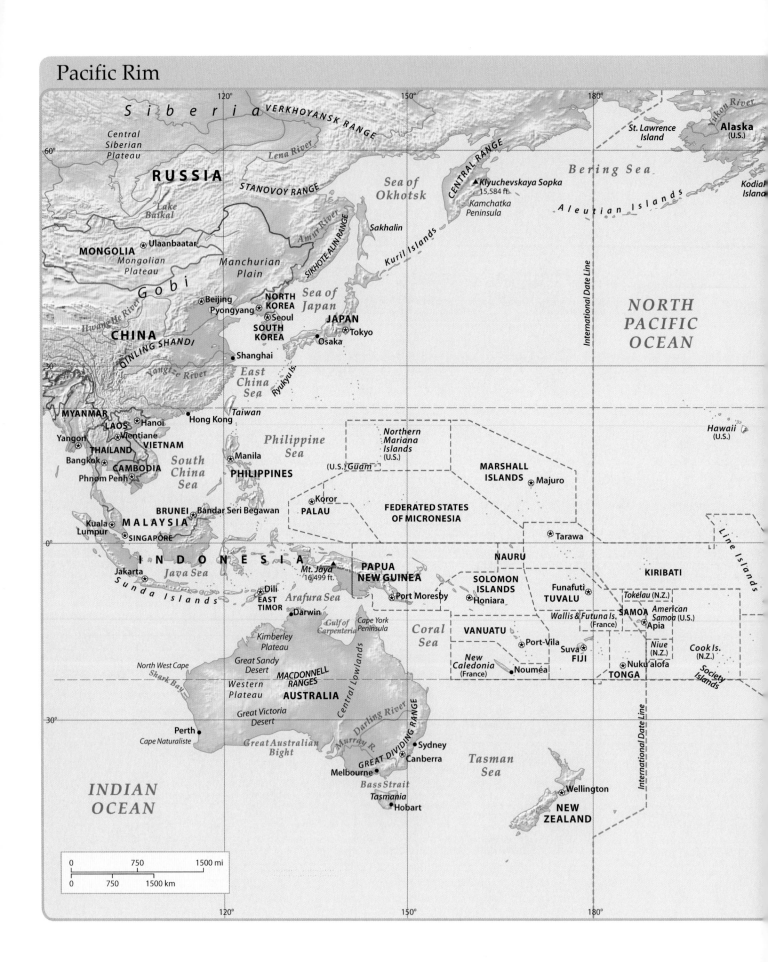

Pacific Rim

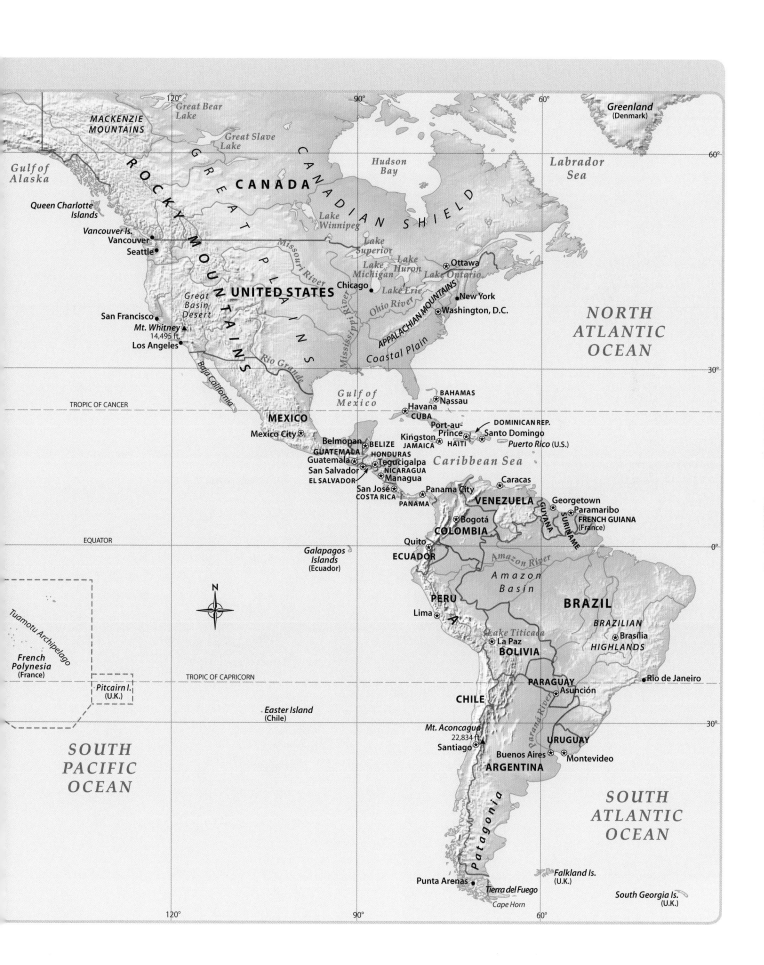

Great Bear Lake
MACKENZIE MOUNTAINS
Gulf of Alaska
Queen Charlotte Islands
Vancouver Is.
Vancouver
Seattle
120°
Great Slave Lake
CANADA
GREAT PLAINS
Missouri River
Lake Winnipeg
CANADIAN SHIELD
Hudson Bay
90°
60°
Greenland (Denmark)
Labrador Sea
60°

Lake Superior
Lake Michigan
Lake Huron
Lake Ontario
Lake Erie
Ottawa
New York
Washington, D.C.
Chicago
UNITED STATES
Great Basin Desert
San Francisco
Mt. Whitney 14,495 ft.
Los Angeles
ROCKY MOUNTAINS
Mississippi River
Ohio River
APPALACHIAN MOUNTAINS
Coastal Plain

NORTH ATLANTIC OCEAN
30°

TROPIC OF CANCER
Baja California
Rio Grande
Gulf of Mexico
BAHAMAS
Nassau
Havana
CUBA
MEXICO
Mexico City
Belmopan BELIZE
GUATEMALA
HONDURAS
Guatemala
San Salvador
EL SALVADOR
Tegucigalpa
NICARAGUA
Managua
San José
COSTA RICA
Panama City
PANAMA
Port-au-Prince
Kingston
JAMAICA HAITI
DOMINICAN REP.
Santo Domingo
Puerto Rico (U.S.)
Caribbean Sea
Caracas
VENEZUELA
GUYANA
Georgetown
Paramaribo
SURINAME
FRENCH GUIANA (France)

EQUATOR
Galapagos Islands (Ecuador)
Bogotá
COLOMBIA
Quito
ECUADOR
Amazon River
Amazon Basin
BRAZIL
0°

SOUTH PACIFIC OCEAN
Tuamotu Archipelago
French Polynesia (France)
Pitcairn I. (U.K.)
N
Easter Island (Chile)
TROPIC OF CAPRICORN
PERU
Lima
Lake Titicaca
La Paz
BOLIVIA
BRAZILIAN HIGHLANDS
Brasília
Rio de Janeiro
PARAGUAY
Asunción
Paraná River
CHILE
Mt. Aconcagua 22,834 ft
Santiago
Buenos Aires
ARGENTINA
URUGUAY
Montevideo
30°

120°
90°
Punta Arenas
Patagonia
Tierra del Fuego
Cape Horn
60°
Falkland Is. (U.K.)
South Georgia Is. (U.K.)
SOUTH ATLANTIC OCEAN

North America

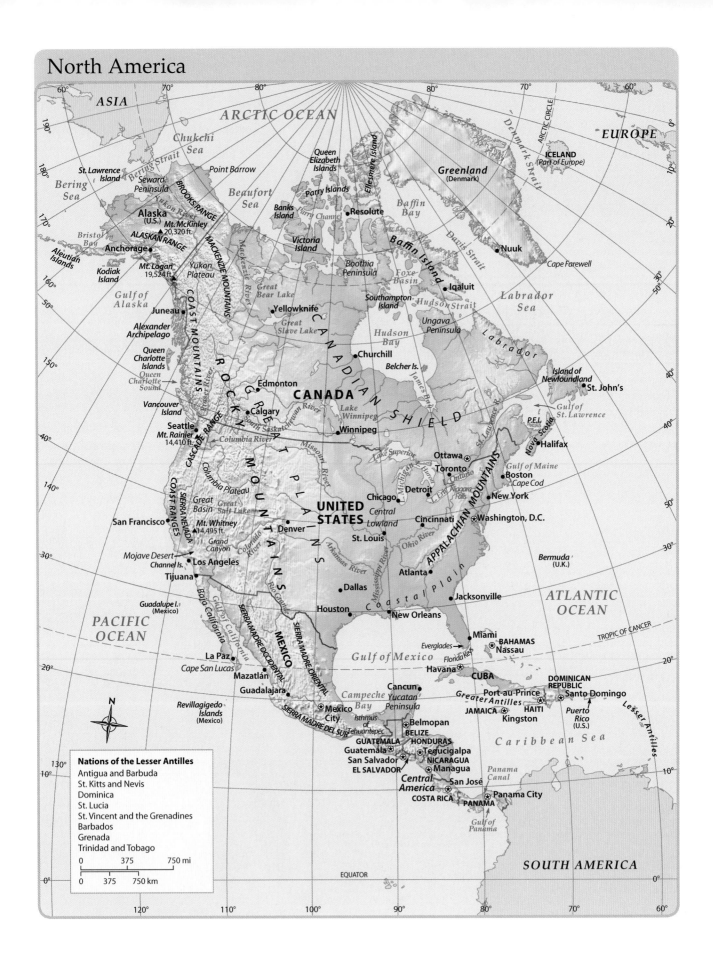

Nations of the Lesser Antilles
Antigua and Barbuda
St. Kitts and Nevis
Dominica
St. Lucia
St. Vincent and the Grenadines
Barbados
Grenada
Trinidad and Tobago

0   375   750 mi
0   375   750 km

South America

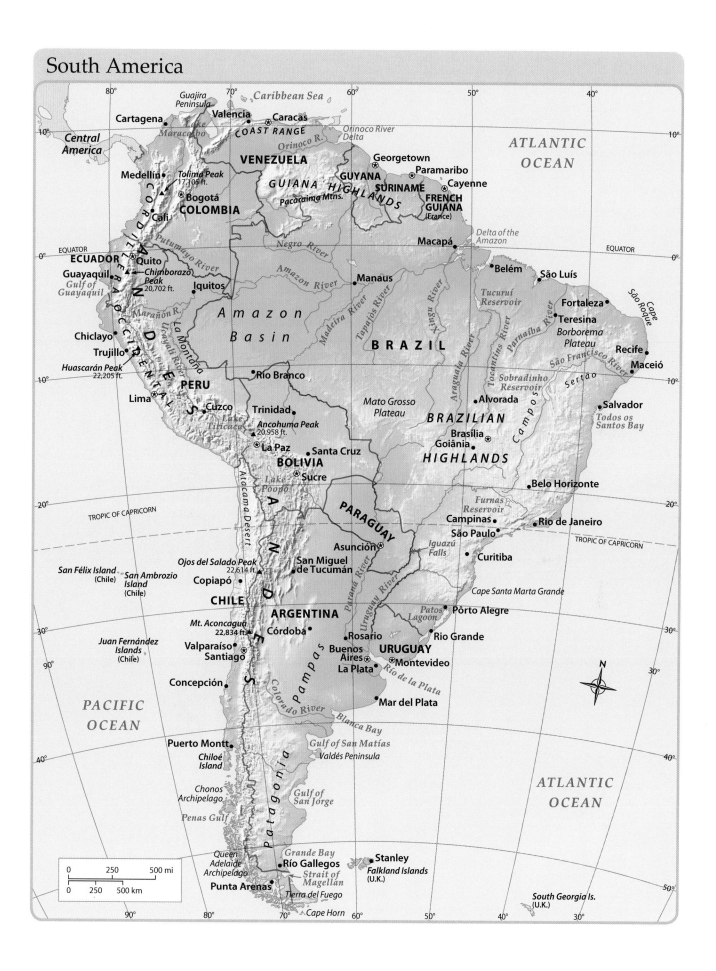

Caribbean Sea

Guajira Peninsula

Cartagena
Valencia • ⊕ Caracas
COAST RANGE
Orinoco River Delta

ATLANTIC OCEAN

Central America

Lake Maracaibo
Orinoco R.

VENEZUELA
Georgetown ⊕
Paramaribo
GUYANA ⊕
Medellín • Tolima Peak 17,105 ft. ▲
GUIANA HIGHLANDS
SURINAME
Cayenne ⊕
⊛ Bogotá
FRENCH GUIANA (France)
Pacaraima Mtns.
COLOMBIA
• Cali

Delta of the Amazon
Negro River
Macapá •

EQUATOR — 0° — EQUATOR

ECUADOR Quito ⊛
Putumayo River
Amazon River
Manaus •
Belém •
São Luís •

Guayaquil • ←Chimborazo Peak 20,702 ft. ▲
Gulf of Guayaquil
Iquitos •
Marañón R.
Ucayali River
La Montaña

Fortaleza •
Cape São Roque
Teresina •
Borborema Plateau
Recife •

Amazon Basin

Madeira River
Tapajós River
Xingu River
B R A Z I L
Tocantins River
Araguaia River
Parnaíba River
São Francisco River

Tucuruí Reservoir

Chiclayo •
Trujillo •
Huascarán Peak 22,205 ft.

Maceió •

10° — Río Branco • — 10°

PERU
Lima ⊛
Cuzco •
Mato Grosso Plateau
Trinidad •
Ancohuma Peak 20,958 ft. ▲
Campos
Sertão

Salvador •
Todos os Santos Bay

Lake Titicaca
Alvorada •
BRAZILIAN

⊛ La Paz • Santa Cruz
BOLIVIA
Brasília ⊛
Goiânia •
HIGHLANDS

⊛ Sucre
Lake Poopó

Belo Horizonte •

Furnas Reservoir

20° — TROPIC OF CAPRICORN — 20°

PARAGUAY
Campinas •
Rio de Janeiro •
São Paulo •

Atacama Desert

San Félix Island (Chile)
San Ambrozio Island (Chile)
Ojos del Salado Peak 22,614 ft. ▲
Asunción ⊛
San Miguel de Tucumán •
Iguazú Falls
Curitiba •

Copiapó •
CHILE

A N D E S

Cape Santa Marta Grande

Mt. Aconcagua 22,834 ft. ▲
ARGENTINA
Paraná River
Uruguay River
Patos Lagoon
Pôrto Alegre •

30° — Córdoba • — 30°
Juan Fernández Islands (Chile)
Valparaíso •
Rosario •
Rio Grande •
Santiago ⊛
URUGUAY
Buenos Aires ⊛
Montevideo ⊛
La Plata •
Río de la Plata

90°
Concepción •
Pampas
Mar del Plata •

PACIFIC OCEAN
Colorado River
Blanca Bay

Puerto Montt •
Gulf of San Matías
Chiloé Island
Valdés Peninsula

40° — — 40°

Chonos Archipelago
Gulf of San Jorge

ATLANTIC OCEAN

Penas Gulf

Patagonia

Queen Adelaide Archipelago
Grande Bay
Río Gallegos •
Stanley •
Falkland Islands (U.K.)

Strait of Magellan
Punta Arenas •
Tierra del Fuego
South Georgia Is. (U.K.)

Cape Horn

| 0 | 250 | 500 mi |
| 0 | 250 | 500 km |

N

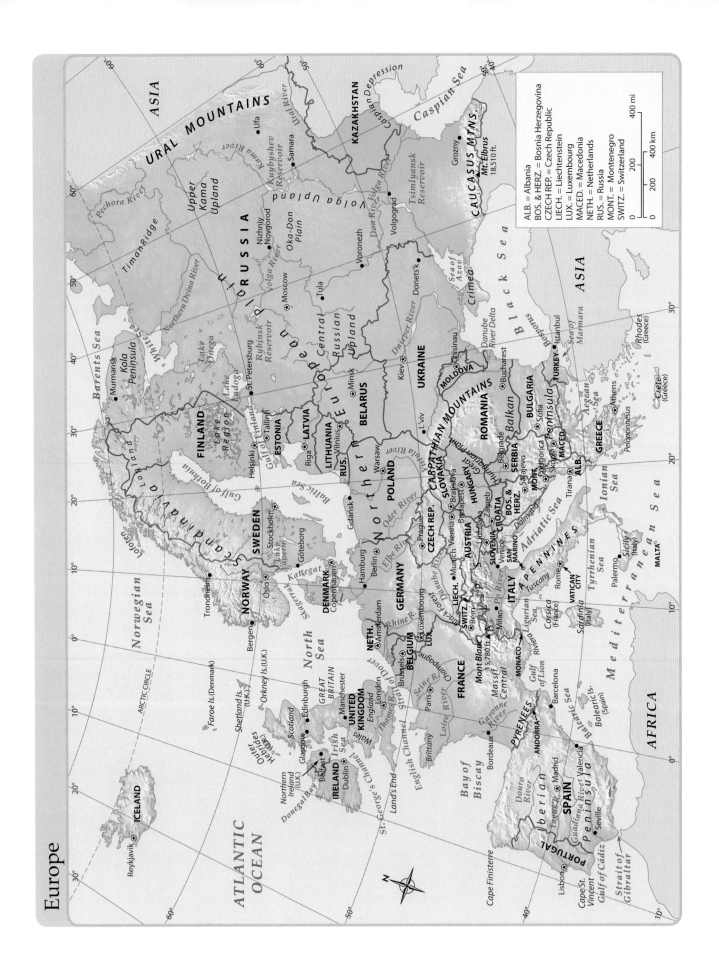

Europe

Africa

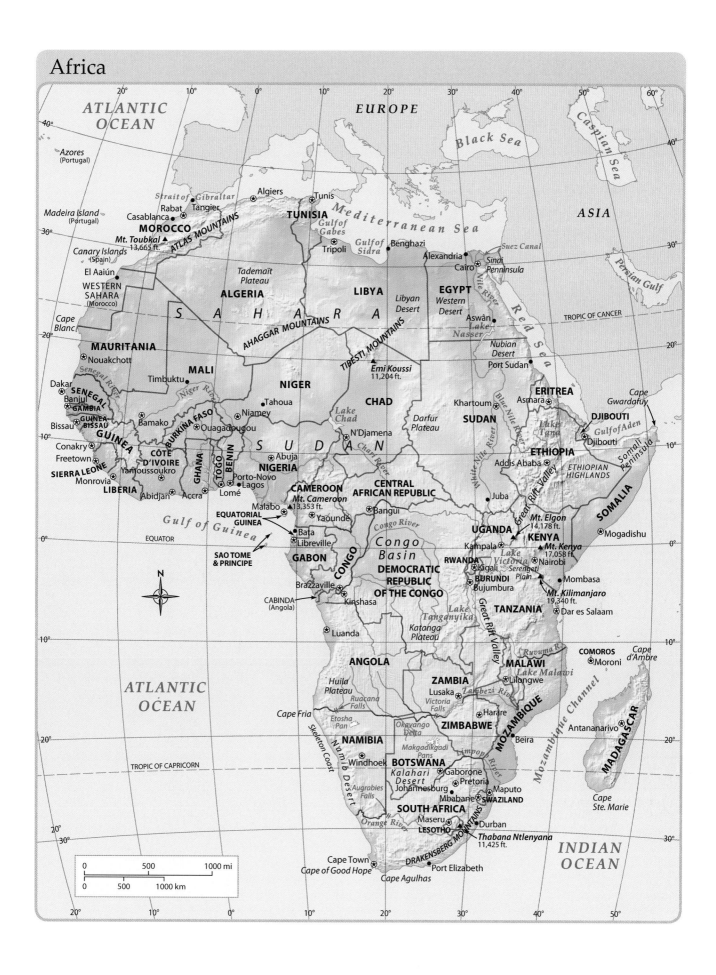

ATLANTIC OCEAN

EUROPE

Black Sea

Caspian Sea

ASIA

Azores (Portugal)

Madeira Island (Portugal)

Strait of Gibraltar

Algiers • Tunis
Rabat • Tangier
Casablanca ⊕

MOROCCO
Mt. Toubkal ▲ 13,665 ft.

ATLAS MOUNTAINS

TUNISIA
Gulf of Gabes

Mediterranean Sea

Tripoli ⊕
Benghazi •

Gulf of Sidra

Alexandria •
Cairo ⊕ Sinai Peninsula

Suez Canal

Persian Gulf

Canary Islands (Spain)

El Aaiún •

WESTERN SAHARA (Morocco)

Cape Blanc

S A H A R A

ALGERIA

Tademaït Plateau

AHAGGAR MOUNTAINS

LIBYA

Libyan Desert

EGYPT
Western Desert

Aswân •
Lake Nasser

TROPIC OF CANCER

Nubian Desert
Port Sudan •

TIBESTI MOUNTAINS

Emi Koussi 11,204 ft.

MAURITANIA
Nouakchott ⊕

Timbuktu •

MALI

NIGER

Tahoua •

CHAD

Lake Chad

Darfur Plateau

Khartoum ⊕

SUDAN

Blue Nile River

ERITREA
Asmara ⊕

Cape Gwardafuy

Dakar •
SENEGAL
Banjul •
GAMBIA
Bissau •
GUINEA-BISSAU
Conakry •
Freetown ⊕
SIERRA LEONE
Monrovia •
LIBERIA

Senegal River

Bamako ⊕

Niger River

Niamey ⊕

Ouagadougou •
BURKINA FASO
Yamoussoukro ⊕
CÔTE D'IVOIRE
Abidjan •

GHANA
TOGO
BENIN
Accra ⊕
Lomé •
Porto-Novo
Lagos •

NIGERIA
Abuja ⊕

S U D A N

N'Djamena •

Chari River

CENTRAL AFRICAN REPUBLIC

Bangui ⊕

DJIBOUTI
Djibouti ⊕
Gulf of Aden

ETHIOPIA
Addis Ababa ⊕

Lake Tana

ETHIOPIAN HIGHLANDS

Somali Peninsula

SOMALIA

Gulf of Guinea

EQUATORIAL GUINEA

Malabo ⊕
Bata •
Libreville ⊕

SAO TOME & PRINCIPE

EQUATOR

CAMEROON
Mt. Cameroon ▲ 13,353 ft.

Yaoundé ⊕

GABON

CONGO

Congo River

Congo Basin

DEMOCRATIC REPUBLIC OF THE CONGO

Juba •

White Nile River

UGANDA
Kampala ⊕

RWANDA
Kigali ⊕
BURUNDI
Bujumbura ⊕

Mt. Elgon 14,178 ft.

Great Rift Valley

Lake Victoria
Serengeti Plain

KENYA
Mt. Kenya ▲ 17,058 ft.
Nairobi ⊕

Mombasa •

Mogadishu ⊕

Brazzaville ⊕
Kinshasa ⊕

CABINDA (Angola)

N

Lake Tanganyika

Katanga Plateau

Great Rift Valley

TANZANIA

Mt. Kilimanjaro 19,340 ft.
Dar es Salaam ⊕

Luanda ⊕

ANGOLA

Huila Plateau

Ruacana Falls

Cape Fria

Etosha Pan

Okavango Delta

Lake Malawi

Zambezi River

ZAMBIA
Lusaka ⊕

Victoria Falls

MALAWI
Lilongwe ⊕

Ruvuma R.

COMOROS
Moroni ⊕

Cape d'Ambre

ZIMBABWE
Harare ⊕

MOZAMBIQUE

Beira •

Mozambique Channel

Antananarivo ⊕

MADAGASCAR

ATLANTIC OCEAN

TROPIC OF CAPRICORN

NAMIBIA

Skeleton Coast

Namib Desert

Makgadikgadi Pans

Windhoek ⊕

Augrabies Falls

BOTSWANA
Kalahari Desert

Gaborone ⊕
Johannesburg •

Pretoria ⊕
Mbabane ⊕
SWAZILAND
Maputo ⊕

Limpopo River

Cape Ste. Marie

SOUTH AFRICA
Maseru ⊕
LESOTHO

Orange River

Thabana Ntlenyana 11,425 ft.

DRAKENSBERG MOUNTAINS

Durban •

Cape Town ⊕
Cape of Good Hope

Port Elizabeth •

Cape Agulhas

INDIAN OCEAN

| 0 | 500 | 1000 mi |
| 0 | 500 | 1000 km |

Eurasia

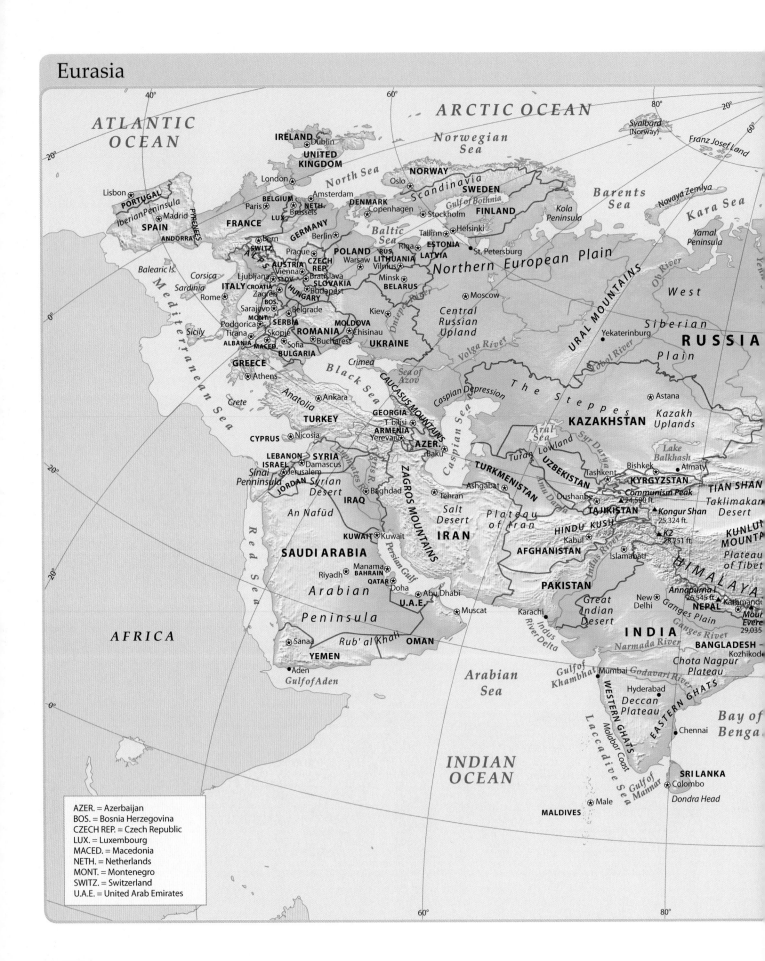

ATLANTIC OCEAN

ARCTIC OCEAN

Norwegian Sea

Svalbard (Norway)

Franz Josef Land

IRELAND
Dublin

UNITED KINGDOM

London

North Sea

NORWAY
Oslo

SWEDEN

Barents Sea

Novaya Zemlya

Kara Sea

BELGIUM
Paris
NETH.
Brussels
LUX.

DENMARK
Copenhagen

Gulf of Bothnia
Stockholm
FINLAND
Helsinki

Kola Peninsula

Yamal Peninsula

Lisbon
PORTUGAL
Iberian Peninsula
Madrid
SPAIN
ANDORRA
FRANCE
PYRENEES

GERMANY
Berlin
Bern
SWITZ.
ALPS

Baltic Sea
Riga
Tallinn
ESTONIA
LATVIA
St. Petersburg

Northern European Plain

URAL MOUNTAINS

Ob River

West Siberian Plain

RUSSIA

Balearic Is.
Corsica
Sardinia
Rome

ITALY

Ljubljana
Vienna
AUSTRIA
CROATIA
Zagreb
BOS.
Sarajevo
MONT.
Podgorica
SERBIA
Belgrade
Tirana
ALBANIA
MACED.
Skopje

PRAGUE
Prague
CZECH REP.
POLAND
Warsaw
Bratislava
SLOVAKIA
Budapest
HUNGARY
ROMANIA
Bucharest
Sofia
BULGARIA

RUS.
LITHUANIA
Vilnius
Minsk
BELARUS

Dnieper River
Kiev

Moscow

Central Russian Upland

Volga River

Yekaterinburg

Tobol River

Siberian

Sicily

GREECE
Athens

Crete

MOLDOVA
Chisinau
UKRAINE

Crimea

Black Sea

Sea of Azov

CAUCASUS MOUNTAINS

Caspian Depression

The Steppes

Astana

Kazakh Uplands

KAZAKHSTAN

Mediterranean Sea

Anatolia
Ankara

TURKEY

CYPRUS
Nicosia

GEORGIA
T'bilisi
ARMENIA
Yerevan
AZER.
Baku

Caspian Sea

Aral Sea

Turan Lowland

Syr Darya

Tashkent

UZBEKISTAN

Lake Balkhash

Bishkek
Almaty
KYRGYZSTAN

TIAN SHAN

LEBANON
ISRAEL
Jerusalem
SYRIA
Damascus

JORDAN
Syrian Desert

Sinai Peninsula

Euphrates R.
Baghdad
IRAQ

ZAGROS MOUNTAINS

Salt Desert

Tehran

IRAN

Plateau of Iran

TURKMENISTAN
Ashgabat

Amu Darya

Dushanbe
TAJIKISTAN

Communism Peak
24,590 ft.

Kongur Shan
25,324 ft.

HINDU KUSH
Kabul

K2
28,251 ft.

Taklimakan Desert

KUNLUN MOUNTAINS

An Nafūd

KUWAIT
Kuwait

SAUDI ARABIA

Riyadh
Manama
BAHRAIN
QATAR
Doha
U.A.E.
Abu Dhabi

Persian Gulf

Arabian Peninsula

Muscat

AFGHANISTAN
Islamabad

PAKISTAN

Indus River

Great Indian Desert

New Delhi

HIMALAYA

Plateau of Tibet

Annapurna
26,545 ft.
NEPAL
Kathmandu

Mount Everest
29,035 ft.

Red Sea

AFRICA

Sanaa
YEMEN

Rub' al Khali

OMAN

Gulf of Aden
Aden

Karachi

Indus River Delta

Ganges Plain

Ganges River

INDIA

BANGLADESH

Kozhikode

Narmada River

Chota Nagpur Plateau

Arabian Sea

Mumbai

Godavari River

Hyderabad

Deccan Plateau

WESTERN GHATS

EASTERN GHATS

Chennai

Bay of Bengal

INDIAN OCEAN

Laccadive Sea

Malabar Coast

Gulf of Mannar

SRI LANKA
Colombo

Male

MALDIVES

Dondra Head

AZER. = Azerbaijan
BOS. = Bosnia Herzegovina
CZECH REP. = Czech Republic
LUX. = Luxembourg
MACED. = Macedonia
NETH. = Netherlands
MONT. = Montenegro
SWITZ. = Switzerland
U.A.E. = United Arab Emirates

ARCTIC
OCEAN

Wrangel
Island

Chukchi
Peninsula

Cape
Navarin

Bering
Sea

80°

60°

40°

160°

120°

North Land

New Siberian
Islands

KOLYMA RANGE

Laptev
Sea

Lena River
Delta

Kolyma
Lowland

Kolyma River

Kamchatka Peninsula

160°

Taymyr
Peninsula

VERKHOYANSK RANGE

Lena River

Central
S I B E R I A
Siberian

Plateau

STANOVOY RANGE

Amur River

SIKHOTE-ALIN RANGE

Sea of
Okhotsk

Sakhalin

Tatar Strait

Kuril Islands

180°

SAYAN MOUNTAINS

Lake
Baikal

Lake Khanka

Manchurian
Plain

Hokkaido
• *Sapporo*

⊕ *Ulaanbaatar*

MONGOLIA *Mongolian*
Plateau

Gobi

Shenyang •

NORTH
KOREA
⊕ *Pyongyang*
⊛ *Seoul*

Sea of
Japan

JAPAN

⊛ *Tokyo*

N

PACIFIC
OCEAN

ALTAY MOUNTAINS

Honshu

Hwang He River

Beijing ⊕

Bo
Hai

SOUTH
KOREA
• *Pusan*

20°

ALTUN SHUN

Qinghai Hu

Mu Us
Desert

North
China
Plain

Yellow
Sea

• *Kitakyushu*
Kyushu

160°

CHINA

QIN LIN

Yangtze River

Shanghai •

East
China
Sea

Naha
•

Ryukyu Islands

▲ *Gongga Shan*
24,790 ft.

WUYI SHAN

Taipei •

Salween River

— BHUTAN

Hongshui River

Guangzhou •
• *Hong Kong*

Taiwan

Luzon Strait

Philippine
Sea

Irrawaddy River

• *Hanoi*

MYANMAR

LAOS

Leizhou
Bay

Gulf of
Tonkin

Hainan

South
China
Sea

Luzon

Yangon ⊛

Indochina

⊕ *Vientiane*

THAILAND *Peninsula*

Bangkok ⊛

CAMBODIA

Phnom Penh
•

VIETNAM

Mekong R.

Manila ⊛

PHILIPPINES

Koror ⊕ PALAU

0°

Andaman
Islands
(India)

Gulf
of
Thailand

• *Ho Chi Minh City*

Palawan

Mindanao

Andaman Sea

Celebes
Sea

Nicobar
Islands
(India)

Malay
Peninsula

Bandar Seri Begawan
BRUNEI

⊛

Borneo
Highlands

Halmahera

MAOKE
MOUNTAINS

Medan •

M A L A Y S I A

⊕ *Kuala Lumpur*

Borneo

Mt. Jaya ▲
16,499 ft.
New Guinea

BARISAN MOUNTAINS

⊛ SINGAPORE

I N D O N E S I A

Celebes

Sumatra

Banda Sea

Torres Strait

Coral
Sea

• *Jakarta*

Java Sea

⊛ *Dili*

EAST
TIMOR

AUSTRALIA

Java

100°

120°

140°

Middle East

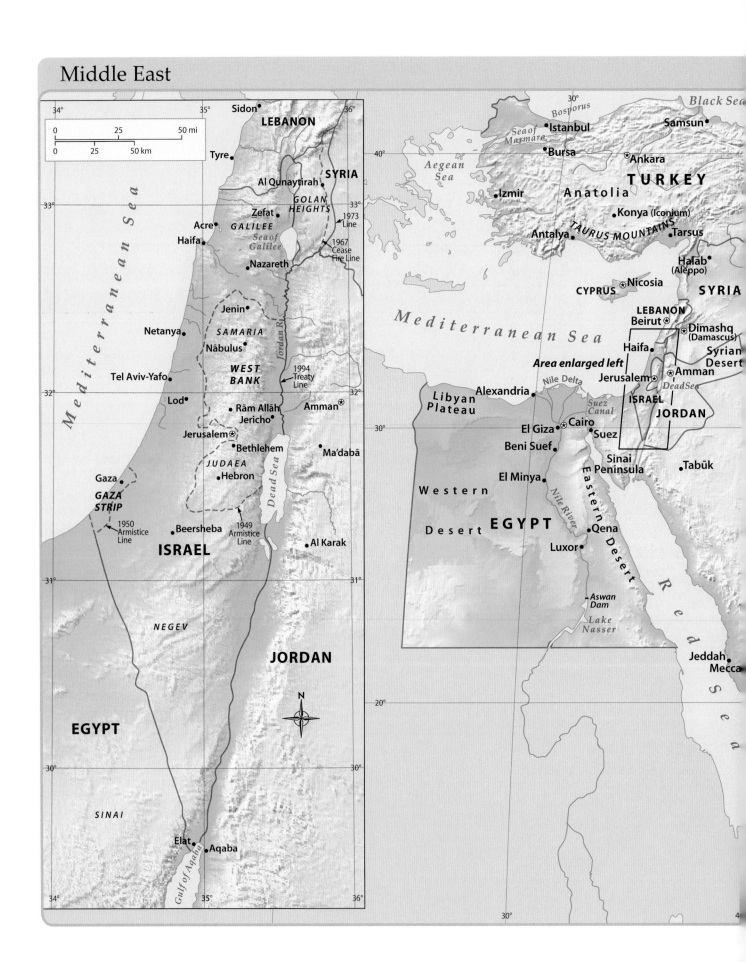

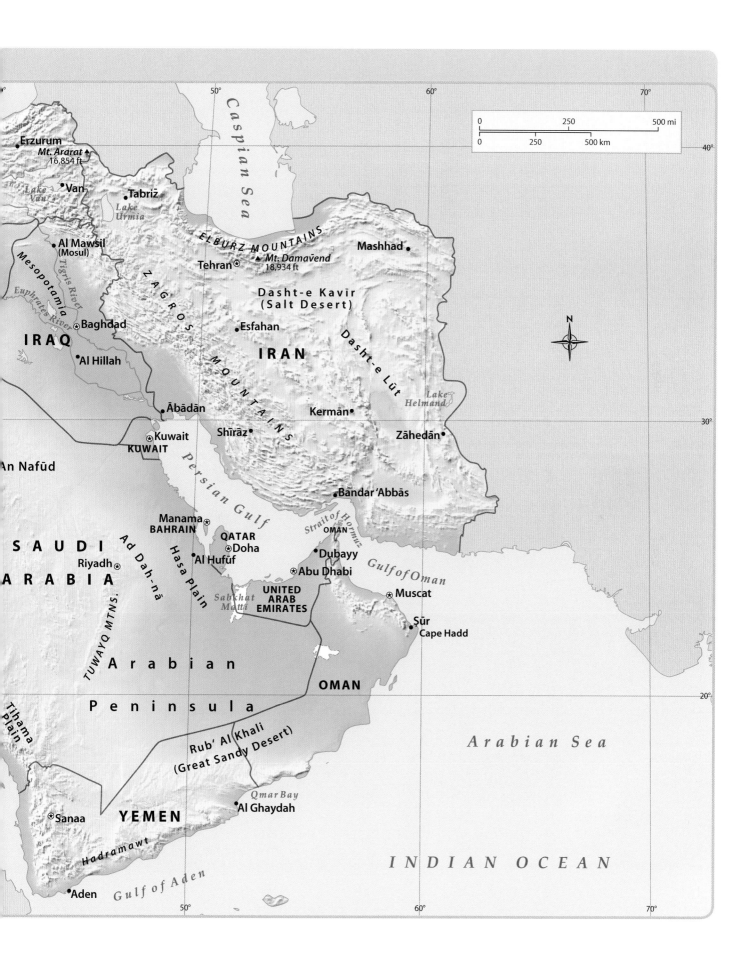

Erzurum
Mt. Ararat ▲
16,854 ft

Van

Lake
Van

Tabrīz

Caspian Sea

Lake
Urmia

ELBURZ MOUNTAINS

Mashhad

Al Mawsil
(Mosul)

Tehran ⊛

▲ Mt. Damavend
18,934 ft

Tigris River

Z
A
G
R
O
S

Dasht-e Kavīr
(Salt Desert)

Mesopotamia

Euphrates River

Baghdad ⊛

Esfahan

IRAQ

M
O
U
N
T
A
I
N
S

IRAN

Dasht-e Lūt

Al Hillah

Kermān

Lake
Helmand

Ābādān

Kuwait ⊛
KUWAIT

Shīrāz

Zāhedān

An Nafūd

Persian Gulf

Bandar 'Abbās

Strait of Hormuz

Manama
BAHRAIN ⊛

QATAR
⊛ Doha

OMAN

Gulf of Oman

SAUDI

Ad Dah-nā

Hasa Plain

Al Hufūf

Dubayy

Riyadh ⊛

UNITED
ARAB
EMIRATES

Abu Dhabi

Muscat ⊛

ARABIA

Sabkhat
Matti

TUWAYQ MTNS.

A r a b i a n

Şūr
Cape Hadd

P e n i n s u l a

OMAN

Tihama
Plain

Rub' Al Khali
(Great Sandy Desert)

Arabian Sea

Qmar Bay

Al Ghaydah

Sanaa ⊛

YEMEN

Hadramawt

INDIAN OCEAN

Aden

Gulf of Aden

0   250   500 mi
0   250   500 km

N

50°   60°   70°

40°

30°

20°

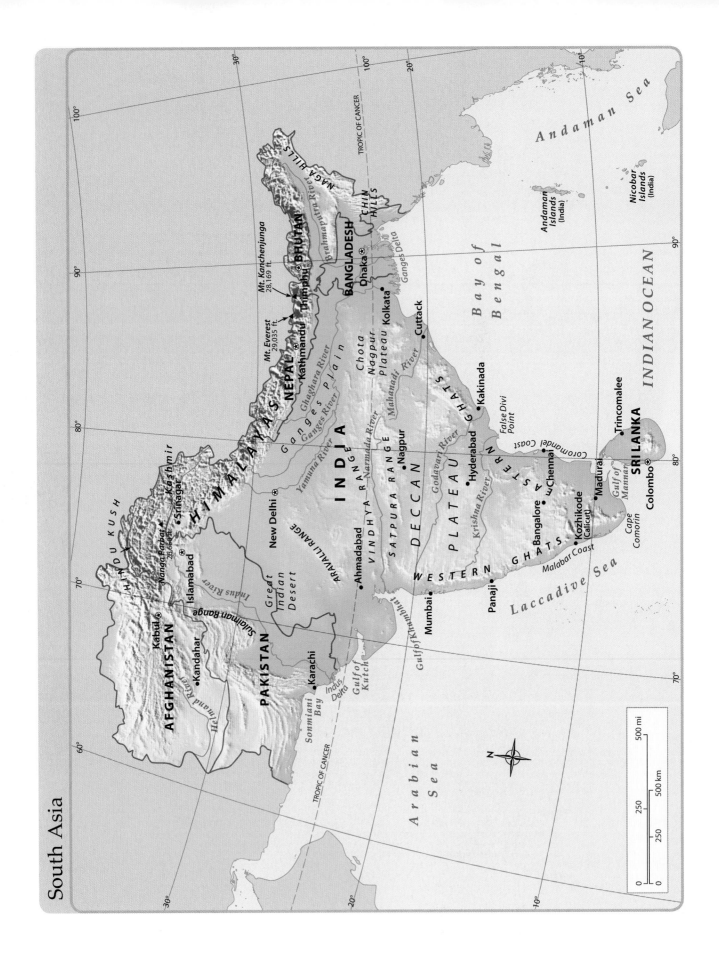

South Asia

North and South Poles

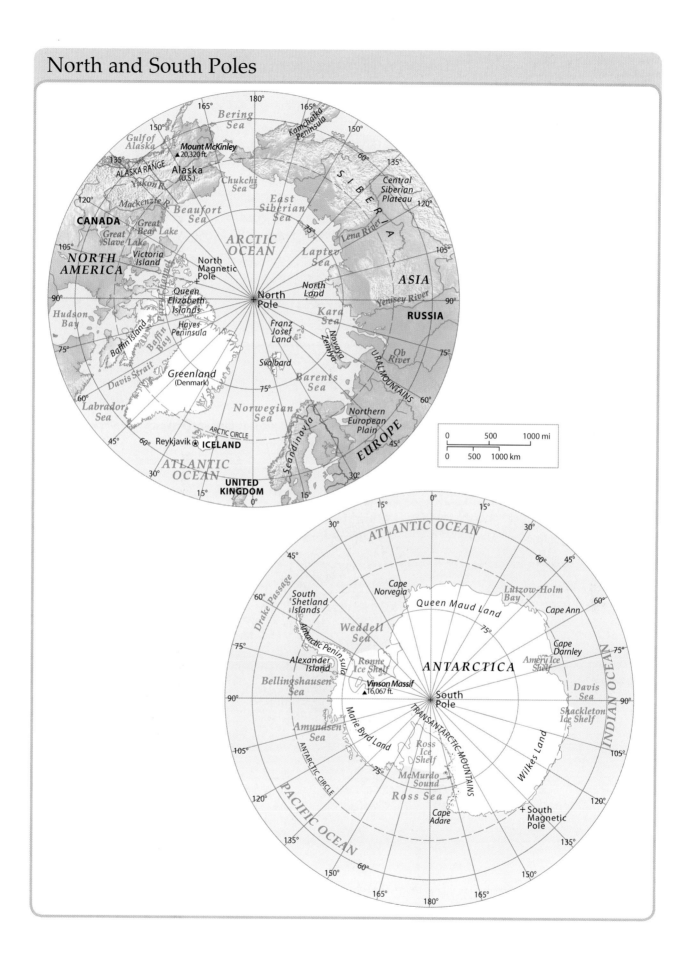

Goode's Interrupted Homosoline Projection

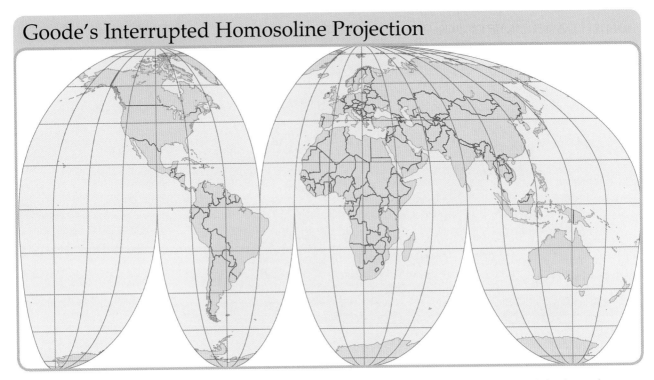

This projection, called interrupted *because it is divided into segments, minimizes distortion of scale and the shape of landforms, but breaks Antarctica, Greenland, and the oceans into pieces.*

Miller Projection

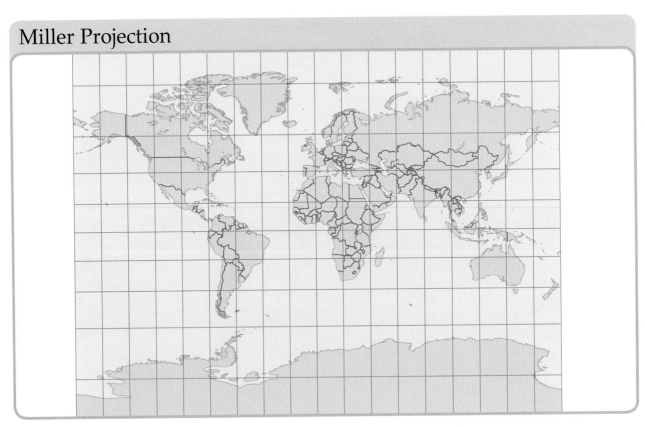

This projection, with straight meridians and parallels that meet at right angles, avoids scale exaggerations, but distorts shapes and sizes.

Mollweide Projection

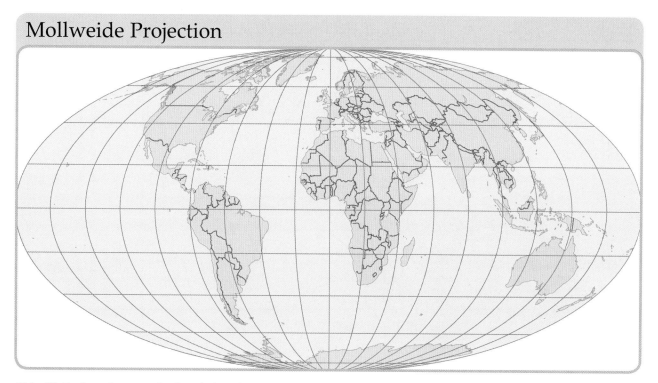

This elliptical equal-area projection, designed in 1805 by German mathematician Carl B. Mollweide, represents the size of landforms quite accurately, but distorts shapes near the edges.

Winkel Tripel Projection

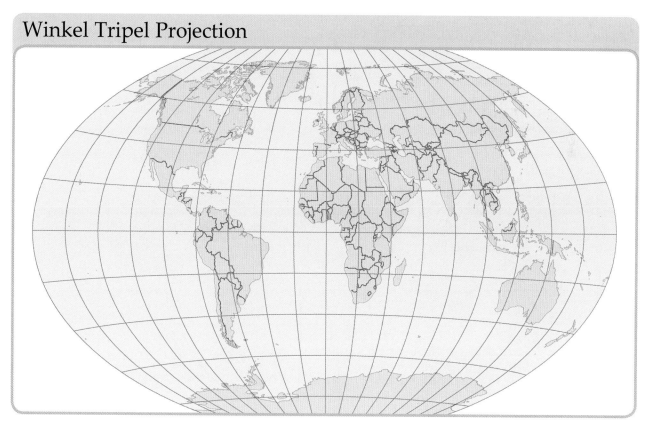

This projection, designed by Oswald Winkel of Germany in 1921, lessens the distortions of scale and shape by presenting the central meridian and equator as straight lines, and the other parallels and meridians as curved lines.

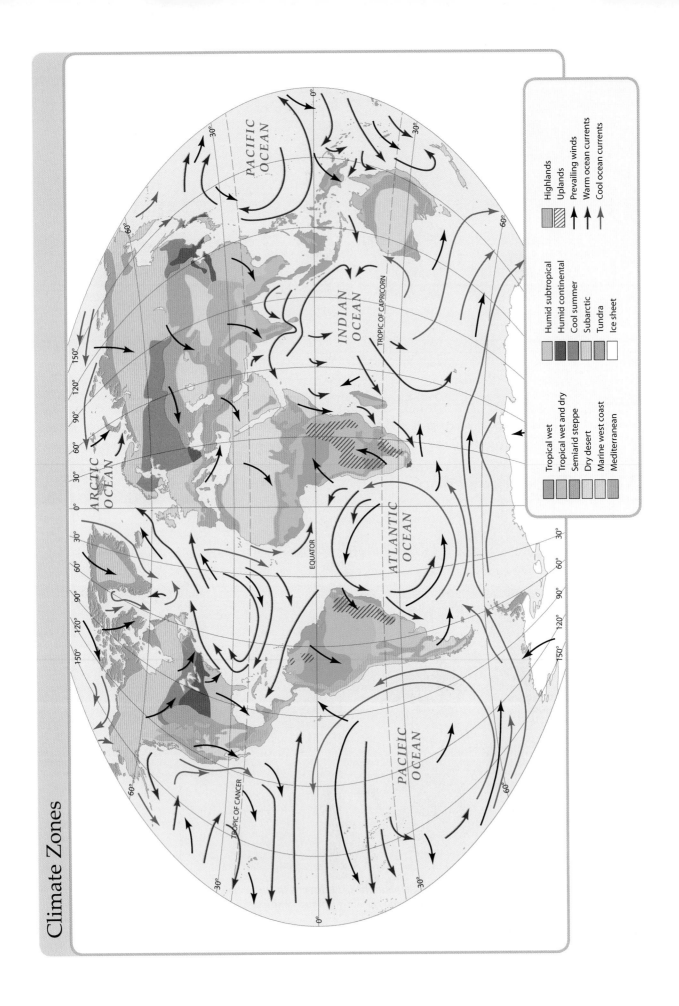

Climate Zones

Legend

Tropical wet
Tropical wet and dry
Semiarid steppe
Dry desert
Marine west coast
Mediterranean

Humid subtropical
Humid continental
Cool summer
Subarctic
Tundra
Ice sheet

Highlands
Uplands
Prevailing winds
Warm ocean currents
Cool ocean currents

PACIFIC OCEAN
INDIAN OCEAN
TROPIC OF CAPRICORN
ARCTIC OCEAN
EQUATOR
ATLANTIC OCEAN
PACIFIC OCEAN
TROPIC OF CANCER

Terrestrial Biomes

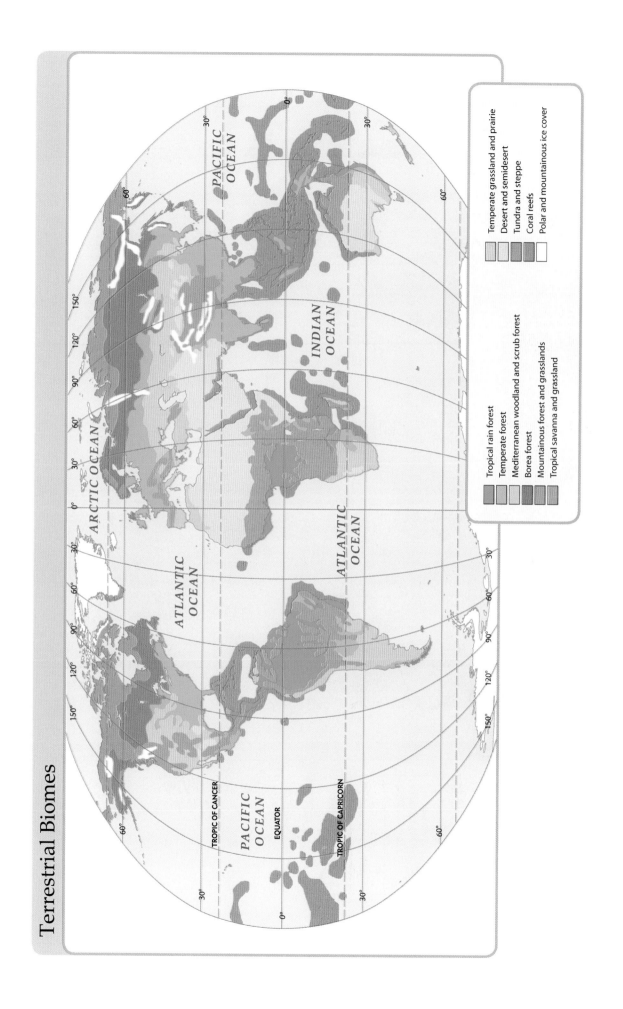

Legend:

- Tropical rain forest
- Temperate forest
- Mediterranean woodland and scrub forest
- Borea forest
- Mountainous forest and grasslands
- Tropical savanna and grassland

- Temperate grassland and prairie
- Desert and semidesert
- Tundra and steppe
- Coral reefs
- Polar and mountainous ice cover

GNI (Gross National Income)

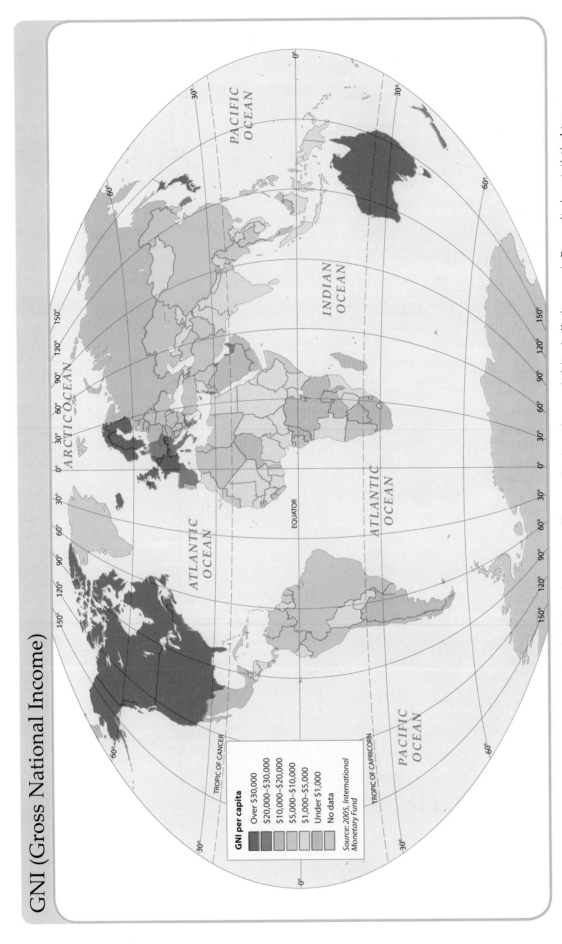

GNI per capita

- Over $30,000
- $20,000–$30,000
- $10,000–$20,000
- $5,000–$10,000
- $1,000–$5,000
- Under $1,000
- No data

Source: 2005, International Monetary Fund

GNI (gross national income) is the total value of goods and services produced by a nation in a given period (typically in a year). Per capita is a statistical term meaning per person.

Population Density

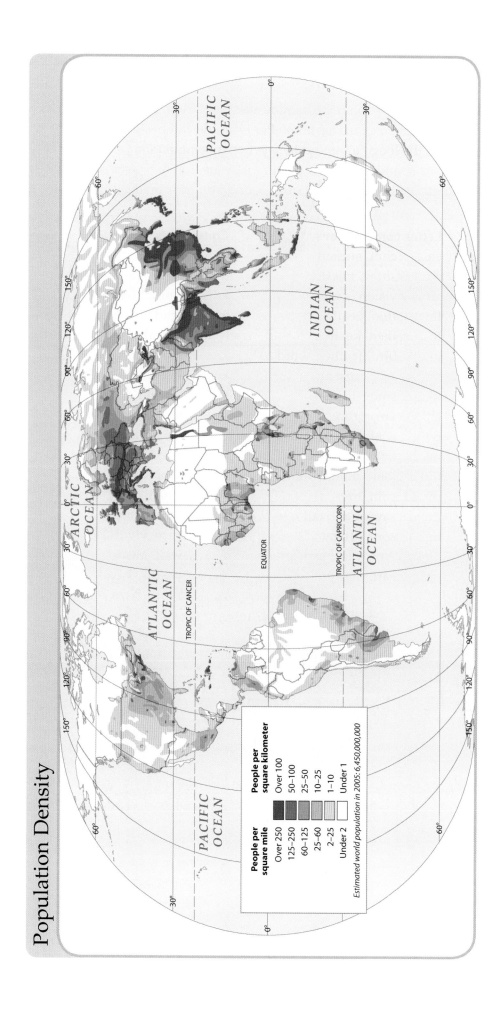

People per square mile

- Over 250
- 125–250
- 60–125
- 25–60
- 2–25
- Under 2

People per square kilometer

- Over 100
- 50–100
- 25–50
- 10–25
- 1–10
- Under 1

Estimated world population in 2005: 6,450,000,000

PACIFIC OCEAN

ATLANTIC OCEAN

INDIAN OCEAN

PACIFIC OCEAN

ATLANTIC OCEAN

ARCTIC OCEAN

TROPIC OF CANCER

EQUATOR

TROPIC OF CAPRICORN

Pronunciation Guide

The table below provides sample words to explain the sounds associated with specific letters and letter combinations used in the respellings in this book. For example, *a* represents the short "a" sound in *cat*, while *ay* represents the long "a" sound in *day*. Letter combinations are used to approximate certain more complex sounds. For example, in the respelling of *proletariat*— PROH-luh-TEHR-ee-uht—the letters *OH* represent the vowel sound you hear in *home* and *throw*.

Vowels

a.......... short a: **apple**, **cat**
ay .... long a: **cane**, **day**
e, eh ... short e: **hen**, **bed**
ee........ long e: **feed**, **team**
i, ih..... short i: **lip**, **active**
iy .... long i: **try**, **might**
ah .... short o: **hot**, **father**
oh .... long o: **home**, **throw**
uh....... short u: **shut**, **other**
yoo ..... long u: **union**, **cute**

Letter combinations

ch .... **chin**, **ancient**
sh........ **show**, **mission**
zh .... **vision**, **azure**
th........ **thin**, **health**
th........ **then**, **heather**
ur........ **bird**, **further**, **word**
us .... **bus**, **crust**
or........ **court**, **formal**
ehr...... **error**, **care**
oo .... **cool**, **true**, **few**, **rule**
ow ...... **now**, **out**
ou .... **look**, **pull**, **would**
oy .... **coin**, **toy**
aw ...... **saw**, **maul**, **fall**
ng .... **song**, **finger**
air....... **Aristotle**, **barrister**
ahr...... **cart**, **martyr**

Consonants

b .... **butter**, **baby**
d .... **dog**, **cradle**
f .... **fun**, **phone**
g .... **grade**, **angle**
h .... **hat**, **ahead**
j .... **judge**, **gorge**
k .... **kite**, **car**, **black**
l .... **lily**, **mile**
m .... **mom**, **camel**
n .... **next**, **candid**
p .... **price**, **copper**
r .... **rubber**, **free**
s .... **small**, **circle**, **hassle**
t .... **ton**, **pottery**
v .... **vase**, **vivid**
w .... **wall**, **away**
y .... **yellow**, **kayak**
z.......... **zebra**, **haze**

Glossary

abolitionism– the movement to end slavery

absolute monarch– a single ruler (such as a king or queen) who governs with unlimited power; sometimes contrasted with a *constitutional monarch*, whose power is limited by a nation's constitution

abstract art– a style of art that does not depict the physical world as we see it, but makes art out of line, color, shapes, light, and texture

Anglican Church– Protestant church set up by England's King Henry VIII after he broke with Rome; also known as the Church of England

armada– a fleet of warships; England's navy defeated the Spanish Armada in 1588

Askia Muhammad (as-KEE-uh moh-HAM-uhd) (died 1538)– king who ruled the Songhai empire from 1493 to 1528, when it reached its greatest size

Atahualpa (ah-tah-WAHL-pah) (c. 1502–1533)– Inca emperor at the time of the Spanish conquest

Bastille– fortress and prison in Paris, and symbol of royal power; its fall on July 14, 1789, marked the beginning of the French Revolution

Beethoven, Ludwig van (BAY-toh-vuhn) (1770–1827)– German composer whose work bridged the Classical and Romantic periods in music

Bell, Alexander Graham (1847–1922)– American (Scottish-born) inventor of the telephone

Bismarck, Otto von (1815–1898)– Prussian chancellor of the German empire, responsible for the unification of Germany

Bolívar, Simón (see-MOHN buh-LEE-vahr) (1783–1830)– Venezuelan-born revolutionary who led successful independence movements in Bolivia, Colombia, Ecuador, Peru, and Venezuela; known as *El Libertador* (The Liberator)

Botticelli, Sandro (boht-ih-CHELL-ee) (1445–1510)– Renaissance artist from Florence; painted *The Birth of Venus*

bourgeoisie (bourzh-wah-ZEE)– the middle class; in Karl Marx's writings, *bourgeoisie* refers to factory and property owners, bankers, and businessmen, in contrast with the *proletariat* (working class)

boyars (BOH-yahrz)– powerful landowning nobles of Russia

boycott– to refuse to do business with a company or group, often to compel it to change in some way

Brunelleschi, Filippo (fee-LEEP-poh broo-nehl-ES-kee) (1377–1446)– Renaissance architect from Florence; designed the dome of Florence's cathedral

bushido (BOU-shee-doh)– meaning "the way of the warrior," the code of behavior of the samurai of feudal Japan, requiring devotion to duty and absolute bravery and loyalty

Calvin, John (1509–1564)– French Protestant reformer who established a church in Geneva, Switzerland, whose followers included French Huguenots, Scottish Presbyterians, and English and American Puritans

capitalism– economic system based on private ownership of land and resources, in which individuals and businesses produce goods and services in order to make money; also known as the free enterprise (or free market) system

caravel– a light sailing ship developed by the Portuguese in the fifteenth century; used for exploration because it sailed well on open seas and in shallow waters

Carnegie, Andrew (1835–1919)– Scottish-born steel producer who helped turn the United States into an economic power

Castiglione, Baldassare (bahl-dahs-SAHR-ay kahs-tee-LYOH-nay) (1478–1529)– author of *The Book of the Courtier*, a Renaissance work describing qualities and standards of behavior for attendants at court

Catherine II (1729–1796)– empress of Russia, known as Catherine the Great, who enlarged her empire and brought Western ideas about art, philosophy, and education to Russia

Catholic Church– the body of Christians who recognize the authority of the pope in Rome as leader of the Church; also called the Roman Catholic Church

caudillos (kaw-DEEL-yohs)– military strongmen who seized power in South American nations after their liberation from Spain

Clarkson, Thomas (1760–1846)– Anglican clergyman and abolitionist who spurred the movement to end slavery and the British slave trade

classical civilization– the civilization of ancient Greece and Rome between about 500 b.c. and a.d. 500

collective bargaining– the process by which groups of workers (such as trade unions) negotiate with employers for changes such as higher wages or better working conditions

Columbus, Christopher (1451–1506)– Genoese navigator who, sailing in the service of Spain, voyaged west in 1492 to reach the Indies and instead reached the Americas

communism– economic system envisioned by Karl Marx in which the government plans the economy and owns most of the land, factories, and other property, and all citizens share in the common wealth

Condorcet, Marquis de (kawn-dor-SAY) (1743–1794)– French Enlightenment philosopher who believed in unlimited human progress

conquistador– "conqueror" in Spanish; Spanish soldiers who conquered native peoples in Latin America in the early sixteenth century

Copernicus, Nicolaus (1473–1543)– Polish astronomer who showed that the Earth (along with the other planets of the solar system) revolves around the sun

Cortés, Hernán (her-NAHN kor-TEZ) (1485–1547)– Spanish conqueror, or conquistador, of the Aztec empire

Counter-Reformation– the Catholic Church's efforts to reverse the spread of Protestantism and reform itself during the sixteenth and seventeenth centuries; also called the Catholic Reformation

courtier– an attendant or official at a royal court

***Creole* (KREE-ohl)–** a person of Spanish descent born and raised in the Americas; socially, *Creoles* ranked beneath *peninsulares*, who were colonists born in Spain

Cromwell, Oliver (1599–1658)– leader of the Puritan parliamentary army during the English civil war and Lord Protector of the English Commonwealth

Cubism– an artistic movement developed by Pablo Picasso and Georges Braque, in which the artist typically breaks objects into geometric shapes and imaginatively reassembles them

da Gama, Vasco (VAHS-koh dah GAH-muh) (c. 1460–1524)– Portuguese explorer who commanded the first expedition to reach India by sea from Europe; he sailed east around the Cape of Good Hope

Daimler, Gottlieb (GAHT-leeb DIYM-lur) (1834–1900)– German engineer who developed some of the first automobiles, including the Mercedes-Benz

Dante Alighieri (DAHN-tay ah-luh-GYEH-ree) (1265–1321)– late-medieval Florentine poet, author of *The Divine Comedy*

Darwin, Charles (1809–1882)– English scientist who formulated the theory of evolution by natural selection; author of *The Origin of Species*

Declaration of Independence– historic document announcing the separation of the American colonies from Great Britain, drafted by Thomas Jefferson and adopted July 4, 1776

Declaration of the Rights of Man and of the Citizen– historic document drawn up by the French National Assembly in 1789 to limit royal power and list rights of the people

democracy– government by the people; originated in the Greek city-state of Athens, where citizens directly took part in government and law-making; also used generally to refer to any representative government based on the will of the people

Descartes, René (ruh-NAY day-KAHRT) (1596–1650)– French mathematician and philosopher whose works greatly advanced the Scientific Revolution

D'Este, Isabella (DES-tay) (1474–1539)– multitalented ruler of the Italian city-state of Mantua, patron of the arts

Dickens, Charles (1812–1870)– one of the greatest English novelists, whose books, such as *Oliver Twist* and *Little Dorrit*, awakened middle-class readers to the plight of the urban poor during the Industrial Revolution

Diderot, Denis (duh-nee DEE-duh-roh) (1713–1784)– French philosopher of the Enlightenment and chief editor of the *Encyclopédie*, a massive collection that sought to organize all knowledge

divine right of kings– the belief that kings receive their power to rule directly from God and therefore are not answerable to the people or to parliament; used to support absolute monarchy

Donatello (dahn-uh-TEL-oh) (c. 1386–1466)– Florentine sculptor whose bronze statue of the biblical hero David was the first large-scale free-standing nude statue in Western Europe since classical times

Drake, Francis (c. 1543–1596)– Elizabethan mariner who raided Spanish treasure ships, became the first Englishman to sail around the world, and helped defeat the Spanish Armada

Dürer, Albrecht (AHL-brekt DYOUR-ur) (1471–1528)– German artist of the Renaissance, known for his finely detailed paintings and engravings

Eastern Orthodox Church– the eastern branch of the Christian Church, which split from the rest of the Church in 1054 and was headed by the bishop of Constantinople (called the patriarch); now the major Christian church of Greece, Russia, Eastern Europe, and the Middle East

Edison, Thomas (1847–1931)– American who invented the first practical light bulb, phonograph, an early movie camera, and many other devices

Elizabeth I (1533–1603)– queen of England whose reign helped establish the nation as a great military and economic power

Enlightenment– seventeenth and eighteenth-century period when philosophers stressed the use of reason; also known as the Age of Reason

Erasmus, Desiderius (DEH-sih-DEER-ee-us ih-RAZ-mus) (c. 1466–1536)– Dutch priest, scholar, and Christian humanist who urged reform of the Church; author of *The Praise of Folly*

Estates-General– French representative assembly that met infrequently before the French Revolution; comprised of three "estates"—the clergy, nobility, and rest of the people

Forbidden City– the walled palace complex in Beijing where Chinese emperors lived and imperial staff worked; few Chinese and almost no foreigners were permitted inside

Ford, Henry (1863–1947)– American automobile manufacturer whose methods of mass production made cars available to millions

Franklin, Benjamin (1706–1790)– American inventor, printer, publisher, scientist, writer, and statesman during the Enlightenment

Franz Josef (1830–1916)– Habsburg ruler of the Austro-Hungarian Empire until his death during the First World War

Freud, Sigmund (1856–1939)– Austrian physician and founder of psychoanalysis who theorized that the mind is divided into conscious and unconscious parts

Fulton, Robert (1765–1815)– American inventor who built the *Clermont*, one of the first commercially successful steamboats

Galileo Galilei (gal-uh-LAY-oh gal-uh-LAY-ee) (1564–1642)– Italian astronomer who helped launch the Scientific Revolution with his experiments and his use of instruments such as the telescope; he was tried by the Church for insisting that the Earth and other planets revolve around the sun

Gandhi, Mohandas (GAHN-dee) (1869–1948)– Indian activist who used nonviolent resistance to win rights for Indians in South Africa and India's independence from Great Britain

Garibaldi, Giuseppe (joo-ZEP-pay gah-ree-BAHL-dee) (1807–1882)– Italian revolutionary who helped unite the Italian peninsula into one nation

George III (1738–1820)– English king at the time of the American Revolutionary War

Giotto (JAWT-toh) (c. 1267–1337)– Florentine painter of the early Renaissance

Glorious Revolution– the bloodless overthrow of England's King James II in 1688, placing William and Mary on the throne; the revolution restricted the king's powers and increased Parliament's powers

Goethe, Johann Wolfgang von (GUR-tuh) (1749–1832)– German poet and novelist, and key figure in German Classical and Romantic literature

Gutenberg, Johannes (GOOT-uhn-burg) (c. 1395–1468)– inventor of the first modern printing press; the Gutenberg Bible is considered the first printed book in the Western world

Habsburg– the ruling family of the Holy Roman Empire and Austria, c. 1438–1918

Hargreaves, James (died 1778)– inventor of the spinning jenny, which could spin 16 strands of thread at once

Henry VIII (1491–1547)– king of England who broke with the pope in Rome to establish the Church of England, also known as the Anglican Church

Henry the Navigator (Prince) (1394–1460)– Portuguese prince who encouraged research in navigation and sent explorers on sea voyages along the coast of Africa

Hidalgo y Costilla, Miguel (ee-DAHL-goh) (1753–1811)– *Creole* priest and the father of Mexican independence

Holbein, Hans (hahns HOHL-biyn) (c. 1497–1543)– German portrait artist of the northern Renaissance; known as Holbein the Younger

humanism– Renaissance educational program that emphasized the classics, stressed the dignity of man, and placed confidence in human potential

Ibn Khaldun (IH-buhn kahl-DOON) (1332–1406)– Muslim scholar from North Africa who wrote a seven-volume study of world civilization

Ieyasu (ee-yeh-yah-soo) (1543–1616)– warlord from the Tokugawa family who united Japan under his rule as shogun; his descendants formed a dynasty known as the Tokugawa shogunate

Ignatius of Loyola (ig-NAY-shuhs of loy-OH-luh) (1491–1556)– Spanish leader of the Counter-Reformation and founder of the Society of Jesus, or the Jesuits

imperialism– empire building; the policy or action by which one country controls another country or territory

Impressionism– an artistic movement in which painters give an "impression" of a scene rather than trying to make their paintings depict reality with photographic accuracy; major Impressionists include Degas, Manet, Monet, Renoir, and Cassatt

Indies– to fifteenth-century Europeans, a large and varied group of lands, including India, China, Japan, Southeast Asia, and the islands of Indonesia

Industrial Revolution– the great changes brought about in the late eighteenth and nineteenth centuries, when power-driven machinery began to produce many goods, which were assembled in factories

Inquisition– a court of the Roman Catholic Church that examined and punished those whose beliefs were thought to go against Church teachings

Islam– world religion based on the teachings of Muhammad; followers are called Muslims

isthmus– a narrow strip of land connecting two larger land areas, such as the Isthmus of Suez or the Isthmus of Panama

Ivan IV (1530–1584)– the first ruler to be crowned tsar of Russia, better known as Ivan the Terrible

Jefferson, Thomas (1743–1826)– American patriot, author of the Declaration of Independence, and third President of the United States

Julius II (1443–1513)– Renaissance pope, known as "the warrior pope," who began the rebuilding of St. Peter's Basilica

Kaiser– title for ruler of the German Empire; the title comes from the German for "Caesar"

kremlin– meaning "fortress," the walled stronghold that protected Russian cities

Las Casas, Bartolomé de (bahr-toh-loh-MAY day lahs KAHS-ahs) (1474–1566)– Spanish missionary who defended rights of the Indians in Latin American colonies and tried to improve their treatment

Leonardo da Vinci (lay-uh-NAHR-doh duh VIN-chee) (1452–1519)– Renaissance painter, sculptor, architect, engineer, scientist, philosopher, visionary

Lesseps, Ferdinand de (lay-SEPS) (1805–1894)– French engineer and builder of the Suez Canal

Lincoln, Abraham (1809–1865)– President of the United States during the Civil War; issued the Emancipation Proclamation

Livingstone, David (1813–1873)– Scottish missionary, physician, and explorer who traveled the African continent and spoke out against the slave trade

Locke, John (1632–1704)– seventeenth-century English philosopher who wrote about the importance of reason and natural law

Louis XIV (1638–1715)– powerful king of France, builder of Versailles, and self-styled "Sun King"

Louis XVI (1754–1793)– king of France at the time of the French Revolution; removed from the throne in 1792 and beheaded the following year

Luther, Martin (1483–1546)– German monk whose criticism of the Church led to the Protestant Reformation

Machiavelli, Niccolò (nee-koh-LOH mah-kyah-VEL-lee) (1469–1527)– Renaissance author of *The Prince* and a founder of modern political science

Machu Picchu– site of ancient Inca city in the Andes mountains of Peru

Magellan, Ferdinand (muh-JEHL-uhn) (c. 1480–1521)– Portuguese seaman whose crew was the first to circumnavigate the world, reaching the Indies by sailing west; Magellan himself died during the voyage

Marconi, Guglielmo (gool-YEL-moh mahr-KOH-nee) (1874–1937)– Italian who invented the wireless telegraph and became known as the Father of Radio

Marie Antoinette (1755–1793)– queen of France during the French Revolution; executed in 1793

Marx, Karl (1818–1883)– critic of capitalism and author of *The Communist Manifesto* and *Das Kapital*; he predicted a revolution of workers and ultimately a communist state

Mazzini, Giuseppe (joo-ZEP-pay maht-SEE-nee) (1805–1872)– Italian revolutionary and founder of Young Italy, a movement that sought to free Italy from foreign rulers

Medici (MED-uh-chee)– powerful Florentine family that dominated European banking; Cosimo de' Medici and his grandson Lorenzo were important patrons of the arts during the Renaissance

Michelangelo Buonarroti (miy-kuh-LAN-jeh-loh) (1475– 1564)– Renaissance sculptor and painter from Florence; his greatest works include his Pietà, statue of David, and fresco of the Sistine Chapel ceiling

Middle Ages– the period between the fall of Rome (c. A.D. 476) and 1400, also known as the medieval era

Middle Passage– the second, or middle, leg of the three-way transatlantic slave trade between Europe, Africa, and the Americas, during which slaves suffered, and often did not survive, terrible conditions on overcrowded ships

Ming dynasty– Chinese dynasty lasting from 1368 to 1644, in which art flourished and Chinese rulers extended their authority over much of Asia

Miranda, Francisco de (mee-RAHN-dah) (1750–1816)– Spanish-American colonist who fought for Venezuelan independence from Spain

Montezuma II (mahnt-uh-ZOO-muh) (1466–1520)– Aztec emperor at the time of the Spanish conquest

modern world– the period in history from the fourteenth century to the present; from the Latin root *modo*, meaning "recently" or "just now"

Montesquieu (mohn-tes-kyou) (1689–1755)– French philosopher whose writings described the importance of separating the executive, legislative, and judicial powers of government to preserve liberty

More, Thomas (c. 1478–1535)– Christian humanist and author of *Utopia* (1516); executed at the order of King Henry VIII

Morse, Samuel (1791–1872)– American inventor who developed the telegraph and Morse code

Mughal Empire (MOO-guhl)– Muslim empire that flourished in India in the sixteenth and seventeenth centuries

Napoleon Bonaparte (nuh-POHL-yuhn BOH-nuh-pahrt) (1769– 1821)– French general who seized control of the revolutionary government, crowned himself Emperor of the French, conquered much of Europe, and spread revolutionary ideas across the continent

Napoleon III (1808–1873)– nephew of Napoleon Bonaparte who came to power after the 1848 revolution; elected president, he abolished the republic and ruled as Emperor of France from 1852 to 1870

Napoleonic Code– code of civil law commissioned by Napoleon; it organized the many regional laws of France into a single code and became a model for the legal systems of many nations

natural law– according to philosophers, the principles of justice that follow from the nature of man and the world, and rank above man-made laws

naturalism– late nineteenth-century literary movement that depicted human beings as mainly shaped by the environments in which they live

nationalism– strong sense of attachment or belonging to one's own country

Newton, Isaac (1643–1727)– astronomer, mathematician, and physicist of the Scientific Revolution; formulated laws of motion, invented calculus

Osman I (aws-MAHN) (1258– c. 1326)– Muslim nomad leader who conquered Asia Minor and is regarded as founder of the Ottoman ("people of Osman") Empire

Ottoman Empire– Muslim empire centered in Asia Minor that became one of the world's most powerful empires in the fifteenth and sixteenth centuries

Panama Canal– canal across the Isthmus of Panama, opened in 1914, connecting the Atlantic and Pacific Oceans

Pankhurst, Emmeline (1858– 1928)– English suffragist who campaigned for the right of women to vote

parliament– a national legislative assembly that includes representatives of the people, such as the British Parliament

Pasteur, Louis (1822–1895)– French chemist who proved that microorganisms cause disease; he developed the process of pasteurization and the first vaccine for rabies

Peter I (Peter the Great) (1672–1725)– tsar and modernizer of Russia, founder of St. Petersburg

Petrarch (1304–1374)– Italian writer and classical scholar whose work prepared the way for the Renaissance; known as the Father of Humanism

***philosophes* (fee-luh-ZAWF)–** from the Greek for "friends of wisdom," the political thinkers of eighteenth-century France who believed that reason and knowledge could bring justice, equality, and freedom

Picasso, Pablo (1881–1973)– Spanish-born painter and sculptor, perhaps the most innovative and influential of all modern artists

Pizarro, Francisco (puh-ZAHR-oh) (c. 1475–1541)– Spanish conqueror, or *conquistador*, of the Inca Empire

proletariat (PROH-luh-TEHR-ee-uht)– factory laborers and others who work for wages; according to Karl Marx, the huge proletariat class would someday overthrow the wealthy owners of businesses

Protestant– a member of one of the Christian churches that rejected the authority of the pope during the Reformation, such as the Anglican, Lutheran, Calvinist, and Presbyterian churches

Puritans– followers of the teachings of John Calvin in England and the American colonies; English Puritans wanted to *purify* the Church of England

Raleigh, Walter (c. 1554–1618)– soldier, sailor, and favorite of Elizabeth I; established the colony of Virginia in honor of the Virgin Queen

Raphael Sanzio (RAHF-ee-uhl) (1483–1520)– Italian Renaissance painter known simply as Raphael, noted for his graceful figures and balanced composition

Reformation– a religious movement of the sixteenth century that rejected the authority of the pope and led to the formation of Protestant churches; the Reformation split Christianity in Europe into Catholic and Protestant branches

Reign of Terror– the bloodiest phase of the French Revolution, in 1793 and 1794, when thousands were guillotined as enemies of the Revolution

Renaissance– period of great European cultural achievement that lasted from the late fourteenth to the early seventeenth century; the term *Renaissance*, which means "rebirth," refers to a renewed interest in classical civilizations

republic– a form of government in which citizens elect representatives to make laws and govern on their behalf

Restoration– the period of English history following the return of the royal family to power in 1660; the reign of King Charles II marked the end of the English Commonwealth and restored the monarchy

Rhodes, Cecil (1853–1902)– British businessman and empire-builder who used his fortune to gain control of much of southern Africa for Britain; he envisioned a string of British colonies "from the Cape to Cairo"

Robespierre, Maximilien (ROHBZ-pyehr) (1758–1794)– French Revolutionary leader who presided over the Reign of Terror in France

Romanticism– a movement in literature and the arts that followed the French Revolution and emphasized an appreciation of nature, feeling, and emotion over reason and intellect, and celebrated the artist as an individual creator

Rousseau, Jean-Jacques (zhahn-zhahk roo-SOH) (1712–1778)– French *philosophe* whose ideas helped pave the way for both the French Revolution and the Age of Romanticism

Safavid Empire (sah-FAH-vuhd)– Muslim empire that flourished in Persia in the sixteenth and seventeenth centuries

***samurai* (SA-muh-riy)–** professional Japanese warriors who served feudal lords

San Martín, José de (hoh-SAY day sahn mahr-TEEN) (1778–1850)– Argentine revolutionary and leader of South American liberation movements

Scientific Revolution– era of great progress in understanding the workings of nature that occurred during the sixteenth and seventeenth centuries; during this period, modern science emerged as a distinct discipline

serfs– peasants obliged to remain on the land of their lord and pay him with labor and rents

shah– title of a ruler in some Asian lands, for example, the Safavid emperor of Persia

Shakespeare, William (1564–1616)– Elizabethan playwright and perhaps the greatest writer in the English language; known as "the Bard"

shogun (SHOH-guhn)– title of the military ruler of Japan from the late twelfth century to mid-nineteenth century

Smith, Adam (1723–1790)– Scottish author of *The Wealth of Nations*, which laid the foundation for modern economics

Stowe, Harriet Beecher (1811–1896)– American author of the antislavery novel *Uncle Tom's Cabin*

Stravinsky, Igor (EE-gor struh-VIN-skee) (1882–1971)– Russian-born composer who, more than any other, is associated with the beginning of modern music; his *The Rite of Spring* shocked the music world when it premiered in 1913

strike– work stoppage by a group of employees with the objective of gaining better wages or working conditions

Suez Canal– canal across the Isthmus of Suez that links the Mediterranean and Red Seas

suffrage– the right to vote, as in the movement for women's suffrage

sultan– title given to some Muslim rulers, for example, the ruler of the Ottoman Empire

Süleyman the Magnificent (SOO-lay-mahn) (c. 1495–1566)– greatest of all the Ottoman sultans; also known as Süleyman the Lawgiver

Sunni Ali (sou-NEE ah-LEE) (died 1492)– warrior king of Songhai who conquered the lands of the crumbling empire of Mali

Sun Yat-sen (soun yaht-sen) (1866–1925)– Chinese nationalist and revolutionary; first president of the Chinese republic

Teresa of Avila (AH-vih-luh) (1515–1582)– Spanish nun who founded 21 convents and was a key figure in the Counter-Reformation

Tokugawa Shogunate (toh-kou-GAH-wah) (1603–1867)– dynasty under which Japan prospered and enjoyed a 250-year period of peace

Toussaint L'Ouverture (too-SEHN loo-vair-tyour) (c. 1743–1803)– former slave who led slaves in Haiti to rebel against their French masters and later became ruler of the French colony

trade union– an organization set up to improve the working conditions of its members

tsar– title used for ruler of Russia; from the Latin word *Caesar*

tyranny– abuse of power; according to John Locke, the actions of a ruler who "makes not the law, but his will, the rule"

Van Gogh, Vincent (van GOH) (1853–1890)– Postimpressionist Dutch painter whose most famous works include *The Starry Night* and *Self-Portrait*

Vatican– Vatican City, or "the Vatican," is both the headquarters of the Roman Catholic Church and the smallest independent country in the world

vernacular– the native language of a place; for example, Martin Luther translated the Bible from Latin into German, the vernacular of Germany

Versailles (vuhr-SIY)– a one-time royal hunting lodge outside Paris that was transformed into a lavish palace by Louis XIV

Vesalius, Andreas (vuh-SAY-lee-us) (1514–1564)– Flemish professor of anatomy at the University of Padua who published the first accurate and detailed study of the human body

Victoria (1819–1901)– queen of England and empress of the British Empire

Voltaire (vohl-TAIR) (1694–1778)– French philosopher and writer who advocated reason as the tool for advance in government, philosophy, and science

Waterloo– 1815 battle in which Napoleon met his final defeat at the hands of the British and the Prussians

Watt, James (1736–1819)– Scottish inventor whose steam engine helped launch the Industrial Revolution

Wilberforce, William (1759–1833)– British abolitionist who worked for an end to the slave trade

Wright brothers (Wilbur and Orville) (1867–1912, 1871–1948)– inventors and builders of the first successful airplane; their flights at Kitty Hawk, North Carolina, began a new era in the history of transportation

yellow journalism– sensational news reporting, frequent in the early newspapers of Joseph Pulitzer and William Randolph Hearst

Zheng He (choung hou) (1371–c.1433)– Chinese explorer and admiral in service of the Ming emperors

Zhu Yuanzhang (joo you-en-jahng) (1328–1398)– military leader who freed China from Mongol rule and founded the Ming dynasty

Zola, Émile (ay-meel ZOH-luh) (1840–1902)– French novelist and naturalist writer; his novel *L'Assommoir* depicts the degrading effect of the slums of Paris

Text Credits and Permissions

34 Petrarch letter to Cicero from LETTERS by Petrarch, translated by James Harvey Robinson and Henry Winchester Rolf. G.P. Putnam's Sons, 1909.

104 Excerpt from UTOPIA by Thomas More, edited with Introduction and Notes by Edward Surtz, Yale University Press, 1964. Reprinted by permission of Yale University Press.

148 Excerpt from THE MUQADDIMAH by Ibn Khaldun. Princeton University Press. Reprinted by permission of Princeton University Press.

163 *The Closing of Japan* excerpt from THE ECONOMIC ASPECTS OF THE HISTORY OF THE CIVILIZATION OF JAPAN by Y. Takekoshi. George Allen & Unwin Ltd., 1930, Vol. II, pp. 28–29. Reprinted by permission of Thompson Publishing Services, UK.

208 Excerpt from THE LOG OF CHRISTOPHER COLUMBUS, translated by Robert H. Fuson, copyright 1987 by Robert H. Fuson. Excerpt used with permission.

220 Excerpt from MAGELLAN'S VOYAGE: A NARRATIVE ACCOUNT OF THE FIRST CIRCUMNAVIGATION BY ANTONIO PIGAFETTA, translated and edited by R. A. Skelton. © Yale University Press, 1969. Reprinted by permission of Yale University Press.

246 Excerpt from FIRST-HAND ACCOUNT OF THE DEATH OF Montezuma–THE TRUE HISTORY OF THE CONQUEST OF MEXICO by Bernal Diaz del Castillo, translated by Maurice Keatinge. Robert M. McBride & Co. First edition, 1800, reprinted, 1927.

257 Excerpt from A BRIEF ACCOUNT OF THE DESTRUCTION OF THE INDIES by Bartolomé de las Casas, translated by Sir Arthur Helps (1813–1875). John Lilburne & Co.

314 Excerpt from *The Starry Messenger* from DISCOVERIES AND OPINIONS OF GALILEO by Galileo Galilei, translated by Stillman Drake, copyright © 1957 by Stillman Drake. Used by permission of Doubleday, a division of Random House, Inc.

375 Excerpt from *The Declaration of the Rights of Man and the Citizen* from TRANSLATIONS AND REPRINTS FROM THE ORIGINAL SOURCES OF EUROPEAN HISTORY, Philadelphia: University of Pennsylvania Press, 1897, Vol. I, No. 5, pp. 6–8.

386 *Napoleon Bonaparte proclamation to his troops in Italy, 1796* from A DOCUMENTARY SURVEY OF THE FRENCH REVOLUTION by John Hall Stewart, 1st Edition, © 1951. Reprinted by permission of Pearson Education, Inc., Upper Saddle River, NJ.

425 *Catherine the Great calls for the election of an assembly to help prepare a new code of laws for Russia, 1767* from DOCUMENTS OF CATHERINE THE GREAT, edited by W.F. Reddaway, copyright 1931 by Cambridge University Press. Used with permission.

496 Excerpt from THE INTERESTING NARRATIVE OF THE LIFE OF OLAUDAH EQUIANO, WRITTEN BY HIMSELF by Olaudah Equiano, 1793, 1794, 1814.

526 *Mazzini Oath to Join Young Italy* from THE LIFE AND WRITINGS OF JOSEPH MAZZINI, Vol. I by Joseph Mazzini, Smith, Elder & Co., 1891, pp. 110–12.

649 Selected short quotes from GANDHI ON NON-VIOLENCE, edited by Thomas Merton, copyright © 1964, 1965 by New Directions Publishing Corp. Reprinted by permission of New Directions Publishing Corp.

While every care has been taken to trace and acknowledge copyright, the editors tender their apologies for any accidental infringement when copyright has proven untraceable. They would be pleased to include the appropriate acknowledgement in any subsequent edition of this publication.

Illustrations Credits

Key: t=top; b=bottom; c=center; l=left; r=right

Maps: Created by Maps.com, Mike Powers, lead cartographer
Front cover, title page: (t) © Erich Lessing/Art Resource, NY; (b) Hulton Archive/Getty Images.
Back cover: (t) The Granger Collection, New York; (b) British Museum, London, UK/Bridgeman Art Library.

Prologue
8–9 © SuperStock. 10 (t) © De Agostini Picture Library/Getty Images; (b) © Royalty-Free/Corbis. 11 © North Wind Picture Archives. 12 (t) akg-images; (b) Derby Museum and Art Gallery, UK/Bridgeman Art Library. 13 The Art Archive.

Part 1
Introduction: 14 (A) The Granger Collection, New York; (B) © Scala/Art Resource, NY; (C) © James L. Stanfield/National Geographic Image Collection. 16 © Archivo Iconografico, S.A./Corbis. 18 The Granger Collection, New York. 21 © Photos12.com-ARJ. 23 © Larry Lee Photography/Corbis.

Chapter 1: 24, 26 Scala/Art Resource, NY. 27 The Granger Collection, New York. 29 © Scala/Art Resource, NY. 30 The Art Archive/Palazzo Ducale Urbino/Dagli Orti. 31 Bibliotheque Inguimbertine, Carpentras, France, Giraudon/Bridgeman Art Library. 33 The Art Archive/Museo Capitolino Rome/Dagli Orti. 34 © Scala/Art Resource, NY.

Chapter 2: 36 Index/Bridgeman Art Library. 39 © Gianni Dagli Orti/Corbis. 40 Musee du Louvre, Paris © SuperStock, Inc./SuperStock. 41 (t) Robert Harding Picture Library Ltd.; (b) Victoria & Albert Museum, London/Art Resource, NY. 42 © Archivo Iconografico, S.A./Corbis. 43 © Bryan Reinhart Palazzo Vecchio Piazza della Signoria Florence, Italy/Masterfile. 44 The Granger Collection, New York. 46 © Archivo Iconografico, S.A./Corbis. 48 Bildarchiv Preussischer Kulturbesitz/Art Resource, NY. 49 Mary Evans Picture Library.

Chapter 3: 50 © Visual&Written/Omni-Photo Communications. 52 Museo de Firenze Com'era, Florence, Italy/Bridgeman Art Library. 53 Scala/Art Resource, NY. 54 (l) © Erich Lessing/Art Resource, NY; (r) © Scala/Art Resource, NY. 55–56 © Scala/Art Resource, NY. 57 © Trevor Wood/Getty Images. 58 © Scala/Art Resource, NY. 59 Galleria degli Uffizi, Florence, Italy/

Bridgeman Art Library. 63 © Erich Lessing/Art Resource, NY. 64 (t) The Granger Collection, New York; (b) Galleria dell' Accademia, Venice, Italy/Bridgeman Art Library. 65 © Erich Lessing/Art Resource, NY.

Chapter 4: 66 © Oxford Scientific (OSF)/Photolibrary.com. 69 Vatican Museums and Galleries, Vatican City, Italy/Bridgeman Art Library. 70 (l) © Graham Tim/Corbis Sygma; (r) © Scala/Art Resource, NY. 72 © Araldo de Luca/Corbis. 73 Bargello, Florence, Italy/Bridgeman Art Library. 75 Vatican Museums and Galleries, Vatican City, Italy/Bridgeman Art Library. 76 © Alinari/Art Resource, NY. 77 © Francis G. Mayer/Corbis. 78–79 Vatican Museums and Galleries, Vatican City, Italy, Giraudon/Bridgeman Art Library.

Chapter 5: 80 © Erich Lessing/Art Resource, NY. 82 Louvre, Paris, France/Bridgeman Art Library. 83, 85 © Erich Lessing/Art Resource, NY. 86 © Scala/Art Resource, NY. 87 Galleria dell' Accademia Carrara, Bergamo, Italy/Bridgeman Art Library. 88 Adam Woolfitt-Woodfin Camp. 90, 91 The Granger Collection, New York. 92 © Scala/Art Resource, NY. 93 The Granger Collection, New York.

Chapter 6: 94 © Erich Lessing/Art Resource, NY. 97 © Julio Donoso/CorbisSygma. 98 National Gallery, London, UK/Bridgeman Art Library. 99 © Scala/Art Resource, NY. 100 © Bildarchiv Preussischer Kulturbesitz/Art Resource, NY. 101 National Gallery of Art, Washington DC/Bridgeman Art Library. 102 © Réunion des Musées Nationaux/Art Resource, NY. 103 © Francis G. Mayer/Corbis. 104 © The New York Public Library/Art Resource, NY.

Chapter 7: 106 Archives Charmet/Bridgeman Art Library. 108 Galleria degli Uffizi, Florence, Italy/Bridgeman Art Library. 110 © Erich Lessing/Art Resource, NY. 111 The Granger Collection, New York. 113 The Art Archive/Nationalmuseet Copenhagen, Denmark/Dagli Orti. 114 The Granger Collection, New York. 115 Retrofile.com. 116 © Foto Marburg/Art Resource, NY. 117 (l) The Art Archive/University Library Geneva/Dagli Orti; (r) © Snark/Art Resource, NY. 118 © National Trust/Art Resource, NY. 119 © Alinari/Art Resource, NY.

Chapter 8: 120, 122 © Archivo Iconografico, S.A./Corbis. 124 The Art Archive/Museo

Tridentino Arte Sacra Trento/Dagli Orti. 125 The Art Archive/Museo Storico Aloisiano Castiglione delle Stiviere/Dagli Orti. 126 akg-images, London. 127 The Granger Collection, New York. 129 © Scala/Art Resource, NY. 130 The Art Archive/Musée des Beaux Arts Lausanne/Dagli Orti. 131, 133 © Scala/Art Resource, NY. 134 Mary Evans Picture Library.

Chapter 9: 136 © Erich Lessing/Art Resource, NY. 138 The Granger Collection, New York. 139 © Bibliotheque Nationale, Paris, France/Bridgeman Art Library. 140 © Lance Nelson/Corbis. 141 © Bibliotheque Nationale, Paris, France, Lauros/Giraudon/ Bridgeman Art Library. 142 Targa © Age Fotostock. 143 © Bildarchiv Preussischer Kulturbesitz/Art Resource, NY. 144 © Victoria & Albert Museum, London/Art Resource, NY. 145 (t) The Granger Collection, New York; (b) © SEF/Art Resource, NY. 146 Private Collection/Bridgeman Art Library, London/SuperStock. 147 © Chris Ryan/Taxi/Getty Images, Inc.

Chapter 10: 150 © Getty Images, Inc. 152 Uniphoto Press/Ancient Art & Architecture Collection. 153 (l) © Réunion des Musées Nationaux/Art Resource, NY; (r) © Artokoloro Quint Lox Limited/Alamy. 154 © Dynamic Graphics/Creatas. 155 © Chinastock. 156–57 © D.E. Cox/Getty Images, Inc. 159 (l) AGE Fotostock/James Montgomery; (r) AGE Fotostock/Doug Scott. 160 akg-images, London. 162 (l) Berlin-Bridgeman Giraudon/Bridgeman Art Library; (r) Age Fotostock/Luis Castaneda.

Chapter 11: 164 © Kurt Scholz/SuperStock. 166 © Scala/Art Resource, NY. 167 © Leonid Bogdanov/Superstock. 168–69 The Granger Collection, New York. 170 © Réunion des Musées Nationaux/Art Resource, NY. 171 Memorial Estate Museum, Kislovodsk, Russia/Bridgeman Art Library. 172 © Jonathan Smith/Lonely Planet Images. 173 © Bettmann/Corbis. 174 © Roger Viollet/Getty Images, Inc. 175 © Kurt Scholz/SuperStock.

Conclusion: 176 (A) Vatican Museums and Galleries, Vatican City, Italy/Bridgeman Art Library; (B) © Creatas; (C) Wayne Walton/© 2000 Lonely Planet Images; (D) © John Wang/Photodisc Green/Getty Images, Inc.; (E) © The Pierpont Morgan Library/Art Resource, NY. 178 The Art Archive/Bibliothèque Universitaire de Mèdecine,

Conclusion: 338 © Scala/Art Resource, NY. 340 © Bildarchiv Preussischer Kulturbesitz/ Art Resource, NY. 341 (t) The Granger Collection, New York; (b) © Bettmann/ Corbis. 342 The Granger Collection, New York. 343 (t) © Topham/The Image Works; (b) MPI/Getty Images. 344 Private Collection, Michael Graham-Stewart/Bridgeman Art Library. 345 (t) The Granger Collection, New York; (b) Bibliotheque de la Comedie Francaise, Paris, France, Peter Willi/ Bridgeman Art Library.

Time Line: 346 (1440) © Ed Simpson/Stone/ Getty Images, Inc.; (1492) Metropolitan Museum of Art, New York/Bridgeman Art Library; (1519) © 2004 by Robert Frerck Odyssey Productions, Inc.; (1522) © Erich Lessing/Art Resource, NY; (1543) © Alinari/Art Resource, NY; (1558) The Granger Collection, New York. 347 (1607) Photo by MPI/Getty Images, Inc.; (1609) © Gustavo Tomsich/Corbis; (1687) The Royal Institution, London, UK/Bridgeman Art Library; (1751) © Erich Lessing/Art Resource, NY.

Part 3

Introduction: 349 (t) The Art Archive/Musée Historique/Dagli Orti; (b) The Granger Collection, New York. 350 akg-images. 351 © Bettmann/Corbis.

Chapter 1: 352 © SuperStock. 354 Washington-Custis-Lee Collection, Washington and Lee University, Lexington, Virginia. 357 (l) The Granger Collection, New York; (r) © Massachusetts Historical Society, Boston, MA/Bridgeman Art Library. 358 © Bettmann/Corbis. 359 North Wind Picture Archives. 360 © Stock Montage. 362 © Bettmann/Corbis. 363 Bibliotheque Nationale, Paris, France, Archives Charmet/ Bridgeman Art Library. 364 © Erich Lessing/ Art Resource, NY. 365 © SuperStock. 366 © Private Collection/Art Resource, NY. 367 © Joseph Sohm; Visions of America/Corbis.

Chapter 2: 368 © Giraudon/Art Resource, NY. 370 (t) © Réunion des Musées Nationaux/ Art Resource, NY; (b) © Giraudon/Art Resource, NY. 371 (t) The Art Archive/Musée du Château de Versailles/Dagli Orti; (b) The Art Archive/Musée Carnavalet Paris/Marc Charmet. 372–73 The Granger Collection, New York. 375 © Erich Lessing/Art Resource, NY. 377 The Granger Collection, New York. 379 (t) © Erich Lessing/Art Resource, NY; (b) © Giraudon/Art Resource, NY. 380 © Giraudon/Art Resource, NY. 381 © Erich

Lessing/Art Resource, NY. 382–83 © Réunion des Musées Nationaux/Art Resource, NY.

Chapter 3: 384 Musee Nat. du Chateau de Malmaison, Rueil-Malmaison, France, Lauros/Giraudon/Bridgeman Art Library. 387 The Art Archive/Musée du Château de Versailles/Dagli Orti. 388 © Timothy McCarthy/Art Resource, NY. 389 © Réunion des Musées Nationaux/Art Resource, NY. 390 (l) © Scala/Art Resource, NY; (r) © Alex Bartel/SuperStock. 391 © Giraudon/Art Resource, NY. 393 © Fine Art Photographic Library, London/Art Resource, NY. 395 (t) © Topham/The Image Works; (b) Christie's Images, London/Bridgeman Art Library. 396 Musee de l'Armee, Brussels, Belgium, Patrick Lorette/Bridgeman Art Library. 397 © Tate Gallery, London/Art Resource, NY. 398 Bibliotheque Nationale, Paris, France, Lauros/ Giraudon/Bridgeman Art Library.

Chapter 4: 400 The Art Archive/Simon Bolivar Amphitheatre Mexico/Dagli Orti. 403 (t) © Réunion des Musées Nationaux/Art Resource, NY; (b) The Art Archive/Museo del Prado, Madrid. 404 The Art Archive/Museo Historico Nacional Buenos Aires/Dagli Orti. 405 The Art Archive/Simon Bolivar Amphitheatre, Mexico/Dagli Orti. 406 The Art Archive/ Museo Bolivar, Caracas/ Dagli Orti. 407 © Museo Nacional de Bellas Artes/Kactus Foto/ SuperStock. 408 Private Collection/Bridgeman Art Library. 409 The Art Archive/Museo Nacional de Historia Lima/Dagli Orti. 413, 415 The Art Archive/National History Museum Mexico City/Dagli Orti.

Chapter 5: 416 © Diomedia/Alamy. 419 © Maximilianeum Foundation, Munich, Germany/A.K.G., Berlin/SuperStock. 421 (t) The Granger Collection, New York; (b) © Sovfoto. 422 © Erich Lessing/Art Resource, NY. 423 The Art Archive/Bibliothèque des Arts Décoratifs Paris/Dagli Orti. 424 akg-images. 425 © Archivo Iconografico, S.A./Corbis. 426 © Réunion des Musées Nationaux/Art Resource, NY. 427 The Art Archive/Bibliothèque Marmottan Boulogne/ Dagli Orti. 428 © Anatoly Sapronenkov/ SuperStock. 429 The Granger Collection, New York.

Chapter 6: 430 © Bildarchiv Preussischer Kulturbesitz/Art Resource, NY. 432 Louvre, Paris, France/Bridgeman Art Library. 434 The Art Archive/Private Collection/Dagli Orti. 435 (t) © Kavaler/Art Resource, NY; (b) © Topham/The Image Works. 436 © H. Stanley Johnson/Superstock. 437 The

Art Archive/Civiche Raccolte Museo L. Bailo Treviso/Dagli Orti. 438 © Bettmann/Corbis. 439 (t) © Art Resource, NY; (b) Louvre, Paris, France, Lauros/Giraudon/Bridgeman Art Library. 440 Louvre, Paris, France/Bridgeman Art Library. 441 © Bildarchiv Preussischer Kulturbesitz/Art Resource, NY. 443 The Art Archive/Beethoven House, Bonn/Dagli Orti.

Chapter 7: 444 The Granger Collection, New York. 446–47 Private Collection/Bridgeman Art Library. 448 Fishmongers' Hall, London, UK./Bridgeman Art Library. 450 akg-images. 451 The Granger Collection, New York. 452 Mary Evans Picture Library. 453 (t) The Granger Collection, New York; (b) © image-BROKER/Alamy. 454 Private Collection, Christie's Images/Bridgeman Art Library. 455 Musee National des Techniques, Paris, France, Lauros/Giraudon/Bridgeman Art Library. 456 © Bettmann/Corbis. 457 (t) © Topham/The Image Works; (b) The Granger Collection, New York.

Chapter 8: 458 © NRM/Pictorial Collection/ SSPL/The Image Works. 460 The Art Archive/British Museum/Eileen Tweedy. 461 Private Collection/Bridgeman Art Library. 462 © Science Museum, London/HIP/The Image Works. 462–63 The Granger Collection, New York. 464–65 Mary Evans Picture Library. 466 (t) © Underwood & Underwood/Corbis; (b) © Bettmann/ Corbis. 468, 471, 473 The Granger Collection, New York.

Chapter 9: 474 © SEF/Art Resource, NY. 475 © Victoria & Albert Museum, London/ Art Resource, NY. 476 (t) © ARPL/HIP/The Image Works; (b) Musee de la Ville de Paris, Musee Carnavalet, Paris, France/Bridgeman Art Library. 477 © Bettmann/Corbis. 478 Guildhall Library, Corporation of London, UK/Bridgeman Art Library. 479 Victoria & Albert Museum, London, UK/Bridgeman Art Library. 480 Mary Evans Picture Library. 482 (l) Mary Evans Picture Library; (r) © Bettmann/Corbis. 483 The Granger Collection, New York. 484 The Art Archive/ Karl Marx Museum Trier/Dagli Orti. 485 © Bildarchiv Preussischer Kulturbesitz/Art Resource, NY. 487 The Granger Collection, New York. 488 Mary Evans Picture Library. 489 © Archivo Iconografico, S.A./Corbis.

Chapter 10: 490, 492 The Granger Collection, New York. 493 The Art Archive/Musée des Arts Africains et Océaniens/Dagli Orti. 495 The Granger Collection, New York. 496 Royal Albert Memorial Museum, Exeter, Devon,

UK/Bridgeman Art Library. **497** © The British Library/HIP/The Image Works. **498** The Granger Collection, New York. **499** © Corbis. **500** © Bettmann/Corbis. **501** © Bettmann/ Corbis. **502** (t) The Granger Collection, New York; (b) © New York Historical Society, New York/Bridgeman Art Library. **503** The Granger Collection, New York. **504** © The British Museum/HIP/The Image Works. **505** The Granger Collection, New York. **506** © Bojan Brecelj/Corbis.

Conclusion: 508 (A) © AAAC/Topham/The Image Works; (B) American Illustrators Gallery, NYC/www.asapworldwide.com/Bridgeman Art Library; (C) © The Granger Collection, New York. **510** © Royalty-Free/Corbis. **511** © Roger-Viollet/Topham/The Image Works. **512** (t) © Science Museum, London/HIP/The Image Works; (b) Mary Evans Picture Library. **513** The Art Archive/Conservatoire des Arts et Métiers Paris/Marc Charmet. **514** The Granger Collection, New York. **515** Wilberforce House, Hull City Museums and Art Galleries, UK/ Bridgeman Art Library.

Time Line: 516 (1762) © Archivo Icono-grafico, S.A./Corbis; (1769) The Granger Collection, New York; (1776) © Bettmann/ Corbis; (1789) © Giraudon/Art Resource, NY; (1800) Musee Nat. du Chateau de Malmaison, Rueil-Malmaison, France, Lauros/Giraudon/ Bridgeman Art Library; (1807) © The British Museum/HIP/The Image Works. **517** (1810) The Art Archive/Simon Bolivar Amphitheatre Mexico/Dagli Orti; (1814) Mary Evans Picture Library; (1837) © Victoria & Albert Museum, London/Art Resource, NY; (1859) © John Reader/Photo Researchers, Inc.

Part 4

Introduction: 518 (A) The Granger Collection, New York; (B) Mary Evans Picture Library; (C) © MPI/Getty Images. **520** The Granger Collection, New York. **521** © Corbis.

Chapter 1: 522 The Granger Collection, New York. **524** © Photodisc/Picture Quest. **525, 527** The Granger Collection, New York. **530** (t) © Archivo Iconografico, S.A./Corbis; (b) © Alinari/Art Resource, NY. **531** The Granger Collection, New York. **533** (t) The Granger Collection, New York; (b) © Archive/Getty Images, Inc. **535** © Hulton-Deutsch Collection/Corbis. **536–37** The Granger Collection, New York.

Chapter 2: 538 Library of Congress, Prints and Photographs Division, LC-USZC4-1732.

541 (t)(b) The Granger Collection, New York. **542** © Hulton-Deutsch Collection/Corbis. **543** The Art Archive/Culver Pictures. **545** (t) © Scala/Art Resource, NY; (b) © Corbis. **546** The Art Archive/Laurie Platt Winfrey. **547** © Archiv for Kunst & Geschichte, Berlin, Germany/SuperStock. **548** © Library of Congress/Getty Images, Inc. **549** (t) © Bettmann/Corbis; (b) © Scala/ Art Resource, NY. **550** Mary Evans Picture Library. **551** © Corbis. **552** © Bettmann/ Corbis. **553** Library of Congress, Prints and Photographs Division, LC3b44035u. **555** © Bettmann/Corbis. **557** The Granger Collection, New York.

Chapter 3: 558 © Schenectady Museum; Hall of Electrical History Foundation/Corbis. **560** The Granger Collection, New York **561** (t) (b) © Corbis. **562–63** The Granger Collection, New York. **564** © Science Museum, London/ Topham-HIP/The Image Works. **565** The Granger Collection, New York. **566** (t) Benelux Press/Retrofile.com; (b) akg-images. **567** Mary Evans Picture Library. **569** © Topham/The Image Works. **571** The Granger Collection, New York.

Chapter 4: 572 The Granger Collection, New York. **574** Guildhall Art Gallery, Corporation of London, UK/Bridgeman Art Library. **576** © Topham/The Image Works. **577, 580** The Granger Collection, New York. **581** Mary Evans Picture Collection. **582** The Granger Collection, New York. **584** © Topham/The Image Works. **585** The Granger Collection, New York. **587** © Snark/Art Resource, NY. **588** The Granger Collection, New York. **590** The Art Archive/Eileen Tweedy.

Chapter 5: 592 © Corbis. **594** The Granger Collection, New York. **595** Mary Evans Picture Library. **596** © Réunion des Musées Nationaux/Art Resource, NY. **597** Mary Evans Picture Library. **598** (t) © Snark/Art Resource, NY; (b) © Hulton Archive/Getty Images, Inc. **599** © Hulton Archive/Getty Images, Inc. **600** © Museum of the City of New York/ Corbis. **601** The Art Archive/ Musée d'Orsay Paris/Dagli Orti. **603** © Bettmann/Corbis. **604** National Archives and Record Administration/ Record Group 102-LH-488. **605–6** The Granger Collection, New York. **607** The Art Archive/ Dagli Orti. **608** © Time & Life Pictures/Getty Images. **609** © Bettmann/Corbis.

Chapter 6: 610 The Fine Art Society, London, UK/Bridgeman Art Library. **612** Private Collection Lauros/Giraudon/Bridgeman Art

Library. **614** The Granger Collection, New York. **615** (t) © SSPL/The Image Works; (b) Private Collection Christie's Images/ Bridgeman Art Library. **616** © SuperStock. **617** (t) © Bettmann/Corbis; (b) Private Collection Archives Charmet British/ Bridgeman Art Library. **618** The Granger Collection, New York. **619** (l) © Bettmann/ Corbis; (r) New York Historical Society, New York/ Bridgeman Art Library. **621** Mary Evans Picture Library. **623** © Bettmann/ Corbis. **624** © Robertstock. **625** Private Collection Archives Charmet American/ Bridgeman Art Library.

Chapter 7: 626 Digital Image © The Museum of Modern Art/Licensed by Scala/Art Resource, NY. **627** Musee de la Ville de Paris, Musee Carnavalet, Paris, France Giradoun/ Bridgeman Art Library. **628** © Bettmann/ Corbis. **630** (t) Musee d'Orsay, Paris, France Lauros/Giraudon/Bridgeman Art Library; (b) © Snark/Art Resource, NY. **633** © Terra Foundation for American Art, Chicago/Art Resource, NY. **634** Musee Marmottan, Paris, France Giraudon/Bridgeman Art Library. **635** © Gianni Dagli Orti/Corbis. **636** Art Institute of Chicago/Giraudon/Bridgeman Art Library © 2005 Estate of Pablo Picasso/ Artists Rights Society (ARS), New York. **637** Vasily Kandinsky *Painting with White Border* (*Bild mit weissem Rand*), May 1913 Oil on can-vas 140.3 x 200.3 cm (55 1/4 x 78 7/8 inches) Solomon R. Guggenheim Museum, New York, Gift, Solomon R. Guggenheim, 1937 37.245 © 2003 Artists Rights Society (ARS), New York/ ADAGP, Paris. **638** © Lebrecht Music and Arts Photo Library/Alamy.

Chapter 8: 640 (A) Private Collection/Archives Charmet/Bridgeman Art Library; (B) The Granger Collection, New York; (C) © DPA/VJ/The Image Works; (D) © Bettmann/Corbis. **642** akg-images. **643** © Kisa Markiza/Getty Images. **645** The Art Archive/Historisches Museum (Museen der Stadt Wien) Vienna/HarperCollins Publishers. **646** (t) The Granger Collection, New York; (b) © Lebrecht Music & Arts Photo Library. **648** The Granger Collection, New York. **649** © DPA/The Image Works. **650** © AP/Wide World Photo. **651** Mary Evans Picture Library. **652** The Art Archive/Dagli Orti. **653** © Hulton-Deutsch Collection/ Corbis.

Chapter 9: 654 (t) © Getty Images, Inc.; (b) © Corbis. **656** 2004 © Image Trader. **657** Mary Evans Picture Library. **659–60** The Granger Collection, New York. **661** ©

Corbis. **662** Mary Evans Picture Library. **663** © Hulton Archive/Getty Images, Inc. **665** The Granger Collection, New York. **666** © Bettmann/Corbis. **667** (t) © ARPL/HIP/ The Image Works; (b) © Underwood & Underwood/Corbis.

Conclusion: 668 (A) © Science Museum, London/HIP/The Image Works; (B) The Granger Collection, New York; (C) Image courtesy of The Advertising Archives. **671** (t) Museum of the City of New York, USA/ Bridgeman Art Library; (b) © Bettmann/ Corbis. **672** Hulton Archive/Getty Images. **673** © The Print Collector/Getty Images. **674** Philadelphia Museum of Art, Philadelphia, PA, USA/Bridgeman Art Library © 2005 Artist Rights Society (ARS), New York/ ADAGP, Paris/Succession Marcel Duchamp. **675** (t) © Hulton Archive/Getty Images; (b) © IWM/Popperfoto/Retrofile.

Time Line: 676 (1860) The Granger Collection, New York; (1869) © Bettmann/ Corbis; (1879) © Science Museum, London/ Topham-HIP/The Image Works; (1885) Mary Evans Picture Library; (1889) Mary Evans Picture Library. **677** (1890) © The Image Works; (1897) © Bettmann/Corbis; (1903) © Bettmann/Corbis; (1907) Art Institute of Chicago/Giraudon/Bridgeman Art Library © 2005 Estate of Pablo Picasso/Artists Rights Society (ARS), New York; (1914) (t) © Hulton Archive/Getty Images, Inc.; (1914) (b) © IWM/ Popperfoto/Retrofile.

Epilogue

678 (A) Museo Real Academia de Bellas Artes, Madrid, Spain, Index/ Bridgeman Art Library; (B) © Corbis; (C) © Brand-X Pictures/Wonderfile Corporation. **680** © Réunion des Musées Nationaux/Art Resource, NY. **681** (t) The Granger Collection, New York; (b) © StockImage/Imagestate.

Appendix: Geographic Terms and Concepts

683 © Maptec International/Photo Researchers, Inc. **685** (t) © Colin Monteath/ Minden Pictures; (c) © Daryl Benson/ Masterfile; (b) © Corbis. **686** (t) © WorldSat International/Photo Researchers, Inc.; (b) © NASA/AFP photo/Getty Images, Inc. **687** (t) Mark Taylor/Warren Photographic/Bruce Coleman USA; (c) © Noboru Komine/Photo Researchers, Inc.; (b) © Tim Davis/Corbis. **688** © Jim Sugar/Corbis. **689** © Dazzo/Getty Images.

Index

A

Abbas I, Shah (Safavid Empire) 144, **144**, 145
Abolition of slavery 408, 502–5, 540, 578
Abstract art 636–37, **637**
Adams, John 367
Adoration of the Magi (Leonardo da Vinci) 62, **63**
Afghanistan 591
African Americans
  during U.S. Civil War 546, **546**
  voting rights 551, 552, **553**
  see also Colonial America: slavery; United States of America: slavery
The Age of Reason, *see* The Enlightenment
Airplanes **654**, 655, 663–66, **666**, 667, **667**, **668**
Akbar, Emperor (Mughal) **146**, 146–47
Alexander I, "Monsieur," Tsar (Russia) 394, 426, **426**, 427–28
Alexander II, Tsar (Russia) 552
Alexander VI, Pope 44, 60, 87, 88, 211, **211**, 212
Allende, Ignacio 412–15
American Revolution 357–65, 353–67
Andes, Army of the 407–8, **408**
Anghiari, Battle of 91
Anglicanism 130
  see also Church of England
Anthony, Susan B. 608
Arc de Triomphe, Paris, France 390, **390**
Argentina **252**, 404, 406–7, 528
Aristocracy 331
Arkwright, Richard
  water frame 452, 453, **453**
Arnold, Matthew 620
Art
  neoclassic **432**, 432–33
  and photography 633
  romantic 432, 433
  see also Abstract art; Cubism; Humanism: in art; Impressionist art; Islamic art; Postimpressionist art; Renaissance: art; Romanticism: and art
Articles of Confederation 365, 366
Askia Muhammad, King (Songhai Empire) 266–67
  tomb **267**

Assembly line production 624–25, **625**
Astronomy 311, 312, 313
  see also Copernicus, Nicholas; Galilei, Galileo
Atahualpa, Emperor (Inca) **248**, 248–49
Australia 575, 578, 582, 605
Austria 97, 392, 395, 399, 485, 525, 529, 530, 532, 534, 535, 536, 642, 643–47, 674
Automobiles 567, 621–25
  manufacturing 567, 622–25, **625**
  tires 583
  see also Model Ts; Quadricycles
Aztec Empire 227–30
  artifacts **229**, **230**, **242**, **341**
  conquered by Spaniards 239–47
  human sacrifice 230, 243, 244
  maps of 224, 240
  pyramids **228**, 228–29, 243, **243**
  see also Tenochtitlán

B

Babur, Emperor (Mughal Empire) 145–46
Bacon, Francis 312, 320
Balboa, Vasco Nuñez de 247, 655–56
Banking 39, 52
Baptistery of the Duomo, Florence, Italy **50**, 53–55, 55, 56, 57
Barnard, Henry 620
Barton, Clara **552**
Baseball 615–16
Bastille, Paris, France **348**, **368**, 374, 383, 608
Beagle, HMS 487, **487**, 488
Beethoven, Ludwig van 442–43, **443**, 645
Beijing, China 153–54, **154**, 155
  see also Dadu (city), China
Belgium 398
  see also Congo Free State
Bell, Alexander Graham 561–62, **562**, 563
Belle Epoque 628
Benin, Kingdom of 267–69, 270
Benz, Karl 567, 622
Berliner, Emile 617
Bessemer, Henry 560
Bible 124, 316
  King James version 293, **293**
  printed by Gutenberg 48, **48**, 49
  translated to German 115, 116
Bicycles 565–66, **566**, 567, 583
Bill of Rights (England) 326–27

Bingham, Hiram, III 234–36, **236**, 237
The Birth of Venus (Botticelli) 59, **59**
Bismarck, Otto von 533, **533**, 534–37, **537**, 550
Blériot, Louis 666, **667**
Bly, Nellie 468, **468**
Boers 586
Bolívar, Simón **400**, 404, **404**, 405–6, **406**, 409–10
Bonaparte, Joseph, King (Spain) 394, 403, 404
Bonaparte, Napoleon *see* Napoleon Bonaparte
Bonfire of the Vanities 59–60
Boniface VIII, Pope 26
The Book of the Courtier (Castiglione) 81–84, 86
Borgia, Cesare 87, **87**, 88, 89, 90
Borgia, Rodrigo 44
Bosnia 647, 674
Boston, Massachusetts 334–35, 336, 357–58, 483
Boston Massacre (1770) 357, **357**, 358
Boston Tea Party 358
Botticelli, Sandro 59, 60, 69
Boucicaut, Aristide 612, 613
Boulton, Matthew 455, 456
Bourgeoisie 484–86
Boxer Rebellion 590, **590**
Boyars 166, 169, 172–75, 419, 420, 428
Bradford, William 301
Branches of government 366–67
Braque, Georges 636
Brazil 214–15, 216, 411, 529
  slavery 271, 493, 497, 498, 552
Brewster, William 301
Bridges 453, **453**, **518**, 598, **598**
Bridgewater Canal, England 461
Britain 395, 399
  abolitionist movement in, 502–5
  attacks on Spanish colonies 403
  canals 460–61
  industrialization 445–57
  invaded by France 392–93, **393**
  labor unions 605, 606
  public education 620
  road improvements 459–60, **460**
  and slavery 498, 502–5, 540, 578
  textile industry 541, 542
  trade 393–94, 446–47, 449, 456–57
  and U.S. Civil War 546, 547
  women's voting rights 609
  see also British Empire; England; Great Britain
British East India Company 575–76

Boldface indicates illustration included on page.

British Empire 278–81, 298–307, 353–54, 574–77, 582–90, 651
Brunelleschi, Filippo 54, 55–56, 57, 58
Buddhism 146, 159, 161
Byron, George Gordon 436–37, **437**, 438, 439
Byzantine Empire 18–19, 42, 49, 139–40, 165, 166

C

Cabot, John 280
    map of travels 199
Cabral, Pedro 214–15
    map of travels 198, 199
California 554, 555–56, 657
Calvert, Cecilius 303
Calvert, Leonard 303
Calvin, John 117, **117**, 118, 121, 293
Canada 280, 354, 575, 578
Canals *see* Bridgewater Canal, England; Erie Canal, New York; Panama Canal, Panama; Suez Canal, Egypt
Capitalism 449, 483, 484–86
Caracas, Venezuela 404–5, 405
Caravels (ships) **192**, 202, **202**, 203
Caribbean *see* West Indies
Carnegie, Andrew 560–61
Carnegie Steel 560–61, **561**, 606
Carolina (colony) 306
Carpenter, Sarah 477–78
Cars *see* Automobiles
Cartesian coordinates 312
Cartier, Jacques 280
Cartwright, Edmund 452, 454
Caruso, Enrico 617
Casement trains 556
Cassatt, Mary
    paintings 633, **633**
Castiglione, Baldassare 81–82, **82**, 83–84
Catalogs by mail 613–14, **614**
Cathedral of St. Sophia, Novgorod, Russia **167**
Catherine II, "the Great," Tsarina (Russia) 422, **422**, 423–25, **425**, 426, 429
Catherine of Aragon 118, 130, 274
Catholic Church *see* Roman Catholic Church
Caudillos 411, 415
Cavaliers 295
Cavour, Count di 529, 530
Central Park, New York City, New York 599–600, **600**

Chadwick, Sir Edwin 482
Chagres River, Panama 656, 661–62
Charles I, King (England) 294, **294**, 295–96, **296**, 303, 304, 324
Charles I, King (Spain) 252, 258
Charles II, King (England) 297, 304, 306, 324–25, 326
Charles V, Holy Roman Emperor 84, 114, 115
Charles X, King (France) 440
Charleston, South Carolina 306, 364, 499, 541, 545, **545**
Child labor 454, 457, 475, 477, **477**, 481, 482, 604, **604**
Chile 404, 407–8
China 151–59
    exploration by sea 155–57, under foreign occupation 589–91, 651–53
    immigrants in U.S. 553, 555–57
    maps 151, 152
    nationalism 651–53
    religion 126, 579, 652
    slavery 552
    treaty ports 651, **651**
    see also Beijing, China; Ming Dynasty
Chivalry, code of 82, 83
Christendom 16–19
Christian Church 67, 101, 102, 103, 107, 110, 111–19
    see also Eastern Orthodox Church; Indulgences; Papacy; Roman Catholic Church; Russian Orthodox Church; The Counter-Reformation; The Reformation
Christian humanism 33, 101–5
Christian missionaries
    in Africa 578–80
    in Asia 146, 157, 162, 579, 590, 591, 652
    in South America 254, 255–56, 258
    see also Jesuits
Christianity 201, 202, 206, 219, 241
    and abolitionism, 503–504
    and art 59–60
    in art 29, **29**
    in literature 27–29
A Christmas Carol (Dickens) 488
Church of England 118–19, 274, 275, 291, 293, 294, 298, 301, 304
    see also Anglicanism; Evangelical Anglicans
Cicero, Marcus Tullius 32, 34–35, 49
Circumnavigations 277, 468

Cities
    disease 594, 600, 603
    industrialization 475–78, 479–82
    population growth 475–76, 593–94
    during Renaissance 37–41, 38–45
    see also London, New York, Paris, Vienna; Parks, urban planning; Suburbs
Civil disobedience 648–50
Civil War (England) 324
Civil War (U.S.) 545–52, 554
Civilization and Its Discontents (Freud) 673
Clarkson, Thomas 503, **503**, 504
Class struggle 484–86
Classical music 441–43
Coleman, Bessie 667
Cold Harbor, Virginia 550
Collective bargaining 604, 605
Colombia 405, 406, 408, 657, 659
Colonial America 354–57
    first English settlements 298–307
    government 302, 303, 307, 354, 356
    independence declared 361–62
    map 305, 355
    slavery 270–71, 354, 492–94, 498–500, 502, 505
    see also American Revolution
Columbus, Christopher 204–9, **205**, **207**, 212
    map of travels 199
Comic strips 619, **619**
Common Sense (Paine) 359–60, **360**, 361
Communication 469–73
    see also Radio; Telegraphs; Telephones
The Communist Manifesto (Marx & Engels) 484–86
Condorcet, Marquis de 332–33, **333**, 364
Confederate States of America 543, 544, 545–50
Congo Free State 583–85, 586, 632
Congress, U.S. 367, 472
Congress of the Confederation 365
Congress of Vienna 399
Conquistadors 239, 255
    see also Cortés, Hernán; Pizarro, Francisco
Conrad, Joseph 632
Constable, John
    paintings 438–39, **439**
Constantine XI, Emperor (Byzantine Empire) 140

Boldface indicates illustration included on page.

Constantinople, Asia Minor 42, 49, **139**, 139–40, 167
  see also Istanbul, Asia Minor
Constitution of the United States 332, 365–67, **367**, 499
  amendments 551, 609
Constitutional Convention, Philadelphia, Pennsylvania 365–66, **366**, 367, 499
Continental Army 359, 362–63, 364
Continental System 393–94
Cook, Thomas 615
Cooper, Peter 466
Copernicus, Nicolaus 311, **311**, 312, 314, 316, 317, 320, 321
  map of universe 308
Cortés, Hernán 239, 241, **241**, 242–44, **244**, 245–47, 252, 255
  map of route 240
Cotton gin 500, **500**, 501
Cotton industry 499–501, 502, 502, 540, 541, **541**, 542
Coubertin, Pierre de 616
The Counter-Reformation 121–30
Courtiers, Renaissance **80**, 81–84
Creoles 253–54, 259, 401, 412, 413, 414
Cromwell, Oliver 295, **295**, 296–97
The Crusades 21, 200
Crystal Palace, London, England 475, **475**
Cuba 241, 242, 245, 591, 660
Cubism 636, **636**
Cuzco, Peru 231, 232, 249
Czech Republic 642, 646

D
da Gama, Vasco 212–13, 214, **214**, 215
  map of travels 198, 199
  stone pillars 212, 213, **213**
da Vinci, Leonardo *see* Leonardo da Vinci
Dadu (city), China 152, 153
  see also Beijing, China
Daimler, Gottlieb 567, **567**, 622
Daimyo 160, 162
Dante 25–26, **26**, 27, **27**, 28–29, 43
Darwin, Charles 486–87, **487**, 488–89, 577–78, 629
Dauphin, The "Lost" 381, **381**
David, Jacques-Louis
  paintings 432, **432**
David (Donatello) **55**
David (Michelangelo) 73, **73**
Davis, Jefferson 542
Decembrist Uprising 428–29, **429**

Declaration of Independence, U.S. 361–62, **362**, 501, 505
Declaration of the Rights of Man and the Citizen (France) 375, **375**, 376–77
Degas, Edgar 633
Deism 331
Delacroix, Eugene 439, **439**, 440–41, 441
Democracy *see* Representative government
Department stores 612, **612**, 613
Descartes, René 312, **312**, 313, 320
Diamond industry 585, 588, **588**
Dias, Bartolomeu 204, 205, 212
  map of travels 199
Díaz del Castillo, Bernal
  writings of 243, 246–47
Dickens, Charles 479, **479**, 480–81, 488
Diderot, Denis 332, **332**, 423, 426, 433
Diet of Worms *see* Worms, Diet of
The Directory (France) 383, 387
Discalced Carmelites 132, 134–35
Diseases 258–59
  see also Scurvy; Smallpox; Vaccines; Yellow fever
Disraeli, Benjamin 577
The Divine Comedy (Dante) 26–29
Divine right of monarchs 292, 294, 324
Division of labor 447–48
Djenné, Mali Empire 265, 266
Dolores (parish), Mexico 412–15
Donatello 56, 58
  sculpture 54–55, **55**
Douglass, Frederick 546
Drake, Sir Francis 276, **276**, 277–78, **280**, 281, 282
  map of travels 198–99
Dreiser, Theodore 607
Dual Monarchy of Austria-Hungary 645–47
Dunlop, Boyd 583
Dürer, Albrecht
  art by 99, **99**, 100, **100**, **182**, **341**
Dutch *see* The Netherlands
Dvořák, Antonín 646

E
East India Company 575
Eastern Orthodox Church 167, 170
  see also Russian Orthodox Church
Economics 447–50
  see also Banking; Capitalism; *The Communist Manifesto*; Marx, Karl; Smith, Adam

Edison, Thomas Alva **558**, 563–65, **565**
  movies 617–18, **618**
Edo, Japan 162
  see also Tokyo, Japan
Edo (people) 267–69
  artifacts **262**, **268**, **269**
Education, public 619–21, **621**
Edward, King (England) 274
Edward, Prince of Wales 570
Edward VI, King (England) **101**
Egerton, Francis, Duke of Bridgewater 461, **461**
Egypt 506, 507, 580–83
Eiffel, Gustave 560
Eiffel Tower, Paris, France **520**, 560, **560**
Elba (island), Italy 395
Electricity 561, 564, 565
  and communication 469–73
  discovered in lightning 336–37
Elevators 598
Elizabeth I, Queen (England) 130, **272**, 273, 274–75, **275**, 276–79, 280, 283, 284, 285, **321**, **343**
Elizabethan Age (England) 273–89
Emancipation Proclamation 546–47, 552
Émile (Rousseau) 434
Empire building *see* Imperialism
Encomienda 254–59
Encyclopédie (Diderot et al.) 332, 369, 423, 433, **446–47**
Engels, Friedrich 483–84
England
  art 438–39, **439**
  coal mining 444, **444**, 446, 454, 455
  conflicts with Spain 280–82, **282**, 283
  constitution 296
  exploration by sea 276–80
  iron industry 446, 453
  labor laws 481–82
  literature 283, 435–38
  maps 279, 326
  monarchy 274, 296, 297, 326, 329, 354, 356
  queens 274
  religion 118–19, 130, 274–76, 291, 293–94, 297, 298, 325, 326
  slave trade 271
  taxes 292–93, 327
  united with Scotland 291
  see also Bridgewater Canal, England; Britain; British Empire; Church of England; Civil War (England); Great

Boldface indicates illustration included on page.

Britain; Industrial Revolution: in England; London, England

English Channel 570
first flight over 666, **667**
English colonies
in North America 278–80, 298–307, 359–61
The Enlightenment 323–37, 431–33, 436
Equiano, Olaudah 494–96, **496**, 497, 504
Erasmus, Desiderius 101–2, 103, 107, 122, 127
Erie Canal, New York 461
Estates (French social classes) 371–75
Ethiopia 588
Europe
invaded by Ottomans 139–40
maps 38, 123
see also places by name
Evangelical Anglicans 504
Evolution 488–89
Experimentation as scientific method 311, 312, 313, 316, 320

F

Factory Laws (England) 481–82
The Faerie Queene (Spenser) 283
Fantasia (film) 639
Ferdinand, King (Spain) 96, **97**, 205, 207, 211
Feudalism 159–62, 371, 375, 391
Filmmaking 639, **639**
see also Movies
Fitch, John 462–63
Florence, Italy 38, 42–43, 51–60, **52**, 73, 87, 90
architecture 43, **43**, **50**, 53, 55–56, **56**, 57, **57**
art 57–58, **58**, 59, **59**, 60, 61–65, 71
language 28
sculpture 53–54, **54**, 55, **55**
Flyer (Wright brothers' plane) 665–66, **666**
Forbidden City, Beijing, China 153–54, **154**, 155
Ford, Henry 621–23, **623**, 624–25
Fort Sumter, Charleston, South Carolina 545, **545**
France 60, 65, 87, 403, 404, 406, 411
and American Revolution 363–64, 364–65
art 439–40, **440**, 633–36
colonies 280, 354, 393, 497, 498, 575, 587–88, 591
executions 379, **379**, 380, 381–82, 382

flight experiments 663, 666, 667, **667**
in Egypt 580–82
invasions of 395, 396, 535–36, 576
laws 390–91
literature 433–34, 629–33
military 364, 382, 391
monarchy 329–30, 331, 369–71, 374–75, 377–78, 399
Napoleonic invasion of Spain 403–4
in Panama 657–59
peasantry 330, **330**, 371–75
religion 117, 118, 129, 330, 331, 371, 376, 378, 388, 390
as a republic 378–79
and slavery 271, 382, 498
taxes 371, 372, 375, 376
trade with Britain 446–47
voting rights 375, 382, 609
see also Bonaparte, Napoleon; Franco-Prussian War; French and Indian War; French Revolution; Paris, France; Versailles, France
Francis I, King (France) 93, 97–98
Franco-Prussian War 535–36
Frankenstein (Mary Shelley) 438
Franklin, Benjamin 334–37, **337**, 462
Franklin stove 335, **335**, 336
Franz Ferdinand, Archduke (Austria) 674
Franz Joseph, Emperor (Austria) 534, 643–46, **646**, 674
Frederick, Prince (Saxony) 115, 116
French and Indian War 354, 363
French Revolution 374–83, 523–24, 608, 619–20
centennial 560, 627–28
Freud, Sigmund 628, **628**, 629, 645, 673
Friedrich, Caspar David
paintings **430**, 441, **441**
Fulton, Robert 461–62, **462**, 463
Fust, Johann 48, 49

G

Galápagos Islands, Ecuador 487, 488
Galen (Greek physician) 310, 311
Galileo 310, 313, **313**, 314–16, **316**, 317, 320, 321, **338**, **345**
Gandhi, Mohandas 647–48, **648**, 649, **649**, 650, **650**
Garibaldi, Giuseppe **522**, 527, **527**, 528–31
Gasoline 561, 566–67, 622–23
Genghis Khan **14**, 151

Genoa, Italy 41, 42
Geocentrism 311, 314, 316–17, 321
George III, King (England) 306, **351**, 354, 364
Georgia 364, 502, **502**, 549
Germany 38, 97, 395, 398
art 441, **441**
automobiles 622
colonies 586, 588
education 620
flight experiments 663, **663**
folktales 533
invasions of France 535–36
labor unions 606
literature 434–35
mercenaries 362
music 442–43
nationalism 531–37
railroads 550
religion 129
steel industry 560
unification of 398, 550, 645
voting rights 535
worker riots 485, **485**
see also Luther, Martin; Bismarck, Otto von
Gettysburg, Pennsylvania
battle of 547–48, 550, **551**
Gettysburg Address 547, 548
Ghana 264, 269
Ghiberti, Lorenzo 54, **54**
Giotto 29, 43
Giovanni Arnolfini and His Bride (Van Eyck) **98**, 99
Gliders **518**, 663, **663**, 664–65
Globe Theatre, London, England 285–86, **286**, 287–88, **288**, 289
The Glorious Revolution 326
Goethe, Johann Wolfgang von 434–35, **435**
Gold 242, 247, 249, 264, 265, 269, 585
Gold Coast, Africa 269, 574
Golden Hind (ship) 277, **277**
Gonzaga family 84
Federico 85
Francesco 82, 85, 86
Ludovico **80**
Good Hope, Cape of, Africa 204, 212, 213, 219
Gorgas, William Crawford 660
Government
and natural rights 326, 327–28, 354
reason as a basis for 333, 359–61
types of 331–32
Gramophones 617

Boldface indicates illustration included on page.

Grand Army (France) 391–96, 397
    in Russia 426–27, **427**
Grant, Ulysses S. 549, **549**
Great Britain
    map 292
    name origin 292
    slavery 502–5
    see also Britain; British Empire;
        England; Scotland
Great Wall of China **156–57**, 157–58
Great Western Railway **458**
Greece **437, 439**
Grimm, Jakob 533
Grimm, Wilhelm 533
Guanajuato (mine), Peru 261
Guatemala 225
Guilds, trade 40, 47, 53
Guillotin, Joseph-Ignace 379
Guillotine 379, **379**, 381, 382, 383
Guinea
    slave market **492**
Gutenberg, Johannes 45–49, **49**

H

Habsburg Empire 643–47, 644
Habsburg family 97, 532, 537
Haciendas 260–61
Hagia Sophia, Istanbul, Asia Minor
    56, 140, **140**, 167
Haiti *see* Saint-Domingue
Hamilton, Alexander 366
Hargreaves, Elizabeth 452
Hargreaves, James 452
Haussmann, Georges-Eugène
    594–97
Haydn, Franz Joseph 442
Hearst, William Randolph 619
Heart of Darkness (Conrad) 632
Heliocentrism 311, 314, 316–17, 318
Henrietta Maria, Queen (England)
    294, 298, 303
Henry the Navigator, Prince 200, **200**,
    201–4
Henry VII, King (England) 97
Henry VIII, King (England) 100, 103,
    118, **118**, 119, 130, 273–74, 275
Hertz, Heinrich 568
Hidalgo y Costilla, Miguel 411–13,
    413, 414–15, **415**
Hinduism 146, 575–76
    see also Gandhi, Mohandas
Hispaniola (island) 207, 256
Holbein, Hans, the Younger 100
    paintings 100–101, **101**, 102, **102**,
    103
Holy Roman Emperor 68, 124, 129,
    532

Holy Roman Empire 97, 531, 532
Hong Kong 574, 575, 582, 651, **678**
Hot-air balloons 663
House of Commons (England) 292,
    294
House of Lords (England) 292
House of Representatives, U.S. 367
How the Other Half Lives (Riis) 672
Hubbard, Gardiner 562, 563
Huguenots 118, 129, 331
Huitzilopochtli (Aztec deity) 227, 228,
    230, 244–45
Human anatomy 310, **310**, 311
Human body
    in Renaissance art 29, **29**
Human nature
    ideas about 628–29
Humanism 32–33, 53, 83
    in art 58, **58**, 59, **59**, 60, 71, 74, 75,
        77–78
    see also Christian humanism
Hungary 643–47
Hus, Jan 109

I

Ibn Khaldun (Muslim scholar)
    148–49
Ieyasu, Tokugawa 161, **161**
Ignatius Loyola 125, **125**, 126, 127
Imperialism 574
    "new" 573–91
    racism as justification for 577–78,
        579, 585–86, 589
Impressionist art 633, **633**, 634, **634**
Inca Empire 230–34, 247–49
    artifacts **233, 237, 249**
    maps 232, 240
    ruins **231, 234**, 235–37
Indentured servants 307
India 213–14, 574
    under British rule 575–78, 649–50
    early European exploration
        213–14, 215
    Mughal princes 575
    under Muslim rule 145–46
    nationalism 649–50
    religion 126, 146, 159, 575–76, 579
    see also Mughal Empire
Indians of North America 206, **207**,
    254–58, **258**, 259–61, 300, **300, 343**
Indies *see* West Indies
Indochina 591
Indulgences 108–10, 111–13, 124, 128
Industrial Revolution 445–57
    "second" 559–71
Inferno (Dante) 27–28

The Inquisition 127–28, **129**, 316–17
*The Interesting Narrative of the Life of
    Olaudah Equiano* (Equiano) 494–97,
    504
Iron industry 453, **541**
Ironbridge, Shropshire, England 453,
    453
Isabella, Queen (Spain) 96, **97**, 205,
    207, 211
Isabella D'Este 84–85, **85**, 86
Isfahan, Persia 145, **145**
Islam 126, 141, 143, 265–67
    in India 575–76
    scholarship 148–49
    study of history 148–49
Islamic art 144–47
Islamic empires 138–147: *see also*
    Mughal Empire, Ottoman Empire;
    Safavid Empire; Slave trade in
    Islamic world
Ismail, Shah (Safavid Empire) 143, **143**
Istanbul, Asia Minor 140, 142, **142**
Italian language 28, 31
Italy 32, 398
    colonies in Africa 588
    conflicts between city-states 40–41,
        52, 55, 82, 85–86
    flag **524**
    invasions of 60, 65, 87, 97
    maps 528, 529
    music 617
    nationalism 524–31
    see also Florence, Italy; Genoa,
        Italy; Mantua, Italy; Milan, Italy;
        Murano, Italy; Rome, Italy;
        Sardinia, Kingdom of; Sicily; The
        Vatican, Rome, Italy; Venice,
        Italy
Ivan III, "the Great," Prince of
    Muscovy (Russia) 168, **168**, 169,
    169, 170
Ivan IV, "The Terrible," Tsar (Russia)
    172–73, **173**, 174–75

J

Jamaica 497, 574
James I, King (England) 291, **291**,
    292–94, 298, 301
James II, King (England) 325, 326
James River, Virginia 298
James VI, King (Scotland) *see* James I,
    King (England)
Jamestown, Virginia 298–99, **299**, 300,
    300, 301
Janissaries 140–41, **141**, 143

Boldface indicates illustration included on page.

Japan 158–63, 590–91
  architecture **159**, **162**
  maps 151
  missionaries **127**
Jefferson, Thomas 361–62, **362**, 380, 393, 403, 491, 501
Jenner, Edward 602
Jesuits 126, 127, **127**, 128, 146, 162, 255, 333
John I, King (England) 356
John II, King (Portugal) 204, 205, 211, 212
Johnson, Eldridge 617
Josephine, Empress (France) **391**
Journalism, wartime 550
Julius II, Pope 44, 69–71, 73, 74, 75–76, **76**, 85, 102, 107, 108
The Jungle Book (Kipling) 577

K

Kandinsky, Wassily
  paintings 636–37, **637**
Keats, John 436
Kiev, Russia 166–67, 168
Kipling, Rudyard 577, **577**
Kinetoscopes 617–18, **618**
Kitty Hawk, North Carolina
  flight experiments 664–66, **666**
The Kremlin, Moscow, Russia **171**, 171, **172**
Kublai Khan 151, 161

L

La Navidad (colony) 207
Labor
  in industrial cities 478–82, 593, 598, 604–9
  work week 614–15
Labor unions 604–6
Lafayette, Marquis de 364, **364**, 365, 369, 470
Lake District, England 435, 436, **436**
Landscape painting **436**, 438–39, **439**, 440, **440**, 441, **441**
Laocoön (sculpture) 70, **70**
Las Casas, Bartolomé de 256, **256**, 257, 412
L'Assommoir (Zola) 630, **630**, 631–33
The Last Supper (Leonardo da Vinci) 65, **65**, 93
Lee, Robert E. 545, **545**, 546, 547
Leisure time 614–21
Leonardo da Vinci 59, 61–65, 77, 86, 90–93, **93**, 97–98, 663
  works of **63–65**, **90–92**
Lenoir, Jean 566
Leo Africanus 267

Leo X, Pope 92, **108**, 108–9, 110, 113, 114
Leopold, King (Belgium) 583–85, 632
Lesseps, Ferdinand de 580–82, 657–58, 660
Liberty Leading the People (Delacroix) 440, **440**, 441
Light
  study of 318, 319, **319**
Light bulbs **558**, **564**, 565
Lightning rods 337
Lighting, gas-powered 597, **597**
Lilienthal, Otto 518, 663, **663**, 664, 665
Lima, Peru 249, 408
Lincoln, Abraham 542–43, **543**, 545, 546–49, 554
Line of Demarcation 212, 215
Livingstone, David 578–80, **580**
Locke, John 323–25, **325**, 326–29, 330, 331, 333, 354, 356, 357, 361, 362
Locomotives **458**, 464–65, **465**, 466, **466**, 468, **508**
London, England 283, 317, **474**, 476, **476**, 477, **477**, 478–82, **485**
  see also Globe Theatre, London, England
Looms 451, **451**, 454
Louis-Charles, Prince (France) 381
Louis XI, King (France) 96
Louis XII, King (France) 65
Louis XIV, King (France) 329, **329**, 330, 331, 369–70
Louis XV, King (France) 370
Louis XVI, King (France) 364, 369, 370, 370, 371, 374, 377–81, **381**
Louisiana Purchase 393, 539
Luther, Martin **106**, 110, **110**, 111, **111**, 112–13, **113**, 114, **114**, 115, **115**, 116, 121, 127, 293

M

Machiavelli, Niccolò 86, **86**, 87–89, 90, 127
Machu Picchu, Peru **222**, 233–37
Magellan, Ferdinand **210**, 216–21
  map of travels 198–99
Mail delivery 466
Mail-order businesses 613–14
Mainz, Germany 44, 45–49
Mali Empire 265, 266
Malindi, Kenya **213**
Malthus, Robert 487–88
Manchu Dynasty (China) 651–52
Manchuria 591
Manet, Edouard 633
Mansa Musa 265, 266

Mantua, Italy 82, 84–86
Manuel, King (Portugal) 212, 214, 215
Marconi, Guglielmo 568–71, **571**, 617
Marie Antoinette, Queen (France) 370, **370**, 377, 381, 381, 382
Marx, Karl 483–84, **484**, 485–86
Mary, Queen (England) 130, 274
Mary II, Queen (England) 326–27, **327**
Maryland 303–4, 545
Masaccio 58–59, 77
Mass entertainment 612, 616–18
Mass production 612, 613, 624–25, **625**
Massachusetts 302, 303, 457, 570, 620
  see also Boston, Massachusetts
Matchgirls' Union
  strike 605, **605**
Mathematics 311, 312, 313, 316, 318–20
Mayan culture 225–27
  artifacts **225**, **227**
  ruins **226**
Maybach, Wilhelm 567
Mayflower Compact 302
Mayflower (ship) 301, **301**, 302
Mazzini, Giuseppe 525, **525**, 526–27, 528
Medici family 43, 52, 53, 60, 87, 88, 98, 316
  Cosimo 52, 53, 54, 56, 62, 71, 108
  crest **179**
  Giovanni 52
  Lorenzo 53, 60, 62, 108, 122
Medicine 310, **310**, 311
  see also Human anatomy; Pasteurization; Vaccines
Meister, Joseph 603
Mendoza, Antonio de 252
Mental illness 628, 629
Mercator, Gerard
  map of the world 220
Mercedes-Benz 567
Mestizos 254, 412, 415
Mexico 229, 404, 411–15
  flag **228**
  see also Aztec Empire; Mayan culture; Olmec civilization
Mexico City, Mexico 245, 259, **259**
Michelangelo 71–76, **76**, 77, 78, **78**
  works of 70, 71–72, **72–74**
Middle class
  emergence and development of 611–25
Middle Passage 271
Milan, Italy 55, 62–64, 82, 125

Boldface indicates illustration included on page.

Ming dynasty (China) 152–58, 651
Mining
    in New World 258, 260, **260**, 261
    see also Diamond industry
Miranda, Francisco de 402–3, **403**,
    404–5, **405**
Model Ts 624, **624**, 625
Modern times
    defined 11
Mona Lisa (Leonardo da Vinci) 92,
    92, 93
Monarchy 331
Monet, Claude
    paintings 633–34, **634**
Mongols 151–52, 157–58, 161, 651–52
    see also Tatars; Yuan dynasty
        (China)
Monks 46, **46**
Montesquieu, Charles de 331–32, **332**,
    357, 366, 369
Montezuma II, Emperor (Aztec) 239,
    241–44, **244**, 245, **246**, 246–47
Moon 313–15, **315**, 318
More, Thomas 102–3, **103**, 104–5, 107,
    118–19, 122
Morse, Samuel 469–71, **471**, 472–73,
    561
Morse code 471–72, 571
Moscow, Russia 168
    in art 637, **637**
    cathedrals **164**, 175, **175**
    fires 173, 394, 427, **427**
Motion, Laws of (Newton) 318, 320
Mott, Lucretia 505
Movies 617–18
Mozart, Wolfgang Amadeus 442
Mughal Empire 145–47
    mosques 147, **147**
Muhammad 143
Murano, Italy 42
Muscovy (city-state), Russia 168–73
    see also Moscow, Russia
Music
    modern 637–39
    see also Classical music;
        Romanticism: and music
Music halls 616–17

N
Nanjing, China 151, 153
Naples, Sicily 530, **531**
Napoleon Bonaparte 383, **384**, 385–87,
    387, 388–89, **389**, 390–93, **393**,
    394–95, **395**, 396, **396**, 397, **397**,
    398–99, 403, **403**, 404, 406, 411,
    426–27, **427**, 428, 523, 524, 531–32,
    580

Napoleon III, Louis, Emperor (France)
    535–36, **536**, 594–97, 600
Napoleonic Code 391, 398, **398**, 399
National Assembly (France) 373–78
National Convention (France)]378–79,
    382–83, 391
Nationalism 524
    see China: nationalism; Germany:
        nationalism; India: nationalism;
        Italy: nationalism; Slavic
        peoples: nationalism
Natural religion 331
Natural rights of mankind 325–26,
    333, 375–77
Natural selection 488–89
Naturalism, literary 629–33
Navigational tools **192**, 203, **203**
Neoclassicism **432**, 432–33, 436
The Netherlands 130, 271, 304, 326,
    398, 586
New Amsterdam, New Netherlands
    see New York City, New York
New Imperialism 574
    in Africa 578–89
    in Asia 574–76, 589–91
New Spain 245, 252–61
New York 304, 363, 461
New York City, New York 351, **521**,
    592, 598, **598**, 599, **599**, 600, **600**,
    617, **672**, **678**
    modernization and growth 563,
        563, 565, 597–600
    poor 483, **483**
    sweatshops 604
    tenements 604
New Zealand 575, 578, 609
News and newspapers 359, 550, 618,
    619
    steam presses **350**, **508**
Newton, Isaac 310, 317–18, **318**, 319,
    319, 320, 330, 489
    telescope **320**
Nicholas I, Tsar (Russia) 428
Nickelodeons 618
Nile River, Africa 579, 580
Ninety-five Theses (Luther) 111–13
Nonviolence 648–50
North America
    earliest human settlers 223–24
    slavery 499–501
    see also Canada; Colonial America;
        Mexico; United States of
        America; West Indies
North Carolina 279, 280, 306
    see also Kitty Hawk, North Carolina
Notre Dame, Cathedral of, Paris,
    France 378, 389, 390, **390**

Novgorod, Russia 166, **167**, 169
Nuremberg, Germany 44, **44**, 45, 99

O
Oakley, Annie **671**
Oath of the Horatii (David) 432, **432**
Oath of Young Italy 526–27
Observation as scientific method 311,
    312, 316, 320
O'Higgins, Bernardo 407, **407**, 408
Olmec civilization 224–25
    artifacts **224**
Olmsted, Frederick Law 599–600
Olympic Games 616, **616**
Organized labor *see* Labor unions
The Origin of Species (Darwin) 489,
    577
Osman, Sultan (Ottoman Empire)
    138, 138–39
Ottoman Empire 138–44, 147, 200,
    437, 439, 641–43
    army 139, **139**, 140–41, **141**, 143
    maps 642
    slavery 506, 507

P
Pacific Ocean
    first seen by Europeans 218, 220–21,
        247
Paine, Thomas 403
Painting with White Border (Kandinsky)
    637, **637**
Panama 247, 248, 276, 408, **656**, 657,
    659
Panama Canal, Panama **654**, 655–57,
    657, 658–59, **659**, 660, **660**, 661,
    661, 662, **662**, 663, 675, **675**
Panama Railroad 657
Pankhurst, Emmeline Goulden 608,
    608, 609
Papacy 32, 44, 52, 67–68, 70, 388
    authority challenged 114–16,
        118, 119
    see also Alexander VI, Pope;
        Boniface VIII, Pope; Julius II,
        Pope; Leo X, Pope; Paul III,
        Pope; Sixtus IV, Pope
Papal States, Italy 43–44, 69, 87,
    524, 529
Paris, France 329, 374, 378, **379**, 381,
    427, **520**, 535–36, **596**, 616
    boulevards 595, **595**, 596, 597,
        597
    disease 600, 603
    modernization of 389–90, 594–97
Parks, urban 599–600, **600**

Boldface indicates illustration included on page.

Parliament, British
    conflicts with monarchy 292–98,
        324–26
    taxation of American colonies
        356–58
Passive resistance 648–50
Pasteur, Louis 600–601, **601**, 602–3
Pasteurization 601
Patagonia, South America 217, 218
Patuxet Indians 302
Paul, Tsar (Russia) 426
Paul III, Pope 75, 122, **122**, 123, 124,
    126
Pedro, King (Brazil) 411
Pedro II, King (Brazil) 562, 563
Peninsulares 253–54, 406, 407, 412,
    415
Penn, William 306, **306**
Pennsylvania 306, 335–36, 361, 563
Perry, Matthew 590–91
Persia 144–45
    see also Safavid Empire
Peru 248–49, 252, 258, 407, 408–9
    see also Inca Empire
Peter I, "the Great," Tsar (Russia)
    418–19, **419,** 420–22, 429
Petrarch 25–26, *30*, 30–34, **34**, 35, 43,
    107
Petroleum 561
Philip II, King (Spain) 125, 128, 130,
    261, 278
Philippines 219, 591
Philosophes 330–33, 422–33
Phonographs 565, 617, **617**
Photography 550, 633
Physics 317–20
Picasso, Pablo
    paintings 636, **636**
Piedmont, Italy 525, 528–30
Pietá (Michelangelo) 72, **72**
Pigafetta, Antonio 216, 219, 220–21
Pilgrims 301–2, 303
Pin-making **446–47**, 447
Pizarro, Francisco **238**, 247, **247**, **248**,
    248–49
    map of routes 240
Plato **33**, 49
Plays *see* Theater
Plymouth, Massachusetts 302, 303
Pocahontas 300
Poetry 26–29, 30–32, 436–38
Polo, Marco 42, 663
Pony Express 466
Pope, Alexander 320
Popes *see* Papacy
Porter, Edwin 618

Portrait of Daniel-Henry Kahnweiler
    (Picasso) 636, **636**
Portugal 411
    colonies 202, 252, 586 (*see also*
        Brazil)
    exploration by sea 197–209,
        200–205, 211–15
    natural disasters 342
    and slavery 203–4, 269–71, 493
    trade 213–14, 269, 271, 277, 393
Portuguese language 215
Postal service 466
Postimpressionist art **626**, 634–35,
    635
"Potemkin villages" 422
Potosí (mine), Bolivia **260**, 261
The Praise of Folly (Erasmus) 102
The Prince (Machiavelli) 88–89
Princes 82–83, 86–87, **87**, 88–89
Printing press 102, 111, 113–16, **180**,
    201, 316, 317
    invention 45–49
Proletariat 484–86
Promontory Point, Utah 553, 557,
    557
Protestantism
    early development of 116–19,
        128
    in England 274, 275, 291, 293–94,
        325
    in France 331, 378
    in Netherlands 130
    in U.S. 303, 304
    see also Pilgrims; Puritans;
        Quakers; The Reformation
Prussia 392, 395, 396, 399, 532,
    533–37
Psychology 628–29
Ptolemy 201, 311, 313, 314
Publishing, mass 619
    see also Printing press
Pulp fiction 619
Purgatory 108–9, 111, 112, 113
Puritans 293–96, 298, 302–3, 304
Pyramids 225–26, **226**, **228**, 243, **243**

Q

Quadricycles 622–23, **623**
Quakers 304, 306, 503
Querétaro, Mexico 413, 414

R

Rabies vaccine 602–3
Racism 501–2, 577–78, 579, 585–86,
    589
Radio 568–71, 617

Railroads 464–65, **465**, 466, **466**, 467,
    468, 472–73, 584
    role in modern warfare 534, 549,
        550
    tracks 466–67, 556–57, 560
    underground 595–96
    see also Locomotives;
        Transcontinental railroad (U.S.)
Rainhill Race 465
Raleigh, Sir Walter 278, **278**, 279, 280,
    283, 298
Raphael 75, 77–78, 82
    works of **77**, **78–79**
Redshirts 528, 530, **530**
The Reformation 107–19
Reign of Terror (France) 381–83
The Renaissance 25–35, 95–105, 108,
    170–71
    architecture **50**, 53, 55–56, **56**,
        57, **57**
    art **42**, 58, **58**, 98–101
    defined 25
Renoir, Pierre-Auguste 633, 634
Representative government
    Athenian democracy 38
    in American colonies 302, 303,
        307
    in England 296, 325–27, 356
    in Renaissance city-states 38, 40,
        52–53
    influence on nationalist
        movements 525, 645–46, 652–53
    Montesquieu 331–32
    spread of 12–13, 351, 509–11, 679,
        681
    spread of after Napoleon 399
    spread of during American
        Revolution 353–67
    spread of during 1848 revolutions
        485
    spread of during French
        Revolution 374–75, 378
    spread of during Latin American
        revolutions 409–11
The Restoration 297–98
Rhodes, Cecil 585, **585**, 587
The Rite of Spring (Stravinsky)
    638–39
Roads 459–60, 625
Roanoke Island, North Carolina
    early colony 279, 280
Robespierre, Maximilien 380, **380**,
    381, 383, 391
Rocket (locomotive) 465, **465**
Roebuck, Alvah Curtis 614
Rolfe, John 300

Boldface indicates illustration included on page.

Roman Catholic Church 116–17, 124–29
  in England 274, 275–76, 293, 298, 325, 326, 327
  in France 330, 331, 371, 378, 388, 389
  in the New World 254, 255–56, 258, 303, 304
  and science 316–17
  see also Eastern Orthodox Church; Indulgences; Papacy; Russian Orthodox Church; Counter-Reformation; Inquisition; Reformation; Vatican, Rome, Italy; St. Peter's Basilica, Vatican City
Romanov family 417–29
  crest **416**
Romanticism
  and art **436**, 438–39, **439**, 440, **440**, 441, **441**
  and literature 431, 433–38
  and music 433, 441–43
  and science 436
Rome, Italy 44, 56, 57, 67–78, 528, 530
Roosevelt, Eleanor **681**
Roosevelt, Theodore 659, **660**, 661–62
Roundheads 295, 324
Rousseau, Jean-Jacques 433–34, **434**
Rubber industry 583–84, **584**, 585, 588
Russia 165–75, 395, 399, 417–29
  architecture 171, **171**, 172, **172**
  art 636–37, **637**
  city-states 166–70
  communism 486
  education 423, 426
  and Enlightenment ideas 422–23, 425, 428, 429
  expansion of 174–75, 420, 422, 591
  invasions of 165–66, 392, 394–95, 426–27, **427**, 591
  law and government 419–20, 425, 428, 486
  literature 423
  maps 166, 418
  music 638–39
  peasant life 173, 174, **174**, **421**, 424, **428**
  religion 167, 170, 171
  and the Renaissance 170–71
  seaports 417, 420–21, **421**
  serfdom 173–74, 417, 418, 421, 423–28, 491, 552, 642, 643

Tatar occupation 168–70
unification of 170
see also Moscow, Russia; Muscovy (city-state), Russia
Russian Orthodox Church 170, 171, 175, 420

S
Sacrifices, human 230, 243, 244
Sacsahuamán (fortress), Peru 231, **231**
Safavid Empire 143–45, 147
  mosques 145, **145**
Sa'id Pasha, Khedive (Egypt) 580
Saint-Domingue 497, 498, 499
St. Basil's Cathedral, Moscow, Russia **164**, 175, **175**
St. Peter's Basilica, Rome, Italy **66**, 70–71, 75, 108, 109, 110
St. Petersburg, Russia 420–21, **421**, 428–29, **429**
Samurai **160**, 160–61, **161**, 163
San Martín, José de 406–9, **409**, 410
San Salvador (island), Bahamas 206, **207**, 209
Santos-Dumont, Alberto 666
Saratoga, Battle of 363, **363**, 364
Sardinia, Kingdom of 524–25, 527–28, 529
Savonarola, Girolamo 59–60
Schiller, Friedrich von 443
The School of Athens (Raphael) 77–78, **78–79**
Schools 619–21, **621**
Science 436
  methods developed 311–13
  modern 486–89
  see also Astronomy; Mathematics; Medicine
Scotland 117–18, 292
Scriptures, Christian *see* Bible
Scurvy 214, 219
Sears, Richard Warren 613–14
Sears catalogs 613–14, **614**
Semaphore system 470
Senate, U.S. 367
Seneca Falls, New York
  first conference for women's rights 505, **505**, 607–8
Separatists 301, 302
Sepoy Mutiny 575–76
Serbia 642, **642**, 643, 647, 674
Sforza, Ludovico 62–65
Shah Jahan, Emperor (Mughal Empire) 147
Shakespeare, William 284, **284**, 285–89, 423

Shanghai, China 651, **651**
Shares of stock 658
Shattuck, Lemuel 483
Shelley, Mary Wollstonecraft 438, **438**
Shelley, Percy 438
Sherman, William Tecumseh 549
Shintoism 158–59, 161
  shrines 158, 159, **159**
Shogun 160, 162
Shopping
  department stores 612, **612**, 613
  mail catalogs 613–14, **614**
Shuttles, flying 451, **451**, 452
Siberia, Russia 174, 424
Sicily **522**, 529–30
Siemens, Charles William 560
Singapore 582
Sister Carrie (Dreiser) 607
Sistine Chapel, Vatican 69
  paintings 73–74, **74**, 77, 78, 91, **182**
Sixtus IV, Pope 68–69, **69**, 107
Skyscrapers **521**, 598–99, **599**
Slater, Samuel
  textile mills 457, **457**
Slave ships 492, 493, 495, **495**, 496–97
Slave trade
  in Africa 492, **492**, 493, **493**, 495, 505–6, **506**, 507, 578, 579
  in Islamic world, 505–6, **506**, 507, 552
  by Britain 498, 504–5
  by Portugal 203–4
  by Spain 241, 243, 270–71, 493
  by the United States 499
  transatlantic 269–71, **270**, 307, 492–97
Slavery 491–507
  in Africa 263–64, 266, 269–70, 492–95
  in Brazil 271, 493, 497, 498, 552
  in Britain 502–5
  in Caribbean 497–98
  in China 552
  in Egypt 506, 507
  in France 382
  in French colonies 498
  in Islamic world 578, 579
  in North America 270–71, 300–301, 307, 354, 492, 493–94, 498–502, 505
  in Ottoman Empire 141, 506, 507
  in Peru 408
  and racism 501–2
  in Venezuela 406
  in West Indies 493

Boldface indicates illustration included on page.

see also Abolition of slavery;
    Russia: serfdom; Slave trade;
    United States of America:
    slavery
Slavic peoples 165, 166, 506, 577
    nationalism 642–47
Smallpox 245, 248, 258, 259, 299, 602
Smith, Adam 446–50, **450**, 486
Smith, Capt. John 299, **299**
Smithsonian Institution, Washington,
    D.C. 663, 664
The Sneeze (kinetoscope) 618, **618**
Songhai Empire 264–67, 269
The Sorrows of Young Werther (Goethe)
    434–35
South Africa 648–49
South America
    earliest human settlers 223–24
    early European exploration 208,
        216–18, **218**
    see also Argentina; Brazil; Chile;
        Colombia; Peru; Venezuela
South Carolina 306, 364, 499, 502
South (region), U.S. see Civil War
    (U.S.); Confederate States of
    America
Spain
    art 636, **636**
    exploration by sea 205–9, 211–12,
        215–21, 241, 276–77
    Napoleonic invasion of 403, **403**,
        404, 406
    religion 125–26, 131–32, 134–35
    slave trade 241, 243, 270–71, 493
    trade with Britain 393–94
    see also Conquistadors
Spanish-American War 591, 618,
    658–59, 660
Spanish Armada 280–81, **281**, 282–83
Spanish colonies 207, 241, 252–61,
    588
Spenser, Edmund 283
Spice Islands 216, 219
Spice trade 200, 205, 214, 215
Spinning jenny 452, **452**
Sports, professional 615–16
Stamp Act (1765) 356–57
Stanley, Henry Morton 579–80, **580**
Stanton, Elizabeth Cady 505, **505**
The Starry Messenger (Galileo) 314–15,
    315
The Starry Night (Van Gogh) **626**
Steam engines 444, **444**, 454–55, **455**,
    456, 566
    see also Locomotives; Steamboats
Steamboats 462, **462–63**, 463–64, **464**,
    512

Steel
    in architecture 560, **560**, 598, 599
Steel industry 559–61, **561**
Stephenson, George 464–65
Stevens, John 462, 465–66, 661–62
Stocks 658
Stores, department 612, **612**, 613
Stowe, Harriet Beecher 542, **542**
Stratford-upon-Avon, England 285
Stravinsky, Igor 638–39
Strikes, labor 605, **605**, 606, **606**
Sturm und Drang (literary movement)
    435
Suburbs 596
Suez Canal, Egypt 580–81, **581**, 582,
    582, 657
Suffrage see Voting rights
Sugarcane production 251, 258, 271,
    271, 493, 497, **497**, 498, 505
Süleyman I "the Magnificent," Sultan
    (Ottoman Empire) **142**, 142–43, 143,
    144
Süleymaniye Mosque, Istanbul, Asia
    Minor 142, **142**, **186**
Summertime (Cassatt) **633**
Sun Yat-sen 652–53, **653**
Sunni Ali, King (Songhai) 265–66
Survival of the fittest 488–89
Sweatshops 604
Swiss Guard 70, **70**
Switchboard operators 607, **607**
Switzerland 117, 398

T

Taino people 206, 207
Taiwan 591
Taj Mahal, Agra, India 147, **147**
Tatars 168–70
Taylor, Zachary 542
Telegraphs 466, 469–73, **512**, 561, **561**,
    562
    wireless 568–69, **569**, 570–71, 612
Telephones 562–63, **563**, 612
    switchboard operators 607, **607**
Telescopes 313, **313**, 314–15
Tennis Court Oath 373, **373**, 374
Tenochtitlán (Aztec city), Mexico **228**,
    228–30, 239, 241–43, **243**, 244–47,
    259
Teresa of Avila 125, 127, 128, 131–32,
    133, 134, **134**, 135
Tetzel, Johann 109–10, 111, 112
Textile industry
    in England 449, 451–46, **456**, 457,
        457, 477, **477**, 478, 481
    machine inventions 451, **451**, 452,
        452, 453, **453**, 456–57

in U.S. 457, **457**, 540, 541
Theater 284–89
    see also Vaudeville
Theaters, movie 618
Ticonderoga, Fort, New York 363
Tierra del Fuego, South America 218
Tikal (Mayan city), Guatemala 225
Timbuktu, Mali Empire 265, 266, 267
Time Lines
    1300–1600 **190–91**
    1400–1800 **346–47**
    1750–1860 **516–17**
    1860–1914 **676–77**
Tin Lizzies see Model Ts
Titanic (ship) 673, **673**
Tobacco 206, 279, 300–301, 306, 307
Tokugawa Shogunate 161–62
Tokyo, Japan 162, 590–91
Tolpuddle Martyrs 605
Tordesillas, Treaty of 212, 215
Tourism 615
Toussaint L'Ouverture, 498, **498**
Trade unions see Labor unions
Trafalgar, Battle of 392–93, **393**
Tramways 464–65
Transcontinental railroad (U.S.) 553–
    55, **555**, 556–57, **557**
Transportation 459–68
    see also Airplanes; Automobiles;
        Bicycles; Canals; Gliders;
        Railroads; Roads; Steamboats;
        Tramways
Trent, Council of **120**, 122–24, **124**,
    128
Turnpikes 460, **460**
Twelfth Night (Shakespeare) 288–89
Two Sicilies, Kingdom of the 529–30
Tyranny 332, 357, 362, 364

U

Uncle Tom's Cabin (Stowe) 542
Unions, trade see Labor unions
United States of America
    early flag **510**
    education 620
    first modern democracy 365–67,
        510
    founding of 365–67
    labor unions 606
    maps 467, 540
    and Panama Canal 658–63
    railroads 465–66, **466**, 467, 468,
        472–73
    slavery 301, 307, 498–500, **500**, 501,
        501, 502, **502**, 540–43, 545–47,
        551–52
    sports 615–16
    states rights 542–43

Boldface indicates illustration included on page.

steel industry 560–61, **561**

telegraphs 471–73, **473**, 554, 557, 561

territorial expansion 422, 539–40, 590, 591

voting rights 551, 552

see also American Revolution; Civil War (U.S.); Colonial America; Constitution of the United States; Declaration of Independence, U.S.; Spanish-American War; Transcontinental railroad (U.S.)

Universal Declaration of Human Rights 681, **681**

Urban planning 594–97, 599–600

Urbino, Italy 77, 82

Uruguay 528, 529

Utopia (More) 102–5

V

Vaccines 601–3

Van Eyck, Jan
paintings **98**, 98–99

Van Gogh, Vincent **635**
paintings **626**, 634–35, **635**

Vasari, Giorgio 56, 93

The Vatican, Rome, Italy 68–69, 70, **70**
see also St. Peter's Basilica, Rome, Italy

Vatican City 530, **530**

Vaudeville 616–17, **617**

Velázquez, Diego 241, 242, 245

Velocipedes 565–66, **566**

Venezuela 208, 403, 404–6, 408

Venice, Italy **36**, 38, 41–42, 49, 82, 85–86, 530, **678**
arts and crafts **41**

Vera Cruz, Mexico 241, 242, 245

Verrocchio, Andrea del 61

Versailles, France 536

royal palace 329, **329**, 370, **371**, 372, 377

Vesalius 310–11, 312, 320

Vespucci, Amerigo 208, **208**

Viceroyalties, Spanish 252

Victor Emmanuel II, King (Sardinia) 528–29, 530

Victoria, Queen (England) 482, **482**, 570, 574, 576, 582

Victoria (ship) 216, **216**, 219, 221

Vienna, Austria 399, 532, 615, 628, 643, 645, **645**, 646

Vikings 165–66, **166**

Virginia 301, 304, 546, 549, 550
colonial map 279, 290

Virginia Company of London 298–301

Vladimir, Prince of Kiev (Russia) 166–67

Voltaire 330–31, **331**, 332, **345**, 364, 369, 374, 422

Voting rights 356, 551, 552, 607–9

W

Warfare, modern
weapons 534, **535**, 549, 550, **550**

Washington, D.C. 472, 546, 663, 664

Washington, George 354, **354**, 359, 363, 364, **365**, 380, 403

Water power 452, 454

Waterloo, Belgium
battle of 396, **396**

Watson, Thomas 562

Watt, James
steam engine 444, **444**, 454, **454**, 455, **455**, 456

The Wealth of Nations (Smith) 447–50

Wellington, Duke of, 396

West Indies 241, 575
slavery 493, 497–98
trade routes to 205–9, 211–21

Wheatley, Phillis 499, **499**

Whitney, Eli 500

Wilberforce, William 504

Wilhelm I, King (Prussia) 533–34, 537

William III, King (England) 326–27, **327**

Women
and education 619
during Civil War 552
during Renaissance 84–86
rights of 505, 593
voting rights 552, 607–9
in the workforce 475, 477–78, 552, 606–7

Women's Social and Political Union (WSPU) 608–9

Wordsworth, William 431, 435, **435**, 436, 437

World War I 674–75

Worms, Diet of 114–15

Wright, Orville **654**, 664–66, **666**

Wright, Wilbur 664–66, **666**

X

Xavier, Francis (Jesuit missionary) 126, 127, **127**, 146

Y

Yellow fever 658, 660–61

Yellow journalism 619

Yorktown, Virginia
surrender at **352**, 364–65, **365**

Young Italy 525–27

Yuan Dynasty (China) 151–52

Z

Zanzibar 493
slave trade 506, **506**, 507

Zheng He **155**, 155–57

Zhu Yuanzhang, Emperor (China) 151–52, **152**, 153

Zola, Émile 629–30, **630**, 631–33